Transformation and Efficiency Enhancement of Public Utilities Systems:

Multidimensional Aspects and Perspectives

Jordan Gjorchev
International Slavic University, North Macedonia

Samoil Malcheski
International Slavic University, North Macedonia

Tamara Rađenović
University of Niš, Serbia

Dejan Vasović
University of Niš, Serbia

Snežana Živković
University of Niš, Serbia

A volume in the Advances in Human Services and Public Health (AHSPH) Book Series

IGI Global
PUBLISHER of TIMELY KNOWLEDGE

Published in the United States of America by
IGI Global
Information Science Reference (an imprint of IGI Global)
701 E. Chocolate Avenue
Hershey PA, USA 17033
Tel: 717-533-8845
Fax: 717-533-8661
E-mail: cust@igi-global.com
Web site: http://www.igi-global.com

Library of Congress Cataloging-in-Publication Data

Names: Gorčev, Jordan, editor. | Malcheski, Samoil, 1983- editor. | Radenovic, Tamara, 1981- editor. | Vasović, Dejan, 1982- editor. | Živkovic, Snezana, 1971- editor.
Title: Transformation and efficiency enhancement of public utilities systems : multidimensional aspects and perspectives / edited by: Jordan Gjorchev, Samoil Malcheski, Tamara Rađenovic, Dejan Vasovic, Snežana Živkovic.
Description: Hershey, PA : Information Science Reference, [2023] | Includes bibliographical references and index. | Summary: "Much remains to be known about public utilities systems organization, efficiency, management, legislation, practices, and solutions worldwide, as well as, the implications for sustainable development in different countries. Thus, a better understanding of the different management practices in public utilities across different contexts is needed to assess their impact on efficiency and sustainability, especially in the changed climate conditions. Authors of this publication will discuss the importance of efficient management of public utilities systems, with respect to the exchange of best practices and knowledge. The publication will certainly add value in sharing knowledge among different stakeholders to provide answers to the ongoing concerns in the changed climate conditions regarding the transformation, development, and sustainability of public utilities systems"-- Provided by publisher.
Identifiers: LCCN 2023019754 (print) | LCCN 2023019755 (ebook) | ISBN 9781668477304 (hardcover) | ISBN 9781668477342 (paperback) | ISBN 9781668477311 (ebook)
Subjects: LCSH: Public utilities--Management. | Sustainable development.
Classification: LCC HD2763 .T663 2023 (print) | LCC HD2763 (ebook) | DDC 363.6068--dc23/eng/20230614
LC record available at https://lccn.loc.gov/2023019754
LC ebook record available at https://lccn.loc.gov/2023019755

This book is published in the IGI Global book series Advances in Human Services and Public Health (AHSPH) (ISSN: 2475-6571; eISSN: 2475-658X)

British Cataloguing in Publication Data
A Cataloguing in Publication record for this book is available from the British Library.

All work contributed to this book is new, previously-unpublished material.
The views expressed in this book are those of the authors, but not necessarily of the publisher.

For electronic access to this publication, please contact: eresources@igi-global.com.

Advances in Human Services and Public Health (AHSPH) Book Series

ISSN:2475-6571
EISSN:2475-658X

Editor-in-Chief: Jennifer Martin, RMIT University, Australia

MISSION

The well-being of the general public should be a primary concern for any modern civilization. Ongoing research in the field of human services and public healthcare is necessary to evaluate, manage, and respond to the health and social needs of the global population.

The **Advances in Human Services and Public Health (AHSPH)** book series aims to publish high-quality reference publications focused on the latest methodologies, tools, issues, and strategies for managing the health and social welfare of the public. The AHSPH book series will be especially relevant for healthcare professionals, policy makers, government officials, and students seeking the latest research in this field.

COVERAGE

- Healthcare Reform
- Social Work
- Social Welfare Policy
- Public Welfare
- Access to Healthcare Services
- Health Policy
- Public Funding
- Poverty
- Domestic Violence
- Medicare and Medicaid

IGI Global is currently accepting manuscripts for publication within this series. To submit a proposal for a volume in this series, please contact our Acquisition Editors at Acquisitions@igi-global.com or visit: http://www.igi-global.com/publish/.

The Advances in Human Services and Public Health (AHSPH) Book Series (ISSN 2475-6571) is published by IGI Global, 701 E. Chocolate Avenue, Hershey, PA 17033-1240, USA, www.igi-global.com. This series is composed of titles available for purchase individually; each title is edited to be contextually exclusive from any other title within the series. For pricing and ordering information please visit http://www.igi-global.com/book-series/advances-human-services-public-health/102256. Postmaster: Send all address changes to above address.

Titles in this Series

For a list of additional titles in this series, please visit:
http://www.igi-global.com/book-series/advances-human-services-public-health/102256

Regulating Human Rights, Social Security, and Socio-Economic Structures in a Global Perspective
Emilia Alaverdov (Georgian Technical University, Georgia) and Muhammad Waseem Bari (Government College University, Faisalabad, Pakistan)
Information Science Reference • © 2022 • 327pp • H/C (ISBN: 9781668446201) • US $215.00

Assessing the Effects of Emerging Plastics on the Environment and Public Health
Sung Hee Joo (University of Seoul, South Korea)
Engineering Science Reference • © 2022 • 441pp • H/C (ISBN: 9781799897231) • US $240.00

Global Dimensions of Democracy and Human Rights Problems and Perspectives
Nika Chitadze (International Black Sea University, Georgia)
Information Science Reference • © 2022 • 345pp • H/C (ISBN: 9781668445433) • US $215.00

Modern Challenges and Approaches to Humanitarian Engineering
Yiannis Koumpouros (University of West Attica, Greece) Angelos Georgoulas (University of West Attica, Greece) and Georgia Kremmyda (University of Warwick, UK)
Engineering Science Reference • © 2022 • 321pp • H/C (ISBN: 9781799891901) • US $240.00

Societal Resilience and Response to Contagious Diseases and Pandemics
Amal Adel Abdrabo (Faculty of Education, Alexandria University, Egypt) and Aly Abdel Razek Galaby (Faculty of Arts, Alexandria University, Egypt)
Information Science Reference • © 2022 • 344pp • H/C (ISBN: 9781799889731) • US $240.00

For an entire list of titles in this series, please visit:
http://www.igi-global.com/book-series/advances-human-services-public-health/102256

IGI Global
PUBLISHER of TIMELY KNOWLEDGE

701 East Chocolate Avenue, Hershey, PA 17033, USA
Tel: 717-533-8845 x100 • Fax: 717-533-8661
E-Mail: cust@igi-global.com • www.igi-global.com

Editorial Advisory Board

Table of Contents

Detailed Table of Contents

Utility services represent economic activities of special social importance, as they determine the quality of people's everyday work and life. The local self-governments need to provide utility services of acceptable scope and quality for their citizens. Among them, supplying the population with hygienically correct drinking water is one of the main tasks, but also an indicator of sustainability. The aim of this chapter is to investigate the current state of the public utility systems in the Republic of Serbia and consider their future perspectives. The secondary goal of this work is the analysis of sustainability trends related to SDG 6 in the Republic of Serbia. The main conclusion of the work is that there is certain significant progress in transformation and reorganization in the water sector, as well as positive progress in reaching the SDG 6 target, but further institutional and legislative reform is necessary as well as an increase in the volume of investments.

This chapter deals with a topic that has been publicly debated in the North Macedonia in the last few years. The public utility companies are constantly in debt and with consistently poor quality of services. Hence, the main focus of the public debate is how to identify the causes of the persistent poor situation and how to overcome these problems facing the public utility systems. The primary aim of this chapter is to give an overview of the state in which public utility systems operate. Also, this chapter gives an overview of the importance of the institutional environment and decentralization and their impact on public utilities systems. At the end of the chapter, the sustainability of public utility companies and the financing of utility services and covering costs are presented.

The chapter provides an overview of the origin and development of the public utility system through different epochs in the development of human civilization. The old century is characterized by the emergence of significant architectural achievements related to the public utility system. The darkest period in the history of human civilization was the Middle Ages, in which there was stagnation in the development of the public utility system. In the new century, the process of planning in cities and equipping them with communal infrastructure all over the world begins. The modern public utility system is characterized by the application of the latest technologies, innovations, and knowledge to improve the quality of life of the population and the effects of environmental protection, which requires monitoring through the development of performance indicators. The methodological framework of this research is based on cluster analysis using Ward's method, where the selected countries will be grouped into clusters.

This chapter discusses best transparency and integrity practices and methods from a literature review of multilateral governments worldwide, emphasizing public utility systems. Corruption and organizational malpractices are commonplace in government and public entities, as well as the private and not-for-profit sectors. This chapter highlights the importance of an adequate understanding and implementation of transparency and integrity methods in the public utility sector. Moreover, it reviews how stakeholders like governments, utility companies, the private sector, not-for-profit entities, and citizens could create an environment of trust and transparency to fight corruption and other unwarranted practices. This chapter also explores the implementation of transparency and integrity programs in countries in South America and Africa.

The city is an invention of human civilization that is distinguished, among other things, by the presence of infrastructure systems that assist public utility management. Globally, there is a growing awareness of the vital role that water and waste management play in sustainable development. The sustainable management of utility systems is unquestionably in the public and state interest. Therefore, this chapter presents current good practices and general ideas that constitute a foundation for beginning sustainable water and municipal waste management efforts in any activity. It also discusses the fundamental ways of improving sustainability in the municipal waste and water supply management sectors.

Transboundary lakes have always played a significant role in the development prospects and welfare of border areas. The international hydrological basin of the Prespa Lake, a protected area in three neighboring countries, Greece, Albania, and North Macedonia, is a typical example of a transboundary lake basin of exceptional importance. The empirical investigation of transboundary water management and sustainability cooperation in the Prespa, which adds to the limited international research in transboundary lakes, was carried out via six structured interviews, two per country, to identify the strengths and weaknesses as well as the opportunities and threats in the Prespa basin, and highlight the significance of transboundary cooperation towards sustainable development and social prosperity between riparian Municipalities. The results obtained have significant implications for all stakeholders in the Prespa basin, as they highlight the need to organize joint actions and generate new development strategies and products, such as alternative forms of tourism.

Since education is the most influential factor of a sustainable society and the fourth UN Sustainable Development Goal (SDG) promotes the importance of the quality of education, the chapter proposes the tripartite research method. Firstly, a qualitative analysis of the sustainability and efficiency of the education system is conducted. Secondly, an assessment of the efficiency of 31 European education systems is provided by applying the benefit of the doubt approach. Thirdly, the ranking of the education systems in question was conducted according to the criterion of their efficiency. The research illuminates that 40% of analyzed education systems are above the threshold when it comes to the indicators of education efficiency. Having in mind that the research database exploited in this research is grounded on the indicators from SDG4, the data-based conclusions from this chapter support education systems' reforms targeted at upbringing their efficiency, inclusion, equality, and finally, sustainability as a public service.

Local governments in Bulgaria have stable property rights regulated by the Constitution (1991) and the Municipal Property Act (1996). Municipalities own and use different types of assets to provide public services to local communities, but the effectiveness of local financial management is a controversial and topical issue. This chapter aims to analyze the financial performance of 18 large municipal companies for the period 2006-2020 by applying the Z-Score model. The results show that most municipal companies achieve profitability while providing a wide range of public services, such as water supply and sanitation, garbage collection, maintenance of urban infrastructure, management of municipal markets, construction supervision, investor and technical control, property management, geodetic services, and security services. At the same time, the municipal companies that provide district heating and urban transport and operate the municipal sports complexes are in poor financial condition and need appropriate measures to improve their financial performance.

In the last two decades, the public utility companies in North Macedonia are becoming more and more dysfunctional, and the services they offer are continuously of lower quality. Subsequently, they became a training ground for political-party employment and calculations. Hence, there is a need to find an efficient model that will overcome the problems faced by public utilities. The purpose of this chapter is to give an overview of the possibilities for public-private partnerships as a solution for improving the services and efficiency of utility companies. Finding an efficient solution for managing public utility companies is of great importance, both for citizens who regularly pay for utility services and do not receive them with adequate quality and for the Government of the Republic of North Macedonia, which at certain intervals must intervene financially with funds from the budget to be able to discharge the over-indebted utility companies.

Public utility service providers are expected to perform positively, with reduced prices and without losses that could put pressure on the local self-government budget. The global energy crisis has had negative impacts on public utility services in the Republic of Serbia. Many public companies, including those in the heating sector, have faced operational problems and rising business costs. The local self-governments, however, are obligated to ensure the availability of utility products and the distribution and supply of heating to their citizens. By considering the fundamental features of fiscal federalism, this chapter will analyze the pricing strategy of the heating company in Leskovac. The main objective of the work is to examine the impact of increasing energy prices on heating prices. Based on the results and indicators, conclusions are drawn, and recommendations are given for further research in the field of operations of public utility companies with the aim of overcoming the consequences of the energy crisis as easily as possible.

In the contemporary circumstances, one of the greatest challenges companies are facing is the identification of environmental costs, both due to the lack of a unique classification and accounting coverage and because they occur when taking or not taking measures related to and relevant to environmental protection. Neglecting the ecological aspect of business increases the risk of a discrepancy between the consumption of natural resources and their limited availability. In order to cope with the constantly growing competition in modern business conditions, companies need an adequate information base. This information base is provided by environmental management accounting. It is focused on the use and management of natural resources and environmental costs as well as identifying the responsibility of individuals and the entire company for activities that are carried out to improve the environment. The aim of the chapter is to point out the role and importance of environmental accounting and especially management accounting for sustainable business development.

The world has seen many pandemics; however, COVID-19 provoked global emergencies at an unprecedented scale in all aspects of life. Despite of recent advances in learning management systems and online education tools, one of the worst disruptions experienced was in the delivery of education. To keep students safe, most educational institutions were closed at the onset of the pandemic. At the peak of the crisis, ~90% of learners worldwide had their education disrupted. The policies were based on social distancing and the use of personal protection. However, the negative impacts of long-term isolation were not articulated. It is likely that there may be similar emergencies in the future. How can we use exponential technologies and innovations for the effective delivery of education? Guided by the lessons learned from the impact of school closures, assessment of remote learning, and the fact that education delivery should be continuous, the authors explore how different research perspectives and evidence gathered can help strengthen policy reflections and future planning for improving efficiency.

The chapter aims to review the existing concepts of the sustainable development within the logistics industry, analyze them, and provide recommendations for further improvement. Special emphasis is placed on the concept of green logistics, together with perspectives on future development in this area. Great potential in solving the sustainability problem is identified in the concept of circular economy and reverse logistics, whose elements and potentials are discussed in detail. The chapter provides answers to the research questions: RQ1: What are the potential ways to improve the sustainability of the logistics sector? and RQ2: What are the risks and threats to implementing sustainable logistics? A key contribution is reflected in the conception of the SWOT matrix for applying the concept of green logistics, highlighting the strengths, weaknesses, opportunities, and threats for the implementation of this concept based on the literature review and current experience.

Waste disposal is one of the main environmental problems facing society today. Environmental impacts of solid waste landfilling include loss of land area, contamination of soil, leaching of hazardous substances to groundwater, as well as emissions of methane to the atmosphere. The world generates over 2 billion tonnes of municipal solid waste (MSW) each year, with at least 33% of that not managed in an environmentally safe manner. In many developed countries, municipal solid wastes (MSW) are dumped in sanitary landfills, while in many developing countries, they are dumped in an inappropriate way which poses a serious threat to the environment. The deficiency of land and the requirement for reuse of the landfill sites demand their rehabilitation. In recent years, phytoremediation has been used as an efficient, environmentally friendly, and cost-effective technology in the remediation and rehabilitation of contaminated sites, including municipal solid waste (MSW) landfills.

Preface

Dysenteria et cholera,

cum parum valetudinis curandae aquae hygiene coniunguntur,

sunt notabiles causae praematura mortalitatis.

This Latin phrase can briefly synthesize the research and conclusions reached by John Snow in the 19th century, analyzing the causes of the frequent occurrence of cholera and dysentery in London. When this famous scientist began to analyze the causes and vectors of transmission of water-borne diseases, he probably did not have in mind that he made an outstanding contribution to the development of modern public utility systems, primarily from the perspective of public hygiene, which somehow lost its importance during the Middle Ages. His research inspired fundamental changes in London's public water supply and sewage system, which led to similar modifications in other cities and paramount improvements in public hygiene worldwide, marking the beginning of modern public utilities.

Bearing the previous statement in mind, an efficient, effective, reliable, continual, and sustainable public utility system is a prerequisite for the social well-being of modern human society, but also for the protection of the living environment in urban areas. This is especially important in the era of intense urbanization, where the percentage of the population in urban agglomerations is constantly growing, which creates new challenges in the domain of meeting essential human needs, on the one hand, and effective environmental protection, on the other. As an adequate mechanism for meeting such dual needs of society, the public utility system has long been recognized as a necessary element of human communities. However, bearing in mind the already mentioned effects of urbanization, climate change, but also changes in the habits and needs of the average member of a modern household, consumerism, new technologies, novel products, and therefore emergent pollutants, the necessity of transformation and reorganization of public utility services in the context of an effective response to modern challenges is a necessity.

Considering that no social activity is perfect, it is important to identify the shortcomings in the public utility system and define the initial steps of its transformation and reorganization. This is primarily important considering that the average share of utility activities within the economic potential of a given country is represented by a significant two to five percent. Also, if we look at households as direct or indirect users of public utility services, we can easily define the conclusion that utility expenses at the level of the household budget can very easily overload the financial stability of the average family. Therefore, it is very important to implement an effective policy of improving the work of public utility services, which can lead to an increase in the contribution of public utility activities to the well-being either of the state in general or individuals, that is, end-users of public utility services and products.

Public utility systems include technical-technological resources, but also organizational and legal elements aimed at improving the quality of life in the territory of a certain local self-government unit. An efficient and effective public utility system is essential in every large city, small municipality, or village (which may also have a certain, rudimentary public utility system, primarily due to burial needs). Moreover, the importance of public utility systems, i.e. public hygiene, became even more important during the pandemic caused by the Covid-19 virus, given that the local self-government unit, among other issues, is obliged to take care of the prevention of the spread of infectious diseases, regardless of the origin, intensity, and virulence of the pathogen.

For several of the previously mentioned reasons, this publication is dedicated to the multidimensional nature of public utility systems and emphasizes the importance of holistic management with a focus on sustainability functions. One of the additional values of this publication is the review of the elements of transformation and reorganization of the public utility system, in order to improve its efficiency. Elements of transformation are especially significant for countries undergoing structural, political, economic, and cultural transition, but also for those that intensify the technical-technological and informational aspects of the modification of public services. No less important is the fact that the organization of the book follows the need of improving the work of communal services from the perspective of social well-being, but also from the standpoint of the protection of the living environment in urban areas above all.

OBJECTIVES OF THE BOOK

Much remains to be known about public utility systems organization, efficiency, management, legislation, practices, and solutions worldwide, as well as the implications for sustainable development in different countries. Thus, a better understanding of the different management practices in public utilities across different contexts is needed to assess their impact on efficiency and sustainability, especially in the changed climate conditions, which represents a scientific gap that is partially filled by the publication of this book.

Contributors of this publication debated the importance of efficient management of public utility systems, with respect to the exchange of best practices and knowledge. The publication certainly adds value in sharing knowledge among different stakeholders to provide answers to the ongoing concerns in the changed climate conditions regarding the transformation, development, and sustainability of public utility systems.

ORGANIZATION OF THE BOOK

The book contains 14 chapters. The chapters in the book are informally organized in such a way that the first half of the book gives the most general guidelines on the organization of communal activities at the level of selected countries, an overview of the history and development as well as the importance of a certain number of concrete communal activities, while the second half of the book provides multidimensional reviews of various influential aspects in this area - economic aspects, decentralization, transition, etc.

Chapter 1, by Dejan Vasović, Tamara Rađenović, and Snežana Živković from Serbia, emphasizes that utility services represent economic activities of special social importance, as they determine the quality of peoples' everyday work and life. The local self-governments need to provide utility services of acceptable scope and quality for their citizens. Among them, supplying the population with hygienically correct drinking water is one of the main tasks, but also an indicator of sustainability. The aim of this chapter is to investigate the current state of the public utility systems in the Republic of Serbia and consider their future perspectives. The secondary goal of this work is the analysis of sustainability trends related to SDG 6 in the Republic of Serbia. The main conclusion of the work is that there is certain significant progress in transformation and reorganization in the water sector, as well as positive progress in reaching the SDG 6 target, but further institutional and legislative reform is necessary, as well as an increase in the volume of investments.

Chapter 2, by Samoil Malcheski and Jordan Gjorcev from North Macedonia, highlights that public utility companies are constantly in debt and with consistently poor quality of services in the Republic of Macedonia. Hence, the main focus of the public debate is how to identify the causes of the persistent poor situation and how to overcome these problems facing the public utility systems. The primary aim of this chapter is to give an overview of the state in which public utility systems operate. Also, this chapter gives an overview of the importance of the institutional environment and decentralization and their impact on public utility systems. At the end of the chapter, the sustainability of public utility companies and the financing of utility services and covering costs are presented.

Chapter 3, by Žarko Vranjanac and Žarko Rađenović from Serbia, provides an overview of the origin and development of the public utility system through different epochs in the development of human civilization. The old century is characterized by the emergence of significant architectural achievements related to the public utility system. The darkest period in the history of human civilization was the Middle Ages, in which there was stagnation in the development of the public utility system. In the new century, the process of planning in cities and equipping them with communal infrastructure all over the world begins. The modern public utility system is characterized by the application of the latest technologies, innovations, and knowledge to improve the quality of life of the population and the effects of environmental protection, which requires monitoring through the development of performance indicators. The methodological framework of this research is based on cluster analysis using Ward's method, where the selected countries are grouped into clusters.

Chapter 4, by Carlos Andrés Merlano from Colombia, discusses best transparency and integrity practices and methods from a literature review of multilateral governments worldwide, emphasizing public utility systems. Corruption and organizational malpractices are commonplace in government and public entities, as well as the private and not-for-profit sectors. This chapter highlights the importance of an adequate understanding and implementation of transparency and integrity methods in the public utility sector. Moreover, it reviews how stakeholders like governments, utility companies, the private sector, not-for-profit entities, and citizens could create an environment of trust and transparency to fight corruption and other unwarranted practices. This chapter also explores the implementation of transparency and integrity programs in countries in South America and Africa.

Chapter 5, by Sandra Stanković and Natalija Petrović from Serbia, highlights that the city is an invention of human civilization that is distinguished, among other things, by the presence of infrastructure systems that assist public utility management. Globally, there is a growing awareness of the vital role that water and waste management play in sustainable development. The sustainable management of utility systems is unquestionably in the public and state interest. Therefore, this chapter presents current good practices and general ideas that constitute a foundation for beginning sustainable water and municipal waste management efforts in any activity. It also discusses the fundamental ways of improving sustainability in the municipal waste and water supply management sectors.

Chapter 6, by Georgios Damianos from Greece, underlines that the transboundary lakes have always played a significant role in the development prospects and welfare of border areas. The international hydrological basin of the Prespa Lake, a protected area in three neighboring countries, Greece, Albania, and North Macedonia, is a typical example of a transboundary lake basin of exceptional importance. The empirical investigation of transboundary water management and sustainability cooperation in the Prespa, which adds to the limited international research in transboundary lakes, was carried out via six structured interviews, two per country, to identify the strengths and weaknesses as well as the opportunities and threats in the Prespa basin and highlight the significance of transboundary cooperation towards sustainable development and social prosperity between riparian Municipalities. The obtained results have significant implications for all stakeholders in the Prespa basin, as they highlight the need to organize joint actions and generate new development strategies and products, such as alternative forms of tourism.

Chapter 7, by Bojan Krstić, Milica Jovanović Vujatović, Ivana Marjanovic, Sandra Milanović, and Georgios Tsaples from Serbia and Greece, highlights that education is the most influential factor of a sustainable society and hence, proposes the tripartite research method. Firstly, a qualitative analysis of the sustainability and efficiency of the education system is conducted. Secondly, an assessment of the efficiency of 31 European education systems is provided by applying the Benefit of the Doubt approach. Thirdly, the ranking of the education systems in question was conducted according to the criterion of their efficiency. The research illuminates that 40% of analyzed education systems are above the threshold when it comes to the indicators of education efficiency. Having in mind that the research database exploited in this research is grounded on the indicators from SDG4, the data-based conclusions from this chapter support education systems' reforms targeted at upbringing their efficiency, inclusion, equality, and, finally, sustainability as a public service.

Chapter 8, by Desislava Stoilova from Bulgaria, aims to analyze the financial performance of 18 large municipal companies in Bulgaria for the period 2006-2020 by applying the Z-Score model. Local governments in Bulgaria have stable property rights regulated by the Constitution (1991) and the Municipal Property Act (1996). Municipalities own and use different types of assets to provide public services to local communities, but the effectiveness of local financial management is a controversial and topical issue. The results show that most municipal companies achieve profitability while providing a wide range of public services, such as water supply and sanitation, garbage collection, maintenance of urban infrastructure, management of municipal markets, construction supervision, investor and technical control, property management, geodetic services, and security services. At the same time, the municipal companies that provide district heating and urban transport and operate the municipal sports complexes are in poor financial condition and need appropriate measures to improve their financial performance.

Chapter 9, by Pavlina Stojanova and Lence Petreska from North Macedonia, focuses on the public utility companies in North Macedonia. Namely, they have become more and more dysfunctional, and the services they offer are continuously of lower quality. Subsequently, they became a training ground for political-party employment and calculations. Hence, there is a need to find an efficient model that will overcome the problems faced by public utilities. The purpose of this chapter is to give an overview of the possibilities for public-private partnerships as a solution for improving the services and efficiency of utility companies. Finding an efficient solution for managing public utility companies is of great importance, both for citizens who regularly pay for utility services and do not receive them with adequate quality and for the Government of the Republic of North Macedonia, which at certain intervals must intervene financially with funds from the Budget to be able to discharge the over-indebted utility companies.

Chapter 10, by Jadranka Đurović Todorović, Marina Đorđević, and Milica Ristić Cakić from Serbia, emphasizes that the public utility service providers are expected to perform positively, with reduced prices and without losses that could put pressure on the local self-government budget. The global energy crisis has had negative impacts on public utility services in the Republic of Serbia. Many public companies, including those in the heating sector, have faced operational problems and rising business costs. The local self-governments, however, are obligated to ensure the availability of utility products and the distribution and supply of heating to their citizens. By considering the fundamental features of fiscal federalism, this paper will analyze the pricing strategy of the heating company in Leskovac. The main objective of the work is to examine the impact of increasing energy prices on heating prices. Based on the results and indicators, conclusions are drawn, and recommendations are given for further research in the field of operations of public utility companies with the aim of overcoming the consequences of the energy crisis as easily as possible.

Chapter 11, by Bojana Novićević Čečević, Milica Đorđević, and Marina Stanojević from Serbia, highlights the importance of environmental accounting and especially management accounting for sustainable business development. In contemporary circumstances, one of the greatest challenges companies are facing is the identification of environmental costs, both due to the lack of a unique classification and accounting coverage and because they occur when taking or not taking measures related to and relevant to environmental protection. Neglecting the ecological aspect of business increases the risk of a discrepancy between the consumption of natural resources and their limited availability. In order to cope with the constantly growing competition in modern business conditions, companies need an adequate information base. This information base is provided by environmental management accounting. It is focused on the use and management of natural resources and environmental costs, as well as identifying the responsibility of individuals and the entire company for activities that are carried out to improve the environment.

Chapter 12, by Ashok Vaseashta, Carmen Maftei, and Dorin Radu from the United States and Romania, points towards the global emergencies provoked by COVID-19 at an unprecedented scale in all aspects of life. Despite recent advances in learning management systems and online education tools, one of the worst disruptions experienced was in the delivery of education. To keep students safe, most educational institutions were closed at the onset of the pandemic. At the peak of the crisis, ~90% of learners worldwide had their education disrupted. The policies were based on social distancing and the use of personal protection. However, the negative impacts of long-term isolation were not articulated. It is likely that there may be similar emergencies in the future. How can we use exponential technologies and innovations for the effective delivery of education? Guided by the lessons learned from the impact of school closures, assessment of remote learning, and the fact that education delivery should be continuous, authors explore how different research perspectives and evidence gathered can help strengthen policy reflections and future planning for improving efficiency.

Chapter 13, by Filip Bugarčić and Vladimir Mićić from Serbia, aims to review the existing concepts of sustainable development within the logistics industry, analyze them and provide recommendations for further improvement. Special emphasis is placed on the concept of green logistics, together with perspectives on future development in this area. Great potential in solving the sustainability problem is identified in the concept of circular economy and reverse logistics, whose elements and potentials are discussed in detail. The paper provides answers to research question RQ1: What are the potential ways to improve the sustainability of the logistics sector? and RQ2: What are the risks and threats to implementing sustainable logistics? A key contribution is reflected in the conception of the SWOT matrix for applying the concept of green logistics, highlighting the strengths, weaknesses, opportunities, and threats for the implementation of this concept based on the literature review and current experience.

Chapter 14, by Tatjana Golubović and Sreten Ilić from Serbia, highlights the fact that waste disposal is one of the main environmental problems facing society today. Environmental impacts of solid waste landfilling include loss of land area, contamination of soil, leaching of hazardous substances to groundwater as well as emissions of methane to the atmosphere. The world generates over 2 billion tonnes of municipal solid waste each year, with at least 33 percent of that not managed in an environmentally safe manner. In many developed countries, municipal solid wastes are dumped in sanitary landfills, while in many developing countries, they are dumped in an inappropriate way which poses a serious threat to the environment. The deficiency of land and the requirement for reuse of the landfill sites demand their rehabilitation. In recent years phytoremediation has been used as a well-efficient, environmentally friendly, and cost-effective technology in the remediation and rehabilitation of contaminated sites, including municipal solid waste landfills.

The target audience for this publication is very diverse. Given the wide range of topics covered in the book, this book provides a paramount resource for managers and engineers of public utility organizations, as well as for competent representatives in local self-government units, other professionals, researchers, students, and end-user organizations. Moreover, this book is exploring different experiences within this area throughout the world, thereby providing potential guidelines for the creation of strategic directions for the transformation and reorganization of communal activities, which the editors and authors are well aware of.

The process of editing this publication was very challenging, but also very inspiring, which gives us confidence that potential users of this publication will have the opportunity to become more familiar with public activities seen from different perspectives.

It is no less important to emphasize our gratitude to the publishing house IGI Global, which had enough patience, understanding, and support for the realization of this publishing project.

Deeply grateful editors of the book:

Jordan Gjorchev
International Slavic University, North Macedonia

Samoil Malcheski
International Slavic University, North Macedonia

Tamara Rađenović
University of Niš, Serbia

Dejan Vasović
University of Niš, Serbia

Snežana Živković
University of Niš, Serbia

Acknowledgment

We would like to express our deep gratitude to the authors, reviewers, Editorial Advisory Board members, and copy editors who devoted their knowledge, time, and efforts to make this book an outstanding piece of literature in the area of Public Utility Systems.

First, our truthful gratefulness goes to the chapters' authors, who devoted their knowledge and expertise to this book project.

Second, we are grateful for the respectful contributions of the reviewers, who provided their competencies and proficiency to advance the chapters' quality, consistency, and clarity.

Third, we would like to acknowledge the profound support of the Editorial Advisory Board, who contributed immeasurable assistance and experience in completing the content of the book.

Fourth, we highly appreciate the continued assistance of the Editorial Department of IGI Global.

Finally, our endless appreciation goes to the copy editors – Assistant Professor Katerina Vidova from the International Slavic University, Faculty of Economics, and Associate Professor Ivana Ćirković Miladinović from the University of Kragujevac, Faculty of Education in Jagodina, who proofread the chapters.

Jordan Gjorchev
International Slavic University, North Macedonia

Samoil Malcheski
International Slavic University, North Macedonia

Tamara Rađenović
University of Niš, Serbia

Dejan Vasović
University of Niš, Serbia

Snežana Živković
University of Niš, Serbia

Chapter 1
Public Utility Systems in the Republic of Serbia:
Current State and Future Perspectives With Particular Regard to Economic Issues and SDG 6 Targets

Dejan Vasović
https://orcid.org/0000-0003-4043-8093
University of Niš, Serbia

Snežana Živković
https://orcid.org/0000-0002-7931-9334
University of Niš, Serbia

Tamara Rađenović
https://orcid.org/0000-0003-1632-7772
University of Niš, Serbia

ABSTRACT

Utility services represent economic activities of special social importance, as they determine the quality of people's everyday work and life. The local self-governments need to provide utility services of acceptable scope and quality for their citizens. Among them, supplying the population with hygienically correct drinking water is one of the main tasks, but also an indicator of sustainability. The aim of this chapter is to investigate the current state of the public utility systems in the Republic of Serbia and consider their future perspectives. The secondary goal of this work is the analysis of sustainability trends related to SDG 6 in the Republic of Serbia. The main conclusion of the work is that there is certain significant progress in transformation and reorganization in the water sector, as well as positive progress in reaching the SDG 6 target, but further institutional and legislative reform is necessary as well as an increase in the volume of investments.

DOI: 10.4018/978-1-6684-7730-4.ch001

INTRODUCTION

Utility services encompass numerous services which are important for the realization of the life needs of citizens and legal entities, where the local self-government is obliged to create conditions for ensuring appropriate quality, scope, availability and continuity, as well as supervision over their performance (Negrut et al., 2023). According to Article 2 of the Serbian Law on Utility Services, public utility services involve:

1) supply of drinking water;
2) purification and drainage of atmospheric and wastewater;
3) production, distribution and supply of thermal energy;
4) municipal waste management;
5) urban and suburban passenger transport;
6) management of cemeteries and burials;
   6a) funeral services;
7) management of public parking lots;
8) provision of public lighting;
9) management of markets;
10) maintenance of streets and roads;
11) maintenance of cleanliness in public areas;
12) maintenance of public green areas;
13) chimney services;
14) zoo-hygiene services.

A utility system is established to satisfy the various utility needs of citizens and other users, thus fulfilling the public interest (Jedynak & Wąsowicz, 2021). It consists of three key components: national regulatory framework, the accountability of the local self-governments, and citizens' needs (Filipović & Krnjeta, 2017). These components need to be aligned to enable the utility system to function properly. Any disturbances in each of these components lead to the utility system disbalance and cause serious problems in regard to the satisfaction of the public utility needs. This implies that utility companies are only one part of the utility system, which is much more complex (European Commission, 2011). Utility system consists not only of the utility companies (which provide the utility services) and decision makers but also of the unsatisfied utility needs of citizens and other users (Filipović & Krnjeta, 2017).

Hence, the local self-governments are obliged to provide the availability of utility services to their citizens and residents. The local self-government establishes a public company to which it assigns the provision of utility services or assigns it to an entrepreneur in accordance with the law or regulations adopted by the assembly of that local self-government (Voorn et al., 2017). When two or more units of local self-government determine interest in the joint provision of utility services, the city council of each of those local self-government units makes a decision to prepare a justification study for such a decision. The chain of accountability is straightforward and clear. Local self-governments are responsible for organizing and developing utility systems, public utility companies are responsible for providing utility services, and citizens and other service users have an obligation and responsibility to make their contribution to the whole system, primarily through bill payment, but also through other activities which are essential for the entire system and its sustainability (Filipović & Krnjeta, 2017).

Many problems in the functioning of the public utility systems in the Republic of Serbia have raised concerns among researchers and practitioners regarding the transformation of these systems towards efficiency and sustainability in the provision of utility services. Thus, this paper sheds some light on the current state and future perspectives of the public utility systems in the Republic of Serbia. In this sense, this chapter is stewarded to the analysis of the current public utility system state and future challenges with particular regard to economic awareness and SDG 6 achievement. The key objectives of this chapter are aimed at a narrative description of emerging challenges, financial issues related to the public utilities and practical experiences with such systems transformation and reorganization in the Republic of Serbia. Also, this paper aims to identify the relationships between the selected SDG 6 targets and national achievements based on a literature review and correlation analysis of the achievements within the SDG 6 targets and indicators for the Republic of Serbia, where the source of data is derived from the national SDGs progress reports.

BACKGROUND

The current system of public utility services in the Republic of Serbia exhibits many problems. The delivery of public utility and communal services does not conform to a decentralized, market environment. The main reason is that the practical autonomy of local self-governments is not sufficient yet. A lack of local experience is needed for autonomy, and regulations do not contain enough incentives. Service providers do not operate in a real market-based system of incentives; thus, market financing methods cannot be applied. Namely, a great part of the utility services is not organized based on the market competition principles. Still, it represents a pure monopoly structure where services are provided "at reduced costs, which is impossible in a situation with several market participants when costs of providing services are much higher" (Radukić et al., 2018, p. 30). Public service providers are obliged to deliver utility services to end users concerning social aspects, that is often in collision with the economic aspects of the business (Hefetz & Werner, 2012). On one side, the public utility service providers are expected to have positive performance, without losses to additionally pressure the local self-government budget, while on the other side, these companies are viewed as the social pillar for the protection of citizens' well-being through the reduced prices of utility services (Filipović & Krnjeta, 2013).

Another issue is the very high entry barriers for the potential utility service providers due to the high sunk costs of founding the water, sewage, heating, etc. infrastructure, thus making establishing competition in this segment of the market impossible or economically totally unjustifiable and puts existing public utility companies practically in the position of a monopolist (Filipović & Krnjeta, 2017). This monopolistic position has a negative impact on the organization of public utility companies, as managers do not put enough effort into the relationship with service users as buyers. As a result, the quality of utility services is diminished. Also, the managers do not have a sense for defining and effective implementation of development plans and programs, as they do not have the need for it.

In relation to the local service providers, the local government system is politically biased, causing significant over-employment and a politically directed price setting. The main obstacle to adequate service delivery is the lack of linkage between local self-governments (as principals) and service providers (as agents). There is a lack of practical knowledge about the output of services and the calculation of a single activity's total cost. Management methods are not appropriate, and the required experience for the formation of economic incentives is missing. Sustainable management of public utility service providers entails a complex set of specific economic, social and environmental constraints, which determine the cost and revenues of both, the utility companies and the end users (Del Borghi et al., 2013; Cabrera et al., 2013). Often, the utility service providers transfer the difficulties they face in the business operations to the end users, who consequently end up with either diminished service quality or increased service prices (Radukić et al., 2018).

REFLECTION ON THE CURRENT STATE OF PUBLIC UTILITIES IN THE REPUBLIC OF SERBIA

As highlighted in the previous section, the double role of public companies in the domain of utility service provision has resulted in (Filipović & Krnjeta, 2013):

- insufficient level and quality of utility services, which not only jeopardize the short-term interest of service users but produce long-term damage through environmental degradation and irrational use of natural resources;

- socialization of losses of the public companies through increased public consumption, which is paid by the citizens and business entities of the local self-government in the final instance, through the local budget expenditures, thus spilling over the development part of the budget in the current consumption;
- incapacity to realize development programs in these companies, as only current liabilities and maintenance are covered by current income, while the system development is transferred to a higher level of responsibility - to the local self-governments or state government.

The current state of the public utility systems in the Republic of Serbia can be best observed through the data provided by the Ministry of Construction, Transport and Infrastructure (MCTI) in its yearly reports. As regards water in 2020, 677 million m^3 per year (about 21 m^3/s) is captured in the Republic of Serbia through the communal water systems, where about 65% of captured water is sent for consumption (437 million m^3 - 14 m^3/s): 48% (328 million m^3 per year ~ 10 m^3/s) for household consumption and 16% (109 million m^3 per year - 4 m^3/s) for consumption by industry and institutions, while about 35% (240 million m^3 - 7 m^3/s) of the captured water represents losses. Households consume about 75%, the industrial sector about 10%, and other users about 15% of the supplied water. The total length of the water supply network in 2020 was 48,337 km. (MCTI, 2021, p. 12).

As regards wastewater, about 4.2 million inhabitants (~61% of the population) are connected to the public systems for the collection, removal and purification of wastewater in the Republic of Serbia. The total length of sewage collectors is about 17,757 km. There are 46 wastewater treatment plants, out of which 30 are working, 3 are in the reconstruction phase, 5 are in trial operation, and 8 are not working due to outdated treatment technology. About 23% of the collected wastewater is purified to varying degrees, but there is also an estimate that less than 15% of the collected wastewater is properly purified. (MCTI, 2021, p. 16).

The average price of water for households in 2020 was 49.76 RSD per m^3, with a service price range of 1:3.6 - the minimum price was 24.6 RSD/m^3. The average price of sewage (collection, removal and purification) of wastewater for households in 2020 was 20.2 RSD per m^3, with a service price range of 1:12 - the minimum price was about 5.2 RSD/m^3. With these prices, water supply and sewerage companies cannot maintain the current level of services, nor withstand the changes awaiting them. (MCTI, 2021, p. 18). According to the research conducted by the KOMDEL in 2019, affordability constraints regarding water and sewage for households are limited to 2.25% of the average monthly household income, while the constraint of 5% of household income is viewed as the acceptable amount of costs that can be recovered from end users (KOMDEL, 2019, p. 4).

Figure 1. Business performance of public water and wastewater companies
Source: MCTI (2021, p. 20)

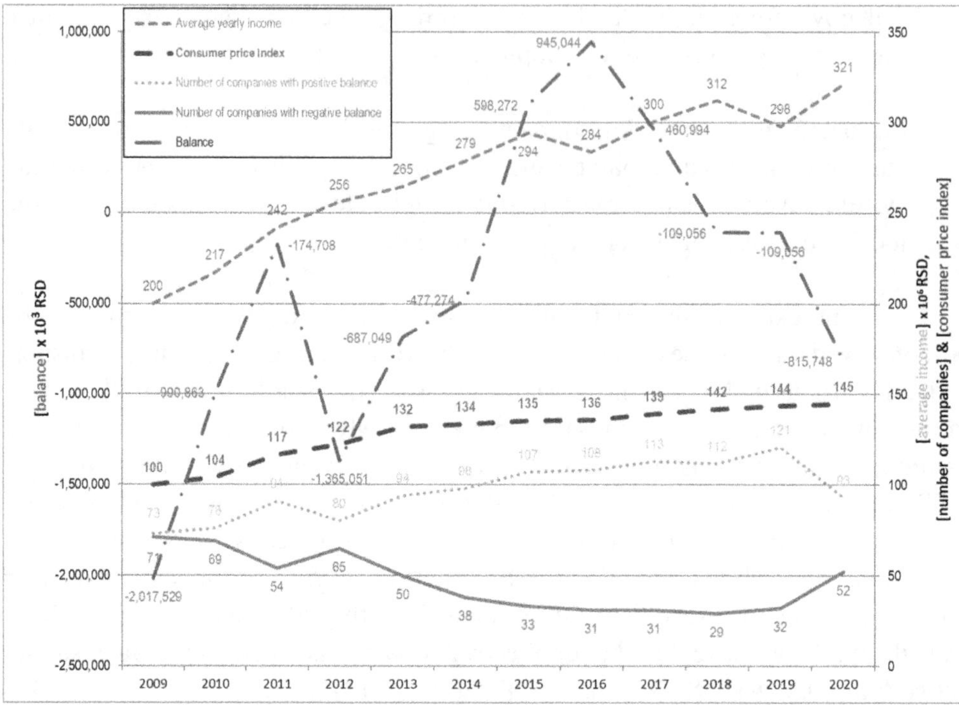

Based on Figure 1, it is evident that the multi-year total negative balance changes to positive in 2015, remains positive until 2017 and is negative again in 2018-2020. In this period, the specific income of the company grew slightly faster than the growth of consumer prices: 1.61 vs 1.45.

Regarding district heating in 2020 in the Republic of Serbia, there were 893,865 users, out of which 638,787 households and 28,822 business entities. The total amount of thermal energy produced was 20,149,747,343 MJ, out of which the total consumption in households was 13,885,992,738 MJ, while the total consumption by legal entities and entrepreneurs amounted to 3,635,322,532 MJ (MCTI, 2021, pp. 25, 29). The functioning of these systems is prone to technical problems that may arise, and the riskiest of them are those that cause halts in operation, which affect a large number of users. The problem in the supply of heat energy is caused by old and used boilers, as well as by the poor condition of the distribution network, which is prone to breakdowns.

The calculation of the delivered thermal energy is performed per square meter of the heating surface, or per consumed thermal energy, as defined by the Law on Energy Efficiency and Rational Use of Energy. Affordability constraints regarding heating prices for households reduced from a historical highest of 12.89% in 2012 to 11.66% in 2018. Although the affordability constraints are hard to determine in this sector, it is evident that the current heating prices are already at the maximum level which household budgets objectively can handle (KOMDEL, 2019, p. 5).

As regards waste management in 2020 in Serbia, there were 2,517,213 users, out of which 1,871,530 households and 112,136 business entities. The amount of collected municipal waste at the national level was 2,090,997 tons per year. The total amount of waste that was primarily or secondary separated for reuse during 2020 was 42,141 tons (MCTI, 2021, pp. 34-35).

Problems in the domain of waste management are mainly related to landfills. Namely, a large number of municipalities and cities still have their own landfills, which are already full, and most of them do not even meet the minimum technical standards. Besides, the land on which the landfills are located is usually owned by the Republic of Serbia. The age of landfills varies from 4 to 60 years. Data on the dimensions and volume of landfills are not reliable, given that there is no appropriate technical documentation for many of them. About 70% of active landfills are not projected in the spatial planning documents, and they do not have an environmental impact assessment study, nor do they have the necessary permits. Further, the uncontrolled discharge of landfill gas, generated by the decomposition of waste in the landfill, can cause fire or explosion. Landfill leachates are not collected or purified, which endangers underground, surface water, and soil due to the high content of organic material and heavy metals. There is no systematic monitoring of emissions, leachate, landfill gas, etc. (MCTI, 2021, p. 44).

The allocation of funds for waste management at the level of only 28 EUR per ton is way below the funds allocated in the EU countries and also in other less developed countries. It is not even enough to cover the operating costs for basic needs. The affordability constraints regarding waste management for households are currently limited at 0.6% of the average monthly household income, while the constraint of 1.5% of household income is viewed as the maximum acceptable amount of costs that can be recovered from end users. Therefore, upon the establishment of regional centers for waste treatment, primary separation networks, sanitary landfills, plants for secondary separation and mechanical biological treatment, prices will necessarily have to increase to at least 40-50 EUR per ton of generated waste in the next few years (KOMDEL, 2019, p. 3).

REFLECTION ON THE PUBLIC WATER SUPPLY AS PRIMARY PUBLIC UTILITY AND SUSTAINABLE DEVELOPMENT GOALS 6

The activity of water management represents a basic, but also very complex, activity of the state institutions responsible for it, most often aligned with the core principles of sustainable development, where the interests of society and the preservation of the functions of aquatic ecosystems are taken into account (Sharma et al., 2016). Integral management of water resources is a complex and difficult task, which includes extensive measures and activities aimed at maintaining and strengthening the elements of the water regime, ensuring the necessary amount of water of the required quality for various purposes (primarily key consumers), protecting water from pollution and protecting it from harmful, water-related events (Stanković et al., 2019). Natural conditions, social and economic frameworks, as well as legal regulations of the republic and local significance, play a dominant role in this system (Janaćković et al., 2018).

An efficient water management system requires appropriate institutional and organizational solutions that can, in terms of structures and capacity, meet the requirements of all stages of sustainable development and functioning of the water sector (Fulazzaky, 2014). Improvement of the situation in the water sector can only be ensured with the adequate implementation of the necessary, sustainable measures aimed at the current but strategic, long-term needs of consumers and the environment. Therefore, regulation, financial means, information systems, international cooperation and participating publics (stakeholders) represent a common basis of sustainability in the water sector (Velasco-Muñoz et al., 2018). The health and safety of drinking water intended for human usage should be achieved by a risk analysis of all elements in the public water supply system and the definition of drinking water quality standards. In the Republic of Serbia, there are several regulations governing water status (Law on public utilities, 2018; Law on water, 2018; Law on environmental protection, 2018). It regulates the legal status of water, integral water management, management of water facilities and water land, sources and methods of financing water activities, and other issues important for water management as aspects of sustainable development.

Nowadays, most countries exert a certain, often unsustainable, pressure on water resources (Vasović et al., 2016). The world's population is growing rapidly, but water resources are not, so estimates show that the world's population will reach a shortfall of about 40% between projected demand and available water supply by 2030 (UN-SDGs, 2022). It is well known that chronic water scarcity, hydrological uncertainty and extreme weather events are considered among the biggest threats to global prosperity and stability (Mancosu et al., 2015; Mekonnen & Hoekstra, 2016). Drinking water resources throughout the world are threatened, not only due to excessive use and inappropriate management but also due to increased environmental pollution and climate change adverse effects (Nhamo, 2018).

The increase in water consumption due to higher living standards, urbanization and industrialization has led to an increase in the amount of wastewater discharged into natural systems (Wada et al., 2011). Rivers and lakes cannot accept waste materials without seriously affecting the natural balance, which leads to intensive pollution of water resources and loss of quality water. Hence, the efficiency of environmental management systems in companies is essential for the minimization and elimination of damaging influences on the environment (Takić et al., 2013; Živković et al., 2013). Also, cleaner production is an efficient way of reducing waste materials and emission levels, while promoting a holistic approach to resources, production, economy and environment (Živković et al., 2016). Pollution of surface water also reduces the amount of hygienically correct underground water, which is most often used for drinking (Vasović et al., 2018b). In order to ensure sufficient quantities of healthy drinking water, it is necessary to make additional efforts related to its protection and saving. The importance of international cooperation in the management of limited water resources in the world must not be underestimated because water pollution knows no borders (Vasović et al., 2018a).

In the context of international relations, one of the most important recognitions of the UN in the field of human rights is the right to water and sanitation (WHO, 2012, 2017). The UN recognizes and acknowledges the right of every person to have access to a sufficient amount of water for personal and domestic use (between 50 and 100 liters of water per person per day), which must be continuous, economically acceptable, hygienically correct and physically available (Fonseca et al., 2020). This is to be achieved by the implementation of various structural and non-structural measures. Having this in mind, it is also necessary to stress the role/importance of education for sustainable water resources management, which is no longer matter of discussion (Kioupi & Voulvoulis, 2019).

So far, seventeen sustainable development goals have been defined, which should be achieved by 2030 through the implementation of global agreements and concrete actions at the level of countries that have accepted these goals. All 17 sustainable development goals are related to the thematic areas of the UNDP Strategic Plan, which are actually:

1. sustainable development,
2. democratic management,
3. peacebuilding, and
4. resilience to climate changes and disasters.

Indirectly, all the goals of sustainable development are related to the preservation of the environment and existing resources, that is, the quality of life that exists today. Their implementation is voluntary and takes into account the different national realities, capacities and levels of development of the member states of the United Nations while respecting national policies and priorities. In order to monitor progress, measurable indicators suitable for all spheres of sustainable development have been introduced. As far as the progress in achieving the goals of sustainable development is concerned, specifically thematic unit 6, which refers to water management, it is extremely important to note that there is no success in achieving the goals of sustainable development without a responsible, reliable and efficient communal system, i.e., communal activities related to the supply of drinking water to the population and removal and treatment of wastewater. In the Republic of Serbia, there are 14 communal activities (public utilities) recognized by the Law of Public Utilities, where public water supply and sewerage system represents one of the basic, essential utilities, whereas observed in terms of environmental performance, the number of employees, financial means, etc.

The methodology for monitoring progress in the field of sustainable development goals in the Republic of Serbia relies on the Eurostat Methodology. Progress is measured through a compound annual growth rate, with the following categories: significant progress, moderate progress, moderate movement away, significant movement away, trend tracking not possible (for example, due to short time series or lack of data), inconsistent trends - progress is registered against one (sub)indicator, while movement away from the goal is registered against another, and goal achieved category (The Statistical Office of the Republic of Serbia - SORS, 2022).

In general, SDG 6 goal calls for the availability and sustainable management of water resources as well as sanitation services for all citizens. This sustainable development goal includes eight targets that should be monitored against eleven indicators. Currently, the progress in the Republic of Serbia can be monitored in relation to six targets against eight indicators. The national reports demonstrate significant progress in achieving the following targets, which are subcomponents of SDG 6:

- 6.1 achieve universal and equitable access to safe and affordable drinking water for all,
- 6.2 achieve access to adequate and equitable sanitation and hygiene for all,
- 6.3 improve water quality by reducing pollution,
- 6.4 substantially increase water-use efficiency,
- 6.a. expand international cooperation and capacity-building support in water- and sanitation-related activities and programmes, and

- 6.b. support and strengthen the participation of local communities in improving water and sanitation management.

The illustrative charts showing the progress within the selected SDG 6 goal and its subcomponents in the Republic of Serbia are shown in Figures 2, 3, 4 and 5, respectively.

Figure 2. Population connected to wastewater treatment with at least secondary treatment, 2010-2019 (%)
Source: Environmental statistics and accounts, SORS

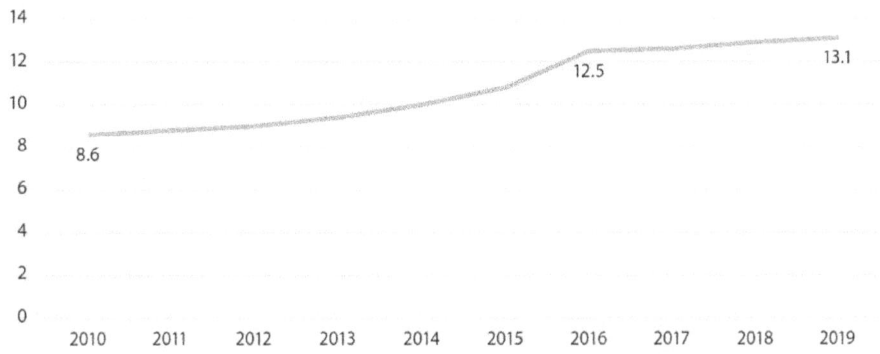

Figure 3. The proportion of bodies of water with good ambient water quality, 2014-2017 (%)
Source: Environmental statistics and accounts, SORS

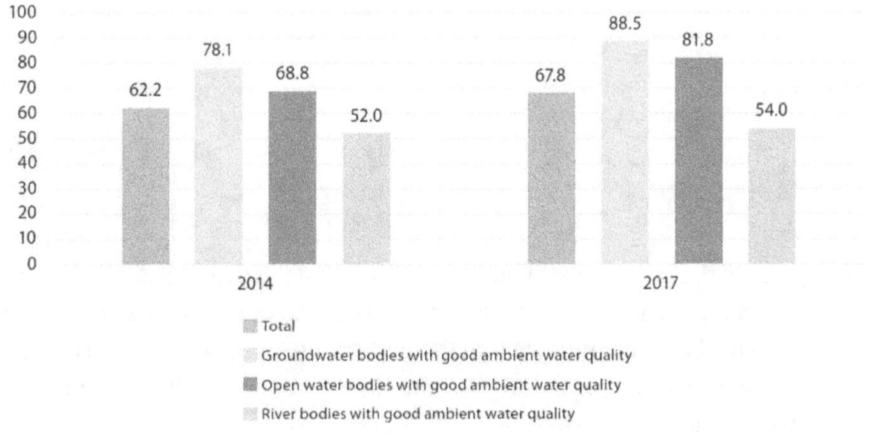

Figure 4. Change in water-use efficiency (WUE) over time indicator, 2015-2019 (RSD/m³)
Source: Environmental statistics and accounts, SORS

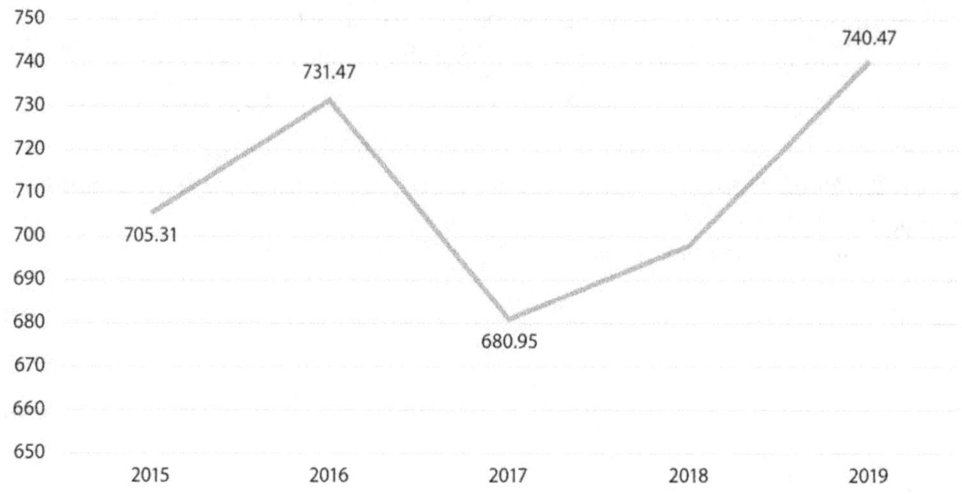

Figure 5. Water exploitation index (WEI), 2010-2019 (%)
Source: Environmental statistics and accounts, SORS

With regards to the percentage of the population connected to wastewater treatment, this percentage has been growing slowly for the last nine years, but there is a tendency for further growth. The data indicate that the percentage of the population connected to wastewater treatment increased in both the long-term (2010-2019) from 8.6% to 13.1% but also in the short-term (SORS, 2022).

The share of total water bodies with good ambient water quality from 2014 to 2017 had a compound annual growth rate of 2.90%, which indicates that significant progress was made towards achieving the goal. In 2014, the share of water bodies with good ambient water quality was 62.2%, while in 2017, the value increased to 67.8% (SORS, 2022).

In the period 2015-2018, changes in the water-use efficiency had a positive trend. A compound annual growth rate of 1.22% was recorded, and thereby it may be concluded that significant progress was made towards the attainment of the goal. Namely, in 2015, WUE amounted to 705.31 RSD/m^3, whereas in 2019, its value increased to 740.47 RSD/m^3 (SORS, 2022).

The Republic of Serbia is wealthy in water resources and uses a relatively small share of them, which is demonstrated in a moderate movement away from the target measured by the water exploitation index (WEI) related to ensuring sustainable water exploitation and freshwater supply in order to respond to water shortages and reduce the number of people facing water shortages. This is indicated by the long-term (2010-2019) compound annual growth rates of 2.71% (the value increased from 2.57% to 3.27%), as well as by the short-term (2016-2019) 6.07% (the value increased from 2.74% to 3.27%) (SORS, 2022).

In general, it could be concluded that, regarding selected SDG 6 targets, the Republic of Serbia has achieved moderate progress concerning target 6.1, envisaging universal and equitable access to safe and affordable drinking water for all. However, this progress was achieved due to a slight increase in the share of the urban population that uses drinking water from the system that is safely managed, while in other settlements such an increase was not registered. Significant progress was made within target 6.3, envisaging improved water quality by reducing pollution and increasing the share of water bodies with good water status, as well as by reducing the proportion of untreated wastewater from households and industry measured by increasing population connected to urban wastewater treatment with at least secondary treatment. Moderate progress was recorded under target 6.4 in terms of change in water-use efficiency over time and moderate movement away from the target based on the water exploitation index (SORS, 2022).

THE FUTURE PERSPECTIVES OF THE PUBLIC UTILITY SYSTEMS

It is evident that an urgent reform in public utility services is needed. However, this is not anything new, as the reform of public utilities in the Republic of Serbia has been an issue on the agenda since the early 2000s (Jovanić, 2017). In 2011, within Municipal Infrastructure Support Program, an EU-funded project, a Strategy for

Restructuring the Public Utility Companies in Serbia was drafted with the goals of (MISP, 2011, p. 7):

- Improving the level of utility service delivery while reducing costs;
- Stimulating capital investments in utility infrastructure to improve the quality of services;
- Creating guarantees for retaining the quality of utility services even when public investments are insufficient;
- Preparing the utility sector for integration into the European Union;
- Encouraging private capital inclusion for improving services and reducing costs;
- Attracting private capital in the public sector to compensate for the lack of public resources.

However, up to now, no systematic steps have been taken toward the operationalization of public utility restructuring, and the lack of a strategic approach imposes a risk for the divergent practice across the local self-governments in the Republic of Serbia (Jovanić, 2017).

Although many regulations in the legal system define the Serbian utility services sector, the two most important are the amended Law on Utility Services, which has enabled private capital participation, and the Law on Public-Private Partnerships and Concessions, as they "offer a partnership between private investors and public partners in launching infrastructure business" (Petrović, 2013, p. 118). The public-private partnerships (PPPs) have been especially interested in the water, wastewater, and waste disposal projects due to the fact that those projects require significant investments and specialized technical knowledge (Benković et al., 2015).

Table 1. PPP project proposals approved by the Commission for PPPs

Utility Services
District Heating: Zrenjanin, Niš, Batočina, Grocka, Vrbas, Pirot, Kragujevac, Gornja Toponica, Mali Iđoš, Kikinda, Sremska Mitrovica, Vrbas, Gornji Milanovac, Belgrade, Kula, Vranje, Negotin, Zaječar, Bor, Bačka Palanka
Waste Management: Topola, Žagubica, Regional Center Keleš, Grocka (co-generation, district heating), Belgrade, Obrenovac, Vrnjačka Banja, Žabari, Svilajnac, Inđija, Sombor, Pančevo
Public Wastewater and Sewage System: Stara Pazova, Zrenjanin
Public Transport: Loznica, Topola, Srbobran, Niš, Jagodina, Šabac, Negotin, Paraćin, Belgrade, Kanjiža, Ruma, Valjevo, Lajkovac, Koceljevo, Pirot, Bačka Palanka, Ćuprija, Knjaževac, Kovin, Smederevo, Zaječar, Kraljevo, Sokobanja, Novi Pazar, Sremska Mitrovica, Pančevo, Pirot, Šabac, Šid, Jagodina, Vladimirci, Mali Zvornik, Ljig, Prokuplje, Prijepolje, Srbobran, Bačka Topola, Požarevac, Bogatić, Užice, Veliko Gradište, Kula, Bor, Aleksinac, Topola, Kanjiža, Kuršumlija, Medveđa, Žagubica, Kruševac
Public Lighting: Topola, Sečanj, Vrbas, Vranje, Varvarin, Žabalj, Ada, Beočin, Plandište, Bor, Petrovac na Mlavi, Kruševac, Nova Crnja, Pirot, Vlasotince, Veliko Gradište, Kovačica, Irig, Kladovo, Požega, Ćićevac, Lapovo, Dimitrovgrad, Stara Pazova, Knjaževac, Bečej, Bogatić, Sremski Karlovci, Zrenjanin, Pančevo, Svilajnac, Pirot, Negotin, Jagodina, Sremska Mitrovica, Leskovac, Majdanpek, Vršac, Vrbas, Šid, Priboj, Sremska Mitrovica, Niš, Subotica, Kikinda, Zaječar, Sombor, Opovo, Smederevo, Kovin, Lajkovac, Knić, Babušnica, Kragujevac, Vranje, Osečina, Trstenik
Maintenance of residential buildings and institutions, public lighting and chimney-sweeping: Novi Sad
Chimney Services: Bečej
Water distribution system and construction of a small hydropower plant: Brus, Novi Bečej
Local road infrastructure construction and maintenance: Stara Pazova, Smederevo, Vršac, Pančevo, Sremska Mitrovica, Kruševac, Krupanj, Srbobran, Mali Zvornik, Sombor, Veliko Gradište, Babušnica, Ada, Brus
Public Parking: Šabac, Belgrade, Svilajnac, Novi Sad, Kruševac, Prokuplje, Užice, Kragujevac
Management of Cemeteries: Topola
Zoo-hygiene: Subotica, Bečej
Other
River port and Road Terminal: Apatin
Highway Concession: E-763 Belgrade-Požega
Building, reconstruction and maintenance of the Airport and the airport operation: Belgrade
Optical Network – Telecommunications: Novi Sad
Selected urban infrastructure property: Belgrade
Pharmaceutical Services: Novi Sad, Zrenjanin, Kruševac, Prokuplje, Rasina district
Public bicycles: Belgrade
Sports and recreation center: Kragujevac, Batočina

Source: Commission for PPPs (2022)

The core rationale of PPPs is that the involvement of private participants in the utility service provision will increase the quality of those services and deliver better value for money (Rakić et al., 2014). Although the key focus of PPPs is on efficiency in public service provision through risk sharing and private sector expertise, they can also relieve pressure on public finance by providing additional capital (Rakić & Rađenović, 2011b). Hence, many governments are interested in this kind of cooperation with the private sector (Rakić & Rađenović, 2014).

Namely, there are two groups of local self-governments in Serbia in terms of financing possibilities (Nenezić & Radulović, 2012): the local self-governments that have reached the upper debt limits set in the Law on Public Debt and those entities with low credit capacity and status, and thus uninteresting for bank financing. Besides the restrictions imposed by the budget constraints, limiting factors for financing stem from the limited government support through the tariff policy, thus making public utility companies more prone to short-term financing (Jovanić, 2017). An additional constraint is related to the provisions set in the Law on Public Property regarding the possibilities for issuing guarantees when assets of public companies are not treated as their assets, but the public company is viewed as the user of the publicly owned assets. This ownership by the state limits public utility companies in providing necessary funds for financing. The inability of local self-governments to issue guarantees due to the Law on Public Debt makes the PPPs viable options for public infrastructure projects financing (Rakić & Rađenović, 2011a).

The Law on PPPs and Concessions defines PPP as long-term cooperation between public and private partners in order to finance, build, reconstruct, manage or maintain infrastructure and other objects of public interest and provide public services, and it can be either contractual or institutional (Article 7). The duration can be set from 5 to 50 years. The Commission for PPPs needs to give a positive opinion to the project proposal, and only those with a positive opinion can enter into the further procedure. From March 2012 till November 10, 2022, the Commission has issued 218 positive opinions for PPPs. As can be observed from Table 1, most of the approved PPPs are within the utility services, especially public transport, public lighting, district heating, and waste management. Further, it is evident that the same municipalities have approved PPPs in various utility services sectors. This trend points to the fact after gaining approval for the first PPP project proposal in any sector, local self-governments are more confident in preparing PPP project proposals in various sectors as their administrative capacities grow.

SOLUTIONS AND RECOMMENDATIONS

The approach to the development of society from the point of sustainability (which is becoming an increasingly present strategic approach to development in the world) arose as a response to the increasing pressure on natural resources. This pressure is particularly pronounced in the domain of water, food, energy and the environment. The problem of water can be singled out as the most serious because the pressure on it as a resource is the greatest since the problems in the other three crisis complexes are largely refracted through water: water is of decisive importance for the production of food and energy, and the protection of the quality of aquatic biotopes and the protection the harmful effect of water becomes a key problem of environmental protection.

The participation of private capital in communal activities is usually represented by the phrase public-private partnership (PPP) and in the Republic of Serbia, for almost twenty years, it has been cited as a potentially good solution to the problem of financing the construction of communal infrastructure. But in practice, it is still rare. It is most present in urban and suburban passenger transportation, street and road maintenance, animal hygiene activities, municipal waste management and public lighting, which means that it is least used in the construction of communal infrastructure and most in the performance of activities. The participation of the private sector in the activity of supplying drinking water is partially limited by law, but not in the activity of purification and removal of atmospheric and other wastewater. Hence the topic of PPP is also important for water supply companies as unique performers of both these activities. In addition, the Serbian National Environmental Protection Program contains a detailed framework of another basic issue of importance for communal activities, namely the system of financing communal activities.

FUTURE RESEARCH DIRECTIONS

In order to improve the utility services at the national level, continuous activities are necessary to be strengthened concerning the capacity and functionality of utility infrastructure, funds for financing the construction of utility infrastructure should be provided (PPPs are proven to be a viable option), and activities monitoring the quality of utility services, as well as measures should be taken for the continuous performance of utility services in order to satisfy the life needs of citizens and business entities (MCTI, 2021 p. 125).

This is particularly important in the field of the public water supply sector, since the usable water resources of the Republic of Serbia are significantly less than the actual water present on its territory due to the unfavorable water regime and limitations in the conditions for use (for instance, very unfavorable transit/domicile ratio of 90/10% poses the need of urgent address in the field of water management issues). In the Republic of Serbia, water resources are scarce and in average values, and water needs in the future can only be met by building integral water management systems. In the Republic of Serbia, there are problems with both a lack of water (drought) and an excess of water (floods). The priority task, i.e., the answer in the context of sustainability and efficiency, should be the provision of water supply according to world standards of quantity and quality (150-200 l/cp/day), which means that the problems of drainage and purification of wastewater must also be solved (an increase of present approx. 13% of the wastewater treatment to at least 30% in next five years), all types of water pollution must be prevented, and water resources must be fully protected.

CONCLUSION

In the pursuit of a better standard of living and during the fulfillment of his ever-increasing needs, humanity has achieved enormous technological development, but at the same time, it has endangered the environment. Solving the problems arising from these human activities is one of the current and future priorities, and starting from the growing demands of the world community, a large number of companies and institutions attach their business strategy to the needs of modern society to preserve the working and living environment.

Through his actions, and in order to satisfy his own needs, humankind makes various changes in the nature that surrounds it and thus disrupts its appearance and changes its characteristics. Through construction, urbanization, exploitation, deforestation, creation of landfills, emission of gases and other activities, man has a negative impact on the environment, climate change, damage to the ozone layer, etc. With increasing and faster technical and technological development, man produces various pollutions and thus constantly degrades the environment.

Consequently, public utilities are actually activities of general interest, and their performance fulfills necessary life functions in a certain territory since more than 90% of the population of the Republic of Serbia is in one or more ways connected with public activities. Public utility systems can positively affect the quality of the environment in terms of reducing physical pollution (solid waste, dust, noise, vibrations...), chemical pollution (aerosols, gases, vapors, smoke...), biological pollution (viruses, bacteria, molds, fungi, parasites, insects, rodents) and partially radiological pollution.

Utility services are activities of general interest and are extremely important for the normal functioning of the community, its residents and business entities. The current state of the public utility systems in the Republic of Serbia is not at a satisfactory level. However, actions in the sense of transformation and reorganization must be taken urgently because this sector is part of the total national economy that employs about 70,000 people and generates about 2% of the Serbian GDP. The problems in these sectors have been accumulated for decades and cannot be solved overnight.

The biggest problems arise due to the politically determined price settings to keep the social peace in the country. Hence, many public utility companies have been cumulating losses in their financial reports while at the same time being subsidized by the state to continue with the minimum acceptable operations in terms of quantity and quality (Radukić et al., 2018). Such a situation has led to serious problems in the public utility systems, resulting in the degradation of the infrastructure and quality of utility services.

Although some utility sectors, such as water and sewage and waste management, have possibilities for increasing pricing within the affordability constraints, other sectors, such as district heating, have already set prices at the maximum affordability by the households (approx. 10% of the average household incomes). Therefore, in order for households to achieve rational consumption and savings of thermal energy, it is necessary to improve energy efficiency in buildings, both by improving the energy properties of buildings and by increasing the share in the use of renewable energy sources for heating, for at least 20% more in next five years (MCTI, 2021 p. 32).

ACKNOWLEDGMENT

This paper is a result of research funded by the Ministry of Science, Technological Development and Innovation of the Republic of Serbia pursuant to agreement No. 451-03-47/2023-01/200148.

REFERENCES

Benković, S., Krivokapić, J., & Milosavljević, M. (2015). Application of the public-private partnership organizational structure in the improvement of business operations of public sector enterprises in Serbia. *Lex Localis*, *13*(3), 397-417. Available at: http://pub.lex-localis.info/index.php/LexLocalis/issue/view/77

Cabrera, B., Pardo, M. A., Cabrera Jr., E. & Arregui, F.J. (2013). Tap water costs and service sustainability, a close relationship. *Water Resource Management, 27*, 239-253. doi:10.1007/s11269-012-0181-3

Commission for PPPs. (2022). *The list of approved projects*. Retrieved from http://jpp.gov.rs/koncesijevesti/spisak

Del Borghi, A., Strazza, C., Gallo, M., Messineo, S. & Nar, M. (2013). Water supply and sustainability: life cycle assessment of water collection, treatment and distribution service. *The International Journal of Life Cycle Assessment, 18*, 1158-1168. doi:10.1007/s11367-013-0549-5

European Commission. (2011). *A Quality Framework for Services of General Interest in Europe*. European Commission. Available at: https://eur-lex.europa.eu/legal-content/EN/TXT/?uri=celex%3A 52011DC0900

Filipović, M., & Krnjeta, L. (2013). *Unique Methodology for Determining Prices of Utility Services*. Standing Conference of Towns and Municipalities of Serbia.

Filipović, M. & Krnjeta, L. (2017). *Guide for Utility Services Pricing Policy in Municipalities and Towns of Serbia*. Conference of Towns and Municipalities of Serbia.

Fonseca, L. M., Domingues, J. P., & Dima, A. M. (2020). Mapping the Sustainable Development Goals Relationships. *Sustainability, 12*(8), 3359. doi:10.3390/su12083359

Fulazzaky, M. (2014). Challenges of Integrated Water Resources Management in Indonesia. *Water, 6*(7), 2000–2020. doi:10.3390/w6072000

Janaćković, G., Vasović, D., Malenović Nikolić, J., Mušicki, S., & Vranjanac, Ž. (2018). Vulnerability assessment of municipality areas to natural disasters based on group fuzzy analytic hierarchy process. *Journal of Environmental Protection and Ecology, Balkan Environmental Association, 19*(4), 1526-1535. https://scibulcom.net/en/journal/1311-5065/issue/2018-19-4/

Jedynak, T., & Wąsowicz, K. (2021). The Relationship between Efficiency and Quality of Municipally Owned Corporations: Evidence from Local Public Transport and Waste Management in Poland. *Sustainability, 13*(17), 9804. doi:10.3390/su13179804

Jovanić, T. (2017). *Liberalization Agenda and the General Framework of Serbian Local Public Utility Services Regulatory Regime. Network Industries Quarterly, 13(3).* https://www.network-industries.org/network-industries-quarterly/

Kioupi, V., & Voulvoulis, N. (2019). Education for Sustainable Development: A Systemic Framework for Connecting the SDGs to Educational Outcomes. *Sustainability, 11*(21), 6104. doi:10.3390/su11216104

KOMDEL. (2019). *Changes in the Prices of Basic Utility Services during the period 2006-2018 and their Impact on the Cost of Living*. KOMDEL.

Law on Energy Efficiency and Rational Use of Energy. (Official Gazette of the Republic of Serbia, no. 40/2021).

Law on Environmental Protection. (Official Gazette of the Republic of Serbia, no. 135/2004, 36/2009, 36/2009, 72/2009, 43/2011, 14/2016, 76/2018, 95/2018 and 95/2018)

Law on Public Debt. (Official Gazette of the Republic of Serbia, no. 61/2005, 107/2009, 78/2011, 68/2015, 95/2018, 91/2019 and 149/2020).

Law on Public-Private Partnerships and Concessions, (Official Gazette of the Republic of Serbia, no. 88/2011, 15/2016 and 104/2016).

Law on Public Property. (Official Gazette of the Republic of Serbia, no. 72/2011, 88/2013, 105/2014, 104/2016 – other law, 108/2016, 113/2017, 95/2018 and 153/2020).

Law on Public Utilities. (Official Gazette of the Republic of Serbia, no. 88/2011, 104/2016, and 95/2018).

Law on Utility Services. (Official Gazette of the Republic of Serbia, no. 88/2011, 104/2016 and 95/2018).

Law on Water. (Official Gazette of the Republic of Serbia, no. 30/2010, 93/2012, 101/2016, 95/2018 and 95/2018).

Mancosu, N., Snyder, R., Kyriakakis, G., & Spano, D. (2015). Water Scarcity and Future Challenges for Food Production. *Water, 7*(12), 975–992. doi:10.3390/w7030975

Mekonnen, M. M., & Hoekstra, A. Y. (2016). Four billion people facing severe water scarcity. *Science Advances*, *2*(2), e1500323. doi:10.1126ciadv.1500323 PMID:26933676

Ministry of Construction, Transport and Infrastructure. (2021). Report of utility services performance on the territory of the Republic of Serbia in 2020. Author.

MISP. (2011). *Strategy for Restructuring the Public Utility Companies in Serbia (draft)*. Municipal Infrastructure Support Programme. Available at: http://www.misp-serbia.rs/wp-content/uploads/2010/05/Strategy-for-Restructuring-the-PUC-Draft.pdf

Negruț, M. L., Muțiu, A., & Mihărtescu, A.-A. (2022). Insights on the Performance of Public Procurement for Water Utilities Works. *Sustainability, 15*(1), 155. doi:10.3390/su15010155

Nenezić, D., & Radulović, B. (2012). The Analysis of possibilities and modalities of financing and financial support measures to public-private partnerships in Serbia. *Quarterly Monitor, 13*, 62-71. Available at: https://fren.org.rs/en/kvartalni-monitor/quarterly-monitor-13/

Nhamo, L., Ndlela, B., Nhemachena, C., Mabhaudhi, T., Mpandeli, S., & Matchaya, G. (2018). The Water-Energy-Food Nexus: Climate Risks and Opportunities in Southern Africa. *Water, 10*(5), 567. doi:10.3390/w10050567

Petrović, M. (2013). Conducting public utilities in Serbia: providing and maintaining services in Kragujevac. *International Journal of Public Sector Management, 26*(2), 116-126. doi:10.1108/09513551311317988

Radukić, S., Perović, D., & Vučetić, D. (2018). Economic and environmental effects from liberalizing utility service prices in the Republic of Serbia. *Industrija, 46*(4), 29-46. . doi:10.5937/industrija46-18444

Rakić, B., Milenković-Kerković, T., & Rađenović, T. (2014). *Infrastructure Development through public-private partnership. Actual Problems of Economics, No. 2.* National Academy of Management.

Rakić, B., & Rađenović, T. (2011a). Risks and Benefits of Private Capital Participation in Public Projects Financing under the Contemporary Economic Crisis Conditions. In B. Krstić (Ed.), *Improving the Competitiveness of the Public and Private Sector by Networking Competences* (pp. 65–83). University of Niš, Faculty of Economics.

Rakić, B., & Rađenović, T. (2011b). The Impact of Global Economic Crisis on Public-Private Partnerships. In E. Petrović (Ed.), *Science and World Economic Crisis* (pp. 51–60). University of Niš, Faculty of Economics.

Rakić, B., & Rađenović, T. (2014). Real Options Methodology in Public-Private Partnership Projects Valuation. *Economic Annals, 59*(200), 91-113. doi:10.2298/EKA1400091R

Sharma, A., Pezzaniti, D., Myers, B., Cook, S., Tjandraatmadja, G., Chacko, P., & Chavoshi, S. (2016). Water Sensitive Urban Design: An Investigation of Current Systems, Implementation Drivers, Community Perceptions and Potential to Supplement Urban Water Services. *Water, 8*(7), 272. doi:10.3390/w8070272

Stanković, S., Vasović, D., & Trajković, S. (2019). Model of sustainable water resources management in the conditions of extreme hydrological phenomena. *Journal of Environmental Protection and Ecology, 20*(3), 1393-1401. Available at: https://scibulcom.net/en/journal/1311-5065/issue/2019-20-3/

Takić, L., Živković, S., & Živković, N. (2013). Improvement of environmental management: a case study. *Fresenius Environmental Bulletin, 22*(12C), 3840-3847. Available at: https://www.prt-parlar.de/download_feb_2013/

The Statistical Office of the Republic of Serbia. (2022). *Progress Report on the Implementation of Sustainable Development Goals (SDG) for the Republic of Serbia for 2021*. The Statistical Office of the Republic of Serbia.

UN-SDGs. (2022). *United Nations Sustainable Development Goals Platform*. Available online: https://sdgs.un.org/goals

Vasović, D., Janaćković, G., Malenović Nikolić, J., Milošević, L., & Mušicki, S. (2018b). Promoting reflective practice in resources protection area: a step to forecast outcomes in uncertainty. *Journal of Environmental Protection and Ecology, 19*(3), 1320-1329. Available at: https://scibulcom.net/en/journal/1311-5065/issue/2018-19-3/

Vasović, D., Janaćković, G., Malenović Nikolić, J., Mušicki, S., & Marković, S. (2018a). Multimodality in the field of resources protection. *Journal of Environmental Protection and Ecology, 19*(4), 1519-1525. Available at: https://scibulcom.net/en/journal/1311-5065/issue/2018-19-4/

Vasović, D., Malenovic Nikolic, J., & Janackovic, G. (2016). Evaluation and Assessment Model for Environmental Management under the Seveso III, IPPC/IED and Water Framework Directive. *Journal of Environmental Protection and Ecology, 17*(1), 356-365. Available at: https://scibulcom.net/en/journal/1311-5065/issue/2016-17-1/

Velasco-Muñoz, J., Aznar-Sánchez, J., Belmonte-Ureña, L., & Román-Sánchez, I. (2018). Sustainable Water Use in Agriculture: A Review of Worldwide Research. *Sustainability, 10*(4), 1084. doi:10.3390/su10041084

Voorn, B., Marieke, L. G., & Thiel, S. (2017). The efficiency and effectiveness of municipally owned corporations: A systematic review. *Local Government Studies, 43*(5), 820–841. doi:10.1080/03003930.2017.1319360

Wada, Y., van Beek, L. P. H., & Bierkens, M. F. P. (2011). Modelling global water stress of the recent past: On the relative importance of trends in water demand and climate variability. *Hydrology and Earth System Sciences, 15*(12), 3785–3808. doi:10.5194/hess-15-3785-2011

WHO. (2012). *Global Costs and Benefits of Drinking-Water Supply and Sanitation Interventions to Reach the MDG Target and Universal Coverage*. Analytical report, WHO/HSE/WSH/12.01, WHO. Available at: https://apps.who.int/iris/handle/10665/75140

WHO, JMP, & UNICEF. (2017). *Progress on drinking water, sanitation and hygiene: 2017 update and SDG baselines*. Available at: https://www.who.int/publications/i/item/9789241512893

Živković, S., Takić, L., & Živković, N. (2013). The improvement of environmental performances by applying ISO 14001 standard: A case study. *Chemical Industry and Chemical Engineering Quarterly/CICEQ, 19*(4), 541-552. Available at: http://www.ache.org.rs/CICEQ/Arhiva/

Živković, S., Todorović, M., & Pejčić, D. (2016). Improvements in Environmental Protection Through Optimization of Production Processes: A Case Study. *FEB-Fresenius Environmental Bulletin, 25*(8), 2725-2735. Available at: https://www.prt-parlar.de/download_feb_2016/

ADDITIONAL READING

Almquist, R., Grossi, G., van Helden, G. J., & Reichard, C. (2013). Public Sector Governance and Accountability. *Crit. Percept. Account., 24*(7-8), 479–487. doi:10.1016/j.cpa.2012.11.005

Directive 2014/25/EU of the European Parliament and of the Council of 26 February 2014 on Procurement by Entities Operating in the Water, Energy, Transport and Postal Services Sectors and Repealing Directive 2004/17/EC Text with EEA Relevance. Off. J. Eur. Union 2014, 94, 243–374.

European Green Deal. European Commission. (2020). Available online: https://commission.europa.eu/strategy-and-policy/priorities-2019-2024/european-green-deal_en

Negruț, M. L., Muțiu, A., & Mihărtescu, A.-A. (2022). Insights on the Performance of Public Procurement for Water Utilities Works. *Sustainability, 15*(1), 155. doi:10.3390/su15010155

Schlör, H., Hake, J., & Venghaus, S. (2018). An Integrated Assessment Model for the German Food-Energy-Water Nexus. *Journal of Sustainable Development of Energy, Water and Environment Systems*, *6*(1), 1–12. doi:10.13044/j.sdewes.d5.0182

Shehu, B., & Nazim, F. (2022). Clean Water and Sanitation for All: Study on SDGs 6.1 and 6.2 Targets with State Policies and Interventions in Nigeria. *Environmental Sciences Proceedings*, *15*(1), 71. doi:10.3390/environsciproc2022015071

Sun, H., Wang, G., Bai, J., Shen, J., Zheng, X., Dan, E., Chen, F., & Zhang, L. (2023). Corporate Sustainable Development, Corporate Environmental Performance and Cost of Debt. *Sustainability*, *15*(1), 228. doi:10.3390u15010228

Sušnik, J., & van der Zaag, P. (2017). Correlation and causation between the UN Human Development Index and national and personal wealth and resource exploitation. *Economic research -. Ekonomska Istrazivanja*, *30*(1), 1705–1723. do i:10.1080/1331677X.2017.1383175

KEY TERMS AND DEFINITIONS

Continuity of Public Services: Lack of interruption, disconnection, or deterioration of quality of any kind of public services in space and time. The focus of the continuity concept refers to the continual needs of the consumers.

Management: Process of planning, decision making, organizing, leading, motivating, and controlling the human resources, financial, physical, and information resources of an organization to reach its goals efficiently and effectively.

Public Utilities: The form of economy utilities that are meant to supply-provide goods/services that are considered essential for human well-being such as: potable water distribution, sewerage systems, waste management, public transport, public heating, public areas management, public lighting, chimney services, funeral services, zoo-hygiene services, public markets, public parking. In some countries, this list also includes gas supply, electricity, telephone, and other communication systems.

Public Utility Company: A special business organization performing a public service subject to special government regulation.

Public Water Supply: The provision of water by public utilities, commercial organizations, community endeavors or by individuals, usually via a system of pumps and pipes. Public water supply systems are crucial to properly functioning societies.

Public-Private Partnership: Long-term arrangement between a government and private sector institutions. Typically, it involves private capital financing government projects and services up-front and then drawing revenues from taxpayers and/or users over the course of the PPP contract.

Safety: Concept that includes all measures and practices taken to preserve the life, health, and bodily integrity of individuals.

Sustainable Development: Development that meets the needs of the present without compromising the ability of future generations to meet their own needs.

Sustainable Development Goals: A universal call to action to end poverty, protect the planet, and ensure that by 2030 all people enjoy peace and prosperity.

System: Group of interacting or interrelated elements that act according to a set of rules to form a unified whole. A public utility system represents a group of entities that provides public goods or services to the general public at the level of concrete local self-government.

Chapter 2
Public Utility Systems in North Macedonia:
State and Perspectives

Samoil Malcheski
https://orcid.org/0000-0001-9357-019X
International Slavic University, North Macedonia

Jordan Gjorcev
International Slavic University, North Macedonia

ABSTRACT

This chapter deals with a topic that has been publicly debated in the North Macedonia in the last few years. The public utility companies are constantly in debt and with consistently poor quality of services. Hence, the main focus of the public debate is how to identify the causes of the persistent poor situation and how to overcome these problems facing the public utility systems. The primary aim of this chapter is to give an overview of the state in which public utility systems operate. Also, this chapter gives an overview of the importance of the institutional environment and decentralization and their impact on public utilities systems. At the end of the chapter, the sustainability of public utility companies and the financing of utility services and covering costs are presented.

DOI: 10.4018/978-1-6684-7730-4.ch002

INTRODUCTION

In the Republic of Macedonia, in July 2005, the process of decentralization was operationalized, and a large number of responsibilities were transferred from the central to the local level. The transfer of competencies, in addition to privileges, meant a great responsibility for the municipalities. Even before the start of the implementation of decentralization, most of the communal activities were under the jurisdiction of the municipalities. But despite that, the services provided by the public utility companies are still not at the desired level of quality, and there is still a big difference in their performance. Also, in large part of the municipalities, unified procedures and forms for providing the services are missing. In many municipalities, there is a lack of unified acts that they should adopt themselves in order to define and establish procedures for providing quality administrative services for public utilities. (Association of Utilities Providers in Macedonia, 2020)

According to the positive legal regulations in the Republic of Macedonia, municipalities can form public utility companies for the following services (Association of Utilities Providers in Macedonia, 2020):

- Arranging and organizing the public local transportation of passengers;
- Construction, maintenance, reconstruction and protection of local roads and other infrastructure facilities;
- Supply of drinking water, delivery of technological water, drainage and purification of wastewater;
- Collecting, transporting and dealing with municipal solid and technological waste;
- Maintenance of graves, cemeteries, and crematoriums and providing funeral services;
- Public cleanliness.

In this chapter, we will give a general overview of the public utility system and the impact of the institutional environment and decentralization on public sector reforms. Financing utility services and covering the cost and sustainability of public utility companies will be presented at the end of this chapter.

BACKGROUND

This chapter reviewed the literature on the public utilities systems in Macedonia, the current state and the perspective. The scholarly studies were searched using Academia.edu, Researchgate.net and Google Scholar platform. (Atanasovski (2006), Angelov

(2005), Allen, Tommasi (2009), CEA (2010), CEA (2006), Jovanovski (2005), OSCE (2009), Spasov, Arsov (2004), Standard & Poor (2010), Todorovski et al. (2004)). Some keywords used were utility companies, public finances, decentralization, and public services. A big challenge faced while writing the chapter is that no one has researched this issue in Macedonia in the last two decades. Hence, the literature available is literature dating from the period between 2008 and 2013, a period in which decentralization was actual. The last Program for public investments adopted by the Government, which foresees investments in public utilities, is for the period 2011-2013. Since then, there has been almost no document that mentions public utility systems.

THE IMPACT OF THE INSTITUTIONAL ENVIRONMENT AND DECENTRALIZATION ON PUBLIC UTILITY SYSTEMS AND THE PUBLIC SECTOR

Effects of Decentralization in the Republic of Macedonia

Modern states are organized into multiple levels or degrees of government. In the unitary states with the simplest arrangement, there are two levels of decision-making - the level of the central government and the level of the local self-government units. Whether a state will be highly centralized or decentralized will depend on the scope of activities, competencies, and functions that the central versus local government has.

Until 1997, Macedonia was a highly centralized state. Centralized financial relations did not correspond to the norms provided by the European Charter for Local Self-Government, which the Republic of Macedonia ratified in 1997. With the ratification, the European norms for the distribution of competencies between the central and local authorities and for the proportions of the local authorities were formally accepted. With that, certain fiscal relations were established between the various levels of government in relation to competencies, the realization of public revenues and the execution of public expenditures for the purpose of efficiency, that is, the optimal realization of the functions of the public sector as a whole (Angelov 2005).

All these relationships, as well as some others such as the distribution of competencies (functions) at each level of government, the financing of the local self-government units as well as the sources of financing, the financial spillover as well as the reasons for decentralization, will be discussed in this chapter. One of the key problems is that no one is monitoring the decentralization process at all. The majority of the municipalities have entered the second phase of the process, but no municipality has started the third phase of the process.

Reasons for Decentralization

There are basically three rational reasons for decentralization, namely (Angelov 2005):

- uses of public goods are generally spatially limited;
- differences in individual preferences for private goods versus public goods, as well as for different types of public goods;
- the mobility of users, which comes to the fore in case of the presence of differences in the volume and quality of public services, as well as in the number of tax rates between local communities.

If you use it, you would not be spatially limited, i.e., if they were of a national character, then the problem would be reduced to choosing, by voting, the level of government that would provide public goods and services. If, on the other hand, consumer preferences were identical, the problem would be reduced to the organization of efficient production of spatially limited public goods. Some public goods are such that the incidence of their use applies to the entire country (for example, the national defense, the supreme court, etc.). Other public goods, on the other hand, are spatially limited in a geographical sense (for example, emergency medical care). Accordingly, only the members of a specific geographical community, which is geographically limited, are beneficiaries of that public good.

The conclusion that is imposed is that the services which, according to the incidence of benefit, refer to the entire national territory, such as national defense, security, the national road network, the national television network, etc., should be provided at the level of the entire country, that is, from by the central government, through its ministries, services, agencies, etc. The services that are of local benefit, such as emergency medical assistance, fire protection, lighting, primary and secondary education, communal activities, etc., should be provided and financed at the level of the respective regional community. Each authority should provide the services whose benefit extends within its borders and must use only such sources of financing that will internalize the costs, which means covering those costs by the users (Community of Local Self-Government Units of the Republic of Macedonia, 2005).

The population of the local government units is divided into two groups. Their choice of a public good is a city park. The demand of the first group is represented by the curve DD and of the second by D_1D_1. The cost of Pc per community member (per capita) is constant. In such a situation, the quantity of the public good preferred by the first group is OQ_1, and the second is OQ_2. If the same public good were to be provided by the central government, the quantity supplied would be, for example, OQ_c. If OQ_c is taken as a parameter, then the first group will have a welfare loss equal to the triangle ABC, which loss actually represents an additional expenditure for each individual to be able to consume more units, that is, Q_1Q_c, compared to his preferred quantity OQ_1.

Figure 1. The benefit in the welfare of users of public goods under decentralized public choice
Source: Angelov G. (2005), Handbook for mayors and members of municipal councils in R. Macedonia,

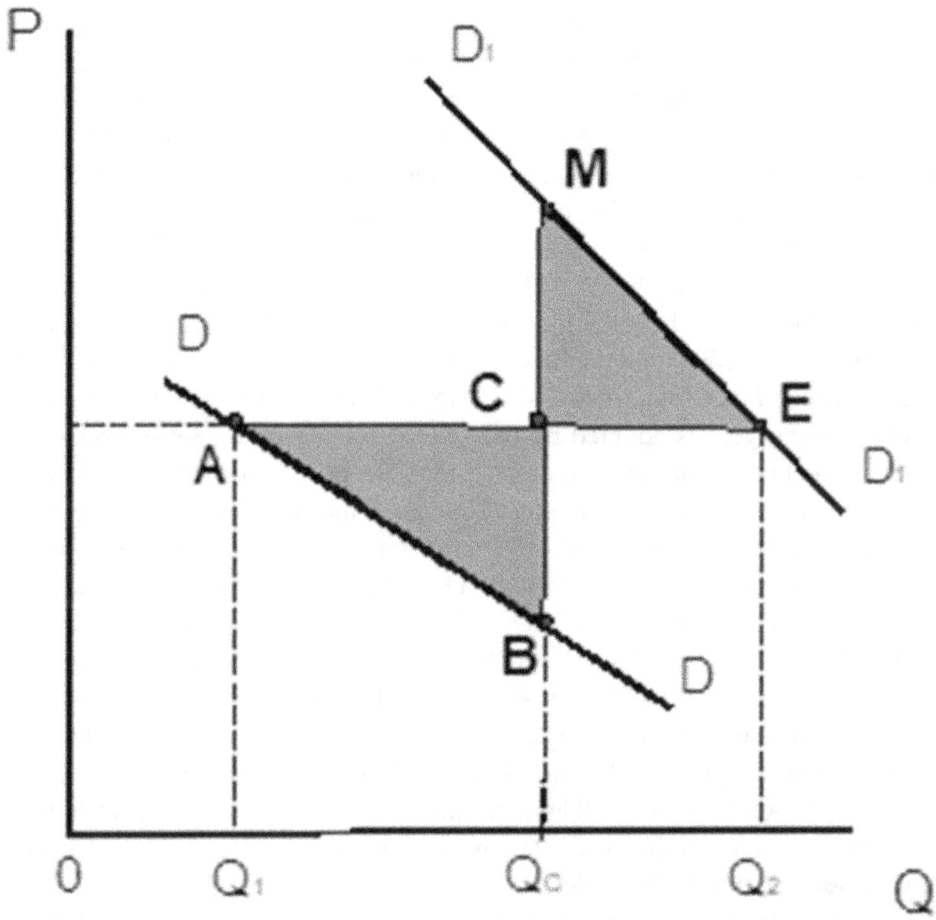

The second group also records a loss equal to CEM, which practically means that it receives less of the public good (OQ_c) than it paid for it (OQ_2). In contrast to the central government, the local authorities are able to adjust the offer of public goods to a greater extent according to the preferences of the buyers, that is, to provide the requested quantities of public goods. This means that the decentralized system of offering public goods allows easier discovery of consumer preferences for different types of goods and services.

Budget and Financing of Local Self-Government Units in the Republic of Macedonia

Local self-government units in Macedonia have their own budget. Issues related to the municipal budget are regulated by law. Local self-government units adopt their budgets independently. The budget is the most important document that the council of the local self-government unit carries during the year. It is an annual plan for financing the functions and obligations of the local self-government units, which consists of an annual assessment of revenues by sources and expenses by purpose, with it the determinations of the local self-government unit specified in numbers. Therefore, the budget not only defines the way money is spent but is also a plan that determines priorities. The local budget consists of a general and a special part.

Based on the Law on Local Self-Government (Official Gazette of the Republic of Macedonia no. 5/2002) and the Law on Financing Local Self-Government Units (Official Gazette No. 61/04, 96/04, 67/07, 156/09, 47/11 and 192/15), the budget for the following year is adopted by the Council of the Local Self-Government Unit on the proposal of the mayor, no later than December 31 of the current year. If for any reason, the council of the local self-government unit does not adopt the budget within the stipulated period, it is obliged to adopt a decision on temporary financing and a financial plan for its implementation in the first quarter of the year. The budget of the local self-government unit is drawn up according to the Law on Budgets (Official Gazette of the Republic of Macedonia, no. 203/2022) and the Instructions given by the Ministry of Finance. It must be balanced, which means it must not contain a budget deficit. The local self-government unit is obliged within 15 days from the adoption of the budget to submit it to the Ministry of Finance for the purpose of monitoring the total public spending in the country. When adopting the budget, the council of the local self-government unit must also adopt a Decision on the implementation of the budget.

The process starts no later than September 30, the deadline by which the Minister of Finance submits a budget circular, which informs the local self-government units about the basic macroeconomic indicators, the main directions for the preparation of the budget and income from various sources. Budgeting takes place in stages, within deadlines established by the budget calendar adopted by the council of the local self-government unit. The mayor submits the main guidelines for the preparation of the budget by the budget beneficiaries. Then the budget beneficiaries submit their financial plans to the mayor, who submits the budget proposal to the council of the local self-government unit. The participation of citizens in the budget process is very important. There is no democratic society without an open local government. After the end of the public discussion and the incorporation of the useful proposals in the text, the Budget proposal is submitted to the council for its adoption. During the fiscal year, if the revenues and expenditures are not realized according to the plan, the mayor proposes to the council amendments and additions to the budget (rebalancing). The mayor is responsible for the implementation of the budget. The budget reserve for financing planned or less planned expenses cannot be greater than 3% of the budget. All budget users submit monthly reports on the execution of their financial plans to the mayor, and the mayor submits quarterly reports on the execution of the budget to the Ministry of Finance and to the council of the local self-government unit. The council of the local self-government unit adopts the annual budget for the previous year at the proposal of the mayor after the end of the fiscal year, and by March 15 at the latest, and submits it to the Ministry of Finance, at the latest by March 31 of the current year.

The council of the local self-government unit also adopts an annual report consisting of the following:

- annual account;
- report on assets, claims, liabilities and sources of assets and their value;
- a report on the implementation of investment programs, on dedicated, capital and block grants for delegated competencies;
- a report from the responsible accountant confirming the accuracy and reliability of the annual account.

Local self-government units are financed from their own sources of income, transfers from the central government and donations. Own sources of revenue are revenues provided by local taxes, local fees, local fees and property income. Local taxes include property tax, inheritance and gift tax, real estate sales tax, and other local taxes established by law. Local fees are communal fees, administrative fees and other local fees established by law. Transfers from the central government are usually reduced to subsidies from the Budget of the Republic of Macedonia and from the budgets of the funds. With these subsidies, additional revenues are provided in the budget of the local self-government unit for financing its competencies determined by law. At the same time, from the Budget of the Republic of Macedonia and from the budgets of the funds, funds are allocated for the following types of grants (Law on Financing of Local Self-Government Units, no. 61/04):

- revenues from value-added tax;
- dedicated grant;
- capital subsidy;

- block grant and
- subsidy for delegated competencies.

In order to achieve their program objectives, local self-government units may also receive grants from third parties. Grants can be received in the form of financial resources and in kind. Grants received as financial assets represent income in the budget of the local self-government unit, while grants received as items represent the property of the local self-government unit and are recorded in that way. (Law on Financing of Local Self-Government Units, no. 61/04)

The Implication of Decentralization on Public Utility Systems at The Municipal Level In The Republic of Macedonia

Public utility systems in the Republic of Macedonia are established (according to the Law on Public Enterprises, Official Gazette of the Republic of Macedonia, no. 38/96, 6/02, 40/03, 49/06) to perform economic activities of public interest.

Figure 2. The institutional environment of public utility systems
Source: Authors' contribution

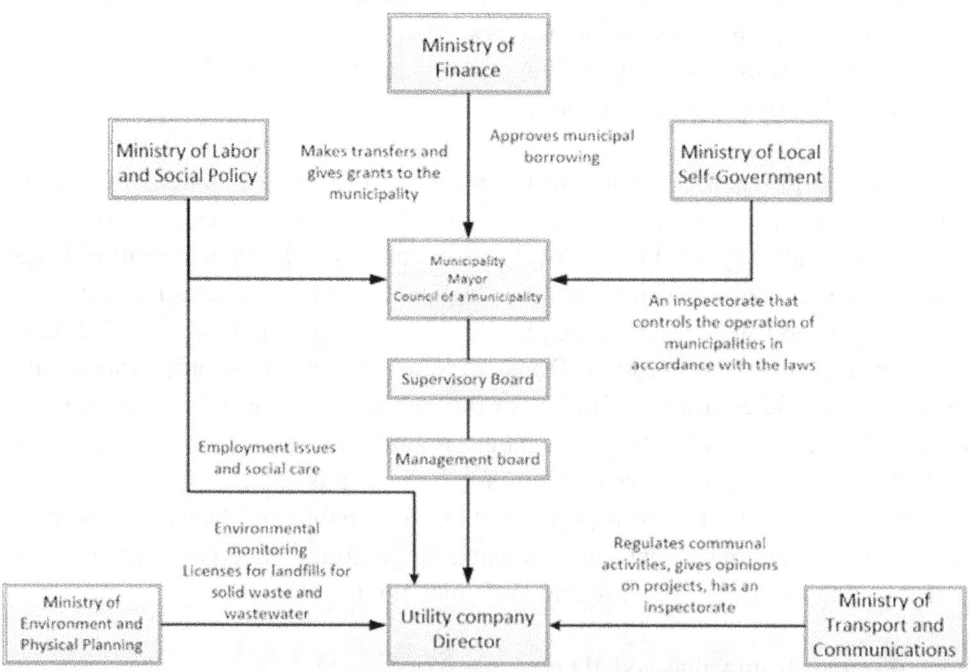

Public utility systems are public enterprises owned and established by local self-government units. Utilities have their own tax number, their own bank account (unlike local government units, which are only allowed to have a treasury account), their own balance sheet and income statement, and use accrual accounting (local government units use cash accounting) and their own legal status. The administration of the utility companies is set by the mayor, and the tariffs (for water, sewage, solid waste and other services) are determined by the council of the local self-government unit. The institutional environment in which public utility systems perform their daily activities is presented in Figure 2.

Other relevant ministries responsible for utility companies in the area of water supply and garbage are (CEA, 2010):

- The Ministry of Agriculture, Forestry and Water Management, which currently issues permits for water resources - in accordance with the new Water Law; from January 2010, this responsibility will be taken over by the Ministry of Environment and Spatial Planning.
- The Ministry of Health, monitors and applies standards for the quality of drinking water and other sanitary conditions through the State Sanitary and Health Inspectorate.

For a utility company, which is established by a local government unit, the most important institutional relationship is that with the local government unit. Table 1 summarizes the close relationship between local government units and the utility company they have established.

Table 1. Relations unit of local self-government - utility company

Item	Local government unit	Utility company
Ownership of fixed assets	Network of fixed assets (if not owned by the state)	Small fixed assets (vehicles, office equipment, etc.)
Appointments	The Council approves the Supervisory and Management Board, the Mayor appoints the General Director	
Tariff regulation	Tariffs are approved by the Council	Tariffs are proposed by utility companies
Financial relations – currently	The council approves the annual accounts of the utility companies	Utility companies invoice the municipality for the services provided (e.g. water used by the municipality); they can get subsidies for public goods (e.g. parks)
Financing of capital investments	The council must approve, and the municipality must issue a guarantee for any indebtedness of the utility company; The Ministry of Finance must approve the guarantee, only the municipality's revenues count towards the debt service limit (not the utility company's revenues)	The utility company can conclude a contract for long-term borrowing only with the approval of the Council of the Municipality and the Ministry of Finance
Accounting practice	The norm in municipalities is cash accounting	The norm in utilities is accrual accounting
Contracts for external cooperation and concessions	Municipalities issue permits / contracts / concessions for communal services	
Technical standards	Municipal inspectorate	

Source: CEA, Republic of Macedonia: Strategy and Action Plan for Reforms in Utilities with Focus on Water Supply, Sewerage and Solid Waste Management, Diagnostic and Strategic Report (2010)

The areas where the influence of local self-government units is most visible to the public are the appointments (of the Supervisory and Management Board and general director) and the determination of tariffs. The council of local government units also approves the annual accounts of the utility companies, guarantees all long-term debts of the utility companies (thereby straining its own debt service limit and legal sources of payment, as already pointed out) and monitors and applies technical standards (which depend on national monitoring by the Inspectorate of the Ministry of Transport and Communications).

Given the managerial intermingling of the local government unit and utility, together with separate accounting, banking and bookkeeping functions, it is apparent that utilities neither operate as independent enterprises nor enjoy the benefits of being an integrated municipal department (no boards etc.). The leading people in the management of utility companies owe all their positions to the Mayor, elected by the people. Therefore, they have no guarantee that they will keep their position. Management is also limited in that their salaries are tied to the public sector wage rate, which leaves no room for incentives.

Table 1 presents the formal relationships as defined in various laws. Anecdotes say that in practice, utilities are dominated by local government units with dubious practices (such as over-employment and hiring people with good connections rather than good qualifications), leading to various types of inefficiencies that end up being paid for by users or through higher prices, higher taxes to finance losses, or poorer service due to insufficient financial resources to effectively maintain capital. (CEA, 2010)

However, it should be noted that this section does not emphasize undue political influence as the main problem. In the majority of focus groups and interviews conducted in recent years for various needs, respondents recognized the political influence as positive, in the sense that local self-government units establish control mechanisms over the work of utility companies. In a small number of cases, negative aspects of political party influence were identified, particularly in relation to maintaining low prices for utility services and employing party loyalists. There was a general consensus among those who participated in focus groups and interviews about the need for reform and restructuring of utility companies, with an emphasis on separating essential from non-essential activities, increasing employee training, and establishing mechanisms for more effective cost control.

Institutional and Regulatory Framework for Treating Communal Activities

Legislation

Main laws relating to communal activities. (CEA, 2010) The legal and institutional framework for communal activities in the Republic of Macedonia is detailed in the legal and financial working documents. In this section, we will specifically refer to the legal regulation.

The main laws relating to water, sewerage and waste utilities and public-private partnerships that are relevant to this paper are as follows:

- Law on Local Self-Government (Official Gazette of the Republic of Macedonia, no. 5/2002)
- Law on balanced regional development (Official Gazette of the Republic of Macedonia, no. 63/07, 187/13, 43/14, 215/15 and 64/18)

- Law on the City of Skopje (Official Gazette of the Republic of Macedonia, no. 55/2004; 158/2011)
- Law on financing of the units of local self-government (Official Gazette of the Republic of Macedonia, 61/04, 96/04, 67/07, 156/09, 47/11 and 192/15)
- Law on communal activities (Official Gazette of the Republic of Macedonia, no. 45/97)
- Law on property and other real property rights (Official Gazette of the Republic of Macedonia, no. 18/01)
- Law on Public Enterprises (Official Gazette of the Republic of Macedonia, no. 38/1996; 9/1997; 6/2002; 40/2003; 49/2006; 22/2007; 83/2009; 97/2010; 6/2012; 119/2013; 41/2014; 138/2014; 25/2015; 61/2015; 39/2016, 64/2018, 35/19 and 275/19.)
- Law on Transformation of socially owned (Official Gazette of the Republic of Macedonia, no. 38/93)
- Law on commercial companies (Official Gazette of the Republic of Macedonia, no. 28/04)
- Environmental Law (Official Gazette of the Republic of Macedonia, no. 53/05)
- Water Law (Official Gazette of the Republic of Macedonia, no. 04/98)
- Law on drinking water supply and urban wastewater disposal (Official Gazette of the Republic of Macedonia, no. 68/04, 28/06 and 103/08)
- Solid waste management law (Official Gazette of the Republic of Macedonia, no. 216/21)
- Law on concessions and other types of public-private partnership (Official Gazette of the Republic of Macedonia, no. 6/2012, 144/2014, 33/2015, 104/2015, 215/2015, 153/2019, 261/2019)

The first four laws (the Law on Local Self-Government, the Law on Balanced Regional Development, the Law on the City of Skopje and the Law on Financing Local Self-Government Units) provide the legal framework for decentralization. The law transfers the competencies to local self-government units, inter alia, for communal services (including water, sewage and solid waste management). Units of local self-government are 84 municipalities and the City of Skopje, which includes 10 municipalities (included in the number of 84). Communal services are regulated by the Law on Communal Activities. This law is an umbrella law that regulates the basic conditions and the way of performing communal activities and how they should be financed. The Law on Property and Other Real Rights allows local self-government units and public enterprises to be the holders of ownership rights over utility infrastructure. The Law on Public Enterprises gives local government units the authority to establish utility companies, to appoint a general director and a supervisory and management board, and to adopt the budgets of the companies. Article 4 allows the founder of the utility company (ie the Council of Local Self-Government Units) to convert the company into a limited liability company or a joint-stock company. In practice, despite the fact that this provision has existed in the statutes since 2002, so far, no utility company has been transformed into a limited liability company or a joint-stock company. Should such a transformation take place, the Law on Transformation of Social Capital Enterprises and the Law on Commercial Companies will provide the legal framework.

The Law on Water and the Law on the Environment cover, among other things, water supply, treatment and disposal of wastewater and solid waste. The special conditions relating to communal activities and the manner of delivery of such services in local government units are also regulated by more specific sectoral laws. They include the Law on Drinking Water Supply and Urban Wastewater Disposal and the Law on Waste Management. As explained in the previous section, the authority to implement these laws lies in the hands of central and local governments.

The law on concessions and other types of public-private partnership was adopted in January 2008. It establishes different forms of public-private partnership agreements, including but not limited to concessions, which should comply with the principles of the European Union directives and the obligations arising from the agreements:

- Transparency
- Equal treatment and non-discrimination of economic operators
- Free movement of goods and services
- Proportionality
- Mutual recognition.

Assessment of the legal framework. As can be seen from the above, one of the main problems with the legal framework is the multiplicity of laws related to the provision of utility services. Laws change frequently. Further changes can be expected as a result of the efforts of the Republic of Macedonia to harmonize the legal framework with the many directives of the European Union relating to communal services. The fact that a special Inspectorate has been opened within the Ministry of Local Self-Government to ensure consistency between the decisions of the local self-government units and the regulations and national laws speaks for the complexity of this issue. (CEA, 2010)

The general assessment is that the legal framework for the provision of communal services is basically good, although there are certain significant anomalies, which partly result from the way in which the laws are applied and partly from the content of the laws. There are also some relatively clear points that need to be addressed at a certain stage. In principle, special attention should be paid to:

- The time periods after which unpaid bills will be considered uncollectible, as well as the time frame for initiating a dispute, should be changed. The proposal is to increase the time frame for disputes with households by the same period that applies to legal entities (e.g. from one to three years).
- Appropriate legal framework should be adopted for providing services to poor families.
- If water supply concession agreements are concluded, an amendment to the Law on Drinking Water Supply and Urban Wastewater Disposal (2004) will be required. The Law on Concessions of 2008 covers the modalities, but the right to grant a concession should be regulated by a sectoral law.

Also, experts, local self-government units and citizens identified the VAT Law (Official Gazette of the Republic of Macedonia, no. 44/99 with changes) as a problem. Utilities pay VAT on invoiced, not billed, services. This represents a financial burden for them when the bills are not paid. There is no provision in the Value Added Tax Law for the refund of tax already paid on invoices that have not been paid. This is most unusual in terms of international VAT application practice, and it is recommended that the law be amended to allow for eventual VAT refunds. At the end of July 2008, the VAT rate for solid waste services was reduced from the standard (18%) to the same preferential rate (5%) as water.

Unclear infrastructure ownership. According to the Law on Local Self-Government, Article 64, the unit of local self-government has the right to property of things, money and rights. The value of the ownership of the unit of local self-government is estimated and expressed during the preparation of the annual account. However, in reality, public enterprises are not shown in the annual account of the local government unit from the fixed assets side. If they were limited liability companies or joint-stock companies, at least the nominal value of the participation or the founding capital would appear on the balance sheet of the owner (ie the local government unit). (CEA, 2010)

Corporatism does not mean private ownership, but the very possibility of corporatism is strongly opposed by a population that fears rising prices. In a post-corporate environment, regular re-evaluation of equity capital would be warranted. Regional experience indicates that utility companies are registered according to book value, and the value in the balance sheet may be higher. Several historical and legal factors explain the bookkeeping/accounting problem described above. One is that large fixed assets such as pipelines and other equipment are actually state-owned and used by local government units/utilities. The reason for this is that when the utilities were established, all fixed assets were owned by the state, and there was no cadastre or other land registration service or other "evidence" to support the entry in the books of account of the balance sheet of the local government units. The argument that the title of the land or the data in the cadastre is not in accordance with the ownership of the units of local self-government is used throughout the former Yugoslavia to deny the ownership rights of the units of local self-government, despite legal provisions such as the Law on Public Enterprises of the Republic Macedonia who claim the opposite. (CEA, 2010)

The problems are compounded by new instruments in the era of decentralization. If the local self-government unit undertakes the expansion or opening of a sanitary landfill, does it own what it builds, or is it a gift to the state? Ambiguity over the ownership and status of fixed assets creates confusion in legal and financial obligations, diluting incentives for local government units and utilities to invest in and maintain the infrastructure necessary to provide adequate services.

Experience in other countries in transition (outside the borders of the former Yugoslavia) indicates that public enterprises in such situations should be transformed into a legal form that will have clear ownership rights and a determined value. Ownership is a way of strengthening responsibility.

Although somewhat ironic, experience in other countries indicates that when the ownership rights of water utilities are accurately established, there is a tendency for them to lose their importance. This occurs due to the nature of fixed assets in the water supply sector, which does not allow them to be given as collateral when borrowing for investments. Fixed assets of water companies cannot be sold like movable plant and equipment, office buildings, and land can, so they cannot be treated as collateral in a conventional way. Most fixed assets in water companies are pipelines, water treatment facilities, pumping stations, etc., which cannot be sold and therefore have no intrinsic value except as a complete package of a business being sold. The importance of ownership in this instance is to bolster the balance sheet and thereby promote its creditworthiness. This does not always require physical fixed assets to be entered on the balance sheet but rather reflects the net present value of the future income stream if there are sufficient assurances to ensure that the projected income stream is a realistic projection.

Successful concession agreements work when the concessionaire does not own the fixed assets but adopts them for a certain period. The fact that the concessionaire does not own fixed assets is not a handicap to the business and its ability to raise capital. What is a handicap for the business is the lack of confidence in the contractual obligations on the part of the grantor and whether the regulatory framework will be fair, and whether they can rely on it. Concession contracts, therefore, require confidence in the regulatory framework that compensation will be determined at realistic cost recovery rates (including capital maintenance provisions – through depreciation or some other economically viable accounting method) and will be able to earn on the principal.

Insufficient financial independence of utility companies. Another significant problem identified during the diagnostic work refers to the provision in the Law on Financing Local Self-Government Units (Article 22), according to which local self-government units should guarantee any long-term indebtedness of utility companies. The effect of this is to undermine the financial autonomy of utilities and incentives for efficient management, but it has even more serious consequences for local government units.

The guarantee provision is fully reflected in the mandatory Guidelines for the method and procedure for borrowing local self-government units and public enterprises in the Republic of Macedonia issued by the Ministry of Finance, published in the first quarter of 2007. These guidelines essentially separate the creditworthiness of the utilities owned by the local government unit from the creditworthiness of the local government unit itself. (CEA, 2010)

As the owner of the enterprise, the local government unit essentially assumes unlimited liability for the operations of the enterprise in contrast to its exposure if the enterprise is organized as a limited liability company. Strangely, the balance sheet of the local government unit is burdened by the presence of the guarantee it provides, but at the same time, the registered capital of the enterprise does not appear on the fixed assets side of the municipal balance sheet. The revenues of the enterprise, regardless of the degree to which they cover the expected debt for servicing, are not sufficient and must be supplemented by a guarantee from the local self-government unit.

The assumption that the guarantee of the local government unit increases the creditworthiness of the enterprise is not always valid. There may be a situation in which a "good" enterprise located in a "badly managed" local government unit does not get access to the credit market. Financial problems at the level of the local government unit do not necessarily threaten the ability of the enterprise to service its debt. The debt of the enterprise, through the mandatory guarantee, burdens the capacity of the local self-government unit to borrow for other purposes.

Regulatory Framework (Licensing, Pricing, Standards)

Technical regulation, in terms of setting and applying standards, exists, but implementation is limited due to the weak capacity of the authorities and the lack of political will for the effective implementation of laws. Economic regulation is less developed and even less effective in the utility sector in the Republic of Macedonia. Economic regulation (https://economy.gov.mk/regulativa.nspx) incorporates the concept that regulation is a tool for policy implementation (as opposed to policy formulation) and is needed when the market is not perfect and external interventions are needed to deliver the desired social balance between price and quality. The purpose of regulation is to ensure that users receive the best service through improved efficiency and better quality of services.

In the water, sewerage and solid waste management sectors, sectors in which there are the most utility companies in Macedonia, the main regulatory interventions are needed in the areas of licensing, pricing and standards. The current situation in each of these areas is briefly described below:

Licensing. Local self-government units are responsible for water supply, transport and wastewater treatment and are responsible for the establishment of utility companies that perform these functions. There is no formal licensing. Contrary to this, licensing is required for solid waste management, and it is the responsibility of the Ministry of Environment and Spatial Planning, not the local self-government units.

Pricing. The compensation is proposed by the utility companies and approved by the Council of the local self-government units. The water tariff should be calculated using a methodology determined by the Ministry of Transport and Communications (Official Gazette of the Republic of Macedonia, no. 68/04). This methodology makes it possible to distinguish the water tariff according to the level of use (block tariffs for average use and for the amount consumed above that) and according to the types of users (households, legal entities). The allowable cost price includes the capital investment allowance.

The methodology does not derive from a well-formulated policy and is given in general frameworks where the necessary specificity is lacking. In practice, it appears that only a few local government units use the methodology to prepare and submit the tariff, and even if they do, the question is whether the councils of the local government units would be able to accurately assess these submitted tariffs. Tariffs are generally too low, and as a result, there are insufficient resources for capital maintenance, let alone expansion. This situation leads to a worse level of service. Rigorous application of the methodology (or rather improved methodology) would be beneficial.

Standards. Standards for drinking water are set out in the Food Safety Act of 2002 and are regulated by the Ministry of Health. Environmental standards regarding the treatment and disposal of wastewater and solid waste are set out in the Environmental Law of 2005 and relevant by-laws. The municipal and the Inspectorate within the Ministry of Environment are responsible for adhering to the standards.

FINANCING UTILITY SERVICES AND COVERING COSTS

Financing of Utility Services

The main source of financing for investments in the past was the central government. In future, under the second phase of the decentralization program, capital requirements will have to be met mainly through loans, plus a combination of central and local government subsidies and retained earnings. Most of the credit financing is expected to be provided by the development partners under favorable conditions. There will also be financing with grants from donors that are usually channeled through the state budget.

According to the government's latest Public Investment Program 2011-2013, 5.49% of all public investment was spent on the water, utility and environment sectors - Table 1.

The majority of these sector expenditures are directed to local utility services. The ambitious investment goals of the Program should be financed from various sources, mainly external borrowings or grants. In the water supply sector, only 25% of the total costs will be financed with public funds, and in relation to public landfills, this percentage is even lower (17%). The collection of funds by the central and local authorities within the foreseen frameworks was a big challenge.

Regarding the financing of current costs, the main source of financing is cost coverage. With the expected increase in investment lending, cost coverage will be even more important in the future as debt servicing costs and running costs will have to be covered. With the introduction of local authority funding for utilities, we note that the ongoing flow of funds between the utility and its founder (the local government unit) is often very non-transparent. One of the goals is to perform a reform which will establish a transparent flow of funds. As a result, the subsidies will be explicitly presented, and a guarantee will be given that the higher tariffs will generate funds that will actually be used to service the debt and not to finance other things in the local government unit.

Movement of funds between local government units and utility companies. Utility managers use explicit, and in some cases, hidden methods to transfer funds to the local government unit of the utility. The flow of cash and services can also take place in the other direction, i.e., from utility companies to the local self-government unit. Given that the budget of the local government unit is based on cash, there is some "synergy" with the balance sheet of utilities and operations that are carried out on a maturity basis. For example, the most explicit movement of funds from the budget of the local self-government unit takes place in the form of subsidies. These subsidies have their own item in the budget and are transferred conditionally, mainly when necessary, or as part of the policy (to cover losses from low tariffs and poor collection). Another clear form of transfer from the budget takes place when a local government unit purchases services from utility companies. The local government unit is not only a big consumer of water, wastewater and other services, but it also buys other planned and ad hoc services like garden maintenance, cleaning after festivals, etc. In these cases, the local government unit pays the utility company on the basis of an invoice, in which VAT has been calculated.

Another non-transparent method of transferring income, if not cash, is the distribution of depreciation allowance. If the fixed assets are on the balance sheet of the local government unit, the utility uses these fixed assets for free or may be charged a usage fee. These fixed assets are not depreciated, as is usually done in the balance sheet of a local government unit. Hence, there is no renovation fund. If utilities do not charge users of the use of the underlying assets and then the users do not pay the owner, the balance sheet of the local government unit subsidizes the services. If the utilities charge a fee for the use of fixed assets but do not transfer those funds to the owner of the fixed assets, then it receives both cash and a subsidy on the balance sheet. If a utility lists fixed assets on its own balance sheet, charges depreciation, and can collect a portion of user fees for depreciation, then its behavior is not distorted.

Each relationship between the unit of local self-government and utilities is unique and deserves to be investigated separately. The interaction of the two types of accounting systems, the unclear policy on the ownership of fixed assets and depreciation, as well as the explicit policy on the lowest possible tariff for water and other services for the sake of political and social services, are fertile ground for unique solutions for the movement of cash or at least for balance sheet impact in directions that are not always economic. Transparency is also needed within utility bills. For example, to ensure proper resourcing of fixed assets it would be useful to open a capital account whereby depreciation provisions can be deposited into the account to fund capital maintenance, infrastructure improvement/level of service improvement and repayment on debt. Access to such an account would need to be controlled by the Public Utilities Supervisory Board to ensure that it is used only for its intended purposes.

Covering Utility Bills

Tariffing – A Comparative Analysis

Table 3 summarizes the tariffs presented by the Association of Utilities Providers in Macedonia for 2020.

Water and sanitation tariffs in many other countries where full cost recovery is achieved are significantly higher, for example, €2.60 in the UK, €1.50 in the USA,

€5.41 in Norway and €3.39 in the Netherlands (source: OECD (2002): Social Issues in the Provision and Pricing of Water Services, Paris). Even after adjustments for purchasing power, cheap labor and other costs, it is evident that the current combined tariffs in the Republic of Macedonia are inadequate to finance services according to EU standards. Longer distances will require triple, quadruple, or even higher magnification.

Table 3 shows that tariffs for water, sewage and garbage vary significantly in the Republic of Macedonia. The conditions for providing the services are different in the Republic of Macedonia, so different prices can be expected, but the big differences that currently exist between local government units are also due to the arbitrariness in determining the tariff. In many, if not most, cases, rates are well below the level needed to cover current costs, while some of the local government units with high rates are debt servicers and have therefore had to raise them significantly.

It is common practice to charge a higher fee to legal entities than to households. Table 3 shows that the prices for water and wastewater are higher for legal entities than for households. In the case of garbage collection, the ratio is even higher. The unit price for serving larger users (mostly companies) is generally lower than the price for serving small users (households), so from an economic point of view, the tariffs should be reversed. However, fairness considerations should continue to use these price differentials because the effect is to help households, a significant majority of whom find it expensive to pay for water, while most (though not all) companies' water bills are only a small item of their expenses. To be able to assess the costs and benefits of mutual subsidization between legal entities and households, it would be useful to quantify this and disclose it to beneficiaries and other stakeholders.

For water and sewage, there are fixed unit fees (MKD per cubic meter) for each category of users. Regarding waste, the Law on Waste Management (2004) provides three methods of calculating fees for users: per square meter, per cubic meter and per kilogram. As can be seen from Table 2, the usual method is to calculate the fee according to the area of the property (for both households and businesses). There is only one exception i.e., a unit of local self-government where the compensation is calculated according to the number of persons in households.

The calculation of the fee according to the area is based on the assumption that the generation of garbage is correlated with the size of the apartment or house. It is relatively easy to measure the basis for this fee, and there is also a hidden idea behind this concept according to which households that use more space are wealthier, so they should pay more for the same service. However, this is not always the case and could cause problems in large houses with poor families or with fewer members in the household. In the case of rural areas, the allowance is calculated as a flat rate per household.

Invoicing and Billing

The utility companies are responsible for invoicing and collecting the fee. Invoices issued by companies often contain a variety of public revenues, not just the fee for services provided by utilities, so local property taxes and street lighting fees could be on the same water and garbage bill. This joint billing technique does not help users understand what services they received for the price on the invoice and makes it difficult for users who do not want to pay for a particular service when they are not satisfied with the delivery. Also, utilities as service providers under the umbrella of a local government unit can easily be confused with local government as a client and local tax authorities.

Against this, it should be noted that joint accounts may result in a more effective collection, partly due to the existence of a stronger legal framework for enforcement than would normally be the case with a single account. If the bill is detailed and each item is clearly indicated, then it is an acceptable method of revenue administration. However, practice shows that the collection of water bills is much higher than that of general utility services in regions where these services are invoiced on separate accounts.

The collection rate differs in all local government units and varies from 52% to about 90%. (Association of Utilities Providers in Macedonia, 2020) Collection is generally better in households compared to businesses and government institutions. It was emphasized in the discussions in the focus groups and the key people who were interviewed that the main factor explaining the higher rate of collection is the generally lower tariffs applied in those local government units. Varying degrees of commitment to pay for utilities are also a factor in determining bill payment.

SUSTAINABILITY OF PUBLIC UTILITY COMPANIES

Basic Rules and Immediate Actions

The core strategy includes a commitment by the government, local government units and utilities to adhere to citizen/user orientation obligations in terms of their competencies and functions, with a reciprocal commitment by the users. Basically, they are the following:

- The key competencies of the government are the establishment of sector policies, the establishment of a national methodology for the water tariff and support for poor households, with appropriate obligations that the policies should be clear and consistent, that the formula for the tariff is based on sound economic principles and that care of poor households without burdening other beneficiaries.

- The responsibilities of the local self-government unit are the appointment of the members of the Boards of the utility companies and the leading people and the approval of the plans and tariffs with the obligation that the appointments are based on skills and integrity, while the approval of the plans and tariffs must be in accordance with the principles of best practices and efficiency standards. With the current structure and legislation, local government units are also responsible for finding funds for investments in which, either directly or by providing a guarantee for the indebtedness of the utility companies.
- The functions of the Government and local self-government units include being users of the services of utility companies, with the obligation to settle bills in a timely manner and to be responsible for the use of those services (e.g. economical use of water and disposal of wastewater taking care for the environment).
- The main competence of utility companies is to manage infrastructure assets (usually owned by local government units or the state) to provide the necessary services, with the obligation to do so in an efficient manner, following sound technical, financial, economic and principles of environmental protection. In the current system, utility companies are responsible for planning and implementing investment projects, but the financing of projects is largely in the hands of the municipality.
- Users have the right to high-quality services at the lowest price and the opportunity to express their opinion and influence the decisions of utility companies. Users are responsible for using water efficiently, disposing of water and waste in an environmentally friendly manner, and paying regularly and promptly for the services they have received.

The Sustainability Policy of Utility Companies

The first important element of the Core Strategy is a national statement on the Policy for the Sustainability of Utilities. This is necessary to provide a clear framework for the arrangements that must take place at the local level in accordance with the decentralization program. (CEA, 2010)

It is recommended that the Utility Sustainability Policy cover three areas explained below:

(a) Clarifying the relationship between local government units, utilities and users:
   - Financial transparency between local government units and utilities and within utilities (through separate accounting for each service);

- User charters, signed between local government units and their utility companies, including all performance requirements, for both parties, and a commitment by users to pay for services
- Clarifying the ownership of the infrastructure;
- System evaluation: regular reporting on the comparative performance of utilities;
- Request for greater accountability to the public and the possibility of involving the public;

(b) Sector policies:

- Commercialization of plumbing, sewage and garbage services;
- Demand to introduce a tariff over time to fully cover costs;
- Subsidy policy for poor households;
- Future direction of the national regulation to support the municipal regulatory functions;
- Investment financing;

(c) Restructuring of utility companies

- Consolidation of utility companies with numerous functions into companies with one sector (or closely related) mandates, either through an external cooperation agreement for non-core activities or through separate companies;
- Regionalization of the provision of services and establishment of joint enterprises;
- Transformation of utility companies into limited liability companies or joint stock companies;
- Preferred forms of private sector participation in water supply, sewage and garbage;

The utility sustainability policy will facilitate the other main elements of the essential reforms, which are (CEA, 2010):

- Formal Role for users that legally defines in a written document the responsibilities and obligations of local self-government units and utility companies towards citizens/users - the goal is to cement the "commitment" and provide a basis for systematic monitoring of performance by the public and to demand accountability;
- Accounting by cost center in order for the economic justification of each service provided by utility companies to be separately analyzed, which is part of the overall improved financial management
- Strengthened price regulation system to provide a more consistent and predictable environment of cost recovery for utility services;

- Utility performance indicators to encourage competitive competition among the best performers and provide a framework for the public to monitor service delivery in an informed manner;
- Raising public awareness (an essential starting point for strengthening the "shortcut to accountability");
- Establishment of a "scheme for social water and garbage" and care for households living on social assistance;
- Minor legal changes to ensure that utility debt is less of a burden on local government units and to extend the time given to utilities to file a dispute against non-paying households.

The Role of Users

Some units of local self-government have made a business plan for the role of users, and in agreement with utility companies, it is a legally binding document. The role of users that is envisaged is based on this concept, but a commitment is required from both the local self-government units and the utility companies.

The role of the users should be formalized in a document that will define the competencies and obligations of the local self-government units and utility companies towards the citizens/users. In the current institutional structure, the form of the envisaged agreement will essentially follow the terms of a lease agreement between the owner of the fixed assets, responsible for investment (in this case, the local government unit), and the service provider authorized to use the basic assets to provide the services (utilities).

It should be noted that the term "Service Agreement" is more often used for documents of this type. However, the term "Role of users" is proposed as a way of directing attention to the ultimate goal of improving services for users and reducing the burden on citizens as national and taxpayers of local government units. The main purpose of the document is to provide a basis for the public to systematically monitor performance and demand accountability from both the local government unit and utility companies.

Although the aim is to make commitments as legally binding as possible, experience from other countries indicates that such documents, although drawn up in legal form, are not treated as binding. However, their formal nature provides a basis and is a reference point for asking questions from the public. Monitoring the extent to which the objectives of local government units and utilities have been achieved will be a major step forward from the current situation. When the public has access to information, and a basis for judging performance, consumer groups and the general public will be able to publicly name local government units and utilities that are not performing satisfactorily and pressure contracting parties to adhere to the document.

The document, which will be called Role of users, should essentially contain: Formal aspects

- Contract duration/extension, modification, termination
- Dispute resolution

Essential aspects

- Management and personnel structure
- Area of coverage
- Service, quality and environmental protection obligations
- Planning, budgeting, reporting and auditing
- Determination of the tariff, adjustment and subsidies
- Fixed assets and investments
- User access, response and objection/complaint mechanisms
- Performance indicators and targets

The above comments specifically apply to documents that do not contain specific incentives to encourage improved performance, in the first instance, by utility managers. Where there are specific incentives, the stakes are higher because the payment is linked to the fulfillment of contractual obligations.

For such a system to be successful, it is necessary to establish strict independent auditing mechanisms. The system should ensure that the benefits of improved efficiency ultimately accrue to users and are not forever appropriated by operators.

With or without incentives, the intent of the document is to introduce greater efficiency (better technical performance and improved financial management) through actions taken by the unit (including its role in infrastructure expansion) and the utilities themselves.

A performance-based document. In a system where the operation and maintenance of the water infrastructure in public ownership are given by contract to an operator (which, in legal terms, is a partnership with the leading persons), monthly payments are made to the operator through 3 elements:

- *Base Fee - Fixed* = 100% of non-controllable fixed operating costs and 75% of controllable performance-related operating costs;
- *Performance fee* - 25% of the balance multiplied by the weighted achievement of 20 minimum performance standards in relation to the 6-month average before the start of the contract - failure to achieve this carries a fine;

- *Incentive fee* – allows the operator to earn excess cash from the operating margin, which is the actual operating margin minus the minimum operating margin, multiplied by the weighted achievement of the "parent" goals. The incentive fee aims to reward the operator's efforts in the field of cost control and revenue generation, reduction of unbilled water, new and active connections and timely collection of bills. This incentive compensation is distributed among the partners and the secondary staff in accordance with their participation in the partnership.

Price Regulation

As already mentioned, according to the current legal framework, the proposals for the tariff are formulated by the utility companies and are approved by the Council of the local self-government unit. The approval of tariffs at the local level is one of the key competencies that were transferred to local self-government units with the decentralization process. Tariffs for water and sewerage, which are closely related to the price of water, have in the past been more politicized and contested than tariffs for garbage.

From December 2005 local political influence was supposed to be eliminated by the national methodology for determining the water tariff that was introduced by the Ministry of Transport and Communications under the Law on Drinking Water Supply and Urban Wastewater Disposal. But this methodology is used by only a few municipalities to prepare tariff submissions, and even when they did, it was questioned whether the councils of local self-government units could accurately evaluate these submissions.

As a result, there is an extremely large and arbitrary divergence in water tariffs and the fear among potential investors that the water tariff could change in an unpredictable manner. There is a strong desire to remove this uncertainty by formulating a clear commitment in pricing policy that will fully cover costs and to use this to develop a well-founded methodology and ensure that it is effectively implemented at the municipal level.

Citizens and authorities in local government units recognize the need for change in the way the price for utility services is determined. It has been suggested for a long time that prices should be determined in a way to reduce the influence of local self-government units and that a possible solution to this problem would be the establishment of a national Regulatory Commission. This approach has been successfully applied in other countries, but only when the committee members are people of integrity and the necessary technical skills. The implementation of the regulation through such a commission could be a long-term option for the Republic of Macedonia, or it could be a temporary solution that could later lead to the establishment of an independent regulatory agency for water or a department within a multi-sectorial regulatory agency responsible for water. In any case, professionalism and independence from everyday political pressures will be essential.

Systematic Evaluation and Rising of Public Awareness

Systematic evaluation is the systematic collection of performance information so that utilities can compare their performance with that of other utilities. The existence of a national system for systemic evaluation of the performance of service providers in the field of water supply, sanitation and solid waste management has many advantages. Combined with an improved accounting system and financial management, system evaluation would be a low-cost addition that would encourage managers to review performance in each area of their operations and strive to compete with the best utilities in each area. Regular reports with the results of the system assessment would also allow the media and the general public to monitor the performance of utilities and apply well-informed pressure for improvements in specific areas.

Considering the starting base of many of the utility companies, the effect of the systemic valuation in the Republic of Macedonia could be very large and very fast.

There are two complementary systems assessment initiatives in the Republic of Macedonia from which to start, first the system assessment by the German Agency for Technical Cooperation and second the workshop organized by the World Bank and Association of Utilities Providers in Macedonia in December 2017 for evaluation of the performance of the water utilities in the Republic of Macedonia according to the International Network for Systemic Evaluation of Water and Sanitary Utilities.

Key indicators for public utilities are:

- Consumption: income stream
- Unbilled losses: potential for improvement and cost reduction
- Measurement rate: forecast accuracy
- Personnel: efficiency of operations
- Unit price for production – the red part of accounting
- Income unit – black part of accounting
- Collection rate – cash flow forecast
- Accumulation of claims from users – potential for improving the accounting balance
- Cost recovery rate

One of the areas of concern for utilities that was frequently raised during the survey was the issue of overemployment. System valuation indicators such as the number of employees per thousand users will immediately single out utilities with chronic overemployment. Many of the other issues that were raised during the research discussions regarding utility management will be more quickly resolved with the introduction of system valuation. Some of these issues are the separation of tariff-based activities from public good activities, the need for more effective cost control, and the need to develop employee skills through merit-based hiring and training programs.

Raising public awareness. The results of the research conducted by Economic Consulting Associates suggest that the general public in the Republic of Macedonia is extremely poorly informed about the delivery of utility services. Raising public awareness and motivating people to be more involved in the process of obtaining better services and thus strengthening the "straight path of accountability" are key elements of the strategy for utilities. (CEA, 2010)

Addressing a lack of awareness is the most obvious way to address some of the most pressing problems in utilities, according to those who participated in focus groups and interviews in a survey conducted by Economic Consulting Associates. For example, interviewees believed that a key to improving billing was raising awareness that water and other utility bills should be paid, just as commercial services such as telephone and electricity are paid. In this direction, the role of local communities as a channel for starting a campaign to increase the collection with regular meetings and discussions was emphasized.

It is difficult to raise awareness directly among utility users. Good knowledge of the situation predicts an approach according to which journalists from the print and electronic media will be worked with at the beginning, and they will be given the necessary information to be more informed and engaged to perform "supervision" of the issues of water supply, sanitation, garbage and public-private partnership. In particular, with the introduction of the Role of Users document, the media will be encouraged to give importance to performance monitoring reports and public disclosure of those whose performance is poor, thereby contributing to local government units and utilities complying with the commitments.

Establishing a national system for systemic evaluation will also be a crucial step in raising public awareness. Regular system assessment reports will be a good basis for writing articles in the media and putting performance and efficiency issues in the public arena, and raising the stakes for utilities to improve their rating until the time for the next system assessment. Public debates will involve not only management but also utility employees, which is another target group for raising awareness. This should help to motivate employees to be more committed to the work of suffering, increase their efficiency, increase collection and reduce losses and costs.

Targeting the media to raise user awareness and encourage their involvement is a short-term item. Permanent information campaigns and raising awareness are part of the responsibilities of local governments and utility companies themselves.

Contracts with consumers are an important starting point for closer direct relations between utilities and their customers. According to the Law on Supply of Drinking Water and Drainage of Urban Wastewater (Article 48), utility companies are in the process of signing formal contracts with their users to ensure the delivery of services and timely payment of bills.

Contracts between users and utilities will gain more weight as other aspects are implemented, such as a pricing mechanism with clear rules and accompanying social policy measures for families receiving welfare.

SOLUTIONS AND RECOMMENDATIONS

Public utility systems in the Republic of Macedonia have been in debt for years and are non-functional, and the services they deliver are not of adequate quality. In that direction, the Government of the Republic of Macedonia and local self-government units:

- They should prepare a National Water Plan and Water Strategy
- In large urban areas, an integrated sewage network and wastewater treatment system should be established
- Feasibility studies should be prepared for the identified regional landfills
- Temporary landfills should be opened, and illegal hotspots should be closed.
- Plan for the economic sustainability of utility companies.
- Employment plan and provision of an estimate for the optimal number of employees.

In the water sector, Macedonia should work on compliance with the following directives:

- Water Framework Directive (2000/ 60/ EC)
- Water quality directive (98/ 83/ EC)
- Directive on urban wastewater treatment (91/ 271/ EC)

In the solid waste sector, the main directive is the Waste Management Directive (2006/12/EC). However, this is a framework directive, with around 15 subsidiary directives relating to specific areas of solid waste management.

FUTURE RESEARCH DIRECTIONS

At least once a year, it is necessary to check surveys of the public's opinion about the problems and satisfaction of consumers with the communal services offered in the units of local self-government. The findings of these surveys should be presented at an annual public hearing with the service providers and the representatives of the larger groups of consumers, the representatives of the Municipal Councils. Plans to improve the situation should be determined at these public hearings. This recommendation does not exclude the implementation of individual service providers' own surveys on the degree of user satisfaction.

Furthermore, research should be carried out continuously, and the indebtedness of the public utility companies should be monitored, as well as the criteria for employment and the number of employment opportunities in the same should be followed.

CONCLUSION

From the aspect of financing the units of local self-government in order to complete the implementation of the Law on financing the units of local self-government, the Government, through the competent ministries, should ensure the following conditions:

- It should enable all municipalities to enter the second phase of fiscal decentralization.
- Established a functional and objective financial monitoring system for the implementation of dedicated, block and capital grants by the municipalities.
- Establish minimum service standards (where they do not currently exist) and review the basis for matching service delivery based on minimum service standards with financial capacity as the most appropriate way to calculate service costs.
- Considered measures to improve grants and will develop an effective fiscal settlement system.

General recommendations for the local self-government units that did not enter the second phase of fiscal decentralization should provide an initial precondition for entering the second phase of fiscal decentralization, which consists of fulfilling the conditions of the first phase of fiscal decentralization, or rather within the municipal administration. To have at least two employed officers who are qualified to work in the field of financial management, preparation and execution of the budget, accounting and preparation of financial reports and at least three employees in the municipal administration who work to determine and collect local taxes, fees and fees. Since most units of local self-government have not fulfilled the conditions of the first phase of fiscal decentralization and therefore do not have sufficient personnel capacities for financial management, in order to fulfill these conditions, the following possible solutions are recommended:

- In local self-government units where there is an opportunity to hire new people in order to fulfill this condition, it is necessary to do the same;
- In local self-government units where, for certain reasons, there is no possibility of new employment and they already have professional staff from this area employed in the municipal administration in other jobs, it is necessary to redistribute existing jobs to jobs that are required, in order to fulfill the conditions of the first phase of fiscal decentralization;
- If there is no possibility of fulfilling the condition according to the proposed solutions described above, in that case, it is necessary for those units of local self-government to make an agreement with another unit for the performance of these obligations or with the Administration of Public Revenues. The positive experiences of the municipalities that have achieved this kind of cooperation can be taken as an example.

The second largest problem facing the Local Government Units for entry into the second phase of fiscal decentralization is the situation with outstanding obligations to suppliers or any other creditors, which exceed the terms of payments that are usual. In a large number of cases, due to non-timely payment of obligations or the lack of sufficient financial means to pay the obligations, the municipality's account is blocked by a court decision. Meeting this requirement has financial implications that make it extremely complex and lengthy to resolve. To overcome this situation, the following measures and activities are proposed:

- Involvement of the Government of the Republic of Macedonia to solve this huge problem by starting a dialogue between the local self-government units that have problems with blocked accounts and the Government of the Republic of Macedonia, with the aim of finding appropriate measures and activities that will be adequate to solve this problem.
- Local self-government units that have blocked accounts exclusively from institutions and public enterprises founded by the Republic of Macedonia are recommended to conclude appropriate agreements for deferred payment of these obligations with the mediation of the Government of the Republic of Macedonia.

- In local self-government units that have determined financial instability, it is necessary to establish a Commission for overcoming financial instability.
- Creation of legal prerequisites for the possibility of local self-government units that have backlogs of unsettled obligations to suppliers or any other creditors, which exceed the terms of payments that are usual or blocked accounts, to borrow specifically from credit and financial institutions for the settlement of the obligations. Borrowing money market interest rates are lower than interest rates on court orders blocking accounts.
- Local self-government units that have outstanding unpaid obligations to suppliers or any other creditors that exceed the terms of payments that are usual, but their account is not blocked need the majority of financial resources obtained from their own sources of income, income from VAT, income from personal income to direct them towards fulfilling these obligations.

In the part of raising the capacities of the municipal administration for the successful performance of the tasks and obligations resulting from the fiscal decentralization (first and second phase), it is noted that there is a serious and necessary need for training in almost all areas that were the subject of research. Special attention needs to be paid to providing training on the management of block grants and property assessment for new taxpayers.

It is recommended that the Local Self-Government Units in the budget planning process achieve more intensive institutional communication with the central government institutions for the purpose of timely and complete information on the amount of dedicated block and capital subsidies, VAT revenues and income tax. In this way, frequent changes and additions to the Budgets will be avoided.

The transfer of knowledge and experience by the municipal administration from the local government units that entered the second phase can significantly help those units that did not enter the second phase of fiscal decentralization to do the same in a fast and efficient way.

REFERENCES

Allen, R., & Tommasi, D. (2009). *Upravljanje javnim izdacima*. OECD.

Angelov, G. (2005). *Handbook for mayors and members of municipal councils in the Republic of Macedonia.* Skopje: Community of Local Self-Government Units of the Republic of Macedonia.

Association of Utilities Providers in Macedonia. (2020). *Annual report 2019.* Association of Utilities Providers in Macedonia.

Atanasovski, Z. (2006). *Public finance.* Faculty of Economics.

Budget Law ("Official Gazette of the Republic of Macedonia", 35/01; 93/01)

CEA. (2006). *The Future of Public Finance at Local Level.* CEA.

CEA, Republic of Macedonia. (2010). *Strategy and Action Plan for Reforms in Communal Enterprises with a Focus on Water Supply, Sewerage and Solid Waste Management, Proposed Diagnostic and Strategic Report.* CEA.

Community of Local Self-Government Units of the Republic of Macedonia, Skopje. (2005). *Report 2002-2004.* Skopje: Community of Local Self-Government Units of the Republic of Macedonia.

Economic Consulting Associates. (2008). *Republic of Macedonia: Strategies and Action Plan for Reforms in Utilities with a Focus on Water Supply, Sewerage and Solid Waste Management.* Economic Consulting Associates.

Environmental Law (Official Gazette of the Republic of Macedonia, no. 53/05).

Government of the Republic of Macedonia. (2008). *Decentralization Implementation Program 2008-2012.* Government of the Republic of Macedonia.

Jovanovski, P. (2005). *Public Finances.* FON.

VAT Law (Official Gazette of the Republic of Macedonia, no. 44/99 with changes).

Law on balanced regional development (Official Gazette of the Republic of Macedonia, no. 63/07, 187/13, 43/14, 215/15 and 64/18).

Law on Budgets (Official Gazette of the Republic of Macedonia, no. 203/2022).

Law on commercial companies (Official Gazette of the Republic of Macedonia, no. 28/04).

Law on communal activities (Official Gazette of the Republic of Macedonia, no. 45/97).

Law on concessions and other types of public-private partnership (Official Gazette of the Republic of Macedonia, no. 6/2012, 144/2014, 33/2015, 104/2015, 215/2015, 153/2019, 261/2019).

Law on determination and collection of public revenues ("Official Gazette of the Republic of Macedonia", no. 13/01, 61/02 and 24/03).

Law on drinking water supply and urban wastewater disposal (Official Gazette of the Republic of Macedonia, no. 68/04, 28/06 and 103/08).

Law on Financing Local Self-Government Units (Official Gazette No. 61/04, 96/04, 67/07, 156/09, 47/11 and 192/15).

Law on Financing of Local Self-Government Units ("Official Gazette of the Republic of Macedonia", no. 61/04).

Law on Local Self-Government ("Official Gazette of the Republic of Macedonia", No. 5/05).

Law on Local Self-Government (Official Gazette of the Republic of Macedonia no. 5/2002).

Law on property and other real property rights (Official Gazette of the Republic of Macedonia, no. 18/01).

Law on Public Enterprises (Official Gazette of the Republic of Macedonia, no. 38/1996; 9/1997; 6/2002; 40/2003; 49/2006; 22/2007; 83/2009; 97/2010; 6/2012; 119/2013; 41/2014; 138/2014; 25/2015; 61/2015; 39/2016, 64/2018, 35/19 and 275/19).

Law on Public Enterprises (Official Gazette of the Republic of Macedonia, no. 38/96, 6/02, 40/03, 49/06).

Law on the City of Skopje (Official Gazette of the Republic of Macedonia, no. 55/2004; 158/2011).

Law on Transformation of socially owned (Official Gazette of the Republic of Macedonia, no. 38/93).

OECD. (2002). *Social Issues in the Provision and Pricing of Water Services*. OECD.

OSCE. (2009). *Report on the process of fiscal decentralization in the Republic of Macedonia*. OECD.

OSCE. (2009). *Review of Decentralization*. OECD.

Solid waste management law (Official Gazette of the Republic of Macedonia, no. 216/21).

Spasov, S., & Arsov, S. (2004). *Financial Management*. Faculty of Economics.

Standard & Poor. (2010). *Public finance system overview, Macedonian municipalities*. Standard & Poor.

The Law on Accounting for Budgets and Budget Users ("Official Gazette of the Republic of Macedonia", no. 61/02, 98/02).

Todorovski, I. (2004). *Functioning of the local self-government system in the Republic of Macedonia*. Institute for Sociological and Political Legal Research, UKIM.

Water Law (Official Gazette of the Republic of Macedonia, no. 04/98).

ADDITIONAL READING

Cilibiu, O. M. (2016). *Public Services and Public Utilities*. SSRN *Electronic Journal*. doi:10.2139/ssrn.2802211

Klass, A. B. (2019). Public utilities and transportation electrification. *Iowa Law Review, 104*(2), 545–617.

Smojver, Ž., Mudronja, G., & Schiozzi, D. (2017). Reorganization of the public utility companies. *Pomorstvo, 31*(1), 53–59. doi:10.31217/p.31.1.11

William, B. (2014). Public Utility and the Low-Carbon Future. *UCLA Law Review. University of California, Los Angeles. School of Law*, *61*(6), 1614–1710.

KEY TERMS AND DEFINITIONS

Budget: Classical economists define the budget as an act of forecasting the revenues and expenditures of the local government unit.

Decentralization: Process of transfer of competencies from central to local authorities.

Evaluation: Critical analysis of the achievements and results of a project, program, policy, or institution.

Legislation: The process of making or enacting laws.

Policy Formulation: Process of creating public policies.

Public Utility: An enterprise established and managed by a local government unit.

Chapter 3
Public Utility System Evolution: Hierarchical Clustering Pricing Procedure

Žarko Vranjanac
https://orcid.org/0000-0002-0893-8330
University of Niš, Serbia

Žarko Rađenović
https://orcid.org/0000-0002-3679-7870
University of Niš, Serbia

ABSTRACT

The chapter provides an overview of the origin and development of the public utility system through different epochs in the development of human civilization. The old century is characterized by the emergence of significant architectural achievements related to the public utility system. The darkest period in the history of human civilization was the Middle Ages, in which there was stagnation in the development of the public utility system. In the new century, the process of planning in cities and equipping them with communal infrastructure all over the world begins. The modern public utility system is characterized by the application of the latest technologies, innovations, and knowledge to improve the quality of life of the population and the effects of environmental protection, which requires monitoring through the development of performance indicators. The methodological framework of this research is based on cluster analysis using Ward's method, where the selected countries will be grouped into clusters.

DOI: 10.4018/978-1-6684-7730-4.ch003

INTRODUCTION

Water right is one of the basic human rights. Globally, for many people, especially those living in the poorest parts of the world, this basic human right is still unavailable. Among other things, water supply systems have not been built everywhere, but also because water reserves are being depleted or have already been completely exhausted in some places. Water as such is, therefore, much more than a simple communal need. It is an overly sensitive and limited resource that needs to be preserved and, to preserve it, should be treated with the utmost care. From the point of view of the local community, regular water supply is the first and most important communal function that should be established not only in urban and urbanized settlements but also in rural areas. In addition to water supply systems that provide the population with the basic prerequisites for life, a system for channeling, removal, and purification of wastewater discharged by consumers should be established. For now, only the most developed countries have established complete control over wastewater, while in most parts of the world, is mostly discharged in an insufficiently controlled manner and without any purification (Vranjanac et al., 2022). Thus, untreated wastewater is "mixed" and pollutes otherwise limited sources of drinking water, thus making the water problem even more difficult. Those extremely significant communal needs for water should be met in a long-term sustainable way. In such a way that water is not viewed only as a communal product and service, but as a particularly valuable resource that, if we do not treat it properly, will simply not exist one day. Public utilities have a significant impact on the quality of life of users in urban areas. Public utility companies provide various products and services to users, which improve their quality of life and environment owing to the fact that utility companies must provide services of satisfactory quality. That quality is significantly decided by the user's requirements, their real possibilities (first financial), and needs (Janaćković et al., 2017). The price of public utilities is of crucial importance for local communities, which is why it is important to take care of when figuring it out it. The methodology for pricing utility services must contain all significant elements in order to achieve efficiency and effectiveness in local communities in a long-term sustainable manner (Vranjanac & Spasić, 2017). This means that utility companies must orient themselves to market conditions, while the local community must devote itself to environmental effects. The local self-government unit must be the mediator in achieving this balance (Filipović & Krnjeta, 2013).

BACKGROUND

In clan communities, we cannot talk about the public utility system because of the way of life following the environment: the use of natural shelters, holes, and caves, making tools from natural materials, etc. With the appearance of the first forms of organized settlements of people, problems arose primarily related to the collective way of life in communities (communal problems) with water, wastewater, waste, heating, etc. Further social and scientific-technological development, in parallel with the emergence of urban human settlements, accompanied the improvement of the public utility system to the level we know today (Pejčić & Vranjanac, 2016). The public utility system is a complex system which consists of subsystems that can function independently. Subsystems of the public utility system are the following public utilities: water supply system, sewerage system, waste management system, district heating system, public lighting, regulation of vehicle parking, burials, animal hygiene, chimneys, management of markets, maintenance of streets and public green areas, transportation of passengers in urban and suburban traffic. Public utilities are of public interest throughout history, they have been related to the protection of the environment and the quality of life of the population. The public utility system operates within the utility economy as part of the social-economic system in public ownership (Simović, 1963). Public utilities are entrusted to utility companies. Regardless of the way of organization and the nature of management of utility companies (state, private, public-private partnership, etc.), in the formal-legal, institutional and legislative sense, utility activities are regulated by the state or local self-government unit. Since it is about municipal activities, hence the name public utilities or communal activities (commune-municipality), i.e., communal (public utility) system (Gancević, 1971).

PUBLIC UTILITY SYSTEMS THROUGHOUT HISTORY

Old-Century Public Utility System

The public utility system of the old century represents the period in which communal problems and solutions appear - it can be said that the old century is the period of development of awareness of the importance of the public utility system. The appearance of the first laws, social divisions in which slave owners could and slaves could not enjoy baths, as well as the construction of large step pyramids and palaces where rulers were buried. As there is general agreement that the appearance of settlements was preceded by a period of domestication of animals and agricultural production, the places for the formation of settlements, in addition to clean water, should have fertile soil and favorable climatic conditions. In addition to the "agricultural revolution", as this period is referred to in the literature, the development of the first settlements is also evidenced by archaeological findings, as well as certain language forms (3000 BC Mesopotamia and Egypt). Also, the development of public green areas next to palaces and residential buildings (Hanging Gardens of Babylon) with the influence of a religion based on respect for animals (Egypt: lion, bull, and cow). The Great Pyramid of Cheops, one of the Seven Wonders of the Ancient World, is in Giza, Egypt. In the East, it is believed that in the period of about 2500 years BC established, settlements in India, as well as around 1800 BC in China. In India, nomadic tribes gradually became settlers, inhabiting the valleys of the Ganges and Indus rivers. In China, settlements began to develop on the banks of the Yellow River and the Yangtze River, whose population was mainly engaged in agriculture. In ancient Greece, the island of Crete became the center of Mycenaean culture, dominated by seafaring, around 2,000 years BC. Ancient Greece gained importance in the Aegean Sea, so the cities had a water supply and underground sewage system, as well as the Agora (the forerunner of today's mixed-use markets). Ancient Rome is characterized by cities with an excellent water and sewage system (Cloaca Maxima), as well as a city traffic network. Later, distinct types of markets appeared - basilicas (Radosavljević, 2010). The water from the thermal baths poured into the drainage pipes, carrying with it dirt and wastewater from the bathroom and toilet. By the way, aqueducts were an imposing part of the public utility system of ancient Rome because their arches (buildings that can be seen from the outside) made up only about 20% of the system, while the greater part was underground. In this way, the system was protected from erosion with minimal damage to the environment.

The fact that before the construction of the aqueduct, engineers assessed the quality of the water by testing its transparency, flow and taste speaks of the elevated level of development of the water supply system of ancient Rome. Attention was also focused on the health of those who drank it and the maintenance of the entire system. Parts of the underground aqueduct could be accessed through shafts, and engineers could temporarily divert the water until the fault was repaired when more intervention was needed. Under the influence of gravity, water arrived in the city and flowed into reservoirs, from which it was directed to other reservoirs or consumers through pipelines. It is believed that the Roman water system was so developed that it could supply over 1000 liters (about 264.17 gals) of water per capita per day. In the Republic of Serbia, archaeological excavations have found remains of Roman waterworks and public baths (Spasić, 2017).

Public Utility System of the Middle Ages

In the Middle Ages, maintaining unsanitary conditions was promoted, as hygiene was considered undesirable during plague epidemics. The disease continued to spread as the infection carried by rodents was more easily transmitted through unsanitary conditions. In addition, residents threw their excrement and waste out of the windows in the middle of the street, and inside the city walls. Hygiene principles were reduced to the saying "Saepe manus, raro pedes, nunquam caput" - hands often, legs rarely, head never (Vranjanac, 2015). The condition that was present in the cities Singer describes in his book "History of Technology" as follows: "Since there was no successful sewage removal and street cleaning, hygienic conditions were far below the standards of imperial Rome, in which water often had to be brought from long distances outside the city limits. The wells, which were usually used to collect rainwater, were often located on low-lying land and near latrines and latrine pits. Because of this, epidemics spread rapidly. The open gutters in the middle of the street were carrying trash and garbage, and the rainwater, which poured from the roofs, was not properly drained. The streets, rarely paved, were often puddles from which the feces of pigs and other animals leaked into wells and onto private lands." (Spasić, 2013). However, after the liberation of the cities from the feudal lords, city administrations (communes) were formed, which, among other things, began to deal with communal issues administratively. The Statute of the city of Dubrovnik from 1272, among other things, regulated communal problems, such as, for example, sewerage and street improvement (Spasić, 2017).

New-Century Public Utility System

The cities of the new century generally did not have the communal infrastructure, so it was necessary to equip them with water and sewage systems, as well as gas pipelines for heating (Clifton, 2013). This situation required the start of the process of spatial planning in cities. Paris, London, and Berlin are building subways for passenger transportation (Milutinović, 2004). An automated public lighting system that activated the flame automatically when the gas supply was turned on was first implemented in the Arab Empire in Córdoba. More modern lamps with the use of kerosene were used in the Austrian Empire starting in 1853. The use of electric "arc lamps" or "electric candles", which were developed and perfected by the Russian Pavel Yablochkov in 1875, was first used in Paris, which is why it was called the "city of light". Later, the same public lighting system was implemented in Great Britain - Newcastle (1879) and in the United States - Cleveland in 1879. The first city in Europe with a modern public lighting system was Timisoara, in Romania. At the end of the 19th century, incandescent light bulbs were invented, and "arc lamps" were then thrown out of wider use (Vranjanac, 2015). Since an indistinguishable situation existed in industrial centers in Europe and the USA, awareness of the importance of the environment and the public utility system began to develop (Clifton, 2013). 1734 in Sweden; the Law on the Protection of Historical Monuments, passed in 1834 in Greece; The law requiring cities to have their site plans, passed in 1874 in Sweden; The Law on the Protection of Water from Pollution and Industrial Waste Water, passed in 1876 in Great Britain (Spasić, 2017).

The Modern Public Utility System

The Law on the Protection of Water from Pollution and Industrial Waste Water was passed in 1876 in Great Britain (Spasić, 2017). An efficient public utility system today implies the functioning of the water supply, sewerage and heating system, the solved problem of municipal waste management, passenger transport, parking lots, public lighting, maintenance of streets and public green areas, as well as animal care, chimney sweep services, market, and funeral activities. The functioning of modern public utility systems and their development requires qualified human resources, the application of modern, cleaner technologies and innovations, artificial intelligence and smart sensors, renewable energy sources, alternative fuels and energy sources, equipment, and machines, as well as the construction of communal infrastructure (Nikitas, 2020). Since 2020, the world has been hit by the pandemic of the Covid-19 virus, in the fight against which the public utility system is also involved, primarily through the disinfection of streets and the provision of quality drinking water to the population (France as an example), but also through the provision of continuity within the performance of vital public utilities. Unmanned aerial vehicles - drones today find application in the municipal system for the performance of the following municipal activities (example: Dubai): identification of damage, malfunctions, and leaks on pipelines and tanks, monitoring of the state of vegetation, determination of the amount of energy and fuel, inspection in non-compliance with the law when disposing of waste, evaluation, management, transport, etc. On the other hand, in some countries (countries in Africa), due to a lack of water, the water supply activity is not regulated. In developing countries (e.g., Serbia), in addition to the occurrence of excessive environmental pollution and endangering the health of the population, there are no sanitary landfills in the largest cities, as well as wastewater treatment facilities. So, the level of development of the public utility system directly depends on several factors, the most important of which are: natural-geographic, socio-economic and cultural-political. Natural-geographical factors include natural conditions (e.g., availability of clean water, environmental quality, etc.) and geographic conditions (terrain slope, relief, etc.). Socioeconomic factors should provide knowledge, qualified human resources, and financial resources to realize significant investments in public utilities. Final decisions on the level of availability, continuity, and quality in the public utility system are made by the state and local political apparatus, while certain cultural understandings and sacred developments can have significant implications for them (e.g., waste management, use of public transport, etc.).

Development Of Performance Measurement in Public Utility Systems

From a modern point of view, the concept of measurement has been widely studied and applied in the scientific literature. The beginnings of measurement are associated with ancient Egypt, 3000 years BC. At that time, the units of measurement were generally the length of the pharaoh's body parts or the length of certain objects from the environment. The first royal "cubit" was defined as the length of the forearm from the elbow to the tip of the extended middle finger of the ruling pharaoh, increased by the width of his hand. This original measure was then transferred and carved from a piece of black granite, whose wooden copies were given to the workers at the construction sites. For measuring larger distances, ropes with knots tied at a certain length were mostly used. Thus, the first thing that was measured was the depth of the Nile River, which was 6 cubits and 1 palm (Howarth, 2008). This shows that man, from the beginning until today, needs to quantify phenomena and objects from nature and the environment. Natural resources have always been the most valuable, therefore, the most important task was to determine the units of measurement for the area (calculation of the surface of the foundations of pyramids, palaces, houses, and other buildings). In ancient Greece, the unit of measure was determined almost identically with the help of the length of body parts and objects, which was classified into smaller and larger. However, measurement is considered to have gained importance with the appearance of goods and their exchange. Not all Romans and Athenians were of the same constitution, so equal exchange of goods, and therefore communication between residents and merchants, was difficult. This shows that the comparison of ancient measures provided a starting point for the development of unified measurement units necessary for understanding various social and natural phenomena. The theory of measurement, according to the literature (Zeković, 2003; Tasić, 2000), developed at the end of the 18th century under the influence of the French bourgeois revolution, when metrology was born. Etymologically, the term metrology comes from the Greek language, from the word metro (Greek μετρο), which means to measure, and the word logia (Greek λογιξα), which means science. Metrology is a science that deals with measurement units and their standards (reference), gauges (measuring instruments), and measurements (procedure). In the same city, two platinum standards were made, the kilogram standard and the meter standard. The first standards of the Kingdom of Serbia, which joined the International Metric Convention in 1879, were the meter and kilogram prototypes from 1891 (Directorate for Measures and Precious Metals, 2019). The development of metrology in the 20th century can be historically divided into the following 5 stages (Stević, 2006, Rowlet, 2005):

- The first stage refers to the period up to 1920, when single standards were introduced into industrial production. Then the first factories of measuring instruments and measuring equipment were opened.
- The second stage refers to the period from 1920 to 1940, when optics were introduced into measurement and control systems. Then several new measuring instruments were developed: an optimeter, interferometer, Schmaltz microscope for roughness measurement, and others.
- The third stage refers to the period from 1940 to 1960, when pneumatics was introduced into measuring systems, and the interference microscope and inductive measuring systems were developed.
- The fourth stage refers to the period from 1960 to 1980, when electronics were introduced into measuring systems and: transistors, integrated circuits, and the beginnings of the application of microprocessors and microcomputers were developed.
- The fifth stage refers to the period after 1980 when the integration of metrological processes with other processes (transport, control, monitoring, etc.) is completed based on computer support.

Metrological systems based on digital photo processing are being developed, and research is being carried out in the field of intelligent metrological systems. As a result of the desire to unify measurement units, the International System of Units was created in 1960 (French Système international d'unités or (SI) English International System of Units). With the further development of science, this system was perfected and universally accepted in science. Metrology has constantly been changing since its inception today, so different classifications of metrology appear in the literature depending on the application (scientific, industrial, legal; general or fundamental and legal), which can be further divided (into medical metrology, technical metrology, etc.) (Terzić, 2017). In the case of natural phenomena, metrology (metrology of temperature, time, etc.) evaluates the values of the quantities that characterize them, which is why a large number of measurement units are in use. Prediction, assessment, and protection of the population from environmental hazards and harms are based on a science that depends on the results of certain measurements.

Indicators in Public Utility System

It is common in multidisciplinary sciences (eg., public utility) for a true value of a measured quantity to remain unknown due to measurement imperfections, which is why the manner or technique of measurement is so vital. The definition of how to decide the values of different objects, or the operationalization of variables, is the establishment of an empirical way to stand for a theoretical variable. Since that case, the empirical variable has been the indicator of the theoretical variable, and it is defined as a showing variable or an indicator (Vranjanac, 2019). The end of the 19th century in the USA and Europe was ridden with conflicts about wages, unemployment, and work conditions. That is when the first institutions dealing with statistics were founded, such as the Bureau of Labor Statistics in Massachusetts (1869) and the American Bureau of Labor (1884) (Cobb, 1998). The early 20th century was marked by an interest in the development of economic, as well as demographic, educational, and health indicators. In the second half of the 20th century, analytical instruments were introduced into politics, so indicators became a major topic of concern in every field. Near the end of the 20th century, books on this topic began to be published extensively, and indicators were finally introduced into institutions such as WHO, OECD, EEA, and many more, which developed the indicators that we know today and that are continuously being improved (Vranjanac, 2019). In multidimensional phenomena, which cannot be covered by only one indicator, individual indicators, together with the corresponding weight coefficients, are integrated into a single composite (Figure 1). Composite indicators are increasingly used to illustrate complex and hard-to-grasp issues, such as public utility systems (Vranjanac, 2019).

Figure 1. Indicators in multidimensional concept
Source: Boulanger, 2008; Vranjanac, 2019.

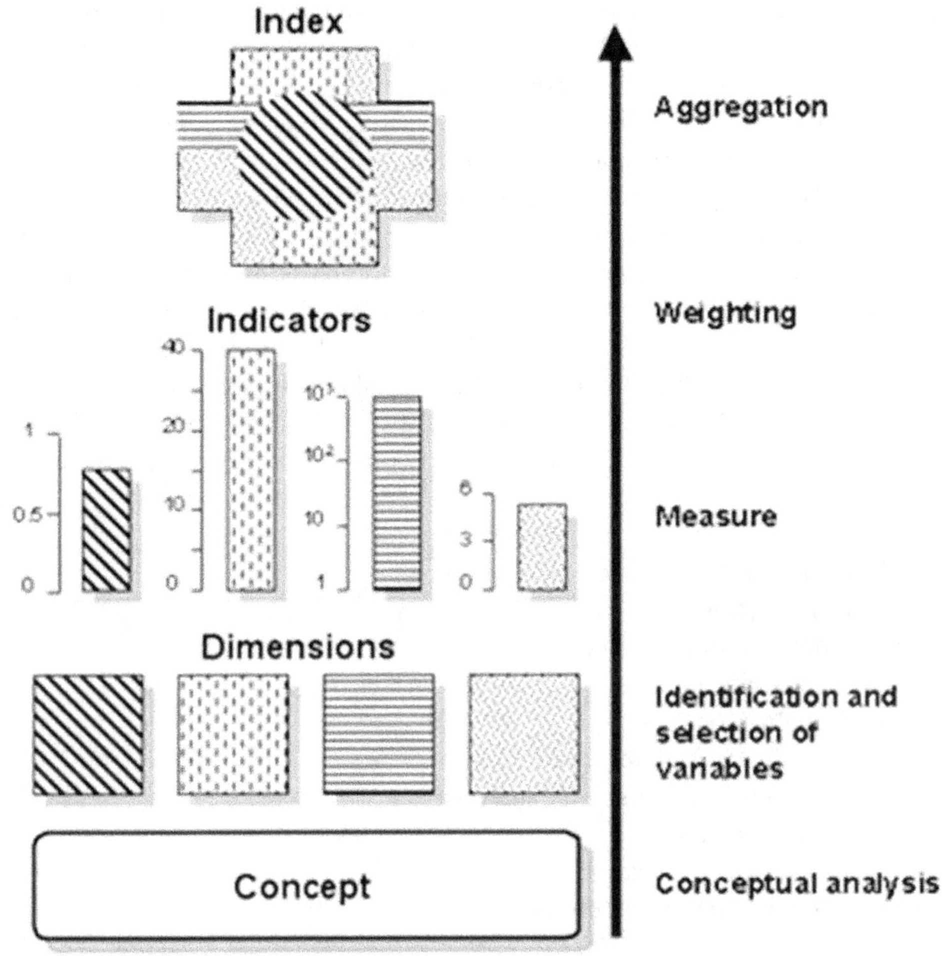

Composite Indicators in Public Utility Systems and Circular Economy

Composite indicators are modern tools for evaluating, comparing, and measuring the performance of multidimensional concepts such as the public utility systems or circular economy among countries, regions, or cities. The core of composite indicators includes the mathematical combination of individual indicators about different dimensions of the observed concept. Importantly, composite indicators are constructed by various mathematical models, primarily multiple-criteria decision analysis, which allows the selection of adequate individual indicators within a composite indicator (Vranjanac et al., 2019). This is followed by selecting a suitable aggregation model and carefully selecting a system for assigning individual indicator weights. Subjectivity during decision-making should be avoided as much as possible, as it could lead to an imprecisely formed indicator (Vranjanac, 2022). According to some authors, composite indicators originated due to globalization, while the reason for their widespread use is that they make collecting, translating, and interpreting shared trends of various phenomena much easier (Salteli, 2007; Adibi, 2017)

In 2015, The European Commission developed a Circular Economy Action Plan, which is intended for monitoring and measuring accomplishments in the circular economy; however, it lacks proper composite indicators on the national level, primarily in EU countries. The list can also include numerous composite indicators that are based on index methods, such as Sustainable Circular Index (SCI), Environmental Performance Index (EPI), Environmental Sustainability Index (ESI), Sustainable Process Index (SPI), Embodied Energy Index (EEI), and many more. According to a group of authors, there are ten key steps in the construction of composite indicators (Dobrota, 2015).

- (1) theoretical framework;
- (2) data selection;
- (3) imputation of missing data;
- (4) multivariate analysis;
- (5) normalization;
- (6) weighting and aggregation;
- (7) uncertainty and sensitivity analysis;
- (8) return to the data;
- (9) links to other indicators;
- (10) visualization of the results.

A model guideline for constructing composite indicators that measure circular economy performance is shown in Figure 2.

Figure 2. Guidelines for constructing circular economy composite performance indicators
Source: Vranjanac et al., 2022.

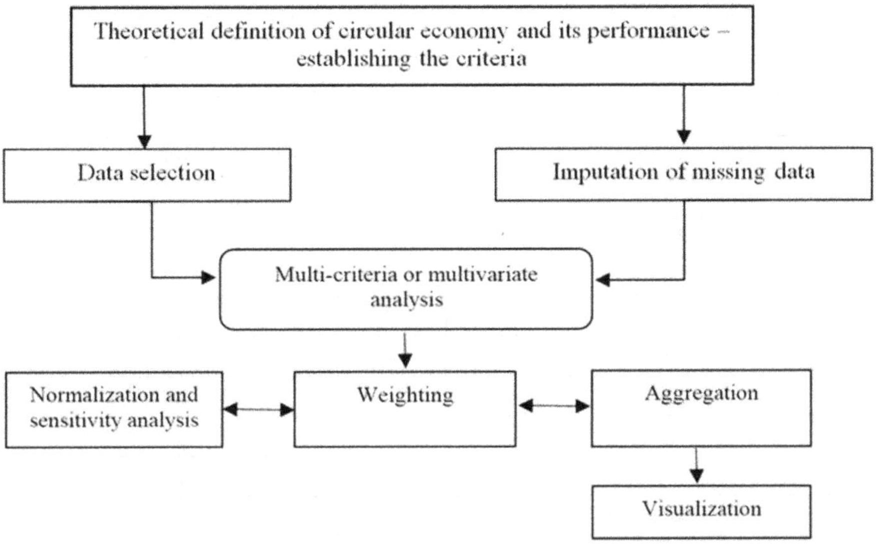

Public Utility Price Clustering: Agglomerative Approach

The research conducted by the magazine "Global Water Intelligence magazine" (GWI) covered several countries of the European continent. It was published under the title - "International monthly data analysis on the world market for the water sector". Through this research, among other things, a cross-section of water and sanitation prices was made, from which we extracted data on the aggregate price of water and sewage in typical European countries (without the associated VAT) (Table 1). The mentioned indicator, called *Public utility price,* was used as a basis for the application of cluster analysis in IBM SPSS 26.0. The methodological framework of the aforementioned cluster analysis based on empirical data obtained by the research of GWI magazine relies on the implementation of a hierarchical agglomerative scheme in the conducted cluster analysis. By applying the agglomerative scheme with cross-iterative operations, the values of the mentioned Public utility price indicator are crossed, whereby the number of clusters in which the analyzed objects are classified is obtained. The methodological framework in this multivariate technique will be procedurally executed by applying Ward's method in Euclidean space, which defines the distance of the analyzed object from the closest belonging to a particular cluster.

Table 1. Public utility prices in selected European countries

Country	Public utility price (in euros/m^3)
Austria	3.58
Belarus	2.76
Bulgaria	3.10
Czechia	0.86
France	0.12
Italy	1.19
Hungary	1.97
Germany	5.15
Poland	2.68
Romania	1.42
Russia	1.09
Serbia	0.53
Spain	1.54
Sweden	1.91
Turkey	1.60
Ukraine	1.60

Source: Global Water Intelligence magazine

The paper also uses cluster analysis, which, as a multivariate technique, aims to group the analyzed countries of the European Union into clusters based on the values of the mentioned indicators. Using the program for statistical data processing - IBM SPSS Statistics 26.0, the authors performed a cluster analysis of the classification of EU member states into homogeneous groups based on the values of the mentioned indicator. The methodology of cluster analysis during the conducted research is based on a hierarchical scheme of agglomeration which, after several iterative steps, shows the last smallest change in the value of the square of Euclidean distance, which defines the number of clusters using the Proximity matrix (Table 2). The agglomerative approach first involves bottom-up analysis and then combines objects and groups until each of them is in a group or cluster (Simović et al., 2020). Euclidean distance is the geometric distance between two data objects (Johnson and Winchern, 2002):

$$d\left(x_i, x_j\right) = \sqrt{\sum\nolimits_{r=1}^{p} \left(x_{ri} - x_{rj}\right)^2}$$

Where: $d\left(x_i, x_j\right)$ distance between *i* and *j*, x_{ri} variable value r in observation *i*, x_{rj} variable value r in observation j, *p*: lots of data variables.

Table 2. Proximity matrix based on Euclidean distance for selected countries and their possible cluster membership

	1	2	3	4	5	6	7	8	9	10	11	12	13	14	15	16
1	0.00	0.67	0.23	7.40	11.97	5.71	2.59	2.46	0.81	4.67	6.20	9.30	4.16	2.79	3.92	3.92
2	0.67	0.00	0.12	3.61	6.97	2.46	0.62	5.71	0.01	1.80	2.79	4.97	1.49	0.72	1.35	1.35
3	0.23	0.12	0.00	5.02	8.88	3.65	1.28	4.20	0.18	2.82	4.04	6.60	2.43	1.42	2.25	2.25
4	7.40	3.61	5.02	0.00	0.55	0.11	1.23	18.40	3.31	0.31	0.05	0.11	0.46	1.10	0.55	0.55
5	11.97	6.97	8.88	0.55	0.00	1.14	3.42	25.30	6.55	1.69	0.94	0.17	2.02	3.20	2.19	2.19
6	5.71	2.46	3.65	0.11	1.14	0.00	0.61	15.68	2.22	0.05	0.01	0.44	0.12	0.52	0.17	0.17
7	2.59	0.62	1.28	1.23	3.42	0.61	0.00	10.11	0.50	0.30	0.77	2.07	0.18	0.00	0.14	0.14
8	2.46	5.71	4.20	18.40	25.30	15.68	10.11	0.00	6.10	13.91	16.48	21.34	13.03	10.50	12.60	12.60
9	0.81	0.01	0.18	3.31	6.55	2.22	0.50	6.10	0.00	1.59	2.53	4.62	1.30	0.59	1.17	1.17
10	4.67	1.80	2.82	0.31	1.69	0.05	0.30	13.91	1.59	0.00	0.11	0.79	0.01	0.24	0.03	0.03
11	6.20	2.79	4.04	0.05	0.94	0.01	0.77	16.48	2.53	0.11	0.00	0.31	0.20	0.67	0.26	0.26
12	9.30	4.97	6.60	0.11	0.17	0.44	2.07	21.34	4.62	0.79	0.31	0.00	1.02	1.90	1.14	1.14
13	4.16	1.49	2.43	0.46	2.02	0.12	0.18	13.03	1.30	0.01	0.20	1.02	0.00	0.14	0.00	0.00
14	2.79	0.72	1.42	1.10	3.20	0.52	0.00	10.50	0.59	0.24	0.67	1.90	0.14	0.00	0.10	0.10
15	3.92	1.35	2.25	0.55	2.19	0.17	0.14	12.60	1.17	0.03	0.26	1.14	0.00	0.10	0.00	0.00
16	3.92	1.35	2.25	0.55	2.19	0.17	0.14	12.60	1.17	0.03	0.26	1.14	0.00	0.10	0.00	0.00

*1-16: The numbers in the first row and column of Table 3 represent the countries from Table 1, from Austria to Ukraine, respectively

Source: Author's calculation based on the cluster analysis output.

Ward's method was applied to form an agglomeration scheme to identify groups of countries that are similar to each other but also different from other groups of countries (Reiff et al., 2018; Reiff et al., 2016). Namely, by applying this approach, the last major change in the value of the cluster combination coefficient determines the total number of clusters (Fanelli, 2018; Fanelli, 2019) (Table 3). Ward's method applied in the agglomerative procedure is based on the analysis of variance to estimate the distance between clusters and thus differs from the others (Simović et al., 2020).Ward's procedure means that (Simović et al., 2020, p. 620): "The average value for each variable (center of the cluster) is calculated for each cluster, and then the square of Euclidean distance from the center of the cluster is calculated for each object, after which the distance for the objects is summed. Using this approach, the cluster analysis tries to find similarities between the analyzed objects, which in this case are represented in the form of EU member states.

Table 3. The hierarchical agglomerative procedure with agglomeration schedule for Public Utility Systems Clustering

Agglomeration Schedule						
Stage	Cluster Combined		Coefficients	Stage Cluster First Appears		Next Stage
	Cluster 1	Cluster 2		Cluster 1	Cluster 2	
1	15	16	.000	0	0	3
2	7	14	.002	0	0	10
3	13	15	.004	0	1	6
4	2	9	.007	0	0	9
5	6	11	.012	0	0	7
6	10	13	.032	0	3	10
7	4	6	.084	0	5	12
8	5	12	.168	0	0	12
9	2	3	.264	4	0	11
10	7	10	.478	2	6	13
11	1	2	.881	0	9	14
12	4	5	**1.506**	7	8	13
13	4	7	**3.791**	12	10	15
14	1	8	**7.386**	11	0	15
15	1	4	**23.974**	14	13	0

Source: Author's calculation based on the cluster analysis output.

The changes that occurred in the agglomeration schedule after the class recomposition could be monitored via dendrogram- the particular cluster analysis output in the form of a tree that represents the number of clusters on its lower "branches". In this way, it could be seen that the country transitioned from one Public Utility Systems pricing group to another. The number of horizontal lines at lower altitudes which are intersected by a vertical line (dashed line) closer to the initial dendrogram shows the actual number of clusters (Rađenović et al., 2022). The dendrogram divides objects into a certain number of groups in vertical sections at a certain height, with one possible solution for grouping (Figure 3).

Figure 3. Dendrogram
Source: Authors' elaboration based on IBM SPSS 26.0

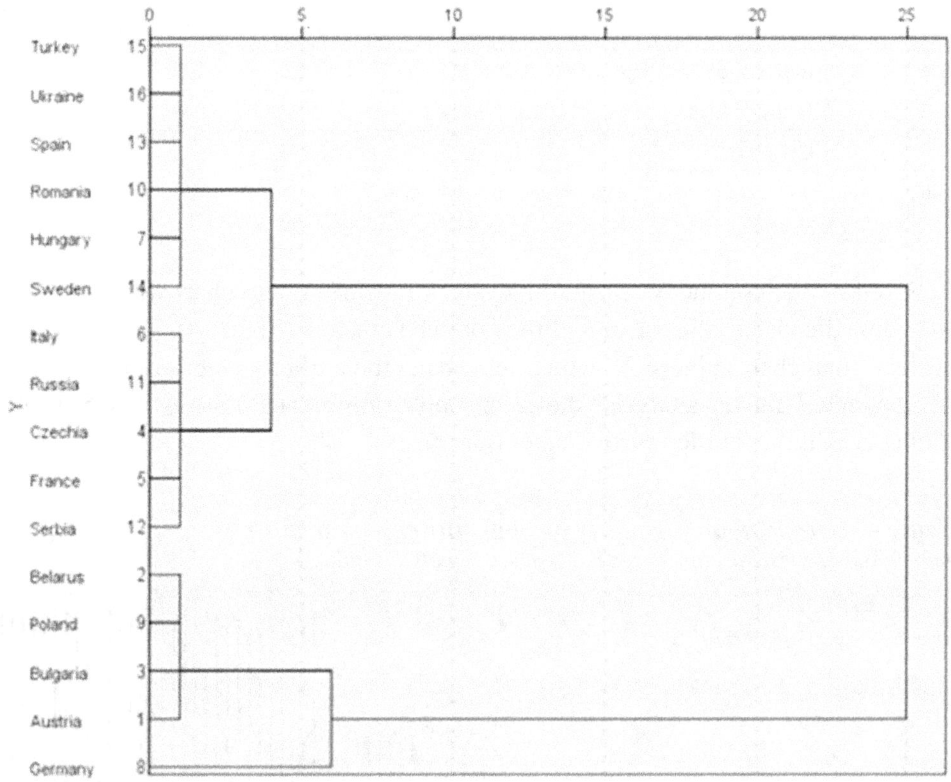

Descriptive statistics among the formed clusters represent one of the output results of the conducted cluster analysis (Table 4). From Table 3, it can be concluded that there are a total of four clusters of selected EU states, which is also confirmed in the previously mentioned agglomeration scheme with the last biggest change in the Coefficients column. Also, Table 4 shows the mean value of the analyzed indicator between the clusters. Country-cluster Germany has the indicators' highest value. Therefore, other countries shouldn't achieve those high public utility prices as Germany. Descriptive statistics of the mean value of indicators within the cluster show that the most dominant is Cluster 4 based on available data.

Table 4. Descriptive statistics among created Public Utility Systems pricing clusters

CLU	N	Countries	Mean	Minimum	Maximum
1	4	Austria, Czechia, France, Poland	3.030	2.68	3.58
2	5	Bulgaria, Belarus, Russia, Italy, Serbia	.758	.12	1.19
3	6	Hungary, Romania, Spain, Sweden, Turkey, Ukraine	1.673	1.42	1.97
4	1	**Germany**	**5.150**	5.15	5.15

Source: Author's calculation based on the cluster analysis output.

Based on the conducted cluster analysis, a European map chart was created to determine the visual relationship of the obtained clusters (Figure 4). The European clusters 'map chart (Figure 2), which represents the author's elaboration based on the conducted cluster analysis, shows the most dominant Public Utility Systems pricing conditions in the fourth cluster (Germany).

Figure 4. European public utility pricing cluster's map chart
Source: Author's visualization based on the cluster analysis output.

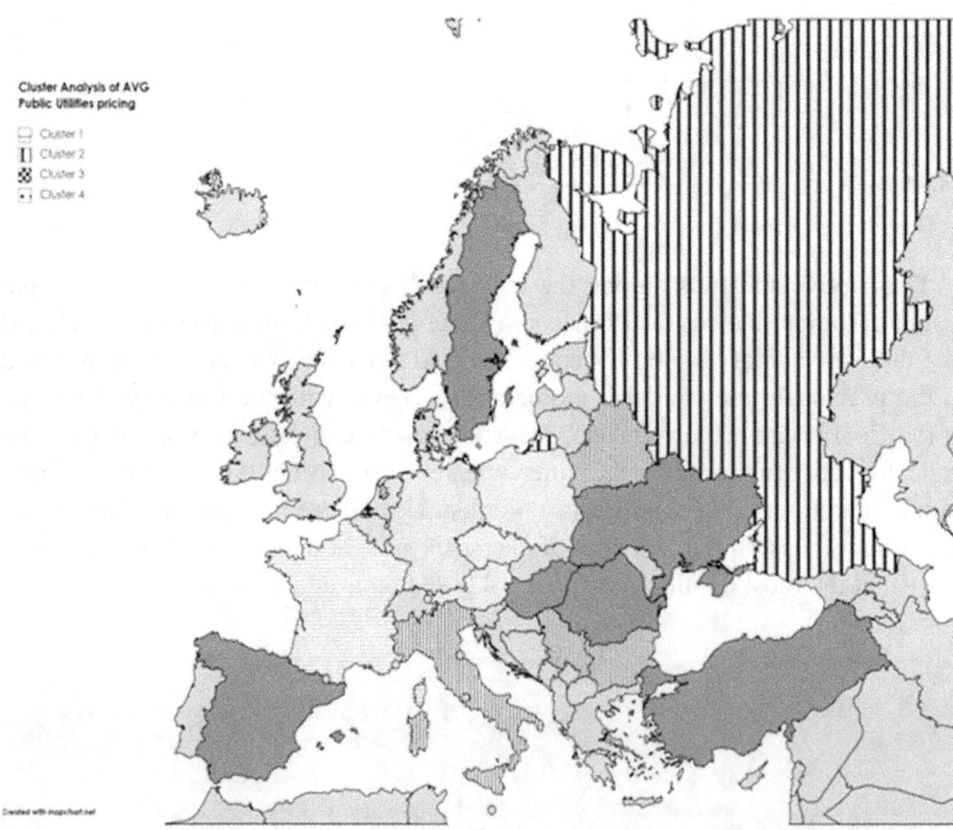

The authors used the ANOVA procedure to check the statistical significance of differences in the average values of indicators among clusters. Based on the conducted ANOVA procedure (Table 5), statistically significant differences in average values can be stated for the analyzed indicator, as seen in the Sig. column where $P < 0.05$ (Rađenović et al., 2022).

Table 5. ANOVA procedure

ANOVA					
AVGUtility_price					
	Sum of Squares	**df**	**Mean Square**	**F**	**Sig.**
Between Groups	22.469	3	7.490	59.685	.000
Within Groups	1.506	12	.125		
Total	23.974	15			

Source: Author's closed on available data.

To check the validity of the hierarchical clustering, the authors have used Levene Statistics. Levene's test is one of the most used, "which starts from the null hypothesis that the variance is the same in all samples if P> 0.05" (Simović et al., 2020, p. 623). "If P > 0.05, the null hypothesis is accepted, i.e., the alternative is rejected, which implies such a situation that the variance is equal for at least one pair of samples" (Simović et al., 2020, p. 623). This can be shown through the following relations:

$$H_0: \sigma_1^{2} = \sigma_2^{2} = \ldots = \sigma_k^{2}, P> 0.05 \quad (1)$$

$$H_1: \sigma_1^{2}{}^{1}\sigma_2^{2}{}^{1} \ldots {}^{1}\sigma_k^{2}, P< 0.05 \quad (2)$$

Testing showed that statistically significant differences do not exist between variations of the given sample, which is recorded in Table 6. The results further indicate that the accepted null hypothesis, i.e., that variance is homogenous for a given variable by groups.

Table 6. Levene statistic

Test of Homogeneity of Variances						Validity Check
		Levene Statistic	**df1**	**df2**	**Sig.**	
Price	Based on Mean	1.566	2	12	.249	Approved
	Based on Median	1.039	2	12	.384	Approved
	Based on trimmed mean	1.501	2	12	.262	Approved

Source: Author's calculation based on available data.

SOLUTIONS AND RECOMMENDATIONS

Databases for the prices of water, sewage, and waste management in the region, compared with prices from other European cities, clearly show the level of prices of basic communal services that should soon be reached in the region of the Western Balkans. Whether this will happen will, of course, depend on the price policy and decisions that will be made in each country individually, but those countries that do not follow that path will certainly bring their utility systems and, with them, the population to serious problems. However, let's see what price level of basic utility services is really necessary. In other words, it begs the question of what is the price level that will allow the communal systems in each country to work smoothly and to develop. So that utility companies from their revenues cover not only current expenses but also finance investments. Without such an approach, it is certain that not a single country from the region, even if it provides grants from EU funds for the financing of certain capital investments, will not be able to reach high EU standards in the field of environmental protection soon. On the other hand, the achieved level of development of each country and the real purchasing power of the population represent an objective limit. Namely, bringing the prices of communal services to the full economic level will not be possible if the majority of the population is objectively unable to pay bills for communal services at those prices. It is more an economic than a political issue, but the answer to it should still come from the political sphere. Namely, the goal and purpose of bringing prices to the economic level are not to take more money from the population but to ensure the functioning of utility systems on a stable and long-term sustainable basis. In any case, users of utility services from most countries in the region should expect that their bills for basic utility services will be significantly higher in the coming years. Among other things, the previous generation is "indebted" to this one by bequeathing a completely neglected communal infrastructure and various types of historical pollution. The only question is if there is a will and that the particulate price of water paid by users can also contain certain fees (taxes) that are revenues of the local or national budget. When it comes to the basic price, it should certainly be sufficient to cover all current production and distribution expenses with depreciation, but also, in addition to depreciation, there should be a certain degree of accumulation from which capital investments and the development of the water supply system will be financed. This means that it is not enough to pay only the salaries and other running costs of the utility company as a distributor from the price of water, but money for investments that will optimize and rehabilitate the entire system should be provided from the price itself: from the water intake, through the main and secondary networks, all the way to measuring instruments and installations of end consumers.

FUTURE RESEARCH DIRECTIONS

Indicators are needed for the conversion from one unit of measure to another, which will enable, on the one hand, the activity provider achieves equal income in terms of volume (so that there is no hidden increase in price or unplanned decrease in price), and on the other hand, the unity of the tariff system should be preserved and prevent excessive burdens of certain groups of users at the expense of other privileged groups. The parameters for price conversion from the basic unit of measure to other known units of measure are:

- St - Specific weight of the garbage in disposal containers, which as a rule, ranges from 0.15 to 0.25 kg/l;
- L - Average daily disposal container volume per household member (in practice, it is 3-5 l/day/member);
- PP - Average number of members of a family household at the local self-government level (in the observed region, the average household in the region has about 3 members);
- Apartment - Average size of residential units (as a rule, it ranges from 55 to 70m2). Ensuring stable financing of the utility company (income) independent of consumption, which is especially important for activities with seasonal oscillations.

There is a possibility (risk) that with the introduction of two components of the sales price, there will be an unwanted covert increase in the price (or decrease in price) of the utility service. Protection of the system and income from users with extremely low or highly seasonal consumption (weekend settlements, vacated households...). For most users, the bills will be less clear and less comprehensible, which can lead to an increased number of complaints and disputing the validity of claims. Equalization ("ironing") of the financial burden between certain groups of consumers where it is not possible to accurately measure the level of utility consumption. Difficulties of a technical nature will especially arise if a large number of utility services are billed together at the utility company level or through a separate company (unified billing). Another truly significant aspect that can improve further analysis in this area of research relates to the formation of composite indicators and the determination of their weighting coefficients using multi-criteria decision-making methods such as PROMETHEE, VIKOR, CRITIC, TOPSIS, and others. Also, to determine the optimal values of the composite indicators for the Public Utility System, it is necessary to rank individual countries/cities in the application of particular solutions to determine the leader in this area. The ranking of research objects using multi-criteria decision-making methods such as AHP, PAPRIKA, FUCOM, MOORA, ARAS, COPRAS, CoCoSo, and others, with adequate sensitivity analyses can significantly contribute to the formation of a strategic framework for determining public utility prices.

CONCLUSION

It can be concluded that the historical heritage, along with the quality of the environment, is another crucial factor for the development and perspective of the public utility system. Utilities, as subsystems of the public utility system, have maintained their function since the beginning of civilization until today to ensure a certain level of comfort for the population and protect the environment. The importance of the public utility system is evidenced, among other things, by architectural achievements from the old age (pyramids) to today (sanitary landfills, water treatment plants, cemeteries, public green areas for various purposes, etc.). Availability, continuity, and quality in the delivery of products and the provision of public utilities, in addition to some factors, also depend on the level of development of society, the state, and the local community. That is why it is important to introduce a unified system for monitoring the level of development of public utilities at the local level. The system of monitoring the performance of the utility system in real-time should become an effective tool for making decisions on the improvement of utilities at the level of local communities and the state. In the world, performance indicators are being formed and introduced in the public utility system, which deals mainly with economic, social, and environmental issues. Within the scope of the chapter, the matter related to the price of basic public utilities (water supply and sanitation) in European countries was presented. The most important results based on the cluster analysis of European countries concerning the prices of water supply and sanitation are the selection of countries within 4 clusters. The first cluster includes the following European countries: Austria, Czechia, France, and Poland, with a 3.03 Mean value of public utility price. Within the second cluster are the following European countries: Bulgaria, Belarus, Russia, Italy, and Serbia, with the lowest price of public utilities (mean value 0.758). The third cluster involves the greatest number of European countries with a 1.673 Mean value of public utility price (Hungary, Romania, Spain, Sweden, Turkey, and Ukraine). The fourth cluster or country cluster is Germany, the European country with the highest Mean value (5.15) for public utility prices. Irrespective of the differences in price and allocation to 4 clusters within the analyzed prices of utility services in selected countries in Europe, there must be an aspiration to achieve local population satisfaction with communal services. First, the municipal unit of local self-government and the city should take care of this to achieve better performance at the state level. The balance between population satisfaction, price, and environmental protection should be achieved to achieve a long-term sustainable perspective of the public utility system (communal system).

ACKNOWLEDGMENT

This research was financially supported by the Ministry of Education, Science and Technological Development of the Republic of Serbia (Contract No. 451-03-47/2023-01/200371).

REFERENCES

Adibi, N., Lafhaj, Z., Yehya, M., & Payet, J. (2017). Global Resource Indicator for life cycle impact assessment: Applied in wind turbine case study. *Journal of Cleaner Production*, *165*, 1517–1528. doi:10.1016/j.jclepro.2017.07.226

Boulanger, M. P. (2008). Sustainable development indicators: A scientific challenge, a democratic issue. *SAPIENS*, *1*(1), 45–59. doi:10.5194apiens-1-59-2008

Clifton, J., Lanthier, P., & Schröter, H. (2013). *The economic and social regulation of the public utilities: An international history*. Routledge.

Cobb, W. C., & Rixford, C. (1998). Lessons learned from the history of social indicators. Redefining progress.

DM. (2019). *Direkcija za mere i dragocene metale [Directorate for Measures and Precious Metals],* Ministarstvo privrede, Beograd. https://www.dmdm.rs/cr/Istorijat.php

Dobrota, M. (2015). *Statistički pristup formiranju kompozitnih indikatora zasnovan na Ivanovićevom odstojanju [A statistical approach to composite indicators construction based on Ivanović distance, doctoral dissertation]*. Doktorska disertacija, Faculty of Organizational Sciences, Belgrade.

Fanelli, R. M. (2018). The Interactions between the Structure of the Food Supply and the Impact of Livestock Production on the Environment. A Multivariate Analysis for Understanding the Differences and the Analogies across European Union Countries. *Quality - Access to Success*, *19*(167), 131–139.

Fanelli, R. M. (2019). The (Un)Sustainability of the Land Use Practices and Agricultural Production in EU Countries. *The International Journal of Environmental Studies*, *76*(2), 273–294. doi:10.1080/00207233.2018.1560761

Filipović, M., & Krnjeta, L. (2013). Jedinstvena metodologija za određivanje cene komunalnih usluga [A unique methodology for determining the price of utility services]. Stalna konferencija gradova i opština – Savez gradova i opština Srbije, Beograd.

Gančević, I. (1971). Community Services-Activities of Special Public Interest. *Zb. Radovalovide*, *8*, 239.

Howarth, P., & Redgrave, F. (2008). Metrology – in short, 3rd edition. EURAMET project 1011.

Janaćković, G., Malenović, J., & Vranjanac, Z. (2017). The importance of user requirements for the quality of communal services, Upravljanje komunalnim sistemom i zaštita životne sredine. Fakultet zaštite na radu u Nišu, Niš, pp.243-250.

Johnson, R. A., & Wichern, D. W. (2002). *Applied Multivariate Statistical Analysis* (5th ed.). Prentice Hall.

Milutinović, S. (2004). Urbanizacija i održivi razvoj [Urbanization and sustainable development]. Fakultet zaštite na radu u Nišu, Niš.

Nikitas, A., Michalakopoulou, K., Njoya, E. T., & Karampatzakis, D. (2020). Artificial Intelligence, Transport, and the Smart City: Definitions and Dimensions of a New Mobility Era. *Sustainability*, *12*(7), 2789. doi:10.3390u12072789

Pejčić, D., & Vranjanac, Ž. (2016). *Environmental impact analysis of hygiene and cleaning products packaging waste, Safety Engineering*. Faculty of Occupational Safety in Niš.

Rađenović, Ž., Krstić, B., & Marković, M. (2022). Economic Performance of Agriculture in the European Union Countries / Wyniki ekonomiczne w rolnictwie w krajach Unii Europejskiej. *Zagadnienia Ekonomiki Rolnej / Problems of Agricultural Economics, 370*(1), 5–21. https://doi doi:org/10.30858/zer/145686

Radosavljević, J. (2010). Prostorno planiranje i zaštita životne sredine [Spatial planning and environmental protection]. Fakultet zaštite na radu u Nišu, Niš.

Reiff, M., Ivanicova, Z., & Surmanova, K. (2018). Cluster analysis of selected world development indicators in the fields of agriculture and the food industry in European Union countries. Agric. Econ. –. *Czech, 64*(5), 197–205. doi:10.17221/198/2016-AGRICECON

Reiff, M., Surmanová, K., Balcerzak, A. P., & Pietrzak, M. B. (2016). Multiple criteria analysis of European Union agriculture. *Journal of International Students, 9*(3), 62–74. doi:10.14254/2071-8330.2016/9-3/5

Rowlett, R. (2005). *A Dictionary of Units of Measurement.* Russ Rowlett and the University of North Carolina at Chapel Hill.

Saltelli, A. (2007). Composite Indicators between Analysis and Advocacy. *Social Indicators Research, 1*(81), 65–77. doi:10.100711205-006-0024-9

Simović, O., Rađenović, Ž., Perović, D., & Vujačić, V. (2020), Tourism in the Digital Age: E-Booking Perspective. *ENTRENOVA – ENTerprise REsearch InNOVation, 6*(1), 616-627. https://hrcak.srce.hr/ojs/index.php/entrenova/ article/view/ 13515/6766

. Simović, V. (1963). *Komunalni sistem i komunalna politika II [Communal system and communal policy II].* Savez studenata Pravnog fakulteta u Beogradu, Beograd, str. 67-84.

. Spasić, D., Vučković, S. (2017). Importance and Role of Public Utilities in the Development of Civilization. XVII naučni skup s međunarodnim učešćem. Čovek i radna sredina. *Fakultet zaštite na radu u Nišu, Niš*, str. 306-315.

Stević, M. (2006). Povećanje tačnosti merenja numerički upravljanih mernih mašina [Increasing the measurement accuracy of numerically controlled measuring machines]. Fakultet tehničkih nauka u Novom Sadu, Novi Sad.

Tasić, D., & Živković, V. (2000). Osnovi metrologije [Basics of metrology]. Savezni zavod za mere i dragocene metale, Beograd.

. Terzić, M., Forkapić, S. (2017). *Uvod u metrologiju i standardizaciju [Introduction to metrology and standardization].* Fakultet tehničkih nauka, Novi Sad, Departman za grafičko inženjerstvo i dizajn, Grafički centar GRID.

Vranjanac, Ž. (2015). Ekonomsko-ekološki uticaj otpada od higijenskih sredstava na životnu sredinu [Economic-Environmental Impact of Household care Products on the environment]. Master rad, Fakultet zaštite na radu u Nišu, Niš.

Vranjanac, Ž. (2015). Quality management of public lighting. *Internacional May Conference on Strategic Management – IMKSM 2015,* pp. 373 - 382, Bor, Serbia.

Vranjanac, Ž. (2019). Overview of indicator development in the fields of sustainable development and environmental protection, Facta Universitatis, Series. *Working and Living Environmental Protection*, *16*(3), 193–198.

Vranjanac, Ž., & Spasić, D. (2017). Economic and Environmental Effects of Collection and Primary Recycling of Packaging Waste from Hygiene and Cleaning Products in Serbia, Serbian. *Journal of Management*, *12*(2), 317–330.

Vranjanac, Ž., Vasović, D., Janaćković, G., Živković, N., & Malenović-Nikolić, J. (2019). Comparative Analysis of Selected Environmental Indicators within Adjusted Savings in Serbia and Romania. *Journal of Environmental Protection and Ecology*, *20*(2), 906–911.

Vranjanac, Ž., Velimirović, L., & Stanković, M. (2022). Guideline for constructing composite indicators that measure circular economy performance, Facta Universitatis, Series. *Working and Living Environmental Protection*, *19*(1), 1–7.

Vranjanac, Ž., Živković, N., Djordjević, A., Janaćković, G., & Vasović, D. (2022). Correlation between Development of the Country and Contribution to Air Pollution an Indicator-based Analysis for EU and WBC. *Fresenius Environmental Bulletin*, *31*(5), 5192–5169.

. Zeković, Lj., Savović, S., Belča I. (2003). *Osnovi metrologije [Basics of metrology].* Prirodno-matematički fakultet Kragujevac.

ADDITIONAL READING

Brunner, P., & Fellner, J. (2007). Setting priorities for waste in developing countries. *Waste Management & Research*, *25*, 234–240. doi:10.1177/0734242X07078296 PMID:17612323

. Franceschini, F., Galetto, M., Maisano, D. (2006). Classification of performance and quality indicators in manufacturing. *Int. J. Services and Operations Management, 2*(3).

Jacobs, R., Goddard, M., & Smith, P. (2006). *Public services: Are composite measures a robust reflection of performance in the public sector?* University of York: Centre for Health Economics, Research Paper 16.

Saitta, S., Raphael, B., & Smith, I. F. C. (2008). A comprehensive validity index for clustering. *Intelligent Data Analysis, 12*(6), 529–548. https://content.iospress.com/articles/intelligent-data-analysis/ida00346. doi:10.3233/IDA-2008-12602

Vujić, G., & Brunner, P. (2009). *Sustainable Waste Management (Održivo upravljanje otpadom), Faculty of Technical Science*. Serbia.

KEY TERMS AND DEFINITIONS

Agglomeration Schedule: The agglomeration schedule shows the amount of error created at each clustering stage when two different objects – cases in the first instance and then clusters of cases – are brought together to create a new cluster. A large jump in the value of the error term indicates that two different things have been brought together and that there is a significant typology at that level of fusion.

Dendrogram: It represents a tree and illustrates the objects grouped.

Hierarchical Clustering: A belief that one's own culture is superior to other cultures.

Indicator: The term indicator originates from the Latin verb *indicare* (show, point to, indicate) and the related Latin noun *indicator* (someone who points out). Indicators are tools that show a specific state or changes in a specific state. Indicators and indexes (Lat. index) are tools meant to reduce a large amount of data to a simple form while preserving the essence of those data with added compactness and clear understanding.

Levene STATISTIC: A situation that the variance is equal for at least one pair of samples.

Performance: The term *performance* refers to a socially constructed performance of an observed phenomenon and pertains to the level of success of a task or operation.

Proximity Matrix: In hierarchical clustering, we have a concept called a proximity matrix. This stores the distances between each point.

Ward Method: This is a special type of agglomerative hierarchical clustering technique that was introduced by Ward in 1963. Unlike the linkage method, Ward's method doesn't define the distance between clusters and is used to generate clusters that have minimum within-cluster variance. Instead of using distance metrics, it approaches clustering as an analysis of the variance problem.

Chapter 4
Transparency and Integrity Methods for Public Utilities Systems

Carlos Andrés Merlano
CECAR, Colombia

ABSTRACT

This chapter discusses best transparency and integrity practices and methods from a literature review of multilateral governments worldwide, emphasizing public utility systems. Corruption and organizational malpractices are commonplace in government and public entities, as well as the private and not-for-profit sectors. This chapter highlights the importance of an adequate understanding and implementation of transparency and integrity methods in the public utility sector. Moreover, it reviews how stakeholders like governments, utility companies, the private sector, not-for-profit entities, and citizens could create an environment of trust and transparency to fight corruption and other unwarranted practices. This chapter also explores the implementation of transparency and integrity programs in countries in South America and Africa.

INTRODUCTION

A globalized or "semiglobalized" world (Ghemawat, 2018) must strive to achieve stable and transparent economic environments. Nations should determine the proper level of regulation to create markets and make externalities visible to the institutional apparatus so national and international businesses or transactions can be fulfilled efficiently and sustainably (Boyd & Martin, 2022). Likewise, the care

DOI: 10.4018/978-1-6684-7730-4.ch004

and good use of public resources and public administration should be encouraged to satisfy political constitutions and laws (Apostolou & Tjortjis, 2019). A stable and transparent economic environment prevents imbalances in the supply and demand of goods and services from distinct economic actors. Unequal relations between market participants may arise from the lack of adequate controls to prevent and detect corrupt practices like transnational enticement and bribery (Bourne, 2022).

Transparency and integrity are two central concepts in corruption and bribery analysis. On the one hand, transparency relates to the degree of an organization's openness to disclosing information to third relevant parties; on the other hand, integrity relates to codes of conduct and values that any society believe and accept. According to the Organization for Economic Co-Operation and Development (OECD, 2020), no country or organization is exempt from transparency and integrity abuse. Addressing this challenge requires the participation of the whole of society and government. The whole of society is an approach in which companies, civil society, and individual citizens reciprocally engage with governments to ensure that society respects ethical values and codes of conduct (OECD, 2020). Doing so guarantees a set of principles related to transparency and integrity that individuals should implement within every type of organization. This crucial approach sets general guidelines within society; however, organizations should also apply methods and standards according to their circumstances. For example, a utility company in the water sector differs from a generator in the energy sector (Llamas et al., 2009). In addition, civil society organization has differing methods for addressing risk. Without general and specific guidelines and standards, the various forms of corruption and their perceptions can eliminate trust in governments, companies, individuals, and markets. Similarly, tolerance of corruption and organizational misconduct by stakeholders and the social fabric of businesses leads organizations to abandon innovation in all its forms, including social and sustainable practices and free competition. This paves the way for corrupt, illegal practices within business activities and interactions with society.

Governments must monitor and supervise society's acceptance of ethical values and codes of conduct and employ policy tools to correct deviations from the norm (Muers, 2020). Moreover, governments should follow the implementation of transparency and integrity standards within all entities to avoid detrimental actions from workers and officials who might be tempted to divert their functions and promote their interests to the detriment of citizens and the community as a whole (Wilkes & Voormeulen, 1989). Therefore, all efforts against corruption related to transparency and ethical methods should strengthen trust in institutions, industries, markets, and a country's economy. This chapter is organized as follows: First, the background section discusses the concept of public utility systems, the legal framework of anticorruption and antibribery activities, and the ideas behind ethical values, transparency, and corruption. Second, the following section defines the transparency and integrity programs and highlights their importance to the public utility system. Third, the solutions and recommendations section explores these programs' implementation stages, standards, and guidelines and delivers real live implementation examples. Finally, this chapter discusses future research directions and provides concluding remarks.

BACKGROUND

A literature review was conducted to comprehend the importance of applying transparency and integrity existing approaches and methods within the public utility system, with an in-depth analysis of studies on public utility systems, international and regional legal frameworks to fight corruption and bribery, and concepts and standards of transparency, ethical values, and accountability. The scholarly studies were searched using the Google Scholar platform (Martín-Martín et al., 2020). Some keywords used were accountability, corruption, integrity, public utilities, risk management, and transparency of recent works.

Public Utility Systems

The public utility system includes services offered by private, public, or other organizations in the public services sector. Examples include water, sanitation, waste disposal, energy, and gas (McNabb, 2018). Public utilities deliver essential services to society to satisfy the public and general interest (Glaeser, 1957; McNabb, 2018). The Encyclopedia of Law and Economics (Geddes, 2000) defined public utilities as various industries, including natural gas, electricity, telecommunications, and airlines. These public utilities exhibit considerable sunk costs and economies of scale due to extensive infrastructures over a specific network (Geddes, 2000). These have been granted concessions from governments. The state oversees public services. Government regulation is critical to avoid negative externalities in the form of discriminatory tariffs or prices and ensure adequate service quality.

A value chain is one essential activity developed by public utilities. This includes production, transmission, and distribution. Some countries and economic sectors exhibit a fourth component, the commercialization service, which creates a link closer to the end consumer of these public services. Moreover, some countries allow for the vertical integration of services in the value chain. Still, others restrict this possibility to avoid noncompetitive practices. Gianfreda (2020, p. 1) stated that vertical integration refers to "the organization of successive stages of production or distribution – i.e., a supplier and a retailer – within a single firm." The two critical aspects of vertical integration are ownership (control in the production or distribution process) and the internal and external exchanges between the firm and third parties (Gianfreda, 2020). In most public utilities, according to Crandall and Ellig (1997), the production stage is competitive; therefore, production could be vertically integrated with the other value chain stages. However, in some instances, the production function could be vertically integrated to a specific limit to avoid noncompetitive practices. In different contexts, the transmission stage is monopolistic. It must, therefore, stand alone in the electrical energy value chain. With the peculiarities of the public utility systems, governments, for instance, regulate where the value chain stages exhibit monopolist conditions. This is the case of transmission and distribution, which allows market forces to define prices in the production stage.

Public utility companies differ from other companies (McNabb, 2018) in the following ways:

- They serve markets without discriminatory practices.
- They exhibit profit and non-for-profit corporate characteristics.
- They receive income from distinct sources.
- They are economic entities that practice price discrimination.
- Prices do not necessarily reflect market forces.

This chapter will explore public utility services and countries' experiences related to water, sanitation, waste disposal, electrical energy, and fuel gas. For example, modern appliances would influence companies and millions of households worldwide. These appliances require electricity, which is attained thanks to electrical energy public utilities. Water utility companies deliver precious liquid so people can drink and bathe. Some companies treat wastewater and collect solid or liquid waste (McNabb, 2018). Without natural or liquid petroleum gas, individuals would be unable to use the water for residential needs (cooking or heating water), industrial processes, or energy production (McNabb, 2018).

LEGAL FRAMEWORKS: ANTICORRUPTION AND ANTIBRIBERY ACTIVITIES

Currently, an international legal framework includes the following conventions and legal agreements to fight corruption and bribery:

- **United Nations Convention Against Corruption (UNCAC):** This convention covers provisions at the organizational level. It promotes a preventive focus and control approach (repressive), delivering guidelines on international cooperation actions (Llamas et al., 2009). According to the World Bank (2003), the UNCAC "is the only legally binding universal anti-corruption instrument with a far-reaching global approach." Moreover, this convention addresses several forms of corruption, such as bribery, abuse of functions, and influence peddling. It also includes acts of corruption in the private sector (World Bank, 2022). The UNCAC convention was embraced in 2003, went into effect in December 2005 (with 140 countries), and was confirmed by 187 nation-states as of February 2020 (World Bank, 2022).

- **OECD Convention on Combating Bribery of Foreign Public Officials:** This convention, which was adopted in 1997, urges member countries to encourage companies to develop and adopt adequate internal controls, as well as ethics and compliance programs or measures to prevent and detect the bribery of foreign public officials (Llamas et al., 2009). The OECD (2022a) noted that this convention will establish "legally binding standards to criminalize bribery of foreign public officials in international business transactions." According to the OECD (2022a), it is the only anti-corruption instrument focused "on the supply side of bribery." To date, 38 OECD countries and six non-OECD countries have signed this convention (OECD, 2022a).

The following regional conventions have been implemented in continents like Europe, Africa, and the Americas:

- **Council of Europe - Criminal Law Convention on Corruption:** This convention seeks the coordinated criminalization and prosecution of corrupt practices (COE, 2022a). The Group of States against Corruption, which started activities in 1999, and includes nonmember states, monitors its implementation.
- **Civil Law Convention on Corruption:** This convention states that those who have suffered acts of corruption can receive appropriate compensation and defend their rights (COE, 2022b). It covers topics from state liability of acts committed by public officials to contract validity, whistleblower protection, and international cooperation (COE, 2022b).
- **African Union Convention on Preventing and Combating Corruption:** This convention was adopted in 2003. Of the 55 African countries, 49 have signed the convention, and 45 have ratified it (African Union, 2021). The convention's main objectives are as follows: (1) prevent, detect, and eradicate corruption in all its forms; (2) promote and facilitate cooperation among states to ensure that actions against corruption have been taken; and (3) coordinate

the harmonization of public policies while promoting socioeconomic development.

- **Inter-American Convention Against Corruption of the Organization of American States (OAS):** The OAS convention seeks to eradicate corruption by promoting mechanisms and state collaboration that prevents, detects, punishes, and eradicates corruption in all forms (OAS, 2022). Some of the preventive measures of this convention are related to standards and mechanisms that enforce this conduct, ethical rules governing personnel activities, revenue collection and procurement of goods and services, oversight bodies, and means to promote participation by civil society and other nongovernmental organizations (OAS, 2022). To date, 30 countries have ratified this convention.
- **Anti-Corruption Initiative for Asia Pacific:** Countries in this initiative collaborate in the battle against corruption with collective action events and regional thematic gatherings. They use specific training, measures, and tools to detect and counter corrupt actions or gather evidence to apply those findings in other regional contexts (OECD, 2022b). Under this initiative, 17 countries endorsed an anticorruption plan in 2001. The plan is committed to fighting corruption and enhancing accountability in the public sector of this region (OECD, 2022b).

The above conventions and agreements promote the adoption of compliance programs and codes of conduct by companies, including the public utility sector. Moreover, these conventions agree that corruption is a reality that requires a united effort across states and with multiple stakeholders.

TRANSPARENCY, ETHICAL VALUES, ACCOUNTABILITY, AND CORRUPTION

Transparency International (TI) is a global society organization that fights corrupt practices. It outlines transparency practices in organizations (i.e., private and public companies, citizens, and other stakeholders) so they openly disclose information (TI, 2022c). According to TI, the board of directors, managers, and public officials must act visibly, predictably, and transparently before third parties to allow the latter to evaluate the former's undertakings. Furthermore, according to the Regulated Industries Commission (2010), transparency is the actions that organizations (both public and private) undertake to publicize accessible information about their economic and corporate activities. Also, Erkkilä (2012) argues that transparency relates to public accountability through the disclosure of data and the publicity of government activities as a critical performance measurable element.

Organizations should be transparent (Berggren & Bernshteyn, 2007) because it strengthens risk management and maintains credibility (Albu & Flyverbom, 2016), (Danker, 2013). Otherwise, the organizations jeopardize their reputation (Men, 2014) and how society and the markets perceive them.

The terms "transparency" and "accountability" (Gaventa & McGee, 2013) are closely connected. However, accountability ensures that influential individuals (Singh & Vutukuru, 2010) within an organization receive proper oversight by an external third party or auditor (Regulated Industries Commission, 2010). According to the Regulated Industries Commission (2010), the accountability process has answerability and enforcement phases. Meanwhile, answerability focuses on an organization's legal obligation to display information to the public. On the other hand, enforcement has to do with oversight entities' ability to implement sanctions on offending institutions (Regulated Industries Commission, 2010).

According to TI (2022b) and Turilli and Floridi (2009), ethical values are standards for how stakeholders, including public and private organizations and society, should conduct themselves through guided choices and actions (Turilli, 2011). For instance, an integrity pact can ensure that third parties agree to a code of conduct (Regulated Industries Commission, 2010). In turn, those involved will conform to avoid unethical behavior like the acceptance of bribes. Common ethical issues include conflict of interest, acceptance of gifts, and preferable treatment.

Furthermore, TI (2022d) defined corruption as "the abuse of entrusted power for private gain." Corruption erodes trust, creating negative externalities like inequality and poverty (TI, 2022d). The corruption perception index ranks and scores international experts' and business executives' perceptions of the public sector (TI, 2022a). According to TI (2022a), the global average index has remained unchanged for the 10th consecutive year, meaning that countries in the sample have not made considerable progress in the fight against corruption. Moreover, the World Bank (2022) issued its governance indicators for corruption control. The aggregate indicators analyzed companies, citizens, and survey responses in developed and developing countries to measure transparency concerning sound public policies and institutional credibility.

TRANSPARENCY AND INTEGRITY PROGRAMS

Transparency and integrity programs are a series of guidelines and tools that aid in detecting, preventing, and managing corrupt practices in public and private companies. As noted, transparency and integrity instruments gather best practices from international legal frameworks. Nation-states support and develop integrity treaties to enhance the quality of life, the rule of law, and sustainable economic development (Llamas et al., 2009). For instance, Llamas et al. (2009) proposed the implementation of integrity tools and an institutional structure to enhance national transparency and integrity (see Figure 1).

Figure 1. The institutional structure of national transparency and integrity
Source: Llamas et al. (2009)

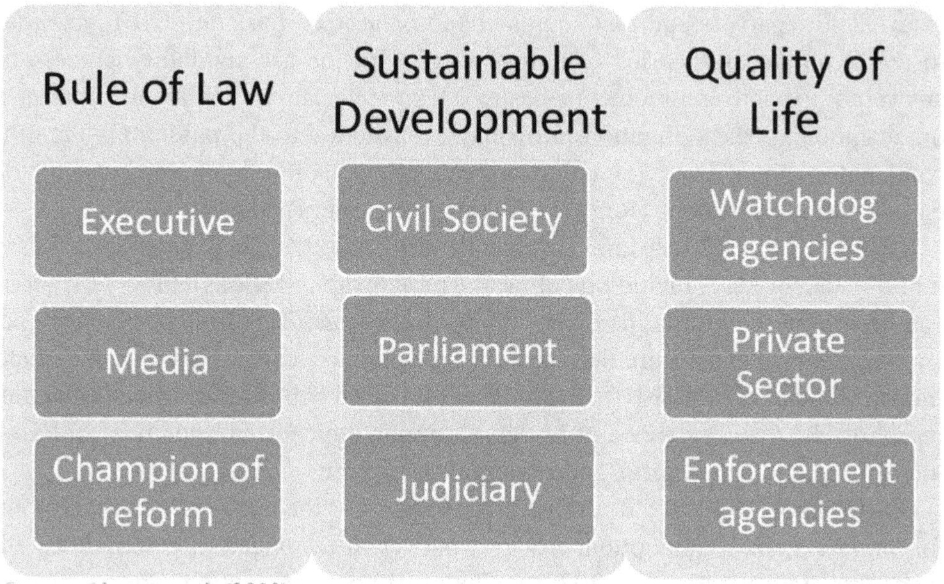

Institutions represented in Figure 1 should be efficient and credible in the eyes of society (Pope, 2000). Citizens play a critical role in ensuring that organizations maintain transparency, integrity, and the values of society. Integrity pacts are tools that communities use to prevent bribery in public contracting (Llamas et al., 2009). According to Llamas et al. (2009), integrity pacts are used in several scenarios, including construction and supply contracts, selections of consultants, in-state licenses, or concessions when selecting beneficiaries. This is the case with water utility companies or privatization processes.

In its whole-of-society approach, the OECD (2020) recognizes the importance of working closely with companies to increase transparency and public integrity. Governments support legislation on transparency, integrity, and ethical values, ensuring that corporate governance structures are in accordance with specific sectors and organizational culture. For example, transparency and integrity programs are different for an organization in the water sector compared to an energy or gas utility company. Differences have to do with unique risks in each of the economic sectors. Types of risk include credit, financial, legal, and systemic.

Considering the above, transparency and integrity programs must be drawn up and developed in accordance with the specific conditions of each public utility company. In any case, a strong transparency and integrity program must ensure that an entity prevents, detects, and corrects situations that may lead to corruption or bribery activities. These programs should collect all the internal rules on the prevention and mitigation of corruption risks and/or transnational bribery risks, as well as the ethical principles and values that each utility entity deems appropriate to conduct business in an ethical, transparent, and honest manner. Consequently, any modification to these transparency and integrity programs must be brought together in detail and rigorously. These methods and tools will be explored in more detail in the guidelines section of this chapter.

The methods and standards of the transparency and integrity programs should suit the needs of each organization within the public utility sector, whether water, energy, or gas. Utility companies must identify and evaluate the risks of corruption and transnational bribery, depending on risk factors like the economic sector, third parties, contractors, intermediaries, advisors, consultants, and type of state contract. This will be discussed in this chapter.

SOLUTIONS AND RECOMMENDATIONS

Transparency and integrity programs for public utility systems should include implementation stages, standards, and guidelines. Table 1 illustrates the implementation stages for transparency and integrity programs, detailed in the following subsections.

Table 1. Implementation stages for transparency and integrity programs

Problem Analysis	Design and Approval	Program Implementation	Monitoring	Evaluating and Improving
Strategy approach within the organization	Definition of strategic objectives	Communicating the program	System review	Feedback from evaluation and improvement activities
Strategy approach with relevant stakeholders	Organizational structure review	Training activities for relevant parties	Gathering knowledge from incidents	Evaluating the effectiveness of the program
Risk identification	Implementation plan and indicators	Internal audits	External verification	Developing improvements to the program
Risk analysis and measurement	Communication and reporting matters	Dealing with incidents	Certification processes	Communicating findings to senior management and acting
Risks mitigation and control	Senior management approval	Project team key characteristics	Whistleblower channels	Disclosing results to relevant stakeholders

The above implementation stages consider the conceptual and theoretical implications of several academic publications and the practical insights from several organizations worldwide (OECD, 2020), (Regulated Industries Commission, 2010).

Problem Analysis

Implementing transparency and integrity programs requires a risk focus and strategic approach (OECD, 2020). Governments and relevant stakeholders should participate in the development of a viable, transparent process. A sound strategic approach must contemplate the crucial stage of problem analysis, including identifying transparency and integrity risks, analysis, control measures, and mitigation. Corruption and transnational bribery are critical risks for transparency and integrity programs. As seen in figure 2, public utility companies should develop a logical process of identifying, measuring, evaluating, controlling, and mitigating these risks.

Figure 2. Risk management framework

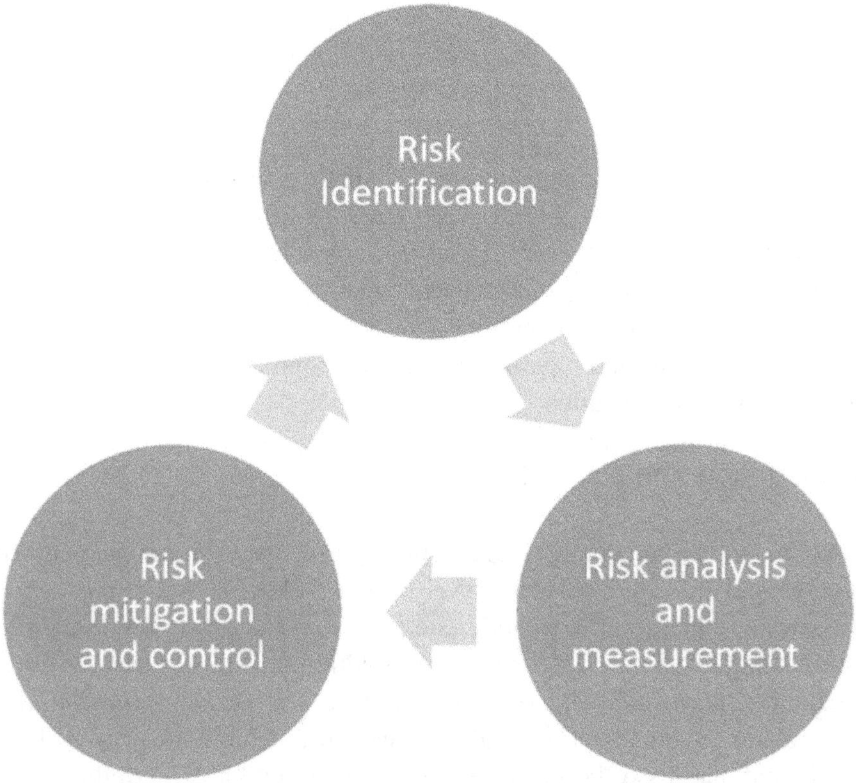

Risk Identification

Organizations should acknowledge the corruption and transnational bribery risks in the identification stage with each utility company's characteristics and social mission. For instance, these risks should not be the same for a tap water company as for electrical energy or gas companies. In addition, larger companies exhibit a different reality compared to smaller organizations. Public utility companies should analyze their internal and external context. The internal context covers business elements, such as day-to-day operations and financial reporting, human resources (HR), and corporate culture. The external context refers to interactions with third parties like providers, consumers, governments, and the socioeconomic context in which utility companies interact. For proper risk identification, the organization should define who is responsible for gathering corporate information. The board members and chief executive officer should provide guidelines for risk data collection.

Transparency and integrity risks are not limited to corruption and transnational bribery. Other risks include nepotism, conflict of interest violations, and procurement fraud (OECD, 2020).

Risk Analysis and Measurement

Risk analysis and measurement consist of estimating the likelihood and impact of corruption and transnational bribery risks (OECD, 2020). Aside from identifying risks, describing those with exact causes and possible outcomes is critical. In this stage, it helps to identify agents that can inhibit the correct functioning of the organization and engage in corruption, such as transnational bribery. The final step of proper risk analysis and measurement is to recognize possible risks and losses related to a utility organization.

Risk Mitigation and Control

The risk mitigation and control stage implement measures to mitigate and control corruption and transnational bribery risks (OECD, 2020). These actions seek to mitigate the likelihood of materializing risks and their impacts. Public utility companies should analyze different elements within this stage, such as gifts offered inside the company or by external third parties. The organization should revise policies related to remunerations and commissions, including expenses like travel, entertainment, and food. Political contributions of any kind, as well as donations from philanthropic organizations, must also be controlled. Lastly, this stage should define internal audit systems, conflict of interest in reporting, sound data conservation systems and internal sanctioning procedures, and reporting channels of suspicious activities with safeguards for those who report corruption.

Additional steps include designing a strategy, developing indicators, drafting an action plan, funding activities, distributing responsibilities, and implementing, monitoring, evaluating, and communicating results. This chapter will outline the standards and procedures that proper transparency and integrity programs should possess.

Design and Approval

Transparency and integrity programs must have a systematic view and a strategic approach in which utility companies define their objectives and create programs with the organization's personnel and relevant stakeholders. Strategic goals must align with the organization's mission and vision and the government's public policies for a specific economic sector. The main strategic objectives should address corruption and transnational bribery risks as indicated in the problem analysis stage. Other objectives, milestones, and targets help achieve the goals of the transparency and integrity programs (OECD, 2020).

Furthermore, the strategic approach requires coordination with stakeholders inside and outside the public utility organizations. Everyone has responsibilities and brings valuable insight to strengthen the transparency and integrity of the programs. Moreover, dialogue between participants must be constructive, with a two-way discourse to guarantee a sense of ownership of the process (Regulated Industries Commission, 2010).

The Regulated Industries Commission (2010) recommended several instances of consultation and approval activities. For example, the organization might use consultation codes that make it mandatory to consult with relevant parties to elaborate on a list of parties affected by the transparency and integrity programs, costs associated with the initiative, and possible impacts on different geographical areas. These are significant considerations because public utility companies are in numerous locations and attend several markets and customers.

Furthermore, the design phase of the transparency and integrity programs must be based on a thorough evaluation of the corruption risk matrix or transnational bribery risk matrix identified and mitigated by each organization, as mentioned in the implementation section. These programs must specify administrator responsibilities within the company, as well as with the compliance officer, in the implementation of the organization's transparency and integrity initiatives.

Information disclosure, an essential step in the design phase of transparency programs (Regulated Industries Commission, 2010), increases a third party's accountability and performance to utility organizations. Disclosed information should be timely, easy to understand, and relevant to stakeholders. The Regulated Industries Commission (2010) noted that corporate Websites could be used to disclose information in a friendly and interactive manner. The sites could also include a section related to transparency and integrity issues.

Llamas et al. (2009) argued that the TI six-step implementation process allows organizations to develop a consistent, detailed anti-bribery program via a thorough review of the ability of internal dependencies to support the program. The transparency program can use the design phase to develop an implementation plan by adapting HR policies and training programs and setting up communication and reporting functions (Llamas et al., 2009).

A vital aspect of the strategic approach is the elaboration of a document with a plan to implement the transparency and integrity program. This action plan should include how the organization will communicate the program, provide training activities to relevant parties, deal with incidents, and deliver internal audits. The plan should also include the main characteristics of the project's team. This stage must also elaborate on strategic indicators to measure and ensure that objectives will be met (OECD, 2020). The organization should define an indicator's baselines, targets, and milestones.

Indicators are not static; therefore, the public utility company should periodically revise them to adapt to internal and external changes. Finally, the utility organization could revise corruption and bribery indicators from international entities (OECD, 2020). It should elaborate on its own indicators in accordance with the service and context in which it delivers its core business. These could eventually serve as a benchmark with peers in the specific sector.

Considerations within the design phase of the transparency and integrity programs require commitment and approval from senior management. Many obstacles will surface without the endorsement of leadership. In turn, subsequent steps will only face challenges once; eventually, they will be disregarded within the organization.

Implementing the Program

The implementation stage of transparency and integrity programs requires several activities from public utility organizations. A crucial function is communicating the transparency integrity program inside and outside the public utility organization. In this regard, the utility company should design appropriate channels, such as an intranet, that allow individuals in the organization to communicate and share information about the program. To avoid corrupt practices in the public utility company, the organization's employees, administrators, associates, and contractors should communicate the importance of the transparency and integrity program. The HR department should train the organization's human talent on antibribery practices and instruments to counter corruption.

The public utility organization must put suitable mechanisms in place for the adequate communication and pedagogy of transparency and integrity programs. Transparency and integrity training is not only for internal personnel; this training should also be provided to relevant third parties like distributors and collaborators with a systemic focus in mind (Llamas et al., 2009). The utility company's image could be compromised if a business partner fails in its antibribery and anticorruption practices and activities.

Implementing compliance audits is necessary because corruption and bribery risks and exposures will change. Therefore, transparency and integrity programs must be dynamic and easily modified. The complexity of a transparency and integrity program will depend on factors like the ones shown in figure 3:

Figure 3. Factors of the complexity of transparency and integrity programs

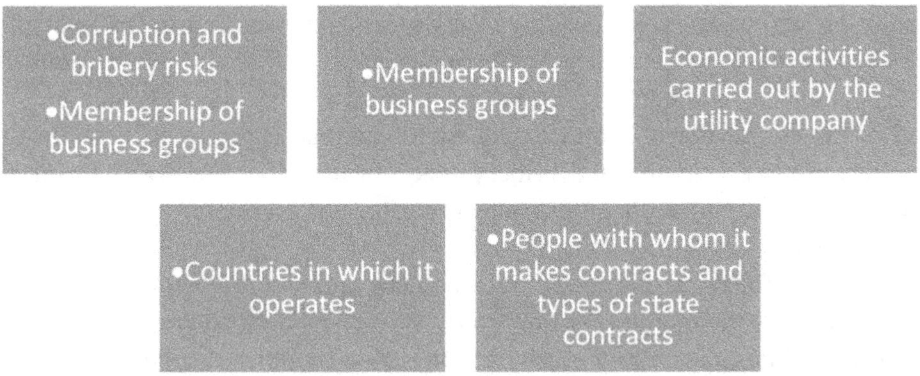

The organization needs a person responsible for the audit and compliance verification of the program. Therefore, a compliance officer should be appointed under the corresponding government agency's transparency and integrity instructions and methods. In short, a sound internal audit system should deter those actors from considering acts of bribery or corruption (Llamas et al., 2009).

At some point, the utility organization will need to address an illegal act. The incident may be insignificant; however, the organization could face significant negative consequences in the form of reputational harm. Hence, the public utility company must act by developing periodical tasks of due diligence (OECD, 2020).

The public utility's transparency and integrity program must specify those individuals (project team) responsible for designing, implementing, and executing the program. This team should acknowledge the most important issues behind antibribery practices and corruption in all its forms. Moreover, the team should understand public utility systems and the implications of wrong approaches toward organizational credibility. Lastly, the individuals responsible should possess admirable qualities and values within the organization.

Monitoring the Program

Monitoring activities are a crucial part of transparency and integrity programs. They determine whether the program works or if guidelines and standards are followed according to the strategic objectives. For example, the organization should monitor its business parents with a sample of crucial companies, deciding when, how, and to what depth it will monitor its activities (Llamas et al., 2009).

There are many businesses upstream and downstream of the value chain within the public system. The utility organization must define how far it will go in its monitoring activities. The due diligence process involves numerous analytical processes. Technology is an essential ally in this regard. At this point, a data warehouse strategy could aid in integrating disparate data from multiple sources (Sharda et al., 2017). Extract, transform, and load techniques can make operational and strategic decisions about corruption and bribery risks. In addition, the organization can develop financial and accounting controls related to procedures, guidelines, and objectives within the utility company.

Aside from the regular review of transparency and integrity systems, the utility company can use the monitoring stage to learn from incidents related to corruption and bribery. Understanding why the risk materialized could strengthen controls and spotlight the root causes of the issues. No system is free of errors and vulnerability; however, monitoring transparency and integrity programs guarantees improvement within the system's checks and balances process.

Furthermore, utility organizations can seek external audits for verification purposes. This external verification will gather information to support the organization's compliance with the transparency and integrity program. Limitations and barriers of external auditing are related to the trustworthiness of the external auditors and potential costs (Dimitrijević et al., 2021). However, public utility companies could decide to certify their business operations with ISO antibribery certifications or BSI 10500 anti-bribery management systems. Nevertheless, organizations should compare the costs of several alternatives with their budgets to make the most cost-effective decisions.

Additionally, the organization should implement whistle-blowing channels, where anyone can confidentially provide information about incidents or wrongdoing. These informant channels should be safe, amicable, and straightforward. Lastly, whistle-blowing channels must abide by the legal norms of specific countries and jurisdictions.

The public utility company should communicate its findings to all relevant stakeholders because it shows reliability and credibility in the transparency and integrity process. It also stimulates an environment of accountability, which enhances the organization's position in the market and society (OECD, 2020). Communication with interest groups should be clear, widely publicized, and timely. There are countless channels to communicate the strategy, such as social media, institutional Websites, and community gatherings.

Evaluating and Improving the Program

The evaluation and improvement phase, the final stage of the transparency and integrity program implementation process, is an integral part of the transparency and integrity programs (Jacob et al., 2015). They seek the continuous improvement of the system, considering that all businesses, including public utility companies, operate in dynamic environments that change accordingly (Llamas et al., 2009). The design and approval stage defines the evaluation and improvement mechanisms (OECD, 2020). Senior management is responsible for guaranteeing the proper functioning of these programs. Although senior management and board members are accountable, employees and other personnel can inform leadership about situations they encounter in the transparency and integrity system. The evaluation and improvement process covers all organizational instances, including external partners.

Feedback from evaluation activities is crucial to program improvements. For instance, the evaluation process takes place in-house or may be outsourced to an external organization (OECD, 2020). The public utility company's decision about the evaluation, whether internal or external, depends on a cost-benefit analysis and capacities assessment. Generally, the in-house evaluation is cheaper and faster because the organization uses its own resources. Still, there is a downside. The company's employees require additional time to perform the evaluation activities. The process also has a learning curve; employees may not possess the required expertise to do a practical monitoring task. Moreover, an independent external evaluator brings transparency to the evaluation process. However, it could be costlier and take more time (OECD, 2020). Public utility companies can experiment with a hybrid alternative (OECD, 2020).

Once the evaluation process is complete, the appointed transparency and integrity team must develop improvements to the transparency and integrity program. The team could work within the corresponding areas of the organization to validate that the actions will improve the system and that the new controls will reduce risks related to future incidences. In addition, the transparency and integrity team should communicate the results to senior management, disclosing any noncompliance findings. They should validate that the actions to improve the system are logical and practical. Some authors argue that revealing the evaluation results and improving the process could be optional (Llamas et al., 2009). Still, revealing ongoing findings increases accountability and trust among relevant parties.

The evaluation and improvement activity of the transparency and integrity program should be done at least once a year, depending on the public utility company's resources and capabilities. Nonetheless, evaluation and improvement tasks are continuous within a quality or risk management system. Controls are taken once an alarm signals an adverse event, which could compromise the system's functioning.

Examples of Implementation of Transparency and Integrity Programs

The following examples show the experience of countries and utility companies in South America and Africa when implementing transparency and integrity programs. They highlight insights to improve the application process in other latitudes and contexts. These two countries were chosen as countries that participate in the implementation of OECD policies and guidelines to improve their governance and reduce their levels of corruption. It is worth mentioning that other practical examples of these types of programs can be found in OECD (2020) and González de Asís et al. (2009).

Program Implementation in Colombia

Colombia, the fourth largest country in Latin America, has around 1,139,000 square kilometers of territory (Colombia.co, 2022). The only South American country that borders the Atlantic and Pacific Oceans. It has 46 million inhabitants and about 10% of the world's biodiversity. Colombia is also a presidential democracy with a bicameral congress (Colombia.co, 2022).

With the promulgation of Law 2195 of 2022, all businesses, including public utility companies, must adopt transparency and integrity programs under inspection, surveillance, and control of government entities. The law demands that the inspection, surveillance, and control of government entities must define the content of these programs, considering the following elements of any supervised organization: the economic sector; risks; total assets; revenues; the number of employees; and social mission. Moreover, the law requires that the guidelines of the transparency and integrity programs be in harmony with the inspection, surveillance, and control of government entities and the transparency secretary of the Colombian government.

Regarding public utility companies in Colombia (Superservicios, 2022), the superintendency of residential and public services drafted a plan of action to develop the minimum guidelines and the transparency and integrity programs with support from the Water Integrity Network (WIN). WIN (2022) supported many organizations worldwide, including private and public organizations, in promoting integrity and fighting corruption while improving the water sector. Although the water sector is WIN's core expertise, the organization has experience in other sectors like energy and gas.

By way of a collaboration agreement with WIN, the superintendency of residential and public services seeks to strengthen the transparency and integrity capabilities of energy and gas, tap water, sanitation, and waste management public utility companies in Colombia by managing knowledge and information about the public utility system.

This agreement designs guidelines and methodologies that utility companies can apply to increase their understanding of transparency, integrity, anticorruption and antibribery practices, and corporate governance.

Agreement objectives aim to enhance diagnostics on the state of maturity and progress of the transparency and utility programs in the utility sector in Colombia. Regarding this first objective, an initial evaluation found that most of the larger companies had transparency and integrity programs and management risk systems. This highlights that governments should verify the maturity level of any economic sector's integrity and transparency before implementing transparency and integrity programs. Another main objective of the agreement between WIN and the superintendency is to gather and share information on the experience of implementing this program to replicate these practices in other contexts.

It is too soon to tell how this agreement will turn out. However, the superintendency has support from WIN. This guarantees ample experience in implementing transparency and integrity initiatives around the globe.

Program Implementation in Morocco

Morocco, a constitutional monarchy with two legislative houses, is in the western part of North Africa, across the Strait of Gibraltar from Spain (Britannica, 2022). Tangier, a coastal city in northern Morocco, has experienced a yearly population growth of 4.4%. In the late 1990s, only 70% of its 700,000 inhabitants had potable water (WIN, 2021). In 2001, the Tangier municipality began working with Amendis, a subsidiary of Veolia, to organize the public utility services of water supply, waste management, and electricity.

The Amendis contract had four levels of control:

1. Supervision by municipality staff on performance indicators and community complaints
2. Expenditure checks and financial accomplishments
3. A committee to supervise the program and make necessary changes
4. A municipal delegate to make and approve decisions within the scope of the contract

As of 2018, 1.2 million inhabitants had achieved full utility services coverage. This 70% increase from 2001 may be attributed to the region's population growth (WIN, 2021).

The above was achievable because Amendis followed a transparency program and strict integrity methods (WIN, 2021). The operator applied several tools and standards, including an anti-corruption code of conduct and an alert system of ethics incidents. Individuals could report ethical breaches to the corporate ethical committee. In addition, the Amendis operator elaborated on procedures and rules concerning the management of external partners, gifts, and donations. Amendis developed a compliance training program, bringing together 100 managers and e-learning campaigns related to anticorruption and anti-competitive practices. Moreover, the operator implemented annual surveys and questionnaires on compliance issues. The Amendis Internal Control Unit gathered and analyzed the data to act as needed. Lastly, the Amendis HR management system complied with international standards, Moroccan national legislation, and French anti-bribery regulations (WIN, 2021).

These examples show that transparency and integrity programs require considerable work in all implementation stages. However, it can bring measurable benefits. Public utility companies may seek aid from specialized, lower-cost organizations. This can enhance the programs and increase transparency and accountability in the eyes of stakeholders and society.

FUTURE RESEARCH DIRECTIONS

The findings in this chapter are subject to constraints, including its tight focus on general standards and methods of mostly multi-lateral and not-for-profit organizations. However, this constraint does not prevent the results in this chapter from contributing to the academic literature as it helps form a broader picture of the research and studies concerning transparency and integrity elements. Future research on transparency and integrity programs should study the effectiveness and impact of applying standards and methods within public utility companies worldwide. Many organizations use data analytical tools to measure business operations, reduce risks, and increase their market reach. Studies should analyze the use of these tools to address corruption and bribery risks.

CONCLUSION

Transparency and integrity programs are vital standards and guidelines in the fight against corruption and bribery. Countless organizations are implementing integrity principles to become more transparent and accountable to their relevant stakeholders. The public utility system has been no exception to this reality. It has implemented risk management systems and anticorruption principles worldwide by developing in-house or outsourced initiatives to abide by international and national legislation. Some of these public utility companies have strategic alliances with specialized entities like WIN, which accelerates the implementation process. There is a long way to go before the public utility system understands the importance of implementing transparency and integrity initiatives within their organizations. Hopefully, the methods, guidelines, and standards outlined in this chapter, which have a solid theoretical and practical background, will facilitate the adoption of transparency and integrity programs by the public utility ecosystem.

REFERENCES

African Union. (2021). *African Union Convention on Preventing and Combating Corruption*. AU. https://au.int/en/treaties/african-union-convention-preventing-and-combating-corruption

Albu, O. B., & Flyverbom, M. (2016). Organizational Transparency: Conceptualizations, Conditions, and Consequences. *Business & Society*, *58*(2), 268–297. doi:10.1177/0007650316659851

Apostolou, K., & Tjortjis, C. (2019). Sports analytics algorithms for performance prediction. *10th International Conference on Information, Intelligence, Systems and Applications (IISA)*. IEEE.

Berggren, E., & Bernshteyn, R. (2007). Organizational Transparency Drives Company Performance. *Journal of Management Development*, *26*(5), 411–417. doi:10.1108/02621710710748248

Boyd, N. M., & Martin, E. C. (2022). *Sustainable Public Management*. Routledge.

.Britannica. (2022). *Economy of Morocco*. Encyclopedia Britannica.

COE. (2022a). *Criminal law convention on corruption*. Impact of the European Convention on Human Rights. https://www.coe.int/en/web/impact-convention-human-rights/cr iminal-law-convention-on-corruption#/

COE. (2022b). *The Civil Law Convention Against Corruption*. Council of Europe. https://justice.gov.mt/en/pcac/Pages/CouncilofEurope.aspx

Colombia.co. (2022). *Así es Colombia [In Spanish]*. Colombia. https://www.colombia.co/pais-colombia/hechos/asi-es-colombia-1/

Crandall, R. W., & Ellig, J. (1997). *Economic Deregulation and Customer Choice: Lessons for the Electric Industry*. Center for Market Processes.

.Danker, M. (2013). Understanding stakeholder activism, managing transparency risk. *Developments in Corporate Governance and Responsibility*, 33–72.

Dimitrijević, D., Jovković, B., & Milutinović, S. (2021). The scope and limitations of external audit in detecting frauds in company's operations. *Journal of Financial Crime, 28*(3), 632–646. doi:10.1108/JFC-11-2019-0155

Erkkilä, T. (2012). Transparency and Institutions of Public Accountability. In: Government Transparency. Public Sector Organizations. Palgrave Macmillan, London.

Gaventa, J., & McGee, R. (2013). The Impact of Transparency and Accountability Initiatives. *Development Policy Review, 31*, 31. doi:10.1111/dpr.12017

Geddes, R. (2000). *Encyclopedia of Law & Economics - 5940 Public Utilities*. Findlaw. https://reference.findlaw.com/lawandeconomics/bibliographies/5940-public-utilities.html

Ghemawat, P. (2018). *Redefining global strategy crossing borders in a world where differences still matter*. Harvard Business Review Press.

Gianfreda, G. (2020). Vertical integration. In A. Marciano & G. Ramello (Eds.), *Encyclopedia of Law and Economics*. Springer. doi:10.1007/978-1-4614-7883-6_672-2

Glaeser, M. G. (1957). *Public Utilities in American Capitalism*. Macmillan.

. González de Asís, M., O'Leary, D., Ljung, P., & Butterworth, J. (2009). *Improving Transparency, Integrity, and Accountability in Water Supply and Sanitation*. World Bank.

Jacob, S., Speer, S., & Furubo, J. (2015). The institutionalization of evaluation matters: Updating the International Atlas of Evaluation 10 years later. *Evaluation, 21*(1), 6–31. doi:10.1177/1356389014564248

Llamas, M. R., Martínez-Cortina, L., Mukherji, A., & O'Leary, D. (2009). Corruption and transparency in the water sector. In *Water ethics*. CRC Press. doi:10.1201/9780203875438-28

Martín-Martín, A., Thelwall, M., Orduna-Malea, E., & Delgado López-Cózar, E. (2020). Google Scholar, Microsoft Academic, Scopus, dimensions, web of science, and OpenCitations' Coci: A multidisciplinary comparison of coverage via citations. *Scientometrics, 126*(1), 871–906. doi:10.100711192-020-03690-4 PMID:32981987

McNabb, D. E. (2018). *Public utilities: Old Problems, New Challenges*. Edward Elgar Publishing.

Men, L. R. (2014). Internal Reputation Management: The Impact of Authentic Leadership and Transparent Communication. *Corporate Reputation Review*, *17*(4), 254–272. doi:10.1057/crr.2014.14

Muers, S. (2020). *Culture and Values at the Heart of Policy Making*. Institute for Policy Research.

OAS. (2022). *OAS: SLA: Department of International Law (dil): Inter-American.* OAS. https://www.oas.org/en/sla/dil/inter_american_treaties_B-58_against_Corruption_signatories.asp

OECD. (2020). *OECD Public Integrity Handbook*. OECD Publishing. doi:10.1787/ac8ed8e8-

OECD. (2022a). *Anti-corruption initiative for Asia Pacific*. OECD. https://www.oecd.org/corruption/anti-corruption-initiative-for-asia-pacific.htm

OECD. (2022b). *OECD convention on combating bribery of foreign public officials in international business transactions*. OECD. https://www.oecd.org/corruption/oecdantibriberyconvention.htm

. Pope, J. (2000). *Confronting corruption: The elements of a national integrity system*. TI (Transparency International).

Regulated Industries Commission. (2010, December). *Improving transparency and accountability in the electricity and water.* RIC. http://www.ric.org.tt/wp-content/uploads/2021/02/Improving-Transparency-and-Accountability-in-the-Electricity-and-Water-Sectors.Main_.2021.pdf

. Sharda, R., Delen, D., & Turban, E. (2017, January 13). *Business Intelligence, Analytics, and Data Science: A Managerial Perspective* (4th ed.). Pearson.

Singh, R., & Vutukuru, V. (2010). *Enhancing Accountability in Public Service Delivery through Social Audits: A case study of Andhra Pradesh. Accountability Initiative*. Centre for Policy Research.

Superservicios. (2022). *Superintendency of Residential Public Services*. Superservicios. https://www.superservicios.gov.co/

Transparency International (TI). (2022a). *2021 corruption perceptions index - Explore the results*. Transparency.org. https://www.transparency.org/en/cpi/2021

Transparency International (TI). (2022b). *Ethics - Corruptionary A-Z.* Transparency.org. https://www.transparency.org/en/corruptionary/ethics

Transparency International (TI). (2022c). *Transparency - Corruptionary A-Z*. Transparency.org. https://www.transparency.org/en/corruptionary/transparency

Transparency International (TI). (2022d). *What is corruption?* Transparency.org. https://www.transparency.org/en/what-is-corruption

. Turilli, M. (2011). Ethical protocols design. *Machine Ethics*, 375–397.

Turilli, M., & Floridi, L. (2009). The Ethics of Information Transparency. *Ethics and Information Technology*, *11*(2), 105–112. doi:10.100710676-009-9187-9

Water Integrity Network (WIN). (2021). *Water integrity global outlook 2021*. WIN. https://www.waterintegritynetwork.net/wigo2021/

Water Integrity Network (WIN). (2022). *About win*. WIN. https://www.waterintegritynetwork.net/about/

. Wilkes, R. G., & Voormeulen, R. (1989). *Improving public sector financial management: Making better use of national resources*. The chartered Institute of public finance and accounting.

World Bank. (2003). *UNCAC*. World Bank. https://star.worldbank.org/focus-area/uncac

World Bank. (2022). *Worldwide governance indicators*. World Bank. https://info.worldbank.org/governance/wgi/

ADDITIONAL READING

Alam, M. M., Said, J., & Abd Aziz, M. A. (2019). Role of integrity system, internal control system and leadership practices on the accountability practices in the public sectors of Malaysia. *Social Responsibility Journal*, *15*(7), 955–976. doi:10.1108/SRJ-03-2017-0051

Alqooti, A. A. (2020). Public governance in the public sector: Literature review. *International Journal of Business Ethics and Governance*, *3*(3), 14–25. doi:10.51325/ijbeg.v3i3.47

. Androniceanu, A. (2021). Transparency in public administration as a challenge for a good democratic governance. *Revista» Administratie si Management Public «(RAMP)*, (36), 149-164.

Beshi, T. D., & Kaur, R. (2020). Public trust in local government: Explaining the role of good governance practices. *Public Organization Review*, *20*(2), 337–350. doi:10.100711115-019-00444-6

Joseph, C., Gunawan, J., Madi, N., Janggu, T., Rahmat, M., & Mohamed, N. (2019). Realising sustainable development goals via online integrity framework disclosure: Evidence from Malaysian and Indonesian local authorities. *Journal of Cleaner Production*, *215*, 112–122. doi:10.1016/j.jclepro.2019.01.057

Sofyani, H., Riyadh, H. A., & Fahlevi, H. (2020). Improving service quality, accountability and transparency of local government: The intervening role of information technology governance. *Cogent Business & Management*, *7*(1), 1735690. doi:10.1080/23311975.2020.1735690

KEY TERMS AND DEFINITIONS

Accountability: A guarantee that any organization will be accountable or evaluated on its performance.

Corruption: A series of dishonest acts and abuse of power to seek private gain.

Governance: This concept goes beyond the typical government within any organization and considers the relationship with other relevant stakeholders.

Integrity: A set of ethical values that organizations and society embrace and act on.

Public Utilities: Organizations that deliver essential services to society, such as tap water, electricity, gas, and waste management.

Risk Management: A set of tools to identify, analyze, manage, and control risks within a system.

Transparency: An organization's openness to sharing information and actions with stakeholders.

Transparency and Integrity Program: A series of standards, guidelines, and tools that aid in detecting, preventing, and managing corruption and bribery practices within organizations.

Chapter 5
Sustainability Enhancement in Water Supply and Municipal Waste Management Utilities

Sandra Stanković
Academy of Applied Technical and Preschool Studies, Niš, Serbia

Natalija Petrović
Academy of Applied Technical and Preschool Studies, Niš, Serbia

ABSTRACT

The city is an invention of human civilization that is distinguished, among other things, by the presence of infrastructure systems that assist public utility management. Globally, there is a growing awareness of the vital role that water and waste management play in sustainable development. The sustainable management of utility systems is unquestionably in the public and state interest. Therefore, this chapter presents current good practices and general ideas that constitute a foundation for beginning sustainable water and municipal waste management efforts in any activity. It also discusses the fundamental ways of improving sustainability in the municipal waste and water supply management sectors.

INTRODUCTION

With the advancement of human society, there was a need for transformation and efficiency to construct regional water supply systems, national and transnational transportation, energy, communication, and waste systems. Once built, the systems not only provide utility services to the area for which they are intended, but they

DOI: 10.4018/978-1-6684-7730-4.ch005

also have a feedback effect on future development by multiplying economic effects and encouraging the overall development of an environment.

Water is a comprehensive and inestimably precious resource as it fills every element of human endeavor. The diversity of water's final applications appears to be so extensive that any attempt at classification or synthesis would be futile. One of the most crucial components of societal infrastructure is the water delivery system, which is significant in both urban and rural locations. Water companies usually have extended planning perspectives as well as lengthy infrastructure maintenance and operation responsibilities (USEPA, 2012). As an example of a good sustainability policy, the EPA's Sustainability Policy is cited, which directs water plant systems to engage in resilient and inclusive planning to ensure that water infrastructure investments are cost-effective throughout their lifecycle, resource-efficient, and consistent with other relevant community goals. It is worth noting that per capita water demand has risen over time. The water volume required by an individual to meet all of their life and hygienic needs in a given period, such as daily, is referred to as per capita water demand. Water demand management is determined by the level of economic development and the ease with which water can be obtained. On the other hand, access to clean water is now largely acknowledged as a fundamental human right (UN General Assembly, 2022). Changes and interruptions to how water utilities operate can seriously disrupt people's lives and jeopardize the hygienic and safe conditions of those who use these services. The water supply sector is required to operate continuously under challenging conditions to ensure seamless utility services (Stanković, Vasović, Petrović, Boričić, & Takić, 2022). One of the numerous, more recent examples that confirm these statements is listed in the Pacific Water and Wastewater Association (PWWW) report. An evaluation of the pandemic's effects on PWWA member utilities was conducted using a COVID-19 survey as part of the data-gathering procedure for the 2021 year. The COVID-19 epidemic put utilities' operations and sustainability to the test. In addition to the evident overall economic impact on all PWWA nations, which included delayed water service payments resulting in a 50% decrease in billing in some member nations, quarantine restrictions also disrupted the supply of spare parts and interrupted chemical supply to many PWWA water providers (Pacific Water and Wastewater Association, 2021).

On the other hand, sustainable municipal waste management refers to a set of actions, judgments, and guidelines for preventing the production of waste, reducing the amount of waste and its detrimental impact on the environment, collecting and sorting waste separately, transporting and recycling waste, disposing of waste, and monitoring all procedures. As there are increasing problems with the proper management of municipal waste, various research has been done in this area all over the world: in China (Khan, Anjum, Raza, Bazai, & Ihtisham, 2022), Hong Kong

(Cheng, Zhu, Thompson, & Zhang, 2021), Russia (Kozlovskiy, Nedoseka, & Tishkov, 2022), Turkey (Cakar, Aydin, Varank, & Ozcan, 2020), Italy (Rusciano, Civero, & Scarpato, 2020), Colombia (Vargas-Terranova, Rodrigo-Ilarri, Rodrigo-Clavero, & Parra-Saad, 2022), and Spain (Rodrigo-Ilarri & Rodrigo-Clavero, 2020). The risk of water, soil, and air pollution, the occurrence of excessive noise, vibration, and unpleasant odors, the endangerment of flora and fauna, the detrimental impact on cultural-historical, aesthetic, and natural values, occurrence of fires, explosions, as well as groundwater contamination due to leachate percolation and other accidents are just a few issues that can arise from improper communal waste management procedures (Tošić & Vasović, 2020). The primary objectives of municipal waste management are to prevent and minimize waste formation, reduce trash's danger factors, reuse waste as a secondary raw material or as a source of energy, and dispose of waste in landfills and other planned and regulated temporary disposal sites (Rodrigo-Ilarri, Rodrigo-Clavero, & Cassiraga, 2020). Municipal waste management can be sustainable if all levels of waste management are conducted in compliance with the legal framework and social norms to safeguard the public's health and the environment. All of this should at the same time, meet requirements for both economy and aesthetics (Počuča N., 2020). According to World Bank data, global waste is expected to grow 70% by 2050. The developed world makes up 15% of its population; it generates 34% of the world's waste. For this reason, the Waste 2.0 initiative was founded to encourage waste management, proposing that, firstly, creation should be avoided, and otherwise created waste should be recovered, reduced, and recycled and discourages the disposal of waste (Farooq et al., 2022).

Quality data is critical for facilitating both water and waste management planning and the necessary infrastructure investments. However, the availability and dependability of waste data are frequently subpar. Although statistical research is done, the precision and response rates are frequently relatively low. Since many landfills still lack weighing equipment, it is difficult to determine the exact amounts of processed waste that were dumped there (ETC/WMGE, 2021). Likewise, water quality data collecting is a crucial aspect of protecting water resources and sustainable water usage. Numerous economic, social, and ecological factors must be taken into account in order to determine whether a water system is sustainable. The generated data assists water resource managers in determining where pollution problems exist, where pollution control efforts should be directed, and where progress has been made.

The key objectives of this chapter are present the contemporary practice in the municipal waste and water supply management field in the world and the Republic of Serbia, as well as to propose potential solutions for sustainable waste and water management.

SUSTAINABILITY IN WATER SUPPLY AND MUNICIPAL WASTE MANAGEMENT SECTORS - GLOBAL PERSPECTIVE

Rising awareness of sustainability in water supply and waste management began in the 1970s, during the first global initiatives in the field of environmental protection. Since the Paris Agreement was signed and the Agenda 2030 entered into force, achieving the Sustainable Development Goals and harnessing the potential they represent have been a challenge for many companies globally. The ambitions of the goals require the coordination and collective efforts of the entire utility sector.

To use water sustainably, one must be able to meet current water demands without endangering the ability of future generations to do the same while also minimizing the environmental effects of catastrophic weather events caused by climate change as floods and droughts. Some broad guidelines may be used to make sustainable use of available water supplies, prolong the life of current water supplies, and spread the advantages of water delivery to a huger segment of the global population (Stanković, Vasović, & Živković, 2019).

Further away, sustainable waste management, at all stages that potentially have an environmental impact, has become indispensable in the last few years (Tošić & Vasović, 2020). As a result, a range of new and existing waste treatment technologies and management strategies are brought together to maintain environmental quality today and to meet sustainable development goals in the future. Waste management is complex as it involves a wide range of activities, waste management technologies and disciplines at different stages of waste management. It includes various analyzes of technological processes related to the properties and production of waste, as well as techniques and technologies of waste disposal, from the collection, through transport, and storage, to the final option of disposal or utilization (Počuča N., 2020). Unsystematic and inadequate handling of waste represents one of the biggest problems of environmental protection policy. This situation is primarily a consequence of society's undeveloped attitude towards waste, lack of understanding of why it is important to manage waste and implement plans, and non-acceptance and neglect of the positive effects of organized collection and utilization of waste.

Water Supply Sector

According to economic classifications, the "water supply sector" refers to water utilities that provide fresh water to buildings and other entities that are connected to the public water supply system (Hoekstra, 2015). Various objects that make up parts of the water supply system can be divided into five groups (Djurdjević, 2009):

- Water catchment facility;

- Water treatment plants;
- Water supply facilities;
- Distribution network;
- Reservoirs.

Water consumption depends on many constant and variable factors such as (Djurdjević, 2009):

- Climate conditions;
- Consumers numbers and specific daily consumption per inhabitant;
- Population's characteristics;
- Number of consumers augmentation;
- Pricing policy;
- Maintenance and functioning of the city water supply and sewage system;
- City needs for street watering and firefighting;
- Number, types and technologies in industrial facilities.

For a new water supply system, it is best to estimate the future consumption based on the experiences of cities that have a similar urban structure, geographic location, economic, social and economic conditions (Djurdjević, 2009).

A total of 148 nations share 276 transboundary basins, which account for 60% of the flow of freshwater global. Similar to this, 300 aquifer systems have a transboundary aspect, and 2.5 billion people depend on groundwater worldwide (The World Bank, 2022). Global freshwater usage, or freshwater withdrawals for agriculture, industry, and municipal uses, has increased approximately six-fold since last century as a result of an expanding world population and an economic shift toward more resource-intensive consumption patterns. Freshwater consumption varies greatly around the world. For instance, India's annual freshwater withdrawals of nearly 760 billion cubic meters in 2014 were the highest. China came in second with a little over 600 billion m^3, while the United States came in third with 480–90 billion m^3 (Ritchie & Roser, 2017). Water withdrawal rates must be lower than freshwater replenishment rates in order to maintain sustainable levels of water resources.

Municipal water is described as water which is utilized for private, domestic, or public uses. Usually, the water is used for drinking, cleaning, washing, and cooking, and it is the most "visible" type of water. According to Ritchie and Roser's data from 2015, the biggest annual domestic water demand, at over 70 billion m^3, is in China. Third-largest municipal water usage is India, which has the world's second-largest population. Due to higher per capita water demands, the United States, while having a far lower population, is the second greatest user. Domestic needs, while the most obvious use of freshwater, are typically insignificant in comparison to agricultural and industrial uses. Around 11% of withdrawals worldwide are used for municipal reasons. Less than 30% of withdrawals are used for domestic purposes in most nations (Ritchie & Roser, 2017).

About 2.1 billion people do not have access to safe drinking water services, while water scarcity already affects four out of every ten people, according to World Health Organization (UN, 2022). In 2020, 74% of the world's population had access to a source of water that was well-managed. One in four individuals lack access to clean water for drinking. Clearly, this will take much longer than 2030 to achieve sustainable development goal target 6. If development keeps moving forward at this pace, it will only reach 82% by 2030 (Ritchie & Roser, 2017). Cities like Cape Town in South Africa, and Cairo in Egypt, are already experiencing or are projected to experience catastrophic water supply shortages, which are making headlines in news outlets all over the world.

To assist focus more attention on water over the next ten years, the United Nations General Assembly unanimously approved the resolution "International Decade (2018-2028) for Action - Water for Sustainable Development" in December 2016. The Decade's goals are focused on advancing cooperation and partnership at all levels to help achieve internationally agreed water-related goals and targets, including those found in the Agenda 2030 for Sustainable Development, as well as on the sustainable development and integrated management of water resources for the achievement of social, economic, and environmental objectives. As part of the water, food, energy, and environment nexus, the Decade also emphasizes the significance of promoting efficient water use at all levels. It also emphasizes the importance of full participation from all relevant parties, including women, children, young people, older people, people with disabilities, indigenous people and local communities (UN, 2022). Among the Member States that are already taking action are 43 countries: Afghanistan, Andorra, Australia, Austria, Bangladesh, Brazil, Cabo Verde, Canada, China, Cyprus, Egypt, El Salvador, Estonia, Ethiopia, Finland, Georgia, Germany, Ghana, Hungary, India, Indonesia, Iran, Ireland, Israel, Italy, Japan, Jordan, Malta, Mongolia, Namibia, Netherlands, Nigeria, Paraguay, Philippines, Romania, Singapore, Slovenia, South Africa, Tajikistan, Thailand, The Russian Federation, United Arab Emirates and Vietnam (UN Water, 2022).

Municipal Waste Management Sector

About 17 billion tons of solid waste are generated annually in the world, and assumptions are that these quantities will amount to around 27 billion tons by 2050. From that 1.3 billion tons of municipal waste are generated in the world's cities, and it is estimated that this amount will increase to 2.2 billion tons by 2025 (Stepanov, 2018).

The rate of municipal waste generation per inhabitant is 1.2 kg per day, and predictions show that by 2025 this amount will increase to 1.4 kg per capita per day. Increase the amount of waste is inextricably linked with the increase in the number of inhabitants, which has increased urbanization and socio-economic development of the country. The United States of America is leading in terms of the amount of generated waste (about 621,000 tons per day), followed by China in which about 521,000 tons of waste is generated per day (Worldwatch, 2012) (Laurent, et al., 2014a).

The United States Environmental Protection Agency (USEPA) (USEPA, 2012), under the Resource Conservation Recovery Act (RCRA), regulates household, commercial, industrial, and hazardous wastes, treatment methods, and efficient management systems (JeyaSundar, Ali, di, & Zhang, 2020). It also promotes plans for nonhazardous and municipal waste monitoring and treatment by the concerned authorities in each state to achieve efficiency.

The generation rate and composition of waste varies greatly between regions, countries, cities and even within cities. A comparison of the morphological composition of municipal waste in relation to the income level of countries is shown in Figure 1. Organic fractions occupy a considerable amount higher share in the middle- and low- income countries, while in high-income countries per inhabitant, a large percentage of municipal waste is occupied by paper and plastic (GWMO, 2015).

Organized collection of municipal waste in countries with low per capita income is 36%, in lower-middle income countries 64%, in in countries with middle-higher income 82%, and in countries with high per capita income residents, organized waste collection services are approaching 100% (Hoornweg & Bhada-Tata, 2012).

Figure 1. Morphological composition of waste
Source: Global Waste Management Outlook, 2015

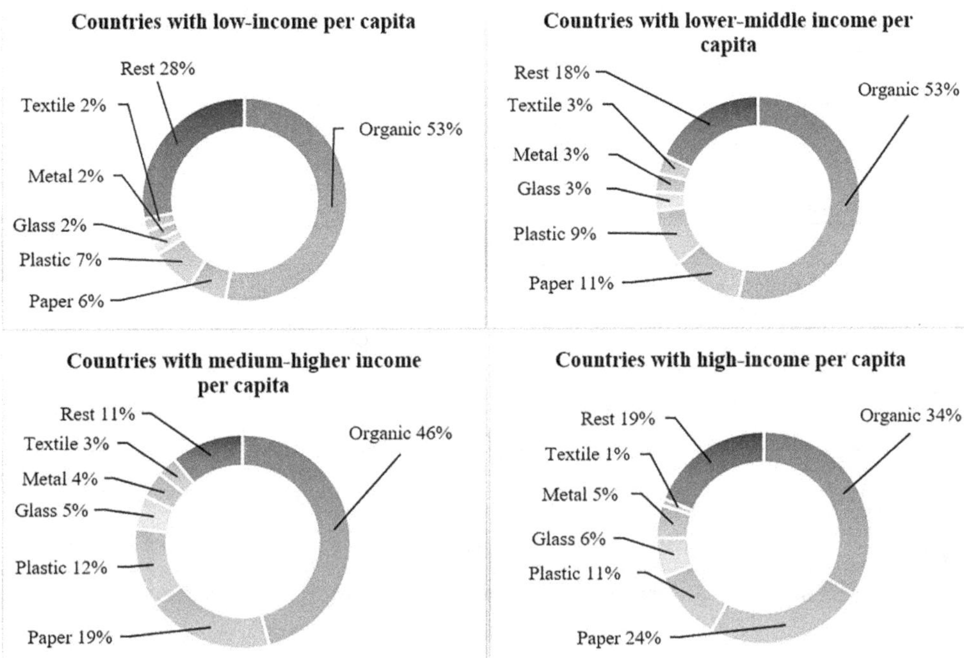

The most represented option for the municipal waste treatment, on a global level, and beyond represents disposal, although according to many strategic documents from the area waste management, this option is considered the least desirable in the waste management hierarchy (Batinić, 2015). Implementation of certain options for the treatment of communal waste to the greatest extent it depends on economic indicators, that is, on the development of a certain country. Table 1 shows the method of waste treatment depending on the level of national income per capita.

Table 1. Municipal waste treatment methods in the world (million t)

Countries with low-income per capita		Countries with lower-middle income per capita	
Illegal landfills	0.47	Illegal landfills	27
Disposal	2.3	Disposal	6.1
Composting	0.05	Composting	1.2
Recycling	0.02	Recycling	2.9
Thermal treatment	0.05	Thermal treatment	0.12
Rest	0.97	Rest	18
Countries with medium-higher income per capita		**Countries with high-income per capita**	
Illegal landfills	44	Illegal landfills	0.05
Disposal	80	Disposal	250
Composting	1.3	Composting	66
Recycling	1.9	Recycling	129
Thermal treatment	0.18	Thermal treatment	122
Rest	8.3	Rest	21

Source: What a waste – A global review of solid waste management, World Bank, 2012

Waste disposal and thermal treatment are the most common methods of municipal waste treatment in countries with high incomes. Countries with low- and middle-income waste mostly dispose of in uncontrolled or partially controlled landfills.

MUNICIPAL WASTE AND WATER SUPPLY MANAGEMENT - EUROPEAN UNION EXPERIENCES

Some of the best environmental standards in the world are advantageous to European members. With the help of dedicated research programs, legislation, and funding, the EU and national governments have set clear objectives to steer European environment policy until 2030 and a vision beyond that. In addition to the energy transition, sustainable water supply and waste management are also important goals of public utility activities.

Municipal Waste Management in EU Countries

The European Union Waste Framework Directive provides legal framework for prompt (JeyaSundar, Ali, di, & Zhang, 2020):

- collection,
- transportation,
- optimal recovery,
- treatment and
- landfilling of wastes along with their proper definition.

This directive acts in the Member States regarding the treatment and disposal of waste related to human health and the environment by improving proper registration, permits and inspections.

EU has strict control of hazardous waste handling, treatment and disposal in accordance with the laws of the Hazardous Waste Regulations and the Batteries Directive, as well as by reducing the waste load on electronic equipment by the Restriction of Hazardous Substances in Electrical and Electronic Equipment (RoHS) Directives. The European Union Landfill Directive suggests the allowable materials for disposal in order to reduce the harmful impact on groundwater and the environment. It also suggests recycling and reusing materials rather than ideal disposal.

In the European Union countries, municipal solid waste constitutes approximately 10% of the total generated solid waste (EEA, 2015). The total amount generated municipal waste for the EU-28 in 2014 amounted to 240 million tons, i.e., 475 kg per inhabitant (Eurostat, 2016a). Largest quantities of municipal waste generated by the inhabitants of Denmark, »759 kg per inhabitant, on an annual basis.

The morphological composition of waste within the EU differs between member states, and for this reason, it is difficult to determine a unique structure of waste. In the morphological composition of municipal waste in more developed countries, member states (Germany, France, Sweden) dominate plastic, cardboard and paper, while the share of organic waste is low. In other member states, among others, Romania, and Bulgaria, which according to economic indicators, belong to developing countries, in the morphological composition of waste, the organic fraction dominates (Batinić, 2015).

Figure 2. Morphological composition of waste in the EU-27
Source: Evaluation model of the municipal waste management system using the life cycle assessment method, 2018.

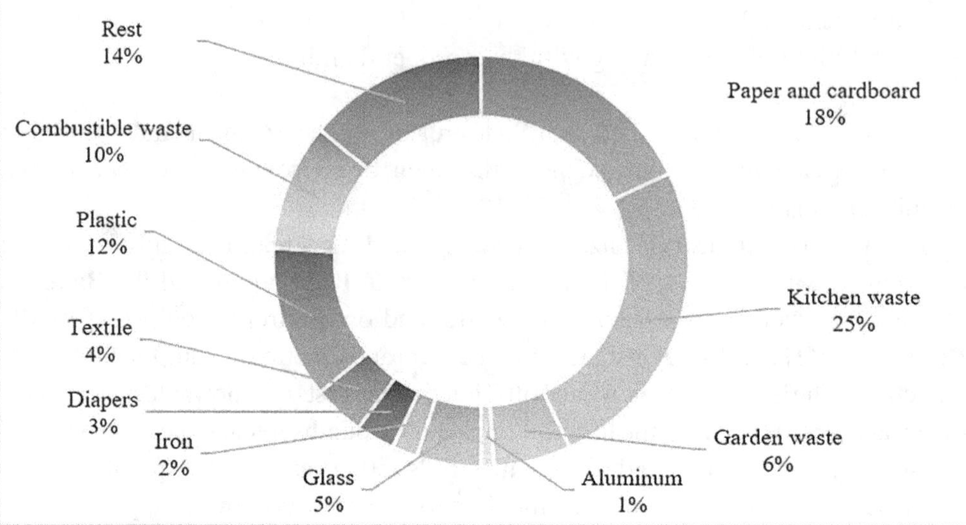

When it comes to the representation of municipal waste treatment options in EU countries the largest percentage is occupied by landfilling and recycling, followed by thermal treatment, and the smallest percentage is represented by composting.

Table 2. Municipal waste treatment methods in EU

Municipal waste treatment method in EU	%
Recycling	28
Thermal treatment	27
Composting	16
Landfilling	28

Source: (EEA, Municipal waste management across European countries, 2016)

Germany, Austria, Belgium, Switzerland, the Netherlands and Sweden recycled at least half of their municipal waste. The highest increase in recycling rates was reported in Lithuania, Poland, Italy, the United Kingdom and the Czech Republic. The rate of municipal waste landfilling for the 32 EEA member countries fell from 49% in 2004 to 34% in 2014. In Austria, Belgium, Denmark, Germany, the Netherlands, Norway, Sweden and Switzerland, virtually no municipal waste is sent to landfill.

On the other hand, Cyprus, Croatia, Greece, Latvia, Malta and Turkey still landfill more than three quarters of their municipal waste. (EEA, 2016)

Separate collection of municipal waste, stimulated by ambitious EU legislation, is steadily increasing over time. New, higher recycling targets were introduced in the amended Waste Framework Directive in 2018, which indicates even higher separate collection in the future. The amended 2018 Directive introduced a target for recycling of 65% by 2035. This is particularly ambitious compared with the estimated maximum potential of 80%. The target refers to final recycled amounts, not to amounts of waste collected for recycling.

Municipal Waste Management in Western Balkan Countries

Since 2015, municipal waste production per capita has increased in Kosovo* (according to UN Security Council Resolution 1244/99), North Macedonia and Serbia, and remained stable in Bosnia and Herzegovina and Montenegro.

Figure 3. Municipal waste generation per inhabitant in the Western Balkan countries, 2015- 2020
Source: (EEA, Municipal waste management in Western Balkan countries, 2022)

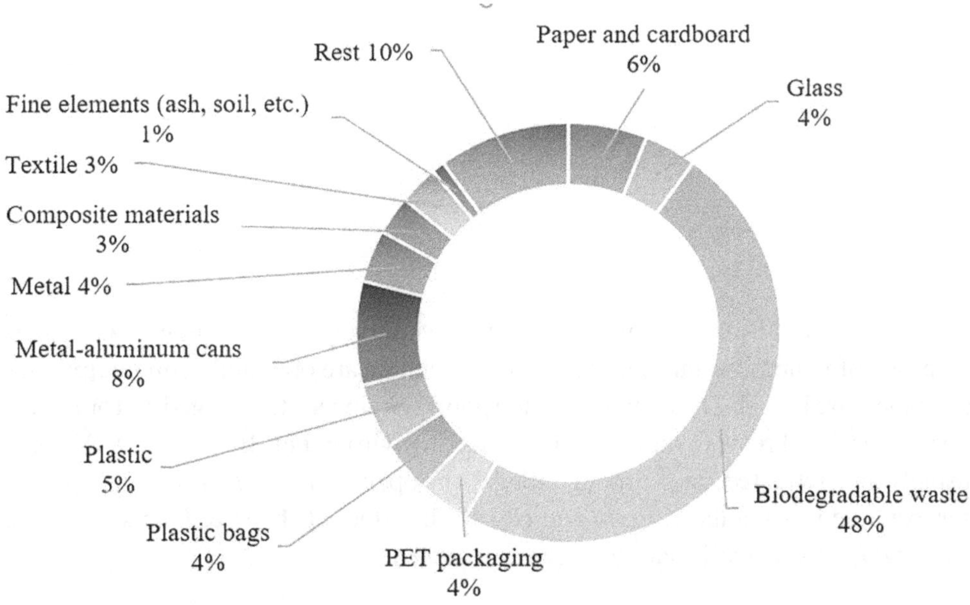

These countries show different levels of municipal waste production, ranging from approximately 250 kg per capita in Kosovo* to almost 500 kg/inhabitant in

Montenegro. All these values are lower than the 2020 EU average of 505 kg per capita and corresponds to household consumption below the EU average in the Western Balkans countries.

All the countries of the Western Balkans continue to deposit waste to a large extent: considerable amounts of waste end up in landfills and recycling is mostly still negligible, with little progress over the years.

Figure 4. Municipal waste treatment in the Western Balkan countries, 2020
Source: (EEA, Municipal waste management in Western Balkan countries, 2022)

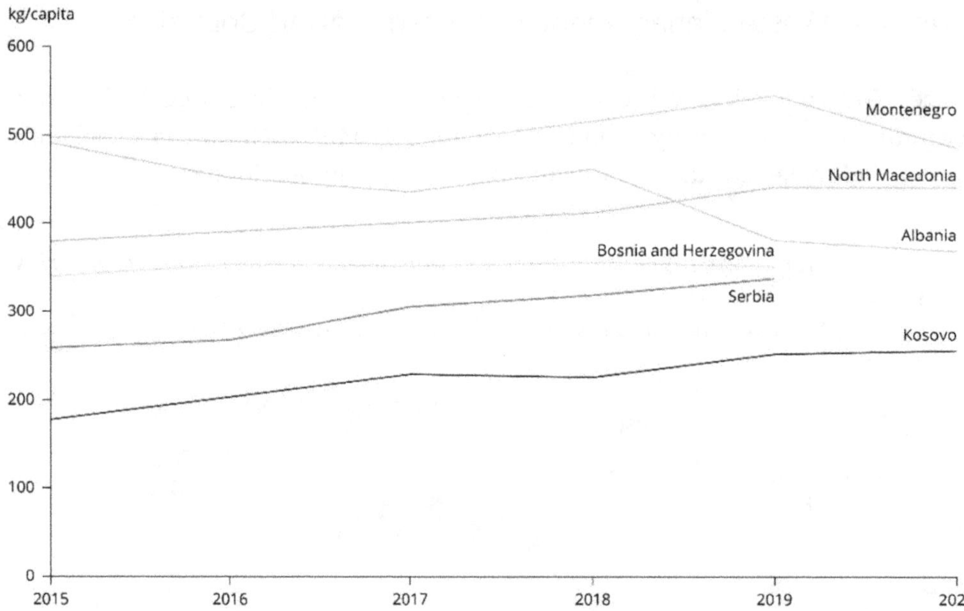

In all Western Balkan countries except for Montenegro, most municipal waste is disposed of in non-sanitary landfills, some of which are operated by municipalities and others are illegal. These sites are often poorly engineered, managed and operated, posing serious threats to human health and the environment (EEA, 2021). Waste is usually not pretreated, and, although illegal, the open burning of waste still happens, for example in Albania, Kosovo and North Macedonia (Shapo & Glanxhi, 2021). Currently, only a small share of waste is recycled.

Water Supply Management in EU Countries

Supplying the population with water is considered the primary branch of water management today. Every year, Europeans consume billions of cubic meters of water for various purposes, including agriculture, manufacturing, heating and cooling, tourism, and other ecosystem services. The amount of freshwater accessible in Europe's lakes, rivers, and underground water sources may appear endless. However, factors such as urbanization, pollution, and extreme hydrological events such as droughts during the summer of 2022 are severely affecting both the quantity and quality of water supply in Europe. For drinking and other purposes, rivers and groundwater provide about 88.2 percentage of Europe's freshwater needs, with lakes and reservoirs providing the remaining portions 10.3 percentage and 1.5 percentage, respectively. As a result, these sources are extremely vulnerable to threats from overuse, pollution, and climate change (EEA, 2021). According to EEA estimates, either permanently or intermittently, about one-third of EU territory is subject to water stress conditions. Water shortage is a problem in northern regions, including sections of the United Kingdom and Germany and has already been a problem in countries like Greece, Portugal, and Spain during the summer months. However, since 1990, total water abstraction has decreased by 19 percentage as a result of advancements in water efficiency and supply management (EEA, 2021).

For instance, the region of Eastern Europe withdraws 81.024 million m^3 of water annually, or 2.0% of global withdrawals. With 248 million m^3, or 0.3%, and 631 million m^3, or 6%, respectively, of the total withdrawals in the region, Latvia and Lithuania have the lowest withdrawal rates. The average amount of water used annually per person is 387 m^3, ranging from 126 m^3 in Latvia to 1.310 m^3 in Estonia (FAO, 2022).

The main hydrological feature in SEE countries is a spatially and temporally uneven distribution of water and a significant lack of water resources in certain areas (parts of Serbia, Kosovo*, and Macedonia). The total intake of freshwater that includes surface and underground water, during the year varies from 328.9x106 m^3 (B&H, period 2011 - 2013), 263.5x106 m^3 (Kosovo*, period 2011 - 2015), 3,710x106 m^3 (Serbia, period 2011 - 2014) up to 109x106 m^3 in Montenegro (2011). Water intake per inhabitant in municipalities in Albania amounts to 177.1 m^3 per year. The use of fresh groundwater dominates in B&H (83.2%), Montenegro (81%), and Albania (75%), while in Serbia it is 13.1% and in Kosovo* 11%. The total number of households in B&H connected to the system water supply is 686,149 and the rest of the population has the individual supply from various sources (shallow wells, springs). Water supply coverage in Albania is about 80.5% in the period 2012 - 2015, 70% in Kosovo*, 89% in Macedonia, 80% in Serbia, and 60% in Montenegro. The urban population in the SEE region has a much higher level of availability of public water supply systems than the rural population. Average water losses are very high in the SEE region, up to 60% in Montenegro and 55% in Kosovo* (Dragović, Ristić, Pilcl, & Volfslehner, 2017).

It is impossible to discuss the sustainable management of water resources in the European Union without mentioning the relevant legislation. The following directives serve as the main codifications of EU water policy:

- the Drinking Water Directive (98/83/EC) - was revised and formally adopted by European Parliament in December 2020,
- the Urban Waste Water Directive (91/271/EEC),
- the Bathing Water Directive (2006/7/EC),
- the Floods Directive (2007/60/EC),
- the Nitrates Directive (91/676/EEC).

The Drinking Water Directive provides for the integration of protection and sustainable water management in all areas of human activity. It gives common grounds for water protection improvement in terms of quality and quantity, promotes sustainable use of water through control over border watercourses, protection of aquatic ecosystems, and improves the use of polluted water discharges by potential water users. A Regulatory Committee was established to oversee the implementation of the Directive. This committee, made up of officials from the Commission and the member nations, has the authority to enact measures, reconcile differences, and provide suggestions for improvements (Počuča N., 2018). From the perspective of water supply, this Directive establishes a framework for behavior and actions in the field of water supply, which is also accepted by countries outside the Union, such as the Republic of Serbia. All distribution systems that serve more than 50 people or provide more than 10 m3 of water per day are covered by the Drinking Water Directive, as are distribution systems that serve fewer than 50 people or provide less than 10 m3 of water per day if the water is provided as part of an economic activity. The directive also applies to water used in the food-processing industry unless the competent national authorities are satisfied that this is not the case (European Comission, 2022). The water policies of the EU encourage Member States to adopt better water management practices, particularly when it comes to water price laws, along with additional measures like public awareness campaigns promoting water efficiency through the use of water-saving equipment (EEA, 2021).

WATER SUPPLY AND MUNICIPAL WASTE MANAGEMENT SECTOR – EXPERIENCES OF REPUBLIC OF SERBIA

There is a prevailing belief that public utility firms need to be owned by the state in the Republic of Serbia. With rare exceptions in the areas of municipal traffic or waste collection, where there is also a private sector in addition to the public sector, the current ownership structure of public utility sector is such that they are publicly owned. From an organizational standpoint, local utilities and services are combined in local directorates for public utilities in smaller cities and municipalities, but only in larger cities such as Belgrade, Novi Sad and Nis.

Water Supply Sector in Republic of Serbia

The Republic of Serbia has an area of 88,361 km^2 and is located in the center of the Balkan Peninsula. The territory is divided into two distinct areas: the large Vojvodina plain in the north and the hilly-mountainous area in the south, separated by the Danube and Sava rivers. The Republic of Serbia is classified as a medium-populated European country. During the last decade, Serbia has been characterized by a decrease in the number of inhabitants, a reduced birth rate and population concentration in urban areas. The availability of water resources is closely related to climatic conditions, especially precipitation and temperature. Although the rainfall of 734 mm is significant, the key problem is the uneven annual distribution of rainfall. The Republic of Serbia is one of the poorer areas of Europe in terms of water resource availability, with an annual distribution of surface water of 1500 m^3 per inhabitant. The lowland areas with the most people and the richest land resources (northern and central Serbia) have the lowest water yield (specific runoff 2-4 $l/s \bullet km^2$), posing a special challenge for water supply (Dragović, Ristić, Pilcl, & Volfslehner, 2017).

A significant part of the water supply system in Serbia is based on the use of water from surface reservoirs. The settlement's water supply is based on the use of local underground and surface water sources, and the shortage is eventually resolved by using water from the regional system. Water bodies are formed to clearly define spatial elements of surface water that have approximately uniform characteristics for planning measures with the ultimate goal of preserving or achieving a certain state of surface water. Water bodies form in watersheds larger than 100 km^2 in size and on all major interstate watercourses, regardless of the basin area. There were 499 water bodies in total, 492 of which were found in the Danube basin. Nearly 70% (342) of the total number of surface water bodies are natural watercourses (mostly rivers), 16 are manmade water bodies, and the remaining 28% are preliminary rated as significantly modified water bodies due to severe hydro-morphological changes. Only five water features are classified as standing water within Serbian territory because there are comparatively few natural lakes there (natural and artificial lakes). The majority of planning documents start with an analysis of the chemical and physical characteristics of formed water bodies. The Environmental Protection Agency, a division of the Ministry, and the Republic Hydrometeorological Institute of Serbia are the agencies qualified to undertake water monitoring (Dragović, Ristić, Pilcl, & Volfslehner, 2017).

Each region has a unique water supply scenario that varies depending on infrastructure development, population density, and water supply reliability (time, amount, and quality). Different densities, levels of economic activity, the availability of water supplies, system losses, and other factors all contribute to this. Over time, a greater proportion of people are now connected to public water delivery networks. Without Kosovo, it was roughly 76% in Serbia in 2000. Today, that percentage exceeds 80%. As a result of people moving from the rural to the city, there is also an upward tendency in connectivity. Over 90% of connections are in Vojvodina and Belgrade, which help with the development of water supply infrastructure. The reality is that major settlements in central Serbia do not have a public water supply system (Dragović, Ristić, Pilcl, & Volfslehner, 2017).

Municipal Waste Management Sector in Republic of Serbia

In Serbia, the Law on waste management aims to transpose the EU waste legislation. Implementation is at an early stage. The Law on waste management and the Law on packaging and packaging waste are the key pieces of legislation steering municipal waste management, both being currently under revision (EEA, 2021). The national waste management strategy is an integral component of the legal framework in Serbia and must be revised every 5 years. Data about waste management in the Republic of Serbia are collected under the Law on Waste Management and in accordance with: Regulation on the Methodology for Creating a National and Local Register of Pollution Sources, and Methodology for Types, Ways and Terms for Data Collection (R. Serbia, 2016), Rule on the Form of the Document on Waste Movement and the Instruction for its Completion (R. Serbia, 2021), Regulation on Forms for the Report on Packaging and Packaging Waste Management (R. Serbia, 2018), Regulation on the form of the Document on the movement of hazardous waste, the template for the previous notification, the manner of its submission and the instructions its completion (R. Serbia, 2017).

Under Serbia's Law on waste management, waste treatment data include the total amount of waste recycled and disposed of. These data are provided by the PUCs based on their annual reports. Between 2015 and 2019 the reported quantities of waste treated increased by 47%, while the amount of waste generated increased by only 28% in the same period (EEA, 2021).

The total amount of produced waste, according to the data submitted to the National Register sources of pollution, is shown in Figure 5.

Figure 5. Total amount of produced waste in Serbia (t)
Source: (Đorđević, Redžić, Radovanović, & Jovanović, 2021)

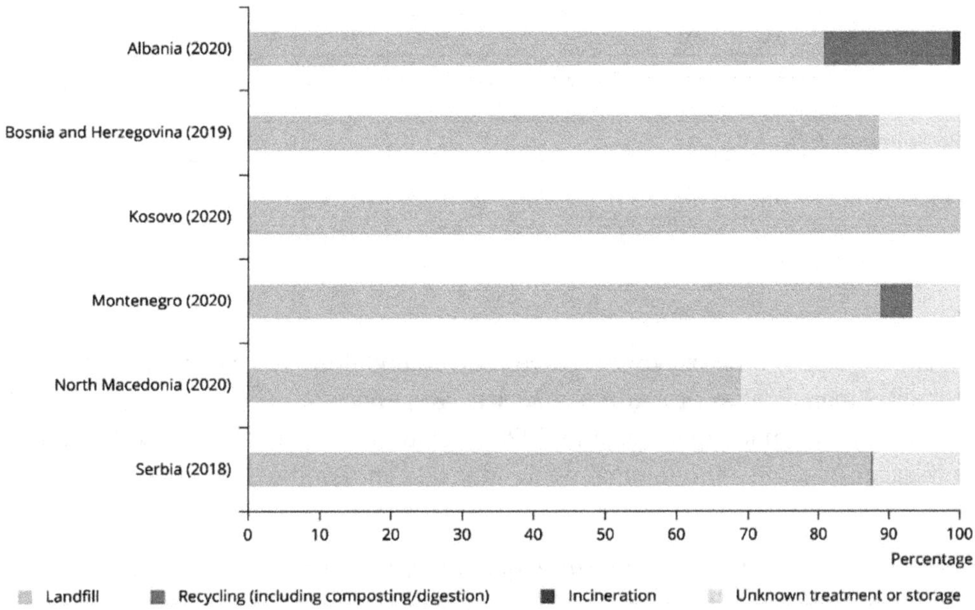

As can be seen from figure 5, the total amount of generated waste during 2020 is in the minority increase compared to the previous year. Municipal waste generation in Serbia decreased from 2.65 million tons of waste generated in 2010 to 1.84 million tons in 2015 but then increased to 2.35 million tons in 2019. The amounts generated correspond to 363 kg per capita in 2010 and 338 kg per capita in 2019, which is roughly 67% of the EU average of 502 kg per capita in 2019.

Table 4 shows the basic indicators that show the quantities of produced utility of waste and they monitor the achievement of the strategic goal - avoiding and reducing the generation waste. Indicators are created on the basis of annual data on the amount of waste reported by utility companies in local self-governments in accordance with the Regulation on form of daily record and annual report on waste and the Instruction for its Completion ("Official Gazette of RS", no. 7/2020 and 79/2021) (R. Serbia, 2021). In accordance with the Regulation on methodology for collecting data on composition and quantities of municipal waste on the territory of the local self-government unit (Official Gazette of RS, No. 61/2010, 14/2020) (R. Serbia, 2021) local governments have the obligation to perform quantity analyzes four times a year and composition of municipal waste in its territory.

Table 4. Municipal waste indicators

	2018	2019	2020
Total amount of generated waste (t)	2.795.296	2.827.910	2.947.496
Amount of waste collected and landfilled by municipal PUCs (t)	2.223.864	2.243.661	2.341.732
Reuse procedure (R1 – R11) (t)	450.112	461.740	477.897
Average scope of waste collection (%)	87.2	86.2	86.4
Average daily amount of municipal waste per capita (kg)	1,10	1,11	1,15

Source: (Đorđević, Redžić, Radovanović, & Jovanović, 2021)

During 2020, the Agency prepared the Methodology for calculating the total amount of municipal waste and recycling in the Republic of Serbia. The morphological composition of municipal waste in 2020 is given in Figure 6 of the collection of individual fractions of municipal waste in local communities.

Figure 6. Morphological composition of municipal waste of Serbia in 2020
Source: (Serbian Government, 2022)

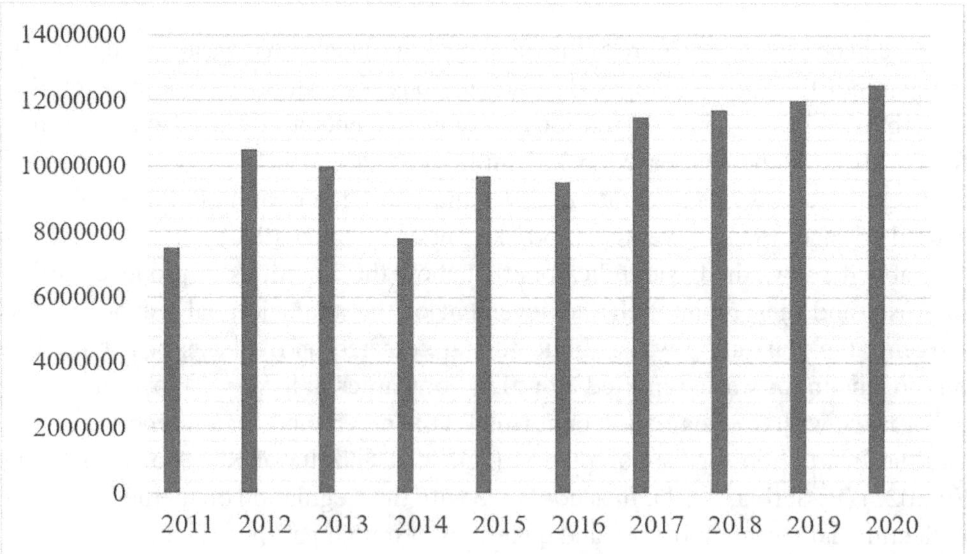

As can be seen from Figure 4, the morphological composition of municipal waste in 2020 indicates to the highest representation of biodegradable waste in the share of 48.4%. Types of waste that are significant less represented are: paper and cardboard, fine elements and others (leather, diapers, rubber, etc.).

The Serbian authorities state that there are no precise data on the total capacity for the treatment of municipal waste. Recycling rates remain low, with the majority of collected and selected considerable quantities of recyclable waste materials by Public-Private-Partnership waste management companies, such as Kappastar Recycling and Hamburger Recycling, Eko Unija Belgrade, Green tech Novi Sad, A.K.O. International, ALWAG in Nova Gajdobra, E-Reciklaža in Niš, etc (Consulting, 2021).

Waste Treatment Methods in Republic of Serbia

In Serbia, the amounts of treated waste are assumed to be equal to the quantities collected. The collection efficiency, i.e. the amount collected divided by the total amount of generated, increased from 71% in 2010 to 86% in 2019 (EEA, 2021). Under Serbia's Law on waste management, waste treatment data include the total amount of waste recycled and disposed of. These data are provided by the PUCs based on their annual reports. Between 2015 and 2019 the reported quantities of waste treated increased by 47%, while the amount of waste generated increased by only 28% in the same period. The amount of recycled waste remained stable (Eurostat, 2021).

In the 2020, 2.14 million tons of waste were subjected to R1-R11 reuse operations (recycle included). From the total amount processed, metals are the most represented waste, followed by slag from thermal processes, waste paper and paper and cardboard packaging (Đorđević, Redžić, Radovanović, & Jovanović, 2021). Procedures R1 - R10 are different types of treatment procedures, while the procedures from R12 - R13 are ancillary activities, related to treatment procedures - waste preparation, storage and they are most commonly used for wood, plastic, paper, cardboard and mixed municipal waste, and R11 refers to utilization waste obtained from any operation from R1 to R10 (Tošić & Vasović, 2020).

Table 6. The amount of reused waste in the Republic of Serbia in the period 2011-2020

Year	Treated with R1-R10 (t)	Treated with R11-R13 (t)	Total treated (t)
2011	1.422.017	31.755	1.453.772
2012	940.662	178.820	1.119.482
2013	1.493.388	294.275	1.787.664
2014	1.660.068	345.319	2.005.387
2015	1.279.231	360.255	1.639.486
2016	1.418.226	261.122	1.679.340
2017	1.479.522	260.609	1.740.131
2018	1.700.470	332.679	2.033.149
2019	1.971.395	299.003	2.270.398
2020	2. 050.048	93.086	2.143.134

Source: (Serbian Government, 2022)

Of the non-hazardous waste, most of it was treated with the R4 process, i.e. metal recycling. The amount of waste that is also important is treated by procedures R5 and R3, i.e. recycling and processing of other inorganic materials and recycling and processing of organic materials that are not used as solvents (including composting and other processes of biological transformation).

There is a pilot composting facility in Čačak with a capacity of 500 tons per year, set up as a public-private partnership, treating bio-waste from the municipality, i.e. mainly garden waste. Also, from 2018 there is a composting company in Smederevo (Composting DOO) with annual treatment capacity that includes more than 10,000 tons of biodegradable waste per year. There are 300 waste operators in Serbia treating 2 million tons of industrial waste and MSW. Furthermore, there are seven operators with a permit for packaging waste management. The largest amount of packaging placed on the market in Serbia was taken care of by national operators (SEPA, 2021)

Every year there is an increase in the amount deposited waste in sanitary landfills. A large part of the generated municipal waste is disposed of in unsanitary landfills outside the control of PUCs, because this is the cheapest option. In 2018, it was estimated that 25% of the waste was sent to one of the sanitary landfills, where entrance fees must be paid. 45% was deposited in registered, but unsanitary municipal landfills, and about 30% of the total waste ended up in uncontrolled landfills (ETC/WMGE, 2021).

There are 11 sanitary landfills in Serbia which are, however, reaching the limits of their capacity. They do not operate completely in accordance with the conditions set out in the EU Landfill Directive. In addition to the 11 sanitary landfills, there are about 100 unsanitary municipal landfills and more than 3 000 illegal dumpsites in Serbia.

There are 11 sanitary landfills in Serbia, which, however, have reached the limit of their capacity. They do not completely operate with the conditions set out in the EU Landfill Directive. In addition to the 11 sanitary landfills, there are about 100 unsanitary municipal landfills and more than 3,000 illegal landfills in Serbia.

Figure 7. Presentation of disposed amounts of waste at sanitary landfills
Source: (Đorđević, Redžić, Radovanović, & Jovanović, 2021)

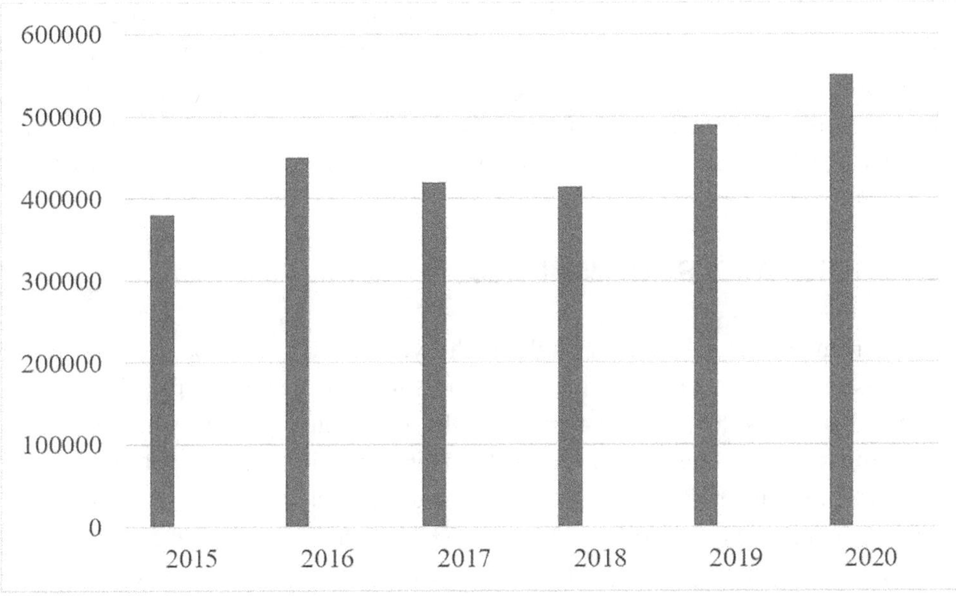

The report on the amount of disposed waste in 2020 was submitted by 30 operators. In 2020, approximately 2 million tons of waste were disposed of, of which 11.6 thousand tons are hazardous waste. Hazardous waste is mostly disposed of at the landfill for disposal of industrial waste, where 11,389 tons of hazardous waste were disposed of, and 269 tons were disposed of at a regional landfill that has a permit for the disposal of hazardous waste. The hazardous waste disposed of at the industrial waste landfill is mainly sludge and filter cakes containing dangerous substances.

Significant amounts of disposed non-hazardous waste are represented by waste from group 20 03, which includes mixed municipal waste, residues from street cleaning and bulky waste that is disposed of in consists of 962 thousand tons, followed by waste from slag processing from thermal processes, waste soil and stone, mixtures or individual fractions of concrete, bricks, tiles and ceramics and mixed waste from construction and demolition.

Mixed municipal waste in Serbia is disposed of in landfills without any prior treatment, and that is a key source of surface and groundwater pollution in the Republic of Serbia (Tošić, Vasović, Nešić, & Petrović, 2020). When the improper management of landfills is present, high leachate leakage, from municipal solid waste which contains a broad mixture of chemical pollutants, can have negative impacts on soils, plants, groundwater, aquatic organisms, and human health (Christensen, et al., 2001) (Rathod, Mishra, & Karmakar, 2013). Leachate represents the entity affected by the complex of factors, both inside the body of the landfill (landfill age, waste morphological composition, moisture content, fluid migration, pre-disposal waste technologies, landfill thickness, waste decomposition stages), and outside of it (meteorological parameters, with emphasis on annual rainfall, change of seasons) (Antić, Adamović, Turk Sekulić, & Radonić, 2018). Because of that the monitoring of leachate and groundwater movement around the landfill becomes a necessity.

SOLUTIONS AND RECOMMENDATIONS

The recurrence of dry spells throughout the year, which have been observed in recent history and can be anticipated in the future, threatens Serbia in light of climate change. Water management must be conducted primarily on the basis of ongoing study on changes in the cycle of precipitation and evapotranspiration using contemporary methodologies such as satellite images, vegetation scenarios, development of measurements, predictions etc. to lessen the negative consequences of droughts, particularly those that affect agricultural production. Investment in blue-green infrastructure is another solution for the water supply sector that promises to be both sustainable and cost-effective. It can reduce floods and urban storm water runoff while also improving water quality and providing triple-bottom-line benefits like urban greening. In many cases, it is also significantly less expensive than traditional 'grey' infrastructure approaches. The analysis of administrative public utility bodies in charge of water treatment and distribution also revealed the need for improvement, as well as a clear definition of the place and role of administrative-planning bodies for water delivery, along with the melioration of work implementation in water supply systems. The examination of the water treatment plant's organizational performance using the process functions technique is one option for such an analysis. Through the evaluation of job implementation in the area of water supply, this strategy increases the effectiveness of operations in water treatment plants (Stanković, Vasović, Petrović, Boričić, & Takić, 2022).

Various researches have shown that most of the groundwater near landfills has been influenced by leachate leakage and its components, including not only conventional but also many kinds of toxic and harmful components such as heavy metals, as well as persistent organic pollutants (POPs). In addition, models and methods for predicting leachate production and leakage, such as the Landfill Water Balance (LWB) model (Pantini, Verginelli, & Lombardi, 2014), the Leachate Assessment Screening Tool (LAST) (Grugnaletti, Pantini, Verginelli, & Lombardi, 2016), as well as models for predicting leachate leakage and environmental impacts, such as Hydrologic Evaluation of Landfill Performance (HELP) (Butt, et al., 2014), have also been developed. These models are used for landfill design optimization, life cycle assessment, and environmental risk assessment (Anders, Simone, Hanna, Steen, & Thomas, 2011), (Leyla, Mohammad, Reza, & Seyed, 2018). Research has shown that the performance of the geomembrane, which is the fundamental landfill engineering barrier, will degrade for various reasons, resulting in the increase of leachate production and leakage. Researchers (Rebecca, Jan, David, & Nikolaos, 2007), (David, Richard, & Nick, 2017), (Mishra, Karmakar, Kumar, & Kadambala, 2017) assumed an idealized geomembrane performance variation with time, and coupled this with the water balance model and one-dimensional advection-diffusion model in order to create LandSim software, which generates long-term prediction of leachate generation, leakage, and environmental impacts. Using this model in conjunction with default aging parameters, it is possible to predict the long-term leakage and pollution of both industrial and household hazardous waste disposed in landfills, and it can be used to evaluate different landfill aftercare strategies from a life cycle perspective.

LandSim simulation model is a probabilistic performance assessment model for predicting the impacts of landfill development on groundwater. It is used to predict leachate concentrations and elevations during the operational phase of the site, including changes in infiltration, declining source term within leachate and deteriorating leachate control systems (Sun, et al., 2019). Since 1996 it has been used as a relatively simple tool to evaluate leakage of leachate from landfills, attenuation in the unsaturated zone, and dilution and contaminant transport in the saturated zone. The model was developed on behalf of the Environment Agency in the UK and can be used as a tool for optimizing design and undertaking impact assessments. The model can deal with a large range of liner configurations and incorporates the concepts of uncertainty throughout. LandSim allows landfill operators and regulators to consider the environmental performance of different liners, leachate collection systems, and to take account of the large variety of geological and hydrogeological regimes. LandSim uses the Monte Carlo simulation technique to create parameters for use in the model calculations by random selection from a pre-defined range of possible input values such as: data on water infiltration into the landfill body, cell geometry, leachate inventory, drainage system, engineered barrier, unsaturated pathway, vertical pathway and aquifer flow. LandSim output can be split into three groups: hydraulic behavior, contaminant travel times and contaminant concentrations in the geosphere. LandSim uses a variety of mathematical techniques to calculate ultimate solute concentration distributions over time. The program combines analytical and semi-analytical models of groundwater flow with analytical models of solute transport. All output from LandSim is in the form of probabilistic plots, expressed as frequency, cumulative or reverse cumulative diagrams and/or tabular summaries printed in report format with the appropriate quality assurance documentation. With the help of software solutions, it is possible to make progress in the area of municipal waste management, predict possible negative impacts on the environment and propose potential measures to reduce them.

FUTURE RESEARCH DIRECTIONS

Both of these public utility sectors play a crucial part in helping humanity to address future challenges including ensuring employment, adequate waste management, required amounts and quality of water, and security for the next generation in a way that is environmentally responsible. Public perceptions, as well as all administrative, financial, legal, environmental, urban, and engineering activities, must be consistent with these public utilities. All of these disciplines should be linked mutually, resulting in successful implementation of the integral water and waste management plan.

CONCLUSION

Almost all collected municipal waste in Serbia is landfilled, either at illegal/uncontrolled dumpsites or at officially designated but unsanitary landfills. Only about 25% of all waste collected is disposed of in managed landfills. As disposal of waste in landfills not compliant with the EU Landfill Directive at a very low cost is still permitted, it is hard for other waste management options to become cost-competitive. The large number of unsanitary landfills with close to zero disposal costs does not provide any incentive to initiate recycling activities higher up in the waste hierarchy. Therefore, increased effort is needed to close Serbia's non-compliant landfills and to invest in waste reduction, separation and recycling. Only a very small share of waste is recycled. As this is mainly done by informal waste pickers, there are no official data on the exact quantities. A new methodology for collecting data for reporting municipal waste data, including recycling, to Eurostat is in the final stages of revision and will consider the requirements of Commission Implementing Decision (EU)

2019/1004. Since the largest percentage of waste treatment in Serbia is disposal in landfills, it is necessary to introduce new technologies in management methods and procedures. Evaluations of leachate regimes based on software simulations are becoming more significant in addition to conventional methods based on field measurements.

The Republic of Serbia has been facing almost the same problems for more than two decades in water management. Certain areas still do not have an adequate solution to the water supply issue. The most common challenges in water supply in the Republic of Serbia are the poor quality of drinking water, and insufficient quantities of quality drinking water and in some areas, there are both problems. Also, it is crucial to note that the current level of wastewater treatment is negligible, which has the effect of endangering drinking water sources, as well as a danger to human health and the environment. The interest of the Republic of Serbia is the preservation of the population's health, water resource protection, and the protection of the environment. It is essential to provide funds for financing the construction and reconstruction of water facilities for water use (Ministry of Agriculture, Forestry and Water Management of Republic of Serbia, 2022). In terms of the institutional features of monitoring, such as the integration of data collection and analysis across sectors, regions, and administrative levels, the collaborative effort around SDG 6 is particularly crucial.

The main conclusions of this chapter are:

- The implementation of new technologies in the field of water and municipal waste management is needed, such as predictions using software tools;
- The regional and national governments will develop sustainable water strategies, which will differ based on a range of variables, including the state of the water infrastructure, climate change impact and risks of climate change, the level of political ambition, legislation, and financial accessibility;
- Blue-green water and waste public utility infrastructure investments are lucrative throughout their existence, resource-efficient, and support nine out of seventeen sustainable development goals.

REFERENCES

Anders, D., Simone, M., Hanna, M., Steen, S., & Thomas, H. (2011). LCA and economic evaluation of landfill leachate and gas technologies. *Waste Management (New York, N.Y.)*, 1532–1541. PMID:21435856

Antić, K., Adamović, D., Turk Sekulić, M., & Radonić, J. (2018). Systematization and comparative review of the legislation of the European Union and the Republic of Serbia in the field of leachate management of municipal solid waste landfills. *1st International conference „The Holistic Approach to Environment*. Sisak.

Batinić, B. (2015). *A model for predicting the amount of packaging and biodegradable waste using neural networks*. University of Novi Sad, Faculty of Engineering.

Butt, T., Gouda, H., Baloch, M., Paul, P., Javadi, A., & Alam, A. (2014). Literature review of baseline study for risk analysis d the landfill leachate case. *Environment International*, *63*, 149–162. doi:10.1016/j.envint.2013.09.015 PMID:24295846

Cakar, B., Aydin, S., Varank, G., & Ozcan, H. (2020). Assessment of environmental impact of FOOD waste in Turkey. *Journal of Cleaner Production*, *244*, 244. doi:10.1016/j.jclepro.2019.118846

Cheng, C., Zhu, R., Thompson, R., & Zhang, L. (2021). Reliability analysis for multiple-stage solid waste management systems. *Waste Management (New York, N.Y.)*, *120*, 650–658. doi:10.1016/j.wasman.2020.10.035 PMID:33243600

Christensen, T., Kjeldsen, P., Bjerg, P., Jensen, D., Christensen, J., Baun, A., Albrechtsen, H.-J., & Heron, G. (2001). Biogeochemistry of landfill leachate plumes. *Applied Geochemistry*, *16*(7-8), 659–718. doi:10.1016/S0883-2927(00)00082-2

.Consulting, A. (2021). *Factsheet: Waste management in the Republic of Serbia.*

David, A., Richard, P., & Nick, D. (2017). Evaluating landfill aftercare strategies: A life cycle assessment approach. *Waste Management (New York, N.Y.)*, 417–431. PMID:27989657

Djurdjević, M. (2009). *Public utilities infrastructure*. College of Civil Engineering and Surveying.

Đorđević, L., Redžić, N., Radovanović, N., & Jovanović, G. (2021). *Waste management in the Republic of Serbia in the period 2011-2020 years*. Agency for Environmental Protection.

Dragović, N., Ristić, R., Pilcl, H., & Volfslehner, B. (2017). Natural resource management in Southeast Europe: Forests, soil and water. Skopje: Nacionalna i univerzitetska biblioteka „Sv. Kliment Ohridski", Skopje.

EEA. (2015). *Waste — municipal solid waste generation and management*. European Environment Agency.

EEA. (2016). *Municipal waste management across European countries*. European Environment Agency.

EEA. (2021). *Municipal waste management country profiles 2021-EEA cooperating countries*. European Environment Agency.

. EEA. (2021). *Municipal waste management in Serbia*. European Environment Agency, European Topic Centre on Waste and Materials in a green Economy.

EEA. (2021, May 11). *Water use in Europe - Quantity and quality face big challenges*. Retrieved from European Environment Agency: https://www.eea.europa.eu/signals/signals-2018-content-list/articles/water-use-in-europe-2014

EEA. (2022). *Municipal waste management in Western Balkan countries*. European Environment Agency.

.ETC/WMGE. (2021). *Municipal waste management in Serbia*. European Environment Agency, European Topic Centre on Waste and Materials in Green Economy.

European Commission. (2022). *Drinking water - Legislation*. Environment. https://ec.europa.eu/environment/water/water-drink/legislation_en.html

.Eurostat. (2016a). *Environmental data centre on waste, key waste streams, municipal waste*. European Commission.

.Eurostat. (2021). *Municipal waste by waste management operations*. Eurostat.

FAO. (2022, November 28). *Aquastat - Water Uses*. Aquastat. https://web.archive.org/web/20190317171236/http://www.fao.org/nr/water/aquastat/countries_regions/profile_segments/EuropeEastern-WU_eng.stm

Farooq, M., Cheng, J., Khan, N. U., Saufi, R. A., Kanwal, N., & Bazkiaei, H. A. (2022). Sustainable waste management companies with Innovative smart solutions: A systematic review and conceptual model. *Sustainability*, *14*(20), 1–19. doi:10.3390u142013146

Grugnaletti, M., Pantini, S., Verginelli, I., & Lombardi, F. (2016). An easy-to-use tool for the evaluation of leachate production at landfill sites. *Waste Management (New York, N.Y.)*, *55*, 204–219. doi:10.1016/j.wasman.2016.03.030 PMID:27033994

GWMO. (2015). *Global Waste Management Outlook*. UNEP-ISWA.

Hoekstra, A. Y. (2015). The water footprint of industry. In *Assessing and Measuring Environmental Impact and Sustainability* (pp. 221–254). Butterworth-Heinemann., doi:10.1016/B978-0-12-799968-5.00007-5

Hoornweg, D., & Bhada-Tata, P. (2012). *What a waste – A global review of solid waste management.* World Bank.

Khan, S., Anjum, R., Raza, S., Bazai, N., & Ihtisham, M. (2022). Technologies for municipal solid waste management: Current status challenges, and future perspectives. *Chemosphere, I*(288), 132403. doi:10.1016/j.chemosphere.2021.132403 PMID:34624349

. Kozlovskiy, V., Nedoseka, E., & Tishkov, S. (2022). Environmental practices of waste management in the small towns of the European part in the Arctic zone of the Russian Federation. *Regionology*, 129-154.

Laurent, A., Bakas, I., Clavreul, J., Bernstad, A., Niero, M., Gentil, E., Hauschild, M. Z., & Christensen, T. H. (2014a). Review of LCA studies of solid waste management systems–Part I: Lessons learned and perspectives. *Waste Management (New York, N.Y.), III*(34), 573–588. doi:10.1016/j.wasman.2013.10.045 PMID:24369845

Leyla, B., Mohammad, S., Reza, A., & Seyed, H. (2018). Sustainability analysis of landfilling and composting-landfilling for municipal solid waste management in the north of Iran. *Journal of Cleaner Production*, 1028–1038.

Ministry of Agriculture. Forestry and Water Management of Republic of Serbia. (2022, July 13). *Arrangement and use of water*. Directorate of Water. https://www.rdvode.gov.rs/lat/uredjenje-koriscenje.php

Mishra, H., Karmakar, S., Kumar, R., & Kadambala, P. (2017). A long-term comparative assessment of human health risk to leachate-contaminated groundwater from heavy metal with different liner systems. *Environmental Science and Pollution Research International*, 1–13. PMID:29147980

Pacific Water and Wastewater Association. (2021). *PWWA: Post-COVID recovery and new frontiers*. Pacific Water and Wastewater Association. https://www.ib-net.org/docs/PWWA_2021_A4s.pdf

Pantini, S., Verginelli, I., & Lombardi, F. (2014). A new screening model for leachate production assessment at landfill sites. *International Journal of Environmental Science and Technology, 11*(6), 1503–1516. doi:10.100713762-013-0344-7

.Počuča, N. (2018). *Water - pollution and purification.* AGM book.

.Počuča, N. (2020). *Municipal solid waste management.* Belgrade: AGM book.

Rathod, M., Mishra, H., & Karmakar, S. (2013). *Leachate characterization and assessment of water pollution near municipal solid waste landfill site*. Int J Chem Phys Sci.

Rebecca, J., Jan, R., David, H., & Nikolaos, V. (2007). Household hazardous waste disposal to landfill: Using LandSim to model leachate migration. *Environmental Pollution*, 501–509. PMID:17046126

Ritchie, H., & Roser, M. (2017). Water Use and Stress. *Our World in Data*. https://ourworldindata.org/water-use-stress

Rodrigo-Ilarri, J., & Rodrigo-Clavero, M.-E. (2020). Mathematical modeling of the biogas production in MSW landfills. Impact of the implementation of organic matter and food waste selective collection systems. *Atmosphere*, *11*(12), 11. doi:10.3390/atmos11121306

Rodrigo-Ilarri, J., Rodrigo-Clavero, M.-E., & Cassiraga, E. (2020). A new decision support model for the real-time management of municipal solid waste bioreactor landfills. *International Journal of Environmental Research and Public Health*, *17*(5), 17. doi:10.3390/ijerph17051675 PMID:32143477

Rusciano, V., Civero, G., & Scarpato, D. (2020). Social and ecological high influential factors in community gardens innovation: An empirical survey in Italy. *Sustainability*, *12*(11), 12. doi:10.3390u12114651

SEPA. (2021). *Questionnaire to Western Balkan countries for providing information regarding municipal waste management and waste prevention and follow-up interview: Serbia*. Serbia Environmental Protection Agency.

.Serbia, R. (2016). Rulebook on the methodology for creating the national and local register of pollution sources, as well as the methodology for the types, methods and deadlines of data collection. *Official Gazette of RS*.

.Serbia, R. (2017). Rulebook on the form of the document on the movement of hazardous waste, the form of prior notification and the method of its delivery and instructions for filling them out. *Official Gazette of RS*.

.Serbia, R. (2018). Rulebook on report forms on packaging and packaging waste management. *Official Gazette of RS*.

.Serbia, R. (2021). Ordinance on the form of daily records and annual reports on waste with instructions for its completion. *Official Gazette of RS*.

.Serbia, R. (2021). Ordinance on the form of daily records and annual reports on waste with instructions for its completion. *Official Gazette of RS*.

.Serbia, R. (2021). Rulebook on the methodology for collecting data on the composition and quantities of municipal waste in the territory of the local self-government unit. *Official Gazette of RS*.

.Serbian Government. (2022, January 28). Waste management program in the Republic of Serbia for the period 2022-2031 years. *Official Gazette of the Republic of Serbia*.

. Shapo, O., & Glanxhi, A. (2021). *Accurate data on municipal waste as basis for policy development and improvement of waste management to citizens- municipal waste data estimation based on weighting at depositing sites*. Deutsche Gesellschaft für Technische Zusammenarbeit (GIZ) and Ministry of Tourism and Environment of Albania.

.Stanković, S., Vasović, D., Petrović, N., Boričić, A., & Takić, L. (2022). Application of process function method for the evaluation of water treatment plant organizational performance – PUC "Naissus" Nis case study. *Facta Universitatis, Working and Living Environmental Protection*, 15-26.

. Stanković, S., Vasović, D., & Živković, N. (2019). Impacts of extreme hydrological events on sustainable water resources management and human well-being. *Safety engineering*, 37-42. doi:10.7562/SE2019.9.01.06

Stepanov, J. (2018). *A model for the evaluation of the municipal waste management system using the life cycle assessment method*. Faculty of Technical Sciences in Novi Sad.

Sun, X., Xu, Y., Liu, Y., Nai, C., Dong, L., Liu, J., & Huang, Q. (2019). Evolution of geomembrane degradation and defects in a landfill:Impacts on long-term leachate leakage and groundwater quality. *Journal of Cleaner Production*, *224*, 335–345. doi:10.1016/j.jclepro.2019.03.200

. Sundar, P. G., Ali, A., & Zhang, Z. (2020). Waste treatment approaches for environmental sustainability. *Microorganisms for Sustainable Environment and Health*, 119-135.

The World Bank. (2022, October 05). *Water resources management*. World Bank. https://www.worldbank.org/en/topic/waterresourcesmanagement

Tošić, N., & Vasović, D. (2020). Analysis of contemporary municipal waste management practice in the Republic of Serbia. *Safety Engineering*, *X*(2), 89–96. doi:10.5937/SE2002089T

Tošić, N., Vasović, D., Nešić, B., & Petrović, N. (2020). Leachate treatmant by reverse osmosis method-regional sanitary landfill "Zeljkovac" case study. *Facta Universitates, Working and Living Environmental Protection*, 175-184.

UN. (2022, December 1). *International Decade for Action on Water for Sustainable Development, 2018-2028*. Retrieved from United Nations: https://www.un.org/en/events/waterdecade/

UN General Assembly. (2022, October 28). *General Assembly Adopts Resolution Recognizing Access to Clean Water, Sanitation as Human Right by Recorded Vote of 122 in Favour, None against, 41 Abstentions*. United Nations. https://press.un.org/en/2010/ga10967.doc.htm

USEPA. (2012). A Handbook for Water and Wastewater Utilities. Seattle, WA 98101: U.S. Environmental Protection Agency.

.USEPA. (2012). *United States environmental protection agency, laws and regulations*. USEPA.

Vargas-Terranova, C.-A., Rodrigo-Ilarri, J., Rodrigo-Clavero, M.-E., & Parra-Saad, A. (2022). Implementing circular economy techniques for the optimal management of recyclable solid waste using the M-GRCT decision support model. *Applied Sciences (Basel, Switzerland)*, *12*(16), 12. doi:10.3390/app12168072

Water, U. N. (2022, November). *Country activities and commitments*. Water Action Decade: https://www.wateractiondecade.org/country-activities/

.Worldwatch. (2012). *Global Municipal Solid Waste Continues to Grow*. Worldwatch Institute.

ADDITIONAL READING

.Anwandter, L., Ozuna, T. Jr., (2002), Can public sector reforms improve the effciency of public water utilities?, *Environment and Development Economics*, pp. 687 – 700, doi:10.1017/S1355770X02000414

Global Water Partnership. (2009). *A Handbook for Integrated Water Resources Management in Basins, Global Water Partnership (GWP) and the International Network of Basin Organizations*. INBO.

Grugnaletti, M., Pantini, S., Verginelli, I., & Lombardi, F., (2016), An easy-to-use tool for the evaluation of leachate production at landfill sites. *Waste Management*, 1-16.

ICF. (2018). *Best practices and resources on climate resilent natural infrastructure*. Canadian Council of Ministers of the Environment.

Margeta, J. (2010). *Vodoopskrba naselja – Planiranje, projektiranje, upravljanje, obrada vode, Sveučilište u Splitu.* Faculty of Civil Engineering and Architecture.

Mishra, H., Rathod, M., Karmakar, S., & Kumar, R. (2016a). A framework for assessment and characterisation of municipal solid waste landfill leachate: An application to the Turbhe landfill, Navi Mumbai, India. *Environmental Monitoring and Assessment, 188*(6), 1–26. doi:10.100710661-016-5356-6 PMID:27194233

Serdarevic, (2018), Landfill leachate management – control and treatment, *Advanced Technologies, Systems, and Applications II*, pp. 618-632.

Stepanov, J. (2018). *Model for evaluating the municipal waste management system using the life cycle assessment method.* University of Novi, Faculty of Technical Sciences in Novi Sad.

KEY TERMS AND DEFINITIONS

Annual Freshwater Withdrawals: Represents total water withdrawals measured in cubic meters (m^3) per year, excluding evaporation losses from storage basins.

Leachate Generation: An occurrence of leachate at the landfill, most often by rain infiltration onto the surface of the landfill (atmospheric precipitation to the active part of the landfill, from the moisture of the waste itself).

Morphological Waste Composition: Represents types of municipal waste are generated at the source (organic, plastic, paper, glass, metal, textile, etc.).

Municipal Waste Generation and Management: Refers to the source of communal waste, most often from households and its handling according to the legal procedure (based on the analysis, consideration and definition of solid waste treatment methods and procedures).

Municipal Water: The amount of water that is annually taken primarily for population consumption.

Renewable Internal Freshwater Flows: Represents internal river flows and groundwater from rainfall in the country.

Safely Managed Drinking Water: Drinking water that is properly managed comes from an on-site, upgraded water source that is always accessible and uncontaminated.

Waste Treatment Approaches: Includes reuse or disposal operations, including prior preparation for waste reuse or disposal. For waste reuse, treatment methods can be mechanical, physical and chemical treatment, biological and thermal. Waste can be disposed of in sanitary or non-sanitary landfills (according to the procedure).

Water Demand Management: Rainwater collection, irrigation, regulatory restrictions, fee increases, and cultural adjustments are all examples of equitable and sustainable water demand management.

Chapter 6
Joint Actions in Water Resources Management in the Transboundary Ecologically Sensitive Area of the Prespa Lakes

Georgios Damianos
https://orcid.org/0000-0001-9789-4570
Aristotle University of Thessaloniki, Greece

ABSTRACT

Transboundary lakes have always played a significant role in the development prospects and welfare of border areas. The international hydrological basin of the Prespa Lake, a protected area in three neighboring countries, Greece, Albania, and North Macedonia, is a typical example of a transboundary lake basin of exceptional importance. The empirical investigation of transboundary water management and sustainability cooperation in the Prespa, which adds to the limited international research in transboundary lakes, was carried out via six structured interviews, two per country, to identify the strengths and weaknesses as well as the opportunities and threats in the Prespa basin, and highlight the significance of transboundary cooperation towards sustainable development and social prosperity between riparian Municipalities. The results obtained have significant implications for all stakeholders in the Prespa basin, as they highlight the need to organize joint actions and generate new development strategies and products, such as alternative forms of tourism.

DOI: 10.4018/978-1-6684-7730-4.ch006

INTRODUCTION

Lakes, typically defined as water systems located in basins, contain more than 90% of the planet's freshwater, thus, attracting scientific and socio-political interest in a wide variety of issues, such as biodiversity, ecosystem goods and services, sustainability, social life and economic growth. In addition, they frequently require efficient management interventions, especially in case they are transboundary lakes, which implies that they are located in cross-border areas, which also makes them susceptible to conflicts in terms of water use (Wolf, 2006; Valvis, 2015).

Overall, the number of transboundary lakes accounts for 204, 53 of which are listed as priority transboundary lakes located in various countries around the globe, and, more specifically, 23 lakes in Africa, 30 in South America, 70 in Europe, 51 in Asia and 20 in North America (ILEC & UNEP, 2016).

In the context of understanding the value of transboundary lakes and considering that a great number of them have been degraded and require more efficient management, various tools and assessment methodologies have been produced, such as the indicator-based Global Environment Facility Transboundary Waters Assessment Programme (GEF TWAP), which aims at identifying and assessing potential changes in transboundary lakes resulting from human intervention and natural processes, as well as the possible consequences for the population in riparian countries (http://geftwap.org/). TWAP is also used for developing relevant strategies and goals for the sustainable development of water resources by 2030.

Transboundary lake assessment enables the collection and understanding of significant information and data about potential opportunities and threats and adds to the relevant research in transboundary lake management and transnational collaborative efforts in transboundary areas, which is rather limited in comparison with equivalent research in transboundary rivers (Wolf, 2006).

Remarkably, transboundary water sustainability and efficient management require cooperation and joint actions between the stakeholders of shared waters, which is perceived as a rather complicated process offering various options and benefits, the assessment of which is critical, especially under the obligations under the UN Water Convention on the Protection and Use of Transboundary Watercourses and International Lakes (Sadoff & Grey, 2005).

In this framework, an investigation and detailed discussion about collaboration and joint actions between riparian countries for water resources management in transboundary basins of eco-sensitive areas, such as the Prespa Lake, highlight the significance of water resources management and the collaborative efforts within transboundary basins. The chapter includes a brief overview of issues related to transboundary lakes and discusses bilateral and multilateral agreements on territorial cooperation. By focusing on the transboundary area of the Prespa Lakes, a globally significant environmental area, it investigates the benefits of transboundary cooperation between the countries (Greece, Albania and North Macedonia) and the local communities involved in sharing the transboundary lake water of the Prespa. In addition, it includes a SWOT analysis of the transboundary area identifying the potential strengths, weaknesses, opportunities, and threats. The rest of the chapter includes a discussion of the empirical research, further research recommendations and conclusions, which demonstrate that the Prespa International basin is part of a major transboundary effort aimed at sustainable development, environmental protection, and social prosperity in the wider area. In addition, it highlights that efficient transboundary management of water resources and the eco-sensitive zone of the Prespa contributes to organizing alternative forms of tourism.

BACKGROUND

Value and Functions of Lakes

Lake basins have been associated with the cosmogenic action of various and varied natural phenomena, such as the action of glaciers or volcanic and seismic actions. The way they were created also determines the details and types of lakes on our planet (Papoutsoglou, 1992). Vegetation in lakes includes both rooted and floating plants, and the fauna includes zooplankton, fish, insects, larvae, as well as waterfowl, mainly ducks, geese and herons (Wright, 2005).

In lakes and, overall, aquatic ecosystems, the functions which are carried out are crucial both to the ecosystem and human beings, depending on their structure and the wider environment in which they are located.

Overall, the surface water of aquatic ecosystems, such as lakes, rivers and wetlands, has greatly contributed to people's lives by providing goods and services, such as drinking water, and non-cost goods, such as biodiversity (Gleick, 1993; Naiman et al., 1997; Postel & Carpenter, 1997).

Lakes are both invaluable and sensitive ecosystems, not only from a conservation perspective but also in terms of their contribution to human communities, despite the fact that a vast number of them have been wasted due to human activities, and several are constantly being degraded. Ecosystem services, by definition, involve "conditions and processes through which natural ecosystems and the species that comprise them sustain and complement human life" (Daily, 1997).

Lakes, like all aquatic ecosystems, ensure basic functions for humans, such as nutrient recycling; in addition, they provide various goods of aesthetic and cultural value (Costanza et al., 1997), distinguished in:

- cost-oriented goods or services, such as drinkable water, transportation, electricity generation and irrigation, and
- non-cost goods, such as biodiversity, plant habitats and animals, as well as the satisfaction offered to humans by aquatic ecosystems (Dorfman & Dorfman, 1993; Freeman, 1993; Costanza et al., 1997; Daily, 1997).

The aesthetic value of lakes makes them ideal for recreational activities, which helps to attract visitors and increase the income of local communities. Apart from any financial benefits, they contribute to people's life quality improvement by offering increased opportunities for sports and recreation, such as hiking, swimming, sailing, and fishing and the possibility of tourism development in natural ecosystems, mainly associated with a great range of tourist activities and services. In addition, the cultural value of lakes is associated with the mythology, history, and cultural heritage of the surrounding area.

It is also worth highlighting the educational function of lakes. High biodiversity, in combination with the presence of many rare plant and animal species, makes them particularly attractive for research and exploration in the framework of various disciplines. The observatories set up in most lakes and other aquatic ecosystems facilitate educational processes, which, apart from their scientific and educational contribution, are also particularly significant in terms of the economy by encouraging an influx of visitors. Nature- and tourist-based activities have a positive impact on the income of the local communities around all types of aquatic ecosystems (Albayrak & Caber, 2018; Osning, & Rahman, 2018).

Despite the benefits, however, biodiversity has been substantially declining, and lakes have been constantly degraded, which implies that enhancing the crucial role of sustainable development must be a major concern for all stakeholders (http://geftwap.org/).

Environmental Degradation of Lakes

As an extensive loss of lakes and wetlands has been observed in all countries, mainly developing ones, and the foreseeable damage is incredibly severe, various area-specific conservation programs have been initiated (Davis et al., 2005).

Typically, the most common cause of lake degradation, which is a condition involving the collapse of many adaptive and developmental mechanisms, is pollution resulting from a multitude of sources, the most significant of which are agricultural and industrial activities (Davis et al., 2005). Changes in land use, which cause and maintain the deposition of pollutants in the lakes, are related to the economic, demographic, and social changes taking place in the surrounding area. Eutrophication is described as probably the most obvious indication of lake degradation (Hasler, 1947; Edmondson, 1969; Harper, 1992).

According to Kousouris & Athanasakis (1992), indirect wetland and lake alterations derive from their watershed and are caused by:

- Destruction of natural vegetation from fires, overgrazing, uncontrolled logging, quarrying activities etc.
- Runoff caused by fertilizers, pesticides and organic material derived from leftovers from farming.
- Changes in the hydrological status of the area due to over-pumping, dams, engineering works etc.
- Disposal of liquid waste, sewage, and solid waste in streams.
- Destruction of natural fences of agricultural crops.
- Sandblasting, embankments, and arrangements of streams and rivers.
- Residential areas, industries, craft units and infrastructure projects without spatial planning.

Bilateral or Multilateral Transboundary Water Management Agreements and Treaties in Greece and the EU

Despite the fact that the different socio-economic levels of development, insufficient infrastructure, and political, administrative and legal issues may frequently prevent joint and effective actions for the management and protection of international watersheds, they can also considerably motivate cooperation on a practical, social, economic and political level (OECD, 2015). Legislative frameworks and, more specifically, transboundary agreements are mechanisms which enhance cooperation, a critical issue in the case of transboundary hydrological basins. The above considerations highlight the significance and the relevant challenges posed for achieving the management of international watersheds internationally.

It is worth emphasizing that in the international literature, the underlying principles of the management of transboundary watersheds are summarized in the phrase 'fair and reasonable exploitation' of common water resources, 'without causing significant damage' and on the premise of 'early notification in view of the projects', which affects watershed level (Tsiropoulos, 2010). Obviously, the application of these principles is difficult when issues of national rights are raised focused on the principle of 'absolute territorial sovereignty'. In this case, the neighboring countries usually apply the principle of 'equivalent use', the right to future use of the same quantity resulting from the already established 'previous use'.

On a global level, the adoption of agreements and treaties between riparian countries on transboundary water management and protection has ensured the quality and sustainability of water resources. There is a number of successful examples of joint actions and implementation of relevant practices of water management, such as joint actions for the Mekong River Basin, the Sava River Basin, and the Baikal Basin (CADRI, 2020).

In the European Union, a significant number of bilateral and multilateral water agreements and treaties have been signed in the past decades under the International water law and Water Convention of the United Nations Economic Commission for Europe (UNECE) as regards transboundary water cooperation. The UNECE Water Convention is a framework agreement which sets out the details of water resource management and has, thus, influenced the formulation and content of a number of bilateral and multilateral agreements on transboundary waters, with a view to providing guidelines for the development and implementation of national policies, programmes and actions (UNECE, 2018). The major objectives of the Water Convention, i.e., the basic obligations of the signatory members, are:

- the protection of transboundary waters (surface and underground) through the prevention, control, and reduction of pollution,
- the rational management of transboundary waters,
- the rational and fair use of transboundary waters, considering actions likely to cause transboundary problems, and
- the preservation/restoration of ecosystems.

The Convention places particular emphasis on the measures to be taken to prevent, control and reduce transboundary pollution, with priority at its source (Bošnjaković, 2001).

Remarkably, the specific agreements, which are compliant with the principles and basic guidelines of UNECE, are fully dependent on the political will of the signatory states and provide for different levels of participation for regional and local authorities. Thus, some focus exclusively on the transboundary cooperation of national authorities, whereas others mainly aim at the establishment of legal foundations for transboundary activities of regions or local authorities located on the territory of the contracting parties (MacCaffrey, 2015).

On a national level, since the 1950s, several intergovernmental agreements and protocols have focused on a specific area of cooperation and the establishment of special organizations. Such agreements have also emphasized specific issues and covered a wide range of daily life in the border areas, such as regional politics, spatial planning, economy and tourism, agriculture, environment, water supply and sanitation, border workers, agricultural issues, education and research, sports, the provision of judicial or administrative assistance, the arrangement and maintenance of common borders, security, fire protection and emergency situations. As early as 1960, bilateral or multilateral agreements concluded by national governments established specific intergovernmental cooperation structures, such as ad hoc working entities or joint institutions ('transnational' or 'intergovernmental commissions'), composed mainly of representatives of central administration in different geographical and specific cooperation areas.

In Greece, which is a riparian country of five Balkan rivers and two lakes, transboundary water cooperation agreements have not been substantive, especially as regards river agreements, despite their environmental, financial, and political significance. Since the 1960s, the relevant water agreements have mainly focused on water resources as a commercial good, thus, emphasizing the principles of 'limited sovereignty' and 'equitable utilization' (Valvis, 2015), whereas there was only one exception, the bilateral agreement for the Nestos River between Greece and Bulgaria in 1995, which involved the sustainable management of the river water resources (Mylopoulos et al., 2004). Overall, the most successful agreement on transboundary water cooperation so far has been the agreement for the Prespa Lakes in 2000, signed by Greece, Albania and North Macedonia, which involved the Declaration on the Environmental Protection and Sustainable Development of the Prespa Lakes and their Surroundings, and the establishment of the Prespa National Park (Bogdanović, 2008). Later, in 2010, another agreement on the Protection and Sustainable Development of the Prespa Park Area was concluded between the three riparian countries, Greece, Albania and North Macedonia, which aimed at protecting the Prespa ecosystem and enhancing sustainable development and cooperation in the area (https://ypen.gov.gr).

MAIN FOCUS: THE TRANSBOUNDARY PRESPA BASIN

Overview

The lakes Mikri and Megali Prespa are amongst the oldest in Europe and are considered invaluable in terms of biodiversity. The Prespa basin is located between the two national parks of Pelister and Galichica. The Lake Megali Prespa, which is the wet border between three countries, Greece, North Macedonia, and Albania, covers an area of 284km^2, with a depth of 54 meters and a surface of 853 meters above sea level. Of the total lake surface, 65% belongs to North Macedonia, 18% to Albania and 17% to Greece.

The specific area includes the Municipality of Prespa in Greece, the Municipality of Resen in North Macedonia and the Municipality of Pustec or Komuna Liqenas in Albania. The area around the Prespa watershed is an environmental center of global importance on account of its high biodiversity in lakes, plains, mountains and forests. Along the northern shores of the Lake Megali Prespa there is the Ezerani Natural Park, covering an area of 1917ha, of which 1066ha are on land and 851ha in water. The specific protected area is a habitat for about 200 species of birds, of which 62 are listed as protected under the Bern Convention; three are also included in the European list of globally threatened species.

Other protected areas within the territory of the Lakes Mikri and Megali Prespa in the three neighboring countries, Albania, Greece and North Macedonia, are The National Park of the Lake Prespa (Government Gazette 19A/75), part of which is a protected wetland by the Ramsar Convention, the Prespa National Park in Albania, which includes the catchment area of both lakes and is subject to a specific zone, and the National Park in Pelister, North Macedonia, which is the oldest national park in the region (1948). In addition, the National Park in Galitsica, North Macedonia, extends partly outside the Prespa basin, on the shore of Lake Ohrid, but covers the largest part of the eastern side of the Megali Prespa basin, and the Strictly Protected Reserve in Ezerani, on the northern shore of the Lake Megali Prespa, re-declared a Natural Park in 2011 and protected under the Ramsar Convention.

In the Prespa sub-basin and the wider area, a set of bilateral, trilateral, and multilateral actions, as well as programs and construction and infrastructure projects, have been implemented both by Greece and the neighboring countries, Albania and North Macedonia (Valvis, 2015). In addition, various other programs have been organized aiming at promoting water management, improving the ecological state of the lakes, adopting best practices, and achieving more efficient waste and pollution control as well as transnational cooperation. This illustrates the considerable efforts for transboundary cooperation towards sustainable development, environmental protection and the welfare of people living in the wider area.

SWOT Analysis

To explore the factors and considerations on which joint actions and programs are based in the international hydrological basin of the Prespa, a SWOT analysis was carried out. SWOT analysis is a framework enabling the assessment of internal and external factors and the current and future potential of organizations (Kenton, 2022). The analysis was applied with a view to identifying the major strengths, weaknesses, opportunities, and threats as regards the Prespa water resources.

The analysis was based on the investigation of the demographic characteristics, economy, and prosperity indicators of the border area of all three countries, focusing on the eco-sensitive system of the Prespa basin. The table below (Table 1) demonstrates the strengths of the transboundary area in the Prespa.

Table 1. Strengths

Topic	Strengths
Geography, Environment & Water Resources	• Abundant water resources (from all three countries). • Large nature reserves and areas of outstanding natural beauty. • Major and valuable ecosystems and natural resources. • Rich natural heritage with numerous protected areas. • Ecosystems provide essential services, including supporting primary and secondary production and biodiversity.
Tourism & Culture	• Valuable Cultural Heritage / UNESCO Monuments. • Rich and unspoiled natural areas. • Attractive natural environment and cultural sites. • Huge potential for development (traditional villages, etc.). • Cultural bonds and bonds in specific thematic areas (religion, rural life and eco-tourism). • Crossing International Mountaineering Pathways. • A large number of tourists in the countries around the lake. • Connection to Northeast and Central Europe. • Thematic tourism promoting unique/typical local products.
Economy	• GDP differences between neighboring countries have been gradually diminished, thus, enabling cooperation. • Enhanced cooperation between neighboring countries in various fields. • Greece is an important investor in the neighboring countries. • Increased awareness of EU strategies and gradual utilization of European grants. • Positive rates of growth in the Albanian cross-border region.
Research & Innovation	• Establishment of Institutions, Universities and Research centers.
Labor Market	• Favorable age structure of the Albanian population.
Social Profile	• Sustainable development. • SDG
Accessibility & Transport System	• Improved road network and critical infrastructure under construction.
Connectivity	• Cooperation experience of potential beneficiaries from previous programs (Interreg). • Significant progress in telecommunications in all three countries in the last 15 years (Internet connection and mobile telephony).

Despite the significant number of strengths, the identification of the underlying weaknesses of the researched area demonstrates several considerations to be taken into account for transboundary cooperation (Table 2).

Table 2. Weaknesses

Topic	Weaknesses
Demographics and Immigration	• Population decline and adverse demographics (age structure). • Internal and external migration.
Geography, Environment & Water Resources	• Large mountainous areas of low accessibility. • Poor environmental infrastructure and insufficient implementation of environmental protection policies. • Poor wastewater treatment in Albania. • Inadequate policies/systems for efficient use of resources in Albania. • Delays due to deficient infrastructure, facilities and control procedures affecting environmental health. • Transport pressures on the environment and natural resources. • Inadequate recycling processes and reuse of solid and liquid waste management. • Increased amount of waste (only a small percentage is recycled or composted). • Protected areas, ecosystems and biodiversity at risk.
Tourism and Culture	• Inadequate planning and management of niche/alternative types of tourism (ecotourism, religious tourism, etc.). • Poor tourism development action plans (no destination branding, no special tourist destinations, etc.). • Tourists do not stay in the cross-border area and offer no added value. • No brand and organization of the local tourist industry. • Borders interrupt the International Mountaineering Pathway crossing.
Economy	• Economic recession. • Significant differences between cross-border regions in terms of economic development and labor productivity. • A wide gap in achieving the Europe 2020 strategy objectives.
Research and Innovation	• Poor performance achievement of small enterprises in the field of technological development and innovation.
Labor Market	• Very high rates of unemployment, especially among the youth and long-term unemployed people. • High rates of unemployment, especially for women. • Low employment rates in Albania.
Social Profile	• Poor hospital, emergency health care and eHealth services. • Aging population exerts more pressure on the health care system.
Education, Lifelong Learning	• Low educational status in Albania. • Low percentage of higher educational status.
Accessibility and Transportation	• Poor direct connection/crossing (border station) road networks from the Greek to the North Macedonian Prespa. • Main accessibility is still provided by the regional road network. • Problems in secondary road networks. • Poor air transport infrastructure (vital for tourist growth). • Problems with information and communication accessibility as regards mobility and transport.
Connectivity	• Outdated networks with relatively low connectivity speed in Albania.

Considering both the strengths and weaknesses of the Prespa basin, the majority of opportunities are mainly focused on technology- and sustainability-based projects (Table 3).

Table 3. Opportunities

Topic	Opportunities
Demographics and Immigration	• Desire of northern Europeans to settle in southern Europe. • Decentralization trends both at home and work (i.e., people take advantage of the possibilities offered by ICT applications).
Geography, Environment & Water Resources	• EU policies to promote activities and manage areas as interconnected natural systems. • Technological developments in water resources management, energy production and renewable sources. • Close cooperation in the field of adaptation to climate change, reducing carbon/water footprint and greenhouse gas emissions and supporting a low carbon economy. • Implementation of Networks and Projects in progress in the framework of Transboundary Cooperation and future funding programs. • Increasing interest in sustainable management of natural resources and protection from natural disasters.
Tourism and Culture	• Recent tourism trends in the Mediterranean. • Increasing preference for alternative tourism. • ICT and digital marketing provide opportunities for direct contact with special interest groups.
Research and Innovation	• Smart specialization strategies. • "Europe 2020-25" strategic objectives. • Significant research and development potential in the cross-border area; prospect for integration into production processes.
Economy	• Similar production systems with prospects for cross-border interconnections, vertical integration of production structures and trade.
Labor Market	• EU policies to increase labor mobility enable the reduction of local unemployment rates.
Social Situation	• Digital applications create opportunities to increase access to health services for vulnerable groups and remote areas.
Education, Lifelong Learning	• Smart specialization strategies create opportunities to link education with the most dynamic parts of local economies.
Accessibility and Transportation	• Technological advances in ICT can improve communication and information on transport networks and facilitate border controls. • Opportunity to switch from energy-consuming and environmentally unfriendly road transport to other transport means (e.g., lake transport & local transport) as a result of the increased fuel price. • Use of Corridor X (E75), Egnatia Road (E90) and Ohrid Airport for transportation between neighboring countries.
Connectivity	• Globally growing digital applications.

Finally, the major potential threats include a reduction in population rates, severe impacts of climate change on the ecosystem and increased unemployment and poverty rates (Table 4).

Table 4. Threats

Topic	Threats
Demographics and Immigration	• Increasing population decline rates (a point of no recovery). • Increased ageing population rates create social problems.
Geography, Environment & Water Resources	• Possible serious impact of climate change on the natural and human environment. • Extreme weather conditions, such as droughts, heat waves, forest fires and floods, have been aggravated in recent decades. • Human activities exert greater pressure on the natural environment and resources.
Tourism and Culture	• Inadequate planning/management of the capacity of natural habitats and tourist attractions. • Natural disasters (i.e., forest fires in rural areas or floods).
Economy	• Slow global economic growth in the 21st century. • Fierce competition due to globalization.
Research and Innovation	• Higher education is dependent on public funding and, thus, lacks incentives for alternative sources of funding (e.g., from the business industry). • Higher education is focused on primary and non-applied research.
Labor Market	• Limited employment opportunities due to a prolonged recession. • Integration of digital technologies (as a means of promoting competitiveness) into the economy sector may limit the number of vacancies.
Society	• Higher poverty rates due to the prolonged recession resulting in increasing economic and social exclusion.
Accessibility and Transportation	• Poor infrastructure resources due to the prolonged economic recession and the underprivileged status of the transboundary area.
Connectivity	• Internet resource demand may grow faster than the capacity of local networks.

EMPIRICAL INVESTIGATION

Methodology

Based on the relevant literature review and with a view to investigating transboundary cooperation in water resources management in the ecologically significant and sensitive Prespa Lakes, an empirical investigation was organized.

As the specific survey was carried out in three countries, and due to the different socio-economic contexts and the nature of the research questions, the collection of data was based on a qualitative survey. Qualitative surveys are mainly used to collect, analyze, and interpret non-numerical data and concepts or experiences and produce detailed information to enable understanding the various dimensions of the topic under research' (Queirós et al., 2017). Maxwell (2013) holds that qualitative methods involve "the universe of meanings, motives, aspirations, beliefs, values and attitudes, which corresponds to a deeper space of relationships, processes and phenomena that cannot be reduced to the operationalization of variables".

The survey, carried out in January 2020, includes six structured interviews (two per country) of the 3 Mayors of the Municipalities within the Prespa hydrological basin and 3 university professors in each surveyed country (opinion leaders). The research questions, based on the extant literature review, involve making a general assessment of transboundary cooperation and the constraining factors to the effective management and protection of international hydrological basins. They also investigate bilateral, trilateral, and multilateral actions, programs and projects about water degradation factors in each country, with a view to developing a shared tourist product (in all three zones) in relation to the Prespa basin. To ensure the effectiveness of the interview meetings and avoid misunderstandings due to the different languages and cultures, a list of questions/questionnaires was drawn up, which was translated into three languages (English, Albanian and Macedonian).

Results and Discussion

The analysis of the interview answers revealed a number of significant findings. As regards the advantage close geographical location of Greece to the two bordering regions, the answers demonstrated that it is a strong advantage for Greece, as it provides a 'way out', given that for decades the researched area has been a border zone, a 'last stop'. It is also worth noting that the Albanian professor gave a positive answer, but the mayor was doubtful; the North Macedonian subjects answered positively.

As far as the cross-border cooperation with the neighboring countries is concerned, the respondents answered that all three Municipalities and local Universities had cooperated in the previous years, except for the Universities of Koritsa and Ohrid. The University of Western Macedonia has promoted cooperation within the framework of funded programs. However, the joint cooperation actions were established and controlled by the central authorities/Universities in each country, despite their regional context and concern.

For Greece, the positive outcomes deriving from the cooperation with the two neighboring countries involve environmental protection and development actions for the Prespa basin, tourism, education, and transboundary cooperation in NSRF and various cross-border programs. The subjects stated that the only negative point is the organizational weaknesses of the administrative services in Albania and, thus, the lack of consistent joint actions and lost funding opportunities.

The positive results that the North Macedonian subjects expect from the cooperation with Greece involve deciding on common solutions to management issues in the Prespa hydrological basin and creating cooperation networks between Universities and Institutes. Similarly, the Albanian subjects answered positively about the cooperation prospects with the neighboring countries but also stated that there will be an added advantage as regards the protection of the National Park in Galicica. Their attitude is not negative as regards cooperation with Greece, whereas it is negative towards Albania, due to the weaknesses identified, such as the inability to commit in the context of joint projects and difficulties in partnership processes and communication.

Potential advantages deriving for Albania from the cooperation with North Macedonia involve improvement of infrastructure, efficient energy use and improvement of lake sanitation. In addition, the Albanian subjects claimed that the common language spoken in the two regions contributes to cooperation, future decision-making and planned actions, whereas they also agreed on the methods applied in North Macedonia to protect biodiversity, as well as investment and development plans. As regards the potential disadvantages, the Albanian mayor answered negatively, whereas the professor was uncertain, as the political context in North Macedonia can affect life in Albania and, due to wage differences, skillful and qualified young people prefer to work in North Macedonia.

In addition, the Albanian subjects were confident that Greece, as a member of the EU, can contribute to promoting Albania's partnership in EU-funded projects, adopting good Greek practices for the protection of aquifers and getting technical assistance from Greek experts in infrastructure and water management projects. As far as the potential disadvantages are concerned, the Albanian mayor gave a negative answer, whereas the professor was uncertain, mainly as regards the fair distribution of European funds, as Albania cannot apply modern and reliable methods like Greece due to poor expertise in specific fields.

As regards sustainable development in the international hydrological basin of the Prespa, the subjects answered that there is a possibility for transboundary cooperation aimed at environmental protection and social welfare in the wider area. Figure 1 below demonstrates the degree of contribution of cross-border cooperation in terms of sustainable development, environmental protection, and social welfare.

Figure 1. Contribution of cross-border cooperation for sustainable development, environmental protection, and welfare in the wider area

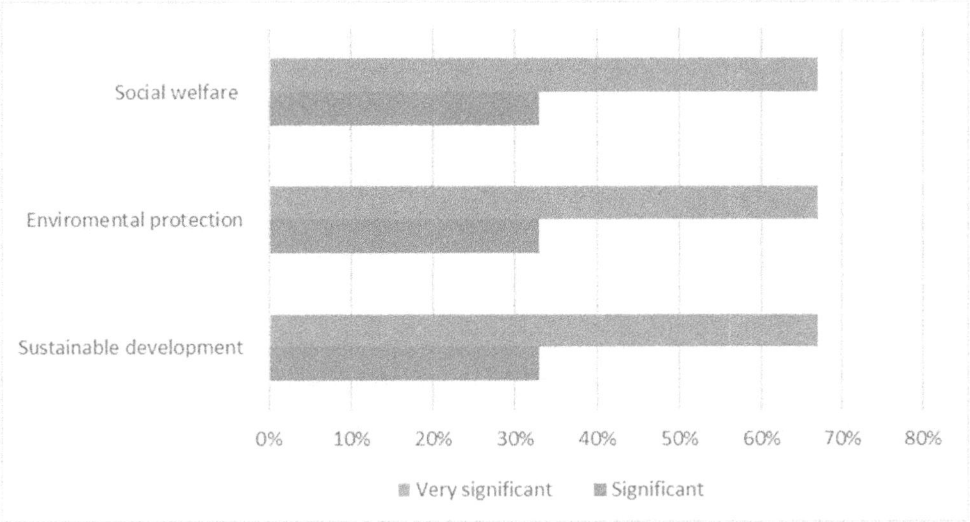

For the protection of the Prespa international hydrological basin, working towards bilateral or trilateral cooperation agreements on the effective management of the transboundary areas is of great importance. For the protection of the hydrological basin, the Greek subjects answered that the nationally funded bilateral or trilateral development programs do not seem to be particularly significant, whereas, in Albania and North Macedonia, development programs for construction works and infrastructure projects aiming at the protection of the Prespa basin receive significant support and are nationally rather than internationally funded. Bilateral or trilateral programs financed by international bodies, such as the EU, the World Bank, and the Organization for Economic Development and Cooperation, also play a very significant role in the effective management and protection of the Prespa basin, water resources management, improvement of the ecological status of the lakes, efficient waste and pollution management, transnational cooperation and the adoption of best practices. The results of the respondents' answers about the significance of water protection agreements are demonstrated in Figure 2.

Figure 2. Significance of water protection agreements

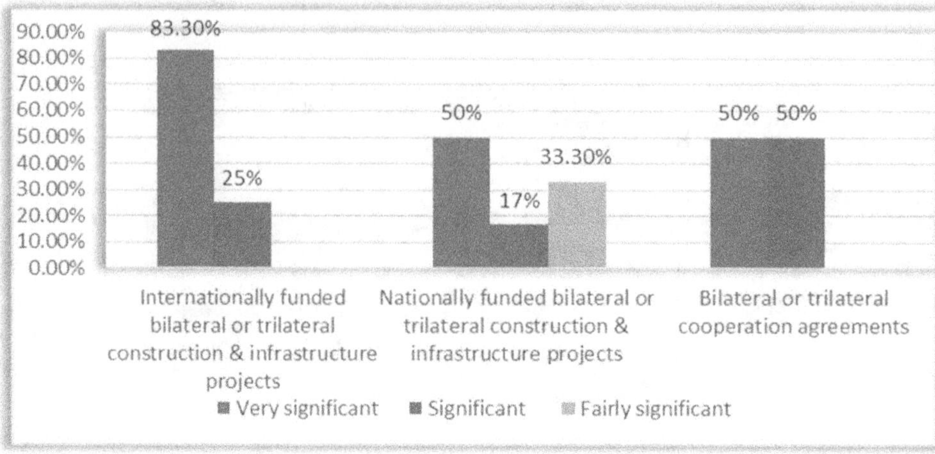

The impacts of the possible constraints to joint effective management and protection of the Transboundary Prespa basin, namely, different social profiles and financial growth status by region, poor infrastructure, political, national, or local issues, different administrative and legal systems, as well as institutional frameworks, are depicted below (Figure 3).

Figure 3. Constraints to joint transboundary management and protection of the Prespa basin

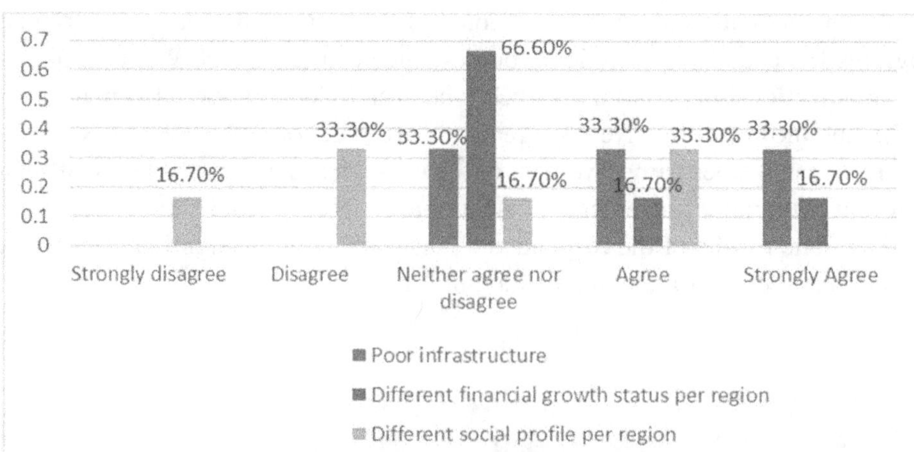

It is also worth noting that despite the various measures against water degradation, the results are rather worrying. According to the Greek and North Macedonian respondents, water degradation is mostly caused by Albanian activities. The specific respondents stated that pollution is mainly caused by the Albanian part of the Prespa lake. Water degradation is caused by sewage networks/urban waste pollution, aquaculture, industrial waste, and the use of fertilizers and pesticides. The lake is also moderately polluted by the water well drilling for irrigation and solid waste.

Regarding the pollution caused by human activities in Greece, both the Albanians and the Macedonians stated that the impact of the use of fertilizers and pesticides, as well as water well drilling for irrigation is significant. A moderate impact is caused by the Greek residents' activities for sewage water/wastewater, industrial liquid waste and solid waste. Finally, the pollution caused by aquaculture and fishing is minimal.

North Macedonia seems to cause the fewest problems in the hydrological basin, as both the Greek and Albanian subjects stated that degradation caused both by sewage water and industrial liquid waste is minimal. In addition, pollution rates caused by the use of fertilizers and pesticides, aquaculture and water well drilling for irrigation are negligible, despite the fact that in North Macedonia, the specific area near the lake is the area with the largest population.

The extent to which ecosystems positively affect primary and secondary production and biodiversity, the answers demonstrated that for Greece, ecosystems are very important, whereas, for Albania and North Macedonia, they are very significant only for primary production. The North Macedonian subjects also stated that the contribution of ecosystems in supporting secondary production is high and moderate in terms of biodiversity. On the other hand, the Albanian subjects believe that biosystems in the researched area are very important for biodiversity and of less significance for secondary production, which is very inadequate.

As regards joint actions with North Macedonia for developing a shared brand name for tourist products focusing on the Prespa Lake in the next five years, the Greek respondents stated it is very likely, whereas the Albanian subjects believed it is likely. Similarly, they stated that it is very likely that they engage in joint actions with North Macedonia for exploiting natural resources for enhancing tourism and developing cultural and other types of bonds (religion, rural life, and eco-tourism). The Greek respondents' attitude seems to be more positive than that of the Albanians, as they believe it is very likely to engage in International Mountaineering Pathway programs in the next five years with North Macedonia, ICT and Digital Marketing for attracting Special Interest Groups as well as in the establishment of new cross-border tourist enterprises, given that border crossing will be possible and will facilitate communication between the two parties.

The Greek mayor, knowledgeable of the local history, insisted on operating the border crossing promised in 2018, as it will enable easy and direct communication and minimize travel distance between the two countries/regions.

In addition, both the Greek and North Macedonian subjects believed that it is unlikely to engage in joint actions with Albania to develop a shared brand name for tourist products in the next five years. In addition, the Greek respondents believe that it is not very likely that they engage in joint actions with Albania for exploiting natural resources for tourism development and cultural and other types of bonds (religion, rural life, and eco-tourism).

The Greek subjects also stated that there are few possibilities to engage in International Mountaineering Pathway programs with Albania in the next five years and in ICT and Digital Marketing applications for attracting Special Interest Groups as well as in the establishment of new cross-border tourist enterprises. The North Macedonian subjects believed that it is likely that they will engage in joint actions with Albania in the next five years to exploit natural resources and establish mixed cross-border enterprises.

Finally, the Albanian subjects stated that it is very likely to develop joint actions with the two neighboring regions in all sectors for tourism growth, i.e., cultural and other bonds (religion, rural life and eco-tourism), the International Mountaineering Paths, ICT and digital marketing applications and the establishment of new cross-border tourism enterprises (Tourist Agencies, etc.).

The interviews demonstrated that, although there are reservations and different attitudes towards bilateral inter-regional cooperation, all subjects agree on trilateral cooperation. More specifically, they stated that they had already engaged in joint actions to create a favorable context for sharing natural resources (lakes and protected areas), cultural bonds and international mountaineering paths with a view to encouraging thematic/niche tourism growth.

As an efficient joint transboundary water management of the eco-sensitive area of the Prespa can promote the development of some alternative forms of tourism, the answers were positive for trilateral cooperation. More specifically, all Mayors considered that trilateral cooperation for water resources protection can create a background for the development of alternative forms of tourism, as demonstrated in the following table (Table 5).

Table 5. Possibilities of development of alternative forms of tourism

Alternative forms of tourism	0%	1-25%	26-50%	51-75%	76-100%
Scientific Tourism			50%	16.7%	33.3%
Agritourism			33.3%	16.7%	50%
Ecological Tourism				50%	50%
Mountain Hiking Tourism			33.3%	33.3%	50%
Religious tourism				66.6%	33.3%
Cultural Tourism				33.3%	66.6%
Nature tourism				50%	50%
Walking Tourism				50%	50%
Off-road Tourism (Off-road: 4X4, Enduro, mountain bike)			16.7%	50%	33.3%
Other					

Potential weaknesses and constraints to transboundary management of the Prespa basin, in terms of cross-border development, include specific considerations, such as poor access and border crossing due to land configuration, possible problems with environmental infrastructure and poor implementation of environmental protection policies, delays due to infrastructure, facilities and control problems affecting environmental health, and poor recycling processes and re-use of solid and liquid waste.

Poor access and border crossing due to the land configuration are considered by all as a weakness for cross-border development. Overall, the relevant answers are demonstrated in Figure 4 below.

Figure 4. Constraints to transboundary alternative forms of tourism

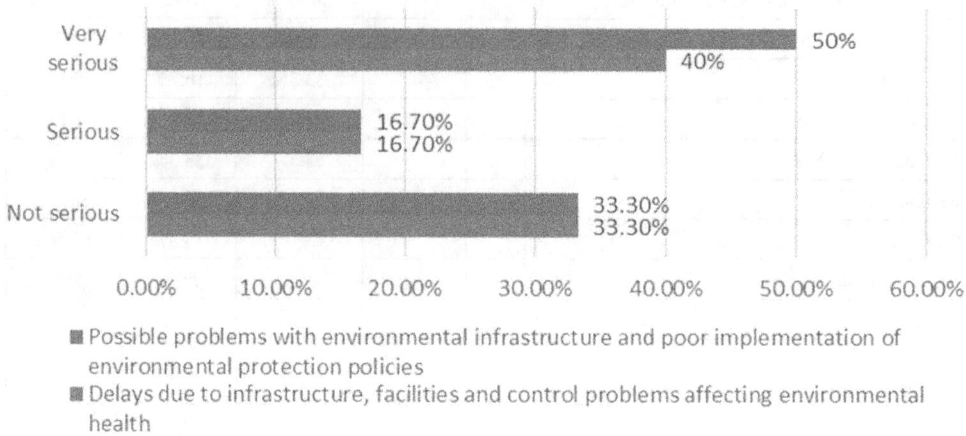

With regard to threats, all subjects believe that protected areas, ecosystems and biodiversity in the Prespa basin are at risk, as recycling and re-use of solid and liquid waste management are poor, despite their significance.

As regards the development of alternative forms of tourism, potential weaknesses include poor planning and management for mild tourism (ecotourism, religious tourism etc.), absence of a joint action plan for tourist growth and development (tourist destinations are not listed etc.), absence of a 'brand name' for the area and poor organization of all aspects of tourism. The specific weaknesses, given a different weight by the subjects, are shown in the following table (Table 6).

Table 6. Significance of weaknesses for developing alternative forms of tourism

Inhibiting Factor - Weakness	Strongly disagree	Disagree	Neither agree nor disagree	Agree	Strongly agree
Poor planning and management for mild tourism		16.7%	50%	33.3%	
Absence of a joint action plan for tourist growth and development (tourist destinations are not listed etc.)	33.3%		16.7%	50%	
Absence of a "brand name" and poor organization of tourism	33.3%	16.7%		50%	
Discontinuous route of International Mountaineering Pathways due to borders				66.6%	33.3%
Discontinuous off-road routes due to borders				66.6%	33.3%

Despite the above-mentioned weaknesses, the researched area also provides a significant number of opportunities for:

- EU policies adoption for creating activities and the possibility of managing the specific areas as interconnected natural systems.
- Role of technological developments in water resources management, energy generation and renewable sources.
- Close cooperation prospects as regards climate change adaptation, reduction of carbon/water footprint and greenhouse gas emissions towards a low carbon economy.
- Application of Networks and Projects in progress during Transboundary Cooperation Programs and future funding.
- Increasing interest in sustainable management of natural resources and protection from natural disasters.
- Recent developments in the tourism industry in the Mediterranean.
- Increasing preferences for alternative forms of tourism.
- ICT and digital marketing to provide opportunities for direct contact with special interest groups.

Regarding the extent to which these opportunities are functional for the transboundary management of the Prespa basin, the surrounding ecologically sensitive environment and the development of alternative forms of tourism, the Greek subjects believe they are very functional, whereas the North Macedonian ones think they are functional. In addition, the Albanian subjects stated that most of the opportunities are very functional, except for the adoption of technological advances in water resources management, energy generation and renewable sources. They also claim that recent developments in the tourism industry in the Mediterranean cannot have a positive impact.

To conclude the result analysis, the participants also stated that:

- The operation of a border station and cross-border crossing between the Greek and North Macedonian areas at the Marco Noga point is extremely important.
- A transboundary park with 15 employees, designed by all three states and the European Union, will also be significant.
- To develop and promote the Prespa cross-border tourist area, each country should invest in infrastructure, protection of the ecological environment, creating paths, tourism growth, etc. However, it is rather doubtful whether the three countries are ready to invest in infrastructure and activities and whether they can claim EU funds.

- Actions to improve the environment and organize joint activities must be enhanced.
- It is desirable to promote volunteering on an international level, to improve attitudes about the protection and preservation of natural and historic cultural attractions.
- In terms of local development, lake tourism and transportation around the lake can be critical.
- To ensure sustainability and promote alternative forms of tourism, measures should be taken to protect traditional architecture, local cuisine, cultural heritage, and natural beauty.
- A Transboundary Park and walking paths, cycling lanes and boat hire on the lake can enhance the attraction of the Prespa basin.

SOLUTIONS AND RECOMMENDATIONS

It is worth noting that, as greater efforts are required towards achieving sustainable development, environmental protection and welfare in the wider area, trilateral cooperation agreements between the three transboundary areas are critical.

However, the potential constraints to such cooperation, such as the different social profile and financial growth status by region, poor infrastructure, political, national, or local issues, different administrative and legal systems, and different institutional frameworks, were emphasized as vital issues for cooperation.

The findings also emphasized that Albania, the weakest partner in administrative and financial terms, seems to expect positive results from such cooperation for infrastructure improvement, efficient use of energy and improvement of lake sanitation.

In addition, it was demonstrated that, despite the various measures to protect water resources in the Prespa basin, lake degradation has been aggravated, as a result of a number of harmful activities, especially in Albania, such as pollution from sewage water/urban sewage, aquaculture, industrial waste, and use of fertilizers and pesticides, and, to a lesser extent, by irrigation and solid waste.

Cooperation for creating a shared attractive tourism product, especially alternative forms of tourism focusing on the lakes in the next five years, is desirable, as it will enable enhancing economic growth and prosperity and raise awareness of sustainability in the Prespa basin. Thus, the joint exploitation of natural resources, cultural bonds, and international mountaineering paths with a view to encouraging thematic/ niche tourism growth, new ICT applications and digital marketing, as well as the establishment of new cross-border tourist businesses, will facilitate communication and strengthen collaboration between the three partners. The research findings demonstrated the necessity of diversification strategies and, thus, underscored the prominent role of tourism.

In addition, despite any reservations and different perceptions of bilateral cooperation, the research emphasized the positive attitude of all subjects towards trilateral cooperation and, more specifically, towards developing alternative forms of tourism focusing on the hydrological basin and the surrounding natural environment.

Weaknesses and inhibiting factors to the transboundary management of the Prespa basin and its eco-sensitive environment involve low accessibility and poor border crossing due to the land configuration of the area, possible problems with environmental infrastructure and poor implementation of environmental protection policies, delays due to infrastructure, facilities and control problems affecting environmental health, and poor recycling processes and re-use of solid and liquid waste.

As regards the potential threats to the specific protected areas, ecosystems, and biodiversity, these are very likely to cause significant damage to the Prespa basin, as recycling and re-use of solid and liquid waste management is poor.

Finally, opportunities involve promoting activities and managing areas as interconnected natural systems, enhancing the role of technological developments in the management of water resources, energy production and renewables, climate change adaptation, reducing carbon/water footprint and greenhouse gas emissions, and supporting a low carbon economy. Opportunities can also be created by applying Transboundary cooperation Programs and Projects and future EU funding, enhancing interest in the sustainable management of natural resources and protection from natural disasters, by the recent developments in the tourism industry in the Mediterranean, the increasing preference for alternative forms of tourism and ICT and digital marketing applications.

In addition, a Transboundary Park with 15 employees, designed and supported by all three states and the European Union, can enhance the protection and management of the Prespa basin.

FUTURE RESEARCH DIRECTIONS

The investigation of transboundary water management and sustainability cooperation between Greece, Albania, and North Macedonia in the Prespa basin focused on transboundary cooperation in all three countries and emphasized the contribution of collaborative efforts to sustainable development, environmental protection, and socio-economic prosperity.

Further research can be focused on specific other aspects of transboundary cooperation and investigate the role of NGOs and other stakeholders in the transboundary cooperation efforts in the research area. It can also explore the significance of trilateral cooperation to enhance lake-based tourism and improve local and national economic growth.

In addition, further quantitative research investigating the local residents' perceptions, views and attitudes from all three countries with different financial, social, political and cultural backgrounds could elicit significant information concerning the promotion and enhancement of transboundary cooperation. Significantly, further quantitative research focused on exploring the Greek local people's approach to transboundary cooperation in comparison with that of Albanian and North Macedonian local residents in the Prespa basin, in terms of equal opportunities for sustainability and tourism growth, would yield interesting results as regards difference in perceptions and intentions.

Finally, a regression analysis exploring the degree and effectiveness of implementing shared ICT tools and models in integrated environmental data management under the Water Framework Directive will identify and address the lack of accurate information and data on the Prespa basin and provide valuable insights into new collaborative strategic planning and objectives setting.

CONCLUSION

Water resources, such as lakes, are fundamental environmental assets, as they greatly affect the majority of terrestrial flora and fauna, the multitude of ecosystems, and humanity and provide important functions for both ecosystems and people. In the context of ensuring economic and social growth and prosperity, transboundary lakes have largely determined the development prospects and welfare of a border area.

Despite their significant benefits, water resources have been continuously degraded, thus, forcing people to promote and enhance sustainable development efforts. The process of European integration promoted the conclusion of bilateral and trilateral agreements in the field of transboundary cooperation, with special emphasis on the external borders of the EU. For the protection of water resources, international treaties have been signed concerning transboundary waters, navigable waters, river and lake basins, and international water resources (UNEP, 2016).

The area around the Prespa hydrological basin (the Mikri and Megali Prespa lakes) is an environmental treasure of global importance and has been declared a protected area in the three neighboring countries, Greece, Albania and North Macedonia. In recent years, the lakes have suffered great damage due to prolonged drought, a decrease in atmospheric precipitation, and underground karst leaks.

The empirical investigation into transboundary water management cooperation for the eco-sensitive Prespa basin, organized via six structured interviews, two per country, demonstrated the strengths and weaknesses as well as the opportunities and threats in the Prespa basin and highlighted the significance of transboundary cooperation between Municipalities and local Universities as part of the effort to integrate policies under the 2030 Agenda for Sustainable Development Goals. Remarkably, the languages spoken in the border areas of all three countries, which are mutually comprehensible, help cooperation, future decision making and implementation of cooperation programs.

Overall, the research demonstrated the positive results of the trilateral cooperation in terms of the environmental protection of the lake, tourism, education, and transboundary cooperation in NSRF and cross-border programs, which enable solving shared management problems arising in the Prespa basin and create networks with Universities and Institutes.

To conclude, the research findings, overall, address a solutions-oriented approach to ensure trilateral cooperation and joint action implementation as well as diversification strategies for water management and socio-economic growth. Such an approach will exploit ICT contribution to developing advanced integrated water resources management methods and tools, such as real-time monitoring networks, cloud-based information systems (Skoulikaris, 2018), as well as decision support systems (DSS) (Gourbesville, 2008).

ACKNOWLEDGMENT

I would like to thank Dr. Efstathios Oikonomou, Assistant Professor, School of Rural and Surveying Engineering, Aristotle University of Thessaloniki, Greece, for his valuable support and comments on the research.

This research received no specific grant from any funding agency in the public, commercial, or not-for-profit sectors.

REFERENCES

Albayrak, T., & Caber, M. (2018). A motivation-based segmentation of holiday tourists participating in white-water rafting. *Journal of Destination Marketing & Management*, *9*, 64–71. doi:10.1016/j.jdmm.2017.11.001

Anderson, J., & O'Dowd, L. (1999). Borders, border regions and territoriality: Contradictory meanings, changing significance. *Regional Studies*, *33*(7), 593–604. doi:10.1080/00343409950078648

Arabiadis, R. (2016). *Investigation of the economy and the environment of Prespa and Proposals for the management of water resources: Criticism of the irrigation network combined with monoculture of beans* [Diploma thesis, Department of Civil Engineering, Aristotle University of Thessaloniki].

Aykaç, A. (1994). *Transborder regionalization: an analysis of transborder cooperation structures in Western Europe within the context of European Integration and decentralization towards regional and local governments*. Libertas Europäische. Sindelfingen.

Bogdanović, S. (2008). Prespa Park Coordination Committee in Transboundary Ecosystem Management. *GWP Toolbox*. https://www.gwptoolbox.org

Bošnjaković, B. (2001). Regulations of International Watercourses under the UN/ECE Regional Agreements. *Water International, 25*.

Brinkhoff, A., Gabbe, J., & Martinos, H. (1997). *VADE MECUM, Cross-Border and Inter-regional Co-operation on External Borders of the European Union. AEBR*. Gronau.

CADRI. (2020). *Good Practices on Transboundary Water Resources Management and Cooperation*. CADRI. https://www.cadri.net/good-practices-transboundary-water_2020.pdf

.CEC, Commission of the European Communities (1995β). *Seventh annual report on the reform of the Structural Funds*. Office for Official Publications of the European Communities.

.CEC, Commission of the European Communities (2008β). INTERACT Handbook, *The European Grouping of Territorial Cooperation (EGTC)*. European Commission. Brussels.

CoE Council of Europe. (1995). *Additional Protocol to the European Outline Convention on Transfrontier Co-operation between Territorial Communities or Authorities*. Explanatory Report, Council of Europe. Strasbourg.

CoR Committee of the Regions. (2007). The European Grouping of Territorial Cooperation. Study carried out by: GEPE (supervision N.Levrat), the Unit for Policy Analysis, Studies & Inter-institutional & Legislative Planning (G.Spinaci, J.Lotarsk & L.Cannellini) & COTER (D.L.Taberner), Committee of the Regions. Brussels.

Costanza, R., d'Arge, R., Groot, R., Farber, S., Grasso, M., Hannon, G., Limburg, K., Naeem, S., O'Neill, R. V., Paruelo, J., Raskin, R. G., Sutton, P., Belt, M., & Belt, H. (1996). The value of the world's ecosystem services and natural capital. Nature. Report of Workshop organized by NCEAS, Santa Barbara, Calif. (1996) 387.

Council of Europe. (1980). *European Outline Convention on Transfrontier Co-operation between Territorial Communities or Authorities Madrid*. Council of Europe.

Creswell, J., & Poth, C. (2017). *Qualitative inquiry and research design: choosing among five approaches*. Sage.

Daily, G. (1997). *Nature's services*. Island Press.

Davis, S., Childers, D., Lorenz, J., Wanless, H., & Hopkins, T. (2005). A Conceptual Model of Ecological Interactions in the Mangrove Estuaries of the Florida Everglades. *Wetlands, 25*(4), 832–842. doi:10.1672/0277-5212(2005)025[0832:ACMOEI]2.0.CO;2

EC Council of the European Union. (2000). *Regulation (EC) No 2666/2000 of 5-12-2000 on assistance for Albania, Bosnia & Herzegovina, Croatia, Federal Republic of Yugoslavia& FYROM, repealing Reg. (EC) No 1628/96 &amending Regulations (EEC) No 3906/89 & (EEC)&No 1360/90 & Decisions 97/256/EC&1999/311/EC*. Office for Official Publications of the European Communities.

EC Council of the European Union. (2006β). Regulation 1082/2006 of the European Parliament and of the Council of 5 July 2006 on a European Grouping of Territorial Cooperation. OJ 2006 L 210. Office for Official Publications of the European Communities.

Gourbesville, Ph. (2008). Integrated river basin management, ICT and DSS: Challenges and needs. *Physics and Chemistry of the Earth Parts A/B/C, 33*(5), 312–321. doi:10.1016/j.pce.2008.02.007

Great Lakes Directory of Universities. (1976). *Research Institutes and Agencies Concerned with Water and Land Resources in the Great Lakes Basin*. Great Lakes Basin Commission. https://play.google.com/books/reader?id=spC7Z77cImgC&hl=el&pg=GBS.PP1

ILEC and UNEP. (2016). *Transboundary Lakes and Reservoirs: Status and Trends, Summary for Policy Makers. United Nations Environment Programme*. UNEP.

IW Learn. (2011). *Integrated Ecosystem Management in the Prespa Basin in Albania, FYROM and Greece*. GEF Project (2006-2011). https://iwlearn.net/iw-projects/1537

Kalokardou, R., & Kradonelli, K. (2005). *Alternative Forms of Tourism and Critical Capacities in Tourist Areas of Western Greece* [Paper presentation]. Heleco Conference.

Kenton, W. (2022). *SWOT Analysis: How to with Table and Example*. Investopedia. https://www.investopedia.com/terms/s/swot.asp

Kousouris, Th., & Athanasakis, A. (1992). *Environment, Ecology, Education*. Savvala Publications.

Maxwell, J. (2013). *Qualitative research design: an interactive approach*. Sage.

Mccaffrey, S. (2015). The 1997 UN Convention: Compatibility and Complementarity. In: Tanzi, A., McIntyre, O., Kolliopoulos, A., Rieu-Clarke, A., Kinna, R. *The UNECE Convention on the Protection and Use of Transboundary Watercourses and International Lakes – Its Contribution to International Water Cooperation, Brill.*

Mekong River Commission (MRC). (2018). *An introduction to MRC procedural rules for Mekong Water Cooperation*. MCR. https://www.mrcmekong.org/assets/Publications/MRC-procedures-EN-V.7-JUL-18.pdf

Mylopoulos, Y., Eleftheriadou, E., & Kampragou, E. (2004). The transboundary catchment of River Nestos and the bilateral agreement between Greece and Bulgaria. [Paper presentation] ECO-Geowater conference, GI for International River Basin Management. Budapest.

Noble, H., & Smith, J. (2015). Issues of validity and reliability in qualitative research. *Evidence-Based Nursing*, *18*(2), 34–35. doi:10.1136/eb-2015-102054 PMID:25653237

O'Dowd, L. (2002). The Changing Significance of European Borders. *Regional & Federal Studies*, *12*(4), 13–36. doi:10.1080/714004774

OECD. (2015). *OECD Principles on Water Governance*. OECD. www.oecd.org/governance/oecd-principles-onwater-governance.h
tmOECD. (2011). *Water Governance in OECD Countries: A Multi-level Approach*. OECD Publishing. doi:10.1787/9789264119284-

. Official Gazette. (1974). *Official Gazette 19A/75 National Park of the Prespa and the Official Gazette 86B/77, The protection of the Prespa Ecosystem where it is recognized as a "Landscape of Special Natural Beauty"*. Official Gazette.

Papoutsoglou, S. E. (1992). *Possible Effects of Climate Change on Fisheries and Aquaculture in Greece*. Bank of Greece.

Perkmann, M. (2007a). Construction of new territorial scales. A framework and case study of the EUREGIO cross-border region. *Regional Studies*, *41*(2), 253–266. doi:10.1080/00343400600990517

Perkmann, M. (2007b). Policy entrepreneurship and multilevel governance: A comparative study of European cross-border regions. *Environment and Planning. C, Government & Policy*, *25*(6), 861–879. doi:10.1068/c60m

. Petrovska, M., Conevski, T., Krstić, S., Blinkov, I., Stavrić, V., Chukaliev, O., Longholt, J., Ristovski, I., Kočovski, Z., Mincev, I., Dinev, Ġ., Mileski, J., Dimov, M., Bojkovska, R., Talevski, T., Talevska, M., Slavevska-Stamenković, V., Stafilov, T., Kaevski, I., Blinkova, M. (2014). *Prespa Lake Watershed Management Plan*. WMP.

. *Program Restoration of Prespa Lake Ecosystem* (2011-2018). (FYROM–UNDP) Approved SD: YD09/00 – SMBE (KYA).

Queirós, A., Faria, D., & Almeida, F. (2017). Strengths and Limitations of Qualitative and Quantitative Research Methods, *European Journal of Education Studies*, *3* (9). www.oapub.org/edu

doi:10.5281/zenodo.887089

Region of Western Macedonia. (2012). *Special Spatial Study of the Prespa area.*

Region of Western Macedonia. (2015). *Spatial Plan of the Region of Western Macedonia.*

Region of Western Macedonia. (2017). *Special Environmental Study of the Prespa Region.*

.RULAND. (2013). *Interactive Farmers Support System for Efficient Water Use Management*. Greece– FYROM (2012-2013).

Sadoff, C., & Grey, D. (2005). Cooperation on International Rivers. A Continuum for Securing and Sharing Benefits. *Water International*, *30*(4), 420–427. doi:10.1080/02508060508691886

Sapuric, Z. (2014). The potentials for bio waste management in macedonia. *International Journal of Ecosystems.*, *4*, 513–520.

Skoulikaris, C., Filali-Meknassi, Y., Aureli, A., Amani, A., & Jiménez-Cisneros, B. E. (2018). *Information-Communication Technologies as an Integrated Water Resources Management (IWRM)*. Tool for Sustainable Development. Achievements and Challenges of Integrated River Basin Management., doi:10.5772/intechopen.74700

Society for the Protection of the Prespa. (2011). *Protection and Sustainable Use of Biodiversity in the Region of the Large Lakes Prespa, Ohrid and Sckoder.* Albania–Fyrom (2011-2014). https://www.spp.gr/

.Technical Task Team (TTT). (2008). *For the collection, assessment and evaluation of national information in support of the Transboundary Diagnostic Analysis (TDA) and development of a Strategic Action Programme (SAP) in the Prespa Lakes Basin (TTT-TDA,2008).*

.Technical Task Team (TTT). (2017). Study for the collection, assessment and evaluation of national information in support of the *Transboundary Diagnostic Analysis (TDA) and development of a Strategic Action Program (SAP) in the Prespa Lakes Basin* (TTT-TDA, 2009), Region of Western Macedonia *Special Environmental Study of the Prespa Region.* Kozani. 2017.

Topaloglou, L., & Petrakos, G. (2008b). The economic geography of borders. A brief literature review. *Research Paper Series, University of Thessaly, 14*(6), 105-118.

. TRABOREMA. (2007). *Concepts for Integrated Transboundary Water Management and Sustainable Socio-Economic Development in The Cross Border Region* of Albania, Former Yugoslav Republic of Macedonia (FYROM) and Greece.

. Transboundary. (2015). *Biosphere Reserve Prespa– Support to the National Park Pres.*

Transboundary Waters Assessment Programme (TWAP), Transboundary Lakes and Reservoirs: Status and Future Trends. http://geftwap.org/

UNECE. (2018). *Identifying, assessing and communicating the benefits of transboundary water cooperation: Lessons learned and recommendations.* UNECE. https://unece.org/environment-policy/publications/identifying-assessing-and-communicating-benefits-transboundary

United Nations. (2008). *Achieving Sustainable Development and Promoting Development Cooperation.* UN. https://www.un.org/en/ecosoc/docs/pdfs/fina_08-45773.pdf

Valvis, A. (2015). *Transboundary Freshwater Resources Management: Greece and its neighbors towards Cooperation or Conflict*, [PhD Thesis, University of Peloponnese, Greece].

van Griensven, A., & Vanrolleghem, P. A. (2006). The CatchMod toolbox: Easy and guided access to ICT tools for Water Framework Directive implementation. *Water Science and Technology*, *53*(10), 285–292. doi:10.2166/wst.2006.323 PMID:16838714

Wilson, M. A., & Carpenter, S. R. (1999). Economic Valuation of Freshwater Ecosystem Services In The United States: 1971-1997. *Ecological Applications*, *9*, 772–783.

Wolf, A. (2006). Conflict and Cooperation Over Transboundary Waters, UNDP (United Nations Development Programme). https://hdr.undp.org/

World Tourism Organization. (2001). *Sustainable Development of Tourism: A Compilation of Good Practices*. World Tourism Organization.

Wright, R. T. (2005). *Environmental Science* (International Edition). Pearson, Prentice Hall Inc.

ADDITIONAL READING

Hector, G., & Amerasinghe, P. Huber-Lee A., (2005). The Effects of Agricultural Irrigation on Wetland Ecosystems in Developing Countries: A Literature Review. International Water Management Institute.

.Klatt, M., Kühl, J. (2006). *National Minorities and Cross-border Cooperation between Hungary and Croatia. A Case-Study of Baranya/Hungary and Osiječko-baranjska County/Croatia*. European Yearbook of Minority Issues (2006/7) 93-210.

Lejeune, Y. (2005). *Le droit des relations transfrontalières entre autorités régionales ou locales relevant d'états disctincts*. Bruylant.

Perkmann, M. (2007a). Construction of new territorial scales. A framework and case study of the EUREGIO cross-border region. *Regional Studies*, *41*(2), 253–266. doi:10.1080/00343400600990517

Perkmann, M. (2007b). Policy entrepreneurship and multilevel governance: A comparative study of European cross-border regions. *Environment & Planning*, *25*(6), 861–879. doi:10.1068/c60m

Sands, P. (2003). *Principles of International Environmental Law*. Cambridge University Press., doi:10.1017/CBO9780511813511

Shimon, C., & Anisfeld, M. (2010). *Water Resources HC*. Island press.

Shroder, F., & Ahmadzai, S. J. (2016). *Transboundary Water Resources in Afghanistan: Climate Change and Land-Use Implications*. Elsevier Science Publishing Co Inc.

Van Houtoum, H., & Struver, A. (2002). Bordering, Ordering and Othering. *Tijdschrift voor Economische en Sociale Geografie*, *93*(2), 143.

Wright, R. T., & Boorse, D. (2005). *Environmental Science: Toward a Sustainable Future* (International Edition). Pearson.

KEY TERMS AND DEFINITIONS

Alternative Forms Of Tourism: All specialized mild local activities that attract tourists.

Economic Indicators: Measures of macroeconomic performance such as gross domestic product (gdp), consumption, investment, international trade, etc.

Lake Degradation: A syndrome that involves the collapse of many adaptive and developmental mechanisms.

Markova Noga: The border crossing between greece and north macedonia in the prespa lake. it was open until the 1960s. it is still closed, but it is going to be reopened.

Prespa Lakes: Two of the oldest lakes in europe, shared between three countries: greece, north macedonia, and albania.

Social Welfare: Good social situation.

The Prespa Agreement: An intergovernmental agreement concluded on june 12, 2018, between the hellenic republic and the republic of north macedonia, under the auspices of the united nations.

Chapter 7
Sustainability of Public Services:
Efficiency Assessment of Educational Systems

Bojan Krstić
https://orcid.org/0000-0003-4597-6819
University of Niš, Serbia

Sandra Milanović
https://orcid.org/0000-0002-0582-045X
University of Niš, Serbia

Milica Jovanović Vujatović
https://orcid.org/0000-0002-6410-0938
University of Niš, Serbia

Georgios Tsaples
University of Macedonia, Greece

Ivana Marjanović
https://orcid.org/0000-0002-9526-0467
University of Niš, Serbia

ABSTRACT

Since education is the most influential factor of a sustainable society and the fourth UN Sustainable Development Goal (SDG) promotes the importance of the quality of education, the chapter proposes the tripartite research method. Firstly, a qualitative analysis of the sustainability and efficiency of the education system is conducted. Secondly, an assessment of the efficiency of 31 European education systems is provided by applying the benefit of the doubt approach. Thirdly, the ranking of the

DOI: 10.4018/978-1-6684-7730-4.ch007

education systems in question was conducted according to the criterion of their efficiency. The research illuminates that 40% of analyzed education systems are above the threshold when it comes to the indicators of education efficiency. Having in mind that the research database exploited in this research is grounded on the indicators from SDG4, the data-based conclusions from this chapter support education systems' reforms targeted at upbringing their efficiency, inclusion, equality, and finally, sustainability as a public service.

INTRODUCTION

While defining Sustainable Development Goals (SDGs), United Nations placed "quality education" as SDG4 out of seventeen important targets to be achieved by 2030. Through education enhancement, it is expected gradual decrease of the poverty level in national economies and help in accomplishing other SDGs. Specifically, Kolb et al. (2017) indicate that SDG4 is directly related to four other SDGs, and afterwards their interrelation leads to innovative solutions and consequences for other SDGs. Therefore, the management of the national educational system toward its efficiency increment will probably have a wider influence not only on the quality of education itself but also on sustainable development as a whole.

Education efficiency not only depends on public policy and measures implemented by various actors but also on activities at the school level. In order to increase the efficiency of education as a public service, there is a need for actions targeted toward basic education indicators such as the number of school leavers or the number of students involved in tertiary education (Reinikka & Svensson, 2011). The efficiency of the educational sector could also be evaluated from the aspect of a production function. The production function refers to the educational output obtained using inputs through the educational process under the influence of environmental factors and relationships among all factors (Thieme et al., 2012).

It is still uncovered how efficient economies are in their education management practices. Thus, the aim of this chapter will be to analyze the efficiency of educational systems through various educational indicators. The performance of the educational systems of 31 European countries was analyzed based on indicators related to SDG4: Quality education such as early leavers from education and training, adult participation in learning by sex, tertiary educational attainment by sex, participation in early childhood education, the share of individuals having at least basic digital skills and low achieving 15-year-olds in reading, mathematics or science. The chapter deploys the quantitative research methodology to the analysis of the efficiency of educational systems using the Benefit of the Doubt approach.

The results of the analysis indicated that over 40% of the analyzed countries achieve a satisfactory level of efficiency in their educational systems. In order to determine the order of countries according to the achieved level of efficiency, the super-efficiency Benefit of the Doubt approach was applied.

The structure of the chapter is as follows: after the introduction, a literature review of the concept of sustainable education as a public service is presented. Afterwards, the efficiency of the educational system is elaborated. The third part of the chapter is devoted to the multicriteria analysis of the 31 European countries' educational system efficiency. Finally, the discussion and recommendations derived from the study and future directions of the analysis are presented at the end of the chapter.

BACKGROUND

Since the publication of 17 SDGs in 2015, United Nations' activities have been devoted to the increase of lifelong learning opportunities for all citizens. Meanwhile, the numbers are not so promising. In 2018 there were 262 million children outside the education system and 617 million persons in their formative years who did not meet the basic level of reading and calculating ability. On the other hand, the COVID-19 pandemic made disruptive changes to the educational systems by affecting 91% of students' learning methods. Therefore, future SDG4 goals are to enable education opportunities for all, eliminate gender disparities in obtaining all educational levels, increase the level of basic literacy and numeracy and promote the acquisition of skills that contribute to employability improvement, and all of that need to be achieved by 2030 (United Nations, 2022).

Therefore, the education for sustainable development (ESD) plays an important role in preparing all citizens through primary, secondary, and tertiary education and lifelong learning process to study how to implement sustainable practices in everyday life without harming the natural and social environment in order to become the main driver of sustainable development in their country. Consequently, United Nations Economic Commission for Europe (UNECE) recognized the importance of the Strategy for ESD, and it was adopted in 2005, while the period from 2005 until 2014 was declared as a decade of the ESD (Žalėnienė & Pereira, 2021). Subsequently, Global Action Program on ESD (2015-2019) and ESD for 2030 were introduced later. The objectives of ESD2030 are to provide supporting conditions and procedures for the implementation of SDG, especially SGD4 and its target 4.7 (UNESCO, 2020), promotion of sustainable development at multiple levels, provide the necessary resources to both teachers and society for ESD and improve cooperation between UNECE members on this topic. By achieving these objectives, national economies will create an enabling learning environment for sustainable development.

Besides ESD, it is immensely important to create sustainable educational systems as a significant member of a broader concept of the public system. Sustainable education is derived from the push, pull, coupling, and integrated education forms and involves the creation of open educational ecosystems whose aim is to maximize learning outcomes through a partnership between all stakeholders in order to create innovation-driven educational systems. In this system, students acquired knowledge is an outcome of the learning process rather than a customer of educational organizations (Embarak, 2021). On the way to becoming sustainable, educational systems should become high-quality systems expressed through adequate curriculums, modern teaching methods, and an encouraging environment for studying and motivating students to collaborate and transformative learning (Didham & Ofei-Manu, 2020).

Firstly, sustainable education must be an efficient public service. From the point of view that education brings positive effects on society and the economy, it is important to be in public service. On the other hand, there are also opinions that it creates benefits only for individuals and because of that, it can be a private service. Since positive outcomes for the wider community prevail, so government mostly finances compulsory education (i.e., primary education attainment) (Johnes et al., 2017). Also, education is viewed as a politically sensitive and economically important service that is provided to citizens as a part of welfare services. The organization and efficiency of educational systems are largely determined by various factors, such as historical, economic, social, and religious factors (Nistor, 2011).

Moreover, education was promoted as one of the essential services that contribute to sustainability through students and transfers to the practical implementation of their obtained knowledge. This is why educational institutions need to serve as examples of good practice by employing postulates of sustainability in their organization and management procedures. For example, the research of Žalėnienė and Pereira (2021) suggests that higher education institutions are the main drivers of numerous SDGs implementation, such as goals devoted to the poverty elimination, lives that incorporate healthiness and welfare of citizens, parity when it comes to genders, decent work, and economic progress, liable consumption and production, actions targeted at climate preservation and peace, justice and strong institutions. Moreover, higher educational institutions are regarded as public entities that, through mutual collaboration, have to be oriented toward the public interest, develop a research base and engage in proactive activities for sustainable development together with policymakers, build know-how based on SDGs in its students, and refining its curriculums and study programs by integrating priorities of sustainable development (Pandey, 2019). Besides higher educational institutions, the aim of all educational organizations should be to develop future experts with substantial knowledge and competencies needed for economic growth powered by sustainable practices.

On the way to accomplishing seventeen SDGs, and especially SGD4: Quality of Education, there is a vast number of obstacles connected with an educational subject. Firstly, poverty, injustice, and inequality issues are aroused by problems such as different learning opportunities for children in war zones, a cultural milieu that propose constraints for women or societies in which low household income forces children to be a member of the labor force. Secondly, the world's population lacks an understanding of sustainability or its definition. Thirdly, students must be perceived as customers of educational organizations that make their decisions on what school to choose with high involvement in the decision-making process, and they request a great deal of information to avoid post-purchase dissonance. What is more, their decisions are driven by culture, demographic characteristics, and emotions. Fourthly, reaction to sustainability and education programs based on it must be advertised in a manner to evoke emotional reaction among the target population rather than a rational reaction. Fifthly, from the point of view of social cognitive theory, each human being has an identity or self-perception based on their membership in some social group. Therefore, members of the group could manifest social exclusion or discrimination against other parties, causing inequality gaps in society. Sixthly, the existence of elitism and lack of diversity is well represented in educational systems. On the one hand, some schools are only attainable for students from a well-to-do family setting. On the other hand, diversity in the context of grander, race, nationality, etc., in educational institutions is less observable than anticipated. In this way, SDG 10: Reduced inequality through the education system is also jeopardized. Seventhly, cognitive dissonance theory indicates that a person can behave in dissonance with their beliefs and in an impulsive manner that is opposingly different to their perceptions (i.e., perception of sustainability) (Richardson, 2019).

What is more, in the literature on environmental and sustainability education or sustainable education, there is a question of what makes competence a term. Competence is somewhere related to the skills and literacy, such as in UK literature, but also to personality traits and qualifications in German scientific papers or with capabilities in the USA and Australian literature. Furthermore, key competencies are those that enable a person's achievements in some fields, such as reading, mathematics, and science literacy. Literacy in all domains contributes to the competencies referred to as performance rather than potential. Expanding the field of literacy is also possible to assess literacy when it comes to sustainable development or environmental literacy (Vare et al., 2022).

Specifically, educational curriculums should be redesigned in order to capture both local circumstances and sustainability issues of one environment. Even though most educational systems are made to achieve global parity (i.e., the Bologna process) and promote the concept of one-size-fits-all, the student's involvement in the learning process and, consequently their literacy could be enhanced through adding the social and ecological context of the society to the learning process (Paige et al., 2022). Moreover, career counselors could identify in which domains students' rights were not respected and when their interests were discriminated against. Afterwards, they can make influence decision-makers to take into account students' needs, especially if they belong to some vulnerable groups in the educational system. By doing so, career professionals could transform the individual problem into local and state issues' level that need to be tackled in order to build social responsibility and sustainability (Nota et al., 2020).

It should be noted that vulnerable groups, such as females, are perceived as contributing members to the sustainable development of a country, but because of existing disparities in their educational opportunities, they lack the know-how to express their full potential, in particular at the labor market and in the decisionmaker's bodies. National economies could benefit from enrolling as many girls as possible in the educational process because there is evidence that females are not just childcare providers and housewives but also the generator of economic, political, and social development (Haruna & Nafisa, 2021). As SDG5, which enlightens gender equality, is also represented in SDG4, while both goals are devoted to ecological, social, and economic development (Mauerhofer, 2023).

As SGD4 stipulates in its core base that, education must be aimed at obtaining competencies for sustainable development (Wiek & Redman, 2022), but, first of all, education must be efficient. On the way to becoming efficient, the national educational systems are contributing to SDGs' accomplishment.

THE EFFICIENCY OF EDUCATIONAL SYSTEMS

Theoretical Framework of the Efficiency of Educational Systems

Efficiency in education can be seen as doing things the right way in the education system. This means that users get adequate value for money, which requires an acceptable level of results from the education system – quality, attainments, and equality of outcomes. It cannot be considered a simple relationship between the results of the educational system and the investment in that system, bearing in mind the social role of education and the multidimensional character and effects of the education sector (Witte & López-Torres, 2017). The principle of efficiency implies achieving the maximum results of educational institutions with the engagement of available resources, that is, inputs that are transformed into outputs in these institutions (Worthington, 2001). There are two key aspects that should be taken into consideration within efficiency analyses. Primarily, it is important to answer the question: How much costs or other non-financial resources may be reduced to maintain the same level of output/outcome? In addition, an output perspective also has an important role – How to maximize the results by maintaining the same input values? (Dincă et al., 2021). If we take into account that the concept of efficiency is related to productivity, which connects inputs and outputs, then the educational institution with the highest productivity in all inputs is also the most efficient, while the percentage of the inefficiency of other institutions can be seen based on a comparison with the most efficient (Casalprim et al., 2013).

Additionally, different concepts of efficiency in the education sector can be distinguished. Thus, technical, allocative, exchange, and (factor) price efficiency are highlighted. Technical efficiency considers the time and resources (such as teaching methods and materials, students' learning activities) used over a while in order to deliver desired outcomes. Price efficiency is based on the relative costs of resources (generally speaking, it is a cost efficiency assessment). Exchange efficiency indicates the ability of the educational system to contribute to other institutions (for example, companies and social communities) and to what extent the acquired skills correspond to the labor market. Allocative efficiency exists if the other three efficiencies are achieved. It is aimed at maximizing satisfaction with scarce resources. As a result of the complexity of the efficiency concept in the educational system, measuring the efficiency of educational institutions is a complex task, as well as considering the complexity of the output and input of educational institutions, concerning which it is difficult to determine the price, bearing in mind that their market price does not exist (Kosor, 2013). It is characteristic of the inputs and outputs of educational institutions that "inputs and outputs are not only qualitatively heterogeneous but sometimes truly incommensurable, the relation between inputs and outputs is not deterministic, the output is lagged but with a non-fixed lag structure, and the relative weight of different types of output is subject to considerable debate and political appreciation" (Bonaccorsi et al., 2007, p. 405).

In addition, it is possible to distinguish between internal and external efficiency in education. Internal efficiency relates learning as a non-monetary output of the educational system to the costs of educational inputs and provides an answer to the question of what is the best way to allocate resources in the educational system. The goal is to achieve the highest educational outputs for any level of spending in the education system. That is why allocative efficiency and price efficiency are used as synonyms for this concept. It can be improved in the following ways: 1) by reallocating resources from inputs that have smaller learning effects to those that have larger effects; 2) by reducing overall educational resources with existing levels of learning. On the other hand, the external efficiency of the education system relates the monetary results of this system to the monetary inputs and raises the question of the justification of the allocation of funds for education and not for some other public or private needs (Lockheed & Hanushek, 1994).

Key Indicators of the Educational System Efficiency

Indicators of the educational system, if we look at education as a process of transformation (production process) of certain inputs into outputs, can be monitored through the following indicators (Witte & López-Torres, 2017):

- **Input indicators:**
  - indicators at students' level (behavior indicators such as motivation or predicted achievement, demographic indicators that include race/ethnicity/minority, age/gender, lifestyle, the presence of educational limitations),
  - family-related indicators (socio-economic status, economic needs, family structure, parents' qualifications, resources available at home such as the internet),
  - education institution indicators (acceptance rate - selectivity, expenditures for teaching, research activities, administrators, supporting staff, ownership - public, private, job satisfaction, mobility index, student/teacher ratio, teacher experience/education/salary), and
  - community-related indicators (the number of educational institutions available, neighborhood characteristics such as taxes and employment, geographical location, urban/rural area).
- **Output indicators:**
  - student achievement (number of graduates, students' scores in different subjects/performance),
  - publications and research activity (citations, patents/prizes, technology transfer, number of doctoral dissertations, publications such as papers published in international journals, number of books/chapters, research income, quality of teaching and research activities based on different rankings and standards),
  - educational results (attendance rate, dropout rate, enrollment, international staff and students, teachers' attitude), and
  - job market/success (employability, graduates with the job, job destination, starting salary, job satisfaction).
- **Environmental indicators** are focused on different types of non-discretionary variables:
  - student level (disabilities, gender, language background, prior achievement, race/ethnicity/minority/nationality),

- ◦ family level (employment, income, level of education, family structure),
- ◦ education institution level (attendance rate/dropout, hiring practices, local/external funding ratio, ownership structure, quality of teaching and research activities – innovation intensity, rate of expulsion or suspension, organizational performance, size, teacher personal characteristics), and
- ◦ community level (competition, GDP per capita, percentage of population with higher education, immigrants, employment opportunities, mortality rate, poverty rate, population size).

Bonaccorsi et al. (2007) suggest that a framework for educational institutions' efficiency indicators is based on the following: 1) human resources, financial resources, and physical infrastructure as input indicators; 2) decision-making process, organization, strategy as processes indicators; and 3) educational activities, research activities and activities of third mission as output indicators.

A complete analysis of the efficiency of the education sector includes an analysis by the level of education - primary education, secondary education, and tertiary education, as well as an analysis of the entire educational system. For each of these levels, it is necessary to monitor input indicators and output indicators. At the level of primary education, expenditure per student, primary (% of GDP per capita) can be used as an input indicator, and as output indicators: school enrollment, primary (% of age group population), pupil-teacher ratio in primary education, primary completion rate, total (% of relevant age group). At the level of secondary education, the input indicator is public expenditure per pupil, secondary (% of GDP per capita), and the output indicators include PISA average, school enrollment, secondary (% of age group population), and pupil-teacher ratio in secondary education. Within tertiary education, as an input indicator, it can be applied expenditure per student, tertiary (% of GDP per capita), and as output indicators unemployment with advanced education (% of the total labor force with advanced education), labor force with tertiary education (% of the total labor force), school enrollment, tertiary (% of age group population). At the level of the entire education sector, efficiency can be analyzed through total expenditure on education (in % of GDP) – input indicator and PISA average – output indicator (Dincă et al., 2021).

The Efficiency of the Education Sector at the Level of the European Union

There are various studies (Murias et al., 2008; Giambona et al., 2011; Aristovnik & Obadic, 2011; Cornali, 2012; Thieme et al., 2012; Agasisti et al., 2019; Dincă et al., 2021) that deal with the efficiency of the education system in the countries of the European Union.

An analysis (Thieme et al., 2012) from 2006 that included 56 countries, including EU countries, indicated that Bulgaria, Greece, Italy, and Romania are the countries with the highest technical inefficiency in the educational system of the EU countries, while Finland is at the opposite side. Finland is the only country that managed to optimize the three factors that determine the efficiency of the educational system (optimal educational system): management, resources, and environmental conditions. Countries with only managerial problems included the Netherlands, Ireland, Belgium, Slovenia, the Czech Republic, Germany, Austria, Poland, Sweden, Denmark, Iceland, Hungary, Norway, Luxemburg, Spain, and Italy. Countries with a mix of managerial and resource endowment problems were Estonia, Slovakia, Latvia, Lithuania, Croatia, Portugal, Greece, Bulgaria, and Romania.

Giambona et al. (2011) concluded in their analysis that there is differentiation among the EU countries regarding the efficiency of the educational systems. The study included the year 2006 and 24 EU countries, where Malta, Cyprus, and Latvia were excluded due to a lack of data. Italy recorded the lowest efficiency score, while the best performance was achieved by the Czech Republic. It was concluded that the Euro-Mediterranean countries achieved worse positions than the Northern ones, and such results have been achieved by some specific characteristics - student's gender, private/public management, educational institution size, and community size.

Agasisti et al. (2019) proved that higher spending in EU countries' educational systems is not enough to guarantee better results, but efficient use of those resources is a precondition for improving the overall qualitative level of the systems. This indicates to the public policymakers in the EU not to allocate public and private funds for the education sector without defining specific activities to improve the efficiency of spending those funds in order to achieve better results in education. This analysis also determined some factors that contribute to greater efficiency of educational systems in the EU – some characteristics of teachers, the state of adults' human capital, and lower expenditures per student.

A study (Dinca et al., 2021) that included 28 EU countries for the period 2006-2018 showed that, with respect to the education expenditure/GDP ratio, the countries of central Europe recorded the highest average allocative efficiency. The western countries achieved slightly above the EU average, while the southern and northern countries reached below EU average scores. The best performers considering the PISA scores, included the six countries from the western group, followed by the northern countries. The central European countries recorded above-the-average technical efficiency results, while the worst PISA scores reached the southern countries.

According to the above-stated, the research model built to assess the efficiency of the educational institutions in the selected European countries is based on the database that gathers the main output indicators of the educational process.

METHODOLOGY AND METHOD DEVELOPMENT

When analyzing efficiency, two classes of approaches can be applied, non-parametric approaches to efficiency measurement and parametric approaches to efficiency measurement. Regarding parametric approaches, one of the most popular techniques is Stochastic Frontier Analysis (SFA), while Data Envelopment Analysis (DEA) is the most popular non-parametric approach. The main difference between these two approaches is the rigor of the initial parameters, where DEA does not require a clearly defined functional form but only the quantity of inputs and outputs, while SFA requires a precise imposition of a concrete parametric functional form (Hossain et al., 2012). Therefore, in this chapter, a variant of the DEA approach, named the Benefit of the Doubt approach, will be applied. DEA represents a mathematical programming technique whose primary goal is to measure the efficiency of different decision-making units (DMUs). Measuring the efficiency of DMUs is done by analyzing certain combinations of input and output quantities. When creating a model, it is necessary to choose the orientation of the model, whereby the model can be input-oriented when the goal is to minimize the input, or output-oriented when the goal is to maximize the output, while recently, the non-oriented model is gaining importance, mainly due to situations when the previous two orientations are infeasible (Ren et al., 2019). The basic DEA model involves considering n DMUs that use m inputs to produce r outputs, where x_{ij} and y_{kj} denote the used quantities of ith input and the produced quantities of kth output for j^{th} DMU, respectively (Contreras, 2020). The ratio of weighted output to weighted input represents the relative efficiency of each DMU:

$$\theta = \frac{\sum_{k=1}^{r} v_k y_{k0}}{\sum_{i=1}^{m} u_i x_{i0}}$$

where u_i and v_k represent the corresponding weights.

When constructing composite indices, the basic DEA model is modified to create a model that contains only outputs (Hermans et al., 2008). In other words, all indicators are treated as outputs, while inputs are not taken into account. Therefore, the denominator of the coefficient consists of weighted inputs of DMUs that contain a dummy variable equal to one, while the numerator consists of a weighted sum of indicators that form the overall composite index (Yang et al., 2018). This approach is known in the literature as the Benefit of the Doubt model, initially presented in the work of Melyn and Moesen (1991).

In order to assess the performance of the educational systems of 31 European countries, data related to Quality education were used. The indicators were obtained from Eurostat (2022) database for the year 2021 and are represented in Table 1.

Table 1. Identification and definition of indicators

Indicator	Code	Definition
Early leavers from education and training	ELeave_E&T	individuals aged 18-24 who have completed at most a lower secondary education and were not in further education or training during the four weeks preceding the labor force survey
Adult participation in learning	Adult_PartL	participation in education and training for adults aged 25-64
Tertiary educational attainment	TEA	the share of the population aged 25-34 who have successfully completed tertiary studies (e.g., university, higher technical institution, etc.)
Participation in early childhood education	P_ErChildEd	the share of children between the age of three and the starting age of compulsory primary education who participated in early childhood education and care
Share of individuals having at least basic digital skills	Share_BDS	the share of people aged 16 to 74 having at least basic digital skills
Low-achieving 15-year-olds in reading	L15_R	the share of 15-year-old students failing to reach level 2 ('basic skills level') on the PISA scale in reading
Low-achieving 15-year-olds in mathematics	L15_M	the share of 15-year-old students failing to reach level 2 ('basic skills level') on the PISA scale in mathematics
Low-achieving 15-year-olds in science	L15_S	the share of 15-year-old students failing to reach level 2 ('basic skills level') on the PISA scale in science

Source: Authors' presentation

However, when the list of selected variables is analyzed, it can be observed that for certain variables, better performance is achieved if their value is lower, that is, in the context of the Benefit of the Doubt model, they represent undesirable outputs (Table 2). Since the Benefit of the Doubt model implies output maximization, it is necessary to transform undesirable outputs into desirable outputs.

Table 2. Desirable and undesirable output variables

Desirable output variables	Adult participation in learning
	Tertiary educational attainment
	Participation in early childhood education
	Share of individuals having at least basic digital skills
Undesirable output variables	Early leavers from education and training
	Low-achieving 15-year-olds in reading
	Low-achieving 15-year-olds in mathematics
	Low-achieving 15-year-olds in science

Source: Authors' presentation

The treatment of undesirable outputs ultimately affects the achieved efficiency of DMUs, so it is necessary to choose the appropriate approach. Four main types of undesirable output treatment within the DEA model have been identified (Halkos & Petrou, 2018; Halkos & Petrou, 2019a, Stanković et al., 2021): (*i*) to omit undesirable outputs; (*ii*) to treat undesirable outputs as inputs; (*iii*) to apply nonlinear models; (*iv*) to apply necessary transformations. When it comes to transformations of undesirable outputs, there are several approaches. Koopmans (1951) proposed the transformation using the relation $(U) = -U$. The second type of proposed transformation is $(U) = -U + \beta$. The third type of transformation proposed in the literature is the application of an inverse function $f(U) = \frac{1}{U}$. As a way of treating undesirable outputs, the authors opted for transformation, where the inverse function will be applied.

RESULTS AND DISCUSSION

In the first step, the assessment of the efficiency of the European educational systems is performed using the Benefit of the Doubt approach on the model with treated undesirable outputs (Figure 1). The results of the analysis indicate that more than 40% of the countries in the sample achieved efficiency in their educational systems. The relatively high efficiency of education systems can be justified by the fact that there are various ways to achieve efficiency (Agasisti et al., 2019).

Figure 1. The efficiency of European educational systems
Source: Authors' presentation

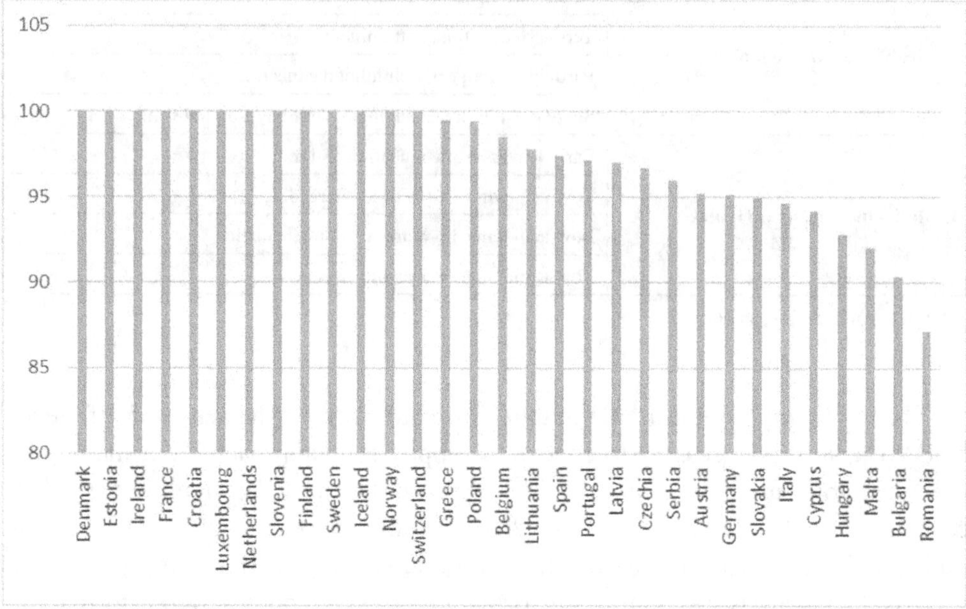

Hence, the results of the Benefit of the Doubt approach indicate that DMUs are efficient if the achieved efficiency is 100%. However, as it often happens that there are several DMUs with maximum efficiency, in that case, in order to obtain the ranks of the DMUs, it is possible to carry out a super-efficiency analysis (Eren et al., 2017). The geographical representation of the super-efficiency results is presented in Figure 2. It can be observed that the highest efficiency of educational systems is achieved by Nordic and Western Europe countries, where at the top of the list is Sweden followed by Ireland and Finland. At the very bottom of the list are Malta, Bulgaria, and Romania, with Romania being the country with the least efficient educational system.

Figure 2. Super efficiency of European educational systems
Source: Authors' presentation

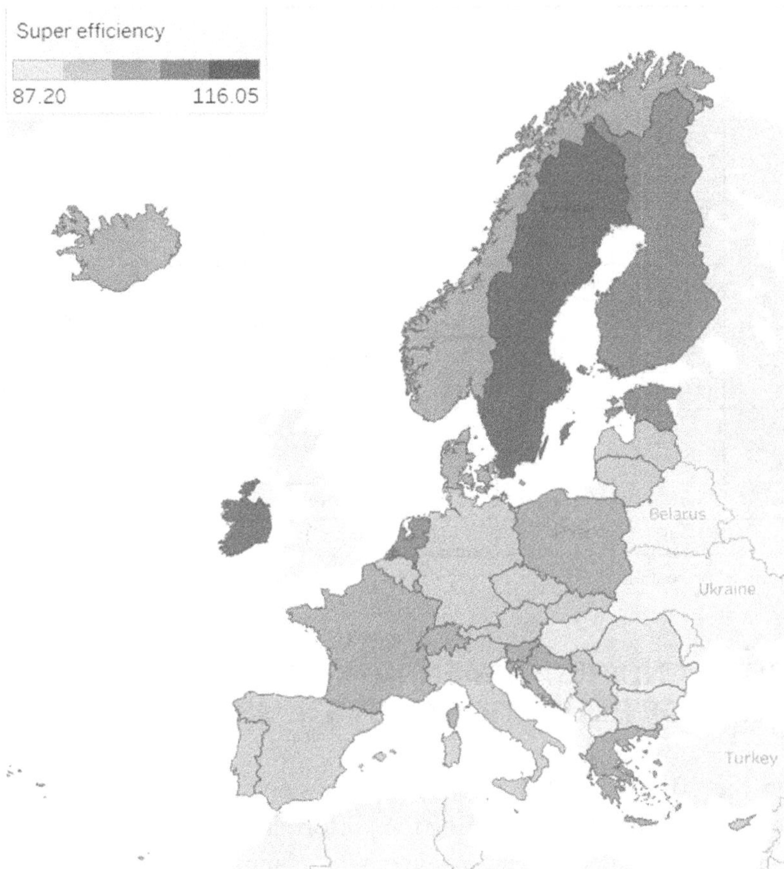

In order to check the robustness of the results, an analysis of the sensitivity of the model to changes in variables was performed. For that purpose, seven additional models were created (Table 3), and the consistency of the results was assessed using correlation analysis (Cylus et al., 2017). The results of the correlation analysis indicate the existence of a significant positive correlation when the results of the original model are compared to each of the additional models. Furthermore, Sweden remained efficient in all models except Model 2, signifying that the educational efficiency of Sweden depends mostly on adult participation in learning. The greatest difference in results is observed compared to Model 1, which could indicate the heterogeneity of European countries in terms of participation of early leavers from education and training. The results of the sensitivity analysis prove the consistency of the efficiency scores relating to changes in output variables due to the fact that similar groups of countries form the efficiency frontiers in all model specifications (Stanković et al., 2021).

Table 3. Results of correlation analysis

	Model 1	Model 2	Model 3	Model 4	Model 5	Model 6	Model 7
Output variables	Adult_PartL	ELeave_E&T	ELeave_E&T	ELeave_E&T	ELeave_E&T	ELeave_E&T	ELeave_E&T
	TEA	TEA	Adult_PartL	Adult_PartL	Adult_PartL	Adult_PartL	Adult_PartL
	P_ErChildEd	P_ErChildEd	P_ErChildEd	TEA	TEA	TEA	TEA
	Share_BDS	Share_BDS	Share_BDS	Share_BDS	P_ErChildEd	P_ErChildEd	P_ErChildEd
	L15_R	L15_R	L15_R	L15_R	Share_BDS	Share_BDS	Share_BDS
	L15_M	L15_M	L15_M	L15_M	L15_M	L15_R	L15_R
	L15_S	L15_S	L15_S	L15_S	L15_S	L15_S	L15_M
Spearman's rho correlation coefficient	.781	.961	.918	1.000	1.000	.988	.997
Sig. (2-tailed)	.000	.000	.000	.000	.000	.000	.000
N	31	31	31	31	31	31	31

Source: Authors' presentation

SOLUTIONS AND RECOMMENDATIONS FOR THE EFFICIENCY OF EDUCATIONAL SYSTEMS' ENHANCEMENT

Improving the efficiency of the educational system as a part of public service should be not only aimed at improving the performance of the educational system but also at improving assessment, management, planning (based on realistic data, long-term, flexible), and research in the educational system which, as a result, has greater efficiency in the use of educational resources (Windham, 1990). As seen in the previous part of the chapter, the output indicators of efficiency and, at the same time, indicators of the accomplishment of the SDG4 target are the level of 40% for the selected European countries. This further implies that the other 60% of analyzed countries must follow the example of the education efficiency leaders. Therefore, the level of analysis should be transferred to the input indicators of the educational systems with lower efficiency. For example, in Spain, which is in the declining part of Figure 1, the efficiency analysis that included input factors has shown that budget restrictions can be reflected in the increase of primary schools' efficiency (López-Torres & Prior 2020). On the other hand, educational systems' budget allocation is also an important issue. The allocation of that budget using the level of efficiency and aim to achieve equality in schools' results as a criterion for allocation could produce two effects. Inefficient schools could see resources allocated in this way as a decrease in a budget and not as a possibility to increase efficiency in order to get larger amounts for financing (Johnes et al., 2017). Lastly, some researches indicate that a combination of management, environmental and financial resources could be the indicators of the efficiency of educational systems. Specifically, educational and human resources management practices could be the driver of efficient education (Thieme et al., 2012).

FUTURE RESEARCH DIRECTIONS

Regarding efficiency in the educational context, it could be enhanced in a threefold manner. Firstly, it is necessary to endorse new indicators in the efficiency assessment procedure to obtain general results and to broaden the researched economies in order to increase the comparability of assessment outputs. Secondly, even though students' results when it comes to literacy or gender imbalance in the educational surroundings are indicative of the calculations of sustainability of an educational system through their efficiency, there is a necessity for overviewing educators' characteristics in the new era of education for sustainable development. Therefore, one of the priorities of ESD for 2030 is to upskill educators as promoters of sustainable development among students of all ages and consequently include the results of their competencies to transfer knowledge to the learners (Rieckmann & Barth, 2020). Thirdly, the research could be broadened by employing Tobit regression analysis aimed at investigating the main determinants of educational systems' efficiency.

CONCLUSION

Although forced, an underprivileged population that is living on the verge of poverty has, at the same time, the most sustainable mode of life because it tries to use up the majority of resources or recycle all commodities as much as possible. On the other hand, sustainability has become a lifestyle symbol of wealth for the population with above-the-average income that perceives ecology, fairness, and equality as representative means for a clear conscience. But, in order to be one step closer to sustainability and development based on it, the education systems are the ones that could broaden the horizons of its users.

In accordance with SDGs, societies must perceive education as a crucial tool for empowering students to be contributing members of the society that fosters sustainability and lives in accordance with the United Nations' SDGs. On the other hand, every SDG and its targeted values for 2030 depend on the level of reached education efficiency of the country's education system. In order to be efficient, policymakers, in synergy with all other interested parties, must enhance education systems' capacities and diminish existing disparities in the educational sphere. Such a process requires, firstly, the assessment of the current situation encountered in educational systems. Therefore, the chapter's aim was derived from the fact that there is no available research on how efficient economies are in the management of education systems.

Furthermore, in this chapter, the authors have applied the Benefit of the Doubt approach to conducting a comparative analysis of the efficiency of 31 educational systems in European countries. The starting point of the analysis was the database created using the secondary data of the SDG database for specific SDG4: Quality of education. According to the used indices of efficiency, 40% of observed societies have satisfactory efficiency of the educational system. Furthermore, the super-efficiency Benefit of the Doubt approach has shown the array of countries when it comes to the efficiency of educational systems. The range of countries is the following: Sweden, Ireland, and Finland are the first three countries, respectively, while the last three countries are Malta, Bulgaria, and Romania. Obtained results indicate that the results on the labor market, the well-being of the society, and the possibilities and limitations of the transition to the knowledge economy will depend on the efficiency of this public service.

ACKNOWLEDGMENT

This chapter is part of a project that has received funding from the European Union's Horizon Europe research and innovation program under grant agreement No 101059994.

REFERENCES

Agasisti, T., Munda, G., & Hippe, R. (2019). Measuring the efficiency of European education systems by combining Data Envelopment Analysis and Multiple-Criteria Evaluation. *Journal of Productivity Analysis*, *51*(2), 105–124. doi:10.100711123-019-00549-6

Aristovnik, A., & Obadic, A. (2011). *The funding and efficiency of higher education in Croatia and Slovenia: a non-parametric comparison with EU and OECD countries*. The William Davidson Institute: University of Michigan.

Bonaccorsi, A., Daraio, C., & Lepori, B. (2007). Indicators for the analysis of higher education systems: some methodological reflections. In A. Bonaccorsi & C. Daraio (Eds.), *Universities and Strategic Knowledge Creation* (pp. 405–432). doi:10.4337/9781847206848.00021

Casalprim, M., Rialp, J., Prior, D., & Sabrià, B. (2013). An assessment of schools' efficiency of different educational systems. *Mediterranean Journal of Social Sciences*, *4*(11), 631–631. doi:10.5901/mjss.2013.v4n11p631

Contreras, I. (2020). A review of the literature on DEA models under common set of weights. *Journal of Modelling in Management*, *15*(4), 1277–1300. doi:10.1108/JM2-02-2019-0043

Cornali, F. (2012). Effectiveness and efficiency of educational measures: Evaluation practices, indicators and rhetoric. *Sociology Mind*, *2*(03), 255–260. doi:10.4236m.2012.23034

Cylus, J., Papanicolas, I., & Smith, P. C. (2017). Using data envelopment analysis to address the challenges of comparing health system efficiency. *Global Policy*, *8*, 60–68. doi:10.1111/1758-5899.12212

Didham, R. J., & Ofei-Manu, P. (2020). Adaptive capacity as an educational goal to advance policy for integrating DRR into quality education for sustainable development. *International Journal of Disaster Risk Reduction*, *47*, 101631. doi:10.1016/j.ijdrr.2020.101631

Dincă, M. S., Dincă, G., Andronic, M. L., & Pasztori, A. M. (2021). Assessment of the European Union's Educational Efficiency. *Sustainability*, *13*(6), 3116. doi:10.3390u13063116

Embarak, O. (2021). A new paradigm through machine learning: A learning maximization approach for sustainable education. *Procedia Computer Science*, *191*, 445–450. doi:10.1016/j.procs.2021.07.055

Eren, M., Eren, M., & Başar, S. (2017). Measuring of human development through the output-oriented super efficiency vs. DEA model without inputs. *Serbian Journal of Management*, *12*(2), 255–270. doi:10.5937jm12-11184

Eurostat. (2022). *SDG4 – Quality education*. Retrieved from: https://ec.europa.eu/eurostat/statistics-explained/index.php ?title=SDG_4_-_Quality_education

Giambona, F., Vassallo, E., & Vassiliadis, E. (2011). Educational systems efficiency in European Union countries. *Studies in Educational Evaluation*, *37*(2-3), 108–122. doi:10.1016/j.stueduc.2011.05.001

Halkos, G., & Petrou, K. N. (2018). *A critical review of the main methods to treat undesirable outputs in DEA*. Retrieved from https://mpra.ub.uni-muenchen.de/id/eprint/90374

Halkos, G., & Petrou, K. N. (2019). Treating undesirable outputs in DEA: A critical review. *Economic Analysis and Policy*, *62*, 97–104. doi:10.1016/j.eap.2019.01.005

Haruna, M. J., & Nafisa, A. (2021). The Challenges of Girl Child Education in Sokoto State, Nigeria and Its Implications for National Development. In J. N. Mojekwu, W. Thwala, C. Aigbavboa, L. Atepor, & S. Sackey (Eds.), Sustainable Education and Development (pp. 32-42). Springer Nature. doi:10.1007/978-3-030-68836-3_4

Hermans, E., Van den Bossche, F., & Wets, G. (2008). Combining road safety information in a performance index. *Accident; Analysis and Prevention*, *40*(4), 1337–1344. doi:10.1016/j.aap.2008.02.004 PMID:18606264

Hossain, M. K., Kamil, A. A., Baten, M. A., & Mustafa, A. (2012). Stochastic Frontier Approach and Data Envelopment Analysis to Total Factor Productivity and Efficiency Measurement of Bangladeshi Rice. *PLoS One*, *7*(10), e46081. doi:10.1371/journal.pone.0046081 PMID:23077500

Johnes, J., Portela, M., & Thanassoulis, E. (2017). Efficiency in education. *The Journal of the Operational Research Society*, *68*(4), 331–338. doi:10.105741274-016-0109-z

Kolb, M., Fr¨ohlich, L., & Schmidpeter, R. (2017). Implementing sustainability as the new normal: Responsible management education – from a private business school's perspective. *International Journal of Management Education*, *15*(2), 280–292. doi:10.1016/j.ijme.2017.03.009

Koopmans, T. C. (1951). *An analysis of production as an efficient combination of activities. Activity analysis of production and allocation*. Cowles Commission, Wiley.

Kosor, M. M. (2013). Efficiency measurement in higher education: Concepts, methods and perspective. *Procedia: Social and Behavioral Sciences*, *106*, 1031–1038. doi:10.1016/j.sbspro.2013.12.117

Lockheed, M. E., & Hanushek, E. A. (1994). *Concepts of educational efficiency and effectiveness*. World Bank.

López-Torres, L., & Prior, D. (2020). Long-term efficiency of public service provision in a context of budget restrictions. An application to the education sector. *Socio-Economic Planning Sciences, 81*, 100946. doi:10.1016/j.seps.2020.100946

Mauerhofer, V. (2023). Gender within sustainable decisions: A 3-D sustainability perspective. In A. Skjerven & M. Fordham (Eds.), *Gender and the Sustainable Development Goals* (pp. 28–45). Routledge., doi:10.4324/9781003174257-4

Melyn, W., & Moesen, W. (1991). Towards a synthetic indicator of macroeconomic performance: Unequal weighting when limited information is available. *Public economics research papers*, 1-24.

Murias, P., de Miguel, J. C., & Rodríguez, D. (2008). A composite indicator for university quality assessment: The case of Spanish higher education system. *Social Indicators Research, 89*(1), 129–146. doi:10.100711205-007-9226-z

Nistor, L. (2011). *Public services and the European Union: healthcare, health insurance and education services*. Springer Science & Business Media. doi:10.1007/978-90-6704-805-7

Nota, L., Soresi, S., Di Maggio, I., Santilli, S., & Ginevra, M. C. (2020). Life Designing for an Inclusive, Sustainable and Equitable Future. In *Sustainable Development, Career Counselling and Career Education* (pp. 41–62). Springer. doi:10.1007/978-3-030-60046-4_3

Paige, K., Haggerty, B., & Comber, B. (2022). Water Literacies: Co-researching, Learning, and Acting for the Wetlands. In M. Häggström & C. Schmidt (Eds.), *Relational and Critical Perspectives on Education for Sustainable Development* (p. 66). Springer. doi:10.1007/978-3-030-84510-0_4

Pandey, P. (2019). Disciplines, Professions and the Sustainable Development Goals (SDGs): Challenges in Higher Education in India. In Implementing the 2030 agenda at higher education institutions: Challenges and responses (pp. 47-53). Springer.

Reinikka, R., & Svensson, J. (2011). The power of information in public services: Evidence from education in Uganda. *Journal of Public Economics, 95*(7-8), 956–966. doi:10.1016/j.jpubeco.2011.02.006

Ren, J., Chen, C., Gao, B., & Zhang, J. (2019). Performance evaluation of pallet rental companies: A non-oriented super-efficiency integer-valued DEA model. *IEEE Access: Practical Innovations, Open Solutions, 7*, 151628–151637. doi:10.1109/ACCESS.2019.2948123

Richardson, C. W. (2019). Obstacles to the implementation of the SDGs: Feelings over facts. In Implementing the 2030 agenda at higher education institutions: Challenges and responses (pp. 54-65). Global University Network for Innovation.

Rieckmann, M., & Barth, M. (2022). Educators' Competence Frameworks in Education for Sustainable Development. In P. Vare, N. Lausselet, & M. Rieckmann (Eds.), *Competences in Education for Sustainable Development* (pp. 27–34). Springer. doi:10.1007/978-3-030-91055-6_3

Stanković, J. J., Marjanović, I., & Stojković, N. (2021). DEA Assessment of Socio-economic Development of European Countries. *Management: Journal of Sustainable Business and Management Solutions in Emerging Economies*, *26*(1), 13–24.

Thieme, C., Giménez, V., & Prior, D. (2012). A comparative analysis of the efficiency of national education systems. *Asia Pacific Education Review*, *13*(1), 1–15. doi:10.100712564-011-9177-6

UNESCO. (2020). *Education for Sustainable Development: A roadmap*. United Nations Educational, Scientific and Cultural Organization.

United Nations. (2022). *Goal 4: Education*. Retrieved from: https://www.un.org/sustainabledevelopment/education/

Vare, P., Rieckmann, M., & Lausselet, N. (2022). Introduction. In P. Vare, N. Lausselet, & M. Rieckmann (Eds.), *Competences in Education for Sustainable Development* (pp. 3–10). Springer. doi:10.1007/978-3-030-91055-6_1

Wiek, A., & Redman, A. (2022). What Do Key Competencies in Sustainability Offer, and How to Use Them. In P. Vare, N. Lausselet, & M. Rieckmann (Eds.), *Competences in Education for Sustainable Development* (pp. 27–34). Springer. doi:10.1007/978-3-030-91055-6_4

Windham, D. (1990). Improving the efficiency of educational systems. In *Stratégie du développement des ressources humaines: communications découlant du séminaire-atelier tenu à Yaoundé, Cameroun, 2-5 fév. 1988*. CRDI. Retrieved from: https://idl-bnc-idrc.dspacedirect.org/bitstream/handle/10625/18253/IDL-18253.pdf?sequence=1

Witte, K. D., & López-Torres, L. (2017). Efficiency in education: A review of literature and a way forward. *The Journal of the Operational Research Society*, *68*(4), 339–363. doi:10.1057/jors.2015.92

Worthington, A. C. (2001). An empirical survey of frontier efficiency measurement techniques in education. *Education Economics*, *9*(3), 245–268. doi:10.1080/09645290110086126

Yang, F. C., Kao, R. H., Chen, Y. T., Ho, Y. F., Cho, C. C., & Huang, S. W. (2018). A common weight approach to construct composite indicators: The evaluation of fourteen emerging markets. *Social Indicators Research*, *137*(2), 463–479. doi:10.100711205-017-1603-7

Žalėnienė, I., & Pereira, P. (2021). Higher education for sustainability: A global perspective. *Geography and Sustainability*, *2*(2), 99–106. doi:10.1016/j.geosus.2021.05.001

ADDITIONAL READING

Cankaya, S., Kutlu, Ö., & Cebeci, E. (2015). The Educational Policy of European Union. *Procedia: Social and Behavioral Sciences*, *174*, 886–893. doi:10.1016/j.sbspro.2015.01.706

Kragten, N., Burgoon, B., & van de Werfhorst, H. (2022). *The Politics of Equity and Efficiency in Educational Reforms in Europe*. Retrieved from: http://www.harryganzeboom.nl/isol/ISOL2016d2%20-%20Kragten%20et%20al%20%20The%20Politics%20of%20Equity%20and%20Efficiency%20in%20Educational%20Reforms%20summary.pdf

Krstić, B., Petrović, J., & Stanišić, T. (2015). Influence of education system quality on the use of ICT in transition countries in the age of information society. *TEME: Časopis za društvene nauke, 39*(3), 747-763.

Krstić, B., & Rađenović, T. (2020). Performance Evaluation System as a Base for Designing the Intellectual Capital Report: The Case of Serbian Public Universities. In V. Babić & Z. Nedelko (Eds.), *Handbook of Research on Enhancing Innovation in Higher Education Institutions* (pp. 261–286). IGI Global. doi:10.4018/978-1-7998-2708-5.ch012

Krstić, B., Stanojević, J., & Stanišić, T. (2015). Education as one of the Core Indicators of Sustainable Development – A Comparative Analysis of the Western Balkans. In *Proceedings IBCM International Conference – The Role of Business in Sustainable Development in the Western Balkans* (pp. 45-52). International Business College Mitrovica.

Krstić, B., & Veselinović, I. (2015). Quality of educational system as a factor of competitiveness of national economy. In K. Bojan & Z. Paszek (Eds.), *Competitiveness of enterprises and national economies* (pp. 115–130). Faculty of Economics: University of Nis.

Krstić, M., & Krstić, B. (2017). Higher education as a factor of competitiveness of Serbian national economy. In B. Krstić (Ed.), *Improving the competitiveness of enterprises and national economies* (pp. 1–28). Faculty of Economics: University of Nis.

Rađenović, T., & Krstić, B. (2018). The Development of Performance Evaluation System of the Higher Education Institutions in the Republic of Serbia with the Aim of Competitiveness Improvement. In B. Krstic (Ed.), *Crucial Aspects of Improving National Competitiveness* (pp. 1–25). Faculty of Economics: University of Nis.

Radukić, S., Petrović-Ranđelović, M., & Kostić, Z. (2019). Sustainability-based goals and achieved results in Western Balkan countries. *Economics of Sustainable Development*, *3*(1), 9–18. doi:10.5937/ESD1901009R

KEY TERMS AND DEFINITIONS

Assessment: Assessment is a systematic process of application of methods and tools for drawing conclusions and recommendations from its output.

Education: Education is a process devoted to giving instruction to children and adults in order to obtain general knowledge.

Education for Sustainability and Development: Education for Sustainable Development (ESD) is aimed at the educational process devoted to building sustainability competencies in students and thus preparing them for future sustainable implementation in practice.

Efficiency: Efficiency, which is doing things with as less resources as possible, is mostly compared with efficacy as an ability to produce the expected result.

Literacy: Literacy is the ability to read, calculate or apply these skills whenever there is a need in the life of an individual.

National Development: National development is a sum of steps through which one nation plans to overcome obstacles and reach the target level of development from which its inhabitants will benefit the most.

Quality of Education: Quality of Education is education free of discrimination and biases for both children and adults during their lifetime.

Chapter 8
On the Effectiveness of Local Financial Management:
Analysis of Municipal Companies in Southwest Bulgaria With the Z-Score Model

Desislava Stoilova
https://orcid.org/0000-0001-6034-4225
Southwest University "Neofit Rilski", Bulgaria

ABSTRACT

Local governments in Bulgaria have stable property rights regulated by the Constitution (1991) and the Municipal Property Act (1996). Municipalities own and use different types of assets to provide public services to local communities, but the effectiveness of local financial management is a controversial and topical issue. This chapter aims to analyze the financial performance of 18 large municipal companies for the period 2006-2020 by applying the Z-Score model. The results show that most municipal companies achieve profitability while providing a wide range of public services, such as water supply and sanitation, garbage collection, maintenance of urban infrastructure, management of municipal markets, construction supervision, investor and technical control, property management, geodetic services, and security services. At the same time, the municipal companies that provide district heating and urban transport and operate the municipal sports complexes are in poor financial condition and need appropriate measures to improve their financial performance.

DOI: 10.4018/978-1-6684-7730-4.ch008

INTRODUCTION

Local governments in Bulgaria have stable property rights regulated by the Constitution (1991), the Local Self-Government and Local Administration Act (1991), and the Municipal Property Act (1996). This legal base stimulates the process of building portfolios of municipal assets, as municipal ownership of various types of property is seen as one of the guarantees of administrative independence and financial autonomy of local governments. In the late 1990s, the central government transferred significant amounts of assets to Bulgarian municipalities in an effort to support the country's financial decentralization. Unfortunately, this process was accompanied by corruption scandals and overall financial mismanagement, revealed in a number of reports by the Center for the Study of Democracy (2006, 2012, and 2017), the Center for Economic Development (2003), and Transparency International Bulgaria (2015).

Two decades later, local authorities have different types of assets used to provide public services, but the effectiveness of local financial management is still a controversial and topical issue. The ongoing process of financial decentralization forces local governments to increase revenues from their sources due to the gradual reduction of subsidies from the central government. Given that raising local taxes and charges is an extremely unpopular decision, the efficient management of municipal property through enterprises emerges as a politically acceptable and easily accessible source of additional own revenues.

Bearing in mind all these assumptions, the main objective of this chapter is to analyze the financial performance of 18 companies owned by the largest municipality in Bulgaria for the period 2006-2020 by applying the Z-Score model. The hypothesis of the study is that most municipal companies can achieve profitability and efficiency while providing a wide range of public services to local communities.

BACKGROUND

Commercial companies are considered the backbone of the economy. Alongside private enterprises, there are some enterprises owned by local authorities that are set up to provide various public services and generate income for local communities. Although economic activities are seen as the domain of the private sector, municipal enterprises are expected to engage in three types of activities, as follows: (1) activities that are beneficial to society but not profitable for private companies, (2) activities that are profitable but private companies fail to perform them, and (3) activities related to the so-called natural monopoly. In theory, the main purposes of municipal enterprises should be to provide essential public services, improve social welfare and promote the development of the local economy, but in practice, municipal enterprises can also strive for economic efficiency by delivering goods and services on a cost-effective basis, thereby generating significant revenue for local budgets. Furthermore, after the liberalization of markets for public service provision, the pressure on local public enterprises to demonstrate their performance in financial and nonfinancial terms has increased. To some extent, expectations and demands on public enterprises are even higher because of their public ownership and mission to protect the public interest (Greiling & Grub, 2015).

A number of authors describe the process of the so-called corporatization of local authorities in Italy, Germany and England (Grossi & Reichard, 2008; Ferry, Andrews, Skelcher & Wegorowski, 2018). The corporatization of local governments, meaning the establishment of municipal companies, is presented as a basis for improving the management and efficiency of local service provision. Tavares & Camões (2007) report a significant increase in municipal enterprises providing public services in Portugal and argue that services involving the collection of user fees are more likely to be transferred to municipal companies. In fact, municipal companies in EU member states operate in a wide variety of sectors. The most common sectors of local corporative activities are social housing, solid waste disposal, urban transport, and supply of power and gas, water and sewage. At the same time, municipal companies also operate in the fields of social services, healthcare, city marketing, economic promotion, and cultural and recreational services, such as museums, operas, theatres, etc. (Dexia Crediop, 2004).

Although local governments in developed countries are increasingly using municipal companies to provide basic public services, research on their role and efficiency is rather scarce. Moreover, there are authors who believe that it is not possible to analyze the performance of municipal corporations with the standard financial ratios measuring liquidity, solvency, efficiency and profitability insofar as the reasons for setting up municipal enterprises are quite different from those of commercial companies (Agh, Vavrek, Dvorak & Papcunova, 2021).

A review of the existing literature reveals both negative and positive perceptions of municipal companies. The positive views highlight the multiple benefits that municipal enterprises provide to the local economy. A study by Geller (2019) outlines the potential positive impacts of municipal companies, emphasizing that these public entities enable local governments to deliver affordable and qualitative goods and services while creating additional jobs and increasing incomes for local residents. In addition, municipal enterprises can support the stability of the local economy by reducing its dependence on private corporations that tend to relocate their business in search of lower costs and maximum profits. Also, municipal companies demonstrate significant potential to provide vital services to local communities, which may be neglected by private providers, thereby enabling the pursuit of social, economic and environmental objectives beyond profit maximization (CLES, 2021). A study by Hanna (2013) describes the negative consequences of the dependence of the United States on large private corporations and argues that public ownership can be a viable alternative, ensuring equitable distribution of resources and local control over economic decisions. Several authors provide evidence that public enterprises can be successful in competing with the private sector (Tan, 1992) and can play an important role in promoting economic development, supporting industrialization and facilitating balanced regional development (Aktan, 1996).

There are authors who have found a relation between the financial performance of local governments and the number of municipal companies. For example, Rubin (1988) explored why some cities in Illinois (USA) have municipal enterprises to deal with garbage collection, parking, and economic development and concluded that cities with fiscal difficulties avoid registering enterprises, while more reformed cities often use enterprises to provide various public services. Tavares & Camões (2010) identified size, financial independence and fiscal surplus as some of the main factors that influence the choice of local governments to use municipal corporations for service delivery. Paul (1999) studied the effect of municipal enterprises on the budgets of local governments across the state of Florida (USA) and concluded that they are often used to supplement insufficient revenues and lessen the effects of fiscal strain.

Voorn, Van Genugten & Van Thiel (2017) reviewed a number of studies on the performance and efficiency of municipally-owned corporations. They concluded that municipal corporations could provide some public goods and services for local communities. Moreover, they found that very often municipal companies are more effective than local bureaucracies in the delivery of some utilities, such as water supply, garbage collection, and transport. This is confirmed by Benito, Bastida & García (2010), who examined the effectiveness of the municipal sector in one of the Spanish regions (Murcia). They found that in the scope of water supply and garbage collection, public management through companies controlled by the local government is more efficient than private management. Also, Romano & Guerrini (2011) performed an analysis of Italian water utilities by reviewing the financial statements of 43 companies and concluded that public enterprises are more efficient compared to mixed companies. Furthermore, Molinos-Senante & Maziotis (2021) assessed the cost efficiency of several Chilean public and private water companies. Their results show that the water industry as a whole demonstrates a high level of cost efficiency and public water utilities perform better than their private counterparts. Cuadrado-Ballesteros, García-Sánchez & Prado-Lorenzo (2012) explored how different modes for provision of local public services affect the quality of life in Spain and found that the quality of life is higher in municipalities where city transport and health services are provided by public enterprises.

At the same time, some authors believe that public ownership is bureaucratic and inherently inefficient, so municipal companies operate with inferior efficiency. For example, Sorensen (2007) combined the principles of political economy and corporate governance and argued that elected politicians can support ineffective solutions to improve their chances of re-election. In this respect, jointly owned companies are expected to perform better than those owned by a single local authority, as local politicians would have less influence. At the same time, he found that in the case of garbage collection in Norway, the cost of dispersed ownership often exceeds the benefits of economy of scale, so the use of jointly owned companies is not always an appropriate response to the inherent efficiency problems typical of a fragmented structure of local government.

Da Cruz & Marques (2011) studied the viability of Portuguese municipal enterprises in providing urban infrastructure services. They concluded that, in theory, the concept of a municipal company is based on high principles and shows advantages over the other means of service provision, but in practice, the expected benefits had not been achieved in Portugal, mainly due to the lack of technical competence and the political patronage of the municipal companies.

Some authors point out that municipal enterprises may indirectly increase the indebtedness of local governments. For example, Junkernheinrich and Micosatt (2007) discussed that 42.3% of local government's debt in Germany at the end of 2005 was related to their companies and was hidden in the various financial statements of those companies. This point of view is shared by Ferry et al. (2018), who found that the process of municipal corporatization in England increased by 50% for the period 2010-2016, especially in the areas of planning and social services. At the same time, they point out that when municipal companies have huge deficits, local authorities face the reputational and financial consequences of service failures.

Grossi & Reichard (2008) study municipal corporatization in Italy and Germany and outline several positive effects, such as closer ties to customers, increased efficiency, extended flexibility and managerial freedom. At the same time, they point out that when local governments transfer the responsibility for the production of public goods and services to municipal corporations, they face a progressive loss of participation and control of the local service provision. In addition, corporatization often leads to significant fragmentation of the local public sector, where different units generate strong centrifugal forces, making it difficult for the political core to control and manage the diverging and conflicting interests of its multiple units. They conclude that the evidence from Germany and Italy demonstrates a conflicting development. Municipal companies are becoming more market-oriented, so that profitability goals are becoming dominant, while reducing the focus on public interests. At the same time, a more commercially oriented utility sector is considered to be politically questionable.

ANALYSIS OF THE FINANCIAL MANAGEMENT OF MUNICIPAL COMPANIES IN SOUTHWEST BULGARIA

Methodology and Data

The Z-Score model is designed to assess the financial stability of different types of companies. Developed and proposed by Edward Altman in 1968, the model is intended to predict the chances of a company going bankrupt in the next years (Altman, 1968). Altman used the methodology of multiple discriminant analysis (MDA) to identify the financial ratios that are most important for detecting the potential for bankruptcy and to specify the different weights attached to the selected coefficients.

The most popular is the original specification of the Z-Score model, which combines five financial ratios as follows *(Formula 1)*:

$$Z = 1.2(X1) + 1.4(X2) + 3.3(X3) + 0.6(X4) + 1.0(X5) \quad (1)$$

where:

Z is the overall Z-score.

X1 is equal to the company's working capital divided by its total assets (WC/TA). The working capital is calculated as the difference between current assets and current liabilities. Therefore, the WC/TA ratio is aimed at assessing the net liquid assets of the company in relation to its total capitalization.

X2 is calculated by dividing a company's retained earnings by its total assets (RE/TA). This ratio aims to estimate the cumulative profitability of the enterprise over time, as well as the leverage of the company. It is expected that companies with higher retained earnings, measured as a percentage of total assets, have paid for their investments through their profits instead of accumulating significant debt.

X3 is equal to the company's earnings before interest and taxes (EBIT) divided by its total assets (EBIT/TA). The purpose of this ratio is to assess the real productivity of the company's assets, i.e., its earning power, independent of any external factors, such as tax rates or interest rates.

X4 is calculated by dividing the market value of a company's equity by the book value of its total liabilities (Eq/TL). This ratio aims to add a notion of market value to the assessment of the company. Also, this ratio shows how easily the company may become insolvent if its liabilities exceed its equity.

X5 is the popular asset turnover ratio calculated by dividing a company's annual sales by its total assets (Sales/TA). This is a standard financial ratio that shows the ability of a company's assets to generate sales.

It is obvious that the original specification of the Z-Score model is based on two data sources that make it inappropriate to use for all types of companies: first, it requires the company to have equity that is publicly traded (as far as X4 requires data for the stock prices) and second, it is mainly applicable for manufacturers (Altman, 2005). Although the most logical modification is to substitute the book value of equity for the market value when calculating X4, Altman (2013) revised the Z-Score model and proposed its adaptation – Z'-Score, which is applicable to companies that are not traded on the stock exchange *(Formula 2)*.

$$Z' = 0.717(X1) + 0.847\ (X2) + 3.107\ (X3) + 0.420(X4) + 0.998(X5)\ \textit{(2)}$$

The adapted Z'-Score model seems quite similar to the original specification, but some of the coefficients have decreased (i.e., the coefficients for X1, X2 and X4), thus diminishing the importance of the respective variables for the overall score.

With more than three decades of experience in testing and using the scoring models for a variety of purposes, Altman (2005, 2013) further improved the original model to make it applicable to non-manufacturers *(Formula 3)* and emerging markets *(Formula 4)*.

$$Z''(\text{Non-Manufacturers}) = 6.56\ (X1) + 3.26\ (X2) + 6.72\ (X3) + 1.05\ (X4)\ \textit{(3)}$$

$$Z''\ (\text{EMS}) = 6.56\ (X1) + 3.26\ (X2) + 6.72\ (X3) + 1.05\ (X4) + 3.25\ \textit{(4)}$$

In the Z"-Score model applicable to non-manufacturers, the asset turnover ratio (X5 = Sales/TA), which was proved to be industry sensitive, was removed from the model, and the coefficients for the other ratios were changed. The Z"-Score model was tested on different samples of both non-manufacturers and manufacturers, demonstrating high accuracy and reliability similar to the previous models (Z-score and Z'-Score). A constant of 3.25 was added to the final Emerging Market Scoring model (EMS) in order to standardize the scores so that a default equivalent rating (D) is consistent with a score below zero. The Z" (EMS) model was also tested and is applicable to both manufacturers and non-manufacturers. Moreover, it is relevant for private and public companies (Altman, 2005, 2013).

Table 1. Z"-scores and equivalent ratings

Z"-Score	Ratings	Zones
> 8.15	AAA	Safe zone
7.60 – 8.15	AA+	
7.30 – 7.60	AA	
7.00 – 7.30	AA-	
6.85 – 7.00	A+	
6.65 – 6.85	A	
6.40 – 6.65	A-	
6.25 – 6.40	BBB+	
5.85 – 6.25	BBB	
5.65 – 5.85	BBB-	Grey zone
5.25 – 5.65	BB+	
4.95 – 5.25	BB	
4.75 – 4.95	BB-	
4.50 – 4.75	B+	
4.15 – 4.50	B	
3.75 – 4.15	B-	Distress zone
3.20 – 3.75	CCC+	
2.50 – 3.20	CCC	
1.75 – 2.50	CCC-	
< 1.75	D	

Sources: Altman, E. (2005, 2013)

Table 1 presents the various Z"-scores and equivalent ratings. The interpretation of the scores follows a simple rule, namely, the higher the score, the better the financial performance of the company. The safe zone (Z" > 5.85) indicates that the company is financially stable and has a very small chance of facing financial difficulties. If the company falls in the grey zone (5.85 > Z" > 4.15,) there is a moderate chance that it will face financial difficulties in the near future. Distress zone (Z" < 4.15) means that the company is in a vulnerable position, so there is a high possibility for the company to face financial difficulties and even bankruptcy in the near future.

A number of studies prove that Altman's Z-score models are accurate and useful tools for predicting the financial difficulties of companies in different countries, business sectors and time periods. For example, Hayes, Hodge & Hughes (2010) calculate Z"-scores for a sample of 17 US public retail companies that filed for bankruptcy in 2007-2008 and find 94% predictive accuracy of the model. Meeampol et al. (2014) used the original Z-score model and the modified Z" (EMS) model to examine the financial distress of 31 companies listed on the Stock Exchange of Thailand in 2010-2011. The findings show that both models are effective in predicting bankruptcy. Diakomihalis (2012) investigates the accuracy of all Altman models in predicting the bankruptcy of 146 private hotels in Greece. The sample includes a wide variety of hotel categories and locations. The study was conducted in 2007, the last year before the economic crisis. The results demonstrate the high predictive power of all Z-score models, which range between 80% and 88.2%.

Duan & Shrestha (2011) test Altman's original Z-score on a data sample of 286 Japanese firms and estimate the model's accuracy to be 87.6%. Authors conclude that such tools are clearly useful in classifying healthy and failed firms. Reisz & Perlich (2007) estimate the probability of bankruptcy of 5784 US industrial corporations in the period 1988-2002. They conclude that Altman's Z and Z"-score models show about 78.0% ability to rank companies correctly, outperforming structural models in short-term bankruptcy predictions but decreasing in relevance as the forecast horizon extends.

A study by Aasen (2011) applies the original Z-score model and the revised Z"-score model to a sample of 180 manufacturing and non-manufacturing companies listed on the Oslo Stock Exchange (Norway) for the period 2004-2009 and concludes that both models prove to be accurate in correctly classifying the companies in financial distress and are relevant even during a crisis. AlAli (2018) applies the Z"-score model to study the financial stability of healthcare companies listed on the Kuwait stock exchange for the period 2013-2016 and finds that both companies faced the risk of bankruptcy. A study by Al-Manaseer & Al-Oshaibat (2018) tests the validity of the Z"-score model on a sample of 21 insurance companies listed on the Amman Stock Exchange (Jordan) over the period 2011-2016 and finds that Z"-score has a high predictive power.

A recent study by Beltrame et al. (2022) tests Altman's Z-Score models on a sample of 43 viable and 43 non-viable Italian small and medium-sized enterprises (SMEs) for the period 2015-2019. They apply Z'-score to the manufacturing SMEs and Z"-score to the rest of the firms, then compare the results with the alert system of the Italian national institute of statistics (NCCAAE). The authors find that both approaches show complementary results, as the Z-scores outperform the alert system in terms of prediction accuracy for the sample of non-viable firms, while the alert system outperforms the Z-scores in terms of prediction accuracy for the sample of viable firms. Kpodoh (2010) tests the predictive power of Altman's Z"-score model on a sample of three private companies and leaders in the mobile telecommunication sector in Ghana for the period 2005-2008. The results of the study confirm the ability of the Z"-score to predict impending business failure.

Bhuvaneskumar et al. (2022) use the Z-score methodology to evaluate the performance of 14 socially responsible companies (SRCs) listed on the Bombay Stock Exchange (India) over the period 2015-2019. Their findings show that most of the companies in the sample are stable and demonstrate consistent performance. Aloy Niresh & Pratheepan (2015) apply the original Z-score model to assess the financial position of seven trading companies in Sri Lanka for the period 2010-2014. They reveal that 71% of companies are in financial distress, while the remaining

29% operate in the grey zone. Ng, Wong & Zhang (2011) use the Z-score modelling methodology to evaluate the performance of 35 construction companies listed on the Shanghai and Shenzhen Stock Exchanges (China). They conclude that the model demonstrated consistent predictability based on three years of data. A discussion paper by Grabski (2019) argues that a close examination of the Z'-score reveals that it affects almost every aspect of firm performance in one form or another and concludes that this model should be considered more frequently in corporate management.

Based on the wide variety of studies that reveal the predictive accuracy and usefulness of Altman Z-scores, this chapter applies the Z" model (EMS) to estimate the financial performance of 18 companies owned by the largest Bulgarian municipality. The model is applicable because the companies included in the sample are non-manufacturing, the data set is from companies operating in an emerging market, and none of the companies is listed on the stock exchange.

RESULTS AND DISCUSSION

The Z"-score analysis is focused on 18 companies entirely owned by Sofia, which is the capital of Bulgaria, as well as the largest, richest and most developed municipality. Moreover, Sofia Municipality is an administrative-territorial unit, which has the status of a region. It is a legal entity with its public and private property and an autonomous budget. The legislative and executive authorities of the municipality are, respectively, the Sofia Municipal Council and the Mayor of Sofia. They are elected by the citizens for a term of 4 years.

Sofia Municipality is located in Southwest Bulgaria and covers an area of 1,311 sq. km. Sofia's inhabitants are 1.3 million, which represents 18.8% of the total country's population. At the same time, the gross domestic product (GDP) produced in Sofia represents 42.8% of the total GDP of Bulgaria (NSI, 2020). This allows Sofia Municipality to develop considerable administrative capacity and a comprehensive system of local public services, as well as to manage different types of municipal properties, including a variety of municipally-owned companies.

According to the data provided by the *Register of municipal, commercial companies with 100% municipal ownership of the capital* (Sofia Municipality, 2022), the municipality is the sole owner of the capital of 55 enterprises. They were established in accordance with the provisions of the Commercial Law (1991). Bulgarian municipalities are legally prohibited from assuming unlimited liability for any economic activity, so municipal companies are registered either as limited liability companies or as joint-stock companies. Municipal enterprises in Bulgaria are expected to cover a wide range of services. According to the legislation in force, municipal hospitals and medical centers are registered as commercial companies with

100% municipal property. This is the reason why 37 out of 55 companies owned by the Sofia Municipality are medical centers and hospitals created to provide general and specialized healthcare services to the population. As healthcare providers are not typical public utilities, these municipal companies are not included in this study. Of the remaining 18 municipal companies, 10 companies were established for the purpose of managing and maintaining various real assets that are private or public municipal property, and 8 of the municipal enterprises provide communal services such as transport, heating, water supply and sewage, refuse collection and disposal, communal laundry, etc. The data on the activity and financial results of the 18 commercial companies owned by the Sofia Municipality are extracted from their financial statements published by the Registry Agency of the Republic of Bulgaria (2022).

The Z"-scores calculated for four municipal companies that provide utility services to the local community are presented in Figure 1. Established in 1949, **"Toplofikacia Sofia" EAD** provides hot water and heating and is the oldest district heating system in Bulgaria. Moreover, in terms of the scale of production and scope of service, this joint-stock municipal company is one of the largest heating power plants on the Balkan Peninsula. Nowadays, the company has over 12,500 subscriber stations and uses natural gas to produce over 3000 MW of thermal power and over 280 MW of electricity. The company has licenses for heat production and transfer, as well as for the production and trade of electricity. At the same time, the company's financial performance is poor. During the period 2006-2017, "Toplofikacia Sofia" EAD operated in the distress zone. The calculated Z"-scores for the company vary within narrow limits (3.70<Z"<4.50) and indicate the low efficiency of the company's financial management. The two financial ratios related to the company's profitability, namely X2 (RE/TA) and X3 (EBIT/TA), are negative in most years, while the values of X1 (WC/TA) and X4 (Eq/TL) are quite low (*Table 1 in the Appendix*). Since 2018, the company's financial performance has further deteriorated, and the Z"-score dropped to 1.24 in the last year of the analyzed period.

Based on the arguments that Sofia's heating system is a kind of natural monopoly and is "too big to fail", it is regularly subsidized by the state and municipal budgets. At the same time, given the desire for cost-effective use of scarce public resources, the Sofia Municipality should make more efforts to improve the company's financial performance. The poor financial results of district heating in Sofia contradict the findings of a recent report by the International Energy Agency (2022), which argues that district heating networks offer great potential for cost-effective, efficient and flexible integration of low-carbon energy sources in the heating energy mix. Moreover, "Toplofikacia Sofia" EAD operates a cogeneration (combined heat and power) plant, which is known to be much more efficient than conventional facilities (Schleup, 2008; COGEN Europe, 2022). This is the reason why the main European institutions promote cogeneration through the Energy Efficiency Directive 2012/27/EU in an attempt to improve energy efficiency within the European Union.

It is obvious that the financial performance of Sofia's heating system can be improved, but this requires significant efforts for a thorough assessment of its operational, investment and financial activities for significant improvement of the energy efficiency of existing networks and inclusion of renewable heat sources, such as solar thermal energy, bioenergy and geothermal energy. Sofia is rich in hot springs, so this geothermal energy can be used in existing networks to save operational costs. It is well known that geothermal energy can provide access to affordable and environmentally friendly heating (Richter, 2021). The management of the company must work to improve its profitability and liquidity and reduce long-term liabilities.

Figure 1. Z"-scores for "Toplofikacia Sofia" EAD, "VIK-Sofia" EAD, "Sofecostroy" EAD and "Lozana" EAD (2006-2020)
Source: Author's calculations

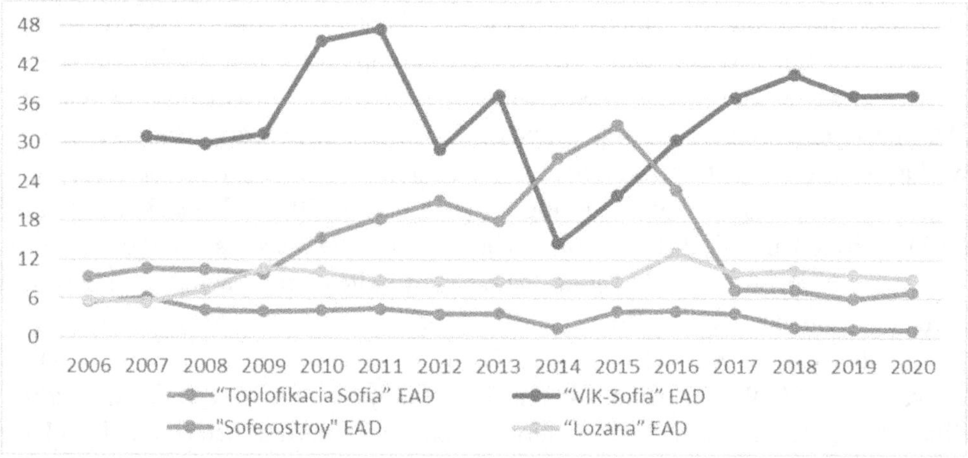

"VIK-Sofia" EAD is a joint-stock company, the successor of the public water supply system established in Sofia in 1884. Nowadays, the company performs various activities, such as maintenance, operation, reconstruction and repair of water supply and sewage systems and facilities. The company is also engaged in the management of mineral waters, construction and operation of small hydropower facilities, and maintenance of the corrected river beds on the territory of Sofia Municipality. The Z"-scores calculated for this company are extremely high, mainly due to the extremely high values of its equity to total liabilities ratio (X4). The ratio of retained earnings to total assets (X2) is negative in some years, which means that the company's profits are not always enough to cover its losses (*Table 2 in the Appendix*). However, the company remains stable due to good liquidity and lack of long-term liabilities. The company needs to take measures to increase revenues and reduce operating costs to improve its profitability in the coming years. Our results are consistent with the findings of Benito et al. (2010), Romano & Guerrini (2011), Voorn et al. (2017) and Molinos-Senante & Maziotis (2021) who conclude that municipal corporations can be a viable means of securing water supply for local communities.

"Sofecostroy" EAD performs a wide range of activities, such as garbage collection, transportation and treatment, construction and operation of landfills and installations for the disposal and processing of solid waste, waste recycling, demolition of buildings and facilities, removal of construction waste, cleaning and maintenance of urban infrastructure (e.g. streets, squares, parks, gardens, green areas and sports grounds), landscaping and afforestation, production of compost and other organic soils, development and implementation of projects in the field of ecology. During the analyzed period, the company has operated entirely in the safe zone and enjoyed good financial health. The highest Z"-scores (22.8 - 32.7) were recorded in the years 2014-2016 due to a significant reduction of the company's liabilities (*Table 3 in the Appendix*). The Z"-score fell sharply to 7.4 in 2017 due to increased short-term and long-term liabilities but did not break out of the safe zone. Management should not increase the company's liabilities further in order to maintain its good financial condition. These findings confirm the views of Rubin (1988), Benito et al. (2010) and Voorn et al. (2017), who conclude that municipal enterprises are efficient in the provision of utility services such as refuse collection and disposal. At the same time, our results contradict the findings of Da Cruz and Marques (2011), who argue that municipal companies are not viable providers of services related to urban infrastructure.

"Lozana" EAD is a social enterprise established in 1995 with the main purpose to ensure employment and integration of disabled people. The company provides various types of services. It owns several salt rooms and offers salt therapies for adults and children. Also, the company manages a communal laundry, a printing house and a bookstore. The company operates in the safety zone, demonstrating sustainability and good financial health, with its Z"-score ranging between 5.8 and 13.1. This is unusual for a social enterprise whose main objectives are to tackle unemployment and social exclusion and is evidence of effective financial management. The company's weakest point is its low liquidity. X1 (WC/TA) is negative in most years, meaning current liabilities outpace current assets (*Table 4 in the Appendix*). These results are consistent with the findings of Taylor (2021), who argues that social enterprises are able to achieve the desired social impact while remaining financially self-sustaining.

The following four municipal companies offer public transport and related services to the citizens and guests of the metropolitan city (*Figure 2*). **"Sofia Electrotransport" EAD** is a joint-stock company that carries out tram and trolley transport in the capital. The idea of using electric transport in Sofia arose as early as 1898 when the Sofia Municipality granted a concession for the construction of tram lines to companies from France and Belgium. The electric transport is cost-effective, suitable for urban environments and meets environmental requirements. Nowadays, the company operates 178 trams, 103 trolleys and a network consisting of 263 km of tram tracks, 257 of km trolley tracks, and a cable network of more than 740 km. During the first half of the analyzed period, the company operated in the safety zone, but since 2012 its financial condition has deteriorated and the Z"-score has collapsed to values between 3.3 and 3.6, characteristic of the distress zone. The ratios X1 (WC/TA), X2 (RE/TA) and X3 (EBIT/TA) become negative, which clearly indicates problems with the liquidity and profitability of the company (*Table 5 in the Appendix*).

"Sofia Avtotransport" EAD is a joint-stock company, the successor of the long-standing tradition of city bus transport in Sofia, which began in 1935. At present, the company operates 563 buses and carries out passenger transport on the mass urban transport routes in the territory of the Sofia Municipality. The total length of the serviced routes is over 860 km, and the total annual mileage of the company is over 33,000,000 km. Also, the company's activities include the storage and maintenance of vehicles in good technical condition, as well as operational management of the transport process. The financial performance of the company during the analyzed period is unstable, with many ups and downs. Since 2013, the values of X2 (RE/TA) and X3 (EBIT/TA) have been mostly negative, so the company remains in the distress zone (*Table 6 in the Appendix*).

Figure 2. Z"-scores for public transport companies (2006-2020)
Source: Author's calculations

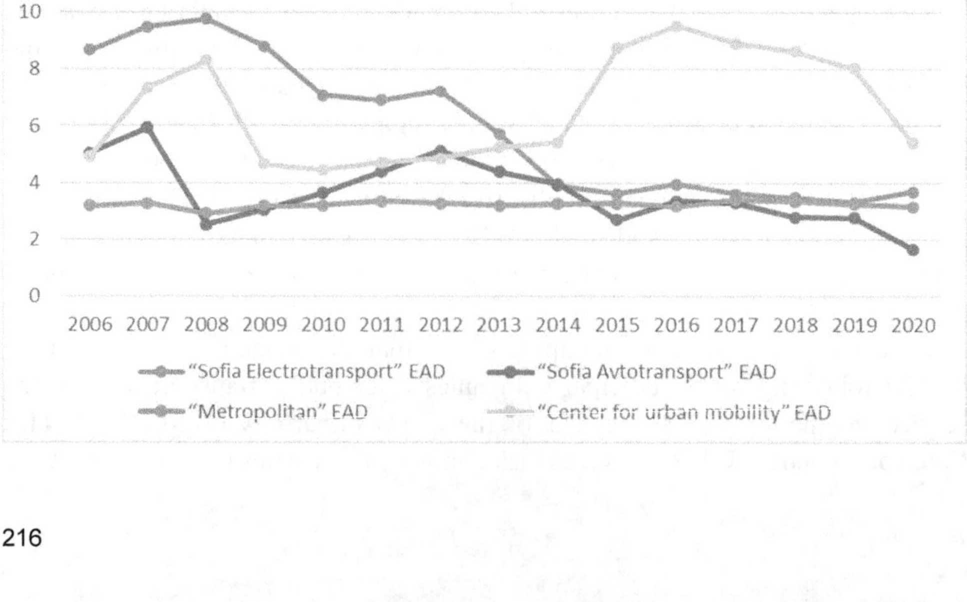

"Metropolitan" EAD was established in 1999 with the decision of the Sofia Municipal Council. The company serves the metro in Sofia, which is the most rapid and modern rail transport. Its main purpose is to provide clean, safe and quick transport for passengers. During the analyzed period, the company's activity is constantly expanding, thanks to the intensive construction of the new metro lines. At the same time, the company's financial performance is weak as it operates in the distress zone (3.0<Z"<3.4). The company does not report substantial losses, nor significant liquidity problems, as far as all ratios from X1 to X4 are mostly positive, but their values are quite low (*Table 7 in the Appendix*).

The only profitable public transport company owned by the Sofia Municipality is the **"Center for urban mobility" EAD.** This is a joint-stock company that has been assigned by the municipality to realize the revenues from urban transport. The company issues transportation documents (tickets and cards), supervises the performance of transport tasks by different transport operators and pays them for the transport services. Also, this municipal company carries out a wide range of activities related to analysis, planning, financing, operation, organization, coordination, management and control in the scope of urban transport. The company analyzes the environmental and operational aspects of urban transport, operates a control and management system based on GPS identification, operates a single automated system for charging passengers, constructs, operates and maintains parking lots, garages and parking spaces, performs advertising and information services for public transport etc. According to the calculated Z"-scores, the company operates in the safe zone and enjoys good financial health and a stable financial position. In 2020, the company's Z"-score declined mainly due to the restrictions related to COVID-19 and the associated reduction in revenues from urban transport. However, its RE/TA ratio (X2) remained positive, so it seems that the company has financial reserves to overcome the difficult period (*Table 8 in the Appendix*).

It is noteworthy that the poor financial performance of the main public transport companies of the Sofia Municipality contradicts the views of Voorn et al. (2017), who argue that very often, municipal companies are more effective than local bureaucracies in providing public transport services. This is further confirmed by Ball (2018), who studies municipal bus operators in the United Kingdom and concludes that bus services provided by the public sector consistently outperform their private counterparts. An empirical study by Wasowicz (2018) investigates the efficiency of enterprises providing local public transport services in Poland and shows that public enterprises provide public utility services with a higher level of economic efficiency compared to other groups of carriers. Another recent paper by the Netherlands Authority for Consumers and Markets (2021) reports on the cost-effectiveness, efficiency and sustainability of three municipal transport companies. Obviously, the Sofia Municipality needs to improve the financial management of all transport companies by improving cost efficiency, revising the pricing policy and increasing the payments made by the "Center for urban mobility" EAD to the transport service providers.

The following five municipal companies operate market sites and facilities located in some of the most attractive areas of the metropolitan city. **"Markets East" EAD, "Markets West" EAD, "Markets North" EAD, "Markets South" EAD and "Markets Vazrazhdane" EAD** are municipal companies established with the purpose to manage, maintain and rent out various facilities, pavilions and premises, grounds and tables for stall trade, owned by the Sofia Municipality. Also, these companies organize so-called "Farmer's Markets" for organic, eco and natural foods and beverages offered directly by their producers. The Z"-scores calculated for municipal markets for the period 2006 – 2020 show that all legal entities demonstrate excellent financial health (*Figure 3*). The stable financial positions of the municipal markets are due to the positive values of the coefficients X1, X2 and X3, which indicate high liquidity and good profitability, combined with high values of X4, which indicate the absence of enormous long-term liabilities (*Table 9, Table 10, Table 11, Table 12 and Table 13 in the Appendix*). The most important competitive advantage of these municipal companies is the possession of lucrative commercial properties in attractive locations. This is the reason why these companies realize good profits and ensure own stable revenues to the municipal budget. The good financial results of municipal markets in Sofia are similar to the findings of Geller (2019), who describes the efficiency of one of the oldest public farmer's markets in the United States, owned and operated by the City of Seattle. A study by Stoilova (2022) shows the good performance of municipal markets in Blagoevgrad (Bulgaria). Also, Harada (2016) describes the vital role of municipal markets in the modernization of retail trade in Japan, while Machell & Caraher (2012) highlight the important social role of municipal markets in Britain as valuable social spaces that provide access to adequate and affordable food for low-income urban communities.

Figure 3. Z"-scores for municipal markets (2006-2020)
Source: Author's calculations

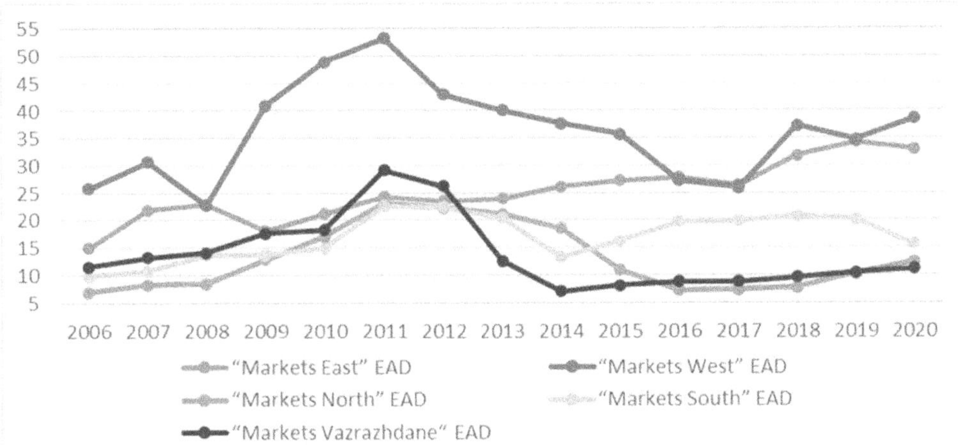

In addition to the municipal markets, there are five other municipal companies that manage municipal property and provide various services to the local community (*Figure 4 and Figure 5*). The first in the line is „**Sofinvest" EAD**, registered in 1989. It carries out a number of activities in the field of construction and investment process, such as independent construction supervision and technical control, development of investment projects, preparation and organization of the design process, a survey of construction sites, legal analyses, procedures for land expropriation and compensation to owners, procedures for transformation, privatization and liquidation of state and municipal enterprises, valuation of real estate, agricultural land, machinery, equipment and entire enterprises, technical, technological and financial analyzes of enterprises, preparation of forecasts and business plans, investor control over the quality, quantity, prices and values of the completed construction works, demolition of buildings and clearing of grounds related to construction activities, etc. The high and growing Z"-scores show that „Sofinvest" EAD is a highly profitable and financially stable company. Constantly decreasing current and long-term liabilities, as well as increasing equity and earnings are the main reasons for the excellent financial performance of the company during the analyzed period (*Table 14 in the Appendix*).

Figure 4. Z"-scores for "Sofinvest" EAD, "Geographical Information System - Sofia" EOOD and "Egida-Sofia" EAD (2006-2020)
Source: Author's calculations

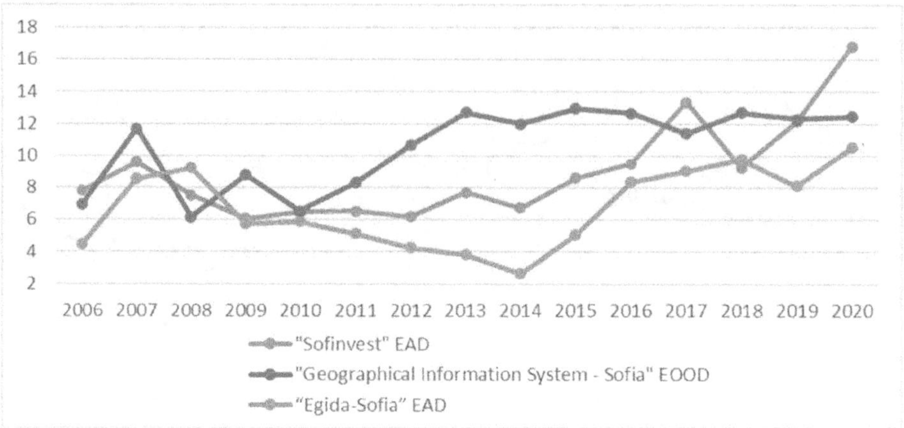

"Geographical Information System - Sofia" EOOD is one of the largest geodetic companies in Bulgaria. For more than 20 years the company has been building, maintaining and managing the information system of the cadastral, regulatory and building plans for the territory of the Sofia Municipality, called SOFCAR. The company offers a rich portfolio of products and services in the field of geodesy, cadaster, urban planning, cartography and photogrammetry. The company enjoys excellent financial health due to a high return on assets (X3), good liquidity (X1) and low indebtedness (X4). In the last three years, retained earnings exceeded 50% of total assets (X2 > 0.5), so the company is a good source of revenue for the municipal budget (*Table 15 in the Appendix*).

"Egida-Sofia" EAD is a municipal company established in 1998 to offer services related to the physical and technical protection of individuals and legal entities and their property. The company is licensed to carry out security activities on the territory of the Republic of Bulgaria. It was created with the main purpose of guarding municipal schools and kindergartens, subways, recreation parks, cemetery plots, municipal enterprises, social homes, tax offices and other municipal objects and structures located in the city of Sofia. In addition, the company guards extremely important objects for the security of the capital, such as the Central Bus Station, the Central Railway Station and the administrative buildings of the Sofia Municipality. Also, the company performs specially assigned tasks in crisis situations, natural disasters and accidents. Despite its important functions, the company's financial position continuously deteriorated during the period 2008-2014 (*Table 16 in the Appendix*). As a result, the company's Z"- score collapsed from 9.2 in 2008 to 2.6

in 2014. Since 2015, the company has carried out non-security activities, renting out 52 commercial premises, included in its capital, by the decision of the Sofia Municipal Council. The increase of the company's assets and the diversification of its activities stabilized its financial performance. The company left the distress zone and entered the safety zone (Z">8.4).

The last two municipal companies show interesting dynamics (*Figure 5*). **„Sofia Properties“ EAD** is known as an established, dynamically developing company for property management and investment projects. The company is fully oriented towards the implementation of the policies and programs of the Sofia Municipality. „Sofia Properties" EAD manages a portfolio of municipal properties and projects, striving to take a leading position among companies with a similar profile on the market. The company owns and manages attractive municipal properties, performs investment analyses and participates in municipal investment projects. The Z"-scores calculated for the company are high (40.2 on average) mainly due to the high values of X4 (Eq/TL) caused by the low liabilities compared to the company's equity. At the same time, the productivity of the company's assets is quite low, as far as in most years, X3 (EBIT/TA) is below 0.03 (*Table 17 in the Appendix*). The company appears to be retaining most of its earnings as X2 (RE/TA) values are high (0.22-0.39) and contribute to the high Z"-scores. In the last two years, the company has taken on significant long-term liabilities, which has reduced its Z"-score to 16.7 – 18.8. In order to maintain the good financial condition of the company, the management should work to improve the efficiency of the company's investments and refrain from further increasing the long-term liabilities.

Figure 5. Z"-scores for „Sofia Properties" EAD and "Sports Sofia - 2000" EAD (2006-2020)
Source: Author's calculations

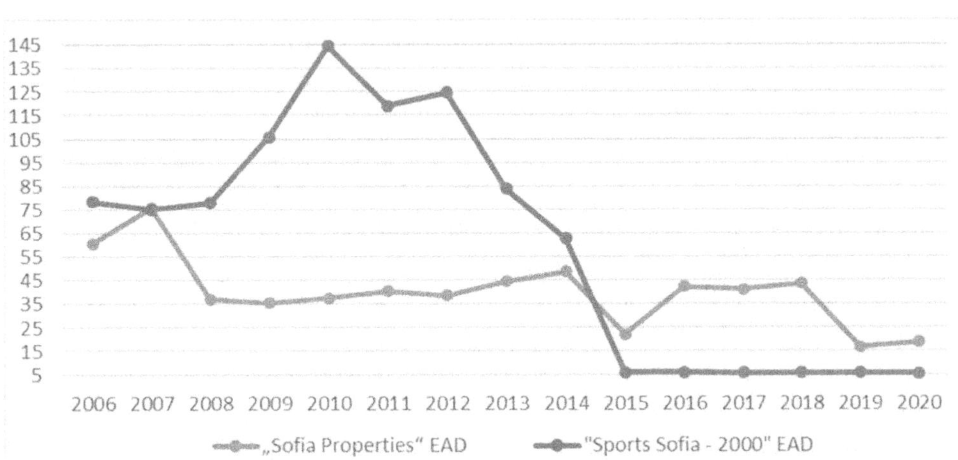

"Sports Sofia - 2000" EAD is a municipal company established in 2000 with the purpose to own, manage, maintain and build sports properties and facilities on the territory of the Sofia Municipality. The company owns and manages three main sports complexes, namely the multifunctional sports complex "Zone B-5", the complex "Boris Garden" and the Horse base. The complex "Zone B-5" covers an area of nearly 24,000 sq. m. and includes four mini football fields, three tennis courts, a volleyball court, a basketball court, an ice rink, a table tennis court, and a children's playground. The complex "Boris Garden" covers an area of 8,000 sq. m., including four football fields, a tennis court, and a table tennis court. The Horse base has an area of 7,000 sq. m. with a 2,000 sq. m. riding arena and 20 horse stables. It offers opportunities for horse sports in a park environment. In addition, the company performs investment analyses and provides expertise and participates in municipal investment projects for sports facilities. During the period 2006-2012, the development of the company followed a positive trend, with the Z"-scores for this period being extremely high and varying between 75.1 and 144.5. After 2013, the company's financial performance deteriorated sharply. Since 2015, the company has operated in the grey zone. The values of X3 (EBIT/TA) have been negative, which means that the company has realized operational losses. In addition, the values of X4 (Eq/TL) have considerably declined due to the significant increase in the company's liabilities. In 2019 and 2020, the company's retained earnings did not cover its losses, resulting in negative values of X2 (*Table 18 in the Appendix*).

The calculations show that the Sofia Municipality, through its municipal company, did not effectively manage the sports complexes. In this regard, it is highly recommended for the municipality to attract private capital and expertise to improve the financial management of "Sports Sofia - 2000" EAD. A possible option is to expand the company's equity by creating a so-called mixed enterprise - a form of limited liability company in which the state or municipality participates as partners of the private capital. Private sector involvement is widely perceived as a solution to the failure of many public enterprises to operate effectively and make the necessary investments to meet community needs. In this regard, mixed companies emerge as a pragmatic middle ground between purely public and purely private production. The efficiency of mixed firms is confirmed by Pérez-López, Prior & Zafra-Gómez (2015), who analyzed the different delivery methods for local public services in 1,058 Spanish municipalities during the period 2001-2010. They found that the mixed company is a delivery form that contributes to improving cost efficiency in municipalities both in times of prosperity and in times of crisis. This is also confirmed by Marra (2007), who carried out an economic analysis of mixed enterprises providing local utility services in Italy and argued that under certain conditions, mixed enterprises could be more effective than public companies and concessions because public authorities can closely monitor and incentivize the efficiency of the private operators in terms of fulfilling their contractual obligations. Bognetti & Robotti (2007) also studied the provision of local public services through mixed enterprises in Italy and concluded that mixed companies are widely used by municipalities as a tool that enables economies of scale and scope without losing control over the management of local utilities.

SOLUTIONS AND RECOMMENDATIONS

The analysis of the financial performance of 18 municipal companies reveals that most of them are viable legal entities capable of effectively providing some local public services, such as water supply and sanitation, garbage collection and disposal, maintenance of urban infrastructure, parking lots and garages, management of municipal markets, public laundry, printing house and bookstore, construction supervision, investor and technical control, municipal property management, geodetic services, security services, etc. There are several recommendations that can be taken into consideration by the management of these companies to further improve their financial positions.

The water supply company "VIK-Sofia" EAD shows low profitability but has good liquidity and a lack of long-term liabilities. The company needs to take measures to increase revenues and reduce operating costs to improve its profitability in the coming years. "Sofecostroy" EAD carries out garbage collection and operates in the safety zone, despite increased liabilities in recent years. The management of the company should not further increase the company's liabilities in order to maintain its good financial condition. Unusual for a social enterprise whose main goals are tackling unemployment and social exclusion, "Lozana" EAD shows resilience and good financial health. The company's weakest point is low liquidity, so the management should take measures to reduce current liabilities.

"Sofia Properties" EAD manages a portfolio of municipal properties and projects. Although the productivity of the company's assets is quite low, the company operates in the safety zone due to the low liabilities compared to the company's equity. In order to maintain the good financial condition of the company, the management should work to improve the efficiency of the company's investments and refrain from further increasing the long-term liabilities. "Egida-Sofia" EAD provides security services and enjoys a stable financial position thanks to the measures taken by the Sofia Municipality to diversify the company's activities. These measures should be further supported by the management of the company, ensuring efficient use of the municipal properties transferred to the company.

The five municipal markets, namely "Markets East" EAD, "Markets West" EAD, "Markets North" EAD, "Markets South" EAD and "Markets Vazrazhdane"

EAD, as well as the geodetic company "GIS - Sofia" EOOD and the construction supervision company "Sofinvest" EAD demonstrate excellent financial performance and stable financial positions. They have good profitability combined with high liquidity and low indebtedness. These municipal companies have specific competitive advantages and are effectively managed by the appointed representatives of Sofia Municipality. The efforts of the management bodies of these companies should be aimed at preserving their competitive positions.

At the same time, the Municipality of Sofia has failed to manage several companies in an efficient manner, so they are rather a burden to the local budget. These are the municipal companies that provide hot water, heating and urban transport and operate the municipal sports complexes.

"Toplofikacia Sofia" EAD provides hot water and heating and is the oldest district heating system in Bulgaria. The Z"-scores indicate low efficiency of the company's financial management. Financial ratios related to the company's profitability are negative in most years, while liquidity and solvency ratios are quite low. Considering that the company operates a cogeneration (combined heat and power) plant, which is known to be much more efficient than conventional facilities, it is obvious that the financial performance of Sofia's district heating system can be improved. This requires significant efforts for a thorough assessment of its operational, investment and financial activities, for significant improvement of the energy efficiency of existing networks and inclusion of renewable heat sources, such as solar thermal energy, bioenergy, and geothermal energy. Sofia is rich in hot springs, so this geothermal energy can be used in existing networks to save operational costs and provide affordable and environmentally friendly heating. The management of the company must work to improve its profitability and liquidity and reduce long-term liabilities.

The results of the analysis point to problems with the profitability and liquidity of the municipal companies providing public transport services, namely "Sofia Electrotransport" EAD, "Sofia Avtotransport" EAD and "Metropolitan" EAD. The only profitable municipal transport company is "Center for urban mobility" EAD, which is assigned by the municipality to realize the revenues from urban transport by issuing transport documents (tickets and cards), monitoring the performance of transport tasks by transport operators and paying them for the transport services. The Sofia Municipality should improve the financial management of all transport companies by improving cost efficiency, revising the pricing policy, and increasing the payments of the "Center for urban mobility" EAD to transport service providers.

"Sports Sofia - 2000" EAD owns, maintains, and manages three large sports complexes on the territory of the Sofia Municipality. The analysis reveals the low efficiency of the company's financial management. Since 2015, the company has realized operational losses combined with a significant increase in its liabilities. In this regard, it is highly recommended for the municipality to attract private capital and expertise to improve the financial management of "Sports Sofia – 2000" EAD. A possible option is to expand the company's equity by creating a so-called mixed enterprise - a form of limited liability company in which the state or municipality participate as partners of the private capital.

FUTURE RESEARCH DIRECTIONS

The scope of the study is limited to the financial performance of 18 companies entirely owned by Sofia, the largest and most developed municipality in Bulgaria. Further research is needed to estimate the operational and investment activities of these municipal companies, as well as to assess the efficiency of the enterprises that are partially owned by the municipality. A more comprehensive study could analyze the financial management of the companies owned by the other large municipalities in Bulgaria.

CONCLUSION

The results demonstrate that most of the municipal companies are viable legal entities capable of effectively providing some local public services, such as water supply and sanitation, garbage collection and disposal, maintenance of urban infrastructure, parking lots and garages, management of municipal markets, public laundry, printing house and bookstore, construction supervision, investor and technical control, municipal property management, geodetic services, security services, etc. At the same time, the Municipality of Sofia has failed to manage several companies in an efficient manner, so they are rather a burden to the local budget. These are the municipal companies that provide heating and urban transport and operate the municipal sports complexes. In this regard, the municipality should take appropriate measures to improve the financial condition of these companies. Since there are various good practices and evidence of efficient public management of district heating systems and transport companies, the municipality should focus its efforts on further analysis and improvement of the operational, investment and financial activities of these companies. As for sports complexes, the municipality should attract private capital and expertise to improve the financial performance of these municipal facilities.

The study has practical and research implications. It is obvious that Z-scores are popular and widely used bankruptcy prediction models, but their application in municipal companies for both practical and research purposes is quite limited. In this regard, the study provides valuable insight into the applicability and utility of Z-score models for municipal corporations. The study supports the increasing use of such models in the performance management of municipal companies. The results of the study would be useful for the policy makers and the management bodies of the municipal companies to determine appropriate organizational and financial interventions.

ACKNOWLEDGMENT

This study received no specific grant from any funding agency in the public, commercial, or not-for-profit sectors.

REFERENCES

Aasen, M. R. (2011). *Applying Altman's Z-Score to the Financial Crisis - An Empirical Study of Financial Distress on Oslo Stock Exchange* [Master thesis]. Norwegian School of Economics, Bergen. Retrieved January 18, 2022, from https://core.ac.uk/reader/30803130

Agh, P., Vavrek, R., Dvorak, M., & Papcunova, V. (2021). Economic Evaluation of the Management of Municipal Firms at the Level of Rural Local Self-Governments (Case Study). *Economies*, *9*(3), 130. doi:10.3390/economies9030130

Aktan, C. C. (1996). Public Enterprises in Turkey. *Annals of Public and Cooperative Economics*, *67*(1), 117–130. doi:10.1111/j.1467-8292.1996.tb01949.x

Al-Manaseer, S. R., & Al-Oshaibat, S. D. (2018). Validity of Altman Z-Score Model to Predict Financial Failure: Evidence from Jordan. *International Journal of Economics and Finance*, *10*(8), 181–189. doi:10.5539/ijef.v10n8p181

AlAli, M. S. (2018). The Application of Altman's Z-Score Model in Determining the Financial Soundness of Healthcare Companies Listed in Kuwait Stock Exchange. *International Journal of Economic Papers*, *3*(1), 1–5. https://www.researchgate.net/publication/325265054_The_Application_of_Altman's_Z-Score_Model_in_Determining_the_Financial_Soundness_of_Healthcare_Companies_Listed_in_Kuwait_Stock_Exchange

Aloy Niresh, J., & Pratheepan, T. (2015). The Application of Altman's Z-Score Model in Predicting Bankruptcy: Evidence from the Trading Sector in Sri Lanka. *International Journal of Business and Management, 10*(12), 269–275. doi:10.5539/ijbm.v10n12p269

Altman, E. (1968). Financial Ratios, Discriminant Analysis and the Prediction of Corporate Bankruptcy. *The Journal of Finance, 23*(4), 589–609. doi:10.1111/j.1540-6261.1968.tb00843.x

Altman, E. (2005). An emerging market credit scoring system for corporate bonds. *Emerging Markets Review, 6*(4), 311–323. doi:10.1016/j.ememar.2005.09.007

Altman, E. (2013). Predicting financial distress of companies: revisiting the Z-Score and ZETA® models. In A. R. Bell, Ch. Brooks, & M. Prokopczuk (Eds.), *Handbook of Research Methods and Applications in Empirical Finance* (pp. 428–456). Edward Elgar Publishing. doi:10.4337/9780857936097.00027

Authority for Consumers and Markets – ACM. (2021). *ACM study: HTM is the most sustainable among the three major municipal public transport companies*. ACM/UIT/567729. Retrieved October 20, 2022, from https://www.acm.nl/en/publications/acm-study-htm-most-sustainable-among-three-major-municipal-public-transport-companies

Ball, J. (2018). Municipal bus companies: can public ownership be profitable? *The New Statesman (UK Edition)*. Retrieved October 20, 2022, from https://www.newstatesman.com/spotlight/2018/06/municipal-bus-companies-can-public-ownership-be-profitable

Beltrame, F., Velliscig, G., Zorzi, G., & Polato, M. (2022). *A revision of Altman's Z-Score for SMEs: suggestions from the Italian Bankruptcy Law and pandemic perspectives*. Department of Management, Università Ca' Foscari Venezia Working Paper No. 9, doi:10.2139/ssrn.4161512

Benito, B., Bastida, F., & García, J. A. (2010). Explaining Differences in Efficiency: An Application to Spanish Municipalities. *Applied Economics, 42*(4), 515–528. doi:10.1080/00036840701675560

Bhuvaneskumar, A., Sivakumar, V., & Pushparaj, N. (2022). Performance assessment and ranking of socially responsible companies in India using FAHP, TOPSIS and Altman Z-score. *Benchmarking*. Advance online publication. doi:10.1108/BIJ-09-2021-0512

Bognetti, G., & Robotti, L. (2007). The Provision of Local Public Services through Mixed Enterprises: The Italian Case. *Annals of Public and Cooperative Economics*, *78*(3), 415–437. doi:10.1111/j.1467-8292.2007.00340.x

Center for Economic Development. (2003). *Corrupt practices in the process of municipal property management.* Retrieved September 5, 2022, from http://ced.bg/uploads/publication/cor_prac.pdf

Center for the Study of Democracy. (2006). *A Painful Shift in Bulgarian Anti-Corruption Policies and Practice.* Policy Brief No. 10. Retrieved September 5, 2022, from https://csd.bg/publications/publication/csd-brief-no-10-a-painful-shift-in-bulgarian-anti-corruption-policies-and-practice/

Center for the Study of Democracy. (2012). *Corruption and Anti-Corruption in Bulgaria (2011– 2012).* Policy Brief No. 35. Retrieved September 5, 2022, from https://csd.bg/publications/publication/policy-brief-no-35-corruption-and-anti-corruption-in-bulgaria-2011-2012/

CLES. (2021). *Municipal Enterprises.* Retrieved September 3, 2022, from https://cles.org.uk/what-is-community-wealth-building/the-principles-of-community-wealth-building/plural-ownership-of-the-economy/municipal-enterprises/

COGEN Europe. (2022). *What Is Cogeneration?* Retrieved December 20, 2022, from https://www.cogeneurope.eu/knowledge-centre/what-is-cogeneration

Commercial Law. (1991). *State Official Journal: 48/1991.* Retrieved September 10, 2022, from https://lex.bg/laws/ldoc/-14917630

Constitution of the Republic of Bulgaria. (1991). *State Official Journal: 56/1991.* Retrieved September 10, 2022, from https://www.lex.bg/laws/ldoc/521957377

Cuadrado-Ballesteros, B., García-Sánchez, I. M., & Prado-Lorenzo, J. M. (2012). Effects of Different Modes of Local Public Services Delivery on Quality of Life in Spain. *Journal of Cleaner Production*, *37*, 68–81. doi:10.1016/j.jclepro.2012.06.008

Da Cruz, N. F., & Marques, R. C. (2011). Viability of Municipal Companies in the Provision of Urban Infrastructure Services. *Local Government Studies*, *37*(1), 93–110. doi:10.1080/03003930.2010.548551

Dexia Crediop. (2004). *Local Public Companies in the 25 Countries of the European Union*. Paris: Dexia. Retrieved September 15, 2022, from https://www.lesepl.fr/pdf/carte_EPL_anglais.pdf

Diakomihalis, M. (2012). The accuracy of Altman's models in predicting hotel bankruptcy. *International Journal of Accounting and Financial Reporting*, *2*(2), 96–113. doi:10.5296/ijafr.v2i2.2367

Directive 2012/27/EU of the European Parliament and of the Council of 25 October 2012 on energy efficiency. Official Journal of the European Union, 14.11.2012, Retrieved December 20, 2022, from https://data.europa.eu/eli/dir/2012/27/oj

Duan, J., & Shrestha, K. (2011). Statistical credit rating methods. *Global Credit Review, 1*, 43–64. Retrieved January 19, 2023, from https://www.econbiz.de/Record/global-credit-review/100101869
46

European Commission. (2022). *Cogeneration of heat and power: The EU promotes cogeneration in order to improve energy efficiency in Europe*. Retrieved December 20, 2022, from https://energy.ec.europa.eu/topics/energy-efficiency/cogeneration-heat-and-power_en

Ferry, L., Andrews, R., Skelcher, C., & Wegorowski, P. (2018). New development: Corporatization of local authorities in England in the wake of austerity 2010–2016. *Public Money & Management*, *38*(6), 477–480. doi:10.1080/09540962.2018.1486629

Geller, S. (2019). *Municipal enterprises are businesses or services owned by local public authorities that provide services or generate revenue for local communities*. The next system. Retrieved September 10, 2022, from https://thenextsystem.org/learn/stories/municipal-enterprise

GrabskiJ. (2019). *The Dynamic Z-Score*. doi:10.2139/ssrn.3509795

Greiling, D., & Grub, B. (2015). Towards Citizen Accountability of Local Public Enterprises. *Annals of Public and Cooperative Economics*, *86*(4), 641–655. doi:10.1111/apce.12098

Grossi, G., & Reichard, C. (2008). Municipal corporatization in Germany and Italy. *Public Management Review*, *10*(5), 597–617. doi:10.1080/14719030802264275

Hanna, T. (2013). Challenging Corporate Domination: The Public Ownership Approach. *The Good Society - PEGS*, *22*(1), 26–43. doi:10.1353/gso.2013.0005

Harada, M. (2016). Japanese modern municipal retail and wholesale markets in comparison with European markets. *Urban History, 43*(3), 476–492. doi:10.1017/S096392681500019X

Hayes, S. K., Hodge, K. A., & Hughes, L. W. (2010). A Study of the Efficacy of Altman's Z to Predict Bankruptcy of Specialty Retail Firms Doing Business in Contemporary Times. *Economics & Business Journal: Inquiries & Perspectives, 3*(1), 122-134. Retrieved January 18, 2023, from https://nebeconandbus.org/journal/EBJI2010HayesHodgeHughes.pdf

International Energy Agency. (2022). *District Heating*. IEA. Retrieved December 20, 2022, from https://www.iea.org/reports/district-heating

Junkernheinrich, M., & Micosatt, G. (2007). *Kommunaler Schuldenreport Nordrhein-Westfalen*. Gütersloh: Bertelsmann Stiftung. Retrieved September 15, 2022, from https://www.bertelsmann-stiftung.de/fileadmin/files/BSt/Publikationen/GrauePublikationen/GP_Kommunaler_Finanz-und_Schuldenreport_Nordrhein-Westfalen_2007.pdf

Kpodoh, B. (2010). *Bankruptcy and Financial Distress Prediction in the Mobile Telecom Industry: The case of MTN-Ghana, Millicom-Ghana and Ghana Telecom* [Master thesis]. School of Management Blekinge Institute of Technology. Retrieved January 19, 2023 from https://www.diva-portal.org/smash/get/diva2:832030/FULLTEXT01.pdf

Local Self-Government and Local Administration Act State Official Journal: 77/1991. Retrieved September 10, 2022, from https://www.lex.bg/laws/ldoc/2132580865

Machell, G., & Caraher, M. (2012). The role of municipal markets in urban food strategies: a case study. In A. M. Viljoen & J. S. C. Wiskerke (Eds.), *Sustainable Food Planning: evolving theory and practice* (pp. 127–136). doi:10.3920/978-90-8686-187-3_10

Marra, A. (2007). Internal Regulation by Mixed Enterprises: The Case of the Italian Water Sector. *Annals of Public and Cooperative Economics, 78*(2), 245–275. doi:10.1111/j.1467-8292.2007.00334.x

Meeampol, S., Lerskullawat, P., Wongsorntham, A., Srinammuang, P., Rodpetch, V., & Noonoi, R. (2014). Applying Emerging Market Z-Score Model to Predict Bankruptcy: A Case Study of Listed Companies in the Stock Exchange of Thailand. *Management, Knowledge, and Learning International Conference*, 1227-1237. Retrieved January 18, 2023 from https://www.toknowpress.net/ISBN/978-961-6914-09-3/papers/ML14-724.pdf

Molinos-Senante, M., & Maziotis, A. (2021). Benchmarking the efficiency of water and sewerage companies: Application of the stochastic non-parametric envelopment of data (stoned) method. *Expert Systems with Applications, 186*, 115711. Advance online publication. doi:10.1016/j.eswa.2021.115711

Municipal Property Act. (1996). *State Official Journal: 44/1996*. Retrieved September, 10, 2022, from https://www.lex.bg/laws/ldoc/2133874691

National Statistical Institute – NSI. (2020). Retrieved December, 11, 2022, from https://www.nsi.bg/en/

Ng, S. T., Wong, J. M., & Zhang, J. (2011). Applying Z-score model to distinguish insolvent construction companies in China. *Habitat International, 35*(4), 599–607. doi:10.1016/j.habitatint.2011.03.008

Paul, G. (1999). Measuring the Effect of Municipal Enterprises on the Budgets of Local Governments. *The Western Journal of Black Studies, 23*(4), 217–228.

Pérez-López, G., Prior, D., & Zafra-Gómez, J. L. (2015). Rethinking New Public Management Delivery Forms and Efficiency: Long-Term Effects in Spanish Local Government. *Journal of Public Administration: Research and Theory, 25*(4), 1157–1183. doi:10.1093/jopart/muu088

Registry Agency of the Republic of Bulgaria. (2021). *Commercial register and register of non-profit legal entities*. Retrieved September 10, 2022, from https://portal.registryagency.bg/CR/reports/ActiveCondition/

Reisz, A., & Perlich, C. (2007). A market-based framework for bankruptcy prediction. *Journal of Financial Stability, 3*(2), 85–131. doi:10.1016/j.jfs.2007.02.001

Richter, A. (2021). *New geothermal district heating system in Höfn, Iceland*. Think Geoenergy. Retrieved December 20, 2022, from https://www.thinkgeoenergy.com/new-geothermal-district-heating-system-in-hofn-iceland/

Romano, G., & Guerrini, A. (2011). Measuring and comparing the efficiency of water utility companies: A data envelopment analysis approach. *Utilities Policy, 19*(3), 202–209. doi:10.1016/j.jup.2011.05.005

Rubin, I. S. (1988). Municipal Enterprises: Exploring Budgetary and Political Implications. *Public Administration Review, 48*(1), 542–550. doi:10.2307/975517

Schleup, J. (2008). How Does Cogeneration Provide Heat and Power? *Scientific American*. Retrieved December 20, 2022, from https://www.scientificamerican.com/article/how-does-cogeneration-provide-heat-power/

Sofia Municipality. (2022). *Register of municipal commercial companies with 100% municipal ownership of the capital*. Retrieved November 06, 2022, from https://www.sofia.bg/register-of-municipal-companies

Sorensen, R. J. (2007). Does dispersed public ownership impair efficiency? The case of refuse collection in Norway. *Public Administration*, *85*(4), 1045–1058. doi:10.1111/j.1467-9299.2007.00681.x

State Property Act. (1996). *State Official Journal: 44/1996*. Retrieved September 10, 2022, from https://www.lex.bg/bg/laws/ldoc/2133874689

Stoilova, D. (2022). Analysis of the financial management of municipal enterprises in Blagoevgrad with Z-score model. *Economics & Law*, *4*(1), 1–14. doi:10.37708/el.swu.v4i1.1

Stoyanov, A., & Gerganov, A. (2017). *Anti-corruption: Implementation and Evaluation of Anti-corruption Measures and Policies*. Center for the Study of Democracy. Retrieved September 15, 2022, from https://csd.bg/publications/publication/anti-corruption-implementation-and-evaluation-of-anti-corruption-measures-and-policies-macpi/

Tan, C. H. (1992). Public Enterprises and Privatization: The Experience of Singapore. *Annals of Public and Cooperative Economics*, *63*(1), 119–125. doi:10.1111/j.1467-8292.1992.tb02081.x

Tavares, A. F., & Camões, P. J. (2007). Local service delivery choices in Portugal: A political transaction costs framework. *Local Government Studies*, *33*(4), 535–553. doi:10.1080/03003930701417544

Tavares, A. F., & Camões, P. J. (2010). New Forms of Local Governance: A theoretical and empirical analysis of municipal corporations in Portugal. *Public Management Review*, *12*(5), 587–608. doi:10.1080/14719031003633193

Taylor, K. M. (2021). Effectiveness of Social Enterprises: Aligning Strategies and Supply Chains for Impact. *Electronic Thesis and Dissertation Repository. 7850*. https://ir.lib.uwo.ca/etd/7850

Transparency International Bulgaria. (2015). *Index of the local integrity system – 2015*. Retrieved September 15, 2022, from http://lisi.transparency.bg/years/2015/

Voorn, B., Van Genugten, M. L., & Van Thiel, S. (2017). The efficiency and effectiveness of municipally owned corporations: A systematic review. *Local Government Studies*, *43*(5), 820–841. doi:10.1080/03003930.2017.1319360

Wasowicz, K. (2018). Assessment of the efficiency of municipal companies based on local collective transport. *Zarządzanie Publiczne*, *44*(2), 56–70. doi:10.15678/ZP.2018.44.2.04

ADDITIONAL READING

Agh, P., Vavrek, R., Dvorak, M., & Papcunova, V. (2021). Economic Evaluation of the Management of Municipal Firms at the Level of Rural Local Self-Governments (Case Study). *Economies*, *9*(3), 130. doi:10.3390/economies9030130

Bognetti, G., & Robotti, L. (2007). The Provision of Local Public Services through Mixed Enterprises: The Italian Case. *Annals of Public and Cooperative Economics*, *78*(3), 415–437. doi:10.1111/j.1467-8292.2007.00340.x

Cuadrado-Ballesteros, B., García-Sánchez, I. M., & Prado-Lorenzo, J. M. (2012). Effects of Different Modes of Local Public Services Delivery on Quality of Life in Spain. *Journal of Cleaner Production*, *37*, 68–81. doi:10.1016/j.jclepro.2012.06.008

Da Cruz, N. F., & Marques, R. C. (2011). Viability of Municipal Companies in the Provision of Urban Infrastructure Services. *Local Government Studies*, *37*(1), 93–110. doi:10.1080/03003930.2010.548551

Ferry, L., Andrews, R., Skelcher, C., & Wegorowski, P. (2018). New development: Corporatization of local authorities in England in the wake of austerity 2010–2016. *Public Money & Management*, *38*(6), 477–480. doi:10.1080/09540962.2018.1486629

Grossi, G., & Reichard, C. (2008). Municipal corporatization in Germany and Italy. *Public Management Review*, *10*(5), 597–617. doi:10.1080/14719030802264275

Molinos-Senante, M., & Maziotis, A. (2021). Benchmarking the efficiency of water and sewerage companies: Application of the stochastic non-parametric envelopment of data (stoned) method. *Expert Systems with Applications*, *186*, 115711. Advance online publication. doi:10.1016/j.eswa.2021.115711

Pérez-López, G., Prior, D., & Zafra-Gómez, J. L. (2015). Rethinking New Public Management Delivery Forms and Efficiency: Long-Term Effects in Spanish Local Government. *Journal of Public Administration: Research and Theory*, *25*(4), 1157–1183. doi:10.1093/jopart/muu088

Romano, G., & Guerrini, A. (2011). Measuring and comparing the efficiency of water utility companies: A data envelopment analysis approach. *Utilities Policy*, *19*(3), 202–209. doi:10.1016/j.jup.2011.05.005

Voorn, B., Van Genugten, M. L., & Van Thiel, S. (2017). The efficiency and effectiveness of municipally owned corporations: A systematic review. *Local Government Studies*, *43*(5), 820–841. doi:10.1080/03003930.2017.1319360

KEY TERMS AND DEFINITIONS

Effectiveness: The ability to be successful and achieve desired results. The extent to which the intended objectives are achieved.

Local Financial Management: The practice of managing local government finances in a way that enables it to be successful and compliant with regulations. It is aimed at optimizing the financial and economic benefits for the local community.

Local Government: The lowest tier of public administration within a particular sovereign state.

Municipal Company: A business owned by a local government that provides services and usually generates revenue for the local community.

Profitability: The ability of the business to generate a high return on investment.

Public Services: Services offered by the government that help all members of the community.

Public Utilities: Government-owned and operated enterprises that provide public goods and services considered essential to the community, such as water, sewage, natural gas, electricity, heating, solid waste disposal, transportation, etc.

Z-Score Model: A model designed to assess the financial stability of various types of companies based on a combination of financial ratios.

APPENDIX A

Table 1. "Toplofikacia Sofia" EAD						*Table 2. "VIK-Sofia" EAD*			
	X1	X2	X3	X4		X1	X2	X3	X4
2006	0.1621	-0.0066	-0.0034	1.1822		0.5035	-0.0242	0.0135	23.1674
2007	0.3178	0.0024	-0.0086	0.9092		0.5030	-0.0231	0.0112	23.2173
2008	0.1881	-0.0890	-0.0852	0.6108		0.5050	-0.0221	0.0164	22.1545
2009	0.1390	-0.1415	-0.0137	0.4325		0.5148	-0.0052	0.0023	23.6205
2010	0.2694	-0.2567	-0.0397	0.3032		0.5463	-0.0053	0.0072	37.0313
2011	0.2101	-0.2129	0.0298	0.3447		0.5476	-0.0001	-0.0512	39.1385
2012	0.1156	-0.1933	0.0036	0.2870		0.4199	-0.1524	0.0056	22.3116
2013	0.0530	-0.1468	0.0054	0.5684		0.3779	-0.1121	-0.1166	31.2500
2014	-0.1303	-0.2161	-0.0757	0.3246		0.3296	-0.1113	-0.0305	9.2329
2015	0.2791	-0.2725	-0.0570	0.2805		0.2786	-0.0366	-0.0883	16.7512
2016	0.3160	-0.3550	-0.0448	0.2543		0.2667	-0.0996	-0.0333	24.7631
2017	0.2826	-0.3894	-0.0383	0.1960		0.3010	-0.0332	0.0074	30.3846
2018	0.0005	-0.5403	-0.0181	0.2667		0.3027	0.0067	0.0025	33.6190
2019	0.0016	-0.5373	-0.0660	0.2777		0.3191	0.0115	0.0127	30.3136
2020	0.0227	-0.6124	-0.0557	0.2025		0.3341	0.0198	0.0107	30.3529

Table 3. "Sofecostroy" EAD						Table 4. "Lozana" EAD			
	X1	X2	X3	X4		X1	X2	X3	X4
2006	0.3216	0.1936	0.2555	1.5526		-0.0855	-0.0153	0.0590	2.6073
2007	0.2613	0.3396	0.3223	2.2764		-0.1402	0.0170	0.0170	2.8361
2008	0.1923	0.3519	0.3007	2.6414		-0.0871	0.0056	0.0184	4.3091
2009	0.2216	0.2546	0.3722	1.7591		-0.0011	0.0223	0.0523	6.6773
2010	0.3361	0.4280	0.4055	5.5950		-0.0155	0.0655	0.0000	6.4493
2011	0.4907	0.5707	0.2172	8.1857		-0.0073	0.0662	-0.0303	5.3409
2012	0.6338	0.5623	0.2498	9.7327		0.0111	0.0354	0.0006	5.0357
2013	0.6408	0.6500	0.2055	6.7001		0.0021	0.0340	0.0010	5.0827
2014	0.8172	0.5890	0.3323	14.1722		-0.0210	0.0336	0.0015	5.0753
2015	0.5890	0.6075	0.2248	21.0494		-0.0104	0.0348	0.0005	5.1341
2016	0.6995	0.6987	0.1195	11.3203		-0.0238	0.0376	0.0026	9.4172
2017	0.2308	0.4175	0.0308	1.0624		-0.0602	0.0395	0.0016	6.6279
2018	0.2233	0.4496	0.0010	1.0734		-0.0268	0.0415	0.0005	6.7264
2019	0.1495	0.4642	-0.0854	0.8116		-0.0404	0.0415	0.0031	6.1991
2020	0.1573	0.4427	0.0104	1.1460		-0.0206	0.0432	0.0025	5.5057

Table 5. "Sofia Electrotransport" EAD						Table 6. "Sofia Avtotransport" EAD			
	X1	X2	X3	X4		X1	X2	X3	X4
2006	0.0468	0.0151	-0.0005	4.8419		-0.1578	-0.0668	0.0001	2.9023
2007	0.0972	0.0130	0.0013	5.2786		-0.1189	0.0000	0.0001	3.2931
2008	0.0621	-0.0406	-0.0152	6.0364		-0.2075	-0.0011	-0.1166	1.3550
2009	0.0985	-0.0429	0.0007	4.8163		-0.1624	-0.1084	0.0018	1.1584
2010	0.1000	0.0163	0.0011	2.9619		-0.1460	-0.0093	0.0004	1.3049
2011	0.1255	0.0259	0.0025	2.6118		-0.1132	0.0007	0.0004	1.7920
2012	0.1667	0.0497	0.0149	2.4973		-0.0046	0.0124	0.0120	1.7066
2013	0.2517	0.0047	-0.0391	1.0258		0.0822	-0.0880	-0.1018	1.5072
2014	0.0004	0.0053	-0.0154	0.7035		0.0842	-0.1041	-0.0431	0.7419
2015	0.0048	-0.0123	-0.0543	0.7031		0.0506	-0.1920	-0.1093	0.4620
2016	0.0170	0.0075	-0.0151	0.6450		0.0286	-0.1477	0.0011	0.3709
2017	-0.0123	-0.0065	-0.0280	0.6263		0.0290	-0.1610	-0.0038	0.3977
2018	-0.0319	-0.0139	-0.0230	0.6195		-0.0311	-0.1393	-0.0130	0.2686
2019	-0.0380	-0.0310	-0.0174	0.5205		-0.0541	-0.1170	0.0025	0.2313
2020	0.0319	-0.0277	-0.0102	0.3725		-0.1202	-0.1859	-0.0559	0.1769

Table 7. "Metropolitan" EAD						Table 8. "Center for urban mobility" EAD			
	X1	X2	X3	X4		X1	X2	X3	X4
2006	-0.0498	-0.0036	0.0000	0.2983		0.1013	0.0967	0.0434	0.3944
2007	-0.0547	-0.0025	0.0000	0.3866		0.2484	0.1695	0.1223	1.0463
2008	-0.0568	-0.0014	0.0000	0.0507		0.3033	0.1985	0.1594	1.2729
2009	-0.0093	-0.0045	0.0011	0.0125		0.0688	0.0945	0.0537	0.2791
2010	-0.0158	0.0022	0.0055	0.0150		0.0662	0.1009	0.0387	0.1621
2011	0.0126	-0.0001	0.0019	0.0116		0.0928	0.1226	0.0382	0.1830
2012	0.0026	0.0014	0.0005	0.0097		0.1258	0.1217	0.0318	0.1696
2013	-0.0071	0.0012	-0.0001	0.0084		0.1416	0.1546	0.0534	0.2113
2014	0.0001	0.0010	0.0002	0.0082		0.1616	0.1749	0.0452	0.2388
2015	0.0053	0.0012	-0.0011	0.0068		0.6491	0.2111	0.0359	0.2982
2016	-0.0120	0.0000	0.0010	0.0073		0.6714	0.2871	0.0707	0.4412
2017	0.0235	0.0009	-0.0022	0.0044		0.4689	0.2450	0.0496	1.3983
2018	0.0187	-0.0010	-0.0012	0.0026		0.4482	0.2532	0.0224	1.4003
2019	0.0031	-0.0021	-0.0004	0.0019		0.3736	0.2543	0.0132	1.3567
2020	-0.0113	-0.0026	0.0006	0.0023		0.2592	0.1308	-0.1224	0.8207

Table 9. "Markets East" EAD

	X1	X2	X3	X4
2006	0.1756	0.0161	0.0503	9.7039
2007	0.4301	0.0169	0.3461	12.7559
2008	0.3024	0.0986	0.0833	15.8868
2009	0.4433	0.1755	0.1311	9.9501
2010	0.5124	0.1886	0.1586	12.2997
2011	0.4907	0.2284	0.1166	15.5132
2012	0.4328	0.2466	0.1095	15.1234
2013	0.4438	0.2673	0.0945	15.4887
2014	0.4616	0.2837	0.0910	17.4413
2015	0.4601	0.3203	0.0710	18.4762
2016	0.3649	0.3744	0.0444	19.6766
2017	0.2865	0.3302	0.0469	18.9283
2018	0.3041	0.3456	0.0597	23.8054
2019	0.3257	0.3848	0.0499	25.9157
2020	0.3601	0.3925	0.0901	24.1797

Table 10. "Markets West" EAD

	X1	X2	X3	X4
2006	0.5385	0.2720	0.1017	16.6968
2007	0.6110	0.3007	0.1226	20.5882
2008	0.6881	0.2506	0.1361	12.6335
2009	0.7815	0.2939	0.1867	28.8710
2010	0.8093	0.3222	0.0918	36.8133
2011	0.8163	0.3663	0.1049	40.7273
2012	0.8011	0.3560	0.0637	31.3077
2013	0.8093	0.3612	0.0700	28.3523
2014	0.8134	0.3658	0.0632	26.0729
2015	0.8279	0.3830	0.0288	24.2653
2016	0.7981	0.4077	0.0158	16.4558
2017	0.7273	0.4004	0.0168	15.7105
2018	0.4409	0.2696	0.0086	28.6767
2019	0.4010	0.2754	0.0075	26.5103
2020	0.4213	0.2833	0.0013	30.0625

Table 11. "Markets North" EAD

	X1	X2	X3	X4
2006	-0.0106	0.0635	0.0021	3.3397
2007	0.0061	0.0852	0.0266	4.2554
2008	0.0179	0.0728	0.0383	4.3721
2009	0.1681	0.0907	0.1941	6.5010
2010	0.2793	0.2648	0.1701	9.3922
2011	0.2093	0.2220	0.1252	16.0094
2012	0.2624	0.2574	0.0869	15.0833
2013	0.3380	0.2594	0.0986	13.4315
2014	0.3304	0.2446	0.0698	11.2485
2015	0.2572	0.2388	0.0561	4.5550
2016	0.1907	0.2001	0.0531	1.6005
2017	0.1753	0.2229	0.0405	1.8405
2018	0.1867	0.2682	0.0202	2.1305
2019	0.1151	0.2127	0.0082	5.1861
2020	0.1033	0.2304	0.0009	7.3257

Table 12. "Markets South" EAD

	X1	X2	X3	X4
2006	0.0716	0.1126	0.0822	4.9704
2007	0.0638	0.1175	0.1324	5.5291
2008	0.2002	0.1188	0.1175	7.5189
2009	0.2731	0.1832	0.1612	6.5996
2010	0.3973	0.2087	0.1961	6.7000
2011	0.2468	0.1265	0.0961	15.8513
2012	0.2658	0.1435	0.0911	15.4886
2013	0.2524	0.1541	0.1042	13.5997
2014	0.2185	0.1434	0.0725	7.2044
2015	0.1683	0.1659	0.0723	10.2859
2016	0.1418	0.2345	0.0358	13.7229
2017	0.1327	0.2549	0.0112	14.0581
2018	0.1472	0.2593	0.0226	14.7294
2019	0.1712	0.2773	0.0090	14.0822
2020	0.0596	0.2692	0.0308	10.3217

Table 13. "Markets Vazrazhdane" EAD						*Table 14. "Sofinvest" EAD*			
	X1	X2	X3	X4		X1	X2	X3	X4
2006	-0.0035	0.1811	0.1381	6.5171		0.0581	0.0139	0.0551	3.5724
2007	0.2517	0.2874	0.2385	5.4688		0.0879	0.0249	0.0925	4.8216
2008	0.4088	0.0739	0.2987	5.5935		0.0390	0.0271	0.1731	2.6213
2009	0.5335	0.1053	0.3573	7.6619		0.0417	0.0519	0.0935	1.6601
2010	0.6114	0.1390	0.3720	7.6953		0.0069	0.0801	0.0734	2.2820
2011	0.2997	0.1128	0.1717	21.3448		-0.0066	0.1045	0.0324	2.6213
2012	0.2665	0.1402	0.1694	18.6793		-0.0421	0.1123	0.0181	2.5771
2013	0.1480	0.1180	0.0423	7.2530		-0.0758	0.1289	0.0163	4.2160
2014	0.0567	0.0629	0.0345	2.8231		-0.0165	0.1218	0.0187	2.9269
2015	0.0852	0.0878	0.0357	3.5770		0.0373	0.1328	0.0322	4.2489
2016	0.1031	0.1211	0.0347	4.0042		0.1745	0.1404	0.1055	3.7517
2017	0.0829	0.1048	0.0344	4.1829		0.2113	0.1662	0.0635	7.3898
2018	0.1068	0.1329	0.0309	4.7234		0.1618	0.1898	0.0465	3.8103
2019	0.1233	0.1574	0.0274	5.3461		0.1980	0.2577	0.0348	6.2209
2020	0.1148	0.1805	0.0030	6.1623		0.2760	0.3093	0.0175	10.1457

Table 17. "Sofia Properties" EAD						*Table 18. "Sports Sofia – 2000" EAD*			
	X1	X2	X3	X4		X1	X2	X3	X4
2006	0.0541	0.2862	0.0090	53.3291		0.1742	0.1284	0.0881	69.6375
2007	0.0334	0.2608	0.0154	68.0144		0.0822	0.0670	0.0294	67.5625
2008	0.0249	0.2229	0.0052	31.3465		0.1161	0.0000	0.0301	70.2639
2009	0.0260	0.2199	0.0032	29.7408		0.0462	0.0056	0.0332	97.1569
2010	0.0205	0.2195	0.0036	31.8566		0.0501	0.0117	0.0139	134.0811
2011	0.0219	0.2212	0.0052	34.6665		0.1582	0.0141	0.0136	109.1333
2012	0.0285	0.2205	0.0094	32.7649		0.1699	0.0163	0.0112	114.3488
2013	0.0480	0.2207	0.0150	38.1415		0.0997	0.0173	0.0253	75.9545
2014	0.0418	0.2098	0.0091	42.2251		0.2202	0.0394	0.0354	54.7474
2015	0.0576	0.2626	0.0135	16.6966		0.0990	0.0377	-0.0103	1.8471
2016	0.1599	0.2439	0.1241	34.6190		0.0851	0.0286	-0.0222	1.8994
2017	0.1025	0.3042	0.0157	34.4554		0.0637	0.0069	-0.0240	1.9240
2018	0.1224	0.3168	0.0240	36.5503		0.0577	0.0000	-0.0245	1.9919
2019	0.0597	0.2766	0.1158	10.8486		0.0428	-0.0079	-0.0290	2.0985
2020	0.0422	0.3932	0.0006	13.3567		0.0451	-0.0385	-0.0258	2.0694

	Table 15. "Geographical Information System – Sofia" EOOD					*Table 16. "Egida-Sofia" EAD*			
	X1	X2	X3	X4		X1	X2	X3	X4
2006	0.0107	0.0621	0.3680	0.9109		0.0990	-0.0562	0.0083	0.6691
2007	0.3166	0.1351	0.5183	2.3312		0.1460	-0.0541	0.0134	4.2055
2008	0.0939	0.2549	0.1084	0.7030		0.0594	0.0037	0.0016	5.2947
2009	0.3053	0.1994	0.2743	1.0000		-0.0353	0.0010	-0.1053	3.2782
2010	0.2463	0.3184	0.0019	0.5752		0.0647	0.0000	-0.1892	3.2976
2011	0.3326	0.2491	0.1729	0.8421		-0.0103	0.0000	-0.1699	2.9347
2012	0.4702	0.2360	0.2646	1.6868		-0.0703	0.0000	-0.1584	2.3960
2013	0.6068	0.3299	0.3041	2.2374		-0.1332	0.0000	-0.1176	2.1368
2014	0.6188	0.4457	0.1778	1.9474		-0.0920	0.0000	-0.3651	2.3260
2015	0.5670	0.3561	0.3288	2.5043		0.0428	0.0000	-0.3390	3.6347
2016	0.5092	0.4600	0.1363	3.4882		0.0781	-0.2642	0.0342	4.9903
2017	0.4680	0.3910	0.1441	2.7063		0.1457	-0.2264	0.0299	5.1073
2018	0.5470	0.5027	0.0975	3.4059		0.1318	-0.1880	0.0103	5.9179
2019	0.5388	0.5056	0.1028	3.0206		0.2178	-0.1441	0.0573	3.3465
2020	0.5364	0.5089	0.1087	3.1345		0.3262	0.0185	0.1123	4.1153

Chapter 9
Public-Private Partnerships as a Way of Financing and Supporting Utility Companies

Pavlina Stojanova
https://orcid.org/0000-0001-9357-019X
International Slavic University, North Macedonia

Lence Petreska
International Slavic University, North Macedonia

ABSTRACT

In the last two decades, the public utility companies in North Macedonia are becoming more and more dysfunctional, and the services they offer are continuously of lower quality. Subsequently, they became a training ground for political-party employment and calculations. Hence, there is a need to find an efficient model that will overcome the problems faced by public utilities. The purpose of this chapter is to give an overview of the possibilities for public-private partnerships as a solution for improving the services and efficiency of utility companies. Finding an efficient solution for managing public utility companies is of great importance, both for citizens who regularly pay for utility services and do not receive them with adequate quality and for the Government of the Republic of North Macedonia, which at certain intervals must intervene financially with funds from the budget to be able to discharge the over-indebted utility companies.

DOI: 10.4018/978-1-6684-7730-4.ch009

INTRODUCTION

For the last twenty years, the public in the Republic of North Macedonia has been dealing with the topic of public utility companies, their efficiency and their economic operation. The public utility companies in the Republic of North Macedonia are continuously in debt, and this seriously affects the services they provide to the citizens. In continuity, the Government of the Republic of North Macedonia, for a certain period of time, pays funds to the municipalities from the state budget so that they can discharge the debts of the utility companies. The last such financial intervention by the Government took place in 2017, which paid all the debts of the municipalities and their utility companies. Unfortunately, only 5 years later, today, the majority of utility companies are again over-indebted, and the topic of the way those companies are managed is being raised again. The possibility of creating public-private partnerships in the area of delivering communal services appears as one of the possible solutions for this situation.

Public-private partnership in the Republic of North Macedonia is regulated by the Law on Concessions and Public-Private Partnership, and such partnership is established by contract. Namely, according to the Law on Concessions and Public-Private Partnership, public-private partnership means a form of contractually regulated, long-term cooperation between the public partner and the private partner, which is characterized by the following:

1. The private partner undertakes the obligation to provide a public service for the end users in areas of the public partner's competence and/or the obligation to provide the public partner with the necessary prerequisites for providing a public service to the end users and/or activities under its competence:
2. In order to fulfill the obligations from point a), the private partner can undertake to:
    - finances, designs, builds and/or reconstructs/renovates a public infrastructure facility, operates and maintains a new facility and/or reconstructed/renovated a public infrastructure facility or
    - uses, manages and maintains an existing facility of public infrastructure or
    - any combination of the above-mentioned obligations as long as the combination of those obligations is aimed at fulfilling the objectives set in point 1);
3. When undertaking the obligation from points 1) and 2), the private partner usually assumes a significant part of the risks related to financing, construction, demand and/or availability and other such actions, management, maintenance

and technical risks, depending on what was agreed upon during establishment the public-private partnership is determined on a case-by-case basis;

4. Each partner in a public-private partnership for the duration of the public-private partnership will take responsibility for risk events that are in his sphere of influence, or the responsibility is shared in order to achieve optimal risk management for the duration of the partnership, among other things, with using management, technical, financial and innovation capabilities of the private partner and by promoting the exchange of skills and knowledge - experience between the public and private partner, without the same being in contradiction with point 3);
5. In exchange for the undertaken obligations, the public partner may grant the private partner a concession for public work or a concession for public service or compensate him through payment;
6. The public partner can also enable the private partner to perform certain commercial, and economic activities, in addition to the obligations from points 1) and 2), determined in the contract, but only if there is no other possible way to ensure the necessary level of cost efficiency of private participation and reasonable return on investment;
7. The public partner can transfer certain real rights to the private partner necessary for the performance of contractual obligations.

Depending on the purpose of the compensation funds by the public partner for the provision of public work and/or public services, as well as the distribution of the key existing risks, the public-private partnership can be established as:

(a) Concession for public work or
(b) Public service concession or
(c) Contract for public procurement of work or
(d) Contract for public service procurement.

In the Republic of North Macedonia, public-private partnership is most often realized in the provision of various types of public services and infrastructure projects, such as transport (roads, railways, airports), telecommunications, drinking water supply and wastewater treatment, waste management, health, facilities intended for education (schools, boarding schools), social protection and environmental protection.

BACKGROUND

During the preparation of this chapter, a literature review was made on the importance of public-private partnerships as a solution for increasing the efficiency of public utility companies, with an in-depth analysis of studies on public-private partnership and their efficiency in delivering public utility services. The scholarly studies were searched using Researchgate.net, Academia.edu, and Google Scholar platform. (Angelov, 2005; Akintola et al., 2003; Akintola, Matthias, 2008; Albert, 2006; Charles, Adrian, 1995; Darrin, Mervyn, 2004; Denton 2006; Gregory 2003; Ellen 2008; Yescombe, 2007; Jovanović, Sredojević, 2016; Levy, 2011; Paolo, 2010; Richard, Esther, 2008). Some keywords used were public-private partnership, investors' equity, loans, bonds, and risk. While writing the chapter, we encountered a more serious problem during the research on the situation with public-private partnerships in North Macedonia. Namely, in the last 15 years, no one has researched this issue either from a scientific or professional point of view.

BASIC CHARACTERISTICS OF PUBLIC-PRIVATE PARTNERSHIPS

There is no precise legal definition for public-private partnerships, despite the fact that the concept is applied in a large number of countries. In general, public-private partnerships represent a complex contractual arrangement between partners from the public and private sectors for joint financing and implementation of a public project or joint performance of a public service. Although it is obviously very broad and covers various forms of cooperation between the public and private sectors, this definition still adequately expresses the essence and characteristics of public-private partnerships. In fact, the concept of public-private partnerships represents a range of arrangements that lie in the middle between:

- The concept of public procurement, where the risk for the realization of the public service is entirely on the side of the public sector and where the private partner has the sole role of contractor according to precisely defined criteria in advance, and
- The concept of concessions and privatization, where the risk for the realization of the public service is completely transferred to the private partner.

In public-private partnerships, the government or municipal authorities and private partners share the investments, costs and obligations of the public service, the revenues from it, as well as the risks related to the realization of the service. In doing so, the main interest is to use the specific advantages of the government or municipal authorities and private partners in relation to the financing, implementation and servicing of public facilities or services. Public-private partnerships combine the advantages and strengths of public and private sector partners and create an optimal complex relationship.

Unlike public procurement and concessions, in public-private partnerships, partners can take initiative and a leadership role in conceiving the services they provide, in providing funds for their implementation, in improving the services they provide, or in all elements simultaneously. This is a key feature and advantage of public-private partnerships as it allows private partners initiative and leadership in areas of their choice. This characteristic gives them important bargaining power and elevates them to the level of equal partners with the government or municipal authorities.

Although we do not abstract the other forms of public-private partnerships, we will mainly focus on the arrangements in which the private partners have a leadership role, i.e., public-private partnerships in which private partners are initiators, developers and main financiers of public services.

The implementation of new public services, in which the private sector has a leadership role in planning, development and financing, is mainly carried out through the model of the so-called "project financing". There is no universal definition even for the concept of project financing, although this model has been widely used in the last few decades in finding solutions that would improve public services.

In general, project financing represents a complex arrangement of deposits and loans and other contractual obligations for the financing of public services in which creditors approve loans solely based on the forecasted future revenues from the operation of public enterprises. In project financing, the return on loans and capital invested depends entirely on the success of the public enterprise and the services it provides. Due to such an approach, project financing is also called financing without or with limited coverage. In theory, project financing represents a model that does not create any other obligation for private investors in addition to their contribution. However, unsecured financing, in the strict sense of the word, is extremely rare because lenders always require additional coverage and guarantees in addition to the profitability of the public service, which is a central element of the collateral. Namely, in practice, creditors insist on various guarantees, deposits or other obligations from private investors or third parties in order to guarantee the loans. The collateral of each specific case of project financing depends on the very nature of the public service, risks during its implementation, i.e., the certainty of achieving sustainable and regular income, as well as the creditworthiness of private investors.

Financial resources provided for the improvement of public services usually consist of loans and equity contributions. Loans are the main source of financing in the project financing model. Loans are granted by commercial banks organized in an association or syndicate of banks. Loans are approved under the condition that their repayment has priority over all other obligations during the realization of the public service.

The second type of capital consists of contributions by private investors who are interested in investing in public services. Contributions represent a smaller part of the total cost in the realization of the public service (usually from 20% to 40%).

In order to secure loans, private investors must guarantee priority payment to lenders and other lenders. The private partners' investment begins to return only after the loans and other debt capitals are repaid. Private investors actually take the biggest risk in the entire venture, but on the other hand, they also receive the biggest part of the profit during the realization of public services after the return of loans and other debt capital.

During the realization of such an investment, the establishment of the project company is beyond doubt. During the establishment of the same government or municipal authorities and private investors, under strictly defined criteria, they agree on the forms and models of cooperation, the distribution of obligations as well as the distribution of profits. The project company is at the center of the project financing structure because it assumes all obligations regarding the financing, implementation and subsequent use of public services, and it has more weight because all participants conclude contractual relations with it. The project company is established in the state or municipality where the public service will be implemented, and the initiative to establish a project company is initiated by the private investor who, by investing in it, becomes its partner. The project company has a different legal personality from its partners, which is why the debts and obligations it assumes are not recorded as debts on the partners' balance sheet, i.e., the government or municipalities and private investors. In addition, according to one of the key provisions of its statute, the project company aims to implement the public service, i.e., it may not undertake other activities that are not directly related to the implementation and use of the public service.

This is a very important feature and advantage of the project financing model because the uniqueness of the project company protects private investors from additional risks. Not writing the debt of the project company on the balance sheet of the private investors limits their potential loss and allows them to take other investments. Limiting the activities of the project company only to aspects directly related to public service limits the chances of it falling into financial difficulties. The form of the project company depends on the obligations arising from the loan, the tax conditions of other aspects of the legislation of the host country and the preferences of the partner. Thus, the project company can be a limited partnership, a limited liability company, a joint-stock company or another form that is a combination of the previous ones.

The only source of income for the project company is the income resulting from the sale of public services. These revenues are the only source for paying off the debt, covering operating costs, returning the investment of the investors and making a profit.

Participants in public-private partnerships vary depending on the specific service, depending on the modality of private sector participation, and depending on the arrangements applied to the financing of the public-private partnership. Typical participants in public services based on public-private partnerships are:

- The public sector. Regardless of the modality of public sector participation in the service, its participation and support are essential.
- Private investors. Private investors invest their own funds in providing public service. They are founders and partners in the project company. Often, the investors themselves or one of their subsidiary companies also take on the role of contractors, operators, suppliers or users of the service.
- The banks. Banks represent the main source of capital in the project financing model. When providing loans for the implementation of a service of a public nature, banks form associations, i.e., syndicates, in order to raise a large amount of financial resources – far greater than an individual bank can provide. The purpose of the bank union is to share loans, share risks and provide a political guarantee for the success of the public-private partnership.
    - At the same time, one or several banks that have the greatest expertise and experience needed for the competitive service of a public nature assume a leadership role in the negotiation with other banks for securing the total amount of loans. The lead bank also facilitates the project company's debt management.
- International financial institutions. The World Bank, the International Finance Corporation and other regional development support banks, such as the European Bank for Reconstruction and Development or the European Investment Bank, often take on the role of lender or promoter of public-private partnerships in developing countries. International financial institutions also provide a certain political guarantee that the domestic government will not take actions that would hinder public-private partnerships. In addition, these institutions assume the role of facilitators of the implementation of new public services based on public-private partnerships by implementing programs to improve the legal environment to support private investments.

- Agencies to support the export of developed countries. Since the improvement of public sector services in developing countries often presupposes the importation of equipment and expertise from developed countries, export support agencies from developed countries take part based on the support of public-private partnerships.

FORMS AND MODELS OF PUBLIC-PRIVATE PARTNERSHIPS

The basic factor that determines the forms of public-private partnerships is the degree of control of the private factor over the public service and its participation in financing, that is, the degree of initiative and risk taken by the private partner (European Commission, 2003).

Public-private partnerships are based on the assumption that partners from the public and private sectors have special advantages in relation to the performance of public services. By enabling each partner to do what they are most capable of, public services are implemented in the most economically efficient way. The challenge of public-private partnerships is to structure the relationship between the partners, which will allow the risks to be taken by the partner who can most effectively control and guarantee them, and the relationship which will allow each partner to make the most of their strengths. If properly designed, public-private partnerships have the potential to deliver significant benefits to the public sector (savings), the private partner (profits) and end users (better services).

The process of developing public services based on public-private partnerships is extremely dynamic. Therefore, there is no general model of public-private partnerships or a model that can be applied in every situation. The choice of the specific model and the specificities of each arrangement are determined by the very needs of public services, partners and the situation. There are many different forms of public-private partnerships, and new modalities are constantly being developed that better suit the specificities of each public service and the conditions imposed by partners from both the public and private sectors. In any case, a number of elements of public-private partnerships are common in many forms.

The terminology used to name the various forms of public-private partnerships is not universal. There are several terms that are used as synonyms, such as, for example, the "turnkey" and "design-build" model or the "build-operate-transfer" (BOT) model and the general form of concession. There are also terms that are used too generally and for cases that are essentially different. For example, BOT is used both in cases of fully private financing and in cases of public financing of infrastructure facilities. Similarly, BOT is used both in cases where a concession fee is paid and in cases where it is not paid. Therefore, the analysis of the models of public-private partnerships should not be satisfied only by defining the term and the concept but should also include an essential analysis of the contractual obligations (European Commission, 2003).

The concept of public-private partnerships is increasingly being applied in the performance of public services with a greater social dimension and which do not offer large opportunities for profit to private partners. This further increases the number of models of public-private partnerships but also creates additional confusion regarding the concept and terminology of public-private partnerships. The various forms of public-private partnerships can be placed on a continuum between public procurement and privatization.

When it comes to public-private partnerships, one cannot help but mention two models that are very similar to public-private partnerships. The first model is public procurement, i.e., governments or municipal authorities call for tenders for some of their needs, and partners from the private sector usually call on them. In that case, the role of private partners is limited to the design or performance of a service. Designing and execution represent separate processes for which different tenders are organized in which two different companies may be selected. In this approach, the public sector is fully responsible for the financing, use and maintenance of the public facility or service for which it fully assumes the risks (European Commission, 2003). As a result, in the investment of the public sector, the entire tender procedure and the selection of a contractor are organized as quickly as possible, but the procedure organized in this way usually results in errors and omissions during conceptualization and design, which are then reflected in the work of the best-rated bidder. Then, due to the additional costs of correcting design errors or performing additional work, the total cost may exceed the highest bid price.

On the other hand, in the case of privatization of infrastructure or public enterprises, full control is transferred to the private sector, in exchange for the value of the entire facility or enterprise or for the management package. This approach is considered not to contribute the best to the public interest as the public sector completely loses control over the management of the facility or enterprise and the income it generates. Privatization is particularly sensitive when it comes to infrastructure or public enterprises of national interest, such as for example, national highways, hydro systems, landfills or energy systems. In addition to ideological difficulties, privatization of public infrastructure or public enterprises can also be problematic from a legal point of view if the constitution and laws do not allow it. However, in the event that domestic investors have the financial and managerial ability to purchase a public infrastructural facility or public enterprise, privatization can be a good model for improving public services while keeping revenues in the national economy (European Commission, 2003).

Tenders and privatization are not forms of public-private partnerships. They are presented in this review solely for the purpose of highlighting the differences in relation to public-private partnerships and for the purpose of showing the extreme points of the continuum within which initiative, participation and risks are transferred to the private partner.

In the following section, we will consider six generally accepted models of public-private partnerships (European Commission, 2003):

- "Design-Build" (DB: Design-Build) or "Turn-key". Unlike public procurement, where the choice of the private partner for design and construction is separate and divided, the "design-build" model unites the design and construction of facilities that will improve the public service in one contract with a fixed price. In this model, the private partner takes full responsibility for design and construction, while the public sector provides full financing. In this model, the designer and the contractor are the same company or a consortium of companies, which offers additional opportunities for saving time, and costs, reducing risks and improving the quality of services.
- "Design-Build-Guarantee" (Design-Build with Warranty). In a similar variant of this model, the private contractor guarantees the performance according to fixed technical specifications and the quality of service performed during a certain period (usually up to 20 years). This approach primarily means transferring the risks to the private partner, i.e., the greater incentive for quality performance of services and, at the same time, freeing the public sector from inspection and maintenance costs.
- Long-term lease or concession. The long-term lease or concession model represents the assignment of the management of an infrastructure facility or public service to a private partner for a certain period of time. Under this approach, the private partner pays the public sector a concession fee in exchange for the right to collect revenue from the provision of the public service over a specified period of time. In addition to the concession fee, the private partner is responsible for the management and maintenance of the facilities and infrastructure, which in certain cases may also mean capital investments. The benefits of the long-term lease or concession consist in transferring the responsibility for charging the public service to the private partner, transferring all risks to the private partner and achieving higher efficiency and quality in the performance of the public service.
- "Build-Operate-Transfer" (BOT: Build-Operate-Transfer). According to this model, the private partner is responsible for the design, construction and management of all facilities used to provide public service during a certain period, after which ownership and management of public facilities

and services are transferred to the public sector. This model may or may not release the private partner from the obligation to provide financial means to implement the infrastructure project.

BOT arrangements are usually concluded for a period of over 10 years. They are suitable for the implementation of large infrastructure systems, highways, railways, energy projects, water and sewage infrastructure, landfills for solid waste management and others. In the BOT model, the private partner can enjoy the privilege of charging the public service directly from the end-users, or the charging can be in the form of regular payments by the public sector. These payments can be fixed but can be calculated in a variable way, for example, based on the level of use of the public facility or service.

- "Build-Own-Operate" (BOO: Build-Own-Operate) or "Build-Own-Operate-Transfer" (BOOT: Build-Own-Operate-Transfer). According to the BOO model, the responsibility for the design, management and maintenance of the facilities is transferred to the private partner. According to the similar BOOT model, the ownership of the facilities is transferred from the private to the public partner after the expiration of the agreed concession period. The main difference between the BOO model and the other described models is that in the case of the BOO, the private partner is the owner of the public facility during the entire operating period.
- "Design-Build-Finance-Operate" (DBFO: Design-Build-Finance-Operate). The DFBO model builds on the previously described models in that the financing, as well as the risks for the return on the investment, are completely transferred to the private partner. According to this model, the private partner has full control over public services and the right to charge for the public service in order to return the investment.

According to the structure of the relations between the partners, public-private partnerships can be contractual or institutional. Contractual public-private partnerships refer to arrangements based on contractual relationships between formally different partners from the public and private sectors. In institutional public-private partnerships, the partnership between the public and private sectors takes place within the framework of a joint legal entity to which certain public powers are transferred. Thus, an institutional public-private partnership can represent:

- Establishment of a new entity with mixed public and private capital for the purpose of performing public works or services or
- Entry of private capital into existing public enterprises that perform public services.

The described forms of public-private partnerships are theoretical models that are rarely found in "pure form" in reality. In reality, each project is planned according to the conditions and needs of the project itself, its participants and the situation, using elements from different models.

FINANCING AND MECHANISMS OF PUBLIC-PRIVATE PARTNERSHIPS

Financial means for the implementation of public services based on public-private partnerships are provided through direct investments by investors, loans by banks or international financial institutions and bonds issued by the project company. This section presents the main sources of capital, as well as the basic mechanisms for providing financial resources for the implementation of public services based on public-private partnerships.

Investors' Equity

Private investors in public services are the first to provide financial means for the implementation of the service, which is also a prerequisite for securing loans and other financial means.

The number of investors, i.e., partners in the project company, is limited. There are usually two to three investors contributing to simplifying the development, management and control of complex contractual arrangements to complete the financial framework. Investors often self-impose a principle according to which an investor, i.e., a partner, must invest at least 15% of the total shares in the project company or at least 10% of the total value of the investment for the improvement of the public service.

In some cases, the investors' strategy may consist in selling their stake in the project company after consolidating it, i.e., after the activities are undertaken to improve the public service prove that it generates revenues as planned. Thus, after the consolidation of the project company, an active secondary capital market is created where other new investors can enter. For example, a secondary investor can buy back part of the shares in the project company from the original investors at a higher share price than the initial one. Unlike primary investors, who expect a higher rate of return on investment due to the higher risks inherent in the initial stages of investment, secondary investors expect a lower rate of return on investment but also lower risks.

An investor who participated with his own capital in the project company from the beginning, in the case of selling his stake to another investor who later joined the investment, aims to receive compensation for taking on the highest degree of risk. It can achieve this by charging a higher price for selling the shares or shares, bundling additional shares or shares at the same price, or charging the project company a commission for developing the service.

The government or municipal authorities in the country where the public-private partnership takes place and the lenders often impose on investors an obligation not to sell their stakes in the project company before the completion of the execution phase because the investor's participation in the project company during the operational period proves their commitment to a successful implementation of the public service. On the other hand, the secondary market of investments in the project company creates liquidity for the initial investments. Liquidity is important because it allows initial investors to reinvest their capital in other public services. Although limiting transfers of initial investments contribute to the long-term reliability and sustainability of the service, the government or municipal authorities also have an interest in allowing a certain level of liquidity of the initial investments, thereby contributing to increasing the value of the service and to reducing financing costs in the future. Conversely, strict restrictions on the liquidity of initial investments contribute to reducing the attractiveness of public-private partnership services from the point of view of private investors and limiting the number of potential investors and competition between them.

Loans From Banks

Loans from banks are the most important source of capital for the implementation of public services based on public-private partnerships. Considering the volume of the investment for the implementation of public service, a loan from only one bank cannot be sufficient to complete the financial framework. In addition, no bank accepts to provide a high amount of loan, especially in an arrangement with high participation of loans and thereby takes a greater risk of non-return of the loan. For this reason, banks join together in associations or syndicates of banks, granting a joint loan for the implementation of public service.

The usual approach when pooling loans to implement public services of a public-private partnership is to designate one or several banks as lead lenders, who will assume the entire debt for the service and then resell it to other banks in the market. The lead lender's experience of previously implemented public services with the help of a public-private partnership, as well as its previous successful relations with one or several investors, are very important factors in the selection of a lead lender.

The costs of the lead lender are paid subject to the successful completion of the financing framework. The Project Company does not assume any risk as to whether the Pooling of Lands is successful or not. Those obligations and risks are assumed by the leading creditors. One of the important issues that investors should focus on is the moment in which the leading lenders will get involved in providing public service. In an ideal case, in order to achieve maximum competition between banks in terms of financing conditions, the entire contractual structure of the service should be finalized and presented to several banks that will submit an offer for financing. This means that investors should hire an advisor to develop the financial model of the service or do it themselves if they have the expertise and experience.

Alternatively, the project company may arrange with a bank in the early development phase of the service to take on the role of both financial advisor and lead lender. In that case, the bank should be recognized for the costs of the financial counseling and the costs of taking over and selling the entire deposit. In practice, taking into account the extensive work of a financial adviser, which is for a relatively low price, banks accept to be financial advisers of the project only if they are also appointed as leading creditors.

The project company, unlike other common corporate borrowers, does not have a financial history that could serve as a basis for a granting loan-granting decision. Therefore, banks should analyze all contracts because they represent the basis for determining construction costs, operating costs, future revenues from the service, as well as risks. For the analysis of the financial, legal and other technical aspects of the service, the banks, and especially the leading banks, should hire financial, legal and other technical consultants, for which they charge an additional commission from the project company.

Bonds

Bonds issued by the project company are similar to a loan from the perspective of the project company. Buyers of bonds for public services are investors who aim for a high rate of return on investment in the long term without bearing the risks characteristic of direct investments in the project company. These are mainly insurance companies and pension or investment funds. The main difference between loans and bonds is the much more pronounced liquidity of bonds. Bonds had a much larger number of potential buyers, unlike loans that are transferred between a much more limited number of banks. On the other hand, the project company has much more limited relations and control over the bondholders.

Bond investors typically do not directly engage in service and bond analysis themselves to the same extent that banks do. They rely on the analysis of investment banks or securities rating agencies.

Public-private partnership public service bonds can theoretically be either public issues or private placements, which are not listed on the stock exchange and are sold to a limited number of large investors who typically hold them until maturity.

The placement of the bonds can be done without the intervention of the investment bank, i.e., the project company can directly issue the bonds to interested investors, but this happens very rarely. The market for bonds of public services based on public-private partnerships is much smaller than the market for loans.

The main factors that influence the project company's decision to finance through loans or bonds are:

- The size: bonds are only used for large services, as investors want the bond issue to be large enough to achieve market liquidity. For many large services, bank loans are achieved, which is why bonds can be a good alternative.
- Debts: Bonds are usually priced lower than equivalent bank loans, mainly due to a large number of potential bond investors.
- Maturity: bonds are always used for long-term financing. Although banks may also grant long-term loans with maturities of up to 20 years or more, bonds are a better alternative for long-term financing.

As a rule, bonds are used for "standard" services. Bonds are also particularly suitable in the case of re-financing a service once it has already been built and is successfully operating. Conversely, the greater adaptability of bank loans makes loans more suitable for building the early operational phase of services, complex services and services in riskier markets.

Mechanisms for the Control of Public-Private Partnerships

Lenders grant loans to improve public services based on public-private partnerships only if the project company, i.e., investors, provide collateral that, in the event that the debt cannot be repaid, will be taken over or sold, and the proceeds will be used to repay the debt.

The collateral i.e., the provision of the loan, is focused on the ownership of the public service. Lenders insist on full collateral relating to all ownership, rights and claims for service. The collateral consists of all tangible property (objects, real estate and other tangible assets) and intangible property of the service (rights and claims from third parties). Permits, operating licenses and service concession agreements also form part of the collateral. It is important that the legislation of the host country allows the transfer of these rights of creditors to the concessionaire, which is often a necessary prerequisite for the very development of the service and granting of the loan. In the opposite case, the permits, licenses and concession agreements are granted in the name of the creditors.

Creditors insist that the project company take out an insurance policy for the physical property of the service and for the right to take over the insurance in case of damage. Guarantees by investors, the government and municipal authorities of the host country, international institutions or third parties are included in the collateral.

By providing collateral in this way, lenders are assured that ownership of the service will not be sold or otherwise made available to third parties without their consent. It guarantees creditors certainty that no other claimant has any rights or claims against the public service. The essence of the collateral is to preserve the integrity and functionality of the service in the material sense and its rights and claims and their transferability to creditors. In addition to the legal analysis of contractual obligations regarding collateral, service developers and lenders should also analyze their practical applicability. The legal and other costs and challenges of taking collateral largely determine its practical value.

Creditors' efforts to acquire the right to foreclose on collateral in the event of service failure for the purpose of debt recovery are mainly defensive in nature. In fact, lenders, by foreclosing or selling the collateral, can hardly recover the value of the loan if the public service improvement fails.

In most of the public services that are based on public-private partnerships, i.e., project financing, debt repayment is only possible if the service improvement succeeds, works and generates revenue. Taking over or selling the collateral in order to repay the loan is difficult in reality. If the project company and investors fail to ensure profitable operation, the chances of finding other partners in exchange for them, who will succeed, are slim. In addition, services that are implemented in developing countries have an even more limited number of potential takers of public services in the event of a collateral sale. It is even more emphasized in developing countries where the political and economic situation has contributed to the failure.

The collateral described in this way is not the lenders' only mechanism for securing their loan. Creditors condition and secure the loan through control over the management of the project company, right over the investors' stakes and through control over the cash flow when providing the service. If a problem arises that threatens the recovery of the debt, creditors must react quickly. In order to optimize the ability to respond quickly, creditors insist on the assumption of rights arising from the investors' stakes in the project company. If the project company is organized as a joint-stock company, this means the right to the investors' shares; if the project company is organized as a limited liability company, this means the right to the investors' shares. In that way, creditors can act much more simply and quickly in order to ensure the repayment of the land than by selling the collateral. The control put in place in this way allows investors the ability to make quick decisions in case of difficulties.

In addition, creditors, in the case of project financing, have almost complete control over the cash flow and accounts of the project company. Lenders' objective is to ensure that service revenues are used to adequately and timely cover project costs and debt repayments.

All revenues from the provision of the public service under the long-term usage agreements are deposited in a separate account over which creditors have full access and control. The income from this account, which represents part of the collateral, is distributed according to a certain priority. The usual priority of payments is: operating expenses, repayment of the principal debt, repayment of subordinated loans (if any) and finally, returns to investors. Investors may ultimately make a profit if all prior priority claims are paid.

This priority of payouts is called "cascading" because the cash flows into successive "pools" before reaching investors. Each pool represents a certain service cost that must be covered. The water from the first pool is intended to cover the operational costs of the service, the second pool is intended to cover the debt and so on. The number, purpose and depth of each pool depend on the type and scale of costs and risks. As the cash flows down, each successive pool fills and overflows, after which the next pool below is filled. When all pools are filled, the excess cash is distributed to investors as profits.

Through this system of priority payments, creditors ensure that the project company adequately covers its claims and repays the debt.

RISKS IN PUBLIC-PRIVATE PARTNERSHIPS

Risk is uncertainty about costs, loss or damage. Under risk is meant any event or development that can prevent, slow down or make impossible the expected results. Although there are risks that are equally serious for all participants, the special risk of each participant is relative and depends on his capacity and the degree and manner of his participation in the implementation of the public service.

In addition to the general identification and analysis of risks, which is usually prepared by investors and creditors, each participant should identify and analyze the specific risks that they will face during the implementation of the public service. Without a detailed analysis and anticipation of risks from the very beginning of implementing the service, the participants cannot have a clear understanding of the obligations and challenges they will face and, therefore, will not be able to take measures to prevent and deal with the risks in time. Thus, if the participants decide how to deal with problems at the moment they arise, the implementation of the service will inevitably run into serious difficulties, delays and additional costs.

This part of the paper presents the main categories of risks in the implementation of public services based on public-private partnerships. The risks can be grouped into risks during the development period, risks related to construction and use, commercial risks, risks related to the fluctuation of exchange rates, political risks and risks of force majeure (UNCITRAL, 2015).

Risks During the Development Period

Risks during the development period are anticipated in the risk analysis, although risks during the development period may be separately expressed. The development of a public service based on a public-private partnership is a very complex and expensive process. Development costs often amount to several million dollars or euros. Development funds are provided through three main sources: government or municipal grants, development loans or equity.

During the development period, any of the following risks may render the further development of the service pointless. These include the loss of the right to implement the service, the failure to agree on support measures or concessions with the government or municipal authorities of the host country, excessive political or public opposition, the inability to secure long-term users on the necessary scale, the implementation of other services that would be competition, unavailability or uncertainty of the mood of basic inputs, political instability, inflation, changes in legislation and the wider context (Hoffman, 2010).

Risks Related to Construction and Use

The main risks during the implementation of the service occur during the performance period, which include the failure to build and modernize the infrastructure facilities within the given period, within the predetermined budget, or the failure to achieve operational capacity. Similarly, during the operational period, investors may face the risk of not meeting the required operational capacity, not achieving the required amount of output from implementing the service, or operating costs being too high. Risks during the performance and operational period do not concern only private investors. The government or municipal authorities of the host country are also particularly affected if the implementation of the service fails to achieve the projected operational parameters or due to any operational problems endanger the environment.

Some of these risks can be directly caused by the project company itself, by the contractors, operator or service providers. Failure to meet projected operating parameters may be due to faulty initial design, the inadequacy of technology application or the inadequacy of equipment used. During the operational period, non-fulfillment of the planned operational plan or frequent work interruptions can be due to inadequate maintenance of infrastructure facilities or inappropriate use of equipment and systems. Operating cost overruns may be due to poor management (UNCITRAL, 2015).

Some of these risks may also be caused by acts of the government or municipal authorities of the host country. Delays and overruns of operating costs may be due to delays by the government or municipal authorities in issuing the necessary permits and licenses for work, failure to provide construction land for the construction of infrastructure facilities or failure to provide access roads to them, insistence on changing a certain aspect from the implementation of the service, interruptions and delays caused by technical inspections, etc. Enhanced standards regarding technical operations or employee social rights can also increase operating costs.

Commercial Risks

Commercial risks refer to the risk of not being able to realize the anticipated revenues from the implementation of the service due to changes in market prices and conditions or due to a decrease in demand for the required output. Commercial risks can seriously prevent the project company from repaying the debt and threaten the financial viability of the service.

Commercial risks vary depending on the infrastructure sector and the type of service. Commercial risks can be negligible if the project company enjoys exclusivity or monopoly in the given sector or if it serves only one user under a long-term usage contract. However, commercial risks can be serious for services that depend on free market revenues, especially where alternative services exist, making it difficult to predict stable demand.

Exchange Rates or Other Financial Risks

The risk related to foreign exchange rates refers to the unfavorable change in the exchange rate of the local currency that contributes to the reduction of revenues when they are converted into hard currency. Service revenues and user charges in the host country are usually denominated in local currency, while loans and most operating costs and inputs are denominated in foreign currency. This risk can be particularly pronounced if the host country's currency is unstable.

In addition to the fluctuation of exchange rates, the project company may also face the risk of non-convertibility of the local currency into hard currency or the risk of increased control of the exchange of local currency into hard currency. Thus, the project company may find itself unable to repay the debt and cover operating costs that are expressed in foreign currency.

Political Risks

Investors, creditors and other participants in the implementation of the public service from the private sector face the risk that certain acts and measures of the government or municipal authorities may have negative consequences on the implementation of the service. These risks are called political risks. Political risks can be grouped into three broad categories:

- Traditional political risks, which include the nationalization or expropriation of part or all of the property of the project company and the imposition of new unfavorable taxes or other charges on the project company and its activity.
- Regulatory risks, including the introduction of stricter standards for clearing public work or services and opening the sector to competition, and
- Quasi-commercial risks, which include the violation or termination of the concession agreement by the government or municipal authorities or termination of contractual support.

In addition to political risks arising from acts of the host country's government or municipal authorities, some political risks can also be caused by acts of foreign governments. These include embargoes or boycotts by third governments or acts of the governments of the participants in the implementation of the service that has a negative effect.

Cases of Force Majeure

Participants in the implementation of the service are faced with the risk of interruption or damage to the service due to unpredictable events beyond the control of any participant. These events are called force majeure and include natural disasters and unpredictable political events. These unforeseeable events can cause temporary or permanent interruption of the provision of the service and cause major delays, damages and other losses.

In the event of a confirmed and recognized event of force majeure, the affected participant in the service is exempted from obligations within a given period necessary for the normalization of the situation and the re-fulfillment of the assumed obligations. The conditions for calling and exemption due to force majeure events and re-fulfillment of the agreed obligations should be clearly foreseen and arranged in the contracts for the implementation of the public service. Insurance against cases of force majeure is provided through international insurance organizations.

PERSPECTIVES OF PUBLIC-PRIVATE PARTNERSHIPS FOR IMPROVING THE SITUATION WITH UTILITY COMPANIES IN THE REPUBLIC OF NORTH MACEDONIA

Interest and Benefits of the Application of Public-Private Partnerships

The Government of the Republic of North Macedonia and the municipalities have a clear interest in applying public-private partnerships and encouraging private initiative because in this way:

- They enable large capital investments without a significant burden on the public budget and without increasing the public debt,
- Release funds from the budget for other purposes and other public goods
- Encourage domestic investments and attract foreign direct investments,
- Encourage and enable technology transfer,
- They acquire new managerial practices,
- They get a faster and better implementation of public services,
- They transfer the risks of the implementation of the services to the private sector,
- They retain participation in the provision of public service and control over it.

Public-private partnerships enable the implementation of public services without increasing public spending and without increasing public debt since the financial resources are provided by the private sector. Non-increasing public spending and non-increasing public debt are important elements for maintaining macroeconomic stability. The limitation of public spending and public borrowing are also key aspects of the European Monetary Union, towards which the Republic of North Macedonia has a long-term strategic aspiration. Therefore, public-private partnerships are the approach of the future and should be applied in many other areas in order to limit public spending and public debt while implementing public services.

The private sector is usually more efficient in implementing public services. Public-private partnerships contribute to faster and better implementation of public services. The private partners have a clear motive to complete the service as quickly as possible because they need the revenue from the service itself to repay the loans and return the deposits. In addition, public-private partnerships also contribute to the reduction of costs for the construction and maintenance of infrastructure facilities and the reduction of costs for the purchase of the necessary equipment for the service. Savings are usually the result of innovative design, technology or better management in the execution phase.

Public-private partnerships contribute to improving the quality of public services. Private operators depend on the collection of the tariff for the public service from the end users, and in conditions of competition, they have a strong incentive to provide quality public services. In addition, since the public sector is freed from the performance of the public service, it can concentrate on meeting the standards in the performance of the service by the private partner. Finally, the Government and municipal authorities have an interest in the application of public-private partnerships because, in this way, they transfer a significant part of the risks to the private sector while retaining the right to participate in the management of the service and internal control over the performance of the public service.

For these reasons, interested private developers of the service based on a public-private partnership should, in principle, find mutual interest from the Government and the municipalities for the implementation of public services based on a public-private partnership.

North Macedonian Legislation on Concessions and Public-Private Partnerships

In 2008, the law on concessions and other types of public-private partnerships was adopted in the Republic of North Macedonia (Official Gazette of the Republic of North Macedonia 7/2008 of 15.01.2008). With this Law, for the first time, public-private partnerships are regulated, which were not subject to the regulation of the previous concession law. The law on concessions and other types of public-private partnerships was adopted in order to enable and promote the private initiative in the financing of public services and facilities of public interest, as well as to regulate the procedure for granting concessions, i.e., the selection of a private partner for the implementation of services based on public-private partnership. The law also regulates issues related to the monitoring of the performance of works and services from the awarded concession, that is, the awarded contracts for public-private partnerships.

According to the concept of the Law, the concession represents the first and main form of public-private partnerships. Most of the law is devoted to the regulation of issues related to concessions, such as the general characteristics of concessions, preparatory actions for the implementation of public service based on a concession, the types of procedures for the selection of a concessionaire, the competence of the commissions for the selection of concessionaire, selection procedure, concession agreement, termination of concession and other issues. Unlike concessions, the law regulates only the general principles of public-private partnerships. In the context of the Republic of North Macedonia, where public-private partnerships are in their infancy, the general and non-exhaustive way of regulating issues related to public-private partnerships is correct because it allows more freedom and flexibility for both the public and private sectors. Otherwise, detailed regulation could contribute to the rigidity of the rules and hinder the development of services based on public-private partnerships.

According to the Law, a public-private partnership represents an undertaking, different from concession and public procurement, which is based on cooperation between the public and private sectors, in which the public and private partners combine resources and professional knowledge for appropriate targeting of resources, risks and profit ensure the performance of certain public service. A public-private partnership agreement is an agreement of financial interest concluded between a public and a private partner whose subject is the design, financing, construction and maintenance of infrastructure facilities, equipping and/or provision of services by a private partner for the purpose of performing a specific public service.

The private partner can be a domestic or foreign legal or natural person or consortium. The law does not impose special conditions regarding the private partner, but he must, in any case, fulfill the special conditions determined by the tender and project documentation.

The law provides for a contractual and institutional concession, that is, a public-private partnership. A contractual public-private partnership is a partnership between the public and the private partner based on contractual relations, while an institutional public-private partnership is a partnership between the public and the private partner in a common legal entity.

The decision to start a public-private partnership procedure is made by the public partner based on a previous study of the undertaking, which determines the efficiency and risks associated with the implementation. In addition, the Law specifies whether the initiative should or can come from a private partner. The study on providing a service based on a public-private partnership should contain an overview of:

- The risks related to the implementation of the undertaking, taking into account the various ways of sharing the risks between the public and private partners and the impact on the budget revenues and expenditures.
- The economic and financial effects of the venture, including a comparison of the costs of the implementation of the venture as a public-private partnership with the costs of its implementation in another form.
- Comparison of the benefits associated with the implementation of the venture as a public-private partnership with the benefits and social consequences of the implementation of the venture in another form, and
- The legal status of the movable and immovable property, if the rights arising from the property should be transferred by the public partner in favor of the private partner.

The awarding of a concession contract, that is, a public-private partnership, is carried out through a public call, an open call, a limited call or a competitive dialogue. The choice of the procedure for awarding a concession contract, i.e., a public-private partnership depends on the complexity and specificity of the subject of the concession, the volume and complexity of the tender documentation for the implementation of the procedure, the number of expected bidders or candidates and the complexity of the offers or requests for participation. In any procedure, the public partner must receive bids from at least three bidders. The decision to start the procedure for awarding a concession, i.e., public-private partnerships, must be properly published in the domestic or foreign public media.

The procedure for awarding a concession, i.e., a public-private partnership, is prepared, organized and implemented by a commission formed by a competent authority from the area for which the concession is awarded or the public-private partnership is concluded, and it consists of a president, at least three members and their deputies, appointed from the employees of the Ministry of Finance and other competent ministries.

Criteria on which the public partner will base the selection of the best offer is the financial or economic most favorable offer. The most economically advantageous offer is evaluated on the basis of criteria related to performance and functional requirements that include quality, price of works and services, technical value, aesthetic and functional characteristics, environmental characteristics, current costs, economic profitability in relation to costs, the technical assistance and period of completion of the performance works.

The public sector can make a decision to terminate the procedure for awarding a concession, i.e., a public-private partnership, if:

- A sufficient number of offers have not been submitted according to the public call,
- The content of the submitted offers does not correspond to the requirements contained in the public call,
- There is no need to implement a procedure as a result of circumstances that were not known, nor could be known at the time of granting the decision to start the procedure; irregularities and irregularities are determined during the implementation of the procedure for granting the concession that cannot be removed without changing the conditions under which the procedure was carried out.
- The first and second-ranked candidates subsequently renounce the conclusion of the concession agreement, that is, a public-private partnership.

The concession agreement, i.e., public-private partnership is concluded by the public partner and the first-ranked candidate within three months from the day of the selection decision. The concession contract or public-private partnership can also be awarded to the second-ranked candidate if the first-ranked candidate does not fulfill the conditions and does not conclude the contract within the stipulated period.

The concession agreement, i.e., public-private partnership is concluded in writing in at least three original copies, of which one is for the contracting parties and the third copy for records in the register of granted concessions maintained by the Ministry of Finance. The provisions of the Law on Obligation Relations shall be applied accordingly to the concession agreement or public-private partnership unless otherwise stipulated by the provisions of the Law on Concessions and other types of public-private partnerships and other special laws.

The public partner carries out constant and regular supervision of the way of performing public works and services and the realization of the awarded contract. The public partner can make recommendations for better execution of works, stop the work when it is a matter of higher public interest and modify the contract in order to adjust the public interest. In that case, the private partner acquires the right to fair compensation adequate compensation, as well as the right to extend the validity of the amended contract.

The public-private partnership agreement must contain the following elements:

- The purpose, subject and term of the public-private partnership agreement,
- The description of the subject of the contract, as well as the description of the existing infrastructure;
- The date of entry into force of the agreement;
- The conditions, method and terms of handing over the object of the contract and termination of the contract;
- The rights and obligations of the parties to the contract, including the terms and deadlines for their fulfillment;
- The amount, terms and method of payment for the realization of the contract;
- The method of dividing the risk;
- The criteria for quality and standards that will be applied in the implementation of the undertaking,
- The types, scale and deadlines for fulfilling the obligation to invest;
- The type, amount, terms and method of delivery of the guarantees and securities established for the fulfillment of the obligations under the contract;
- The responsibility for non-fulfillment of the obligations under the contract, the conditions and the method of performing the supervision of the implementation of the contract, including provisions for the performance of special professional supervision by authorized third parties, as well as the

method of reimbursement of the expenses for the implementation of the professional supervision,
- The method of resolving disputes regarding the contract;
- Other obligations stipulated by the Law, other laws and the regulations adopted on the basis of those laws;
- The method and conditions for acquiring and using the location where the necessary infrastructure facility will be built;
- The installations and stops that will be built and/or upgraded and/or reconstructed at the risk of the private partner;
- The obligations of the private partner to regulate the legal and property issues related to the insurance of the construction site;
- The role of subcontractors, if any, is involved.

In order to create an efficient policy in the field of concessions and public-private partnerships, the Law provides for the establishment of a Council for concessions and public-private partnerships. The Council aims to study issues related to the policy of managing services in the field of concessions and public-private partnerships and the problems arising from inadequate and insufficient regulation of this matter. The Council should prepare proposals. Opinions and initiatives that will be the basis for the development of a Strategy for the realization of services based on concessions and public-private partnerships.

The Council for Concessions and Public-Private Partnerships consists of representatives from the Ministries of Economy, Finance, Transport and Communications, Health, Education and Science, Environment and Spatial Planning, as well as representatives of the Secretariat for Legislation, two representatives from the Community of Local Self-Government Units, as well as two experts from the field of economics and law. The establishment of the Council is in accordance with the positive experiences of the existence of such a coordinating body at the national level.

Readiness for Public-Private Partnerships

The "clean" institutional structure foresees wide participation of the private sector in the provision of services. Well-structured public-private partnerships could be one means through which utilities could achieve greater autonomy as well as achieve other benefits (competition, new skills, increased efficiency, etc.). There are two prerequisites for these benefits to materialize. Both need to be strengthened before broad private-sector participation can be advocated. These prerequisites are:

- A more transparent, predictable and stable operational and regulatory environment than the existing one, especially in relation to the determination of tariffs in the network service and other activities with characteristics of a natural monopoly. These are water supply, sewerage and disposal of solid waste – tariff regulation is not required for the collection of solid waste if it is tendered.
- High level of public acceptance for the private sector to participate in water supply, sanitation and solid waste services.

In terms of public acceptance, the perception based on previous experiences of privatization in the Republic of North Macedonia is not very positive, and one of the unheard-of examples of bad privatization in the solid waste management sector is the terminated contract for the management of the sanitary landfill near Veles. The research, which dealt with the attitudes towards "alternative" service providers, provides a basis for a much more precise characterization of the attitudes towards the participation of the private sector in water supply, sewage and solid waste management.

Focus groups and interviews with key people revealed different views on alternative service providers, from acceptance to strong skepticism that alternative service providers could be a positive solution. On the positive side, public-private partnerships in the public utility sector (especially solid waste management) are seen as:

- A more efficient way to limit or prevent the influence of politics in the field of public utilities
- Way to get better services, especially in relation to
  - More efficient provision of services;
  - Better quality of services;
  - Higher collection rate;
- Increased flexibility;
- Closer relations with users.

As a counterweight to these possible advantages, several negative factors were also identified:

- Probability of price increase;
- Risk that services will not really improve;
- The risk that few of the large investments in water supply and sewerage will actually be made when private companies are in control.

SOLUTIONS AND RECOMMENDATIONS

A public-private partnership has gained importance in the last twenty years, and in this period, it is at the peak of actuality, which is explained by several factors: the problem of insufficient budget funds for the realization of large projects is overcome, the effort to achieve greater benefit based on the use of the knowledge (know-how) and working methods of the private sector and the change of the role of the public sector from a direct participant to a subject that appears in the role of organizer, controller and regulator.

The objectives to be achieved with public-private partnership are agreement and execution of a larger number of projects, natural market division of risk between the private and public sector, more efficient and economical use of taxpayers' funds, use of the higher productivity of private entrepreneurs in the construction and greater efficiency in the management of facilities, the creation of additional value by combining financial and human resources and stimulating economic growth.

The private sector has a dominant role in the design, engineering, construction, reconstruction, maintenance, financing and management of the project, while the public sector basically focuses on defining the basic objectives to be achieved, above all, the quality of services and their prices and compensation. The essence of public-private partnership is also seen in risk allocation because for the success of the project, it is important to correctly establish the risks associated with each component and phase of the project and then to allocate them so that the balance ensures the best value (for the invested resources) in relation to the risk assumed by the partner who can manage those risks in the best way, thereby minimizing the overall costs. Public-private partnership improves the employment situation, that is, the number of realized public-private partnerships is a directly proportional factor in increasing the number of employees, and thus improving the standard of living of the basic political subject - the citizen.

The current legislation in the Republic of North Macedonia enables the creation of public-private partnerships for the delivery of communal services. Hence, it is one of the possible solutions that would be in function of efficient and quality delivery of utility services and reduction of debts of public utility companies.

FUTURE RESEARCH DIRECTIONS

Public-private partnership is one of the frequent political, economic, media and social topics, both in the world and in the Republic of North Macedonia. The partnership of the public and private sectors, which is aimed at providing public services or fulfilling some duty (function) of the public sector, is increasing at all levels of public authority - both central and local. In many developed countries, but also in those that are going through the transition process, roads, railways, airports, prisons, schools, dormitories, hospitals, sports facilities, schools, devices for the needs of the public sector, water and drainage systems, systems for environmental protection, etc. are realized by applying some of the forms of public-private partnership.

With the public-private partnership in the Republic of North Macedonia, the private initiative in the financing of public services is promoted; equal access and transparency are established in the procedure for awarding contracts for public-private partnership, as well as for ensuring quality and efficient performance of the works and services that are the subject of the awarded contracts.

Analyzes and practice show that there is support for private businesses, the Government of the Republic of Moldova, in the past few years, has gradually tended to develop the concepts of public-private partnership. Also, the efforts of the European institutions are included here, which more and more clearly impose their rules for the development of the private sector, and public-private partnerships are presented as one of the basic segments of these efforts. Of great importance to this economic, legal institute - PPP is that the legal regulation in the Republic of Moldova is in constant reform in order to be contemporary and unified with the legal regulation of the EU.

Hence, further research should be focused on finding an acceptable model for public-private partnerships, as well as appropriate legislation that will be in function for those public-private partnerships. Studies should analyze the efficiency of public-private partnerships in the delivery of quality and timely utility services.

CONCLUSION

An effective and efficient public-private partnership, as well as a sustainable public-private partnership, means a well-prepared feasibility study, tender documentation and a public-private partnership agreement. Two-way communication between stakeholders in the formulation of the public-private partnership project can increase the application of public-private partnerships. Most of the data (agreement notices and tender documentation with a template agreement) should be available to all interested private partners. When deciding on a public-private partnership as a means of managing public utilities, the potential long-term gains in efficiency and effectiveness, as well as the public interest, should be considered. When taking into account real effectiveness, a good cost and revenue analysis must be done to test investments in public-private partnerships. This can also be achieved through the concept of value for money.

From what has been said so far, it can be concluded that the establishment of public-private partnerships for the delivery of communal services in the Republic of North Macedonia significantly improves the quality of services, as well as the efficiency in their timely delivery. Such an approach in the management of public utility companies will also be beneficial for the Government, as it will reduce the need for occasional financial interventions from the Budget for debt relief of indebted public utility companies, something that has been a practice for the past twenty years.

REFERENCES

Akintola, A., & Matthias, B. (2008). *Policy, Management and Finance for Public-Private Partnerships (Innovation in the Built Environment).* Wiley-Blackwell. doi:10.1002/9781444301427

Akintola, A., Matthias, B., & Cliff, H. (2003). Public-Private Partnerships: Managing Risks and Opportunities. Blackwell Science Ltd.

Albert, N. L. (2006). *Public private partnerships: innovation strategies and policy alternatives*. Birkhäuser.

Angelov, G. (2005). *Handbook for Mayors and Members of Municipal Councils in the Republic of North Macedonia.* Association of Local Self-Government Units of the Republic of North Macedonia.

Charles, T. W., & Adrian, J. S. (1995). *Privatized Infrastructure: The Build Operate Transfer Approach.* Thomas Telford. doi:10.1680/pitba.20535

Darrin, G., & Mervyn, K. L. (2004). *Public Private Partnerships: The Worldwide Revolution in Infrastructure Provision and Project Finance.* Edward Elgar Pub.

Denton W. S. LLP. (2006). *Public Private Partnerships: Bot Techniques and Project Finance*. Euromoney Books.

Ellen, P. (2008). Public Private Partnerships. Elsevier Ltd.

European Commission. (2003). *Guidelines for Successful Public-Private Partnership*. Author.

Gregory, C. S. (2003). *Defending Interests: Public-Private Partnerships in W.T.O. Litigation*. Brookings Institution Press.

Hoffman, S. L. (2010). *The Law and Business of International Project Finance*. Academic Press.

Jovanović, T., & Sredojević, S. (2016). *Strengthening the Determinants of the Local Government Capacities for the Successful PPP Implementation in the Western Balkans*. The Political Economy of Local Regulation.

Levy, S. M. (2011). *Public-Private Partnerships - Case Studies on Infrastructure, DevelopmentAmericanSocietyofCivilEngineers*. ASCE. doi:10.1061/9780784410134

Paolo, U. (2010). *Public-Private Partnerships: Success and Failure Factors for In-Transition Countries*. University Press of America.

Richard, F., & Esther, G. (2008). *Regulating Water and Sanitation for the Poor: Economic Regulation for Public and Private Partnerships*. Earthscan Publications Ltd.

UNCITRAL. (2015). *Legislative Guide*. Author.

Yescombe, E. R. (2007). *Public-Private Partnerships: Principles of Policy and Finance*. Elsevier Ltd. doi:10.1016/B978-075068054-7.50025-3

KEY TERMS AND DEFINITIONS

Bonds: A fixed-income instrument that represents a loan made by an investor to a borrower (typically corporate or governmental).

Exchange Rates: The value of one currency for the purpose of conversion to another.

Legislation: Legislation is the process or result of enrolling, enacting, or promulgating laws by a legislature, parliament, or analogous governing body.

Loans: A loan is a sum of money that one or more individuals or companies borrow from banks or other financial institutions so as to financially manage planned or unplanned events.

Public-Private Partnerships: Public-private partnerships involve collaboration between a government agency and a private-sector company that can be used to finance, build, and operate projects, such as public transportation networks, parks, and convention centers.

Risk: Possibility of loss or injury.

Chapter 10
Fiscal Federalism and Local Public Utility Policy in the Conditions of Uncertainty by the Energy Crisis:
An Empirical Review

Jadranka Đurović Todorović
University of Niš, Serbia

Milica Ristić Cakić
University of Niš, Serbia

Marina Đorđević
University of Niš, Serbia

ABSTRACT

Public utility service providers are expected to perform positively, with reduced prices and without losses that could put pressure on the local self-government budget. The global energy crisis has had negative impacts on public utility services in the Republic of Serbia. Many public companies, including those in the heating sector, have faced operational problems and rising business costs. The local self-governments, however, are obligated to ensure the availability of utility products and the distribution and supply of heating to their citizens. By considering the fundamental features of fiscal federalism, this chapter will analyze the pricing strategy of the heating company in Leskovac. The main objective of the work is to examine the impact of increasing energy prices on heating prices. Based on the results and indicators, conclusions are drawn, and recommendations are given for further research in the field of operations of public utility companies with the aim of overcoming the consequences of the energy crisis as easily as possible.

DOI: 10.4018/978-1-6684-7730-4.ch010

INTRODUCTION

One of the important utility services is the production, distribution, and supply of heating, a function that is delegated to public utility companies in the area of heating. Thus, these public utility companies faced a big problem at the beginning of the world's Energy crisis. The world is facing rising energy costs and a huge challenge in reducing their effects on production. "By contrast, the need to adapt to rising energy costs is neither widely accepted nor widely understood" (Kreps, 2020, p. 696). High energy costs have a significant impact on public utility companies, especially in developing countries where public utility services have been assigned to municipalities, raising questions about the efficiency of the provision of these services. Many affected local communities are struggling with energy problems. The energy markets have experienced significant disruptions since the outbreak of the Russia-Ukraine conflict. In late 2022, soaring energy prices triggered the risk of energy supply shortages, propelling the issue of energy costs to the forefront. The pricing strategy for the heating company has become very important in order to analyze its business strategy.

The implemented pricing strategy is crucial for public revenues, especially in light of the continuous growth in heating energy costs. It is important to strike a balance between meeting the needs of the population and covering costs, given that there is a degree of freedom in determining the price of heating at the decentralized level. In the cities of the Republic of Serbia, energy costs mainly consist of coal and fuel oil expenses. Natural gas presents a challenge for most cities in the Republic of Serbia, making it imperative to implement an adequate heating strategy before its introduction. Research has shown that "the efficient and clean use of coal through district heating systems can help curb the growing demand for heating energy" (Guo & Xiao, 2022). This system has been successful in China, reducing emissions from heating while providing heat to growing areas. It is important to find an optimal business approach that leads to sustainable heating and improves the efficiency of local self-government. Strategic management of public revenues and expenditures is also a key factor in improving the quality of life in cities worldwide.

This paper presents the results of the operation of a public utility company during the ongoing energy crisis, a problem typical of the heating sector in Serbia. It analyzes the performance of a heating company in Leskovac to study the negative impact of the energy crisis. Examining the key principles of fiscal federalism, this paper will examine the rising energy costs and their effect on pricing strategy. This chapter is devoted to analyzing the consequences of the energy crisis and offering recommendations for future challenges. The study is based on statistical data analysis methods applied at the level of local self-government to examine the changes in local policy. The ultimate goal is to achieve sustainable heating and enhance the efficiency of local self-government. By analyzing reports from the public utility company, the paper examines the revenue and expenses to determine the potential impact on the business performance of public utility companies providing heat energy services. The results of the work should create a basis for considering this policy in other countries as well. In order to fulfil the aim of the study, the following hypothesis is tested.

H1. The increase in heating prices of public utility services in the Republic of Serbia is significantly determined by the increasing energy costs as a consequence of the global energy crisis.

We analyze the developing region of the Republic of Serbia and the problems it faces during the period of the current crisis. Based on the relevant data obtained from the primary and secondary reports of the heating company in the city of Leskovac, an appropriate methodology that involves appropriate statistical techniques is implemented. Based on the results and indicators, conclusions are drawn, and recommendations are given for further research in the field of operations of public utility companies with the aim of overcoming the consequences of the energy crisis as easily as possible. Bearing in mind that there is a limitation regarding the availability of data during the research, special recommendations are directed toward the research of thermal energy consumption through district heating and gas.

BACKGROUND

Theoretically, the need for decentralized management appeared as early as the 1950s, when the arguments in Thibu's model stated that local self-governments could better and better manage public goods. That is when fiscal decentralization gained particular importance. It was believed that local self-government could best influence economic development and social well-being. Financial theory believed that public functions should be left to narrower territorial units (Anđelković, 2009).

The main goal of public utility companies is to operate with a profit. Otherwise, if it were to happen that their business records a loss, the budget would be burdened. Therefore, it is very important that local governments achieve the greatest possible efficiency in the provision of public utility services. This task is very difficult precisely because these services are decentralized, and individual local governments cannot cope with the problems of the modern market. In addition, when providing public utility services, it is necessary to provide a price for these services that will be acceptable from the consumer's point of view and have a social dimension, but also a price that will ensure the company's business with a profit (Filipović & Krnjeta, 2013).

Decentralization in the Republic of Serbia refers to the powers of different levels of government in establishing, introducing and determining the amount of certain public revenues. It represents the relationships established between local communities that are related to public revenues. (Đurović-Todorvić & Đorđević, 2011). Fiscal decentralization implies the responsibility of local self-government for costs. Local self-governments in the Republic of Serbia, therefore, strive to achieve greater efficiency and effectiveness in the management of public resources. Due to inadequate management, fiscal decentralization can threaten local budgets. Research conducted on a sample of 143 local governments in the Republic of Serbia in 2012 showed that the "average" local government in the Republic of Serbia produces public services, i.e., production costs that are approximately 23 percent higher than "best practice" (Radulović & Dragutinović, 2012).

Public utilities must maintain a balance between economic and social goals. They have an obligation to provide services to local users based on the social aspect, which can sometimes collide with the economic aspect of business (Hefetz & Werner, 2012). The majority of public utility companies in the Republic of Serbia in the field of heating face significant problems, among which the following stand out: unclear ownership, politicized management, insufficient funds for investment, and dominant market positions (Petrović, 2013). Because of that, public companies generally increase their service prices to improve their profitability rather than cutting costs.

Since oil reserves in the Republic of Serbia are limited, the Republic of Serbia is dependent on oil imports (Bajić et al., 2015). A new Energy Development Strategy of Serbia, with projections to 2030, involves prioritizing Serbian energy policy with the aim of increasing the energy security supply, further developing the energy market, and providing sustainable energy development (Maricic, 2018; Jovanović, 2017). After the start of the war between Russia and Ukraine and due to efforts to recover from the consequences caused by the coronavirus, the energy crisis put pressure on policymakers to focus on managing the impacts of fuel supply and price disruptions (Frilingou et al., 2023). All these developments have led researchers to focus on the efficiency of energy policy (Zhang & Chen, 2022). The results of the research conducted by Pavlović et al. (2021) show that in Serbia, there is an outdated household heating system, low efficiency, insufficient investment in thermal insulation in the past, and a lack of financial resources for investing in sustainable heating. Wang et al. (2022) indicate that before the onset of these crises, research in this area mainly examined the consumption of renewable energy and investments in infrastructure with the aim of attracting foreign direct investment.

Public utility companies in the area of heating represent a unique kind of monopoly called "pure monopoly" (Radukić et al., 2018). These companies represent a determinant of sustainable development (Alkaff et al., 2016; Radukić et al., 2018; Ziemele et al., 2021). Therefore, the sustainability of the heating sector is essential for reaching sustainable development targets and improving the quality of life (Živković et al., 2016).

LOCAL SELF-GOVERNMENT AND PUBLIC UTILITY COMPANIES IN THE HEATING AREA

The interest of every state is to enable adequate production of public goods. However, when decentralization occurs, certain problems arise. It is also necessary to abide by certain principles, including the principles of efficiency, accuracy, economy, and fiscal responsibility. Adherence to these principles is undoubtedly difficult and complex, whereby management at the decentralized level should not be performed haphazardly (Đurović Todorović & Đorđević, 2019).

The challenges of decentralization are undoubtedly different when comparing developed and developing countries. The finances on the basis of which the problems that arise at the decentralized level would be solved depend a lot on the local economic development. Local self-government must take care to ensure the supply of public goods. It must also ensure the appropriate volume, quality, but also the appropriate price. As each local self-government is different, each strives to be competitive.

In the Republic of Serbia, local self-government is characterized by great freedom in decision-making. "Local self-government is free to decide on the instruments for revenue collection, but also the fees for the use of public goods (Ranđelović & Vukadinović, 2021, p. 210). The effects of fiscal decentralization are present in the domain of increased autonomy in financial management, and the way funds are spent. There is a sense of responsibility for public utility companies and competition, which naturally encourages the improvement of services and the reduction of service prices.

The functions and responsibilities of local self-governments in the Republic of Serbia are regulated by the Law on Local Self-Government and the Law of Utility Services, which regulates all activities of public utility services (Radukić et al., 2018). Most companies in the Republic of Serbia determine their costs based on the costs required to provide the service, including in the heating sector. However, a small number of companies follow a full-cost policy, which reduces the income of the population. This is one of the reasons why public utility companies in the heating sector incur losses in their operations, which represent a significant problem for the state. Covering these losses can affect the inflation rate as it requires an increase in public utility service prices, and a careful approach to price analysis is necessary (Radukić et al., 2018).

As Figure 1 shows, if public utility companies in the heating sector want to cover their energy source costs and operate profitably, the increase in the price of their services will have a significant impact on inflation (0.7982%). Furthermore, these price changes will affect the living standards of the population."

Figure 1. Inflation effects in a model of full cost policy for public utility companies in the Republic of Serbia for the 2008 – 2016 period
Source: Radukić et al., 2018.

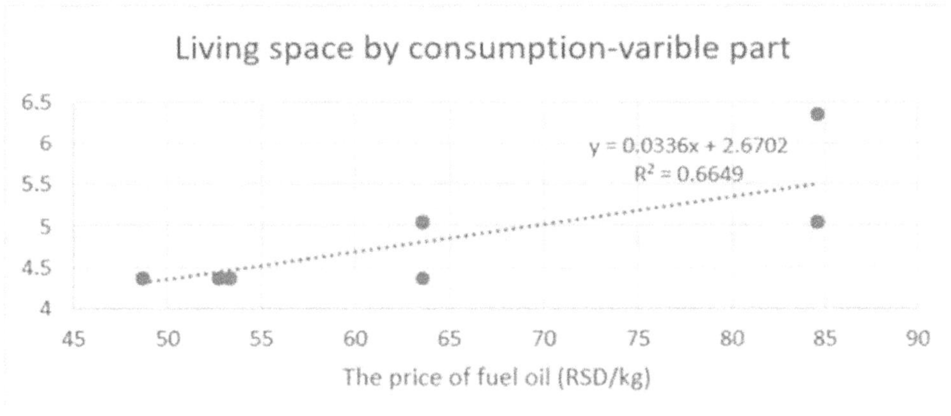

Although the consequences of the crisis caused by the coronavirus are still being felt, the Russia-Ukraine war has further affected the already existing instability in the market. Namely, in 2023 there will be bigger problems and price instability. Energy prices were additionally increased, which undoubtedly represented an energy shock. Also, energy supplies are at very low levels. The crisis in the energy market had an impact on the increase in disruptions on the supply side and, consequently, on the disruptions of production cycles. The combination of shocks facing the Eurozone - war, energy, disrupted supply chains, and redistribution of demand - indicate that inflation is likely to remain above target for some time to come (Lagarde, 2022). The negative effects can best be seen with natural gas. Given that the supply of gas was already limited due to the consequences of the COVID-19 crisis, additional negative reflections of the war. Gas prices have increased drastically. In the same year, in August, gas prices ranged from €155-232/MWh (ECB, 2022).

Current inflation has the fastest growth recorded since the creation of the European Monetary Union. Worrying data indicate that gas and electricity prices rose by 237% in Europe in July. As inflation has reached double-digit values in many countries, a further trend of its growth is expected. The graph shows how inflation moved by month (Jan-Dec, 2022) in the European Union.

Figure 2. Monthly movements of the inflation rate on the Energy market (in %), 2022
Source: Eurostat

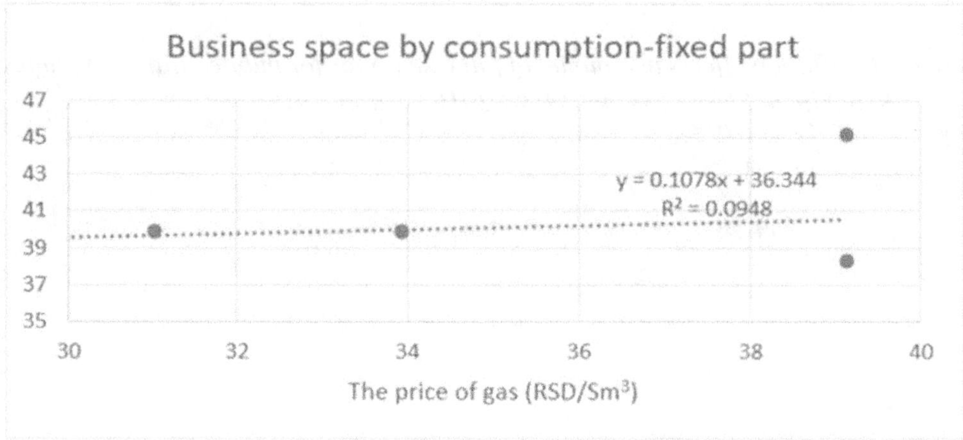

There is a long-term trend of decreasing gas production in the European Union. Given that gas imports in Europe are mostly (about 40%) from Russia, the war has influenced the reduction of imports. The decrease in the supply of energy products was also reflected in other markets. The rise in energy prices also affected the food market, as well as many other markets.

For the above reasons, it can be concluded that local governments are facing a big challenge. Disruptions in the energy market lead to worrying public revenue and public expenditure plans. Especially the operations of public utility companies, which are highly dependent on the state of the energy market. Therefore, in the further part of the work, a detailed analysis of the performance of the heating company in the city of Leskovac was carried out with the aim of providing recommendations and measures to overcome these challenges.

ANALYSIS OF THE REVENUES AND HEATING PRICES: THE CASE OF LESKOVAC, SERBIA

We investigated a heating company in the city of Leskovac. We investigated the revenues and heating prices of the public utility company to indicate the harmful effects of the current energy crisis. We analyzed the operations of this public utility company over the last five years. Monthly changes in energy costs were observed.

Since 2013, the analyzed public utility company has not had a single loss in its operations. As a result of the coronavirus crisis, this company recorded a loss in 2019. In a detailed report on the causes of the reported result, the management of

Toplana cited a large difference in the price of heating and the price of energy as one of the main factors of the loss. In other words, there is a mismatch between the heating price and energy costs. Therefore, compared to other cities in the territory of the Republic of Serbia, Leskovac belongs to the group of cities that have the lowest heating costs, while energy costs tend to increase. It is important to note that income from regular operations in 2019 was at a satisfactory level. In 2018, business revenues amounted to 387,347,000 dinars, while in 2019, they amounted to 325,337,000 dinars. Toplana also expanded the number of users of its services, which gives indications of positive business in the future if the main causes of its business loss are resolved.

The price of heating in Leskovac is not an often changing variable. But in order to solve the problem of the loss, this public utility company made a decision to increase the price of thermal energy in 2019. According to the methodology prescribed by the Ministry of Mining and Energy, its increase should reach up to 20% after corrections, but this increase was significantly smaller. However, this increase was significantly smaller. The goal of the city was to solve the problem of the heating company's loss-making business with a decision on the price of heating, but also to ensure that the price of heating in Leskovac remains among the lowest prices in Serbia in order not to endanger the position of the users of this service.

We start the research by looking at the basic performance of the heating company. As can be seen in Table 1, there are differences in operating results. The table shows deviations between planned and realized revenues.

Table 1. Business performance of the public heating company

SUMMARY				
Groups	*Count*	*Sum*	*Average*	*Variance*
Business revenue	5	0.082945	0.016589	0.001687
Financial revenue	5	0.474571	0.094914	0.096919
Other revenue	5	0.81537	0.163074	0.152806

Source: Authors' calculations

Figure 3. Movement of business, financial and other revenues
Source: Authors' presentation

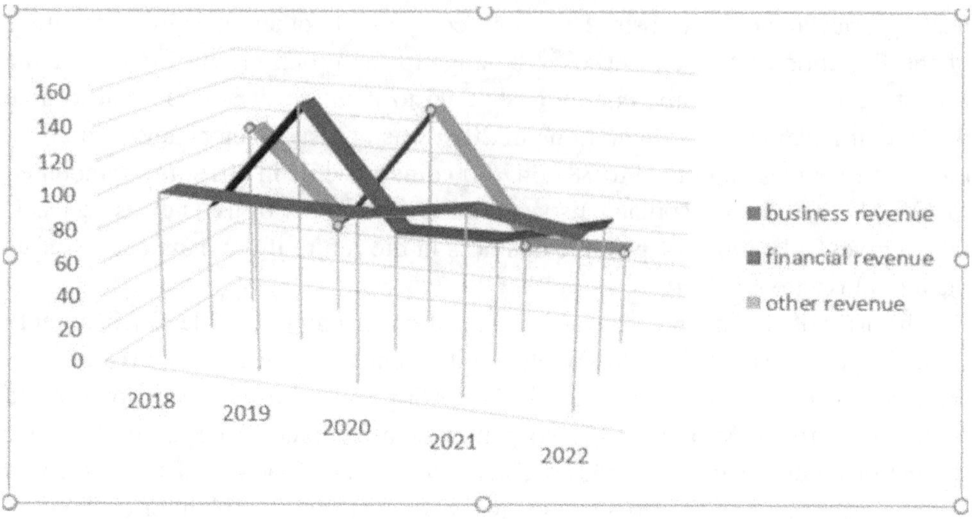

Based on Figure 3, it can be seen that the financial revenue and other income both experienced a sharp decline in 2020 and 2019, respectively. The company's regular business revenue has shown a downward trend over time. The highest business income was recorded in 2022, while the lowest was in 2019.

Considering the discrepancies in the analyzed incomes, the following conclusions can be drawn:

- The deviation between planned and actual revenue is equalized.
- The average is highest for other revenue, followed by financial revenue and finally, business revenue.

Table 2. Analysis of the results for the heating company in the city of Leskovac

Source of Variation	*SS*	*df*	*MS*	*F*	*P-value*	*F crit*
Between Groups	0.053731	2	0.026865	0.320574	0.73176	3.885294
Within Groups	1.005648	12	0.083804			
Total	1.059378	14				

Source: Authors' calculations

Table 2 shows that there are variations in the movement of analyzed revenues. However, variations in business, financial and other revenues are uniform.

When it comes to the consumption of energy sources of a heating system, their price is an important variable in determining the price of heating. Figure 4 illustrates the trend of energy costs for the period of 2018-2022. The consumption of energy sources, coal, fuel oil, and gas, were calculated based on available data in the heating system over the analyzed period. The data is presented in Figure 4.

Figure 4. Consumption of energy sources of a heating system
Source: Authors' presentation

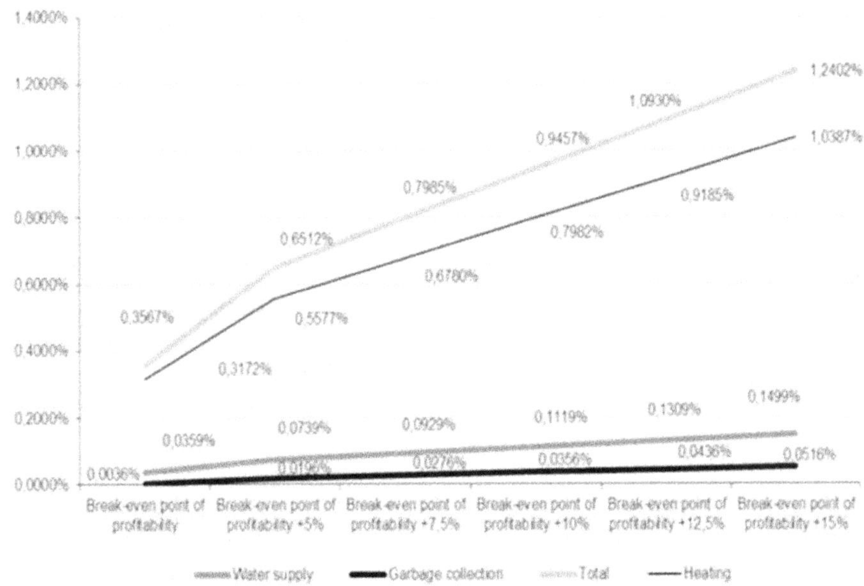

Based on Figure 4, it can be concluded that the costs of fuel oil and the price of coal have increased. On the other hand, gas consumption showed a downward trend in the analyzed period.

Given that there is empirical evidence that the liberalization of utility prices in the Republic of Serbia affects inflation and the standard of living of the population in the Republic of Serbia (Radukić et al., 2018), we investigate the impact of energy prices on the price of heating in the city of Leskovac.

In the further part of the work, an analysis was made to what extent energy prices influenced the creation of the heating price. Heating prices were analyzed according to the following groups:

1. Living space per area;
2. Living space by consumption-variable part;
3. Living space by consumption-fixed part;
4. Business space per area;
5. Business space by consumption-variable part and
6. Business space by consumption-fixed part.

The prices for the following energy sources were analyzed: fuel oil, coal, and gas. Price changes were observed for the period from 2018-2022 by month (January-December). All these data were taken from the company responsible for the operation of the heating system in the city of Leskovac. In order to calculate the effects of these costs on the heating price, it is necessary to say that this is a pure monopoly. The primary heat consumers are apartments and industrial buildings.

Table 3. Correlation matrix of energy and heating prices

		Living space per area;	*Living space by consumption-variable part;*	*Living space by consumption-fixed part;*	*Business space per area;*	*Business space by consumption-variable part*	*Business space by consumption-fixed part*
Fuel oil	*Pearson Correlation*	*.713***	*.815***	*.495***	*.633***	*.783***	*.124*
	Sig. (2-tailed)	*.000*	*.000*	*.000*	*.000*	*.000*	*.344*
	N	*60*	*60*	*60*	*60*	*60*	*60*
Coal	*Pearson Correlation*	*.687***	*.751***	*.525***	*.630***	*.733***	*.221*
	Sig. (2-tailed)	*.000*	*.000*	*.000*	*.000*	*.000*	*.090*
	N	*60*	*60*	*60*	*60*	*60*	*60*
Gas	*Pearson Correlation*	*.475***	*.467***	*.437***	*.467***	*.474***	*.308**
	Sig. (2-tailed)	*.000*	*.000*	*.000*	*.000*	*.000*	*.017*
	N	*60*	*60*	*60*	*60*	*60*	*60*

Source: Authors' calculations

Table 4. Correlation matrix of energy prices

		Fuel oil	*Coal*	*Gas*
Fuel oil	*Pearson Correlation*	*1*	*.962***	*.634***
	Sig. (2-tailed)		*.000*	*.000*
	N	*60*	*60*	*60*
Coal	*Pearson Correlation*	*.962***	*1*	*.727***
	Sig. (2-tailed)	*.000*		*.000*
	N	*60*	*60*	*60*
Gas	*Pearson Correlation*	*.634***	*.727***	*1*
	Sig. (2-tailed)	*.000*	*.000*	
	N	*60*	*60*	*60*

Source: Authors' calculations

Based on Table 3, we can conclude that there is a statistically significant correlation between energy prices and the price of heating (except for the fixed part of business premises). And the energy prices (Table 4) themselves are in a statistically significant correlation with each other. The influence of energy prices on heating prices is modeled by regression models. In order to avoid the problem of multi correlation of predictors, the Stepwise model was used.

Table 5. Regression analysis

Model		Unstandardized Coefficients		Standardized Coefficients	t	Sig.	R2	sig
		B	Std. Error	Beta				
Living space per area	(Constant)	51.312	3.980		12.894	0.000	.508	0.000
	Fuel oil	**0.498**	0.064	0.713	7.744	0.000		
Living space by consumption-variable part	(Constant)	2.670	0.194		13.780	0.000	.665	0.000
	Fuel oil	**0.034**	0.003	0.815	10.728	0.000		
Living space by consumption-fixed part	(Constant)	17.775	2.972		5.981	0.000	.276	0.000
	Coal	**0.001**	0.000	0.525	4.698	0.000		
Business space per area	(Constant)	71.351	4.735		15.070	0.000	.401	0.000
	Fuel oil	**0.476**	0.076	0.633	6.227	0.000		
Business space by consumption-variable part	(Constant)	3.782	0.213		17.769	0.000	.613	0.000
	Coal	**0.033**	0.003	0.783	9.589	0.000		
Business space by consumption-fixed part	(Constant)	36.344	1.395		26.058	0.000	.095	0.017
	Gas	**0.108**	0.044	0.308	2.465	0.017		

Source: Authors' calculations

The results of the regression analysis show the following. If the price of fuel oil were to increase by 1 dinar per kg, the price of heating residential space would increase by 0.498 dinars per m^2. If the price of fuel oil were to increase by 1 dinar per kg, the price of heating the living space per consumption would increase by 0.034 dinars per m^2. If the price of coal were to increase by 1 dinar per ton, the cost of heating residential space would increase by 0.001 dinars per m^2. If the price of fuel oil were to increase by 1 dinar per kg, the price of heating business premises would increase by 0.476 dinars per m^2. If the price of fuel oil were to increase by 1 dinar per kg, the heating price for a business proctor would increase by 0.033 dinars per m^2. If the price of gas were to increase by 1 dinar per Sm^3, the price of heating for a business proctor per consumption would increase by 0.108 dinars per m^2.

Figures 5, 6, 7, 8, 9, and 10 show how energy prices affected heating prices according to different groups. The pictures show the effects of energy price changes on heating prices in the city of Leskovac.

Figure 5. Change in price of fuel oil, 2018-2022 (RSD/kg)
Source: Authors' calculations

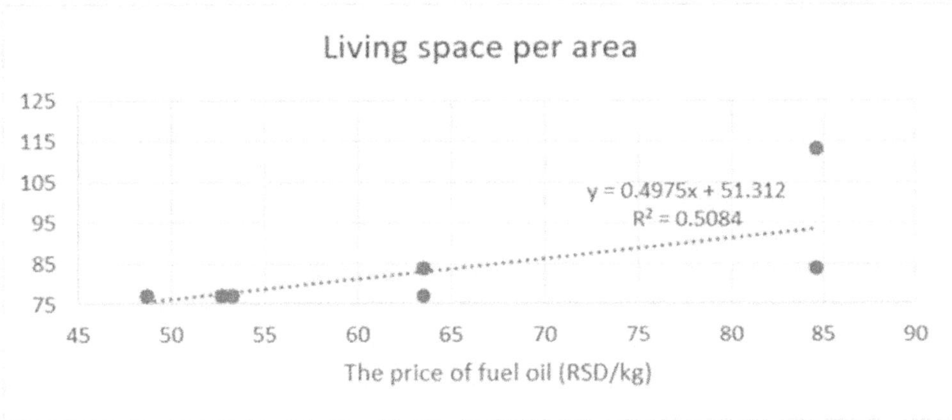

Fuel oil explains 50.8% of the variance in the heating price of Living space per area.

Figure 6. Change in price of fuel oil, 2018-2022 (RSD/kg)
Source: Authors' calculations

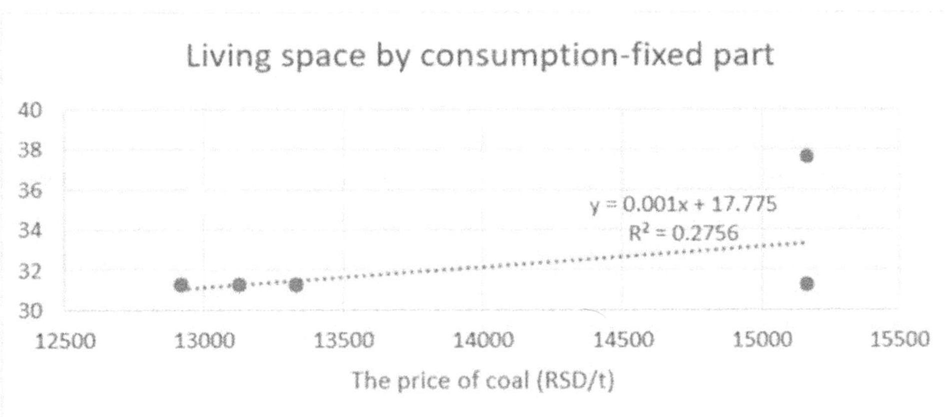

Fuel oil explains 66,4% of the variance in the heating price of Living space by consumption-variable part.

Figure 7. Change in price of fuel oil, 2018-2022 (RSD/kg)
Source: Authors' calculations

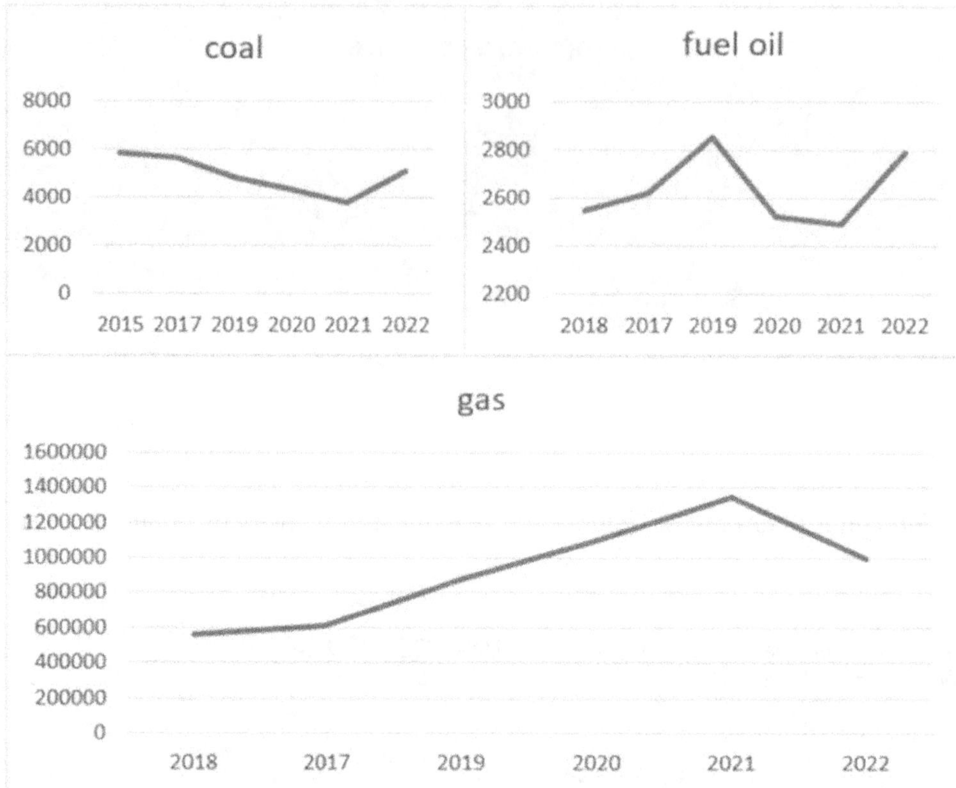

Coal explains 27,5% of the variance in the heating price of Living space by consumption-fixed part.

Figure 8. Change in price of fuel oil, 2018-2022 (RSD/kg)
Source: Authors' calculations

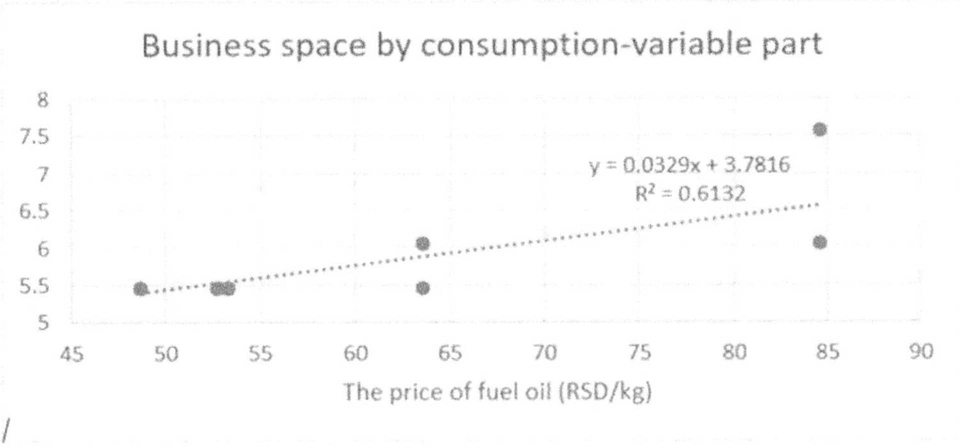

Fuel oil explains 40% of the variance in the heating price of Business space per area.

Figure 9. Change in price of fuel oil, 2018-2022 (RSD/kg)
Source: Authors' calculations

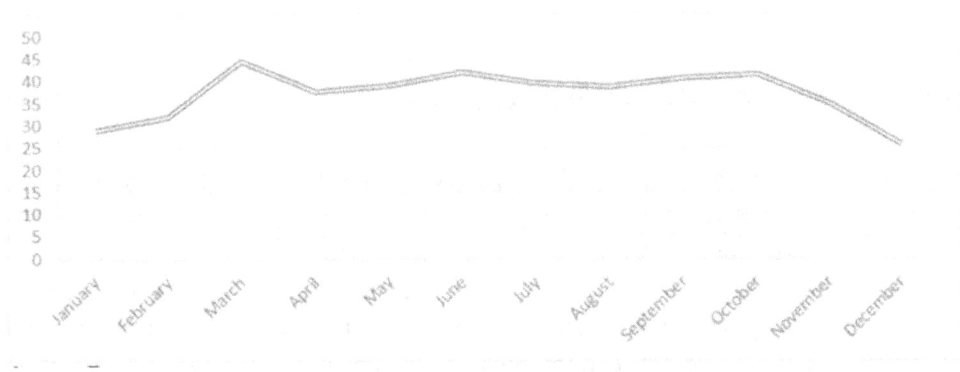

Fuel oil explains 61,3% of the variance in the heating price of Business space by consumption-variable part.

Figure 10. Change in price of gas, 2018-2022 (RSD/Sm3)
Source: Authors' calculations

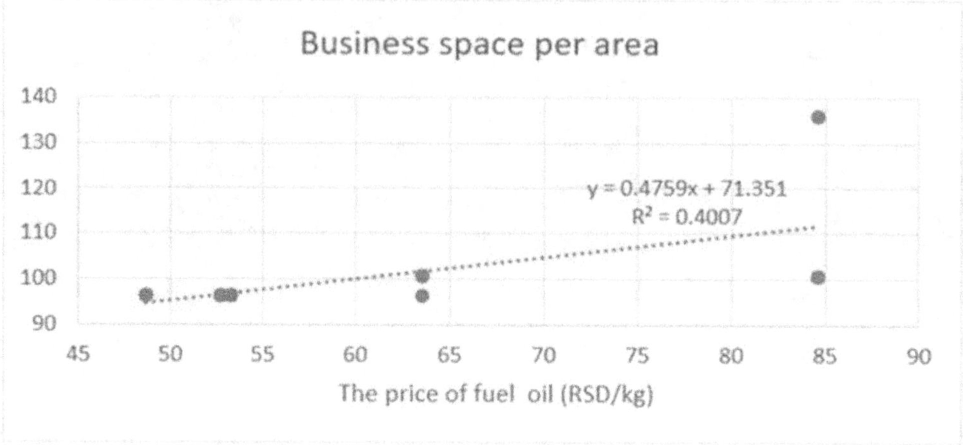

Gas explains 9,4% of the variance in the heating price of Business space by consumption-fixed part.

It can be concluded that the change in the price of fuel oil stands out. It has the greatest influence on price formation in the domain of living space per area, living space by consumption - variable part, business space per area and business space by consumption - variable part.

SOLUTIONS AND RECOMMENDATIONS

What affects heating prices? Lack of energy sources, rising energy prices, inadequate infrastructure, production disruptions, political factors, and global influences such as the energy crisis undoubtedly impact heating prices. Ways to reduce production costs include increasing energy efficiency, utilizing renewable energy sources, diversifying energy sources, regularly monitoring market prices, improving infrastructure, and investing in energy-efficient technologies (such as district heating). These factors can contribute to reducing energy prices.

To efficiently operate public utility companies and address the energy crisis, a sustainable approach to heating public utilities is needed (Vasiljević, 2017). District heating provides an opportunity for price liberalization to lead to sustainable technology. Careful cost-benefit analysis and pricing in accordance with the services provided are necessary. The continuous increase in prices highlights the company's significant problems with losses and impacts the Republic of Serbia's budget. Loss-making public utility companies can pose significant difficulties for the Republic of Serbia. The authors recommend that local governments prioritize sustainable development, given infrastructural limitations in certain cities.

The authors advocate for directing the management of public utility companies towards sustainable development. Solutions should balance economic, social, and ecological goals and consider district heating and increased use of gas heating, ultimately promoting energy savings and sustainability.

FUTURE RESEARCH DIRECTIONS

It is necessary to investigate the consumption of heat energy through district heating and gas in more detail (Perović & Radukić, 2017; Savickas, 2019; Stevanović & Pucar, 2012; Vasić, 2018). Empirical research shows that consumers are most motivated to save energy if they use electricity and gas as energy sources. There is evidence that the highest costs and energy consumption are in the district heating system (Lukić et al. 2015). Heating systems in the Republic of Serbia in urban areas are mainly district heating, gas and electricity. Gas should be a strategic priority of the local government in Leskovac.

Pavlović et al. (2022) gave the base for further research on the effects of different heating system prices, energy prices, and the efficiency of the transition to sustainable heating. Therefore, a recommendation is given for further research and testing of the efficiency of switching to sustainable heating using the example of Leskovac. "Sustainability transformation of the heating sector is recognized as being essential for reaching environmental targets while improving the quality of life in cities worldwide" (Zivkovic et al., 2016, p. 1758).

A comparison of present tariff systems shows that consumers in residential buildings are the most motivated for energy savings if they use electricity or gas as an energy source (Bećirović et al., 2013; Cvetinović et al., 2013; Lukić et al., 2015). "Efficiency for the green future" designed for implementation in the city of Niš included high standards of energy efficiency in buildings, increased share of renewables in the heating energy mix, expanding the district heating system, deploying smart technologies and green architecture (Živković et al., 2016). That scenario may be relevant also for the city of Leskovac.

CONCLUSION

Based on the financial parameters of the heating company, results show that this public enterprise is facing negative consequences from the crisis, including a significant increase in energy prices. This consequence affects the price of heating energy and leads to increased heavy reliance on local government assistance. It can be concluded that the change in the price of fuel oil stands out. The change in fuel oil price has the greatest impact on pricing for both residential and business spaces.

"The price in the public utility sector can have various economic, environmental and social effects that local and state authorities should seriously consider" (Radukić et al., 2018). These "Pure monopolies" are monopolies where fixed costs only fall with the increase in utility users. Given that this is a pure monopoly and that there was a conflict between the economic aspect of business and the provision of services to local users, it is necessary to increase the number of services. In this way, a public utility company that cannot achieve maximum efficiency in production due to the consequences and effects of the market situation can realize business with a loss. Given that the activities of communal services in the area of heating have a great impact on the standard of the population and inflation, the heating price should not be frequently variable. However, negative effects on the energy market initiate price variability. Therefore, in order for the performance of the public utility company not to threaten the local budget, it is necessary to approach their increase with great reserve and with a precise assessment of costs.

Also, this area of public utility companies is quite different from other utility activities. Public-private partnership in this area is currently impossible due to high initial costs, infrastructure, and many other factors. Although, in the direction of increasing the economy and encouraging solutions for the improvement of services and infrastructure, it would be useful. Therefore, it is suggested that local authorities devote more attention and investments to the economy of communal services and the improvement of infrastructure. The improvement of production during the provision of services will enable the reduction of costs and, thus, the reduction of prices.

ACKNOWLEDGMENT

This paper is a result of research funded by the Ministry of Science, Technological Development and Innovation of the Republic of Serbia pursuant to agreement No. 451-03-47/2023-01/200100.

REFERENCES

Alkaff, S. A., Sim, S. C., & Efzan, M. E. (2016). A review of underground building towards thermal energy efficiency and sustainable development. *Renewable & Sustainable Energy Reviews*, *60*, 692–713. doi:10.1016/j.rser.2015.12.085

Anđelković, M. (2009). *Public finances and financial law*. Center for Publications of the Faculty of Law in Nis.

Bajić, B. Ž., Dodić, S. N., Vučurović, D. G., Dodić, J. M., & Grahovac, J. A. (2015). Waste-to-energy status in Serbia. *Renewable & Sustainable Energy Reviews, 50*, 1437–1444. doi:10.1016/j.rser.2015.05.079

Bećirović, S. P., & Vasić, M. (2013). Methodology and results of Serbian energy-efficiency refurbishment project. *Energy and Building, 62*, 258–267. doi:10.1016/j.enbuild.2013.03.027

Cvetinović, D., Stefanović, P., Marković, Z., Bakić, V., Turanjanin, V., Jovanović, M., & Vučićević, B. (2013). GHG (Greenhouse Gases) emission inventory and mitigation measures for public district heating plants in the Republic of Serbia. *Energy, 57*, 788–795. doi:10.1016/j.energy.2012.09.063

Đurović-Todorović, J., & Đorđević, M. (2011). Characteristics of the fiscal federalism of Bosnia and Herzegovina. *Ekonomika (Nis), 57*(2), 39–54.

Đurović Todorović & Đorđević. (2019). *Public finance-Theory and practice*. Faculty of Economics.

ECB. (2022). Economic, financial and monetary developments. *Economic Bulletin*, (6), 2022.

Frilingou, N., Xexakis, G., Koasidis, K., Nikas, A., Campagnolo, L., Delpiazzo, E., Chiodi, A., Gargiulo, M., McWilliams, B., Koutsellis, T., & Doukas, H. (2023). Navigating through an energy crisis: Challenges and progress towards electricity decarbonisation, reliability, and affordability in Italy. *Energy Research & Social Science, 96*, 102934. doi:10.1016/j.erss.2022.102934

Guo, X., & Xiao, B. (2022). How can pricing strategy for district heating help China realize cleaner residential heating? *Energy Economics, 110*, 106035. doi:10.1016/j.eneco.2022.106035

Hefetz, A., & Warner, M. E. (2012). Contracting or public delivery? The importance of service, market, and management characteristics. *Journal of Public Administration: Research and Theory, 22*(2), 289–317. doi:10.1093/jopart/mur006

Kreps, B. H. (2020). The Rising Costs of Fossil-Fuel Extraction: An Energy Crisis That Will Not Go Away. *American Journal of Economics and Sociology, 79*(3), 695–717. doi:10.1111/ajes.12336

Lagarde, C. (2022, November 4). *Monetary policy in a high inflation environment: Commitment and clarity*. European Central Bank.

Lukić, N., Jurišević, N., Nikolić, N., & Gordić, D. (2015). Specific heating consumption in the residential sector of Serbia—Example of the city of Kragujevac. *Energy and Building*, *107*, 163–171. doi:10.1016/j.enbuild.2015.08.012

Pavlović, B., Ivezić, D., & Živković, M. (2022). Transition pathways of household heating in Serbia: Analysis based on an agent-based model. *Renewable & Sustainable Energy Reviews*, *163*, 163. doi:10.1016/j.rser.2022.112506

Perović, D., & Radukić, S. (2017). Comparative analysis of sustainable development components for the Republic of Serbia and neighbouring countries. *Teme – Journal for Social Sciences*, *41*(3), 747–765.

Petrovic, M. (2013). Conducting public utilities in Serbia: Providing and maintaining services in Kragujevac. *International Journal of Public Sector Management*, *26*(2), 116–126. doi:10.1108/09513551311317988

Radukic, S., Perovic, D., & Vucetic, D. (2018). Economic and environmental effects from liberalizing utility service prices in the Republic of Serbia. *Industrija, 46*(4).

Radulovic, B., & Dragutinovic, S. (2015). Efficiency of local self-governments in Serbia: An SFA approach. *Industrija*, *43*(3), 123–142. doi:10.5937/industrija43-8846

Ranđelović, S., & Vukanović, S. (2021). Fiscal decentralization and local public investment policy in the Republic of Serbia. *Ekonomski horizonti, 23*(3), 197-213.

Savickas, R. (Ed.). (2019). *Guidelines for Introduction Heat Metering in the City of Belgrade*.

Stevanović, S., & Pucar, M. (2012). Financial measures Serbia should offer for solar water heating systems. *Energy and Building*, *54*, 519–526. doi:10.1016/j.enbuild.2012.02.054

Vasić, G. (2018). Application of multi criteria analysis in the design of energy policy: Space and water heating in households – City Novi Sad, Serbia. *Energy Policy*, *113*, 410–419. doi:10.1016/j.enpol.2017.11.025

Vasiljević, Z. (2017). The Legal Regime of Utility Services and Public-Private Partnership in Bosnia and Herzegovina. *Network Industries Quarterly.*, *19*(1), 1–34.

Wang, C. H., Padmanabhan, P., & Huang, C. H. (2022). The impacts of the 1997 Asian financial crisis and the 2008 global financial crisis on renewable energy consumption and carbon dioxide emissions for developed and developing countries. *Heliyon*, *8*(2), e08931. doi:10.1016/j.heliyon.2022.e08931 PMID:35243057

Zhang, Q., Wu, X., & Chen, Y. (2022). Is economic crisis an opportunity for realizing the low-carbon transition? A simulation study on the interaction between economic cycle and energy regulation policy. *Energy Policy*, *168*, 113114. doi:10.1016/j.enpol.2022.113114

Ziemele, J., Talcis, N., Osis, U., & Dace, E. (2021). A methodology for selecting a sustainable development strategy for connecting low heat density consumers to a district heating system by cascading of heat carriers. *Energy*, *230*, 120776. doi:10.1016/j.energy.2021.120776

Živković, M., Pereverza, K., Pasichnyi, O., Madžarević, A., Ivezić, D., & Kordas, O. (2016). Exploring scenarios for more sustainable heating: The case of Niš, Serbia. *Energy*, *115*, 1758–1770. doi:10.1016/j.energy.2016.06.034

ADDITIONAL READING

Frigo, G. (2017). Energy ethics, homogenization, and hegemony: A reflection on the traditional energy paradigm. *Energy Research & Social Science*, *30*, 7–17. doi:10.1016/j.erss.2017.06.030

Jovanović, B., Filipović, J., & Bakić, V. (2017). Energy management system implementation in Serbian manufacturing–Plan-Do-Check-Act cycle approach. *Journal of Cleaner Production*, *162*, 1144–1156. doi:10.1016/j.jclepro.2017.06.140

Lapillonne, B., Sebi, C., Pollier, K., & Mairet, N. (2012). *Energy efficiency trends in buildings in the EU. Lessons from the ODYSSEE/MURE project. ADEME, Supported by Intelligent Energy Europe.* Online at: http://www. odysseeindicators. org/publications/PDF/Building s-brochure-2012. pdf

Madžarević, A., Ivezić, D., Živković, M., Tanasijević, M., & Ivić, M. (2018). Assessment of vulnerability of natural gas supply in Serbia: State and perspective. *Energy Policy*, *121*, 415–425. doi:10.1016/j.enpol.2018.06.037

Maricic, V. K., Danilovic, D., Lekovic, B., & Crnogorac, M. (2018). Energy policy reforms in the Serbian oil sector: An update. *Energy Policy*, *113*, 348–355. doi:10.1016/j.enpol.2017.11.011

Matic, D., Calzada, J. R., Eric, M., & Babin, M. (2015). Economically feasible energy refurbishment of prefabricated building in Belgrade, Serbia. *Energy and Buildings, 98*, 74-81.

Oka, S., Sedmak, A., & Đurović-Petrović, M. (2006). Energy efficiency in Serbia: Research and development activity. *Thermal Science*, *10*(2), 5–32. doi:10.2298/TSCI0602005O

Pavlović, B., Ivezić, D., & Živković, M. (2021). State and perspective of individual household heating in Serbia: A survey-based study. *Energy and Building*, *247*, 111128. doi:10.1016/j.enbuild.2021.111128

Pavlović, B., Ivezić, D., & Živković, M. (2022). Transition pathways of household heating in Serbia: Analysis based on an agent-based model. *Renewable & Sustainable Energy Reviews*, *163*, 112506. doi:10.1016/j.rser.2022.112506

Stevanović, S., & Pucar, M. (2012). Financial measures Serbia should offer for solar water heating systems. *Energy and Building*, *54*, 519–526. doi:10.1016/j.enbuild.2012.02.054

KEY TERMS AND DEFINITIONS

Energy Costs: Energy costs refer to the expenses associated with obtaining and using heating, such as the cost of fuel oil, gas and coal.

Energy Crisis: An energy crisis is a situation in which the supply of energy sources (e.g., fuel oil, coal, gas) is insufficient to meet demand, leading to widespread price increases and shortages. This can be caused by factors such as the war between Russia and Ukraine.

Fiscal Federalism: Fiscal federalism refers to the financial relationship between different levels of government, especially the central government and the sub-national governments such as states or provinces.

Heating Company: A heating company is a business that specializes in providing heating services and products to residential and commercial customers.

Heating Price: Heating price refers to the cost of heating a home or building.

Public Utility Company: A public utility company is a business that provides essential services such as electricity, gas, water, and telecommunications to the public.

Chapter 11
The Role and Significance of Environmental Accounting for Sustainable Business Development

Bojana Novićević Čečević
https://orcid.org/0000-0002-4269-0586
University of Niš, Serbia

Milica Đorđević
University of Niš, Serbia

Marina Stanojević
University of Niš, Serbia

ABSTRACT

In the contemporary circumstances, one of the greatest challenges companies are facing is the identification of environmental costs, both due to the lack of a unique classification and accounting coverage and because they occur when taking or not taking measures related to and relevant to environmental protection. Neglecting the ecological aspect of business increases the risk of a discrepancy between the consumption of natural resources and their limited availability. In order to cope with the constantly growing competition in modern business conditions, companies need an adequate information base. This information base is provided by environmental management accounting. It is focused on the use and management of natural resources and environmental costs as well as identifying the responsibility of individuals and the entire company for activities that are carried out to improve the environment. The aim of the chapter is to point out the role and importance of environmental accounting and especially management accounting for sustainable business development.

DOI: 10.4018/978-1-6684-7730-4.ch011

INTRODUCTION

Modern companies conduct their business in a dynamic environment and in conditions of constant business uncertainty caused, on the one hand, by market conditions, and on the other hand, by determined factors of the natural environment. Therefore, in order to achieve and maintain a competitive advantage, today's companies, in addition to the key factors of success, must also take into account the environmental aspect of their business and eco-efficiency. The eco-efficiency strategy is one of the strategies of sustainable development that aims to design and implement cleaner production and business in general. After the appearance of the concepts of business sustainability and eco-efficiency in the 1980s, they have gained significant attention among the scientific and professional public from various fields of research and business. Numerous debates and seminars were organized on this topic with the aim of gathering both theoreticians and practitioners interested in these concepts, their main postulates, conceptualization, and practical implications. The fact is that for the success of a company's operations in the modern business environment, it is necessary to carefully consider all three pillars of sustainability: environmental, social, and economic part. In this sense, it is necessary to incorporate the aspect of business sustainability into the accounting information system.

The traditional accounting information system does not adequately support the necessity to care for environmental protection and the constantly growing need to preserve natural resources. This mismatch of accounting information systems with the requirement to preserve natural resources can destabilize business and the relationship between economic performance and growth, leading to the depletion of natural capital and threatening the environment. The fact that the environmental aspect is not covered by traditional accounting is also shown by the fact that professional accounting regulations do not cover this part. Taking into account the growing importance of environmental issues and sustainable development, it is necessary for traditional accounting to include an ecological aspect in addition to economic ones and to adapt to modern business philosophy.

Accounting can successfully respond to the mentioned request by creating and adopting environmental accounting. Environmental accounting can be applied both in the manufacturing and service sectors, regardless of the size and organizational structure of the company. Today, managers need appropriate information support coming from concepts, tools, and techniques of modern management accounting (Novićević Čečević et al., 2021). In this sense, environmental accounting incorporates an external dimension that is covered by environmental and financial accounting and an internal dimension that is covered by environmental management accounting.

Therefore, the paper is divided into five parts. In the first part, the parts of environmental accounting and its specificities at the national and company level are explained. The second part deals with the issue of classification of environmental costs as a key element for making business decisions, planning, and controlling. In the end, the stages of application of environmental accounting for the purposes of sustainability are pointed out, as well as solutions and recommendations, and further research directions.

ENVIRONMENTAL ACCOUNTING AS AN INTEGRAL PART OF BUSINESS

Ecological accounting, or as it is also called *green accounting* or *environmental protection accounting*, is a modern type of accounting with the task of providing an adequate information base aimed to enable company managers to carry out a cost-benefit analysis and, based on this, to make proper decisions on the company's ecological activities in the future. It refers to the collection, systematization, recording and reporting of the company's activities in the field of investing in the preservation of natural resources and the environment (UNCTAD, 2002).

Multidisciplinarity is one of the important characteristics of ecological accounting, which includes (Grinnel & Hunt, 2010): positioning of ecological policy in the overall business policy and strategy, a compilation of ecological accounting reports and auditing of compliance with ecological rules. Therefore, multidisciplinarity is necessary due to the existence of different users of information and numerous stakeholders.

Ecological accounting is important both from broader international and national aspects, as well as from the level of the business system, because responsibility towards the environment belongs to everyone, regardless of the form in which they are organized. The lack of cooperation between these levels, as well as the neglect of certain environmental aspects and impacts, will lead to a scarce information base for the needs of ecological decision-making. In this sense, ecological accounting implies all areas of accounting that can adapt to the new requirements of the business system due to its orientation towards environmental protection down to the lowest level of eco accounting so that each level provides data and information for an appropriate approach to the creation of an eco-balance sheet, observing macroeconomic and microeconomic level (Gajić et al. 2010).

Disclosure of information on the usage and condition of renewable and non-renewable sources of energy and natural resources is an aspect that is considered most at the macroeconomic level but with the goal of effective management of natural resources and the environment. On the other hand, obtaining data on the impact of the company's business processes on the environment refers to the microeconomic level. In order for managers to get precise information about the costs, benefits, and consequences of the company's economic activity, they need a relevant and reliable information base. As ecological accounting is part of the accounting information system, it is necessary to be considered the financial and management aspects.

Environmental Financial Accounting refers to the recording and reporting of environmental obligations, costs, and effects of implemented ecological activities. Therefore, special attention should be given to identifying, evaluating, and systematizing eco-costs in order to provide that business decisions of high quality can be made. The information produced by financial ecological accounting is primarily intended for external users. Environmental Management Accounting (EMA) is an approach developed in order to help company managers to conduct calculations, implement budgets and make decisions related to environmental issues. Therefore, the information on ecological management accounting gains a kind of internal character, as well as the information on traditional management accounting.

Company managers will be able to plan and control the entire activity of the company in the area of rational usage and management of limited resources and adjust it to the needs of sustainable development based on data on the costs of environmental protection, ecological risks, eco products and the effects of eco-activities. The concept of ecological management accounting includes (Perišić, 2003):

- Environmental resource accounting
- Accounting of environmental protection costs and
- Accounting of responsibility.

Environmental resource accounting (Materials Accounting) provides information on the usage, flow, and effects of energy, water, materials, and waste in order to monitor their usage efficiency and the possibility of improving environmental protection. Accounting of ecological costs involves the identification, classification, and grouping of ecological costs and their allocation to places and cost bearers. Responsibility accounting has the task of generating information on the basis of which management's responsibility is assessed in order to establish an optimal relationship between economic and ecological performance. Therefore, the EMA provides information that is important for making decisions about prices, budgeting, control of general costs, or information that is of broader public interest (Novićević et al., 2021).

Based on the existing knowledge of the basic characteristics of the business process, the organizational structure of the company and the activities performed, as well as the necessary inputs (raw materials, energy, etc.) and outputs, the company's managers are the key help to accountants in the process of design and organization of a new accounting information system. It is also necessary to establish this cooperation due to the fact that by carrying out its business activities for the purpose of realizing the company's goals, it may inadvertently endanger the environment through waste, polluting water, air, soil, etc. Managers are the ones who have to establish a balance between the company's long-term strategy and goals, on the one hand, and the need to preserve and protect the environment, on the other. Managers must convey key facts about this relationship to lower organizational levels and raise awareness among all employees.

ENVIRONMENTAL COSTS AND THEIR IMPACT ON ENTERPRISE'S PERFORMANCE

One of the challenges that today's managers are facing due to the need for ecological accounting is identifying the costs of environmental protection. Observing professional, legal, and internal regulations, traditional accounting does not recognize in an adequate manner the costs of environmental protection as a separate category, rather, these costs are hidden and present within the scope of general costs. In that sense, activities-based costing, starting from its original model and all the improvements done, becomes unavoidable information bases for decision making a connection with an increasing quality of the produced products and the services provided, increased profit, and preservation and improvement of competitiveness The formation of natural types of environmental protection costs is conditioned by two different types of factors, such as (Gajić et al., 2010):

- The type of business the company is operating.
- Selection of technological process and use of equipment in order to achieve the goals of sustainable development.

The complexity of identifying ecological costs stems from the fact that these costs arise with the aim of protecting the environment and as a result of not undertaking activities in the field of adequate investment in its protection. Therefore, environmental protection costs can be defined and classified in various ways. In some countries, environmental protection costs include labor costs, eco-equipment costs, waste costs, landfill formation costs, and more.

One of the classifications of environmental protection costs is based on the type of activities that they include and could be identified as (Hansen & Mowen, 2003):

- prevention costs – costs that arise during the design, development and production phase of the product, but are aimed at protecting the environment and preventing a negative impact on it, such as environmental planning costs, environmental harmonization costs in product design, recycling costs, eco-friendly packaging costs, environmental management costs, waste control, elimination or treatment costs are within the scope of prevention costs.

- *detection costs* incurred when undertaking activities to control process and product compliance with environmental standards;
- *the costs of internal defects* refer to the costs of activities that arise due to the fact that pollution and waste have occurred but have not yet reached the environment, and their goal is to prevent pollution and waste materials from being released into the environment or to reduce the level of pollution to the prescribed level
- *the costs of external deficiencies* are the costs incurred due to the implementation of activities that are carried out after pollution and waste have reached the environment in order to treat them, i.e., pay the fines incurred by the company due to non-compliance with regulations (e.g., cleaning polluted lakes, restoring land, etc.) (Jugović, 2019)

Particular attention should be given to the fact that environmental protection costs have two dimensions. One dimension is internal and refers to costs caused by activities carried out in the company, while the other is external, which includes social costs for which the company is not responsible. These external costs fall on the burden of the wider society, but the role of the state is of special significance, as legal regulations must regulate this part of the company's operations (Todea et al., 2011). In accordance with this, the generally accepted classification of these costs is shown in Figure 1.

Figure 1. Classification of environmental costs
Source: Todea, N. Stanciu, I. C. & Udrea, A-M. (2011). Accounting Policies on Environmental Costs And Their Calculation Method In The Entity, Annals of DAAAM & Proceedings of the 22nd International DAAAM Symposium, Vol. 22, 653-654

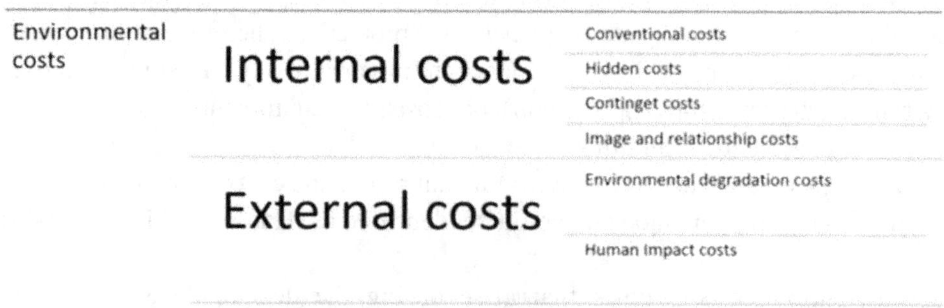

Traditional (conventional) costs are the costs arising from existing items for a regular process of production or service providing (machinery and equipment, raw materials and consumer goods).

Hidden costs represent the indirect environmental costs or the dependent costs which may occur in the future. Within the hidden costs, environmental costs resulting from legal obligations and voluntary actions are included. These costs are the costs that arise during the execution of the activities of a process, system or facility. Many companies treat these costs as an expense in the period and do not give the necessary importance to them in their business decisions and daily activities.

Dependent costs represent the costs that may arise in the future depending on the environmental effects. For example, penalties to be paid for the oil spills caused by various accidents and expenses related to the solution of environmental damage caused are dependent costs.

Image and relationship costs have a more abstract structure than other costs. They are more difficult to identify and measure compared to other environmental costs as they are based on the subjective perception of managers, customers, employees, the public and the governments. Examples of these costs are the costs associated with annual environmental reports, relations with the local population and environmental activities carried out on a voluntary basis.

External costs include the costs that businesses are not directly responsible for, but they arise from activities which have adverse effects on the environment and certain negative consequences that cannot be prevented by law. In addition, measuring the real values of the external costs is difficult. However, modern companies are trying to involve these costs as an item of costs within the environmental accounting systems (Duman et al., 2013).

As the need for the implementation of the environmental protection management system grew, it was necessary to better understand the relationship between the ecological aspect and financial indicators, as well as to emphasize the advantages of its practical application. This was greatly contributed by research that pointed to the final linkage between the environmental aspect and the profitability and financial position of the company.

In order for the company to be able to take care of the environmental aspect and the aspect of sustainability, it is necessary to have operational teams that will be composed of managers, heads of the production department, product designers, engineers, chemists and other professionals. All of them must keep environmental awareness in mind during working processes in order to comply with all the requirements of sustainability, eco-efficiency and cleaner production. When possible, the recommendation is to establish an independent environmental department within the company and to ensure its effective communication with other departments.

Environmental accounting has a large number of usage areas and benefits. In general, they can be expressed under three headings (IFAC, 2005):

- Compatibility: EMA supports the cost-effectiveness of environmental protection by ensuring compliance of the business with environmental policies, laws and regulations.
- Eco-efficiency: EMA supports the use of energy, water and resources more efficiently and effectively in the activities within the business and in final products by reducing operating costs at the same time.
- Strategic status: EMA supports guaranteeing the long-term strategic status of the enterprise. In addition, it is used in the measurement of the cost-effectiveness of the business and in the evaluation of environmental interest programs.

Today, considering environmental performance as one of the most important criteria for measuring the success of companies, identification, consideration, and control of environmental costs are receiving more and more attention (Solovida & Latan, 2017). This is because environmental costs are the starting point for applying the concept of sustainability and eco-efficiency. Also, environmental accounting focuses on the process of measuring, verifying, and determining the prices and costs of assets such as energy, raw materials, waste, etc. These assets are identified in accounting, and then activities are implemented in order to reduce the harmful effects they may have on the environment.

In the literature, a certain number of researches about the relationship between ecological costs and performance and business performance of enterprises as a whole could be founded and examined. Ramamurti (2004) states that environmental accounting enables organizations to track their environment and facilitates environmental reporting to provide sustainability-related data that is comprehensive, auditable, and timely to advance and strengthen the interdependent and mutually reinforcing pillars of sustainable development - economic development, social development and environmental protection in Nigeria. Especially interesting research is carried out by Fasua (2020) on the 18 manufacturing companies on the Nigerian Stock Exchange. The study employed the panel data econometric model adapted in order to establish the relationship between the independent variable firm performance (Return on Assets (ROA), Net Profit Margin (NPM), Earnings per Share (EPS)) and the Dependent variable (EAD disclosure index). The model for this study can be expressed as follows:

EAD = f (ROA, NPM, and EPS)

The econometric form of the model is expressed as:

$$Y = \beta 0 + \beta 1x1 + \beta 2x2 + \beta 3x3 + \mu$$

That is, $EADIt = \beta\, 0 + \beta 1\ ROAit + \beta 2\ NPMit + \beta 3EPSit + \mu it$.

The correlation coefficients showed a relationship between the environmental accounting disclosures and corporate performance of manufacturing companies in Nigeria with a 95% confidence level. In that sense, there is a positive relationship between observed variables. In the end, research reveals that an increase in return on assets and net profit margin will result in an increase in the environmental accounting disclosure. But the reduction in earnings per share leads to increased disclosure of environmental accounting. The authors conclude that enterprises should use environmental accounting practices as part of their strategy for corporate performance.

If some company wants to become more productive, profitable and sustainable, it is necessary to build a strong relationship between business activities and environmental issues. Business activities must be performed in the best possible way, and the results of it should be measured with quantity ratio as one of the measures of company's overall financial health in a specific period of time. Environmental costs are an integral part of business activities with an aim to reduce the environmental impact of performed activities. Solomon (2019) examined the state of the financial health of companies with an Altman Z- Score model. He used primary data from the management and other employees and secondary data from audited annual reports.

The model is specified below:

$$Z = 1{,}2\ X1 + 1{,}4\ X2 + 3{,}3X3 + 0{,}6\ X4 + 1\ X5$$

Where:

X1 = Working Capital / Total Assets

X2 = Retained Earnings / Total Assets

X3 = Earnings Before Interest and Taxes / Total Assets

X4 = Market Value of Equity / Total Liabilities

X5 = Sales / Total Assets.

The study shows that environmental cost is significant and positively related to the financial performance of enterprises in Nigeria. Also, it is shown that product price must include environmental costs as a pathway to innovation and an efficient means to lower costs. Management of enterprises in Nigeria should increase their involvement in environmental cost activities for improved financial performance.

The research that is carried out in Istanbul was examined: Does environmental accounting have an effect on business performance? What is the level of environmental accounting activities of the businesses? What is the output of companies' environmental accounting activities? What is the return of environmental accounting to businesses (Şimşek & Öztürk, 2021)? Obtain results of the study presents that there exists a close and linear relationship between the performance indicators included in the model and environmental accounting activities.

THE RELATIONSHIP BETWEEN ENVIRONMENTAL ACCOUNTING AND SUSTAINABILITY

The concept of sustainability implies the existence of three basic elements, which are the environmental, social, and economic aspects. The main task of sustainability is the efficient use of limited resources in such a way that they can be used by future generations, too. For success in the modern business environment, a combination of all these parts is necessary because if ecology, society, and economy are not in harmony, the growth and development of the entire economy of a country can be threatened in a huge manner. A special place in sustainability is occupied by enterprises and companies that operate on the territory of one country. This is because these companies use natural resources to meet the constantly growing needs of the population.

Many companies have recognized the importance of air pollution prevention and what effect the implementation of these activities will have on the company's image in society. In order to be competitive in that field, they made an effort to integrate this aspect as part of the environmental protection management system into making business decisions that ultimately meet the principles of sustainability. In addition to this, managers must constantly review and assess the potential impact on the environment in every business process, measure it and manage it in an effective manner. Also, it is necessary to measure and evaluate the environmental costs of processing contained in the products, as well as whether cost reduction is aligned with socially responsible behavior.

The difficulties that arise when applying the environmental management system can be systematized as follows (Seetharaman et al., 2007):

- Lack of environmental awareness - a large number of company managers believe that the activities carried out in their company have no impact on the environment, therefore, they consider it unnecessary to measure those costs.
- Lack of visible benefits - a large number of managers believe that investing in the environmental aspect of business does not provide opportunities for cost savings and does not lead to improved performance. Also, only a small number of companies included reporting on the environmental aspect in their annual reports.

- Lack of government pressure - the government, through its institutions, must legally regulate and introduce a mandatory practice of reporting on the environmental aspect of the business. For non-compliance with government regulations, it is necessary to prescribe a penalty, this way that company managers will be forced to deal with this problem and realize that consideration of environmental performance is not an unnecessary expense.
- Environmental audit - an environmental audit encompasses a range of activities related to management and reporting verification, including compliance audits and environmental risk assessments. Environmental auditing can also be viewed as a systematic and documented process of verification, objective acquisition and evaluation of audit evidence in order to determine correctness and compliance with regulations and standards.

The environmental protection management system is an integral part of the management system of the enterprise as a whole and has its own goals, responsibilities, procedures, and activities and is supported by the company's organizational structure. This system manages the environmental aspect of the business. By implementing an environmental protection management system, it is possible to improve environmental performance in many ways, such as: preventing air pollution, reducing costs, complying with environmental laws, and building the image of a socially responsible company.

For the complete application of environmental accounting for the needs of sustainable development, it is necessary to go through four stages (Duman et al., 2013). In the first phase, it is necessary to create the business policy and strategy of the company according to the requirements of sustainability. Identifying environmental costs is done in the second phase. Consideration of environmental costs is important for business sustainability purposes for the following reasons (Rounaghi, 2019):

- ''Environmental costs may be ambiguous in the overhead account or may not be considered at all.
- Many environmental costs can be removed by gaining income from the sale of useless by-products or receiving "green technology" certification.
- Better management of environmental costs can cause the development of environmental performance and has major benefits for human health and, on the other hand, can cause the success of the business unit.
- Understanding environmental costs and the performance of product manufacturing processes can cause more detailed costing and more accurate pricing and thus can help companies to design their process of production of goods and services with more emphasis on environmental issues.

- Environmental accounting and environmental performance can support the development of a company and its operations in terms of the environmental management system''.

In the third phase, it is necessary to compile reports on environmental protection in order to obtain the necessary data on where costs are incurred, whether actions have been taken to reduce them, whether they are taken in the right way and what their effects are. Also, the process aimed to raise the awareness of all employees about the importance of environmental protection should be conducted in order to plan ecological activities and practices in the future (Senn & Giordano-Spring, 2020). The last stage of applying environmental accounting is providing technical and legal support to all participants in the sustainability process and passing on experience in that area to young generations who are the perpetrators of the development of this part of accounting in the future.

By implementing environmental accounting, the company's operations will make a proper contribution to the environmental issues and will get some benefits through the environmental accounting policies they follow. These are (Duman et al., 2013):

- Resource efficiency improvement and management of environmental costs,
- Ensuring compliance with environmental legislation,
- Reduction of environmental costs,
- More knowledge-based decision-making,
- Revealing opportunities,
- Pricing the products better,
- Internal and external reporting assistance,
- To increase the reputation/credibility of the business,
- Employee loyalty and attracting staff,
- The production of social benefits,
- Determination of environmental costs and better management/ monitoring of the problems related to the environment,
- The production of knowledge needed for the environmental impacts of investments.

In this way, environmental accounting enables company managers to control their environment in terms of energy and natural resource consumption and pollution in accordance with the requirements of the adopted ecological standards. As the economic aspect is no longer the only aspect that is observed at the company level, by applying environmental accounting, high environmental performances can be achieved, and a competitive advantage based on environmental protection can be achieved and maintained.

SOLUTIONS AND RECOMMENDATIONS

Environmental or ecological accounting is considered a useful tool for businesses to measure and manage their environmental impact. First of all, it is necessary to set sustainability goals that align them with existing business strategies and stakeholder expectations. These goals should be specific, measurable, achievable, relevant, and time-bound. By setting sustainability goals, companies can prioritize sustainability and track progress towards achieving their overall goals. Implementing a circular economy approach by minimizing waste and maximizing the use of resources includes reducing, reusing, and recycling materials, as well as implementing closed-loop systems that recover and reuse resources.

As businesses become more aware of the environmental impacts of their business operations, they are increasingly looking for ways to reduce their environmental footprint. This includes investing in renewable energy sources and reducing pollution and negative environmental impacts. Since environmental accounting has become more complex, businesses are also increasingly turning to software solutions to help them track and report their environmental performance. This kind of software can help businesses identify areas of improvement, track progress, and report on their environmental performance. It is also necessary to implement business eco-efficiency measures such as energy and water conservation, waste reduction, and pollution prevention. This can lead to cost savings, improved environmental performance, and increased competitiveness.

Engaging stakeholders such as employees, customers, suppliers, and local communities is essential for promoting sustainable business development goals of the company. They can involve stakeholders in sustainability initiatives, seek their feedback and suggestions, and collaborate with them to address sustainability challenges. Therefore, companies should report their sustainability performance to stakeholders regularly. This includes reporting on environmental metrics such as greenhouse gas emissions, water and energy consumption, waste generation, and recycling rates. Reporting on sustainability performance demonstrates the business's commitment to sustainability and helps build trust and credibility with stakeholders.

In conclusion, environmental accounting can play a vital role in promoting sustainable business development. By adopting the above solutions and recommendations, the company can measure and manage its environmental impact, set sustainability goals, implement eco-efficient measures, engage stakeholders, report on sustainability performance, and invest in renewable energy. These efforts can lead to improved environmental performance, cost savings, and increased competitiveness as well.

FUTURE RESEARCH DIRECTIONS

Environmental accounting is an accounting approach that includes environmental costs and benefits in financial statements and decision-making processes. It provides useful information to organizations and stakeholders about their environmental performance, helping them to measure, monitor, and manage their environmental impacts. In an attempt to adapt to changes in the business environment and to successfully respond to the requirements of different stakeholders, companies change their production systems and organizational structure, implement new production information technology, new cost management, business process management, and company management concepts and methods (Antić, Novićević Čečević, 2015). Here are some future trends and concepts in environmental accounting towards which further research could be conducted:

- Technology-enabled and based environmental accounting - contemporary technology is significantly changing the way we collect, analyze, and report data on the environmental performance of the company. For example, remote sensing technologies can be used to monitor land use and deforestation, while blockchain can be used to track the supply chain of limited resources and commodities. As technology continues to evolve, it will provide new opportunities for environmental accounting.
- Circular economy accounting - the circular economy is an economic model that aims to minimize waste and maximize resource use. Circular economy accounting involves tracking the flow of resources through the economy, from production to consumption and back again. This approach can help organizations to identify opportunities to reduce waste and improve resource efficiency.
- Social and environmental impact reporting - in addition to financial reporting, organizations are increasingly being asked to report on their social and environmental impacts. This includes reporting on issues such as labor practices, community engagement, and environmental performance. Social and environmental impact reporting can help organizations demonstrate their commitment to sustainability and engage with stakeholders on these issues of high importance.
- Natural capital accounting - Natural capital refers to the world's stocks of natural resources, such as water, air, and biodiversity. Therefore, natural capital accounting is the process of measuring and valuing the benefits that these resources provide to society. This approach recognizes that natural resources have economic value and that their depletion or degradation can have strong economic consequences.

- Carbon accounting - As the world becomes more focused on climate change, carbon accounting is becoming more critical and could be a method of measuring and reporting an organization's greenhouse gas emissions. Companies are being pressured to reduce their carbon footprint, and carbon accounting can help them to identify where they need to focus their efforts.

Overall, environmental accounting will continue to evolve and gain importance as organizations and stakeholders become more aware of the importance of environmental sustainability. As a result, environmental accounting will play an increasingly important role in financial reporting and decision-making processes in companies.

CONCLUSION

Today, the main goal of a company's business is to maximize profits in the short term and maximize benefits for stakeholders in the long term. In the era of significant climate change and increasing environmental pollution, the question is what constitutes a benefit for stakeholders. If we take into account that the operation of a company can have harmful consequences for the environment, which in the end can threaten the survival of stakeholders themselves, should we take into account only the economic aspect of the business? Namely, sustainable business requires cooperation in the environmental, as well as in the economic and social aspects. In recent years, more and more attention has been given to the protection of the environment and its preservation.

In order to be able to harmonize and adjust the economic and social aspects of business, company managers need an appropriate information base that will provide support for decision-making and point out this aspect of the business. This information base could be provided by accounting. Accounting has been considered an open system that cannot remain indifferent to business conditions and the needs of society. Having this in mind, environmental accounting was designed as an integral part of the accounting information system. Due to the constantly growing need to preserve the environment and make business decisions in accordance with the required standards of eco-efficiency, this accounting can grow into a separate and independent information system.

Environmental accounting provides the necessary information on environmental costs that represent the basis for making business decisions. Also, it produces information for the purposes of planning and reducing costs of environmental protection. Finally, environmental accounting identifies, groups, allocates and measures environmental costs for the purposes of business control and achieving adequate environmental performance.

Environmental costs can no longer be ignored and considered secondary and considered together with other costs. Namely, dedication and concern for environmental costs can ultimately lead to significant savings and quality improvement. This is supported by the fact that there is a positive and significant relationship between information on the environment, savings and monitoring of environmental costs, and compliance with legal requirements on the one hand and financial performance and sustainability on the other.

In order to achieve the goals of preservation of the environment and its protection, it is necessary to create a balance between the wishes and needs of customers, that is, the output they receive through the production or service process and the requirements for the preservation of not only the limited natural resources that are consumed in the production process but also the requirements for the preservation of the health of the customers themselves. Environmental accounting, as an integral part of a company's operations, takes care of all these aspects, providing necessary information basis for managers, policymakers and other relevant stakeholders.

REFERENCES

Antić, Lj., & Novićević Čečević, B. (2015). Lean Concept Techniques for Overcoming Constraints of Business. *Themes*, *39*(3), 905–923.

Antić, Lj., & Novićević Čečević, B. (2016). Time driven activity based costing in hospitality enterprises. In *International thematic monograph Modern management tools and economy of tourism sector in present era* (pp. 302–316). UDEKOM.

Duman, H., İçerli, Y., Yücenurşen, M., & Apak, I. (2013). Environmental cost management within the sustainable business. *The Online Journal of Science and Technology*, *3*(2).

Fasua, H. K., & Osifo, O. I. U. (2020). Environmental Accounting and Corporate Performance. *International Journal of Academic Research in Business & Social Sciences*, *10*(9), 142–154. doi:10.6007/IJARBSS/v10-i9/7711

Gajić, Lj., Medved, I., Rac, L. (2010). Obračun troškova i ekologija – novi pristip unapređenju poslovanja. *Škola biznisa, 4*, 76-85.

Grinell, D. J., & Hunt, H. G. (2000). Development of an Integrated Course in Accounting: A Focus on Environmental Issues. *Issues in Accounting Education*, *15*(1), 19–42. doi:10.2308/iace.2000.15.1.19

Hansen, R., & Mowen, M. (2003). *Cornerstones of Cost Management.* South-Western, Cengage Learning.

IFAC. (2005). *Annual report*. IFAC.

Jugović, J. (2019). Upravljanje troškovima ekološke zaštite u funkciji unapređenja konkurentnosti preduzeća. *Ekonomske ideje i praksa, 33*, 43-59.

Novićević, B., Antić, Lj., & Milenović, J. (2021). *Uticaj industrije 4.0 na ekološko upravljačko računovodstvo*. International Scientific Conference - Limen.

Novićević Čečević, B., Antić, Lj., & Milenović, J. (2021). Application of the concept of target costing in hospitality. In V. Bevanda & S. Štetić (Eds.), *International thematic monograph Modern management tools and economy of tourism sector in present era* (pp. 93–108). UDEKOM. doi:10.31410/tmt.2021-2022.93

Perišić, M. (2003). *Računovodstvo okoliša i održivi razvoj turizma*. Academic Press.

Ramamurti, R. (2004). Developing countries and MNEs: Extending and enriching the research agenda. *Journal of International Business Studies, 35*(4), 277–283. doi:10.1057/palgrave.jibs.8400087

Rounaghi, M. (2019). Economic analysis of using green accounting and environmental accounting to identify environmental costs and sustainability indicators. *International Journal of Ethics and Systems, 35*(4), 504–512. doi:10.1108/IJOES-03-2019-0056

Seetharaman, A., Ismail, M., & Saravanan, A. S. (2007). Environmental Accounting as a Tool for Environmental Management System. *Journal of Applied Science & Environmental Management, 11*(2), 137–145.

Senn, J., & Giordano-Spring, S. (2020). The limits of environmental accounting disclosure: Enforcement of regulations, standards and interpretative strategies. *Accounting, Auditing & Accountability Journal, 33*(6), 1367–1393. doi:10.1108/AAAJ-04-2018-3461

Şimşek, H., & Öztürk, G. (2021). Evaluation of the relationship between environmental accounting and business performance: The case of Istanbul province. *Green Finance, 3*(1), 46–58. doi:10.3934/GF.2021004

Solomon, A., & Ayodeji, O. (2019). Environmental Cost and Financial Performance: Analysis of Cement Companies in Nigeria. *International Journal of Academic and Applied Research*, 60-65.

Solovida, G., & Latan, H. (2017). Linking environmental strategy to environmental performance. *Sustainability Accounting. Management and Policy Journal, 8*(5), 595–619.

Todea, N., Stanciu, I. C., & Udrea, A-M. (2011). Accounting Policies On Environmental Costs And Their Calculation Method In The Entity. *Annals of DAAAM & Proceedings of the 22nd International DAAAM Symposium*, *22*, 653-654.

ADDITIONAL READING

Antić, L., Novićević Čečević, B., & Milenović, J. (2022). Measuring company performance using the integrated indicator. *Sixth International Scientific Conference on Economics and Management - EMAN 2022 – Selected Papers* (pp. 71-81). Udekom. 10.31410/EMAN.S.P.2022.71

Baumüller, J., & Grbenić, S. (2021). Moving from Non-Financial to Sustainability Reporting: Analyzing the EU Commission's Proposal for a Corporate Sustainability Reporting Directive (CSRD). *Facta Universitatis, Series. Economics and Organization*, *18*(4), 369–381. doi:10.22190/FUEO210817026B

Berber, N., Slavić, A., & Aleksić, M. (2021). Corporate Social Responsibility in Contemporary Organizations: Evidence from Serbian Processing Industry. *Economic Themes.*, *59*(2), 227–241. doi:10.2478/ethemes-2021-0013

Bojović, V. (2011). Sustainable Development – Multiple Meanings Yet Unambiguous Necessity. *Economic Themes*, *49*(2), 175–192.

Jones, J. M. (2010). Accounting for the environment: Towards a theoretical perspective for environmental accounting and reporting. *Accounting Forum*, *34*(2), 123–138. doi:10.1016/j.accfor.2010.03.001

Ligonie, M. (2021). Sharing sustainability through sustainability control activities. A practice-based analysis. *Management Accounting Research*, *50*(1), 100726. Advance online publication. doi:10.1016/j.mar.2020.100726

Novićević Čečević, B., Antić, Lj., & Milenović, J. (2021). Impact of Industry 4.0 on Environmental Management Accounting. *7th International Scientific-Business Conference: Leadership, Innovation, Management and Economics – LIMEN 2021.*

Sekulić, V., Antić, Lj., & Novićević Čečević, B. (2019). The impact of management accounting disclosure on corporate government efficiency. Contemporary economic trends: Technological development and challenges of competitiveness, 277-286.

KEY TERMS AND DEFINITIONS

Circular Economy: Economic system that is restorative and regenerative by design and which aims to keep products, components, and materials at their highest utility and value at all times, based on the principles of designing out waste and pollution, keeping products and materials in use, and regenerating natural systems.

Cost Accounting: It is an integral part of management accounting and is considered the process of tracking and analyzing the costs associated with producing goods and services.

Environmental Costs: Costs associated with the damage to the environment caused by human activities. These costs can include the costs of cleaning up pollution, restoring damaged ecosystems, and mitigating the effects of climate change.

Environmental Management Accounting: The process of measuring, analyzing, and reporting the economic costs and benefits of an organization's environmental activities and also a tool and practice of incorporating principles of environmental management and conservation into reporting in order to provide the basis for managerial decision-making.

Management Accounting: It is a field of accounting that focuses on providing financial information to managers within an organization to help them make decisions and involves analyzing financial data, creating budgets, and forecasting the future financial performance of the company.

Managerial Decision Making: It is the process of making decisions in an organization or business, which involves identifying and analyzing problems, gathering, and evaluating information, and developing and implementing solutions.

Sustainability: A concept that encompasses economic, environmental, and social aspects in order to ensure that current and future generations can continue to benefit from the resources available to them.

Sustainable Development: A concept that aims to meet the needs of the present without compromising the ability of future generations to meet their own needs. It is based on the principles of environmental protection, social equity, and economic efficiency.

Chapter 12
Exploring Disruption Trajectories From COVID-19 on Education and the Impact of Policies:
Lessons Learned and Path Forward

Ashok Vaseashta
https://orcid.org/0000-0002-5649-0067
International Clean Water Institute, USA

Dorin Radu
https://orcid.org/0000-0001-5043-2723
Transilvania University of Brasov, Romania

Carmen Maftei
https://orcid.org/0000-0002-7150-608X
Transilvania University of Brasov, Romania

ABSTRACT

The world has seen many pandemics; however, COVID-19 provoked global emergencies at an unprecedented scale in all aspects of life. Despite of recent advances in learning management systems and online education tools, one of the worst disruptions experienced was in the delivery of education. To keep students safe, most educational institutions were closed at the onset of the pandemic. At the peak of the crisis, ~90% of learners worldwide had their education disrupted. The policies were based on social distancing and the use of personal protection.

DOI: 10.4018/978-1-6684-7730-4.ch012

However, the negative impacts of long-term isolation were not articulated. It is likely that there may be similar emergencies in the future. How can we use exponential technologies and innovations for the effective delivery of education? Guided by the lessons learned from the impact of school closures, assessment of remote learning, and the fact that education delivery should be continuous, the authors explore how different research perspectives and evidence gathered can help strengthen policy reflections and future planning for improving efficiency.

INTRODUCTION

Around December 2019, a novel coronavirus disease emerged in Wuhan, Hubei province, China (Zhou et al. 2020; Cheng and Shan 2020; Wu and McGoogan 2020). A cluster of patients with severe respiratory illnesses, such as viral pneumonia and lung failure, were observed around that time in that region. The causal agent, unidentified at that time, has since been named the "Severe Acute Respiratory Syndrome Novel Coronavirus" - (SARS-nCoV-2) virus or simply COVID-19, being originated in the year 2019. While initially, there were few reports that person-to-person transmission was occurring, it became clearly evident that transmission from asymptomatic individuals to others was observed to be quite likely (Pan et al. 2020; Bai et al. 2020; Rothe et al. 2020). Due to high transmissivity, the SARS-nCoV-2 (or COVID-19) disease disseminated rapidly regionally and across the borders of many nations in less than six months from its first discovery and led to its global spread in 2020 (Holshue et al. 2020; Lee et al. 2020; Huang et al. 2020; Burke et al. 2020). Immediately, COVID-19 was declared a global pandemic by the World Health Organization (WHO) on 11 March 2020 (WHO 2020), causing many countries to ban flights from, initially, China but later from many other countries, as well. The causal agent, SARS-CoV-2, was initially confirmed via genome analysis to be a close relative of zoonotic coronaviruses and of a prior outbreak strain, SARS-CoV, which triggered an earlier epidemic in 2003. Clinical observations of SARS-CoV-2 infections normally manifested themselves as respiratory syndromes, although there is a degree of intestinal involvement, and the most severe symptoms were interstitial pneumonia and acute respiratory distress syndrome (ARDS) (Hamming et al 2004; Lamers et al. 2020).

Early in the outbreak, the taxonomy and language employed were not finalized, and hence "Novel Coronavirus", "2019-nCOV", SARS-nCoV-2, and sometimes "COVID-19" were used interchangeably to describe the virus, that is, now known as SARS-nCOV-2 or simply COVID-19. For the purposes of discussion here, we will designate the recent coronavirus disease as COVID-19 and will define it for any number of coronavirus viral strains that may cause it. The COVID-19 syndrome is to be considered associated with the critical complication, interstitial pneumonia associated with ARDS at varying rates, with ARDS being considered a major driver in mortality and morbidity. Due to the immense spread of COVID-19 in the first year of its first observation in Wuhan, the pandemic resulted in enormous human casualties and caused serious social, economic, educational, and productivity losses. Large field hospitals were seen under construction to house many incoming patients. Due to its fast spread, many organizations, such as the World Health Organization (WHO), John Hopkins University (JHU) Medical Center, Institute for Health Metrics and Evaluation (IHME), and many others started websites for tracking patients and associated information, such as age, co-morbidity factors, race, gender, etc. to discern evolving trends. Figure 1(a) and (b) show confirmed cased of COVID-19 in (a) and confirmed deaths in (b) for the period between Jan 1, 2020 – Jan 1, 2023. The data is available at OurWorldInData.org (Mathieu, E. et al, 2020). Although data is available for almost all countries, the data is shown for China, India, North and South Americas, Africa, Asia, and its comparison to the entire world. The data shown below indicates measures against 7-day rolling average counts of confirmed cases and deaths reported.

Figure 1. COVID-19: (a): Confirmed cases and (b): Confirmed deaths between Jan 1, 2020 – Jan 1, 2023 (using data from OurWorldInData.org)

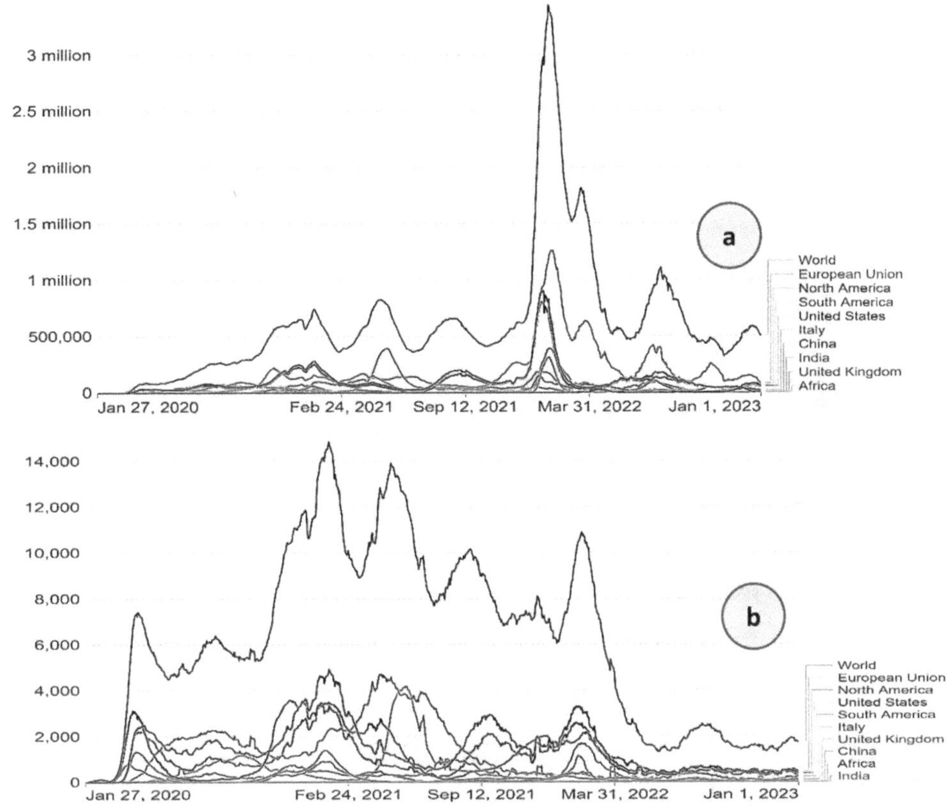

A global spread of SARS-nCOV2 was recorded at the height of the peak, initially around mid-2020, with second and third waves appearing at staggered rates, in U.K. and India with different variants, as shown in figure 2. With over 90 different variants currently reported, especially in second and third waves around many countries, causing widespread disruptions in terms of transportation, employment schedules, the service industry, the medical community, and even the delivery of education. The disruption to various sectors of society was enormous and devastating since the world was not prepared for widespread disruption, despite having gone through several pandemics in the recent past, such as the Ebola virus disease (EVD), Severe acute respiratory syndrome (SARS), Creutzfeldt-Jacob disease (CJD), also known as mad cow disease, and Middle East Respiratory Syndrome (MERS), also called as MERS-CoV, first reported in Saudi Arabia in 2012 and has since spread to several other countries. Hence, it is critical to have a holistic understanding of the ongoing situation and the development of strategies not only to cope with the current but also the future spread of the virus. Such an approach is critical for us to be better prepared to deal with similar situations in the future.

Figure 2. Infection by different variants for selected countries. (using data from OurWorldInData.org)

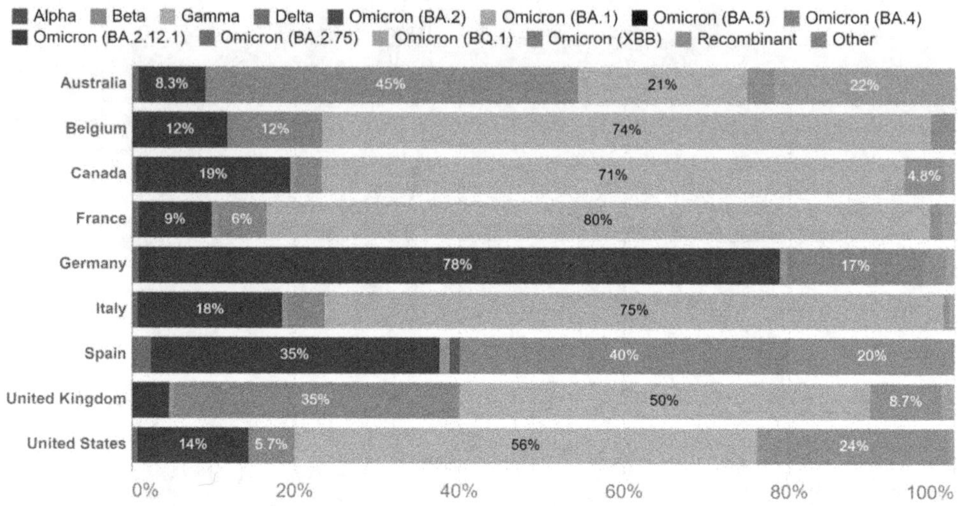

PREVENTING COVID-19 TRANSMISSION: RATIONAL AND LESSONS LEARNED

The impact of COVID-19 due to system-wide lockdown, viz., the world economy, medical community, service industry, and even education delivery, has been massive and will likely be felt for a long time. Although the world is slowly recovering from such a massive shock, a few facts remain worth noting, viz. COVID-19 created a global recession that has been the most severe since the end of World War II, the global economy contracted significantly, according to the World Economic Outlook Report published by the International Monetary Fund (IMF)), and while virtually every country covered by the IMF posted negative growth, the downturn was more pronounced in the poorest parts of the world. In addition to the overall economy, the impact on human health – physical as well as mental, social well-being, and global education have been pronounced.

The policies implemented at the time were designed to stop the spread of the virus by "flattening the curve". Without any vaccine for COVID-19, the only alternatives were to create social distance and use personal protective equipment, such as a face shield and/or mask. In doing so, organizations allowed employees to work remotely, education institutions were shuttered, restaurants were not allowed to serve meals on premises, personal services which required close contact were not allowed, and even many medical services were provided online, and the ones requiring physical contact were postponed. To some extent, these exercises to prevent transmission seemed to work to reduce the spread and or "flatten the curve". These directives were based on simple estimates of the probable distance a virus or virus-like particle (VLP) would travel. A distance of approximately 6ft (~1.5 meters) was considered optimal, and the use of masks (preferably N95) or even simple cloth was assumed to provide a certain level of protection against COVID-19. There were some extreme examples to reduce the number of severe COVID-19 cases by limiting contact between individuals at higher risk of developing the severe disease ("high-risk") and the general population ("low-risk"), viz. the high-risk individuals would be temporarily relocated to safe or "green zones" established at the household, neighborhood, camp/sector, or community level depending on the context and setting. They would have minimal contact, even with family members and other low-risk residents. Parallel to these efforts, a fast-track operation called "operation Warp-speed" (OWS) was announced as a public–private partnership to facilitate and accelerate the development, manufacturing, and distribution of COVID-19 vaccines, therapeutics, and diagnostics. The program promoted the mass production of multiple vaccines and different types of vaccine technologies based on preliminary evidence, allowing for faster distribution if clinical trials confirm one of the vaccines is safe and effective. Within a year, five of the six OWS vaccine candidates entered phase 3 clinical trials, two of which—Moderna's and Pfizer/BioNTech's vaccines received an emergency use authorization (EUA) from the Food and Drug Administration (FDA). Three primary platforms viz. mRNA, Replication-defective live-vector, and Recombinant-subunit adjuvanted protein were supported under the OWS and the general accounting office (GAO's) analysis of these vaccine candidates' technology readiness levels (TRL)—an indicator of technology maturity— showed that COVID-19 vaccine development under OWS generally followed traditional practices, with some adaptations. All the above-mentioned efforts were to stop a fast-spreading virus since there was no precedence to such a highly transmissive pandemic. Once the spread began to ease, it provided time to reflect and analyze which policy worked and, if so, how effective were they. It is, obviously, outside of the scope of this article to elaborate on all of these aspects. However, for this writing, we will focus on the educational aspects and analyze which policies should be implemented in the future for optimal results should there be another pandemic in the future.

A partial list of public policies implemented during the recent pandemic included the following. Policies adopted at educational institutions are italicized below.

1. *Wearing of facial masks or coverings* (with options as follows):

- No mask.
- Recommended wearing masks in any setting.
- Require wearing masks in some settings (e.g., public transport, classroom, restaurants, stores, etc.).
- Require wearing masks in all settings.

2. Adapting or closing educational institutions (with options as follows):
    - No rules.
    - Recommend/Require adapting in-person teaching (hybrid format, physical distancing, staggered arrival, separate entrances, lanes within corridors, hand hygiene, staff with plastic shields, etc.).
    - Recommend suspension of in-person teaching (transition to online or distance learning).
    - Require suspension of in-person teaching on some levels or categories (e.g., only grade schools).
    - Require suspension of in-person teaching on all levels.
3. Adapting or closing offices, businesses, institutions, and operations (with options as follows):
    - No measures.
    - Recommend closing (or working from home) and/or recommend/ require adapting (e.g., implementing sanitary measures).
    - Require closing (or work from home) for some sectors or categories of workers.
    - Require closing (or work from home) for all-but-essential services (e.g., grocery stores, pharmacies, and doctors)
4. Restrictions on gatherings (with options as follows):
    - No measures.
    - Some restrictions on gatherings.
    - Restricted all gatherings.
5. Restrictions on domestic movement (with options as follows):
    - No measures.
    - Recommend not leaving the house and/or recommend limited domestic movement.
    - Restriction on domestic movement (e.g., travel ban between or into certain regions or outside a certain radius from a given location).
    - Partial curfews in place.
    - Stay-at-home orders or full curfews.
    - Population not allowed out from their primary locations for any reason (some exemptions may apply, e.g., seeking medical care);
6. Restrictions on international travel
    - Entry bans, border closures, and/or visa restrictions.

- No entry bans or visa restrictions.
- Entry bans and/or visa restrictions for a single country.
- Entry bans and/or visa restrictions for multiple countries.
- Entry bans and/or visa restrictions for all countries.

7. Quarantine and/or COVID-19 test (on entry or before entry)
    - No quarantine and negative COVID-19 test for any country.
    - Required quarantine and/or negative COVID-19 test for one or more countries.
    - Required quarantine and/or negative COVID-19 test for all countries.

It should be noted that these guidelines were not based on physical or mathematical modeling but simply based on the estimated time of flight and residence time and estimated diffusion length of VLPs. Additionally, estimates from plume modeling were not available, perhaps in a rush to contain the pandemic from spreading. Although the initial estimates were based on the spread of VLPs from the aerosol transmission and high-touch surfaces, COVID-19 virus was also discovered in wastewaters later on, and of course, a separate set of rules needed to be put in place to contain the spread by other means. In the following section, we describe results from the literature on aerosol modeling, which might provide some additional insight into policy guidelines for future pandemics.

Aerosol Modeling

Upon observing COVID-19's second wave and third waves, and from the logarithmic explosion of cases in a matter of few weeks, one can only postulate mechanisms other than direct contact, viz. by aerosolized droplets – giving credence to "patient zero" theory, also discussed in the context of Wuhan, either at the Wuhan Institute of Virology (WIV) or wet markets in Wuhan, as suggested in the news media. Speculations aside, considering the respiratory nature of the virus, it is plausible to consider diffusion by aerosol to understand the social distancing protocols and also if any personal protective equipment (PPE), such as masks or face shields, should be used as a preventive measure. In general, microbial aerosols are generated in indoor and outdoor environments due to a variety of natural and anthropogenic activities. Wind, rain, waves splash, spray irrigation, waste-water treatment activity, cooling towers, air handling water spray systems, and agricultural processes are all examples of activities that generate (bio-) aerosols outdoors. A bio-aerosol is an airborne collection of biological- material comprised of bacterial cells and cellular fragments, fungal spores and fungal hyphae, viruses, VLPs, and by-products of microbial metabolism. Pollen grains and other biological material can also be airborne as a bio-aerosol. Table 1 below provides typical particle size and natural background concentration of bioaerosols.

Table 1. Bioaerosol particles size and natural background concentration

Bioaerosol Type	Typical size (μm)	Background concentration (per m^3)
Viruses	0.02-0.3	
Bacteria	0.3-10	0.5-1000
Pollen	10-100	0-1000
Spores (fungal)	0.5-30	0-10,000
Cell debris/biofilms	0.001-5	0-10,000
Microalgae	1-200	Varies widely

Corona Viruses (CoVs) are large enveloped non-segmented positive-sense RNA viruses. Viral- envelopes consist of proteins and lipid components, and such enveloped viruses require the fusion of their lipid envelope with the host cell membrane to enter the infected cells. Interaction of the SARS-CoV-2 envelope with a particulate matter (PM) is possible in the aqueous surrounding. After drying, PM can serve as a carrier for transmission of SARS-CoV-2 immobilized at their surface. The lipid-constituents of the viral envelope can be very important for the unspecific interaction of viral particles with different surfaces, including air-pollution PM. It should be emphasized that this interaction capability can be inherent mainly to enveloped viruses. Several research investigations have been conducted to study the diffusion of aerosolized particles with varying % RH (relative humidity), temperature, and other parameters. In a controlled study conducted by Alford et al, volunteers were exposed to carefully titrated aerosolized influenza-virus suspensions by inhaling through a face- mask. The demonstration of infection in participants of the study was achieved by recovery of infectious viruses from throat swabs taken daily or by seroconversion, that is, the development of neutralizing antibodies. The use of carefully titrated viral stocks enabled the determination of the minimal infectious dose by aerosol inoculation. The approximate 50% human-infectious dose (HID50-50% human infectious dose) of virus per volunteer was from 1 to 126 TCID50 (the tissue culture infectious dose at 50%). The dose for half of the volunteers was 5 TCID50. The other half of the volunteers, who had very low or non-detectable pre-inoculation antibody titers, were infected with 0.6 to 3 TCID50. The study reliably shows that the human-infectious dose of the influenza-A virus, when administered by aerosol to subjects free of serum-neutralizing antibodies, is approximately 3 TCID50. The approaches used in this study allow the precise number of infectious particles in the total number of particles to be determined and demonstrate infection by aerosolized particulate matter. A detailed lung-particle interaction is necessary for a complete study, however, based on earlier experiments, it is irrefutable to note that there is a significant potential for inhalation exposure to viruses in microscopic respiratory droplets at short to medium distances (up to several meters, or room scale).

Based on this study, it is thus recommended to use preventive measures to mitigate airborne- transmission, especially in indoor and heavily occupied settings, realizing that viruses are released during exhalation, talking, sneezing, sniffles, and coughing in micro-droplets which are small enough to remain aloft in the air and pose a risk of exposure at distances beyond 1–2 m from an infected- individual. at typical indoor-air velocities. A 5-μm droplet will travel tens of meters, much greater than the scale of a typical room, while settling from a height of 1.5 m to the floor. Hence, while a social distance of 1 meter may not be ideal, it is still somewhat better prevention than none. Increasing circulation air velocity and reduction in relative humidity may reduce the probability somewhat, as is evident from Table 2 below, which shows the effect of relative humidity on the infectivity of the airborne virus.

Table 2. Effects of RH relative humidity on the infectivity of selected airborne viruses

Virus	Relative Humidity for max. infectivity	Family	Genetic material	Size (nm)	Envelope
Human corona-virus 229E	Mid-range	*Coronaviridae*	ssRNA (+)	120-160	Yes
Influenza virus	Low	*Orthomyxoviridae*	ssRNA (−)	80-120	Yes
Newcastle disease	Low	*Paramyxoviridae*	ssRNA (−)	150	Yes
Vesicular stomatitis	Low	*Rhabdoviridae*	ssRNA (−)	60 × 200	Yes
Japanese encephalitis	Low	*Flaviviridae*	ssRNA (+)	40-60	Yes
Semliki Forest	Low	*Togaviridae*	ssRNA (+)	70	Yes
Rotavirus	Mid-range	*Reoviridae*	dsRNA	100	No
Pseudorabies	Mid-range	*Herpesviridae*	dsDNA	200	Yes
Rhinovirus	High	*Picornaviridae*	ssRNA (+)	25-30	No
Poliovirus	High	*Picornaviridae*	ssRNA (+)	25-30	No
Picornavirus	High	*Picornaviridae*	ssRNA (+)	25-30	No
T3 coliphage	High	*Podoviridae*	dsDNA	60 (capsid)	No
Rhinotracheitis	High	*Herpesviridae*	dsDNA	200	Yes
St. Louis encephalitis	All	*Flaviviridae*	ssRNA (+)	40-60	Yes

*Data from experiments of sampling airborne viruses performed using a chamber and artificially produced aerosol of viruses. The data shows a more pronounced stabilizing effect of low temperature, however, the role of the environment on the persistence of viruses in the air may be more complex and significant than previously thought.

Social Distancing and Personal Protective Equipment

Public health and social measures (PHSM) are data-driven actions taken by individuals, institutions, communities, local and national governments, and international bodies to suppress or stop the spread of disease. Hence, in response to COVID-19, several countries implemented a set of procedures, which were calibrated in the context of local and regional epidemiology of the disease. Such actions included individual, environmental, social, and physical distancing, disease surveillance and response, business practices, and movement and travel restrictions. However, having no previous guidance, the response was reactionary in nature. If weekly cases of COVID-19 reported were high, the measures were stricter, with the condition that the cases must drop by a certain percentage and for a certain period of time before the restrictions would ease. WHO and CDC also produced public health and social guidance of procedures in the context of COVID-19. One of the restrictions implemented was on public gatherings, for example, in educational institutions, hospitality industries, public transportation, workplaces and other locations of public gathering Figure below shows 4 snapshots of time and global restrictions on public gatherings. The dates reflect (a): 25 February 2020 – almost at the beginning of COVID-19, when only China had major restrictions on social gatherings; (b): 20 August 2020 – restrictions at the height of the pandemic; (c): 6 July 2021 – restrictions in the US due to 2ns and 3rd wave and in India and Middle East; and (d): 1 August 2022, when a steep decline in cases was observed. The restrictions, hence, were reactionary to the disease epidemiology. In view of unprecedented social, economic, and education-related losses, the objective is to adopt a data-driven and science-based proactive approach to minimize overall losses.

Figure 3. Restrictions on the public gathering (a): 25 February 2020, (b): 20 August 2020, (c): 6 July 2021, and (d): 1 August 2022. Clearly, the regulations lagged behind the pandemic, indicating that the response was reactionary (using data from OurWorldInData.org).

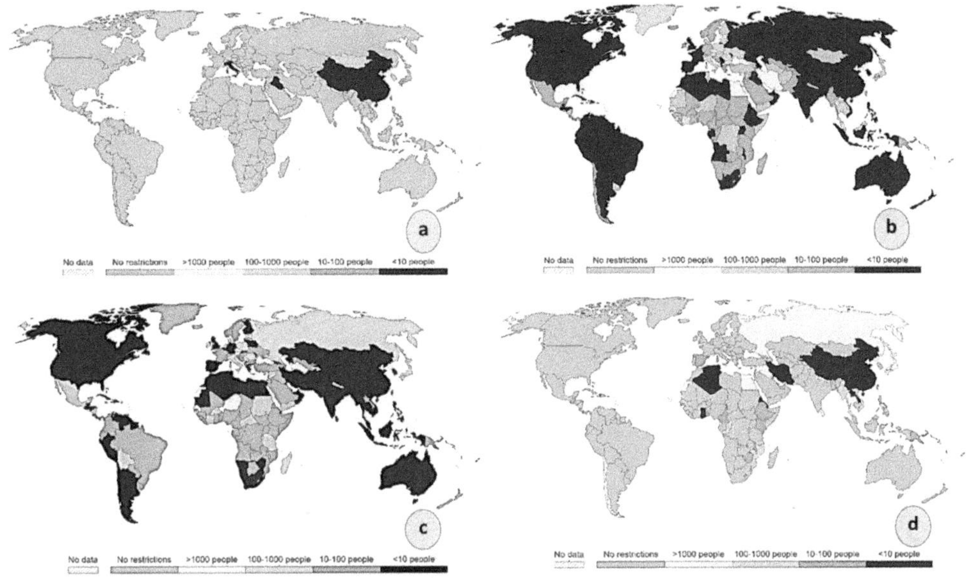

In general, there were six types of PHSM recorded as indicators and calculated from an ordinary scale, corresponding to the response policy's degree of intensity and scope. Scope corresponds to whether the policy was implemented regionally, across the entire country, or if applied to a group of people. The overall severity of the measure is reduced if it applies only to a select group or location as opposed to the whole of the country or general population. The average of these six indicators forms the composite PHSM severity index score. Yet another policy was on face covering, which was applied across most countries and was one of the most controversial policies (after vaccination). The applicability of uniform masking policy was not well articulated due to age, pre-existing health conditions, coverage of nose and mouth or just mouth, type of masks, one or two masks, discarding of masks, frequency of change, etc., were noted as some of the most common complaints. A well-established policy based on all these factors would provide mask guidance for a future pandemic. By the end of December, most countries have removed restrictions on face coverings, with some countries recommending optional face covering, as shown in Figure 4. The data for this graph is available in the open domain at OurWorldInData.org, along with IHME, CDC, and a few other sites tracking various other aspects of the COVID-19-related data.

Figure 4. Face covering policies ending on December 31st, 2022. Policies may vary at the subnational level. (using data from OurWorldInData.org).

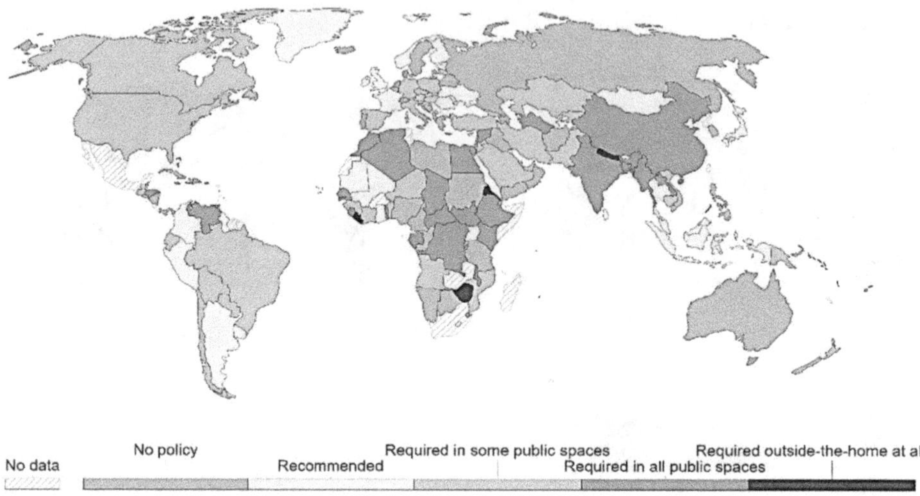

GLOBAL IMPACT ON EDUCATION

During the 2019-2022 period, a review of literature on the topic of the "impact of COVID-19 on education" yielded 831,721 research communications consisting of 9431 journal articles, 542 books (including manuscripts, short reports, etc.), and 821,746 sources such as technical reports, conference papers, etc. The studies were conducted practically in almost all countries, for almost all disciplines, and consisting of all socioeconomic backgrounds - for both students and educators. Conclusively, the impact of COVID-19 on education across the world has been unprecedented and devastating. A few examples are cited here to highlight the point, viz., over 1.6 billion learners in 190 countries had been affected by school closures, which happened on a scale never seen before. Disruption to education on a global scale resulted in millions of children having significantly missed out on academic learning had they been in the classroom. This was more prominent in younger and more marginalized children who experienced the greatest loss of education. According to the web-based resources, learning losses in the U.S. were observed in many states, including Texas, California, Colorado, Tennessee, North Carolina, Ohio, Virginia, and Maryland. In Texas, for example, two-thirds of children in grade 3 tested below their grade level in math in 2021, compared to half of the children in 2019. In Brazil, around 3 in 4 children in grade 2 were off-track in reading, up from 1 in 2 children pre-pandemic. Also, 10% of students aged 10-15 reported that they were not planning to return to school once their schools reopen. In South Africa, around 75% of children were a full school year behind their normal schedule, and about 500,000 students reportedly dropped out of school altogether between March 2020 and July 2021. In low- and middle-income countries, ~70% of 10-year-olds were unable to read or understand a simple text, up from 53% cent pre-pandemic. Also, many children missed school meals, which for some children have been the only reliable source of food and daily nutrition.

The health impact, including mental health, of COVID-19 has been direct as well as indirect. The direct health impacts resulted from coronaviruses spread among people through droplets dispersion from coughs, sneezes, breathing, sniffles, and even talking. The droplets may diffuse to another person or on an item such as a door handle. If someone else touches the handle, the virus may pass on to them if they touch their mouth, nose, or eyes. Once inside the body, coronaviruses mostly affect the respiratory system, including the nose and lungs. However, some viruses and the immune reaction they trigger can have wider health impacts. Indirect health impacts include obesity, inactivity, high blood pressure (HBP), and computer vision syndrome (CVS), resulting in eye strain and discomfort. Research shows that between 50% and 90% of people who work at a computer screen have at least some symptoms. The isolation created several mental health consequences, as shown in figure 5. Although a detailed discussion is beyond the scope of this article, it is widely agreed that the lockdowns due to COVID-19 have resulted in an adverse impact on social and behavioral interactions globally.

Figure 5. Detrimental influences of the pandemic COVID-19 on mental health

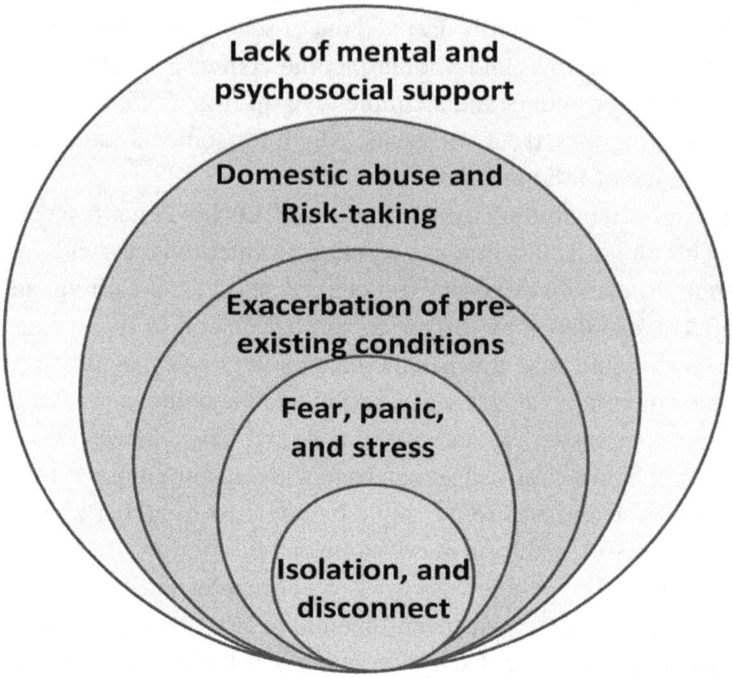

As per Centers for Disease Control and Prevention, "Younger adults, racial/ethnic minorities, essential workers, and unpaid adult caregivers reported having experienced disproportionately worse mental health outcomes, increased use of controlled substances and elevated suicidal ideation." Studies show that this pandemic is also associated with distress, anxiety, fear of contagion, depression, and insomnia in the general population and even among healthcare professionals. Social isolation, anxiety, fear of contagion, uncertainty, chronic stress, and economic difficulties may lead to the development or exacerbation of depression, anxiety, substance use, and other psychiatric disorders in vulnerable populations, including individuals with pre-existing psychiatric disorders. Stress-related psychiatric conditions, including mood and substance use disorders and, are associated with suicidal behavior. Furthermore, the outbreak has affected all segments of the population and is particularly detrimental to members of social groups in the most vulnerable situations, including people living in poverty, older persons, persons with disabilities, youth, and indigenous peoples.

The long-term impact of lockdowns will not be fully known for quite some time to come. While *ad hoc* solutions were implemented to address the sudden need for remote and online education, the pandemic highlighted how unprepared international education systems were to offer education in emergencies as a means of disaster preparedness. However, being unprepared and without previous experience and guidance, the difficult decisions regarding public health were to shutter the business and other services with severe economic and social impacts, along with widespread school closures. After almost over 2.5 years of the lockdowns, as we transition out of the pandemic, it is vital to consider longer-term implications and actively seek support and collaboration in finding long-term solutions to address wider issues that society seemed to be so unprepared. As established earlier in this article, quite likely, there may be another pandemic in the future. From the lessons learned from COVID-19, the world may be somewhat better prepared to counter another pandemic in the future. It takes a while to effectively establish policies and guidelines for alternate means to offer education and conduct work remotely for those employees who may be able to contribute remotely (please note that authors consider all employees as "essential employees" since during the pandemic, the employees were classified as non-essentials vs. essential), and ways to address social issues. Needless to point out, during the pandemic, one policy that superseded all others was how to prevent transmission.

Hence it is critical to conduct aerosol modeling to understand dispersion modalities in an effort to reduce the probability of transmission. This may reduce, if not eliminate, the probability of transmission, which, coupled with masks and other personal hygiene protocols, will minimize the probability of inhaling any variant of the COVID-19 virus. The authors have prepared survey questionnaires for real-time DELPHI studies. Such surveys, based on the active response, can help design not only different perspectives but also help develop horizontal and vertical priorities.

From the survey, it is instructive to address several questions, such as:

- Do masks make any difference?
- What kind of masks are necessary?
- For social distancing, what is an optimum social, spatial distance?
- Should only persons sick with flu or COVID-19 isolate himself/herself and not the whole class/group?
- Does the honor system of reporting work efficiently?
- Should younger children be forced to wear masks?
- Should some age groups, religious groups, military, and emergency persons be exempted from vaccination, should they choose to do so?
- What other precautions must be taken to prevent transmission – such as personal hygiene, and what is the optimum?
- Is there an alternative to distance learning tools?
- Should distance learning tools be gradually introduced to develop emotional maturity among younger students?

- What are the choices for vaccines? How many vaccine shots must be administered, and at what interval? Do the vaccines account for some or all variants?
- How do we develop immunity without vaccination?

There are many more variations, and more can be added based on individual experiences.

Disease Surveillance: Bioinformatics, Contact Tracing

Disease surveillance is an information-based activity involving the collection, analysis, and interpretation of large volumes of data originating from a variety of sources. The information gathered is used in a variety of ways, such as to evaluate the effectiveness of control and preventative health measures, monitor the propagation of infectious agents, support health planning and the allocation of appropriate resources within the healthcare system, identify high-risk populations or areas to target interventions, and provide a valuable progression of disease activity for archive and future reference. Bioinformatics is an essential methodology in forecasting and responding to disease outbreaks and incidents of regional, national, and international significance. To be effective, the collection of surveillance data must be standardized on a national basis and made available at local, regional, and national levels. The authors, Baldwin et. al. 2019, reported an automated sequencing analytics methodology suited for the detection/identification and classification of mixtures of Chemical, Biological, Radiological, and Nuclear (CBRN) agents of concern. The method provides simplified answers (or Go/No Go) responses), especially suited for a kinetic environment. The method operates regardless of the sequencer vendor, and no special user skill or foreknowledge is required. Its operation in a standalone or cloud environment, coupled with artificial intelligence (AI) decision support, is likely to improve its readiness in disease surveillance and contact tracing – a close contact evaluation and monitoring hierarchy. Different protocols are in place, but in general, contact tracing is the process used to identify those who came into contact with people who have tested positive for many contagious diseases – such as measles, HIV, and COVID-19. It is not the same as "exposure notification" or "digital alerting" tools. The consumer apps, such as those created with Google and Apple's API, are not contact tracing tools. These apps function as a way for the public to track if they have come into contact with a person who has tested positive and entered that information into their phone. Throughout the active period of COVID-19, several contact tracing protocols were adopted, and some of them remain active to this day. Figure 6 below shows countries with active contact tracing as of Dec 31, 2022.

Figure 6. Countries with active contact tracing as of Dec 31, 2022. (using data from OurWorldInData.org).

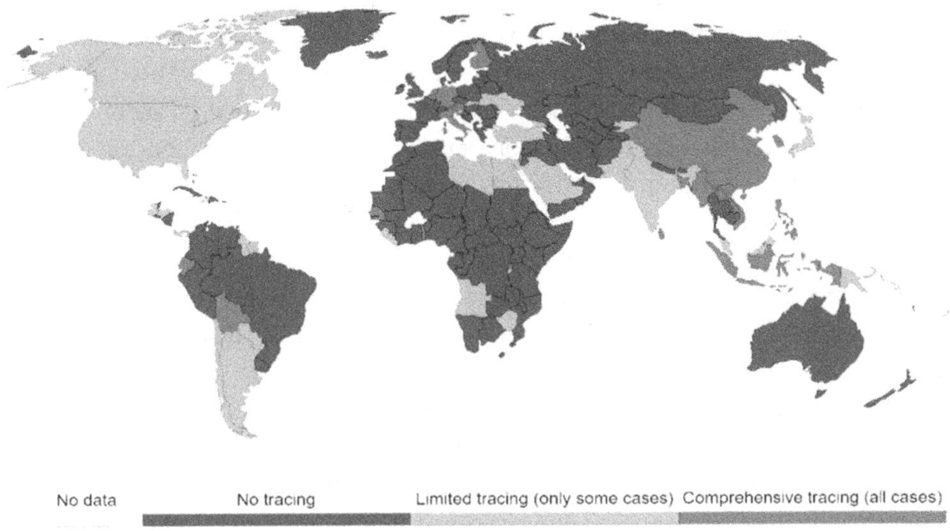

Although the city of origin for COVID-19 is well documented, there is still a lot of discussion on the exact source and mode. The discussion has ranged from accidental release from WIV to wet markets around Wuhan and also if the virus was zoonotic or non-zoonotic in nature. There have been swirling congressional debates over gain-of-function research, in which laboratory-engineered functionality into existing viruses renders them more potent to make such viruses as "super-viruses". In fact, the Intercept produced new evidence (Intercept, 2023) that the WIV and the nearby Wuhan University Center for Animal Experiment, along with their collaborator, the U.S.-based nonprofit EcoHealth Alliance, engaged in the "gain-of-function research of concern," as defined by the U.S. government in intentionally making viruses more pathogenic or transmissible in order to study them, despite stipulations from a U.S. funding agency that the money not be used for that purpose. This is also categorized under dual-use research of concern (DURC). In relation to the tracing source and mode in the context of disease surveillance, *in-silico* bioinformatic analyses are needed to analyze and interpret whole-genome sequence data generated from sequencing to take full advantage of the power of whole-genome sequencing. The *in-silico* analyses can easily be implemented in a laboratory setting and, in some cases, without the need for intensive computing resources and infrastructure.

Path Forward

The emergence of novel pathogens is a well-known epidemiological risk, however, the unexpected emergence of a truly novel coronavirus-mediated pandemic, SARS-nCOV2 (COVID-19), underscored the significance of understanding this contagion. Many researchers are examining how the new environment affects learners' mental, physical, and social health to help compensate for any losses incurred by this pandemic and to better prepare for future pandemics. There is a paucity of data at this juncture, but some investigators have extrapolated from earlier school shutdowns owing to hurricanes and other natural disasters. Inclement weather closures are estimated in some studies to lower middle school math grades by 0.013 to 0.039 standard deviations, and natural disaster closures by up to 0.10 standard deviation decrease in overall achievement scores. The data from inclement weather closures did show a more significant decrease for children dependent on school meals, but generally, the data were not stratified by socioeconomic differences. Math scores are impacted overall more negatively by school absences than English language scores for all school closures. These existing modalities can be integrated into calculations for quantifying the impact of a pandemic, with the intention that proactive approaches will diminish adverse impacts in the future. One thing is for sure, viz., blended or hybrid learning will be an integral part of higher education, henceforth, colleges and universities have made tremendous strides to improve their curriculum, adapt their pedagogy, and embrace technology to address student and faculty needs. However, the core challenges still revolve around student engagement, accessibility, and assessment. The areas that need special attention are successfully engaging students across all learning platforms and student preparedness. In addition, Guillen et al demonstrated that emotional intelligence was related to engagement and, consequently, resulted in better academic performance. Building emotional intelligence is key to resilience and successful delivery of education for sustainable development (ESD). Many educational entities have adopted initiatives to bridge the learning gaps through strategic course design and hybrid and asynchronous learning as part of their curriculum to inculcate emotional intelligence and self-discipline needed for remote learning.

DATA ANALYTICS FOR INFORMED PUBLIC HEALTH DECISION MAKING

With the recent advances in computation capabilities, artificial intelligence (AI) has transformed the world and produced capabilities that have led to numerous innovations. Complex algorithms have advanced using logic rules and reasoning that mimic human thought processes. The establishment of decision-support tools provided complex and hierarchical reasoning capabilities, however, unlike humans, such tools cannot learn new rules to evolve and expand their decision-making capability. Biologically inspired software, also known as "neural networks," provided the additional capability to recognize complex patterns and complete such tasks. These new capabilities are complemented by big data and data analytics – the process of examining raw datasets to find trends, draw conclusions and find the capacity for improvement. Healthcare analytics uses current and historical data to gain insights and support decision-making at both the patient and business levels. There are a variety of tools that gather and analyze health data gathered through various means, viz. Electronic Health Records (EHRs), Personal Health Records (PHRs), Electronic Prescription Services (E-prescribing), Patient Portals, Master Patient Indexes (MPI), Health-Related Smart Phone Apps, and more. With digital data collection, there is a vast amount of data to be studied in real-time. In fact, big data and health data analytics have played an integral role in the fight against COVID-19 by analyzing data in real-time, thus allowing a better understanding of trends, supply of PPEs, medical care availability, and hence decision-making in healthcare. The data analytics capability in conjunction with the wide-spectrum bio-threats identification and classification scheme (Baldwin, 2019), promises a tremendous capability to fight against such pandemics in the future.

The Whole-of-Government Approach in Providing Proactive Solutions

Building resilience is a strategic task that requires mapping pre-crisis assessment of nations' (and organizations') capabilities to deal with grand challenges. These capabilities include critical infrastructure, public health, cyber-space, and social domains. Improving resilience is critically important for a large community of stakeholders, including Public-Private Partnerships, local, state, and the whole of government approach, and through system-wide policy adaptations. As states, societies, and economies become more interdependent, resilience requires joint action of all relevant actors – including whole-of-society and international partners with the understanding that only cooperation will enable resilience. Implementation of agreed strategies and legislation are critical initial steps, thus, concrete actions must be established to reinforce these efforts for resilience to manifest. Resilience, as a philosophy and methodology, must aim better to prepare complex systems for a variety of challenges – both known and unknown – by reviewing interdependencies across systems, where disruptions trigger lasting and consequential losses and disharmony, to quickly recover from any pandemic or other domains of interest (DOI).

In section 2, several *ad-hoc* policies guidance was provided, viz. wearing of facial masks or coverings, adapting to social distancing, or closing educational institutions and/or work environments, businesses, institutions, operations, restrictions on gatherings, domestic movement, and air travel – domestic and international travel, quarantine and/or COVID-19 test. In addition to this guidance, a set of vaccines were made mandatory. The policy provided no exemptions for federal workers and military personnel, causing massive layoffs - should they choose not to get vaccinated. Without vaccination, travel was not allowed, and people could not visit many state and federal facilities. The authors concur that although the policies were implemented on the fly, *ad-hoc*, and without any previous experience, the implementation saved many lives. However, considering the economic, educational, social, and other losses suffered by the global population, the natural question is "are there better solutions?". With the use of exponential technologies, bioinformatics-based disease surveillance capabilities (Baldwin et al, 2019), nanotechnology-based solutions (Vaseashta, 2013; Vaseashta, 2021) to create resilience, remote sensor platforms (Monea, 2017; Vaseashta, 2021), and strategic decision-making analytical capability allowing for next-generation solutions to address current and future societal and technical challenges (Vaseashta, 2014), it is possible to offer the whole-of-government approach in providing proactive solutions (Vaseashta, 2022) to such pandemics.

The solutions may consist of:

- Technology and support to track and surveil symptomatic and asymptomatic patients.
- Use of AI in data mining.
- De-centralized social networks for monitoring.
- HUMINT (Human Intelligence) to identify the source.
- Academic-private partnerships.
- Enhance awareness through unbiased media.
- Technologically advanced infrastructure.
- Resilience by design (RbD).
- Information literacy.
- Use of the Internet of Things and the Internet of Behaviors.
- Enhanced cooperation.
- Use of masks only for symptomatic and asymptomatic patients.
- Limited disruption of education – may be limited only to symptomatic and asymptomatic patients.
- Limited use of masks - may be limited only to symptomatic and asymptomatic patients.
- Honors-based policies – a reward for honesty.
- Regular drills and practice for pandemics.

- Policies should be well documented and kept along with the institutional operational manual.
- Federal and State policies mandate that such policies are documented and kept on file through the registry.

Furthermore, the approaches to enhance resilience can be divided into three distinct categories:

Technology

- Convergence of interdisciplinary fields to address challenges.
- Paradigm shift using nexus of technological innovations.
- Integration of new platforms.
- Use of emerging and disruptive technologies.

Dissemination

- Balance in publication and dissemination.
- Education, training, certifications, and information sharing.

The COVID-19 pandemic was an unprecedented event, although there were several pandemics in the past, in the sense that it impacted education, travel, the economy, and almost every aspect of our lives. For an event to occur, the response has been primarily from the local, state, and Federal entities, including utilities. Private enterprises play a major role in the coordination of such activities with local, state, and federal entities. It is conceivable that based on lessons learned, any subsequent pandemic will have a much more informed and calculated response in close coordination with private and public entities, based on this and similar research on other aspects of life that were impacted due to the pandemic. Informed decision-making by the inclusion of knowledge base, analytical capability, foresight, and guidance plays a major role in futures-oriented analytical methodologies, including heuristics, data mining, scientometrics, scenario development, and modeling and simulation to provide solutions and analyze their potential for integrated, novel and/or unconventional manifestations. Using a "framework by design" of emerging scientific and technological advances and trends, Vaseashta et al. developed a systematic and strategic methodology and decision support tools to understand current, future, and varying challenges, as well as opportunities to create fully integrated solutions pathways which include challenges to critical issues.

CONCLUSION AND PATH FORWARD

Collectively, it is estimated that approximately 10% of the world had been exposed to COVID-19 during the peak period (around October 2020), and consequently, over 90% of the globe remained susceptible to COVID-19. With such a large parity, the future recommendations must emphasize building on the innovative solutions generated by the response to the crisis, especially to make education systems more resilient, whilst solutions support learners and teachers, as well as governments, throughout the recovery process. The suggestions made in the article conclude that the recent crisis was an opportunity for stronger international collaborations to foster a better focus and deliver solutions, including digital tools. Resilience and adaptability will be crucial for the next generations to navigate through any future pandemic. Realizing that COVID-19, SARS-nCoV-2, is an emerging disease, various diagnostics, therapeutics, and treatment platforms became available. Some of the vaccines are still considered experimental, casting doubts in the minds of many people about administering such vaccines. Hence many pharmaceutical companies, in partnership with research institutions worldwide, have announced the clinical trials of vaccines, and some of them are in phase 3 clinical trials, many have passed phase 3 trials and are administered worldwide. There has been a lot of progress in the treatment of disease, and death rates have fallen significantly all across the globe. However, there is still much to do. Furthermore, as the pandemic still continues to remain a problem and the infection still continues to evolve, it seems that this will be a multiple-year event. With the progression of time, a certain percentage of the population will see their antibody profile wane each month and potentially become susceptible again. If this occurs in months and is frequent, herd immunity cannot be established naturally, and there will be a steady state of sporadic recurrences until a confirmed vaccine is widely available and more people get vaccinated. Thus, either through the duration of the SARS-COV-2 pandemic itself or through natural common cold COVID strains, we are likely to investigate the theory of secondary COVID. It will be critical to accurately assess if prior coronavirus exposure will alter the impact (be protective, neutral, or harmful) with respect to the expected continued infections of SARS-COV-2. This will be critical for educational institutions to continue year-round education without interruptions. The most important impact if secondary COVID syndrome is proven to exist is the immediate need to make a continuous coronavirus vaccine program based perhaps on the influenza vaccine program framework and release an annual or periodical COVID vaccine and or required boosters, such as periodic influenza vaccines, based on medical history or Ig titer testing. Thus, while theoretical secondary COVID syndrome is concerning, this should not change our vaccine trajectory in the short term. If the outbreak lasts the theoretical drop of coronavirus antibodies may also complicate things with required boosters. We may need to add a global, ongoing program for the development of vaccines against COVID-19 and any future strains of this virus group to eradicate this disease. This may require a new annual or semiannual vaccination program to boost public immunity and provide protection, so we can once again reduce our social distance and regain our collective economic prosperity. However, for this pandemic to end, enormous funding and long-term clinical research studies will be required to compensate for the short and long-term impacts. This also raised a question, however, can we as humans prepare for the unknown? Regardless of the technology, we as humans need to be able to detect novel pathogens routinely in this highly mobile world to avert much of the risk of future pandemics.

REFERENCES

Alford, R. H., Kasel, J. A., Gerone, P. J., & Knight, V. (1966). Human Influenza Resulting from Aerosol Inhalation. *Proceedings of the Society for Experimental Biology and Medicine*, *122*(3), 800–804. doi:10.3181/00379727-122-31255 PMID:5918954

Bai, Y., Yao, L., Wei, T., Tian, F., Jin, D. Y., Chen, L., & Wang, M. (2020). Presumed asymptomatic carrier transmission of COVID-19. *Journal of the American Medical Association*, *323*(14), 1406–1407. doi:10.1001/jama.2020.2565 PMID:32083643

Baldwin, J., Noorali, S., & Vaseashta, A. (2019). *Development of a Wide-spectrum, Cloud Based Tool to Detect, Identify and Classify nCOV-SAR2*. NDIA CBRN Defence Conference and Exhibition.

Burke, R. M., Midgley, C. M., Dratch, A., Fenstersheib, M., Haupt, T., Holshue, M., Ghinai, I., Jarashow, M. C., Lo, J., McPherson, T. D., Rudman, S., Scott, S., Hall, A. J., Fry, A. M., & Rolfes, M. A. (2020). Active monitoring of persons exposed to patients with confirmed COVID-19 - United States, January-February 2020. *MMWR. Morbidity and Mortality Weekly Report*, *69*(9), 245–246. doi:10.15585/mmwr.mm6909e1 PMID:32134909

Center for Disease Control and Prevention. (2021). *CDC Recommends Use of Johnson & Johnson's Janssen COVID-19 Vaccine Resume*. CDC.

Centers for Disease Control (CDC). (2017). https://www.cdc.gov/dotw/sars/index.html

Centers for Disease Control (CDC). (2020a). Https://www.cdc.gov/nchs/nvss/vsrr/covid19/excess_deaths.htm

Centers for Disease Control (CDC). (2020b). Https://www.cdc.gov/nchs/nvss/vsrr/covid19/excess_deaths.htm

Centers for Disease Control (CDC). (n.d.). *Moderna COVID-19 Vaccine Overview and Safety*. https://www.cdc.gov/coronavirus/2019-ncov/vaccines/different-vaccines/Moderna.html

Cheng, Z. J., & Shan, J. (2020). 2019 Novel coronavirus: Where we are and what we know. *Infection*, *48*(2), 155–163. doi:10.100715010-020-01401-y PMID:32072569

Guillén, E. M., Tirado, D. M., & Sánchez, A. R. (2022). The impact of COVID-19 on university students and competencies in education for sustainable development: Emotional intelligence, resilience, and engagement. *Journal of Cleaner Production*, *380*(2), 135057. doi:10.1016/j.jclepro.2022.135057 PMID:36348962

Hamming, I., Timens, W., Bulthuis, M. L. C., Lely, A. T., Navis, G. V., & van Goor, H. (2004). Tissue distribution of ACE2 protein, the functional receptor for SARS coronavirus. A first step in understanding SARS pathogenesis. *The Journal of Pathology: A Journal of the Pathological Society of Great Britain and Ireland*, *203*(2), 631-637.

Holshue, M. L., DeBolt, C., Lindquist, S., Lofy, K. H., Wiesman, J., Bruce, H., Spitters, C., Ericson, K., Wilkerson, S., Tural, A., Diaz, G., Cohn, A., Fox, L. A., Patel, A., Gerber, S. I., Kim, L., Tong, S., Lu, X., Lindstrom, S., ... Pillai, S. K. (2020). First case of 2019 novel coronavirus in the United States. *The New England Journal of Medicine*, *382*(10), 929–936. doi:10.1056/NEJMoa2001191 PMID:32004427

Huang, W. H., Teng, L. C., Yeh, T. K., Chen, Y. J., Lo, W. J., Wu, M. J., Cin, C. D., Tsan, Y. T., Lin, T. C., & Chai, J. W. (2020). 2019 novel coronavirus disease (COVID-19) in Taiwan: Reports of two cases from Wuhan, China. *Journal of Microbiology, Immunology, and Infection*, *53*(3), 481–484. doi:10.1016/j.jmii.2020.02.009 PMID:32111449

IHME. (2022). https://covid19.healthdata.org/global?view=cumulative-deaths&tab=trend

Intercept. (2022). https://theintercept.com/2021/09/09/covid-origins-gain-of-function-research/

JHU. (2022). https://www.jhu.edu/

Lamers, M. M., Beumer, J., van der Vaart, J., Knoops, K., Puschhof, J., Breugem, T. I., ... van Donselaar, E. (2020). SARS-CoV-2 productively infects human gut enterocytes. *Science*, *369*(6499), 50–54. doi:10.1126cience.abc1669 PMID:32358202

Lee, P. I., & Hsueh, P. R. (2020). Emerging threats from zoonotic coronaviruses-from SARS and MERS to 2019-nCoV. *Journal of Microbiology, Immunology, and Infection.*

Mathieu, E., Ritchie, H., Rodés-Guirao, L., Appel, C., Giattino, C., Hasell, J., Macdonald, B., Dattani, S., Beltekian, D., Ortiz-Ospina, E., & Roser, M. (2020). *Coronavirus Pandemic (COVID-19).* Retrieved from: https://ourworldindata.org/coronavirus

Monea, B. F., Ionete, E. I., Spiridon, S. I., Leca, A., Stanciu, A., Petre, E., & Vaseashta, A. (2017). Single Wall Carbon Nanotubes Based Cryogenic Temperature Sensor Platforms. *The Lancet. Infectious Diseases, 20*(4), 410–411. doi:10.1016/S1473-3099(20)30114-6

Rothe, C., Schunk, M., Sothmann, P., Bretzel, G., Froeschl, G., Wallrauch, C., Zimmer, T., Thiel, V., Janke, C., Guggemos, W., Seilmaier, M., Drosten, C., Vollmar, P., Zwirglmaier, K., Zange, S., Wölfel, R., & Hoelscher, M. (2020). Transmission of 2019-nCoV Infection from an asymptomatic contact in Germany. *The New England Journal of Medicine, 382*(10), 970–971. doi:10.1056/NEJMc2001468 PMID:32003551

Vaseashta, A. (2013). Ecosystem of Innovations in Nanomaterials Based CBRNE Sensors and Threat Mitigation. In A. Vaseashta & S. Khudaverdyan (Eds.), *Advanced Sensors for Safety and Security. NATO Science for Peace and Security Series B: Physics and Biophysics* (pp. 3–25). Springer. doi:10.1007/978-94-007-7003-4_1

Vaseashta, A. (2014). Advanced sciences convergence-based methods for surveillance of emerging trends in science, technology, and intelligence. *Foresight, 16*(1), 17–36. doi:10.1108/FS-10-2012-0074

Vaseashta, A. (2021). Nexus of Advanced Technology Platforms for Strengthening Cyber-Defense Capabilities. NATO Science for Peace and Security Series. doi:10.3233/NHSDP220003

Vaseashta, A. (2021). Advanced Sensors for Real-time Infrastructure Integrity and Structural Health Monitoring. *Proceedings of the 16th International Scientific Conference CIBv - Civil Engineering and Building Services.*

Vaseashta, A. (2022). Applying Resilience to Hybrid Threats in Infrastructure, Digital, and Social Domains Using Multisectoral, Multidisciplinary, and Whole-of-Government Approach. NATO Science for Peace and Security Series - D: Information and Communication Security. Vol. 61: Building Cyber Resilience against Hybrid Threats, 42-59. doi:10.3233/NICSP220017

WHO Director-General's opening remarks at the media briefing on COVID-19. (2020, Mar. 11). https://www.who.int/dg/speeches/detail/who-director-general-s-opening-remarks-at-the-media-briefing-on-covid-19

World Health Organization. (2003). *Update 49 - SARS case fatality ratio, incubation period*. https://www.who.int/csr/sars/archive/2003_05_07a/en/

World-Health-Organization. (2019). *Middle East respiratory syndrome coronavirus (MERS-CoV)*. https://www.who.int/emergencies/mers-cov/en/

Wu, Z., & McGoogan, J.M. (2020). *Characteristics of and important lessons from the coronavirus disease 2019 (COVID-19) outbreak in China: Summary of a report of 72314 cases from the Chinese Center for Disease Control and Prevention*. Academic Press.

Zhou, F., Yu, T., Du, R., Fan, G., Liu, Y., Liu, Z., Xiang, J., Wang, Y., Song, B., Gu, X., Guan, L., Wei, Y., Li, H., Wu, X., Xu, J., Tu, S., Zhang, Y., Chen, H., & Cao, B. (2020, March). Clinical course and risk factors for mortality of adult inpatients with COVID-19 in Wuhan, China: A retrospective cohort study. *Lancet*, *395*(10229), 1054–1062. doi:10.1016/S0140-6736(20)30566-3 PMID:32171076

ADDITIONAL READING

Lopes Pinheiro, S., & Pasquier, F. (2023). Consciousness and Environmental Education: Transdisciplinary Urgencies from the Post-pandemic Context. *Transdisciplinary Journal of Engineering & Science*, *14*. Advance online publication. doi:10.22545/2023/00223

Smith, J. E., & Vaseashta, A. (2013). *Advanced Sciences Convergence to Analyze Impact of Nanomaterials on Environment*. Health and Safety. doi:10.1007/978-94-007-7003-4_7

Yulita, I. N., Hariz, F. A., Suryana, I., & Prabuwono, A. S. (2023). Educational Innovation Faced with COVID-19: Deep Learning for Online Exam Cheating Detection. *Education in Science*, *13*(2), 194. doi:10.3390/educsci13020194

Chapter 13
Analysis of the Sustainable Development Concepts in the Logistics Industry

Filip Bugarčić
https://orcid.org/0000-0002-4573-9082
University of Kragujevac, Serbia

Vladimir Mićić
https://orcid.org/0000-0002-0719-8481
Univeristy of Kragujevac, Serbia

ABSTRACT

The chapter aims to review the existing concepts of the sustainable development within the logistics industry, analyze them, and provide recommendations for further improvement. Special emphasis is placed on the concept of green logistics, together with perspectives on future development in this area. Great potential in solving the sustainability problem is identified in the concept of circular economy and reverse logistics, whose elements and potentials are discussed in detail. The chapter provides answers to the research questions: RQ1: What are the potential ways to improve the sustainability of the logistics sector? and RQ2: What are the risks and threats to implementing sustainable logistics? A key contribution is reflected in the conception of the SWOT matrix for applying the concept of green logistics, highlighting the strengths, weaknesses, opportunities, and threats for the implementation of this concept based on the literature review and current experience.

DOI: 10.4018/978-1-6684-7730-4.ch013

INTRODUCTION

The concept of a green economy implies the realization of economic activities and the achievement of economic growth and development in accordance with the principles of environmental protection. In this sense, green growth can be defined as "growth that is efficient in the use of natural resources, minimizes pollution and environmental impacts, and takes into account natural hazards and the role of environmental management in preventing natural disasters" (World Bank, 2012, p. 30). In order to ensure the realization of the long-term sustainable development, it is necessary to encourage innovation in the sense of "green economic growth", whereby innovation, green investment and improvement of the concept of the green economy through finding new models of environmental protection, can increase economic well-being in the long term (Jänicke, 2012). In the context of modern trends and principles of the green economy, international trade and logistics must find their role in the model of sustainable development and rise the opportunities to reduce global pollution and carbon dioxide emissions, which largely depend on logistics activities, such as international and local transport (Mariano et al., 2017).

Sustainable development, as a long-term, complex, and continuous process, is determined by a combination of economic, social, and environmental factors (Šulskytė, 2019). The logistics sector enables the efficient functioning of national, regional, and international trade (Bugarčić et al., 2020; Zaninović et al., 2020), with the growing volume of activities at the global level requiring the analysis of logistics in the context of sustainable development. The contribution of logistics to the model of sustainable development can be seen through the concept of green logistics, which respects the requirements related to environmental protection and the reduction of harmful gas emissions due to the transportation of goods. Also, it is necessary to look at the long-term perspective of logistics development in the future and analyze the possibilities for implementing innovative solutions in the transportation of goods, which would directly enable the realization of sustainable development goals in terms of reducing pollution and increasing the efficiency of transport. Requirements for the full use of potential by the principles of the circular economy impose the need for reverse logistics analysis, which represents a model for efficient use of resources and optimization of processes and activities, whereby the role of reverse logistics can be considered as a component and potential factor of industrial development in the future.

For this reason, green logistics represents a possible way in which countries could redirect their existing industrial and trade strategies in order to enable an ecologically acceptable model of development of the entire economy. In the realization of that goal, it is necessary to raise awareness among companies in the logistics sector about the importance of environmental sustainability (Lieb & Lieb, 2010). With the growing interest in advanced services, logistics providers face the challenge of providing environmentally sustainable services, which poses the problem of how to put the trends towards the development of green logistics concepts into practice in an efficient and purposeful way. The solution to this can be found in the development of green strategies at the national level, which would enable the realization of sustainable development goals related to logistics and increase the awareness of service users about the effects of green initiatives (Evangelista, 2014; Centobelli et al., 2020). Additionally, countries' trade policies must be committed to urgently reducing greenhouse gas emissions. The fight against climate change and the prevention of harmful effects on the planet and society requires significant changes at the global level in production, international trade, and the logistics industry. The identified gap in the current literature refers to the lack of research that analyses the possibilities of the logistics system in achieving the goals of sustainable development.

The subject of the research is the consideration of different sustainability models in the logistics industry with the aim to answer the following research questions:

RQ1: What are the potential ways to improve the sustainability of the logistics sector?

RQ2: What are the risks and threats to implementing sustainable logistics?

Apart from the introduction and conclusion, the paper consists of three parts. In the first part, the framework of green logistics was presented with recommendations in the form of the implementation of trade logistics instruments for the function of reducing global pollution. A special contribution is provided by the formulation of the SWOT matrix for the application of the green logistics concept, which, for the first time in the scientific and professional literature, highlights the strengths, weaknesses, opportunities, and threats of that concept. The second part of the article refers to the analysis of the future perspectives for global logistics development and the consideration of potential innovations in the transportation of goods while taking into account political, social, technological, and structural factors. Within this part, various scenarios for the future development of the logistics industry are considered. The third part is dedicated to the broader concept of sustainable development of the logistics industry, which concerns and analyses the implementation effects of the circular economy and reverse logistics.

BACKGROUND

In accordance with the subject of research within this chapter and defined goals, the current principles for sustainable logistics and international trade identified by the World Economic Forum (WEF, 2021) represent the basis for further elaboration of this concept:

- Identifying and analyzing traditional tariff and non-tariff trade barriers and production standards is important for reducing costs and bureaucracy related to reducing international transport pollution;
- Reducing market distortions caused by emission-intensive activities, such as fossil fuel subsidies, can encourage investment in environmentally sound alternatives. It is also important to ensure that businesses are not disadvantaged when they take the lead in the fight against pollution;
- Harmonization of standards for measuring emissions of harmful gases, achieved during the transport of traded goods, must be a key priority of trade policy. This issue is the focus of the proposed EU Carbon Border Adjustment Mechanism (CBAM) and enables the premiere of the green economy concept through the development of quality standards;
- Facilitating the efficient spread of new technologies in different markets is of key importance for the sustainable development of international transport and logistics;
- Trade agreements should be used to improve climate action. The scope of issues covered by trade agreements has increased over time to take into account a wide range of new issues. The critical importance of climate change for all stakeholders means that trade agreements should include ambitious, binding and enforceable commitments on climate change and environmental protection.

Many of these priorities, such as reducing and eliminating tariffs on environmentally friendly goods, reducing non-tariff distortions, and phasing out fossil fuel subsidies, build on existing initiatives and could be implemented quickly in theory, with the potential to increase participation in the long term. Other priorities, such as harmonizing emissions measurement standards and harmonizing trade policies and trade agreements, are more complex and require dialogue to develop the foundations for a sustainable and unified global system of international trade and climate policy. Table 1 presents different trade policy options for reducing greenhouse gas emissions. In this way, the implementation and development of international trade logistics activities can be enabled in accordance with the concept of green logistics and the goals of sustainable development.

Table 1. Trade policy in the function of reducing global pollution

The goal of trade policy	Trade policy instruments	
Reducing costs of environmentally friendly technology	Reduction of customs duties on certain products	Harmonization of pollution reduction standards
Encourage investments in green technologies and services	Easier access to the market	A predictable and stable environment
Neutralization of inadequate market mechanisms	Abolition of fossil fuel subsidies	Development and application of methodologies for reducing carbon dioxide emissions
Providing an environment for the possibility of a positive impact of trade policy on climate change	Linking market access requirements with climate commitments	Protection against discrimination of environmentally responsible market participants

Source: World Economic Forum (WEF). (2021). Clifford Chance, Delivering a Climate Trade Agenda: Industry Insights, 2021.

Trade policy can be of crucial help in the transition to a sustainable economy, whose role is important in accelerating climate action by reducing transport sector pollution and overall greenhouse gas emissions. According to a survey by the World Economic Forum (WEF, 2021) on the example of 30 companies that are dependent on global supply chains in their business and that rely heavily on international trade, most of them have developed their own strategies to reduce pollution within their supply chains. At the same time, they highlight the need for appropriate support from the regulatory environment and economic policy. The survey identified that companies want to ensure that national trade-related climate policies are based on transparent, open and non-discriminatory approaches, with the flexibility to respond to changing circumstances and leave open opportunities for consensus. However, the optimal approach to achieving global solutions also depends on unilateral and multilateral mechanisms that play a key role in motivating and encouraging actions, as well as the development of innovative approaches to climate challenges related to the international movement of goods and services.

Based on a broad literature review, Centobelli et al. (2017) identified key factors in the context of green logistics which need to be analyzed in future research. It includes the impact of green initiatives on logistics services, the assessment of environmental sustainability factors, the perspective of participants in supply chains in the context of the green economy, and the application of information technologies that support the green initiative. The concept and further development of green logistics can be formed within these guidelines. At the same time, Mariano et al. (2017) point out that a significant part of harmful gases emission at the global level is a consequence of transport activities, where the authors analyze the relationship between the performance of logistics, measured through the LPI (Logistics performance index), and carbon dioxide emissions from the transport sector. The contribution of this research is the construction of a new logistics performance index that considers the requirements of the green economy to reduce pollution (Low carbon logistics performance index, LCLPI). The proposed composite index and ranking of countries in terms of logistics performance and carbon dioxide emissions can help to identify countries with the best performance in logistics with low emissions, which is especially important for industrialized countries that record significant pollution from the transport sector. Green logistics performance indicators provide a combination of traditional logistics components and levels of harmful gas emissions. In this way, a quantitative expression of the value of this indicator was made possible, which, in addition to assessing the quality of customs procedures, logistics services, and the quality of infrastructure, also reflects the level of sustainability of all logistics operations within a country (Fan et al., 2022).

Certain research (Zaman & Shamsuddin, 2017) concludes that logistics performance is significantly related to indicators of national economic development that affect green supply chain management. Therefore, the timeliness of delivery has a significant impact on energy consumption; the quality of transport infrastructure emphasizes the need for renewable energy to alleviate environmental problems, while other components of the logistics performance index are also related to the emission of harmful gases and require active management at the macroeconomic level. There is also the identification of the relationship between green logistics and social-economic-environmental factors that can help in realizing the goals of green logistics. Liu et al. (2018) confirm that logistics performance is significantly related to environmental performance. The growth of international delivery within LPI reduces CO2 emissions, while the timeliness of logistics increases emissions of harmful gases in the analyzed Asian economies. Other logistics components, such as shipment tracking and service quality, infrastructure, and customs efficiency, also show a significant impact on the environment in different sub-regions of Asia. The conclusion is that industrialization and urbanization increase the emission of carbon dioxide, while trade openness has a positive effect on reducing emissions. These results also indicate a significant connection between logistics performance and the environment and highlight the priorities of environmental sustainability and green supply chain management in Asian countries, which represent one of the leading actors in the process of international trade. Khan et al. (2017) point out that a long-term and sustainable policy is needed to minimize the effects of carbon dioxide emissions and create sustainable global supply chain management practices. Realization of these effects is possible through strengthening the logistics sector and increasing its efficiency, which will consequently enable support in the realization of sustainable international transport of goods and the achievement of "sustainable green growth".

The connection between the intensity of international transport and logistics performance gives reason to appreciate the impact of green logistics in order to see the effects on foreign trade flows in different countries (Wang et al., 2018). One of the possible ways to encourage green logistics is the development of intermodal transport systems and green corridors, with the aim of reducing transport pollution (Beškovnik & Twrdy, 2012). Global logistics service providers are interested in environmental issues, partly due to external pressures and partly because they see the concept of green logistics and transport as a potential source of competitive advantage (Bask et al., 2018). However, due to the lack of widely accepted methods for measuring the environmental impact of transport, companies cannot easily share the costs and benefits of environmental initiatives among the various participants in the supply chain nor realize the benefits of such initiatives as a marketing argument to differentiate their offering. Therefore, due to the inconsistency of application, the contribution of green logistics at the economic level may be missing. The solution for problems related to reducing pollution is more difficult to implement in underdeveloped countries due to a large number of obstacles (Licastro & Sergi, 2021). Nevertheless, the perspective of the logistics sector in the pollution problem unequivocally gives positive results in achieving the goals of sustainable economic development, which can be seen even in the example of less developed countries (Karaduman et al., 2020).

Recent research confirms the previously presented evidence of a high degree of connection between logistics performance and sustainable development, pointing out that the performance dimensions of green logistics can foster a circular economy while promoting the overall economic development of countries (Wichaisri & Sopadang, 2018; Lu et al., 2019; Karaman et al., 2020; Khan et al., 2020). Larson (2021) adds that the solution to sustainable economic progress, viewed from the aspect of the logistics industry, is the development of new technologies and an increase in energy efficiency, as well as fewer emissions caused by the transport sector. By acting on the decomposition and optimization of existing models of goods transport, using an intermodal approach and more environmentally friendly transport alternatives and more efficient use of transport capacities, it is possible to reshape the functioning of the transport system within global supply chains, with the aim of reducing the harmful emission. In addition, efforts for more efficient transport of goods, through the application of the principle of timeliness and quality of delivery, must also consider the reduction in energy consumption, which would have a direct impact on the implementation of the concept of green logistics at the global level. The location factor of industry and distribution centers alike can be decisive in reducing distances when transporting goods internationally. The latest research in this field especially emphasizes the importance of green logistics as the future direction of development in this industry and its connection with the level of trade and service quality, the requirements of the circular economy, as well as the assessment of the effectiveness of this concept from the future development point of view (Yingfei, 2022; de Souza, 2022; Gan, 2022).

SOLUTIONS AND RECOMMENDATIONS

In accordance with the presented theoretical consideration of previous research and with the aim of clearly identifying the concept of green logistics, the SWOT methodology was used to construct the strengths, weaknesses, opportunities, and threats of the application of this concept (Table 2). The applied methodology on the example of green logistics enables an accurate description of all segments for the implementation of this initiative, giving an overview of the positive and negative sides when considering the justification and application of the sustainable concept in the logistics industry. The connection of the identified elements within the SWOT matrix with green logistics activities can be found through all logistics operations, both at the level of industrial logistics and international transport and in the domain of international trade logistics and its elements. The applied methodology enables an accurate description of all segments for the implementation of this initiative, giving an overview of the positive and negative sides when considering the justification and application of the sustainable concept in the logistics industry. This opens up space for future research in this area, mainly through the application of techniques to determine the empirical contribution of this initiative.

Table 2. SWOT matrix for applying the concept of green logistics

Strengths	**Weaknesses**
Reduction of harmful gases emissions	The impossibility of accurately measuring the level of pollution from the logistics and transport sector
Preservation of the environment	Reduced possibility of emitted pollution coordination due to the realization of economic activities on a global level
Realization of sustainable development goals	The problem of raising awareness and motivating market participants to reduce pollution
Opportunities	**Threats**
Development of "green strategies" and improvement of trade agreements by introducing a "green clause"	Cost pressure of implementing technology and means of transport that reduce the emission of harmful gases
Application of ecological innovations in logistics operations and transportation of goods	The risk of reducing the efficiency and speed of goods transportation on a global level
Practical implementation of the circular economy concept	Unequal position of countries in the process of international trade due to different environmental regulations

Source: Authors

Identified strength in applying the concept of green logistics is the long-term sustainability and support for achieving the goals of "green growth" with the ultimate goal of reducing global pollution. The potential opportunities of this initiative contribute through the development of strategies and clauses in order to create a suitable environment for the implementation of green logistics and the application of environmentally friendly ways of goods transportation and contribute to the development of the circular economy principles. On the other hand, the weaknesses of this concept primarily relate to the problematic control and coordination of pollution from the logistics and transport sector on a global level, as well as the problem of motivating market participants. Potential threats are the costs of applying modern technology to reduce pollution, which, despite modern solutions, could disrupt the efficiency of the international transport process, with pressure on less developed countries that generally lag in terms of green initiatives. In addition, the continuous growth of foreign trade flows at the global level requires the urgent application of ecologically designed trade policy instruments and the development of international logistics models that are in accordance with the principles of the green economy. Recommendations for the further development and practical implementation of the green logistics concept are the perspective for the future sustainable development of the logistics industry. The practical realization of this goal requires analysis of innovative ways of goods transportation and consideration of the circular economy and reverse logistics principles.

FUTURE DEVELOPMENT PERSPECTIVES ON GLOBAL LOGISTICS

The future development of the global logistics industry depends on various circumstances, including obstacles and development opportunities, primarily at the global level. The growing importance of international trade logistics and its potential impact on the development of industry, competitiveness, intensification of foreign trade flows, and economic growth rates in different economies faces the challenges of a complex and dynamic environment. Ubiquitous globalization, growth in the level of industrial and global competitiveness, as well as greater customer demands, the lack of certain resources, and their unequal worldwide distribution are some of the factors that lead to a dynamic and uncertain environment. In addition to respecting the concept of a green economy, the future development of international logistics must be in accordance with the long-term trends and needs in various international markets and industries, with the intensive implementation of new technologies with the aim of reducing pollution and increasing the efficiency of transport and the availability of various products on global markets. Innovations in the transportation of goods, as an indispensable part of the progress of international logistics, are primarily conditioned by needs, which is why it is necessary to harmonize the systems of transportation of goods so that the logistics system can keep up with development trends and market demands.

The development of the logistics industry in the future is determined by numerous political, social, technological, and industrial factors, of which the following can be distinguished (Heiko & Darkow, 2010, pp. 55-57):

- Growing demands for quality and personalized logistics services;
- Merger of small and medium-sized logistics companies into global systems in order to be more competitive on international markets;
- Growing demand for consulting services in the field of logistics due to the growing complexity and dynamism of the market;
- Digitalization of documentation flow;
- Development of alternative distribution networks and the growing importance of the CEP industry;
- Increase in the volume of traditional logistics activities;
- Growth in employment and business volume of companies from the logistics sector;
- Aspiration of service users for environmentally friendly options of international logistics and transport;
- The need to relocate traditional logistics activities (outsourcing);
- The flow of documentation is integrated into the portfolio of logistics services;
- Providers of various services are more significantly involved in the accompanying activities of logistics, thus disappearing the classic divisions between certain industries.

Among the other factors, which have not yet realized their full potential or are encountering obstacles in development, we can single out the desire for social and environmental responsibility, the full implementation of all world economies in the global production system, the lack of qualified logistics professionals, the continuous change in consumer demands and requests with the aim of increasing practicality, simplicity as well as digitization of business. These factors have a significant impact on the perspective of logistics development and shape its impact on the macroeconomic environment and industry structure. For this reason, continuous development of strategies and plans for improvement and adjustment of international logistics activities according to future needs are necessary. Logistics systems are becoming a central element of global business structures and a driver of social well-being. Therefore, greater interest and funding directed toward innovative research in logistics are needed, thus reflecting the broad expectations towards this sector in providing economically profitable and sustainable production and transport chains. The challenge is to ensure greater availability of goods with fewer resources and minimize the impact on the environment. This goal will be crucial for various industrial and developing countries that are trying to access international markets as cheaply and efficiently as possible and thereby take advantage of globalization.

The application of trade policy instruments aimed at reducing global pollution is primarily justified given that the intensity of exports has a negative impact on carbon dioxide emissions in the long term (Veselinović et al., 2020). An ecologically motivated model of trade policy thereby leads to a better understanding, coordination, and monitoring of harmful gas emissions reproduced in the transport activities of global and regional supply chains. The development of an appropriate architecture for long-term sustainable supply chains requires the identification and application of modern technology and the setting of clear goals for reducing the emission of harmful gases. Therefore, the concept of green logistics must support its role to become a factor of sustainable industrial and economic development. The analysis of green logistics creates the potential for further theoretical development of the green economy as an integral concept and enables the practical realization of sustainable development goals. Additionally, logistics in terms of sustainability, which is mainly identified with the process of international transport, must also include, and consider internal and local logistics activities within the application of the green logistics concept.

The practical application of pollution reduction strategies is particularly focused on ship and container transport as the dominant form of international transport of goods. Solving the problem of harmful gases emissions requires long-term development strategies with clear goals and recommendations, as well as a series of innovative technical-technological and organizational procedures during the transportation and handling of goods that would achieve the set of sustainability goals (Wang et al., 2015; Lee et al., 2019). In addition to international transport, the emission is also a problem within local logistics activities and last-mile delivery (Deckert & Görs, 2019). A possible solution to this problem lies in the optimization of logistics activities and the creation of standardized places for picking up goods in order to eliminate the negative effects of last-mile delivery. To reduce emissions from a logistics perspective, it is necessary to apply a holistic approach and look at various factors, such as the volume of economic activity, the intensity of transport and traffic, energy sources and the volume of gas emissions (Nilsson et al., 2013). Based on that, certain recommendations for reducing pollution can be identified (Mariano et al., 2017, p. 171):

- Reducing the intensity of transport without affecting the volume of transported goods;

- Reduction in the volume of traffic;
- Reduction of energy consumption;
- Reduction of CO2 emissions from the transport sector.

In accordance with the requirements for predicting the future trends of logistics development, the analysis of the DHL company, one of the leading logistics providers that perform international delivery services in various markets, presented models for the development of the global logistics industry until 2050 (DHL, 2012). This analysis connects logistics trends, innovations, and expectations, considering the needs, goals, and structure of logistics while developing alternative models. Based on that, five potential scenarios for the future development of logistics were identified:

The first scenario assumes a lack of resources and increased demands for sustainable development. Growth in logistics services will lead to the intensive development of logistics companies. Due to the change in the financing model, states will begin to resort to infrastructure privatization, so larger logistics companies will begin to invest more intensively and relocate certain activities to other markets in order to meet greater demands on a global level. According to this scenario, the importance of recycling and reverse logistics will increase;

The second scenario predicts the emergence of mega-cities as centers of social, economic, and political development. In this case, rural regions will significantly lag, so international trade will primarily be conducted between large centers. One of the characteristics of this scenario is the increased demand for automation of transport, the intensification of e-commerce and logistics innovations;

The third scenario emphasizes the increased requirements for security, as well as the growth of innovative technologies and the application of various systems for monitoring and improving the transport and telecommunication infrastructure;

The fourth scenario predicts the need to adapt logistics to uneven population growth in the future. Global imbalances can threaten macroeconomic development, and international trade flows can have a more pronounced regional character. Strong regional logistics providers play the role of a strategically important industry and are a strong factor in the international competitiveness of economies. Also, there will be an increase in the need to hire additional labor in the logistics sector;

The fifth scenario emphasizes the safety of delivery instead of speed as the main goal of logistics, and large industrial hubs will be replaced by numerous regional centers. The application of information technologies and the strong need for processing and analyzing a large amount of information will come to the fore.

In accordance with these trends, Klumpp et al. (2013) made suggestions for the development of international logistics in the future. The proposals concern the formation of a flexible logistics system, including the continuous improvement of the quality of logistics services and the creation of an urban logistics system.

In addition, sophisticated management of transport systems, sustainability, and development of the concept of green logistics, management of innovations in this area, and utilization of logistics in order to improve competitive advantages impose the imperative of further development of this industry. Zijm and Klumpp (2017) state that the achievement of competitive advantage is the key motive for the improvement of trade logistics, with the simultaneous need for the development and implementation of modern technology. The quality of the workforce and its adequate implementation and coordination with modern technologies (Sgarbossa et al., 2020), adaptability, flexibility, and creativity can be singled out as the main determinants of the development of the logistics industry in the future. E-commerce, which heavily relies on the development of innovative technologies in logistics and transport, plays a significant role in the improvement of this sector. Improvements are needed at the systemic, operational, and decision-making levels, given that e-commerce is developing significantly due to different circumstances and the development of new business models. The growth of e-commerce at the global level puts great pressure on the logistics development model, which must take this trend into account when formulating development strategies, both at the micro and macro level (Yu et al., 2017).

The analysis of different dimensions of logistics with the emphasis on macroeconomic and systemic perspectives (Havenga, 2018), also represents a model of the future development of logistics through the examination of its contribution to the development of the national economy and international trade in different economies and economic circumstances. In addition to the requirement to improve the determinants of international trade logistics as a function of economic and industrial development and the analysis of their individual impact on various macroeconomic dimensions (D'Aleo & Sergi, 2017), the trend of logistics development in the future must respect the principles of the digital economy (Lukiyanchuk et al., 2020) and the requirements of Industry 4.0. Additionally, the need for further improvement of logistics and distribution centers was identified to increase their efficiency (Kostrzewski et al., 2021). The successful functioning of distribution centers, their number, and spatial distribution are important for the realization of regional and international trade. A key component and method of further development of spatial connection in different markets is the examination of ways to increase the efficiency of international transport. In addition to the impact on the efficiency of goods transportation, the pursuit of innovation in this area has a direct impact on the environment, as a key argument for the concept of green logistics and sustainable development.

Development policies aimed at the synergy of innovation and transport have the goal of achieving sustainable economic development. Help in realizing that goal can be provided by the systematic application of innovations in transport means and technologies, as well as increasing the efficiency of transport services (von Schönfeld et al., 2018). Various initiatives aim to improve the transport system and optimize the flow of materials and energy consumption by increasing the efficiency of mobility services (Deloison & Wolff, 2020). The primary goal is the reduction of harmful gas emissions from the transport sector, but also the contribution of innovations to increase the efficiency of local and international transport. Modern transport systems such as autonomous vehicles and "smart" infrastructure corridors and roads could contribute to the realization of this goal, which requires a high level of technical and operational innovation aimed at the logistics and transport sector. This trend has proven to be a successful model of international trade development in the past. The use of modern transport technologies in the process of international trade has resulted in faster, more efficient, and safer transport of goods from the producer and sender to the recipient. An example of this is the emergence of container transport of goods, which with the advent of digitization and increased demands on various markets, is exposed to further challenges in container transport of goods and their manipulation in logistics terminals. An important factor and necessary support for the more efficient functioning of container transport is adequate and high-quality infrastructure and the support of modern technologies (Skender et al., 2019).

As key innovations in the field of transport, where a large part has positive implications for the sustainable development of the logistics sector, the literature singles out alternative fuels, e-commerce platforms, Blockchain technology, data security, Innovative systems in ports and terminals, optimization of ship size, robotics, Big Data analysis; smart shipping and autonomous vehicles (Koukaki & Tei, 2020).

The EU development plan and the "European Green Deal" have set a goal of climate neutrality by 2050, which will require, among other things, a reduction in transport emissions. To this end, digital technologies, together with automation are transforming traditional concepts of mobility, with a potential impact on decarbonization and the introduction of new digital platforms for the organization and optimization of transport. Analyzing the success of certain digital strategies in the transport sector helps in the decision-making process related to the allocation of funds for future research and development programs in this area (Tsakalidis et al., 2020). However, the results of some empirical research (Çakar et al., 2021) show that an increase in the level of innovation in developing countries has a positive impact on the emission of carbon dioxide from transport if the increase in innovation is the result of an increase in the number of patents. This effect is more pronounced in developed countries, which are also carriers of innovation. Godil et al. (2021) find that economic growth, technological innovation, and renewable energy significantly affect carbon dioxide emissions in the transportation sector in China, which plays the role of a leading actor in the international commodity exchange. The results indicate that due to increased renewable energy and innovation, carbon dioxide emissions in the transport sector are likely to decrease, however, an increase in a country's GDP still drives carbon dioxide emissions in the transport sector. Due to the complexity and multidimensionality of this issue, further research and new policies are needed to introduce innovations in the transport sector to reduce emissions.

As potential future solutions in the transportation of goods, the use of sophisticated transport solutions based on the application of modern technology and renewable energy sources can be singled out, while the bearers of these initiatives are large multinational companies that heavily depend on global logistics operations. In this way, logistics providers contribute to the improvement of the circulation of goods in different markets and consequently cause positive externalities in other industries within the national economy. Sustainable development of logistics should be focused on reducing emissions of harmful gases, optimizing cargo space by using software solutions to fill empty capacities, and adequate routing of certain international corridors, with the selection of optimal transport solutions. A large contribution can still be expected from the intermodal transport system, and innovative strategies must pay attention to the improvement of various forms of infrastructure and services through the digitization of international logistics processes. The continuous development of the identified determinants in the logistics industry would enable the potential for the sustainable improvement of international transport activities.

Reverse Logistics Concept

One practical solution within the circular economy in the context of sustainable industrial development is the reverse logistics system (Bernon et al., 2018). The idea of the circular economy represents a broader concept than reverse logistics, which primarily includes activities related to the return flow of certain resources and unused parts of products with the aim of further industrial processing and recycling. The extent to which each principle of the circular economy can be adopted depends on the type of logistics operations, where these two concepts coincide in the context of economic optimization, environmental awareness, the pursuit of renewable energy sources, the orientation towards the reverse production cycle, the elimination of waste and the requirements for the improvement of technology and innovation (Ripanti et al., 2015). Reverse logistics refers to all operations involved in returning products and materials from the point of use to the point of reuse. It includes managing the return flow of products at the end of their use, as well as defective and damaged items or materials. Companies have different motives for being active in reverse logistics. Primarily, they can make a profit through more efficient use and cheaper procurement of certain resources and materials. Additionally, due to legal obligations that force them to focus on such functions and due to social and environmental responsibilities, these factors are usually intertwined (Alumur et al., 2015).

In addition to individual companies, the reverse logistics process requires an active role in economic policies and legislation to encourage these activities. The quality of the national logistics infrastructure can be decisive in the implementation of the reverse logistics process, which, along with ecological and social motives, can realize long-term economic utility by intensifying industrial development conditioned by more efficient use and manipulation of resources and materials obtained from the process of reverse logistics. Responsibilities within this concept can be divided between different participants, such as manufacturers, distributors, suppliers, logistics service providers, and national strategies for designing and managing the reverse logistics system. This concept also faces challenges within international supply chains that imply greater complexity and more requirements (Sathish & Jayaprakash, 2017). For this reason, the interest in reverse logistics as a critical component in the supply chain management process is gaining importance in terms of strategic importance. Wang et al. (2017) highlight green logistics and sustainability, product life cycle management, product return, re-production based on previous raw materials, connection with different industrial areas, and creation of a return network as the key challenges and directions for the development of reverse logistics and its involvement in global supply and value chains.

In practical terms, the emergence of stricter environmental regulations and the growing environmental awareness of customers have forced various industries to start thinking about managing environmental operations with the help of reverse logistics (Govindan & Bouzon, 2018), while at the same time, the goals of increasing productivity and efficiency of industrial production can be achieved with cost reduction. Considering the perspectives of the circular economy and reverse logistics as its integral element is crucial for creating a comprehensive sustainable and long-term industrial strategy. Sathish (2019) states that the development of a strategy for increasing profits can be singled out as a key argument in favor of reverse logistics. As part of this goal, it is necessary to reduce the time during the implementation of these activities and, through adequate optimization, influence the reduction of costs in various segments of the processing industry. The level of development of the logistics infrastructure and the determinants of international trade logistics can be adequate support for the function of reverse logistics, which creates a new dimension of the impact of logistics on industrial development. The quality of logistics performance can enable the realization of the reverse flow of products and thus achieve some of the main goals of the circular economy, while the aspect of international logistics can contribute to the implementation of reverse logistics within the system of global supply chains. Global implementation requires the improvement of various forms of infrastructure, bureaucratic procedures and the growth in the level of competence of logistics service providers at the international level.

The rising need for reverse logistics implementation is also conditioned by the rapid growth of e-commerce and the increase in the demand for the return of goods by customers. This requires the development of an appropriate logistics model that can meet the growth of various demands flexibly, considering economic, environmental, social, and legal aspects. This requires the development and improvement of technologies focused on the concept of reverse logistics, storage, distribution, and processing of industrial products after their return (Dutta et al., 2020). Reverse logistics flows are dynamic and complex, especially in food supply chain activities where they can significantly contribute to environmental management and food loss minimization (Kazancoglu et al., 2021), which reflects its consequences on different industries. In the context of the Fourth Industrial Revolution, Wilson et al. (2021) indicate the importance of applying artificial intelligence in order to implement more effectively the concept of circular economy and reverse logistics. The application of the artificial intelligence system provides significant advantages for all functions and tasks of this process, with the inevitability of precisely shaping the necessary model. Based on that, the specific requirements of Logistics 4.0 must include the improvement of the reverse logistics system as an integral part that enables the realization of sustainable development goals. The complexity of this process application is particularly pronounced due to the dominant influence of global supply chains and the complexity of international trade, which requires the coordination and the implementation of the reverse logistics system globally.

CONCLUSION

The importance of sustainable development is present in many social and economic spheres, including the logistics and transport sectors. The need for a quick response to reduce the emission of harmful gases and the long-term environmental protection imposes the imperative of analyzing the current situation while giving recommendations and initiatives to solve these problems. Within the logistics industry, special attention is focused on the consideration of the identified concepts of sustainability in this area, where, based on previous considerations, a conclusion can be drawn about the lack of a holistic, coordinated approach to this problem and the need for precise guidelines for the further implementation of sustainable solutions. Based on that, recommendations can be made in terms of further development of the concept of green logistics with an increase in the number of initiatives that would enable its practical application. The future development of global logistics is moving in the direction of increasingly intensive activities at the international, regional, and local levels, as well as the growing importance of this area for all economic entities and, therefore, it is having an impact on the sustainable development. This requires greater commitment from consumers, companies, and economic policymakers to the sustainability of the logistics and transport industry. One of the possible recommendations and the solution for this problem can be derived from the concept of circular economy and the associated more intensive implementation of reverse logistics, which would enable more efficient use of resources and thus give room for the reduction of the negative impact on the environment.

The main contribution of this article is reflected in the answers to the previously posed two research questions. The answer to the first question (RQ1: What are the potential ways to improve the sustainability of the logistics sector?) is contained in the consideration of the mentioned concepts of sustainable development of logistics while emphasizing the imperative for their further development and implementation of green and reverse logistics systems. The concrete consequences of the initiative for sustainable development within this industry, which can be applied to the wider context of sustainable development, are given within the created SWOT matrix. In this way, the strengths and opportunities for applying the concept of sustainable logistics development are identified through the reduction of harmful gas emissions, preservation of the environment, and realization of sustainable development goals (Strengths), as well as through the development of "green strategies" and improvement of trade agreements by introducing a "green clause", application of ecological innovations in logistics operations and transportation of goods, and practical implementation of the circular economy concept (Opportunities). At the same time, attention is drawn to the negative aspects of the implementation of this concept, namely: the impossibility of accurately measuring the level of pollution from the logistics and transport sector reduced possibility of emitted pollution coordination due to the realization of economic activities on a global level, and the problem of raising awareness and motivating market participants to reduce pollution (Weaknesses), together with cost pressure of implementing technology and means of transport that reduce the emission of harmful gases, the risk of reducing the efficiency and speed of goods transportation on a global level, and unequal position of countries in the process of international trade due to different environmental regulations (Threats). Those statements highlight the risks and threats of this initiative, thus providing an answer to the second research question (RQ2: What are the risks and threats to implementing sustainable logistics?).

As a shortcoming of the paper, given the applied methodology, no empirical evidence can be drawn on the real impact of the proposed measures nor the concrete effects of sustainable logistics on the reduction of total pollution. Future research aimed at solving these problems can include statistical data on the level of pollution from this sector and calculate the concrete contribution resulting from the proposed measures to increase the level of sustainability.

REFERENCES

Alumur, S. A., Kara, B. Y., & Melo, M. T. (2015). *Location and Logistics. In Location Science*. Springer. doi:10.1007/978-3-319-13111-5_16

Bask, A., Rajahonka, M., Laari, S., Solakivi, T., Töyli, J., & Ojala, L. (2018). Environmental sustainability in shipper-LSP relationships. *Journal of Cleaner Production, 172*, 2986–2998. doi:10.1016/j.jclepro.2017.11.112

Bernon, M., Tjahjono, B., & Ripanti, E. F. (2018). Aligning retail reverse logistics practice with circular economy values: An exploratory framework. *Production Planning and Control, 29*(6), 483–497. doi:10.1080/09537287.2018.1449266

Beškovnik, B., & Twrdy, E. (2012). Green logistics strategy for South East Europe: To improve intermodality and establish green transport corridors. *Transport, 27*(1), 25–33. doi:10.3846/16484142.2012.663731

Bugarčić, F. Ž., Skvarciany, V., & Stanišić, N. (2020). Logistics performance index in international trade: Case of Central and Eastern European and Western Balkans countries. *Business: Theory and Practice, 21*(2), 452–459. doi:10.3846/btp.2020.12802

Çakar, N. D., Gedikli, A., Erdoğan, S., & Yıldırım, D. Ç. (2021). A comparative analysis of the relationship between innovation and transport sector carbon emissions in developed and developing Mediterranean countries. *Environmental Science and Pollution Research International, 1*(33), 45693–45713. Advance online publication. doi:10.100711356-021-13390-y

Centobelli, P., Cerchione, R., & Esposito, E. (2017). Environmental sustainability in the service industry of transportation and logistics service providers: Systematic literature review and research directions. *Transportation Research Part D, Transport and Environment, 53*, 454–470. doi:10.1016/j.trd.2017.04.032

Centobelli, P., Cerchione, R., Esposito, E., & Shashi. (2020). Evaluating environmental sustainability strategies in freight transport and logistics industry. *Business Strategy and the Environment, 29*(3), 1563–1574. doi:10.1002/bse.2453

D'Aleo, V., & Sergi, B. S. (2017). Does logistics influence economic growth? The European experience. *Management Decision, 55*(8), 1613–1628. doi:10.1108/MD-10-2016-0670

de Souza, E. D., Kerber, J. C., Bouzon, M., & Rodriguez, C. M. T. (2022). Performance evaluation of green logistics: Paving the way towards circular economy. *Cleaner Logistics and Supply Chain, 3*, 100019. doi:10.1016/j.clscn.2021.100019

Deckert, C., & Görs, N. (2019, March). Transport carbon footprint in the German courier, express and parcel industry (CEP industry). In NachhaltigkeitsManagementForuml Sustainability Management Forum (Vol. 27, No. 1, pp. 23-30). Springer Berlin Heidelberg. doi:10.100700550-018-0471-1

Deloison, T., & Wolff, C. (2020). *The Road Ahead: A policy research agenda for automotive circularity. Circular cars initiative policy workstream*. World Economic Forum.

DHL. (2012). *Delivering Tomorrow: Logistics 2050*. DHL.

Dutta, P., Mishra, A., Khandelwal, S., & Katthawala, I. (2020). A multiobjective optimization model for sustainable reverse logistics in Indian E-commerce market. *Journal of Cleaner Production*, *249*, 119348. doi:10.1016/j.jclepro.2019.119348

Evangelista, P. (2014). Environmental sustainability practices in the transport and logistics service industry: An exploratory case study investigation. *Research in Transportation Business & Management*, *12*, 63–72. doi:10.1016/j.rtbm.2014.10.002

Fan, M., Wu, Z., Qalati, S. A., He, D., & Hussain, R. Y. (2022). Impact of green logistics performance on China's export trade to regional comprehensive economic partnership countries. *Frontiers in Environmental Science*, *10*, 544. doi:10.3389/fenvs.2022.879590

Gan, W., Yao, W., & Huang, S. (2022). Evaluation of green logistics efficiency in Jiangxi Province based on Three-Stage DEA from the perspective of high-quality development. *Sustainability*, *14*(2), 797. doi:10.3390u14020797

Godil, D. I., Yu, Z., Sharif, A., Usman, R., & Khan, S. A. R. (2021). Investigate the role of technology innovation and renewable energy in reducing transport sector CO 2 emission in China: A path toward sustainable development. *Sustainable Development*, *29*(4), 694–707. doi:10.1002d.2167

Govindan, K., & Bouzon, M. (2018). From a literature review to a multi-perspective framework for reverse logistics barriers and drivers. *Journal of Cleaner Production*, *187*, 318–337. doi:10.1016/j.jclepro.2018.03.040

Havenga, J. H. (2018). Logistics and the future: The rise of macrologistics. *Journal of Transport and Supply Chain Management*, *12*(1), 1–10. doi:10.4102/jtscm.v12i0.336

Heiko, A., & Darkow, I. L. (2010). Scenarios for the logistics services industry: A Delphi-based analysis for 2025. *International Journal of Production Economics*, *127*(1), 46–59. doi:10.1016/j.ijpe.2010.04.013 PMID:32288260

Jänicke, M. (2012). "Green growth": From a growing eco-industry to economic sustainability. *Energy Policy*, *48*, 13–21. doi:10.1016/j.enpol.2012.04.045

Karaduman, H. A., Karaman-Akgül, A., Çağlar, M., & Akbaş, H. E. (2020). The relationship between logistics performance and carbon emissions: An empirical investigation on Balkan countries. *International Journal of Climate Change Strategies and Management*, *12*(4), 449–461. doi:10.1108/IJCCSM-05-2020-0041

Karaman, A. S., Kilic, M., & Uyar, A. (2020). Green logistics performance and sustainability reporting practices of the logistics sector: The moderating effect of corporate governance. *Journal of Cleaner Production*, *258*, 120718. doi:10.1016/j.jclepro.2020.120718

Kazancoglu, Y., Ekinci, E., Mangla, S. K., Sezer, M. D., & Kayikci, Y. (2021). Performance evaluation of reverse logistics in food supply chains in a circular economy using system dynamics. *Business Strategy and the Environment*, *30*(1), 71–91. doi:10.1002/bse.2610

Khan, S. A. R., Qianli, D., SongBo, W., Zaman, K., & Zhang, Y. (2017). Environmental logistics performance indicators affecting per capita income and sectoral growth: evidence from a panel of selected global ranked logistics countries. Environmental Science and Pollution Research, 24(2), 1518–1531. doi:10.100711356-016-7916-2

Khan, S. A. R., Zhang, Y., Kumar, A., Zavadskas, E., & Streimikiene, D. (2020). Measuring the impact of renewable energy, public health expenditure, logistics, and environmental performance on sustainable economic growth. *Sustainable Development*, *28*(4), 833–843. doi:10.1002d.2034

Klumpp, M., Clausen, U., & ten Hompel, M. (2013). Logistics research and the logistics world of 2050. In *Efficiency and logistics* (pp. 1–6). Springer. doi:10.1007/978-3-642-32838-1_1

Kostrzewski, M., Filina-Dawidowicz, L., & Walusiak, S. (2021). Modern technologies development in logistics centers: The case study of Poland. *Transportation Research Procedia*, *55*, 268–275. doi:10.1016/j.trpro.2021.06.031

Koukaki, T., & Tei, A. (2020). Innovation and maritime transport: A systematic review. *Case Studies on Transport Policy*, *8*(3), 700–710. doi:10.1016/j.cstp.2020.07.009

Larson, P. D. (2021). Relationships between logistics performance and aspects of sustainability: A cross-country analysis. *Sustainability*, *13*(2), 623. doi:10.3390u13020623

Lee, P. T. W., Kwon, O. K., & Ruan, X. (2019). Sustainability challenges in maritime transport and logistics industry and its way ahead. *Sustainability, 11*(5), 1331. doi:10.3390u11051331

Licastro, A., & Sergi, B. S. (2021). Drivers and barriers to a green economy. A review of selected Balkan countries. *Cleaner Engineering and Technology, 100228*. Advance online publication. doi:10.1016/j.clet.2021.100228

Lieb, K. J., & Lieb, R. C. (2010). Environmental sustainability in the third-party logistics (3PL) industry. *International Journal of Physical Distribution & Logistics Management, 40*(7), 524–533. doi:10.1108/09600031011071984

Liu, J., Yuan, C., Hafeez, M., & Yuan, Q. (2018). The relationship between environment and logistics performance: Evidence from Asian countries. *Journal of Cleaner Production, 204*, 282–291. doi:10.1016/j.jclepro.2018.08.310

Lu, M., Xie, R., Chen, P., Zou, Y., & Tang, J. (2019). Green transportation and logistics performance: An improved composite index. *Sustainability, 11*(10), 2976. doi:10.3390u11102976

Lukiyanchuk, I., Panasenko, S., Kazantseva, S., Lebedev, K., & Lebedeva, O. (2020). Development of online retailing logistics flows in a globalized digital economy. *Revista Inclusiones*, 407-416. https://revistainclusiones.org/index.php/inclu/article/view/329

Mariano, E. B., Gobbo Jr, J. A., de Castro Camioto, F., & do Nascimento Rebelatto, D. A. (2017). CO2 emissions and logistics performance: A composite index proposal. *Journal of Cleaner Production, 163*, 166–178. doi:10.1016/j.jclepro.2016.05.084

Mariano, E. B., Gobbo Jr, J. A., de Castro Camioto, F., & do Nascimento Rebelatto, D. A. (2017). CO2 emissions and logistics performance: A composite index proposal. *Journal of Cleaner Production, 163*, 166–178. doi:10.1016/j.jclepro.2016.05.084

Nilsson, L. J., Khan, J., Andersson, F. N. G., Klintman, M., Hildingsson, R., Kronsell, A., Pettersson, F., Pålsson, H., & Smedby, N. (2013). *I ljuset av framtiden: Styrning mot nollutsläpp 2050*. Lund University. https://www.lth.se/lets2050/aktiviteter/visa-nyhet/article/i-ljuset-av-framtiden/

Ripanti, E. F., Tjahjono, B., & Fan, I. S. (2015, September). Circular economy in reverse logistics: relationships and potential applications in product remanufacturing. *20th Logistics Research Network (LRN) Conference*.

Sathish, T. (2019). Profit maximization in reverse logistics based on disassembly scheduling using hybrid bee colony and bat optimization. *Transactions of the Canadian Society for Mechanical Engineering*, *43*(4), 551–559. doi:10.1139/tcsme-2019-0017

Sathish, T., & Jayaprakash, J. (2017). Optimizing supply chain in reverse logistics. *International Journal of Mechanical and Production Engineering Research and Development*, *7*(6), 551–560. doi:10.24247/ijmperddec201763

Sgarbossa, F., Grosse, E. H., Neumann, W. P., Battini, D., & Glock, C. H. (2020). Human factors in production and logistics systems of the future. *Annual Reviews in Control*, *49*, 295–305. doi:10.1016/j.arcontrol.2020.04.007

Skender, H. P., Zaninović, P. A., & Srića, E. (2019). Review of Modern Transportation Technologies with focus on Containerization. *Annals of Maritime Studies/Pomorski Zbornik*, *57*(1), 111-121. DOI: doi:10.18048/2019.57.08

Šulskytė, D. (2019). The impact of logistics sector on sustainable development. *Vilnius University Open Series*, (2), 75–81. doi:10.15388/OpenSeries.2019.18407

Tsakalidis, A., Gkoumas, K., & Pekár, F. (2020). Digital transformation supporting transport decarbonisation: Technological developments in EU-funded research and innovation. *Sustainability*, *12*(9), 3762. doi:10.3390u12093762

Veselinović, N., Bugarčić, F. Ž., & Radonjić, Lj. (2020, December). Innovation, export, CO2 emission and economic growth: Panel analysis of selected Central and Eastern European countries. *6th International Scientific Conference on Contemporary Issues in Economics, Business and Management (EBM 2020)*, 233-244.

von Schönfeld, K., Ferreira, A., & Pinho, P. (2018). The dialectics between social acceleration and the growth paradigm: Innovation and transport in neoliberal planning. *Proceedings of the Institutionalisation of Degrowth & Post-growth: The European level*, 17-19.

Wang, D. F., Dong, Q. L., Peng, Z. M., Khan, S. A. R., & Tarasov, A. (2018). The green logistics impact on international trade: Evidence from developed and developing countries. *Sustainability*, *10*(7), 2235. doi:10.3390u10072235

Wang, J.-J., Chen, H., Rogers, D. S., Ellram, L. M., & Grawe, S. J. (2017). A bibliometric analysis of reverse logistics research (1992-2015) and opportunities for future research. *International Journal of Physical Distribution & Logistics Management*, *47*(8), 666–687. doi:10.1108/IJPDLM-10-2016-0299

Wang, K., Fu, X., & Luo, M. (2015). Modeling the impacts of alternative emission trading schemes on international shipping. *Transportation Research Part A, Policy and Practice*, *77*, 35–49. doi:10.1016/j.tra.2015.04.006

Wichaisri, S., & Sopadang, A. (2018). Trends and future directions in sustainable development. *Sustainable Development*, *26*(1), 1–17. doi:10.1002d.1687

Wilson, M., Paschen, J., & Pitt, L. (2021). The circular economy meets artificial intelligence (AI): Understanding the opportunities of AI for reverse logistics. *Management of Environmental Quality*. Advance online publication. doi:10.1108/MEQ-10-2020-0222

World Bank. (2012). Inclusive Green Growth: The Pathway to Sustainable Development. Technical Report. World Bank Publications.

World Economic Forum (WEF). (2021). *Clifford Chance, Delivering a Climate Trade Agenda: Industry Insights, 2021*. Retrieved from: https://www.weforum.org/agenda/2021/09/how-can-policymakers-and-the-business-community-deliver-a-climate-focused-trade-policy-agenda-clifford-chance/

Yingfei, Y., Mengze, Z., Zeyu, L., Ki-Hyung, B., Avotra, A. A. R. N., & Nawaz, A. (2022). Green logistics performance and infrastructure on service trade and environment-measuring firm's performance and service quality. *Journal of King Saud University. Science*, *34*(1), 101683. doi:10.1016/j.jksus.2021.101683

Yu, Y., Wang, X., Zhong, R. Y., & Huang, G. Q. (2017). E-commerce logistics in supply chain management: Implementations and future perspective in furniture industry. *Industrial Management & Data Systems*, *117*(10), 2263–2286. doi:10.1108/IMDS-09-2016-0398

Zaman, K., & Shamsuddin, S. (2017). Green logistics and national scale economic indicators: Evidence from a panel of selected European countries. *Journal of Cleaner Production*, *143*, 51–63. doi:10.1016/j.jclepro.2016.12.150

Zaninović, P. A., Zaninović, V., & Skender, H. P. (2020). The effects of logistics performance on international trade: EU15 vs CEMS. *Economic Research-Ekonomska Istraživanja*, 1-17. doi:10.1080/1331677X.2020.1844582

Zijm, H., & Klumpp, M. (2017). Future Logistics: What to expect, how to adapt. Dynamics in logistics, 365-379. doi:10.1007/978-3-319-45117-6_32

ADDITIONAL READING

Buntak, K., Kovačić, M., & Mutavdžija, M. (2019). Internet of things and smart warehouses as the future of logistics. *Tehnički glasnik, 13*(3), 248-253.

Centobelli, P., Cerchione, R., & Esposito, E. (2020). Pursuing supply chain sustainable development goals through the adoption of green practices and enabling technologies: A cross-country analysis of LSPs. *Technological Forecasting and Social Change, 153*, 119920. doi:10.1016/j.techfore.2020.119920

Dong, J., Xu, Y., Hwang, B. G., Ren, R., & Chen, Z. (2019). The impact of underground logistics system on urban sustainable development: A system dynamics approach. *Sustainability, 11*(5), 1223. doi:10.3390u11051223

Lam, J. S. L., & Li, K. X. (2019). Green port marketing for sustainable growth and development. *Transport Policy, 84*, 73–81. doi:10.1016/j.tranpol.2019.04.011

Majerník, M., Daneshjo, N., Malega, P., Drábik, P., & Barilová, B. (2022). Sustainable development of the intelligent industry from industry 4.0 to industry 5.0. *Advances in Science and Technology Research Journal, 16*(2), 12–18. doi:10.12913/22998624/146420

Sinha, E. (2022). Circular economy—A way forward to sustainable development: Identifying conceptual overlaps and contingency factors at the microlevel. *Sustainable Development, 30*(4), 771–783. doi:10.1002d.2263

Wang, X., Yuen, K. F., Wong, Y. D., & Li, K. X. (2020). How can the maritime industry meet Sustainable Development Goals? An analysis of sustainability reports from the social entrepreneurship perspective. *Transportation Research Part D, Transport and Environment, 78*, 102173. doi:10.1016/j.trd.2019.11.002

Zarbakhshnia, N., Govindan, K., Kannan, D., & Goh, M. (2022). Outsourcing logistics operations in circular economy towards to sustainable development goals. *Business Strategy and the Environment.*

Zhang, W., Zhang, M., Zhang, W., Zhou, Q., & Zhang, X. (2020). What influences the effectiveness of green logistics policies? A grounded theory analysis. *The Science of the Total Environment, 714*, 136731. doi:10.1016/j.scitotenv.2020.136731 PMID:32018959

KEY TERMS AND DEFINITIONS

Circular Economy: An economic system that emphasizes circular flow of goods and materials and the full use of all resources within the supply chain in order to increase efficiency and protect the environment.

Green Logistics: This concept requires the realization of logistics activities without negative environmental impacts.

Industrial Development: An improvement in production processes within the economy that is determined by natural and social factors.

Logistics Industry: Represents all activities related to the planning, implementation, and control of the storage and distribution processes.

Reverse Logistics: Operations related to the return flow of products from end users to sellers and producers at the end of product's lifecycle with the aim of the potential reuse of resources.

Sustainable Development: Meeting the needs of current generations without compromising the ability of future generations to meet their own needs.

SWOT Analysis: A technique for structured observation, connection and understanding of strengths, weaknesses, opportunities, and threats.

Trade Policy: It includes a combination of strategies and policies intended for the realization of international trade goals, including regulations, tariffs, and non-tariff instruments.

Chapter 14
Phytoremediation of Municipal Solid Waste Landfills:
Challenges and Opportunities

Tatjana Golubović
University of Niš, Serbia

Sreten Ilić
Military Technical Institute, Belgrade, Serbia

ABSTRACT

Waste disposal is one of the main environmental problems facing society today. Environmental impacts of solid waste landfilling include loss of land area, contamination of soil, leaching of hazardous substances to groundwater, as well as emissions of methane to the atmosphere. The world generates over 2 billion tonnes of municipal solid waste (MSW) each year, with at least 33% of that not managed in an environmentally safe manner. In many developed countries, municipal solid wastes (MSW) are dumped in sanitary landfills, while in many developing countries, they are dumped in an inappropriate way which poses a serious threat to the environment. The deficiency of land and the requirement for reuse of the landfill sites demand their rehabilitation. In recent years, phytoremediation has been used as an efficient, environmentally friendly, and cost-effective technology in the remediation and rehabilitation of contaminated sites, including municipal solid waste (MSW) landfills.

DOI: 10.4018/978-1-6684-7730-4.ch014

INTRODUCTION

Municipal solid wastes (MSW), known as trash or garbage, are a heterogeneous mixture of residential, commercial, and industrial products (product packaging, grass clippings, furniture, clothing, bottles, food scraps, newspapers, appliances, paint, and batteries). While the composition of municipal solid wastes (MSW) could be highly variable, it is commonly accepted that organic fraction is the most abundant component (Vergara & Tchobanoglous, 2012).

Municipal solid waste (MSW) is an increasing concern due to rapid urbanization and industrialization. The most prevalent way of disposing of municipal solid waste (MSW) in developing countries is open dumping, which is the easiest and is considered to be the cheapest way of waste removal. In developed countries, landfills are engineered disposal sites that receive a wide range of materials (Kamaruddin et al., 2017). As previously mentioned, disposal of waste to landfill remains the most usual method of waste management. Despite the fact that landfilling provides a simple and beneficial means of waste disposal, if it is not appropriately managed can cause serious environmental risks relating to gaseous and particulate emissions, leaching, etc. (Vaverková, 2019).

The composition of landfill gas varies. The major constituents are methane and carbon dioxide. Carbon monoxide, hydrogen, oxygen, nitrogen and hydrogen sulphide are present in significant amounts. Landfill leachate forms as a result of waste decomposition and transportation of resulting products by water percolating through the soil profile (Licht & Isebrands, 2005; Qasim & Chiang, 1994). Leachate composition depends on the waste types and the phase of waste decomposition. Leachate contains high concentrations of dissolved and suspended organic matter and inorganic substances and poses a potential risk to the environment.

Establishing vegetation on the landfill has multiple significance: removal of contaminants, erosion prevention and control, as well as aesthetic effects. Phytoremediation is a promising technology for landfill remediation, as it can stabilize soil and, at the same time, remediate landfill leachate. Namely, phytoremediation, plant-based technologies, use green plants and their rhizospheric microorganisms to remediate contaminated sites (Sadowsky, 1999). Successful application of any phytoremediation system implies the selection and establishment of appropriate vegetation. Phytoremediation is evolving into a cost-effective means of managing wastes, especially excess petroleum hydrocarbons, polycyclic aromatic hydrocarbons, explosives, organic matter, nutrients and heavy metals (Nagendran, 2006). Phytoextraction, rhizofiltration, phytovolatilization, phytodegradation, rhizodegradation, hydraulic pumping, phytosorption and phytocapping are different types of phytoremediation based on the used mechanism (Nagendran, 2006).

Phytoextraction refers to the reduction of metal concentrations by cultivating plants with a high capacity for metal accumulation in shoots. Plants used for this purpose should ideally combine high metal accumulation in shoots and high biomass production (Pathak et al., 2012; Pathak et al., 2020).

Rhizofiltration is used for cleaning contaminated surface waters or wastewater by adsorption or precipitation of metals onto roots or absorption by roots or other submerged organs of metal-tolerant aquatic plants. For this purpose, plants must not only be metal-resistant but also have a high adsorption surface and must tolerate hypoxia (Pathak et al., 2012; Dushenkov et al., 1997; Horne, 2000; Poschenrieder & Coll, 2003).

Phytovolatilization is the process of the uptake of pollutants and their conversion to less harmful volatile forms. Volatile organic compounds may be volatilized from stems or leaves (direct phytovolatilization) or from the soil due to plant root activities (indirect phytovolatilization). Organic pollutants absorbed by plants are released into the atmosphere by transpiration, either in their original form or after metabolic modification. Also, this approach can be applied to the detoxification of some heavy metals and metalloids like Se, Hg, and As (Yan et al., 2020).

Phytodegradation which is also known as phytotransformation, is the breakdown of contaminants taken up by plants through metabolic processes within the plant or the breakdown of contaminants surrounding the plant through the effect of enzymes produced by the plants. Plants are able to produce enzymes that catalyze and accelerate degradation. Hence, organic pollutants are broken down into simpler molecular forms and are incorporated into plant tissues to aid plant growth.

Rhizodegradation, also known as phytostimulation, is the degradation of contaminants in the rhizosphere by means of microbial activity which is enhanced by the presence of plant roots.

In phytostabilization, plants are used for immobilizing contaminant metals in soils or sediments by root uptake, adsorption onto roots or precipitation in the rhizosphere. By decreasing metal mobility, these processes prevent leaching and groundwater pollution. Bioavailability is reduced, and fewer contaminants enter the trophic web (Poschenrieder & Coll, 2003).

Hydraulic control uses plants that absorb large amounts of water and thus prevent the spread of contaminated wastewater into adjacent uncontaminated areas. Plants act as natural pumps when their roots reach down towards the water table and establish a dense root mass that takes up large quantities of water (http://www.cpeo.org/techtree/ttdescript/lanassm.htm; Quinn et al., 2001 Poschenrieder & Coll, 2003).

Phytosorption is the adsorption of pollutants by plant roots and leaves and the prevention of pollutant movement.

Phytocapping is the process of establishing perennial vegetation on a layer of soil placed over the waste, such that the soil stores the water during rainfall events, and the plants remove the water via transpiration. When the soil depth and plant density are optimised, it is possible to balance the rainfall input with the evapotranspiration rate to avoid excessive percolation of water into the buried waste (Ashwath & Venkatraman, 2010).

Phytorestauration is the revegetation of barren areas by fast-growing resistant species that efficiently cover the soil, thus preventing the migration of contaminated soil particles and soil erosion by wind and surface water run-off. This technique reduces the spread of contaminants and also visual impact. However, previous soil conditioning is required to enable plants to colonize the polluted substrate (Mench et al., 2000; Vangronsveld et al., 1998; Poschenrieder & Coll, 2003).

Landfills and dumpsites used for the disposal of municipal solid wastes demand periodical rehabilitation. Rehabilitation measures and strategies must provide environmental protection, particularly in terms of groundwater contamination resulting from the migration of leachate, emission of gaseous pollutants and volatile organic pollutants, as well as the aesthetic of the environment.

BACKGROUND

Municipal Solid Waste Management

Municipal solid waste management is a serious challenge for countries worldwide, primarily for developing countries. In many countries, according to the national environmental policy, waste management is defined as one of the most important issues of environmental protection. In practice, the

circumstances are significantly different. An increase in municipal solid waste production in urban and rural areas puts pressure on the management system. The collection service, due to the lack of transportation, is mainly prioritized in areas with well-established infrastructure (Pheakdey et al., 2022). The limitation of public awareness also poses a challenge to the environmentally sound management of municipal solid waste. The deficiency of waste treatment technologies and infrastructures implies that most municipal solid waste is directly disposed on landfills without intermediate treatment. Recently, governments have made many efforts to increase municipal solid waste management by adopting new regulations, policies, strategies, and guidelines. However, the question is how such instruments can be effectively implemented towards the sustainable management of municipal solid waste by taking into account environmental, economic, and social aspects (Spoann, 2019).

Landfill as a Potential Source of Pollution

The requirement for the collection and sanitary disposal of municipal solid waste was not recognized until lately (Vaverková, et al., 2018). In other words, most municipal solid waste was disposed of in open dumpsites. Open dumpsites are those where solid waste is deposited without planning and consideration for environmental and health standards and are illegal from the aspect of establishment and operation (Figure 1). In contrast, sanitary landfills are designed both to store and treat wastes (Figure 2).

Figure 1. Open dumpsite
(Source: Milošević, 2016)

The potential risk from municipal solid waste landfills originates from the migration of contaminated leachate, landfill gas and landfill fires; consequently, the environmental impacts of the landfills must not be ignored.

As water percolates through the landfill, contaminants are leached from the solid waste. The quality of the leachate is variable and depends on the composition of the solid waste, depth of waste, presence of oxygen, temperature conditions, hydrology, etc. Leachates are complex mixtures of dissolved substances such as organic matter, inorganic components including heavy metals and metalloids and a wide range of xenobiotic organic compounds. Landfill leachate is an important source of pollutants. Great content of these substances is hazardous and toxic to humans and the environment (Vaverková, 2019; Živković et al., 2019; Krstić et al., 2018).

Figure 2. Regional sanitary landfill "Muntina Padina", Pirot
(Source: Milošević, 2016)

One of the products of biological processes occurring in municipal solid waste landfills is landfill gas or biogas (Chen et al., 2012; Parker, 1986). Landfill gas is a natural by-product of the decomposition of organic material in landfills. Main factors affecting the amount of landfill gas are waste composition, moisture content, temperature, landfill age etc. When municipal solid waste is first deposited in a landfill, it undergoes an aerobic decomposition stage when a small amount of methane is generated. Then, in most cases, within less than one year, anaerobic conditions are established, and methane-producing bacteria begin to decompose the waste and generate methane. Landfill gas is composed of approximately 50 percent methane (the primary component of natural gas), about 50 percent carbon dioxide (CO_2) and a small amount of non-methane organic compounds. Municipal solid waste (MSW) landfills are the third-largest source of human-related methane emissions in the United States, accounting for approximately 14.5 percent of these emissions in 2020 (https://www.epa.gov/basic-information-about-landfill-gas).

The emission of methane, carbon dioxide, nitrous oxide, and halogenated organic compounds, which have the capacity to absorb infrared radiation, has a major extent on the landfill's environmental impact, contributing to both climate change and global warming. Methane emissions from landfills are considered to represent the main source of climate impact in the waste sector. It should be emphasized that when landfill gas is captured and used to generate electricity, fugitive methane leaks from the landfill gas collection system, further contributing to total landfill greenhouse gas (GHG) emissions (Pawlowska, 2014; W&CC, 2010). It is estimated that global biogenic CO_2 emissions from landfills are equivalent to 0.04–0.06% of fossil fuel emissions of CO_2 (Lima et al., 2002). Municipal solid waste (MSW) landfills can be an important anthropogenic source of N_2O emissions, one of three major greenhouse gases and the dominant ozone-depleting substance. N_2O is produced mainly by microbial processes in soils as a by-product of nitrification (the oxidation of ammonia to nitrate via nitrite) and as an intermediate product of denitrification (the reduction of nitrate to molecular nitrogen via nitrite, nitric oxide, and nitrous oxide). Nitrous oxide (N_2O), as well as other nitrogen oxides, including NO and NO_2 (products of landfill gas burning), are involved in the creation of photochemical smog. The non-methane organic compounds released from landfills contribute to photochemical smog formation (Zhang et al., 2009).

The olfactory nuisance, due to the emissions of active molecules, is mainly associated with improperly managed waste disposal. The substances that are mainly responsible for odour nuisance are hydrogen sulphide, alkylated benzenes, esters, dimethyl sulphide (DMS), butyric acid, thiols (mercaptans), such as methanethiol and propanethiol (Parker et al., 2002), terpenes (*p*-cymene, limonene, α-pinen), carbon disulphide (Stretch et al., 2001; Sadowska-Rociek et al., 2009) and ammonia. Although an odorous compound may represent a nuisance rather than a health risk, long-term exposure to a mixture of volatile compounds may represent a risk for different diseases. The health effects of the individual chemical are well known, while the interactions among molecules with different functional groups have still to be extensively studied (Piccardo et al., 2002).

Migration of landfill gas into the surrounding soils can also result in the deterioration of plant growth. The lack of oxygen, caused by its displacement of landfill gas, contributes to the damaging the root system in plants.

Dust particles which have migrated to the environment from landfill sites also pose a danger to human health. The amount of dust lifted from the surface of the landfill and the distance of their relocation depends on particle size, the condition of the surface and wind speed (Glisovic et al., 2017; Jia et al., 2013).

Landfills pose additionally a microbiological risk for the environment in view of the fact that they are the place of origin of bioaerosols. Bioaerosols are defined as aerosols or particulate matter of microbial, plant or animal origin. Bioaerosols consist of pathogenic or non-pathogenic live or dead bacteria and fungi, viruses, high molecular weight allergens, bacterial endotoxins, mycotoxins, pollen, etc. (Douwes et al., 2003). The total number of bacteria cells in the air on the landfill under the operation phase and in the waste sorting station ranged from 10^2 to 10^4 colony forming unit (CFU) m^{-3} (Pawlowska, 2014; Breza-Boruta, 2016; Kalwasińska & Burkowska, 2013). The number of microorganism cells in the air above the landfill was higher in winter than in other seasons.

The major cause of the fire is methane, as it is highly flammable (Figure 3a). A high number of landfill fires sometimes are active for days (Downard et al. 2015). A greater risk is noticed in the case of wild landfills, which do not have appropriate isolation from the ground. One of the risks that can occur from illegal landfills is fire, which can be caused by intentional arson or spontaneous combustion resulting from the chemical reactions of waste, reactive materials, lightning strikes, heated waste etc. (Rykala et al., 2022). Landfill fires pose a significant threat to the environment as they cause the migration of pollutants to the atmosphere, soil and water. Risk factors depend on the type of burning waste, on the geographical location of the landfill and on the type of fire. Mainly, these fires occur at low temperatures and under anoxic conditions. Some of the most significant polluting substances that arise during a fire, depending on the mentioned conditions, are dioxins/furans, polycyclic aromatic hydrocarbons (PAHs), respirable particulates (PM) and heavy metals (HM), as well as other harmful compounds (Vassiliadou et al., 2009). The smoke produced during the landfill fire may contain toxic gases such as CO, H_2S, CH_4 etc. (Milošević, 2022; Vaverková, 2019).

Figure 3. a) Fire occurrence probability map due to maximum methane emission from the non-sanitary landfill "Bubanj", Niš b) Explosion occurrence probability map due to maximum methane emission from the non-sanitary landfill "Bubanj", Niš (Source: Milošević, 2016)

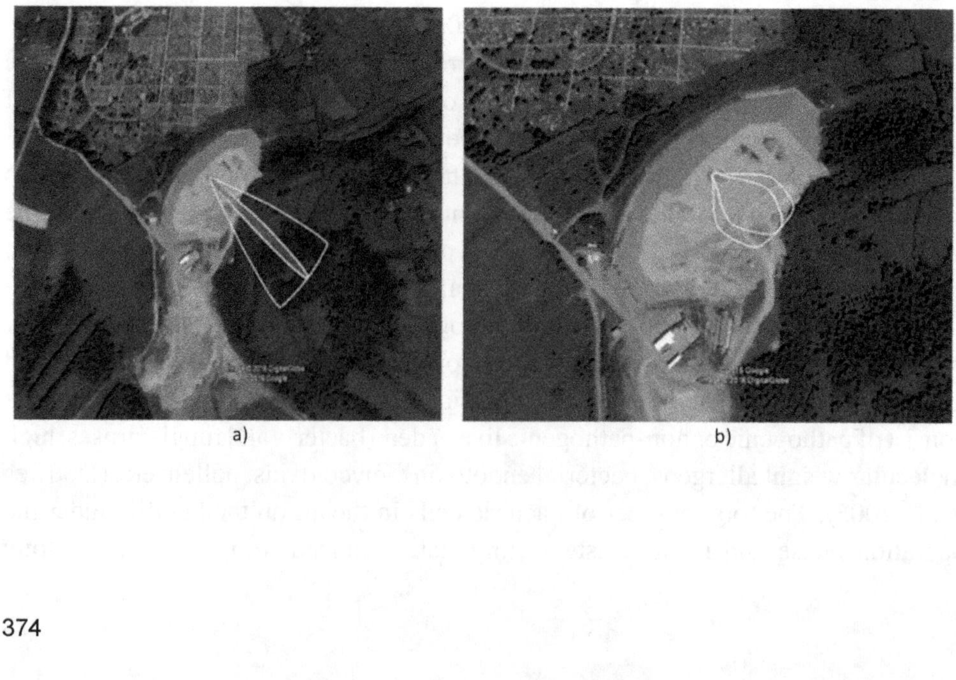

Landfill gas becomes explosive when it escapes from the landfill and mixes with oxygen (Figure 3b). The lower explosive limit is 5% methane, and the upper explosive limit is 15% methane. There are many reports regarding gas explosions at landfills, which had serious consequences (Vaverková, 2019).

PHYTOREMEDIATION

Phytoremediation, collectively referring to all plant-based technologies, uses green plants to remediate contaminated sites (Sadowsky, 1999). It can be used for the removal of heavy metals and radionuclides as well as for organic pollutants (such as polycyclic aromatic hydrocarbons, polychlorinated biphenyls, explosives, pesticides, etc.). This technology is a promising alternative to many of the currently practiced remediation technologies. Phytoremediation is a common term, including several processes, depending on the plant-soil-atmosphere interactions. It is based on certain natural processes carried out by plants, including:

- uptake of metals and certain organic compounds from soil and water;
- accumulation or processing of these chemicals via lignification, volatilization, metabolization, mineralization (transformation into carbon dioxide and water);
- use of enzymes to breakdown complex organic molecules into simpler molecules (ultimately carbon dioxide and water);
- increasing the carbon and oxygen content of the soil around roots (and so promoting microbial/fungal activity) through the release of chemicals (exudates) and decay of root tissue;
- capture of groundwater (even contaminated groundwater) and utilization for plant processes (Miller, 1996).

As previously mentioned, compounds taken up by plants may be metabolised, accumulated, or volatilised into the air. Based on these processes, several phytoremediation methods have been developed: phytoextraction, rhizofiltration, phytostabilisation, rhizo and phytodegradation, land farming, phytovolatilisation, hydraulic control and more.

As it is a relatively new technology, phytoremediation is still mainly in its testing phases and, as such, has not been used in many places as a full-scale application (Raymond, 2011).

The advantages of phytoremediation compared with other remediation options are:

(i) phytoremediation is suitable for a wide range of organic and inorganic contaminants, including some metals with limited alternative options,
(ii) *in situ* as well as *ex situ* application is possible. When it comes to soil remediation, soil can be left at the site after remediation, further disposition or isolation is not needed,
(iii) *in situ* applications reduce the degree of soil degradation compared to conventional methods; consequently, topsoil remains in a usable condition and may be reclaimed for agricultural use,
(iv) reduces the quantity of waste to be landfilled (up to 95%). Plant biomass containing accumulated hazardous substances (e. g., heavy metals) can be combusted to get energy, and the remaining ash is considered as ''bio-ore'',
(v) phytoremediation does not require expensive equipment or highly specialized personnel. Also, it is cost-effective for large areas having low to moderately contaminated surface soils (Schwitzguébel et al., 2002; Ghosh & Singh, 2005).

Despite the fact that a phytoremediation is a promising approach for the remediation of contaminated soils, it also suffers from some disadvantages and limitations. Some of the most important are:

i. a long time is often required for clean-up,
ii. there is a risk of food chain contamination in case of mismanagement and lack of proper care,
iii. restricted to sites with contamination within the rooting zone of remediate plants,
iv. it is applicable to sites with low to moderate levels of contamination owing to the fact that plant growth is not sustained in heavily polluted soils,
v. climatic conditions are a limiting factor. Actually, climatic or hydrologic conditions may restrict the rate of growth of plants that can be used,
vi. introduction of non-native species may affect biodiversity,
vii. phytoremediation efficiency of most metal hyperaccumulators is usually limited by their slow growth rate and low biomass,
viii. limited bioavailability of the contaminants in the soil,
ix. harvested plant biomass from phytoextraction may be classified as hazardous waste; consequently, the disposal should be proper (Ali et al., 2013; Ghosh & Singh, 2005).

PHYTOREMEDIATION OF MUNICIPAL SOLID WASTE LANDFILLS

Phytoremediation is an attractive technology for landfill remediation. Landfill vegetation contributes to establishing erosion and hydraulic control by minimizing infiltration of rainfall and simultaneously remediate landfill soil and leachate.

Phytoremediation of Landfill Soils

Two different approaches can potentially be used for phytoremediation of landfill sites: (1) contaminant extraction/degradation and (2) stabilization (Kim & Owens, 2010).

The first option refers to the uptake of contaminants by plant roots from the soil and their translocation into harvestable plant biomass. It is suitable for heavy metal contaminated soils. Also, plants can accumulate organic xenobiotics from polluted soil and detoxify them through their metabolic activities. Phytodegradation is used for the removal of organic pollutants (heavy metals are nonbiodegradable). The second approach can be considered from the aspect of prevention, concerning runoff and dust blow. Namely, the transfer of contaminated soils to surrounding areas can cause significant environmental risks, hence, vegetation establishment will prevent runoff and dust blowing from the site. Plants can stabilize inorganic contaminants around the root zone and prevent contaminants from leaching into groundwater (Alvarenga et al., 2008). The selected plant species with phytoremediation potential have some limitations, such as slow growing, which limit rapid and large-scale applications of these plants (Sarwar et al., 2017), and adaptation to a variety of environmental conditions like nutrient-poor soils (Gerhardt et al., 2017). Due to the inappropriate physico-chemical characteristics, landfill soils are usually poor for plant growth. As a result, the soil needs to be improved by the application of biosolids and other soil amendments (Gerhardt et al., 2017). Biosolids have been used successfully to establish sustainable vegetation, reduce the bioavailability of toxic substances often found in soils, control soil erosion, and regenerate soil layers at sites that have damaged soils. Soil regeneration is very important for reclaiming sites with little or no topsoil (https://www.epa.gov/biosolids/basic-information-about-biosolids).

All biosolids can be used for their fertilizer value. Biosolids normally contain a high amount of macronutrients (N, P, S, Ca, and Mg), as well as micronutrients essential for plant growth (e.g., B, Cl, Cu, Fe, Mn, Mo, and Zn). As a consequence, biosolids can be applied on micronutrient-deficient soils (e.g., alkaline soils and sandy soil). As regard K concentrations, they are usually low, and additional K fertilizers are needed (Kim & Owens, 2010). N and P concentrations in biosolids and chemical fertilizers are 1–11% N and 0.7–7.5% P and 5–82% N and 8–76% P, respectively. Regardless of lower concentrations of N and P in biosolids, soil organic matter content in biosolids is likely to be of benefit, providing slow-release pools of N and P. Increase in plant production after biosolid application has been the subject of previous research (De Andres et al., 2007; Navas et al., 1998).

Soil's physical properties are recognized for their important role in supporting plant growth. Essential requirements include storage and supply of water and nutrients, aeration, and ease of penetration for roots (Rezaei & Gilkes, 2005). Biosolids-treated soil is less sensitive to compaction than untreated soil due to the improved pore volume. Improved pore size distribution by long-term application of biosolids in soil may be related to the increased volume of micropores or micropores, depending on the texture of the soil (Lu et al., 2012). As biosolids are generally 50% organic matter, biosolids application can improve the physical properties of the soil. The addition of biosolids to soil lowers bulk density and increases porosity, moisture retention, and organic carbon (De Andres et al., 2007). Elevated organic matter contents resulting from sustained biosolid application, improved soil aggregation, and soil moisture-holding capacity enables landfill vegetation to be established even with very low annual rainfall.

Biosolids have the advantage of high organic matter content and have been used to remediate sites previously contaminated with trace metals by binding and converting the metals to less soluble fractions (Lu et al., 2012; Shammas & Wang, 2007).

Due to the beneficial effects of biosolids on soil structure, interest in using biosolids on degraded soils, such as metal-contaminated mine tailings, disturbed urban soils, landfill cover soils, and eroded land to reestablish the vegetation and the ecosystem, which is on the rise (Lu et al., 2012).

Regardless of the significant potential of biosolids as a soil amendment, there are two major concerns with biosolid application to land (transport of harmful substances through the food chain and environmental contamination from runoff and leaching).

Continual application of biosolids to agricultural soils may cause the accumulation of some toxic substances (e. g., heavy metals) in plant tissues. This issue is not important when it comes to non-edible plant crops. Hence, the application of biosolids to landfills to increase phytoremediation is more acceptable than agricultural applications (Kim & Owens, 2010).

Despite the fact that the macronutrients (particularly nitrogen and phosphorus) within biosolids are a source of nutrients for plants, the release of these elements in enormous amounts by runoff and leaching can cause contamination of the groundwater and streams. Increased content of nitrates and phosphates leads to eutrophication, a serious threat to water quality. Applications of biosolids on land reclamation sites from 1972 to 2002 at high loading rates with adequate runoff and soil erosion control had only a minor impact on surface water quality in terms of

NO_3^-, NH_4^+, and total P, and little or no impact in terms of Cd, Cu, and Hg (Kim & Owens, 2010; Tian et al., 2006).

Phytoremediation of Landfill Leachate

Leachate formation is one of the most important parts that is considered in municipal solid waste management.

The composition of landfill leachate varies, primarily depending on the type of waste, climatic variations, and age of the landfill. Regardless of climatic conditions, precipitation intensifies the saturation of waste in the landfill with the following production of leachate (Kumarathilaka et al., 2017). Leachate release into the soil and groundwater probably undergoes natural attenuation processes such as dilution, sorption, volatilization, biodegradation in order to effectively reduce contaminant toxicity, mobility, or volume to permissible levels (Kumarathilaka et al., 2017).

Leachates contain both organic (e. g., xenobiotic organic compounds) and inorganic pollutants (e. g., heavy metal(loid)s), out of which some are highly toxic and pose a threat to the environment. Most of the pollutants exist in the leachate as complex matrices such as organic-metal(loid) derivatives. Also, microbial species and their toxins may be considered as pollutants since some of these species, such as eubacteria and archaea, are found to be dominated by landfill leachate (Kumarathilaka et al., 2017).

Leachate from landfills can be treated by various methods. One potential remediation option for leachate is phytoremediation.

Applying phytoremediation to landfills associated with leachate treatment has some possible advantages:

(1) providing a water and nutrient source for enhanced plant performance (Nagendran et al., 2006);
(2) reduction of leachate volume and consequently mitigation of the migration of groundwater containing elevated levels of contaminants (Dickmann et al., 2001); and
(3) removal of the contaminants in the leachate and hence an improvement of the quality of leachate (Nagendran et al., 2006; Phytolink, 2003; Kim & Owens, 2010).

Water obtained from leachate can be used to irrigate plants, consequently, the amount of leachate that might migrate, carrying hazardous substances to the groundwater and surrounding water bodies, can be reduced. Also, leachate containing a high quantity of nutrients can be utilized by plants. Regardless of landfill leachate being valuable as a water and nutrient source for plants, permanent application of leachate to the land would negatively influence plant growth due to the accumulation of toxic compounds (Bowman et al., 2002; Cureton et al., 1991).

Over the last few decades, constructed wetland (CW) system has been recognized as an appropriate and practical alternative for landfill leachate treatment, making it safe to discharge into the surrounding environment (Kumarathilaka et al., 2017; Zalesny et al., 2006; Ogata et al., 2015; Justin et al., 2010). Constructed wetland system is mostly classified into free water surface system (FWS) and subsurface flow system (SSFS). In the free water surface system (FWS), oxygen is usually introduced into the wetland via atmospheric diffusion and algal photosynthesis. In the subsurface flow system (SSFS), leachate flows underneath and through the plant rooting media, and subsequently, the leachate level is maintained below the tip of the substratum. In terms of fewer issues arising from odors, disease-related vectors, and public exposure, a subsurface flow system (SSFS) is highly recommended for landfill leachate treatment (Kumarathilaka et al., 2017).

Considering that the efficiency of the remediation process depends on qualitative and quantitative characteristics of the leachate, and plant species properties, the choice of plants is of great importance. Typical natural wetland plant species such as cattail (*Typha latifolia* L.), reed (*Phragmites australis*), rush (*Juncus effuse* L.), yellow flag (*Iris pseudacorus* L.), and mannagrass (*Glyceria maxima*) are used in a constructed wetland. The phytoremediation potential of wetland plant species are generally evaluated by their extremely high transpiration rates, frost resistance, disease resistance, and tolerance to high heavy metal(loid) concentrations. Additional characteristics, including quick growth, extensive rates of photosynthesis, ease of rooting, fast establishment, and elevated usage of water, make them successful in CW systems (Kumarathilaka et al., 2017).

When it comes to leachate phytoremediation, it is necessary to emphasize phytocapping technology. Phytocapping encompasses phytoremediation technology that includes phytoextraction (rhizoextraction), phytovolatilization, and phytostabilization (Table 1).

Table 1. Applications of phytoremediation

Application	Process
Phytoextraction/Rhizoextraction	Removal of organic or inorganic contaminants from soil and water and their storage in harvestable tissue
Phytovolatilization	Uptake contaminants and volatilization from soil water and groundwater; Conversion of Se and Hg to volatile chemical species
Phytostabilization	Stabilization of contaminants by binding, holding soils, and/or decreased leaching

Source: Authors

Phytocapping as a phytoremediation subdiscipline implies the use of higher plants to minimize percolation into a waste of landfill sites and stabilize and mitigate off-site migration of soil or gaseous environmental contaminants. Phytocovers are planned to store and eliminate water from the soil using water balancing processes (surface evaporation and transpiration by plants for removal of stored water and controlling soil moisture). Phytocovers enhance soil aeration by increasing porosity and reduce water percolation, which decreases the quantity of leachate, resulting in more diffusion of oxygen into the soil, which helps in biological CH_4 oxidation and reduces the possibility of groundwater contamination. Phytocovers prevent infiltration of water through the canopy interception of rainfall, moisture retention in the soil profile, and evapotranspiration, where rainwater gets evaporated into the environment directly.

Suitable selection of the species is important forsustainable phytocapping. Usually, the plant species are selected depending on their adaptability to the local climate, capping soil, and their abilities to modify transpiration rates according to the moisture available in the phytocover soil. It is very important that selected plant species are incorporated into a diverse community of plant species that will complement each other in order to provide the existence of the established plant species and their continuation in regulating transpiration rates (Kumarathilaka et al., 2017). The role of plants in phytocapping, involving related microflora, especially in the soil rhizosphere, directly correlates with environmental landfill site management. Plants having higher biomass energy are preferred for the phytocapping, provided they meet other criteria (water storage at the capping site, biodiversity, etc.). Due to canopy interception and transpiration, rainwater water infiltration through the waste buried in the landfill is significantly reduced. Selected plant species should be able to control their rate of transpiration as per season and the type of soil/substrates (Lamb et al., 2012; Venkatraman & Ashwath, 2016).

Results from the investigation demonstrate that the selection of the right species is very important for the sustainability of the phytocapping system. The tree species grew very well in the harsh landfill environment demonstrating good adaptability characteristics and performance with respect to growth, canopy interception and transpiration, which grossly contributes to the prevention of rainwater in to the buried waste (Venkatraman & Ashwath, 2009).

CHALLENGES AND OPPORTUNITIES

The investigation of the properties of plant species in cleaning up polluted municipal solid waste landfills has revolutionized the field of phytoremediation.

Due to a number of benefits, like being natural, relatively simple, efficient, and having low establishment costs, phytoremediation has emerged as a suitable alternative approach to other conventional techniques.

Phytoremediation is favorable over other conventional methods of remediation, still, there is a demand to study and address the limitations and challenges of this plant-based remediation technology to apply it successfully and secure its future as a sustainable remediation technique.

A number of authors have suggested that phytoremediation is the ideal technology for mitigating landfill environmental problems, including soil and ground water contamination, leachate generation and gas emissions (mostly if inappropriate post-closure treatment of landfills or deterioration of the conventional clay landfill capping occurs) (Kim & Owens, 2010; Gomes, 2012).

Phytoremediation is an attractive technology for landfill remediation, as it can stabilize soil and simultaneously remediate landfill leachate. In addition, landfill phytoremediation systems can potentially be combined with landfill covers (phytocapping) for hydrological control of infiltrated rainfall. However, for the successful application of any phytoremediation system, the effective establishment of appropriate, desired vegetation is critical. This is because the typically harsh and sterile nature of landfill capping soil limits the sustainable establishment of vegetation. Therefore, the physicochemical properties of landfill capping soils often need to be improved by incorporating soil amendments. Biosolids are a usual soil amendment that includes a number of plant nutrients, as well as a great amount of organic matter. In addition, biosolids improve the physical properties of the capping soils by increasing porosity, moisture content, and soil aggregation. Contaminants which potentially originate from biosolids can be remediated by plants and plant-associated microorganisms (rhizosphere microorganisms) (Kim & Owens, 2010).

Despite the fact that there is some public concern regarding biosolids continuous application to agricultural soils, due to the potential contaminants in the biosolids, application of biosolids to landfills (an already contaminated site) is publicly more acceptable since risks for food chain contamination are insignificant.

Leachate, which is considered to be the most problematic substance generated from landfills, could be simultaneously treated and remediated and provide an additional water source for plant irrigation.

Coyle et al. are of the opinion that irrigation with leachate from municipal solid waste has negative impacts on soil micro- and meso-fauna, which are known to be essential in healthy ecosystem functioning (Coyle et al., 2011).

Phytoremediation may obtain high public acceptance owing to the aesthetic pleasant landscapes that emerge as a result of landfill site treatment.

Recently, much attention has been focused on researching the disposal of agricultural and municipal wastes (as a source of nitrates and other nutrients) on energy crops (Justin et al., 2010). This potentially provides organic matter and nutrients needed for crop growth at a low cost, enabling at the same time-controlled disposal of wastes on non-food crops (Britt et al., 2002).

Several studies reported the positive effects of leachate irrigation on tree growth and showed its fertilizing potential (Abedi & Moghaddami, 2015). Justin et al. detected that the use of landfill leachate treatments increased considerably aboveground biomass compared to the control tap water treatment, but the growth and biomass accumulation in compost wastewater treatments were reduced compared to tap water and landfill leachate treatments (Justin et al., 2010).

The concentrations and amounts of leachate that could be used depending on the constituents of the leachate and soil, as well as the nutrient demands of the genotypes tested (Zalesny & Bauer, 2007b).

The recent development of transgenic plants and bacteria that increase phytodegradation of contaminants could also be a great opportunity for bioenergy production through phytoremediation of municipal solid waste landfills (Gomes, 2012).

SOLUTIONS AND RECOMMENDATIONS

The waste-related pollution of soil, water surface, groundwater, and air exposes humans to a huge health hazard (Al-Ghouti & Dib, 2020).

Principally, the methods and technologies applicable in remediation are very important to realize cleaning, elimination, containment, reclamation as well, as restoration of polluted environment. In order to achieve the best results is necessary to select the most suitable remediation method. Therefore, before choosing a remediation method for any polluted environment (e. g., municipal solid waste landfills) a site survey must be conducted. As well, an understanding of all associated parameters, such as chemical, physical, and biological properties of the pollutants, is necessary for achieving better results.

As previously mentioned, phytoremediation is a sustainable technology due to its cost-effectiveness and utilization of environment-friendly methods for remediating the pollution in soil, water and air. This technology utilizes plants to remediate contaminated media through different mechanisms like phytoextraction, phytostabilization, rhizofiltration, phytovolatilization and phytodegradation. There is a wide range of applications for remediating diverse pollutants such as heavy metals, organic pollutants, radionuclides, pesticides, petroleum wastes, and antibiotics. However, plants differ in their remediation capacity depending on the target contaminants. Hence, the selection of plants per the contaminants and site conditions is crucial (Kafle et al., 2022). Plants suitable for phytoremediation should possess a series of characteristics: (1) fast growth and high biomass, (2) tolerant to toxic effects of metals and contaminants, (3) high absorption capacity, (4) widespread highly branched root system, (5) easy harvestability, (6) non-attractive for herbivory etc.

Additionally, the financial plan, regulatory framework, and existing policies are crucial factors to be painstakingly analyzed before selecting any remediation method (Bello et al., 2022).

Lately, risk-based assessment is a way to evaluate the potential hazards of contaminated landfill sites and is based on considering linkages between pollution sources, pathways, and receptors. These linkages can be broken by source reduction, pathway management, and modifying exposure of the receptors (Lai et al., 2010).

FUTURE RESEARCH DIRECTIONS

The primary idea of using plants in remediating the pollution from the environment is not new, but despite that, the field is still emerging.

Phytoremediation is one of the most favorable techniques for the eco-rehabilitation of polluted sites, but further investigations and research are also required to increase knowledge in efficient phytoremediation of municipal solid waste landfills. The limitations of phytoremediation (long time required for clean-up, limited efficiency of most plants due to their slow growth rate and low biomass, applicability to sites with low to moderate levels of contaminants since plant growth is not sustained in heavily polluted soils, etc.), pose challenges for its implementation and acceptance.

Limitations such as site-specificity, climate-specificity, and contaminant-specificity will continue to restrict its development. However, the results of investigations have contributed significantly in that field and continue to make progress in overcoming the limitations (Kafle et al., 2022).

Having in mind that the addition of amendments can enhance nutrient and water uptake and consequently increase plant growth, research in terms of improving their application deserves attention. Long-term application of some amendments (e. g., biosolids) as possible sources of heavy metals, organic pollutants, and pathogens may cause a threat to the environment and human health. In that sense, long-term monitoring is needed to evaluate the potential impacts of biosolids on soil quality and the environment, including surface and groundwater, air, and plant/animal health (Kafle et al., 2022). As well, improvement of legislation is expected based on scientific monitoring and assessment data.

Phyto techniques (phytocapping) are recently developed effective, economical and environment-friendly techniques for landfill recovery. Phytocap effectiveness depends on communication between the local climate, the substrate (soil) and the established plant community. The landfill caps can be used to: prevent vertical infiltration of water into the landfill that creates leachate, control gaseous emissions from underlying waste, create a land surface that can support vegetation etc. (Kafle et al., 2022). Based on the above facts, future research regarding the application of phytocaps at landfills should be directed towards the identification of additional plant species which can survive in toxic conditions and can be applied on the landfill sites; generation of plant biomass at phytocapping sites having a high concentration of heavy metals that can be used as feedstock for production; application of phyto covers on the closed landfills to mitigate the methane gas emission and leachate formation; utilization of high CO_2 sequestration plant species as phyto caps over the contaminated sites in order to reduce detrimental effects of GHGs in the area; as well as to direct consideration towards the economic benefits since the phytocaps do not require any skilled supervision. Life cycle analysis and techno-economic analysis of phytocapping technology should be underlined in future research to find its eco-friendly nature and cost-effectiveness (Prasad et al., 2022).

The application of heavy metal hyperaccumulators is the most commonly used method for phytoremediation, and hundreds of hyperaccumulator plants have been identified so far (Wuana & Okieimen, 2011). Even so, phytoremediation with natural hyperaccumulators still has a few limitations, such as a time-consuming process, which takes a long time to clean up heavy metal-contaminated soil, particularly in moderately and highly contaminated sites. The possible reasons are the slow growth rate and low biomass production of these hyperaccumulators (Ali et al., 2013). As a consequence, improving plant performance is a crucial step for developing highly effective phytoremediation. Fortunately, the genetic engineering approach has been emerging as a potent tool to modify plants with desired traits. Genes involved in heavy metal uptake, tolerance, sequestration, and translocation can be manipulated to improve either heavy metal accumulation or tolerance in plants. Additionally, chelating agents and rhizosperic microorganisms can be used to improve plant performance for phytoremediation either to increase heavy metal bioavailability or to improve soil conditions and further plant growth (Prasad et al., 2022). Practically, a single approach is neither possible nor sufficient for the successful remediation of heavy metal-polluted soil. The combination of different approaches, including genetic engineering, microbe-assisted and chelate-assisted approaches, is needed for highly effective and comprehensive phytoremediation in the future (Prasad et al., 2022).

In spite of the many challenges, phytoremediation of heavy metals is perceived as a green remediation technology with an expected great potential. It is one of the most advantageous options for the remediation of polluted sites, but additional investigations are needed to boost knowledge in efficient phytoremediation of heavy metals. To avoid any failure during landfill site remediation, it has become an essential requirement to tend toward future ways to clarify mechanisms, metabolites and genes using the latest omic techniques. These methods can assist in defining new metabolites and pathways included in the stabilization or extraction of heavy metals by hyper-accumulator plants. Utilization of hyper-accumulator plants to remove heavy metals from soil and water requires novel strategies for its progress. This can be accomplished either by finding and valorizing a broad diversity of new hyper-accumulator species or by genetic engineering (Prasad et al., 2022).

CONCLUSION

The disposal of municipal solid waste is one of the significant global issues, especially in developing countries. The most prevalent way of disposing of municipal solid waste is open dumping, which is the easiest and is considered to be the cheapest way of waste removal. In developed countries, landfills are engineered disposal sites that receive a wide range of materials. Improper and inefficient handling of waste disposal causes an adverse impact on the environment and human health. It is revealed that landfilling is associated with several environmental pollution problems, such as underground water pollution due to the leaching of organic, inorganic, and various other substances of concern contained in the waste; air pollution due to suspension of particles; and odor pollution from the deposition of municipal solid waste. Additionally, health impacts may occur through the pollution of the underground water and the emissions of gases, causing carcinogenic and non-carcinogenic effects on the exposed population living in the surrounding area. The deficiency of land and the requirement for reuse of the landfill sites demand their rehabilitation. In recent years phytoremediation has been used as a well-efficient, environmentally friendly, and cost-effective technology in the remediation and rehabilitation of contaminated sites, including municipal solid waste landfills.

ACKNOWLEDGMENT

This research was supported by the Ministry of Science, Technological Development and Innovation of the Republic of Serbia - Agreements on the implementation and financing of scientific research in 2023 [number 451-03-47/2023-01/ 200148].

REFERENCES

Abedi, T., & Moghaddami, S. (2015). Phytoremediation concept: biomass production and growth of *Populus deltoides* under compost leachate irrigation. *Journal of Forest Science, 61*(6), 250–254. doi:10.17221/121/2014-JFS

Al-Ghouti, M., & Dib, S. (2020). Utilization of nano-olive stones in environmental remediation of methylene blue from water. *Journal of Environmental Health Science & Engineering*, *18*(1), 63–77. doi:10.100740201-019-00438-y PMID:32399221

Ali, H., Khan, E., & Sajad, M. A. (2013). Phytoremediation of heavy metals - Concepts and applications. *Chemosphere*, *91*(7), 869–881. doi:10.1016/j.chemosphere.2013.01.075 PMID:23466085

Alvarenga, P., Gonçalves, A. P., Fernandes, R. M., de Varennes, A., Vallini, G., Duarte, E., & Cunha-Queda, A. C. (2008). Evaluation of composts and liming materials in the phytostabilization of a mine soil using perennial ryegrass. *The Science of the Total Environment*, *406*(1-2), 43–56. doi:10.1016/j.scitotenv.2008.07.061 PMID:18799197

Ashwath, N., & Venkatraman, K. (2010). Phytocapping: An alternative technique for landfill remediation. *International Journal of Environment and Waste Management*, *6*(1-2), 51–70. doi:10.1504/IJEWM.2010.033983

Bello, A. S., Al-Ghouti, M. A., & Abu-Dieyeh, M. H. (2022). Sustainable and long-term management of municipal solid waste: A review. *Bioresource Technology Reports*, *18*, 101067. doi:10.1016/j.biteb.2022.101067

Bowman, M. S., Clune, T. S., & Sutton, B. G. (2002). Sustainable Management of Landfill Leachate by Irrigation. *Water, Air, and Soil Pollution*, *134*(1/4), 81–96. doi:10.1023/A:1014114500269

Breza-Boruta, B. (2016). The assessment of airborne bacterial and fungal contamination emitted by a municipal landfill site in Northern Poland. *Atmospheric Pollution Research*, *7*(6), 1043–1052. doi:10.1016/j.apr.2016.06.011

Britt, C., Bullard, M., Hickman, G., Johnson, P., King, J., Nicholson, F., Nixon, P., & Smith, N. (2002). Bioenergy crops and bioremediation–a review. Department for Food, Environment and Rural Affairs.

Chen, Y., Xu, X., & Zhan, L. (2012). Analysis of solid-liquid-gas interactions in landfilled municipal solid waste by a bio-hydro-mechanical coupled model. *Science China. Technological Sciences*, *55*(1), 81–89. doi:10.100711431-011-4667-7

Coyle, D. R., Zalesny, J. A., Zalesny, R. S. Jr, & Wiese, A. H. (2011). Irrigating poplar energy crops with landfill leache negatively affects soil micro-and meso-fauna. *International Journal of Phytoremediation*, *13*(9), 845–858. doi:10.1080/15226514.2011.552927 PMID:21972508

Cureton, P. M., Groenevelt, P. H., & McBride, R. A. (1991). Landfill leachate recirculation: Effects on vegetation vigour and clay surface cover infiltration. *Journal of Environmental Quality*, *20*(1), 17–24. doi:10.2134/jeq1991.00472425002000010005x

de Andrés, F., Walter, I., & Tenorio, J. L. (2007). Revegetation of abandoned agricultural land amended with biosolids. *The Science of the Total Environment*, *378*(1-2), 81–33. doi:10.1016/j.scitotenv.2007.01.017 PMID:17306339

Dickmann, D. (Ed.). (2001). *Poplar culture in North America*. NRC Research Press.

Douwes, J., Thorne, P., Pearce, N., & Heederik, D. (2003). Bioaerosol health effects and exposure assessment: Progress and prospects. *The Annals of Occupational Hygiene*, *47*(3), 187–200. doi:10.1093/annhyg/meg032 PMID:12639832

Downard, J., Singh, A., Bullard, R., Jayarathne, T., Rathnayake, C. M., Simmons, D. L., Wels, B. R., Spak, S. N., Peters, T., Beardsley, D., Stanier, C. O., & Stone, E. A. (2015). Uncontrolled combustion of shredded tires in a landfill—Part 1: Characterization of gaseous and particulate emissions. *Atmospheric Environment*, *104*, 195–204. doi:10.1016/j.atmosenv.2014.12.059 PMID:25663800

Dushenkov, S., Kapulnik, Y., Blaylock, M., Sorochisky, B., Raskin, I., & Ensley, B. (1997). Phytoremediation: A novel approach to an old problem. *Stud. Environ. Sci*, *66*, 563–572. doi:10.1016/S0166-1116(97)80071-4

Gerhardt, K. E., Gerwing, P. D., & Greenberg, B. M. (2017). Opinion: Taking phytoremediation from proven technology to accepted practice. *Plant Science*, *256*, 170–185. doi:10.1016/j.plantsci.2016.11.016 PMID:28167031

Ghosh, M., & Singh, S. P. (2005). A Review on Phytoremediation of Heavy Metals and Utilization of Its Byproducts. *Applied Ecology and Environmental Research*, *3*(1), 1–18. doi:10.15666/aeer/0301_001018

Ghosh, M., & Singh, S. P. (2005). A Review on Phytoremediation of Heavy Metals and Utilization of Its Byproducts. *Applied Ecology and Environmental Research*, *3*(1), 1–18. doi:10.15666/aeer/0301_001018

Glisovic, S., Pesic, D., Stojiljkovic, E., Golubovic, T., Krstic, D., Prascevic, M., & Jankovic, Z. (2017). Emerging technologies and safety concerns: A condensed review of environmental life cycle risks in the nano-world. *International Journal of Environmental Science and Technology*, *14*(10), 2301–2320. doi:10.100713762-017-1367-2

Gomes, H. I. (2012). Phytoremediation for bioenergy: Challenges and opportunities. *Environmental Technology Reviews*, *1*(1), 59–66. doi:10.1080/09593330.2012.69 6715

Horne, A. J. (2000). Phytoremediation by Constructed Wetlands. In N. Terry & G. Banuelos (Eds.), *Phytoremediation of Contaminated Soils and Waters* (pp. 13–39). CRC Press LLC.

Jia, M. S., Wang, X. J., & Chen, S. H. (2014). Nitrous oxide emissions from municipal solid waste landfills and its measuring methodology: A review. *Ying Yong Sheng tai xue bao = Journal of Applied Ecology*, *25*(6), 1815–1824. PMID:25223043

Jia, Q., Huang, Y., Al-Ansari, N., & Knutsson, S. (2013). *Dust Emissions from Landfill Deposition: A Case Study in Malmbetget Mine, Sweden.* Environmental Science.

Justin, M. Z., Pajk, N., Zupanc, V., & Zupancic, M. (2010). Phytoremediation of landfill leachate and compost wastewater by irrigation of *Populus* and *Salix*: Biomass and growth response. *Waste Management (New York, N.Y.)*, *30*(6), 1032–1042. doi:10.1016/j.wasman.2010.02.013 PMID:20211551

Kafle, A., Timilsina, A., Gautam, A., Adhikari, K., Bhattarai, A., & Aryal, N. (2022). Phytoremediation: Mechanisms, plant selection and enhancement by natural and synthetic agents. *Environmental Advances*, *8*, 100203. doi:10.1016/j.envadv.2022.100203

Kalwasińska, A., & Burkowska, A. (2013). Municipal landfill sites as sources of microorganisms potentially pathogenic to humans. *Environmental Science. Processes & Impacts*, *15*(5), 1078–1086. doi:10.1039/c3em30728j PMID:23563361

Kamaruddin, M. A., Yusoff, M. S., Rui, L. M., Isa, A. M., Zawawi, M. H., & Alrozi, R. (2017). An overview of municipal solid waste management and landfill leachate treatment: Malaysia and Asian perspectives. *Environmental Science and Pollution Research International*, *24*(35), 26988–27020. doi:10.100711356-017-0303-9 PMID:29067615

Kim, K. R., & Owens, G. (2010). Potential for enhanced phytoremediation of landfills using biosolids: A review. *Journal of Environmental Management*, *91*(4), 791–797. doi:10.1016/j.jenvman.2009.10.017 PMID:19939550

Krstić, I., Zec, S., Lazarević, V., Stanisavljević, M., & Golubović, T. (2018). Use of Sintering to Immobilize Toxic Metals Present in Galvanic Sludge into a Stabile Glass-Ceramic Structure. *Science of Sintering*, *50*(2), 139–147. doi:10.2298/SOS1802139K

Kumarathilaka, P., Wijesekara, H., Bolan, N., Kunhikrishnan, A., & Vithanage, M. (2017). Phytoremediation of Landfill Leachates. In Phytoremediation. Springer. doi:10.1007/978-3-319-52381-1_17

Lai, H. Y., Hseu, Z. Y., Chen, T. C., Chen, B. C., Guo, H. Y., & Chen, Z. S. (2010). Health Risk-Based Assessment and Management of Heavy Metals-Contaminated Soil Sites in Taiwan. *International Journal of Environmental Research and Public Health*, *7*(10), 3595–3614. doi:10.3390/ijerph7103596 PMID:21139851

Lamb, D. T., Heading, S., Bolan, N., & Naidu, R. (2012). Use of Biosolids for Phytocapping of Landfill Soil. *Water, Air, and Soil Pollution*, *223*(5), 2695–2705. doi:10.100711270-011-1060-x

Licht, L. A., & Isebrands, J. G. (2005). Linking phytoremediated pollutant removal to biomass economic opportunities. *Biomass and Bioenergy*, *28*(2), 203–218. doi:10.1016/j.biombioe.2004.08.015

Lima, R., Nolasco, D., Meneses, W., Salazar, J., Hernandez, P., & Perez, N. (2002). *Global Biogenic Emission of Carbon Dioxide from Landfills*. American Geophysical Union, Fall Meeting.

Lu, Q., He, Z. L., & Stoffella, P. J. (2012). Land Application of Biosolids in the USA: A Review. *Applied and Environmental Soil Science*. doi:10.1155/2012/201462

Mench, M., Vangronsveld, J., Clijsters, H., Lepp, N. W., & Edwards, R. (2000). In situ metal immobilisation and phytostabilisation of contaminated soils. In N. Terry & G. Bañuelos (Eds.), *Phytoremediation of Contaminated Soil and Water* (pp. 323–358). Lewis Publishers.

Milošević, L. (2016). *Methodological Approach to Landfill Fire Risk Assessment for the Purpose of Air Pollution Evaluation* [PhD Thesis]. University of Niš, Faculty of Occupational Safety in Niš.

Milošević, L. (2022). Emisija deponijskog gasa kao faktor opasnosti nastanka požara. Fakultet zaštite na radu u Nišu.

Nagendran, R., Selvam, A., Joseph, K., & Chiemchaisri, C. (2006). Phytoremediation and rehabilitation of municipal solid waste landfills and dumpsites: A brief review. *Waste Management (New York, N.Y.)*, *26*(12), 1357–1369. doi:10.1016/j.wasman.2006.05.003 PMID:17064886

Navas, A., Bermudez, F., & Machin, J. (1998). Influence of sewage sludge application on physical and chemical properties of Gypsisols. *Geoderma*, *87*(1-2), 123–135. doi:10.1016/S0016-7061(98)00072-X

Ogata, Y., Ishigaki, T., Ebie, Y., Sutthasil, N., Chiemchaisri, C., & Yamada, M. (2015). Water reduction by constructed wetlands treating waste landfill leachate in a tropical region. *Waste Management (New York, N.Y.)*, *44*, 164–171. doi:10.1016/j.wasman.2015.07.019 PMID:26209341

Parker, A. (1986). Landfill gas-a potential environmental hazard. *Disasters*, *10*(1), 65–69. doi:10.1111/j.1467-7717.1986.tb00569.x PMID:20958628

Parker, T., Dottridge, J., & Kelly, S. (2002*). Investigation of the composition and emissions of trace components in landfill gas*. R&D Technical Report P1-438/TR. Environment Agency.

Pathak, A. K., Singh, M. M., Kumar, V., & Trivedi, A. K. (2012). Phytoremediation of municipal solid waste landfill site: A review. *J. Chem. Chem. Sci.*, *2*(1), 77–92.

Pathak, S., Agarwal, A. V., & Pandey, V. C. (2020). *Phytoremediation—a holistic approach for remediation of heavy metals and metalloids. Bioremediation of Pollutants*. doi:10.1016/B978-0-12-819025-8.00001-6

Pawłowska, M. (2014). *Mitigation of landfill gas emissions*. CRC Press. doi:10.1201/b16791

Pheakdey, D. V., Quan, N. V., Khanh, T. D., & Xuan, T. D. (2022). Challenges and Priorities of Municipal Solid Waste Management in Cambodia. *International Journal of Environmental Research and Public Health*, *19*(14), 8458. doi:10.3390/ijerph19148458 PMID:35886307

. Piccardo, M. T., Geretto, M., Pulliero, A., & Izzotti, A. (2022). Odor emissions: A public health concern for health risk perception. *Environmental Research, 204*(Pt B), 112121. . doi:10.1016/j.envres.2021.112121

Poschenrieder, C., & Coll, J. B. (2003). Phytoremediation: Principles and perspectives. *Contributions in Science*, *2*, 333–344.

Prasad, K., Kumar, H., Singh, L., Sawarkar, D., Kumar, M., & Kumar, S. (2022). Phytocapping technology for sustainable management of contaminated sites: case studies, challenges, and future prospects. Phytoremediation Technology for the Removal of Heavy Metals and Other Contaminants from Soil and Water, 601-616 doi:10.1016/B978-0-323-85763-5.00041-6

Qasim, S. R., & Chiang, W. (1994). *Sanitary Landfill Leachate: Generation, Control and Treatment*. doi:10.1201/9780203740217

Rezaei, S. A., & Gilkes, R. J. (2005). The effects of landscape attributes and plant community on soil physical properties in rangelands. *Geoderma*, *125*(1–2), 145–154. doi:10.1016/j.geoderma.2004.07.011

Rykala, W., Fabianska, M. J., & Dabrowska, D. (2022). The Influence of a Fire at an Illegal Landfill in Southern Poland on the Formation of Toxic Compounds and Their Impact on the Natural Environment. *International Journal of Environmental Research and Public Health*, *19*(20), 13613. doi:10.3390/ijerph192013613 PMID:36294191

Sadowska-Rociek, A., Kurdziel, M., Szczepaniec-Cięciak, E., Riesenmey, C., Vaillant, H., Batton-Hubert, M., & Piejko, K. (2009). Analysis of odorous compounds at municipal landfill sites. *Waste Management & Research*, *27*(10), 966–975. doi:10.1177/0734242X09334616 PMID:19710115

Sadowsky, M. J. (1999). Phytoremediation: past promises and future practices. In *Proc. 8th Int. Symp. on Microbial Ecology*. Atlantic Canada Society for Microbial Ecology.

Sarwar, N., Imran, M., Shaheen, M. R., Ishaque, W., Kamran, M. A., Matloob, A., Rehim, A., & Hussain, S. (2017). Phytoremediation strategies for soils contaminated with heavy metals: Modifications and future perspectives. *Chemosphere*, *171*, 710–721. doi:10.1016/j.chemosphere.2016.12.116 PMID:28061428

Schwitzguébel, J. P., van der Lelie, D., Baker, A., Glass, D. J., & Vangronsveld, J. (2002). Phytoremediation: European and American trends successes, obstacles and needs. *Journal of Soils and Sediments*, *2*(2), 91–99. doi:10.1007/BF02987877

Shammas, N. K., & Wang, L. K. (2007). Land Application of Biosolids. In L. K. Wang, N. K. Shammas, & Y. T. Hung (Eds.), *Biosolids Treatment Processes. Handbook of Environmental Engineering* (Vol. 6). Humana Press. doi:10.1007/978-1-59259-996-7_23

Spoann, V., Fujiwara, T., Seng, B., Lay, C., & Yim, M. (2019). Assessment of public-private partnership in municipal solid waste management in Phnom Penh, Cambodia. *Sustainability*, *11*(5), 1228. doi:10.3390u11051228

Stretch, D., Laister, G., Strachan, L., & Saner, M. (2001). Odour trails from landfill sites. *Proceedings of the 8th International Waste Management & Landfill Symposium*, 709-718.

Tian, G., Granato, T. C., Pietz, R. I., Carlson, C. R., & Abedin, Z. (2006). Effect of long-term application of biosolids for land reclamation on surface water chemistry. *Journal of Environmental Quality*, *35*(1), 101–113. doi:10.2134/jeq2004.0354 PMID:16391281

Vangronsveld, J., & Cunningham, S. (1998). *In situ Inactivation and Phytorestoration of Metal-Contaminated Soils*. Landes Biosciences.

Vassiliadou, I., Papadopoulos, A., Costopoulou, D., Vasiliadou, S., Christoforou, S., & Leondiadis, L. (2009). Dioxin contamination after an accidental fire in the municipal landfill of Tagarades, Thessaloniki, Greece. *Chemosphere*, *74*(7), 879–884. doi:10.1016/j.chemosphere.2008.11.016 PMID:19101012

Vaverková, D. M. (2019). Landfill Impacts on the Environment-Review. *Geosciences*, *9*(10), 431. doi:10.3390/geosciences9100431

Vaverková, D. M., & Adamcová, D. (2018). Case study of landfill reclamation at Czech landfill site. *Environmental Engineering and Management Journal*, *17*(3), 64. doi:10.30638/eemj.2018.065

Venkatraman, K., & Ashwath, N. (2009). Phytocapping: Importance of Tree Selection and Soil Thickness. *Water, Air, and Soil Pollution*, *9*(5-6), 421–430. doi:10.100711267-009-9236-8

Venkatraman, K., & Ashwath, N. (2016). Canopy Rainfall Intercepted by Nineteen Tree Species Grown on a Phytocapped Landfill. *International Journal of Waste Resources*, *6*(1), 202. doi:10.4172/2252-5211.1000202

Vergara, S. E., & Tchobanoglous, G. (2012). Municipal Solid Waste and the Environment: A Global Perspective. *Annual Review of Environment and Resources*, *37*(1), 277–309. doi:10.1146/annurev-environ-050511-122532

W&CC. (2010). *Waste and Climate Change - Global Trends and Strategy Framework*. https://wedocs.unep.org/20.500.11822/8648

Wuana, R. A., & Okieimen, F. E. (2011). Heavy Metals in Contaminated Soils: A Review of Sources, Chemistry, Risks and Best Available Strategies for Remediation. International Scholarly Research Notices. doi:10.5402/2011/402647

Yan, A., Wang, Y., Tan, S. N., Mohd Yusof, M. L., Ghosh, S., & Chen, Z. (2020). Phytoremediation: A Promising Approach for Revegetation of Heavy Metal-Polluted Land. *Front. Plant Sci.*, *11*, 359. doi:10.3389/fpls.2020.00359 PMID:32425957

Zalesny, R. S. Jr, & Bauer, O. E. (2007b). Selecting and utilizing Populus and Salix for landfill covers: Implications for leachate irrigation. *International Journal of Phytoremediation*, *9*(6), 497–511. doi:10.1080/15226510701709689 PMID:18246776

Zalesny, R. S. Jr, Wiese, A. H., Bauer, E. O., & Riemenschneider, D. E. (2006). Sapflow of hybrid poplar (*Populus nigra* L.×*P. maximowiczii* A. Henry 'NM6') during phytoremediation of landfill leachate. *Biomass and Bioenergy*, *30*(8-9), 784–793. doi:10.1016/j.biombioe.2005.08.006

Zhang, H., He, P., & Shao, L. (2009). N_2O emissions at municipal solid waste landfill sites: Effects of CH_4 emissions and cover soil. *Atmospheric Environment*, *43*(16), 2623–2631. doi:10.1016/j.atmosenv.2009.02.011

Živković, N., Takić, L., Djordjević, L., Djordjević, A., Mladenović-Ranisavljević, I., Golubović, T., & Božilov, A. (2019). Concentrations of Heavy Metal Cations and a Health Risk Assessment of Sediments and River Surface Water: A Case Study from a Serbian Mine. *Polish Journal of Environmental Studies*, *28*(3), 2009–2020. doi:10.15244/pjoes/89986

ADDITIONAL READING

Golubović, T. (2020). *Zagađivanje i zaštita zemljišta* [Pollution and soil protection]. University of Nis, Faculty of Occupational Safety in Nis.

Koda, E., Pachuta, K., & Osinski, P. (2013). Potential of Plant Applications in the Initial Stage of the Landfill Reclamation Process. *Polish Journal of Environmental Studies*, *22*(6), 1731–1739.

Lee, A. H., Nikraz, H., & Hung, Y. T. (2010). Characterization of Acetogenic and Methanogenic Leachates Generated from a Sanitary Landfill Site. *Civil and Environmental Engineering Faculty Publications. 376*. https://engagedscholarship.csuohio.edu/encee_facpub/376

Popović, F. J., Filipović, J. V., & Božanić, V. N. (2013). Paradigm shift needed-municipal solid waste management in Belgrade, Serbia. *Hemijska Industrija*, *67*(3), 547–557. doi:10.2298/HEMIND120620087P

KEY TERMS AND DEFINITIONS

Dumpsite (Open Dumpsite): Open dumpsites are those where solid waste is deposited without planning and consideration for environmental and health standards and are illegal to establish or operate.

Environmental Impacts: Changes in the natural or built environment, resulting directly from an activity, that can have adverse effects on the air, land, water, fish, and wildlife or the inhabitants of the ecosystem.

Landfill (Sanitary Landfill): An engineered structure consisting of bottom liners, leachate collection and removal systems, and final covers. Landfills are designed both to store and to treat wastes.

Landfill Gas: Gas produced by the anaerobic decomposition of solid wastes, and includes primarily methane and carbon dioxide, with lesser amounts of other gasses such as hydrogen, hydrogen sulphide, and numerous volatile organic compounds.

Leachate: Liquid and suspended materials which it contains, which has percolated through or drained from a municipal solid waste disposal facility.

Municipal Solid Waste: Municipal solid wastes (MSW), trash or garbage, are heterogeneous mixture of residential, commercial, and industrial products (product packaging, grass clippings, furniture, clothing, bottles, food scraps, newspapers, appliances, paint, and batteries).

Phytoremediation: The use of plants and the associated microorganisms, along with proper soil amendments and agronomic techniques to either contain, remove or render toxic environmental contaminants harmless.

Sustainable Environmental Technology: Sustainable environmental technology is an umbrella term that describes innovation that considers natural resources and fosters economic and social development. The goal of these technologies is to drastically reduce environmental and ecological risks and to create a sustainable product.

Compilation of References

Aasen, M. R. (2011). Applying Altman's Z-Score to *the Financial Crisis - An Empirical Study of Financial Distress on Oslo Stock Exchange [Master thess]. Norwegian* School of Ecoomics, Bergen. Retrieved January 18, 2022, from https://core.ac.uk/reader/30803130

Abedi, T., & Moghaddami, S. (2015). Phytoremediation concept: biomass production and growth of Populus deltoides under compos*t leachate irriga*tion. Journal of Forest Science, 61*(6), 250–254. doi:10.17221/121/*2014-JFS

Adibi, N., Lafhaj, Z., Yehya, M., & Payet, J. (2017). Global Resource Indicator for life cycle impact assessment: Applied in wind turbine case study. Journal of Cleaner Production, *165, 1517–1528. doi:10.1016/*j*.jcl*epro.2017.07.226

African Union. (2021). African Union Convention on Pr*eventing and Combating Corruption. AU. https://au.int/en/treati*es/african-union-convention-preventing-and-combating-corruption

Agasisti, T., Munda, G., & Hippe, R. (2019). Measuring the efficiency of European education systems by combining Data Envelopment Analysis and Multiple-Criteria Evaluation. Journal of Productivity Analys*is, 51(2), 105–124. doi:10.10071*1123-019-00549-6

Agh, P., Vavrek, R., Dvorak, M., & Papcunova, V. (2021). Economic Evaluation of the Management of Municipal Firms at the Level of Rural Local Self-Governments (Case Study). Economies, 9(3), 130. doi:10.3*390/econo*mi*es*9030130

Akintola, A., & Matthias, B. (2008). Policy, Management and Finance for Public-Private Partnerships (Innovation in the Built Environment). Wiley-Blackwell. doi:10.1002/9781444301427

Akintola, A., Matth*ias, B., & Cliff, H. (2003). Public-Private Partnerships: Managing Risks and Opportunities. Blackwel*l Science Ltd.

Aktan, C. C. (1996). Public Enterprises in Turkey. Annals of Public and Cooperati*ve Economics, 67(1), 117–130. doi:10.1111/*j*.14*67-8292.1996.tb01949.x

Al-Ghouti, M., & Dib, S. (2020). Utilization of nano-olive stones in environmental remediation of methylene blue from water. Journal of Environmental Health Science & Engineerin, 18(1), 63–77. *doi:10.100740201-019-00438-y PMID:*32399221

Al-Manaseer, S. R., & Al-Oshaibat, S. D. (2018). Validity of Altman Z-Score Model to Predict Financial Failure: Evidence from Jordan. International Journal of Economics and Finance, 10(8), 181–189. doi:10.5539/ijef.v10n8p181

AlAli, M. S. (2018). The Application of Altman's Z-Score Model in Determining the Financial So*undness of Healthcare Companies Listed in Kuw*ait Stock Exchange. International Journal of Economic Papers, 3(1*), 1–5. https://www.researchgate.net/publication/325265054_The_Appli cati*on_of_Altman's_Z-Score_Model_in_Determining_the_Finania l_Soundness_of_Healthcare_Companies_Listed_in_Kuwait_Stock_E xchange

Albayr*ak, T., & Caber, M. (*2018). A motivation-based segmentation of holiday tourists participating in white-water rafting. Journal of Destination Marketing & Management, 9, 64–71. doi:10.*1016/j.jdmm.2017.11.001*

*Albert, N. L. (2006). Public private pa*rt*ner*ships: innovation strategies and policy alternatives. Birkhäuser.

Albu, O. B., & Flyverbom, M. (2016). Organizational Transparency: Conceptualizations, Conditions, and Consequences. B*usiness & Society, 58(2), 268–297. doi:10.1177/00076*503*16*659851

Alford, R. H., Kasel, J. A., Gerone, P. J., & Knight, V. (1966). Human Influenza Resulting from Aerosol Inhalation. Proceedings of the Society for Exper*imental Bio*logy and Medicine, 122(3), 800–804. doi:10.3181/00379727-122-31255 PMID:5918954

Ali, H., Khan, E., & Sajad, M. A. (2013). Phytoremediation of heavy metals - Concepts and applications. Chemosphere, 91(7), 869–881. doi*:10.1016/j.chemosphere.2013.01.075 PMI*D:*23*466085

Alkaff, S. A., Sim, S. C., & Efzan, M. E. (2016). A review of underg*round building towards ther*mal energy efficiency and sustainable development. Renewable & Sustainable Energy Reviews, 60, 692–713. doi:10.1016/j.rser.2015.12.085

Allen, *R., & Tommasi, D. (2009). Upravljanje javnim iz*d*ac*ima. OECD.

Aloy Niresh, J., & Pratheepan, T. (2015). The Application of Altman's Z-Score Model in Predicting Bankruptcy: Evidence from the Trading Sector in Sri Lanka. International Journal of Busin*ess and Management, 10(12), 269–275. doi:10.5539/ijb*m.v10n12p269

Altman, E. (1968). Financial Ratios, Discriminant Analysis and the Prediction of Corporate Bankruptcy. The Journal of Finance, 23(4), *589–609. doi:10.1111/j.15*40-6261.1968.tb00843.x

Altman, E. (2005). An emerging market credit scoring system for corporate bonds. Emerging Markets Review, 6(4), *311–323. doi:10.1016/j.em*emar.2005.09.007

Altman, E. (2013). Predicting financial distress of companies: revisiting the Z-Score and ZETA® models. In A. R. Bell, Ch. Brooks, & M. Prokopczuk (Eds.), Handbook of Research Mthods a*nd Applications in Empirical Finance (pp. 428–456). Edward Elgar* Publishing. doi:10.4337/9780857936097.00027

Alumur, S. A., Kara, B. Y., & Melo, M. T. (2015). Location and Logistics. In Loc*ation Science. Springer. doi:10.1007/978-3-*319-13111-5_16

Alvarenga, P., Gonçalves, A. P., Fernandes, R. M., de Varennes, A., Vallini, G., Duarte, E., & Cunha-Queda, A. C. (2008). Evaluation of composts and liming materials in the phytstabilization of a mine soil using perennial ryegrass. The Science of the Total Envir*onment, 406(1-2), 43–56. doi:10.1016/*j.*sc*itotenv.2008.07.061 PMID:18799197

Anders, D., Simone, M., Hanna, M., Steen, S., & Thoma*s, H. (2011). LCA and economic ev*aluation of landfill leachate and gas technologies. Waste Management (New York, N.Y.), 1532–1541. PMID:21435856

Anderson, J., & O'Dowd, L. (1999). Borders, border regions and territoriality: Con*tradictory meanings, changing si*gnificance. Regional Studies, 33(7), 593–604. doi:10.1080/00343409950078648

Angelov, G. (2005). Handbook for mayors and members of municipal councils in t*he Republic of M*aced*o*nia. Skopje: Community of Local Self-Government Units of the Rep*ublic of Macedonia.*

*Angelov, G. (2005). Handbook for Mayors and Members of Municip*al Councils in the Republic of North Macedonia. Association of Local Self-Government Units of the Rep*ublic of North Macedonia.*

*Antić, K., Adamović, D., Turk Sekulić, M., & Radonić, J. (201*8). Systematization and comparative review of the legislation of the European Union and the Republic of Serbia in the field of leachate management of municipal solid waste landfills. 1st International conference „The Holistic Appoach to Environment. Sisak.

Antić, Lj., & Novićević Čečević, B. (2015). Lean Concept Techniques *for Overcoming Constraints of Business. Themes, 39(3), 905–923.*

Antić, Lj., & Novićević Čečević, B. (2016). Time driven activity based costing in hospitality enterprises. In Internat*ional* th*em*atic monograph Modern management tools and economy of tourism sector in present era (pp. 302–316). UDEKOM.

Anđelković, M. (2*009). Public finances and financial law. Center for Publications of the Faculty of Law in Nis.*

Apostolou, K., & Tjortjis, C. (2019). Sports analytics algorithms for performance prediction. 10th International Conference on Information, Intelligence, Systems and Applications (IISA). IEEE.

Arabiadis, R. (2016). Investigation of the economy and the environment of Prespa and Proposals for the management of water resources: Criticism of the irrigation network combined with monoculture of beans [Diploma thesis, Department of Civil Engineering, Aristotle University of Thessaloniki].

Aristovnik, A., & Obadic, A. (2011). The funding and efficiency of higher education in Croatia and Slovenia: a non-parametric comparison with EU and OECD countries. The William Davidson Institute: University of Michigan.

Ashwath, N., & Venkatraman, K. (2010). Phytocapping: An alternative technique for landfill remediation. International Journal of Environment and Waste Management, 6(1-2), 51–70. doi:10.1504/IJEWM.2010.033983

Association of Utilities Providers in Macedonia. (2020). Annual report 2019. Association of Utilities Providers in Macedonia.

Atanasovski, Z. (2006). Public finance. Faculty of Economics.

Authority for Consumers and Markets – ACM. (2021). ACM study: HTM is the most sustainable among the three major municipal public transport companies. ACM/UIT/567729. Retrieved Otober 20, 2022, from https://www.acm.nl/en/publications/acm-study-htm-most-sustainable-among-three-major-municipal-public-transport-companies

Aykaç, A. (1994). Transborder regionalization: an analysis of transborder cooperation structures in Western Europe within the context of European Integration and decentralization towards regional and local governments. Libertas Europäische. Sindelfingen.

Bai, Y., Yao, L., Wei, T., Tian, F., Jin, D. Y., Chen, L., & Wang, M. (2020). Presumed asymptomatic carrier transmission of COVID-19. Journal of the American Medical Association, 323(14), 1406–1407. doi:10.1001/jama.2020.2565 PMID:32083643

Bajić, B. Ž., Dodić, S. N., Vučurović, D. G., Dodić, J. M., & Grahovac, J. A. (2015). Waste-to-energy status in Serbia. Renewable & Sustainable Energy Reviews, 50, 1437–1444. doi:10.1016/j.rser.2015.05.079

Baldwin, J., Noorali, S., & Vaseashta, A. (2019). Development of a Wide-spectrum, Cloud Based Tool to Detect, Identify and Classify nCOV-SAR2. NDIA CBRN Defence Conference and Exhibition.

Ball, J. (2018). Municipal bus companies: can public ownership be profitable? The New Statesman (UK Edition). Retrieved October 20, 2022, from https://www.newstatesman.com/spotlight/2018/06/municipal-bus-companies-can-public-ownership-be-profitable

Bask, A., Rajahonka, M., Laari, S., Solakivi, T., Töyli, J., & Ojala, L. (2018). Environmental sustainability in shipper-LSP relationships. Journal of Cleaner Production, *172, 2986–2998. doi:10.1016/j.jcl*epro.2017.11.112

Batinić, B. (2015). A model for predicting the amo*unt of packaging and biodegradable waste using neural networks. University of Novi Sad, Facu*lty of Engineering.

Bello, A. S., Al-Ghouti, M. A., & Abu-Dieyeh, M. H. (2022). Sustainable and long-term management of municipal solid waste: A review. Bioresourc*e Technology Report*s, *1*8, 101067. oi:10.1016/j.biteb.2022.101067

Beltrame, F., Velliscig, G., Zorzi, G., & Polato, M. (2022). A revision of Altman's Z-Score for SMEs: suggestions from the Italian Bank*ruptcy Law and pandemic perspec*tives. Department of Management, Università Ca' Foscari Venezia Working Paper No. 9, doi:10.2139/ssrn.4161512

*Benito, B., Bastida, F., & García, J. A. (2010). Explaining Differences in Efficiency: An Application to Sp*anish Municipalities. Applied Economics, 42(4), 515–528. doi:10.1080/00036840701675560

Benković, S., Krivokapić, J., & Milosavljević, M. (2015). Application of the public-private partnership organizational structure in the improvement *of business oper*atio*ns of public sector enterprises in Serbia. Lex Localis, 13(3), 397-417. Available at: http://pub.lex-localis.info/index.php/LexLocalis/issue/view/77

Berggren, E., & Bernshteyn, R. (2007). Organizational Transparency Drives Company Performance. Journal of *Management* Development, 26(5), 411–417. doi:10.1108/02621710710748248

Bernon, M., Tjahjono, B., & Ripanti, E. F. (2018). Aligning retail reverse logistics practice with circular economy values: An expl*oratory framework. Production Pla*nning and Control, 29(6), 483–497. doi:10.1080/09537287.2018.1449266

Bećirović, S. P., & Vasić, M. (2013). Methodology and results of Serbian energy-efficiency refurbishment project. Energy and Buil*ding, 62, 258–267. doi:10.1016/j.en*build.2013.03.027

Beškovnik, B., & Twrdy, E. (2012). Green logistics strategy for South East Europe: To improve intermodality and establish green transport corridors. Transport, 27(1), 25–33. doi:1*0.3846/16484*142.2012.663731

Bhuvaneskumar, A., Sivakumar, V., & Pushparaj, N. (2022). Performance assessment and ranking of socially responsible companies in India using FAHP, TOPSIS and Altman Z-score. Benchmarking. Advance online p*ublication.* doi:10.1108/BIJ-09-2021-0512

Bogdanović, S. (2008). Prespa Park Coordination Committee in Transboundary Ecosystem Management. GWP Toolbox. https://www.gwpto*olbox.org*

*B*ognetti, G., & Robotti, L. (2007). The Provision of Local Public Services through Mixed Enterprises: The Italian Case. Annals of Public and Cooperat*ive Economics, 78(3), 415–43. doi:10.1111/*j.*14*67-8292.2007.00340.x

Bonaccorsi, A., Daraio, C., & Lepori, B. (2007). Indicators for the analysis of higher education systems: some methodological reflections. In A. Bonaccorsi & C. Daraio (Eds.), Universities and Strategic Kno*wledge Creation (pp. 405–432). doi:10.4337/9*781847206848.00021

Boulanger, M. P. (2008). Sustainable development indicators: A scientific challenge, a democratic issue. SAPIENS, 1(1), 45–59. doi:10.*5194apiens-1-59-200*8

*B*owman, M. S., Clune, T. S., & Sutton, B. G. (2002). Sustainable Management of Landfill Leachate by Irrigati*on. Wat*er, Air, and Soil Pollution, 134(1/4, 81–96. doi:10.1023/A:1014114500269

Boyd, N. M., & Martin, E. C. (2022). Sustainable Public Management. Routledge.

Bo*šnjaković, B. (2001). Regulatio*n*s o*f International Watercourses under the UN/ECE Regional Agreements. Water Interna*tional, 25.*

Breza-Boruta, B. (2016). The assessment of airborne bacterial and fungal contamination emitted by a municipal landfill site in Northern Poland. Atmospheric Pollution Researc*h, 76), 1043–1052. doi:10.1016/*j.apr.2016.06.011

Brinkhoff, A., Gabbe, J., & Martinos, H. (1997). VADE MECUM, Cross-Border and I*nter-regional Co-operation on External Borders of the European Union. AEBR. Gronau.*

Britt, C., Bullard, M., Hickman, G., Johnson, P., King, J., Nicholson, F., Nixon, P., & Smith, N. (2002). Bioenergy crops and bioremediation–a review. Department for Food, Envirnment and Rural Affairs.

Budget Law ("Official Gazette of the Republic of Macedonia", 35/01; 93/01)

Bugarčić, F. Ž., Skvarciany, V., & Stanišić, N. (2020). Logistics performance index in international trade: Case of Central and Eastern European and Western Balkans countries. Bsiness: Theory and Practice, *21(2), 452–459. doi:10.3846/*btp.2020.12802

Burke, R. M., Midgley, C. M., Dratch, A., Fenstersheib, M., Haupt, T., Holshue, M., Ghinai, I., Jarashow, M. C., Lo, J., McPherson, T. D., Rudman, S., Scott, S., Hall, A. J., Fry, A. M., & Rolfes, M. A. (2020). Active monitoring of persons exposed to patients with confirmed COVID-19 - United States, January-February 2020. MMWR. Morbidity and Mortality *Weekly Report, 69(9), 245–246. doi:10.15585/*m*mw*r.mm6909e1 PMID:32134909

Butt, T., Gouda, H., Baloch, M., Paul, P., Javadi, A., & Alam, A. (2014). Literature review of baseline study for risk analysis d the landfill leachate case. Environment International, 63, *149–162. doi:10.1016/j.e*nv*in*t.2013.09.015 PMID:24295846

Cabrera, B., Pardo, M. A., Cabrera Jr., E. & Arregui, F.J. (2013). Tap water costs and service sustainability, a close relationship. Water Resource Management, 27, *239-253. doi:10.1007/s11269*-012-0181-3

CADRI. (2020). Good Practices on Transboundary *Water Resources Management and Cooperation. CADRI. https://www.cadri.net/*good-practices-transboundary-water_2020.pdf

Cakar, B., Aydin, S., Varank, G., & Ozcan, H. (2020). Assessment of environmental impact of FOOD waste in Turkey. Journal of Cleaner Production, *244, 244. doi:10.1016/j.jcl*e*pro.*019.118846

Casalprim, M., Rialp, J., Prior, D., & Sabrià, B. (2013). An assessment of schools' efficiency of different educational systems. Mediterranean Journal of Social Sciences, 4(11), 631–631. doi:10.5901/mjss.2013.v4n11p631

CEA, Republic of Macedonia. *(2010). Strategy and Action Plan for Reforms in Communal En*te*r*prises with a Focus on Water Supply, Sewerage and Solid Waste Management, Proposed Diagnostic and Strategic Report. CEA.

CEA. (2006). The Future of Public Finance at Local Level. CEA.

Center for Disease C*ontrol and Prevention. (2021). CDC Recom*men*d*s Use of Johnson & Johnson's Janssen COVID-19 Vaccine Resume. CDC.

Center for Econ*omic Development. (2003). Corrupt practices in the process of municipal property management. Retrieved September 5, 2022, from http://ced.bg/uploads/publication/cor_pra*c.pdf

Center for the *Study of Democracy. (2006). A Painful Shif*t in Bulgarian Anti-Corruption Policies and Practice. Polic*y Brief No. 10. Retrieved September 5, 2022, from https://csd.bg/publica*tions/publication/csd-bref-no-10-a-painful-shift-*in-bulgarian-anti-corruption-policies-and-practice/*

Center for the Study of Democracy. (2012). Corruption and Anti-Corruption in Bulgaria (2011– 2012). Policy Brief No. 35. Retrieved Septe*mber 5, 2022, from https://csd.bg/publications/publication/policy-b*rief-no-35-corruption-and-anti-corrupion-in-bulgaria-2011-2012/

Centers for Disease Control (CDC). (2017). https://www.cdc.gov/dotw/sars/index.html

Centers for Disease Control (CDC). (2020a). Https://www.cdc.gov/nchs/nvss/v*srr/covid19/excess_deaths.htm*

*Centers for Disease Contr*ol (CDC). (2020b). Https://www.cdc.gov/nchs/nvss/vsrr/covid19/excess_deaths.htm

Centers for Disease Control (CDC). (n.d.). Moderna COVID-19 Vaccine Overview and Safety. https://www.cdc.gov/coronavirus/2019-ncov/vaccines/different-vaccines/Moderna.html

Centobelli, P., Cerchione, R., & Esposito, E. (2017). Environmental sustainability in the service industry of transportation and logistics service poviders: Systematic literature review and research directions. Transportation Research Part D, Transport n*d Environment, 53, 454–470. doi:10.1016/j.tr*d.2017.04.032

Centobelli, P., Cerchione, R., Esposito, E., & Shashi. (2020). Evaluating environmental sustainability strategies in freight transport and logistics industry. Business Strategy and the Environment, 29(3), 1563–1574. doi10.1002/bse.2453

Charles, T. W., & Adrian, J. S. (1995). Privat*ized Infrastructure: The Build Operate Transfer Approach.* T*ho*mas Telford. doi:10.1680/pitba.20535

Chen, Y., Xu, X., & Zhan, L. (2012). Analysis of solid-liquid-gas interactions in landfilled municipal solid waste by a bio-hydro-mechanical coupled model. Science *China. Technological Sciences, 55(1), 81*–89. doi:10.100711431-011-4667-7

Cheng, C., Zhu, R., Thompson, R., & Zhang, L. *(2021). Reliability analysis for multiple-stage solid waste* management systems. Waste Management (New York, N.Y.), 120, 650–658. doi:10.1016/j.wasman.2020.10.035 PMID:33243600

Cheng, Z. J., & Shan, J. (2020). 2019 Novel coronavir*us: Where we are and what we kno*w. *In*fection, 48(2), 155–163. doi:10.100715010-020-01401-y PMID:32072569

Christensen, T., Kjeldsen, P., Bjerg, P., Jensen, D., Christensen, J., Baun, A., *Albrec*hts*e*n, H.-J., & Heron, G. (2001). Biogeochemistry of landfill leachate plumes. Applied Geochemistry, 16(7-8), 659–718. doi:10.1016/S0883-2927(00)00082-2

CLES. (2021). Municipal Enterprises. Retrieved September 3, 2022, *from https://cles.org.uk/what-is-co*mmu*n*ity-wealth-building/the-principles-of-community-wealth-building/plural-ownership-of-the-economy/municipal-enterprises/

Clifton, J., Lanthier, P., & Schröter, H. (2013). The economic and social regulation *of the public utiliti*es*:* An international history. Routledge.

Cobb, W. C., & Rixford, C. *(1998). Lessons lear*ned from the history of social indicators. Redefining progress.

COE. (2022a). Criminal law convention on corruption. Impact of the European Convention on Human Rights. https://www.coe.int/en/web/impact-convention-human-rights/criminal-law-c*onvention-on-corruption#/*

COE. (2022b). The Civil Law Convention Against Corruption. Council of Europe. https://justice.gov.mt/en/pcac/Pages/CouncilofEurope.aspx

CoE Council of Europe. (1995). Additional Protocol to the European Outline C*onvention on Transfrontier Co-operation between Territorial Communities or Authorities. Explanatory Report, Council o Europe. Stras*bourg.

COGEN Europe. (2022). What Is Cogeneration? Retrieved Decemb*er 20, 2022, from https://www.cogeneu*rope.eu/knowledge-centre/what-is-cogeneration

Colombia.co. (2022). Así es Colombia [In Spanish]. Colombia. https://www.colombia.co/pais-colombia/hechos/asi-es-colom*bia-1/*

*Commercial Law. (1991). State Offic*ial Journal: 48/1991. Retrieved September 10, 2022, from https://lex.bg/laws/ldoc/-14917630Commission *for PPPs. (2022). Th*e list of approved projects. Retrieved from http://jpp.gov.rs/koncesijevesti/spisak

Community of Local Self-Government Un*its of the Republic of Maced*onia, Skopje. (2005). Report 2002-2004. Skopje: Community of Local Self-Government Units of the Repbl*ic of Macedonia.*

Constitution of the Republic of Bulgaria. (1991). State Official Journal: 56/1991. Retrieved September 10, 2022, fr*om https://www.lex.bg/laws/ld*oc/521957377

Contreras, I. (2020). A review of the literature on DEA models under common set of weights. Journal of Modelling in Management, 15*(4), 1277–1300. d*oi:10.1108/JM2-02-2019-0043

CoR Committee of the Regions. (2007). The European Grouping of Territorial Cooperation. Study carried *out by: GEPE (supervision N.Lev*rat), the Unit for Policy Analysis, Studies & Inter-institutional &Legislative Planning (G.Spinaci, J.Lotarsk & L.Cannellini) & COTER (D.L.Taberner), Committee of the Re*gions. Brussels.*

*Cornali, F. (201*2). Effectiveness and efficiency of educational measures: Evaluation practices, indicators and rhetoric. Sociology Mind, 2(03), 255–260. doi:10.4236m.2012.23034

Costanza, R., d'Arge, R., Groot, R., Farber, S., Grasso, M., Hannon, G., Limburg, K., Naeem, S., O'Neill, R. V., Paruelo, J., Raskin, R. G., Sutton, P., Belt, M., & Belt, H. (1996). The value of the world's ecosystem services and natural capital. Nature. Report of Workshop organized by NCEAS, Santa Barbara, Calif. (1996) 387.

C*ouncil of Euro*pe. (1980). European Outline Convention on Transfrontier Co-operation between Territorial Communities or Authorities Madrid. Council of Europe.

Coyle, D. R., Zalesny, J. A., Zalesny, R. S. Jr, & Wiese, A. H. (2011). Irrigating poplar energy crops with landfill leache negatively affects soil micro-and meso-fauna. International Journal of Phytoremediation, 13(9), 845–858. doi:10.1080/15226514.201*1.552927 PMID:21972508*

Crandall, R. W., & Ellig, J. (1997). Economic Deregulation and Customer Choice: Lessons for the Electric Industry. Center for Market Processes.

Creswell, J., & Poth, C. (2017). Qualitative inquiry and research design: choosing among five approaches. Sage.

Cuadrado-Ballesteros, *B., García-Sánchez, I. M., & Prado-Lorenz*o, *J.* M. (2012). Effects of Different Modes of Local Public Services Delivery on Quality of Life in Spa*in. Journal of Cleaner Production, 37, 68–81. doi:10.1016/j.jclepro.2012.06.*008

Cureton, P. M., Groenevelt, P. H., & McBride, R. A. (1991). *Landfill leachate recirculation: Effects on vegetation vigour and clay* surface cover infiltration. Journal of Envionmental Quality, 20(1), 17–24. doi:10.2134/jeq1991.00472425002000010005x

Cvetinović, D., Stefanović, P., Marković, Z., Bakić, V., Tur*anjanin, V., Jovanović, M., &* Vučićević, B. (2013). GHG (Greenhouse Gases) emission inventory and mitigation measures for public district heating plants in the Republic of Serbia. Energy, 57, 788–795. doi:10.1016/j.energy.202.09.063

C*ylus, J., Papanicolas, I., & Smi*th, P. C. (2017). Using data envelopment analysis to address the challenges of comparing health system efficiency. Global Policy, 8, 60–68. doi:10.1111/1758-5899.12212

Da Cruz, N. F., & Marques, R. C. (2011). Viability of Municipal Companies in the Provision of Urban Infrastructure Services. Local *Governmen*t Studies, 37(1), 93–110. doi:10.1080/03003930.2010.548551

Daily, G. (1997). Nature's services. Island Press.

Darrin, G., & Mervyn, K. L. (2004). Public Private Partnerships: The Worldwide Re*volution in I*nf*r*astructure Provision and Project Finance. Edward Elgar Pub.

David, A., Richard, P., & Nick, D. (2017). Evaluating landfill aftercare strate*gies: A life cycle* as*se*ssment approach. Waste Management (New York, N.Y.), 417–431. PMID:27989657

Davis, S., Childers, D., Lorenz, J., Wanless, H., & Hopkins, T. (2005). A Conceptual Model of *Ecological Interactions* in *t*he Mangrove Estuaries of the Florida Everglades. Wetlands, 25(4), *832–842. doi:10.*1672/0277-5212(2005)025[0832:ACMOEI]2.0.CO;2

de And*rés, F., Walter, I., & Tenorio, J. L. (2007). Revegetation of abandoned agricultural land amended wit*h biosolids The Science of the Total Environment, 378(1-2), 81–33. doi:10.1016/j.scitotenv.2007.01.017 PMID:17306339

Deckert, C., & Görs, N. *(2019, March). Transport carbon* footprint in the German courier, express and parcel industry (CEP industry). In NachhaltigkeitsManagementForuml Sustainability Management Forum (Vol. 27, No. 1, pp. 23-30).Springer Berlin Heidelb*erg. doi*:1*0.*100700550-018-0471-1

Del Borghi, A., Strazza, C., Gallo, M., Messineo, S. & Nar, M. (2013). Water supply and sustainability: life cycle assessment of water collection, treatment and dist*ribution service. The International* Journal of Life Cycle Assessment, 18, 1158-1168. doi:10.1007/s11367-013-0549-5

Deloison, T., & Wolff, C. (2020). The Road Ahead: A policy research agenda for automotive circularity. Circular cars initiative policy workstream. W*orld Economic Forum.*

Denton W. S. L*LP.* (2006). Public Private Partnerships: Bot Techniques and Project Finance. Euromoney Books.

de Souza, E. D., Kerber, J. C., Bouzon, M., & Rodriguez, C. M. T. (2022). Performance evaluation of green logistics: Paving the way towards circular economy. Cleaner Logistics and Supply Chain, 3, 100019. doi:10.1016/j.clscn.2021.100019

Dexia Crediop. (2004). Local Public Companies in the 25 Countries of the European Union. Paris: Dexia. Retrieved September 15, 2022, from https://www.lesepl.fr/pdf/carte_EPL_anglai*s.pdf*

*DHL. (2012). Delivering Tomorrow: Logistics 205*0. DHL.

Diakomihalis, M. (2012). The accuracy of Altman's models in predicting *hotel bankruptcy. International Journal of Accounting and Financial Reporting, 2(2), 96–113. doi:10.5296/ijaf*r. v2i2.2367

Dickmann, D. (Ed.). (2001). Poplar cul*ture in North America. NRC Research Press.*

*Didham, R. J., & Of*ei-Manu, P. (2020). Adaptive capacity as a*n educational goal to advance policy for integrating DRR into qu*ality education for sustainable development. International Jornal of Disaster Risk Reduction, 47, 101631. doi:10.*1016/j.ijdrr.2020.101631*

*Dimitrije*vić, D., Jovković, B., & Milutinović, S. (2021). The scope and limitations of external audit in *detecting frauds in company's operations. Journal of Financ*al Crime, 28(3), 632–646. doi:10.1108/JFC-11-2019-0155

Dincă, M. S., Din*că, G., Andronic, M. L., & Pasz*tori, A. M. (2021). Assessment of the European Union's Educational Efficiency. Sustainability, 13(6), 3116. doi:10.3390u13063116

Directive 2012/27/EU of the European Parliament and of the Coun*cil of 25 October 2012 on energy efficiency. Offici*al Journal of the European Union, 14.11.2012, Retrieved December 20, 2022, from https://data.europa.eu/eli/dir/2012/27/oj

Djurdjević, M. (2009). Public utilities infrastructure. College of C*ivil Engineering and Surve*ying.

DM. (2019). Direkcija za mere i dragocene metale [Directorate for Measures and Precious Metals], Ministarstvo privrede, Beograd. https://www.dmdm.rs/cr/Istorijat.php

D*obrota, M. (2015).* Statistički pristup formiranju kompozitnih indikatora zasnovan na Ivanovićevom odstojanju [A statistical approach to composite indicators construction based on Ivanović distance, octoral dissertation]. Doktorska disertacija, Faculty of Organizational Sciences, Belgrade.

doi:10.5281/zenodo.*887089*

Douwes, J., Thorne, P., Pearce, N., & Heederik, D. (2003). Bioaerosol health eff*ects and exposure assessment: Progress and prospects. The Annals of Occupational H*ygiene, 47(3), 187–200. doi:10.1093/annhyg/meg032 PMID12639832

Downard, J., Singh, A., Bulla*rd, R., Jayarathne, T., Rathnayake, C. M., Simmons, D. L., Wels, B. R., Spak, S. N., Peters, T., Beardsley, D., Stanier, C. O., & Stone, E. A. (2015). Uncontrolled combustion of shredded tires in a lan*dfill—Part 1: Characterization of gaseous and particulate emissions. Atmospheric Environment, 104, 195–204. doi:10.1016/j.atmosenv.2014.12.*059 PMID:25663800*

Dragović, N., Ristić, R., Pilcl, H., & Volfslehner, B. (2017). Natural resource management in Southeast Europe: Forests, soil and water. Skopje: Nacionalna i univerzitetska biblioteka „Sv. Kliment Ohridski", Skopje.

Duan, J., *& Shrestha, K. (2011). Statistical cre*dit rating methods. Global Credit Review, 1, 43–64. Retrieved January 19, 2023, from https://www.econbiz.de/Record/global-credit-review/10010186946

Duman, H., İçerli, Y., Yücenurşen, M., & Apak, I. (2013). Environmental cost management within the sustainable business. The Online Journal of Science and Technology, 3(2).

Dushenkov, S., Kapulnik, Y., B*laylock, M., Sorochisky, B.,* Raskin, I., & Ensley, B. (1997). Phytoremediation: A novel approach to an old problem. Stud. Environ. Sci, 66, 563–572. doi:10.1016/S0166-1116(97)80071-4

Dutta, P., Mishra, A., Khandelwal, S., & Katthawala, I. (2020). A multiobjective optimization model for sustainable reverse logistics in Indian E-commerce market. Journal of Cleaner Producti*on, 249, 119348. doi:10.*1016/j.jclepro.2019.119348

D'Aleo, V., & Sergi, B. S. (2017). Does logistics influence economic growth? The European experience. Management Decision, 55(8), 1613–1628. doi:10.1108/MD-10-2016-0670

ECB. (2022). Economic, financ*ial and monetary developments. Economic Bull*etin, (6), 2022.

EC Council of the European Un*ion. (2000). Regulation (EC) No 2*666/2000 of 5-12-2000 on assistance for Albania, Bosnia & Herzegovina, Croatia, Federal Republic of Yugoslavia& FYROM, repealing Reg. (EC) *No 1628/96 &ame*nd*in*g Regulations (EC) No 3906/89 & (EEC)&No 1360/90 & Decisions 97/256/EC&1999/311/EC. Office for Official Publications of the European Communities.

EC Council *of the European Uni*on. (2006β). Regulation 1082/2006 of the European Parliament and of the Council of 5 July 2006 on a European Grouping of Territorial Cooperation. OJ 2006 L 210. Office for Official Publications of he European Com*munities.*

*Economic Consult*ing A*s*sociates. (2008). Republic of Macedonia: Strategies and Action Plan for Reforms in Util*ities with a Focus on Water Supply, Sewerage and Solid Waste Management. Economic Consulting Associates.*

EEA. (2015). Waste—municipal solid waste generation and management. European Environment Agency.

EEA. (2016). Municipal waste management across European countries. European Environment Agency.

EEA. (2021). Municipal waste management country profiles 2021-EEA cooperating countries. European Environment Agency.

EEA. (2021, May 11). Water use in Europe - Quantity and quality face big challenges. Retrieved from European Environment Agency: https://www.eea.europa.eu/signals/signals-2018-content-list/articles/water-use-in-europe-*2014*

EEA. (2022). Municipal waste management in Western Balkan countri*es. European Environment Agency.*

Ellen, P. (2008). Public Private Partnerships. Elsevier Ltd.

*Embarak, O. (2021). A new paradigm through ma*chine learning: A learning maximization approac*h for sustainable education. Procedia Computer Science,* 191, 445–450. doi:10.1016/j.procs.2021.07.05*5*

*Environmental Law (Official Gazette of the Republ*ic of Macedonia, no. 53/05).

Eren, M., Eren*, M., & Başar, S. (2017). Measuring of human development through the outpu*t-oriented super efficiency vs. DEA model without inp*uts. Serian Journal of Management, 12(2), 255–270. doi:10.5937j*m12-11184

Erkkilä, T. (2012). Transparency and Institutions of Public Accountability. In: Government Transparency. Public Sector Organizations. Palgrave *Macmillan, London.*

*European Commission. (2003). Guide*lines for Successful Public-Private Partnership. Author.

European Commission. (2011). A Quality Framework for Services of General Interest in Europe. European Commission. Availabe at: https://eur-lex.europa.eu/le*gal-content/EN/TXT/?uri=c*elx*%3*A52011DC0900

European Commission. (2022). Cogeneration of heat and power: The EU promotes cogeneration in order to improve energy efficiency in Europe. Retrieved December 20, 2022, from https://energy.ec.europa.eu/topics/energy-efficiency/cogeneration-heat-and-power*_n*

European Commission. (2022). Drinking water - Legislation. Environment. https://ec.europa.eu/environment/water/water-drink/legislation_en.html

Eurostat. (2022). SDG4 – Quality education. Retrieved from: https://ec.europa.eu/eurostat/statistics-explained/*index.php?title=SDG_4_-_Quality_education*

*Evangelis*ta, P. (2014). Environmental sustainabi*lity practices in the transport and logistics service industry:* An exploratory case study investigation. Research in Trnsportation Business & Management, 12, 63–72. doi:10.1016/j.rtbm.2014.10.002

Fan, *M., Wu, Z., Qalati, S. A., He, D., & Hussain, R. Y. (2022). Impact of green logistics performance on China's* export trade to regional comprehensive economic partnership countries. Frontiers in Environmental Science, 10, 544. doi:10.3389/fenvs.2022.879590

Fan*elli, R. M. (2018). The Inte*ractions between the Structure of the Food Supply and the Impact of Livestock Production on the Environme*nt. A Multivariate Analy*sis for Understanding the Differences and the Analogies across European Union Countries. Quality - Access o Success, 19(167), 131–139.

Fanelli, R. M. (2019). The (Un)Sustainability of the Land Use Practices and Agricultural Production in EU Countries. The Internati*onal Journal of Environmental Studies, 76(2), 273–29*4. doi:10.1080/00207233.2018.1560761

FAO. (2022, November 28). Aquastat - Water Uses. Aquastat. https://web.archive.org/web/20190317171236/http://www.fao.org/nr/water/aquastat/countries_regions/profile_segments/EuropeEastern-WU_eng.stm

Farooq, M., Cheng, J., Khan, N. U., Saufi, R. A., *Kanwal, N., & Bazkiaei, H.* A. *(*2022). Sustainable waste management companies with Innovative smart solutions: A systematic review and conceptual model. Sustainabilit*y, 14(20), 1–19. doi:10.3390u142013146*

Fasua, H. K., & Osifo, O. I. U. (2020). Environmental Accounting and Corporate Performance. International Journal of Academic Research in Business & Social Sciences, 10(9), 142–154. doi:10.6007/IJARBSS/v10-i9/7711

Ferry, L., Andrews, R., Skelcher, C., & Wegorowski, P. (2018). New development: Corporatization of local authorities in England in the wake of austerity 2010–2016. Public Money & Management, 38(6), 477–480. doi:10.1080/09540962.2018.1486629

Filipović, M. & Krnjeta, L. (2017). Guide for Utility Services Pricing Policy in Municipalities and Towns of Serbia. Conference of Towns and Municipalities of Serbia.

Filipović, M., & Krnjeta, L. (2013). Jedinstvena metodologija za određivanje cene komunalnih usluga [A unique methodology for determining the price of utility services]. Stalna konferencija gradova i opština – Savez gradova i opština Srbije, Beograd.

Filipović, M., & Krnjeta, L. (2013). Unique Methodology for Determining Prices of Utility Services. Standing Conference of Towns and Municipalities of Serbia.

Fonseca, L. M., Domingues, J. P., & Dima, A. M. (2020). Mapping the Sustainable Development Goals Relationships. Sustainability, 12(8), 3359. doi:10.3390/su12083359

Frilingou, N., Xexakis, G., Koasidis, K., Nikas, A., Campagnolo, L., Delpiazzo, E., Chiodi, A., Gargiulo, M., McWilliams, B., Koutsellis, T., & Doukas, H. (2023). Navigating through an energy crisis: Challenges and progress towards electricity decarbonisation, reliability, and affordability in Italy. Energy Research & Social Science, 96, 102934. do:10.1016/j.erss.2022.102934

Fulazzaky, M. (2014). Challenges of Integrated Water Resources Management in Indonesia. Water, 6(7), 2000–2020. doi:10.3390/w6072000

Gajić, Lj., Medved, I., Rac, L. (2010). Obračun troškova i ekologija – novi pristip unapređenju poslovanja. Škola biznisa, 4, 76-85.

Gan, W., Yao, W., & Huang, S. (2022). Evaluation of green logistics efficiency in Jiangxi Province based on Three-Stage DEA from the perspective of high-quality development. Sustainability, 14(2), 797. doi:10.3390u14020797

Gančević, I. (1971). Community Services-Activities of Special Public Interest. Zb. Radovalovide, 8, 239.

Gaventa, J., & McGee, R. (2013). The Impact of Transparency and Accountability Initiatives. Development Policy Review, 31, 31. doi:10.1111/dpr.12017

Geddes, R. (2000). Encyclopedia of Law & Economics - 5940 Public Utilities. Findlaw. https://reference.findlaw.com/lawandeconomics/bibliographies/5940-public-utilities.html

Geller, S. (2019). Municipal enterprises are businesses or services owned by local public authorities that provide services or generate revnue for local communities. The next system. Retrieved September 10, 2022, from https://thenextsystem.org/learn/stories/municipal-enteprise

Gerhardt, K. E., Gerwing, P. D., & Greenberg, B. M. (2017). Opinion: Taking phytoremediation from proven technology to accept*ed practice. Pla*nt Science, 256, 170–185. doi:10.1016/j.plantsci.2016.11.016 PMID:28167031

Ghemawat, P. (2018). Redefining global strategy cr*ossing borders in a world whe*re differences still matter. Harvard Business Re*view Press.*

Ghosh, M., & Singh, S. P. (2005). A Review on Phytoremediation of Heavy Metals and Utilization of Its Byproducts. Applied Ecology and Environmental Research, 3(1)*, 1–18. doi:10.15666/aeer/0301_001018*

*Giambona, F., Vassallo, E., & Vassiliadis, E. (2011). Educational systems efficiency in European Union coun*tries. Studies in Educational Evaluation, 37(2-3), 108–122. doi:10.1016/j.stueduc.2011.05.001

Gianfreda, G. (2020). Vertical integration. In A. Marciano & G. Ramello (Eds.), Encyclopedia of Law and Economics. Springer. doi:10.1007/978-1-4614-7883-6_672-2

Glaeser, M. G. (1957). Public Utilities in American Capitalism. Macmillan.

Glisovic, S., Pesic, *D., Stojiljkovic, E., Golubovic, T., Krstic, D., Prascevic, M., & Jankovic, Z. (2017).* Emerging technologies and safety concerns: A condensed review of environmental life cycle risks in the nano-world. International Journal of Envir*onmental Science and Technology, 1(10), 23*01–2320. doi:10.100713762-017-1367-2

Godil, D. I., Yu, Z., Sharif, A., Usman, R., & Khan, S. A. R. (2021). Investigate the role of technology innovation and r*enewable energy in reducing trans*p*ort* sector CO 2 emission in China: A path toward sustainable development. Sustainable Development, 29(4), 694–707. doi:10.1002d.2167

*Gomes, H. I. (2012). Phytoremedia*tion for bioenergy: Challenges and opportunities. Environmental Technolog*y Reviews, 1(1), 59–66. doi:10.1080/09*593330.2012.696715

Gourbesville, Ph. (2008). Integrated river basin management, ICT and DSS: Challenges and needs. Physics and Chemistry of the Earth Parts A/B/, 33(5), 312–321. doi:10.1016/j.pce.2008.02.007

Government of the Republic *of Macedonia. (2008). Decentralization Implementation Progra*m *20*08-2012. Government of the Republic of Macedonia.

Govindan, K., & Bouzon, M. (2018). From a literature review to a multi-perspective framework for reverse logistics barriers and drivers. Journal of Cleaner Production, 187, 318–337. doi:10.1016/j.jclepro.2018.03.040

Grabski*J. (2019). The Dynamic* Z-*Sc*ore. doi:10.2139/ssrn.3509795

Great Lakes Directory of Universities. (1976). Research Institutes and Agencies Concer*ned with Water and Land Resourc*es in the Great Lakes Basin. Great Lakes Basin Commission. https://play.google.com/books/reader?id=spC7Z77cImgC&hl=el&pg=GBS.PP1

Gregory, C. S. *(2003). Defending Interests: Public-Private P*art*n*erships in W.T.O. Litigation. Brookings Institution Press.

Greiling, D., & Grub, B. (2015). T*owards Citizen Accountability of Local Public En*terprises. Annals of Public and Cooperative Economics, 86(4), 641–655. doi:10.1111/apce.12098

Grinell, D. J., & Hunt, H. G. (2000). Development of an Integrated Course in Accounting*: A Focus on Environmental I*ssue*s.* Issues in Accounting Education, 15(1), 19–42. doi:10.2308/iace.*2000.15.1.19*

*Gross*i, G., & Reichard, C. (2008). Municipal corporatization in Germany and Ital*y. Public Management Review, 10(5), 597–617. doi:10.1080/14719030802264275*

*Grugnaletti, M., Pant*ini, S., Verginelli, I., & Lombardi, F. (2016). An easy-to-use tool for the evaluation of leachate production at landfill sites. *Waste Management (New York, N.Y.), 55, 204–219. doi:10.1016/j.wasma*n.2016.03.030 PMID:27033994

Guillén, E. M., Tirado, D. M., & Sánchez, A. R. (2022). The impact of COVID-19 on university st*udents and competencies in education for s*us*ta*inable deelopment: Emotional intelligence, resilience, and engagement. Journal of Cleaner Production, 380(2), 135057. doi:10.1016/j.jclepro.2022.135057 PMID:363*48962*

Guo, X., & Xiao, B. (2022). How can pricing strategy for district heating help China realize cleaner residential heating? Energy Economics, 110, 106035. *doi:10.1016/j.eneco.2022.1*0*6*035

GWMO. (2015). Global Waste Management Outlook. UNEP-ISWA.

Halkos, G., & Petrou, K. N. (2018). A critical review of the main methods to treat undesirable outputs in DEA. Retrieved from https*://mpra.ub.uni-muenchen.de/id/epr*in*t/*90374

Halkos, G., & Petrou, K. N. (2019). Treating undesirable outputs in DEA: A critical review. Economic Analysis and Policy, 62, 97–104. doi:10.1016/j.eap.2019.01.005

Hamming, I., Timens, W., Bulthuis, M. L. C., Lely, A. T., Navis, G. V., & van Goor, H. (2004). Tissu*e distribution of ACE2 protei*n, *th*e functional receptor for SARS coronavirus. A first step in understanding SARS pathogenesis. The Journal of Pathology: A Journal of the Pathological Society of Great Britain and Irelan*d, 203(2), 631-6*37.

Hanna, T. (2013). Challenging Corporate Domination: The P*ublic Ownership Approach. The G*ood Society - PEGS, 22(1), 26–43. doi:10.1353/gso.*2013.0005*

*Hansen, R., & Mowen, M. (2003). Cornerstones of Cost Managemen*t. South-Western, Cengage Learning.

Harada, M. (2016). Japanese modern municipal retail and wholesale markets in comparison with European markets. Urban Hist*ory, 43(3), 476–492. doi:10.*10*17*/S096392681500019X

Haruna, M. J., & Nafisa, A. (2021). The Challenges of Girl Child Education in Sokoto State, Nigeria and Its Implications for National Development. In J. N. Mojekwu, W. hwala, C. Aigbavboa, L. Atepor, & S. Sackey (Eds.), Sustainable Education and D*evelopment (pp. 32-42). Springer Nature. doi:10.1007/978-3-030-68836-3_4*

Havenga, J. H. (2018). Logistics and the future: The rise of macrologistics. Journal of Transport and Supply Chain Manage*ment, 12(1), 1–10. doi:*10.*4*102/jtscm.v12i0.336

Hayes, S. K., Hodge, K. A., & Hughes, L. W. (2010*). A Study of the Efficacy of A*ltman's Z to Predict Bankruptcy of Specialty Retail Firms Doing Business in Contemporry Times. Economics & Business Journal: Inquiries & Perspecti*ves, 3(1), 122-13*4. Retrieved January18, 2023, from https://nebeconandbus.org/journal/EBJI2010HayesHodgeHughes.pdf

Hefetz, A., & Warner, M. E. (2012). Contracting or public delivery? The importance of service, market, and management characteristics. Journal of Public Administration: Research and Theory, 22(2), 289–317. doi:10.1093/jopart/mur006

Heiko, A., & Darkow, I. L. (2010). Scenarios for the logistics services industry: A Delphi-based analysis for 2*025. International Journal of Production Economi*cs, 127(1), 46–59. doi:10.1016/j.ijpe.2010.04.013 PMID:32288260

Hermans, E., Van den Bossche, F., & Wets, G. (2008). Combining road safety information in a performance index. Accident; Analysis and Prevention, 40(4), 13*37–1344. doi:10.1016/j.aap.2008.02.004 PMID:18606264*

*Hoe*kstra, A. Y. (2015). The water footprint of industry. In Assessing and Measuring Environmental Impact and Sustainability (pp. 221–254). Butterworth-Heinemann., doi:10.1016/B978-0-12-799968-5.00007-5

Hoffman, S. L. (2010). The Law and Business of *International Project Finance. Academic Press.*

*Holsh*ue, M. L., DeBolt, C., Lindquist, S., Lofy, K. H., Wiesman, J., Bruce, H., Spitters, C., Ericson, K., Wilkerson, S., Tural, A., Diaz, G., Cohn, A., Fox, L. A., P*atel, A., Gerber, S. I., Kim, L., Tong, S., L*u, *X*., Lindstrom, S., ... Pillai, S. K. (2020). First case of 2019 novel coronavirus in the United States. The New England Journal of Medicine, 382(10), 929–936. doi:10.1056/*NEJMoa2001191 PMID:32004427*

*Hoor*nweg, D., & Bhada-Tata, P. (2012). What a waste – A global review of solid waste management. World Bank.

Horne, A. J. (2000). *Phytoremediation by Constructed Wetlands. In N. Terry & G. Ba*nuelos (Eds.), Phytoremediation of Contaminated Soils and Waters (pp. 13–39). CRC Press LLC.

Hossain, *M. K., Kamil, A. A., Baten, M. A., & Mustafa, A. (201*2). Stochastic Frontier Approach and Data Envelopment Analysis to Total Factor Productivity and Efficiency Measurement of Bangladeshi Rice. PLoS One, 7(10), e46081. di:10.1371/journal.pone.0046081 PMID:23077500

Howarth, P., & Redgrave, F. (2008). Metrology – in short, 3rd edition. EURAMET project 1011.

Huang, W. H., Teng, L. C., Yeh, *T. K., Chen, Y. J., Lo, W. J., Wu, M.* J., Cin, C. D., Tsan, Y. T., Lin, T. C., & Chai, J. W. (2020). 2019 novel coronavirus disease *(COVID-19) in Taiwan: Reports of two cases from Wuhan, Ch*ina. Journal of Microbiology, Immunology, and Infection, 53(3), 481–484. doi:10.1016/j.jmii.2020.02.009 PMID:321*11449*

IFAC. (2005). Annual report. IFAC.

IHME. (2022). https://covid19.healthdata.org/global?view=cumulative-deaths&tab=trend

ILEC and UNEP. (2016). Transboundary Lakes and Reservoirs: Status and Trends, Summary for Policy Makers. United Nations Environment Programme. UNEP.

I*ntercept. (*2022). https://theintercept.com/2021/09/09/covid-origins-gain-of-function-research/

International Energy Agency. (2022). District Heating. IEA. Retrieved December 20, 2022, from https://www.iea.org/reports/district-heating

IW Learn. (2011). Integrated Ecosystem Management in the Prespa Basin in Albania, FYROM and Greece. GEF Project (2006-2011). https://iwlearn.net/iw-projects*/1537*

Jacob, S., Speer, S., & Furubo, J. (2015). Th*e* institutionalization of evaluation matters: Updating the International Atl*as of Evaluat*ion 10 years later. Evaluation, 21(1), 6–31. doi:10.1177/1356389014564248

Janaćković, G., Malenović, J., & Vranjanac, Z. *(2017). The importance of user reqirements for the quality of communal services, Upravljanje komunalnim sistemom* i zaštia životne sredine. Fakultet zaštite na radu u Nišu, Niš, pp.243-250.

Janaćković, G., Vasović, D., Malenović Nikolić, J., Mušicki, S., & *Vranjanac, Ž. (*2018). Vulnerability assessment of municipality areas to natural disasters based on group fuzzyanalytic *hierarchy process. Journal of Environmental Protection and Ecology, Balkan Envir*onmental Association, 19(4), 1526-1535. https://scbulcom.net/en/journal/1311-5065/issue/2018-19-4/

Jedynak, T., & Wąsowicz, K. (2021). The Relationship between Efficiency and Quality of Municipally Owned Corporations: *Evidence from* Local Public Transport and Waste Management in Poland. Sustainability, 13(17), 9804. doi:10.3390/su13179804

JHU. (2022). https://www.jhu.edu/

Jia, M. S., Wang, X. J., & Chen, S. H. (2014). Nitrous oxide emissions from municipal solid waste landfills and its measuring methodology: A review. Ying Yong Sheng tai xue bao = Journal of Applied Ecology, 25(6), 1815–1824. PMID:25223043

Jia, Q., Huang, Y., Al-Ansari, N., & Knutsson, S. (2013). Dust Emissions from Landfill Deposition: A *Case Study in Malmbetget Mine, Sweden. Environmental Science.*

Johnes, J., Portela, M., & Thanassoulis, E. (2017). Efficiency in education. The Journal of the Operational Research Society, 68(4), 331–338. doi:10.105741274-016-0109-z

Johnson, R. A., & Wic*hern, D. W. (20*02). Applied Multivariate Statistical Analysis (5th ed.). Prentice Hall.

Jovanić, T. (2017). Liberalization Agenda and the General Framework of Serbian Local Public Utility Services Regulatory Regime. Network Industries Quarterly, *13(3). https://www*.network-industries.org/network-industries-quarterly/

Jovanović, T., & Sredojević, S. (2016). Strengthening the Determinants o*f the Local Government Capacities for the Successful PPP Implementation in the* Western Balans. The Political Economy of Local Regulation.

Jovanovski, P. (2005). Public Finances. FON.

Jugović, J. (2019). Upravljanje troškovima ekološke zaštite u funkciji *unapređenja konkurentnosti preduzeća. Ekonomske ideje i* praksa, 33, 43-59.

Junkernheinrich, M., & Micosatt, G. (2007). Kommunaler Schuldenreport Nordrhein-Westfalen. *Gütersloh: Bertelsmann Stiftung. Retrieved Sept*ember 15, 2022, from https://www.bertelsmann-stiftung.de/fileadmin/files/BSt/Publikatio*nen/GrauePublikationen/GP_Kommunaler_Fina*nz-und_Schuldenreport_Nordrhein-Westfalen_2007*.pdf*

Justin, M. Z., Pajk, N., Zupanc, V., & Zupancic, M. (2010). Phytoremediation of landfill leachate and compost wastewater b irrigation of Populus and Salix: Biomass and growth response. Waste Management (New York, N.Y.), 30(6), 1032–1042. doi:10.1*016/j.wasman.2010.02.013 PMID:20211551*

*Jänicke, M. (2012). "Green growth": From a growing eco-industry to economic sustainabi*lity. Energy Policy, 48, 13–21. doi:10.1016/j.enpol.2012.04.045

Kafl*e, A., Timilsin*a, A., Gautam, A., Adhikari, K., Bhattarai, A., & Aryal, N. (2022). Phytoremediation: Mechanisms, plant selection an*d enhancement by natural and* synthetic gents. Environmental Advances, 8, 100203. d*oi:10.1016/j.envadv.2022.100203*

Kalokardou, R., & Kradonelli, K. (2005). Alternative Forms of Tourism and Critical Capacities in Tourist Areas of Western Greece [Paper presentation]. Heleco Conference.

Kalwasińska, A., & Burkowska, A. (2013). Municipal landfill sites as sources of microorganisms potentially pathogenic to humans. Environmental Science. Processes & Impacts, 15(5), 1078–1086. doi:10.1039/c3em307*28j PMI*D:*23563361*

Kamaruddin, M. A., Yusoff, M. *S., Rui, L. M., Isa, A. M., Zawa*wi, M. H., & Alrozi, R. (2017). An overview of municipal solid waste management and landfill leachate treatment: Malaysia and Asian perspectives. Environmental Science and Pollution Research International, 24(35), 26988–27020. doi:10.100711356-017-03*03-9 PMID:29067615*

*Ka*ra*d*uman, H. A., Karaman-Akgül, A., Çağlar, M., & Akbaş, H. E. (2020). The relationship b*etween logistics performance and carbon emissions: An empirical investigation on Balkan* countries. International Journal of Climate Change Strategies and Management, 12(4), 449–461. doi:10.1108/IJCCSM-05-2020-0041

Karaman, A. S., Kilic, M., & Uyar, A. (2020). *Green logistics performance and sustaina*bil*i*ty reporting practices of the logistics sector: The moderating effect of corporate governance. Journal of Cleaner Production, 258, 120718. doi:10.1016/j.jclepro.2020.120718

Kazancoglu, Y., Ekinci, E., Mangla, S. K., Sezer, M. D., & Kayikci, Y. (2021). Performan*ce evaluation of reverse logistics in food supply chains i*n *a* circular economy using system dynamics. Business Strategy and the Environment, 30(1), 71–91. doi:10.1002/bse.2610

Kenton, W. (2022). SWOT Analysis: How to with Table and Example. Investopedia. https://www.investopedia.com/terms/s/swot.asp

Khan, S., *Anjum, R., Raza, S., Bazai, N., & Ihtisham, M. (2022). Technologi*es *f*or municipal solid waste management: Current status challenges, and future perspectives. Chemosphere, I(288), 132403. doi:10.1016/j.chemosphere.2021.132403 PMID:34624349

Khan, S. A. R., Qianli, D., SongBo, W., Zaman, K., & Zhang, Y. *(2017). Environmental logis*tics performance indicators affecting per capita income and sectoral growth: evidence from a panel of selected global ranked logistics countries. Environmental Science and Pollution Research, 24(2) 1518–1531. doi:10.100711356-016-7916-2

K*han, S. A. R., Zhang, Y., Kumar, A.,* Zav*a*dskas, E., & Streimikiene, D. (2020). Measuring the i*mpact of renewable energy, public health exp*enditure, logistics, and environmental performance on sustainable economic growth. Sustainable Development, 28(4), 833–843. doi:10.1002d.2034

Kim, K. R., & Owens, G. (2010). Potential for enhanced phytoremediation of landfills using biosolids: A review. Journal of Environmental Management, 91(4), 791–797. doi:10.1016/j.jenvman.2009.10.017 PMID:19939550

Kioupi, V., & Voulvoulis, N. (2019). Education for Sustainable Development: A Systemic Framework for Connecting the SDGs to Educational Outcomes. Sustainability, 11(21), 6104. doi:10.3390/su11216104

Klumpp, M., Clausen, U., & ten Hompel, M. (2013). Logisti*cs research and the log*isti*c*s world of 2050. In Efficiency and logistics (pp. 1–6). Springer. doi:10.1007/978-3-642-32838-1_1

Kolb, M., Fr¨ohlich, L., & Schmidpeter, R. (2017). Implementing sustainability as the new normal: Res*ponsible ma*nagement education – from a private business school's perspective. International Journal of Management Education, 15(2), 280–292. doi:10.1016/j.ijme.2017.03.009

KOMDEL. (2019). Chang*es in the Prices of Basic Utility S*er*v*ices during the period 2006-2018 and their Impact on the Cost of Living. KOMDEL.

Koopmans, T. C. (1951). An analysis of production as an efficient combination of activities. Activity analysis of production and *allocation. Cowle*s Commission, Wiley.

Kosor, M. M. (2013). Efficiency measurement in higher education: Concepts, methods and perspective. Procedia: Social an*d Behavioral Sciences, 1*06, 1031–1038. doi:10.1016/j.sbspro.2013.12.117

Kostrzewski, M., Filina-Dawidowicz, L., & Walusiak, S. (2021). Modern technologies development in logistics centers: The case study of Poland. Transportation Research Procedia, 55, 268–*275. doi:10.1016/j.trpro.2021.06.031*

Koukaki, T., & Tei, A. (2020). Innovation and maritime transport: A syste*matic review. Case Studies on Transport Policy, 8(3), 700–710. doi:10.1016/j.cstp.2020.07.009*

Kousouris, Th., & Athanasakis, A. (1992). Environment, *Ecology, Education. Savvala Publications.*

Kpodoh, B. (2010). Bankruptcy and Financial Distress Prediction in the Mobile Telecom Industry: The case of MTN-Ghana, Millicom-Ghana and Ghana Telecom [Master thesis]. School of Management Blekinge *Institute of Technology. Retrieved Janua*ry *19*, 223 from https://www.diva-portal.org/smash/get/diva2:832030/FULLTEXT01.pdf

Kreps, B. H. (2020). The Rising Costs of Fossil-Fuel Extraction: An Energy Crisis That Will Not Go Away. Americ*an Journal of Economics and Soc*iology, 79(3), 695–717. doi:10.1111/ajes.12336

Krstić, I., Zec, S., Lazarević, V., Stanisavljević, M., & Golubović, T. (2018). Use of S*intering to Immobilize Toxic Met*al*s* Present in Galvanic Sludge into a Stabile Glass-Ceramic Structure. Science of Sintering*, 50(2), 139–147. doi:10.2298/S*OS1802139K

Kumarathilaka, P., Wijesekara, *H., Bolan, N., Kunhikrishnan, A., & Vithanage, M. (2017). Phytoremediation of Landfill Leachates. In Phytoremediation. Springer. oi:*10.1007/978-3-319-52381-1_17

Lagarde, C. (2022, November 4). Monetary policy in a high inflation environment: Commitment and clarity. European Central Bank.

Lai, H. Y., Hseu, Z. Y., Chen, T. C., Chen, B. C., Guo, H. Y., & Chen, Z. S. (2010). Health Risk-Based Assessment and M*anagement of Heavy Metals-Contaminated Soil Sit*es in Taiwan. International Journal of Environmental Research and Public Health, 7(10), 3595–3614. doi:10.3390/ijerph7103596 PMID:21139851

Lamb, D. T., Heading, S., Bolan, N., & Naidu, R. (2012). Use of Biosolids for Phytocappin*g of Landfill Soil.* Wat*e*r, Air, and Soil Pollution, 223(5), 2695–2705. doi:10.100711270-011-1060-x

Lamers, M. M., Beumer, J., van der Vaart, J., Knoops, K., Puschhof, J., Breugem, T. I., ... van Donselaar, E. (2020). SARS-CoV-2 productively infects human gut enterocytes. Science, 369(649*9), 50–54. doi:10.1126cience.abc1669 PMID:32358202*

Larson, P. D. (2021). Relationships between logistics performance and aspects of sustainability: A cross-country analysis. Sustainability, 13(2), 623. doi:10.3390u13020623

Laurent, A., Bakas, I., Clavreul, J., Bernstad, A., *Niero, M., Gentil, E., Hauschild, M. Z., & Christensen, T. H. (*2014*a*). Review of LCA studies of solid waste management systems–Part I: Lessons learned and perspectives. Waste Management (New York, N.Y.), III(34), 573–588. doi:10.1016/j.*wasman.2013.10.045 PMID:24369*845

Law on balanced regional development (Official Gazette of the Republic of Macedonia, no. 63/07, 187/13, 43/14, 215/15 and 64/18).

Law on Budgets (Official Gazette of the Republic of Macedonia, no. 203/2022).

Law on c*ommerci*al *co*mpanies (Official Gazette of the Republic of Macedonia, no. 28/04).

Law on communal activities (Official Gazette of the Republic of Macedonia, no. 45/97).

Law on concessions and *other types o*f *pu*blic-private partnership (Official Gazette of the Republic of Macedonia, no. 6/2012, 144/2014, 33/2015, 104/2015, 215/2015, 153/2019, 261/2019).

Law on determination and collection of public revenues ("Official Gazette of the Republic of Macedonia", no. *13/01, 61/02 and 24/03).*

*Law o*n *dri*nking water supply and urban wastewater disposal (Official Gazette of the Republic of Macedonia, no. 68/04, 28/06 and 103/08).

Law on Energy Efficiency and Rational Use of Energy. (Official Gazette of the Republic of Serbia, no. 40/2021).

Law on Environmental Protection. (Official Gazette of the Republic of Serbia, no. 135/2004, 36/2009, 36/2009, 72/2009, 43/2011, 14/2016, 76/2018, 95/2018 and 95/2018)

Law on Financing Local Self-Government Units (Official Gazette No. 61/04, 96/04, 67/07, 156/09, 47/1 and 192/15).

Law on Financing of Local Self-Government Units ("Official Gazette of the Republic of Macedonia", no. 61/04).

Law on Local Self-Government (Official Gazette of the Republic of Macedonia no. 5/2002).

Law on Local Self-Government ("Official Gazette of the Republic of Macedonia", No. 5/05).

Law on property and other real property rights (Official Gazette of the Republic of Macedonia, no. 18/01).

Law on Public-Private Partnerships and Concessions, (Official Gazette of the Republic of Serbia, no. 88/2011, 15/2016 and 104/2016).

Law on Public Debt. (Official Gazette of the Republic of Serbia, no. 61/2005, 107/2009, 78/2011, 68/2015, 95/2018, 91/2019 and 149/2020).

Law on Public Enterprises (Official Gazette of the Republic of Macedonia, no. 38/1996; 9/1997; 6/2002; 40/2003; 49/2006; 22/2007; 83/2009; 97/2010; 6/2012; 119/2013; 41/2014; 138/2014; 25/2015; 61/2015; 39/2016, 64/2018, 35/19 and 275/19).

Law on Public Enterprises (Official Gazette of the Republic of Macedonia, no. 38/96, 6/02, 40/03, 49/06).

Law on Public Property. (Official Gazette of the Republic of Serbia, no. 72/2011, 88/2013, 105/2014, 104/2016– other law, 108/2016, 113/2017, 95/2018 and 153/2020).

Law on Public Utilities. (Official Gazette of the Republic of Serbia, no. 88/2011, 104/2016, and 95/2018).

Law on the City of Skopje (Official Gazette of the Republic of Macedonia, no. 55/2004; 158/2011).

Law on Transformation of socially owned (Official Gazette of the Republic of Macedonia, no. 38/93).

Law on Utility Services. (Official Gazette of the Republic of Serbia, no. 88/2011, 104/2016 and 95/2018).

Law on Water. (Official Gazette of the Republic of Serbia, no. 30/2010, 93/2012, 101/2016, 95/2018 and 95/2018).

Lee, P. I., & Hsueh, P. R. (2020). Emerging threats from zoonotic coronaviruses-from SARS and MERS to 2019-nCoV. Journal of Microbiology, Immunology, and Infection.

Lee, P. T. W., Kwon, O. K., & Ruan, X. (2019). Sustainability challenges in maritime transport and logistics industry and its way ahead. Sustainability, 11(5), 1331. doi:10.3390u11051331

Levy, S. M. (2011). Public-Private Partnerships - Case Studies on Infrastructure, Development American Society of Civil Engineers. ASCE. doi:10.1061/978084410134

Leyla, B., Mohammad, S., Reza, A., & Seyed, H. (2018). Sustainability analysis of landfilling and composting-landfilling for municipal solid waste management in the north of Iran. Journal o Cleaner Production, 1028–1038.

Licastro, A., & Sergi, B. S. (2021). Drivers and barriers to a green economy. A review of selected Balkan countries. Cleaner Engineering and Technology, *100228. Advance online publication doi:10.1016/j.*clet.2021.100228

Licht, L. A., & Isebrands, J. G. (2005). Linking phytoremediated pollutant removal to biomass economic opportunities. Biom*ass and Bioene*rgy, 28(2), 203–218. doi:10.1016/j.biombioe.2004.08.015

Lieb, K. J., & Lieb, R. C. (2010). Environmental sustainability in the third-party logistics (3PL) industry. International Journal of Physical Distribution & Logistics Management, 40(7), 524–533. doi:10.1108/09600031011071984

Lima, R., Nolasco, D., Meneses, W., Salazar, J., Hernandez, P., & Perez, N. (2002). Global Biogen*ic Emission of Carbon Dioxide* from Landfills. American Geophysical Union, Fall Meeting.

Liu, J., Yuan, C., Hafeez, M., & Yuan, Q. (2018). The relationship betw*een environment and logistics perf*ormance: Evidence from Asian countries. Journal of Cleaner Production, 204, 282–291. doi:10.1016/j.jclepro.2018.08.310

Llamas, M. R., Martínez-Cortina, L., Mukherji, A., & O'Leary, D. (20*09). Corruption and tran*sparency in the water sector. In Water ethics. CRC Press. doi:10.1201/9780203875438-28

Local Self-Government and Local Administration Act State Official Journa*l: 77/1991. Retrieved September 10, 2022, from https://www.lex.bg/laws*/ldoc/2132580865

Lockheed, M. E., & Hanushek, E. A. (1994). Concepts of educational efficiency and effectiveness. World Bank.

Lu, *M., Xie, R., Chen, P., Zou, Y., & Tang, J. (2019). Green* transportation and logistics performance: An improved composite index. Sustainability, 11(10), 2976. doi:10.3390u11102976

Lu, Q., He, Z. L., & Stoffella, P. J. (2012). Land Application of B*iosolids in the USA: A Review. App*lied and Environmental Soil Science. doi:10.1155/2012/201462

Lukiyanchuk, I., Panasenko, S., Kazantseva, S., Lebedev, K., & Lebedeva, O. (2020). Development of online ret*ailing logis*tics flows in a globalized digital economy. Revista Inclusiones, 407-416. https://revistainclusiones.org/index.php/inclu/article/view/329

Lukić, N., Jurišević, N., Nikolić, N., & Gordić, D. (2015). Specific heating consumption in the residenti*al sector of Serbia—Example of the city of Kragujeva*c. Energy and Building, 107, 163–171. doi:10.1016/j.ebuild.2015.08.012

López-Torres, L., & Prior, D. (2020). Long-term efficiency of public service provision in a context of budg*et restrictions. An application* to *t*he education sector. Socio-Economic Planning Sciences, 81, 100946. doi:10.1016/j.seps.2020.100946

Machell, G., & Caraher, M. (2012). The ro*le of municipal markets in urban food* strategies: a case study. In A. M. Viljoen & J. S. C. Wiskerke (Eds.), Sustainable Food Planning: evolving theory and practice (pp. 127–136). doi:10.3920/978-90-8686-187-3_10Mancosu, N.*, Snyder, R., Kyria*k*akis*, G., & Spano, D. (2015). Water Scarcity and Future Challenges for Food Production. Water, 7(12), 975–992. doi:10.3390/w7030975

Mariano, E. B., Gobbo Jr, J. A., de Castro Camioto, F., & do Nascimento Rebelatto, *D. A. (2017). CO2* emissions and logistics performance: A composite index proposal. Journal of Cleaner Production, 163, 166–178. doi:10.1016/j.jclepro.2016.05.084

Marra, A. (2007). Internal Regulation by Mixed Enterprises: The *Case of the It*a*lia*n Water Sector. Annals of Public and Cooperative Economics, 78(2), 245–275. doi:10.1111/j.1467-8292.2007.00334.x

Martín-Martín, A., Thelwall, M., Orduna-Malea, E., & Delgado López-Cóz*ar, E. (2020). Google Scholar, Microsoft Academic, Scop*us, dimensions, web of science, and OpenCitations' Coci: A multidisciplinary comparison of coverage via citations. Scientometrics, 126(1), 871–906. doi:10.100711192-020-*03690-4* PMID:32981987

Mathieu, E., Ritchie, H., Rodés-Guirao, L., Appel, C., Giattino, C., Hasell, J., Macdonald, B., Dattani, S., Beltekian, D., Ortiz-Ospina, E., & Roser, M. (2020). Coronavrus Pandemic (COVI*D-19). Retrieved from: https://our*worldindata.org/coronavirus

Mauerhofer, V. (2023). Gender within sustainable decisions: A 3-D sustainability perspective. In A. Skjerven & M. F*ordham (Eds.), Gender and the Sustainable* Dev*e*lopment Goals (pp. 28–45). Routledge., doi:10.4324/9781003174257-4

Maxwell, J. (2013). Qualitative research design: an interactive approach. Sage.

Mccaffrey, S. (2015). The 1997 UN Convention: Compatibility and Complementarity. In: Tanzi, A., McIntyre, O., Kolliopoulos, A., Rieu-Clarke, A.*, Kinna, R. Th*e *UNE*CE Convention on the Protection and Use of Transboundary Watercourses and International Lakes – Its Contribution to International Water Cooperation, Brill.

McNabb, D. E. (2018). Public utilities: Old Problems, New Chall*enges. Edward Elgar Publishing.*

Meeampol, S., Lerskullawat, P., Wongsorntham, A., Srinammuang, P., Rodpetch, V., & Noonoi, R. (2014). Applying Emerging Market Z-Score Model to Predict Bankruptcy: A Case Study of Listed *Companies in the Stock Exchange of Thailand.* Management, Knowledge, and Learning International Conference, 1227-1237. *Retrieved January 18, 2023 from https://www.toknowpr*ess.net/ISBN/978-961-6914-09-3/papers/ML 14-724.pdf

Mekong River Commission (MRC). (2018). An introduction to MRC procedural rules for Mekong Water Cooperaion. MC*R. https://www.mrcmekong.org/assets/Publications/MRC-procedures -EN-V.7-JUL-18.pdf*

Mekonnen, M. M., & Hoekstra, A. Y. (2016). Four billion people facing severe water scarcity. Science A*dvances, 2(2), e1500323. doi:10.1126ciadv.1500*323 PMID:26933676

Melyn, W., & Moesen, W. (1991). Towards a synthetic indicator of macroeconomic performance: Unequal weighting when limited information is available. Public conomics research papers, 1-24.

Men, L. R. (2014). Internal Reputation Management: *The Impact of Authentic Leadership and Transparent Communica*tion. Corporate Reputation Review, 17(4), 254–272. doi:10.1057/crr.2014.14

Mench, M., Vangronsveld, J., Clijsters, H., Lepp, N. W., & Edwards, R. (2000). In *situ metal immobilisation and phytostabilisation of contaminated soi*ls. In N. Terry & G. Bañuelos (Eds.), Phytoremediation of Contaminated Soil and Water (pp. 323–358). Lewis Publishers.

Milošević, L. (2016). Methodological Approach to Landfill Fi*re Risk Assessme*nt for the Purpose of Air Pollution Evaluation [PhD Thesis]. University of Niš, Faculty of Occupational Safety in Niš.

Milošević, L. (2022). Emisija deponijskog gasa kao faktor opasnosti nastanka požara. Fa*kultet zaštite na radu u Nišu.*

Milutinović, S. (2004). Urbanizacija i održivi razvoj [Urbanization and sustainable development]. Fakultet zaštite na radu u Nišu, Niš.

Ministry of Agriculture. Forestry and Water Management of Re*public of Serbia. (2022, July 13). Arrangement* and use of water. Directorate of Water. https://www.rdvode.gov.rs/lat/uredjenje-koriscenje.php

Ministry of Construction, Transport and Infrastructure. *(2021). Report of utility ser*v*i*ces performance on the territory of the Republic of Serbia in *2020. Author.*

Mishra, H., Karmakar, S., Kumar, R., & Kadambala, P. (2017). A long-term comparative assessment of human health risk to leachate-contaminated groundwater from heavy metal with different liner systems. Environmental Science and Pollution Research International, 1–13. PMID:29147980

MISP. (2011). Strategy for Restructuring the Public Utility Companies in Serbia (draft). Municipal Infrastructure Support Programme. Availableat: http://www.misp-serbia.rs/wp-content/uploads/2010/05/Strateg y-for-Restructuring-*the-PUC-Draft.pdf*

Molinos-Senante, M., & Maziotis, A. (2021). Benchmarking the efficiency of water and sewerage companies: Application of the stochastic non-parametric envelopment of data (stoned) method. Expert Systems with Applications, 186, 115711. Avance online publication. doi:10.1016/j.eswa.2021.115711

Monea, B. F., Ionete, E. I., Spiridon, S. I., Leca, A., Stanciu, A., Petre, E., & Vaseashta, A. (2017). Single Wall Carbon Nanotubes Based Cryogenic Temperatur*e Sensor Platforms. The Lancet. Infectious Diseases, 20(4)*, 410–411. doi:10.1016/S1473-3099(20)*30114-6*

*Muers, S. (2020). Culture and Values at the Heart of Policy Maki*ng. Institute for Policy Research.

Municipal Property Act. (1996). State Official Journal: 44/1996. Retrieved September, 10, 2022, from https://www.lex.bg/laws/ldoc/2133874691

Murias, P., de Miguel, J. C., & Rodríguez, D. (2008). A composite indicator for university quality assessment: The case of Spanish higher education system. Social Indica*tors Research, 89(1), 129–146.* doi:*10.*100711205-007-9226-z

Mylopoulos, Y., Eleftheriadou, E., & Kampragou, E. (2004). The transboundary catchment of River Nestos and the bilateral agreement between Greece and Bulgaria. [Paper presentation] ECO-Geowater conference, GI for International *River Basin Management. Budape*st.

Nagendran, R., Selvam, A., Joseph, K., & Chiemchaisri, C. (2006). *Phytoremediation and rehabilitation of municipal* solid waste landfills and dumpsites: A brief review. Waste Manage*ment (New York, N.Y.), 26(12),* 1357–1369. doi:10.1016/j.wasman.2006.05.003 PMID:17064886

National Statistical Institute – NSI. (2020). Retrieved December, 11, 2022, from https://www.nsi.bg/en/

Navas, A., Bermudez, F., & Machin, J. (1998). Influence of sewage sludg*e application on physical* an*d* chemical properties of Gypsisols. Geoderma, 87(1-2), 123–135. doi:10.1016/S0016-7061(98)00072-X

Negruț, M. L., Muțiu, A., & Mihărtescu, A.-A. (2022). Insights on the Performance of Public Procurement for Water Utilities Works. Sustainability, 15(1), 155. doi:10.3390/su15010155

Nenezić, D., & Radulović, B. (2012). The Analysis of possibilities and modalities of financing and financial support measures to public-private partnerships in Serbia. Quarterly Monitor, 13, 62-*71. Available at: https://fren.o*rg.*rs*/en/kvartalni-monitor/quarterly-monitor-13/

Ng, S. T., Wong, J. M., & Zhang, J. (2011). Applying Z-score model to distinguish insolvent construction companies in China. Habitat International, 35(4), 599–607. doi:10.1016/j.habitatint.2011.03.008

Nhamo, L., Ndlela, B., Nhemachena, C., Mabhaudhi, T., Mp*andeli,* S., & Matchaya, G. (2018). The Water-Energy-Food Nexus: Climate Risks and Opportunities in Southern Africa. Water, 10(5), 567. doi:10.3390/w10050567

Nikitas, A., Michalakopoulou, K., Nj*oya, E. T., & Kara*mpatzakis, D. (2020). Artificial Intelligence, Transport, and the Smart City: Definitions and Dimensions of a New Mobility Era. Sustainability, 12(7), 2789. doi:10.3390u12072789

Nilsson, L. J., Khan, J.*, Andersson, F. N. G.*, Klintman, M., Hildingsson, R., Kronsell, A., Pettersson, F., Pålsson, H., & Smedby, N. (2013). I ljuset av framtiden: Styrning mot nollutsläpp 2050. Lund University. https://www.lth.se/lets2050/aktiviteter/vis*a-nyhet/article/i-lj*us*t*-av-framtiden/

Nistor, L. (2011). Public services and the European Union: healthcare, health insurance and education services. Springer Science & Business Media. doi:10.1007/978-90-6704-805-7

Noble, H., & Smith, J. (2015). *Issues of* validity and reliability in qualitative research. Evidence-Based Nursing, 18(2), 34–35. doi:10.1136/eb-2015-102054 PMID:25653237

Nota, L., Soresi, S., Di Maggio, I., Santilli, S., & Ginevra, M. C. (2020). Life Des*igning for an* In*cl*usive, Sustainable and Equitable Future. In Sustainable Development, Career Counselling and Career Education (pp. 41–62). Springer. doi:10.1007/978-3-030-60046-4_3

Novićević, *B., Antić, Lj., & Milenović, J. (2021). Uticaj indu*strije 4.0 na ekološko upravljačko računovodstvo. International Scientific Conference - Limen.

Novićević Čečević, B., Ant*ić, Lj., & Milenović, J. (2021). Application of the concept of target costing in hospitalit*y. In V. Bevanda & S. Štetić (Eds.), International thematic monograph Modern management tools and economy of tourism sector in present era (pp. 93–108). UDEKOM. *doi:10.31410/tmt.20*21-2022.93

OAS. (2022). OAS: SLA: Department of International Law (dil): Inter-American. OAS. https://www.oas.org/en/sla/dil/inter_american_treaties_B-58_against_Corruption_signatories.asp

OECD. (2002). *Social Issues in the Provision and Pricing of Water Services. OE*CD.

OECD. (2015). OECD Principles on Water Governance. OECD. www.oecd.org/governance/oecd-principles-onwater-governance.h
tmOECD. (2011). Water Governance in OECD Countries: A Multi-level Approach. OECD Publish*ing. doi:10.1787/9789264119284-*

*OECD. (2020). OECD Public Integrity Handbook. OECD Publishing. doi:1*0.1787/ac8ed8e8-

OECD. (2022a). Anti-corruption initiative for Asia Pacific. OECD. https://www.oecd.org/*corruption/anti-corruption-initiative-for-asia-pacific.htm*

OECD. (2022b). OECD convention on combating bribery of foreign public officials in international business transac*tions. OECD. https://www.o*ecd.org/corruption/oecdantibriberyconvention.htm

O*gata, Y., Ishigaki, T., Ebie, Y., Sutthasil, N., Chiemchaisri, C.*, & Yamada, M. (2015). Water reduction by constructed wetlands treatin waste landfill leachate in a tropical region. *Waste Management (New York, N.Y.), 44, 164–171. doi:10.101*6/j.wasman.2015.07.019 *PMID:26209341*

OSCE. (2009). Report on the process of fiscal decentralization in the Republic of Macedonia. OECD.

OSCE. *(2009). Review of Decentralization. OECD.*

*O'Dowd, L. (20*02). The Changing Significance of European Borders. Regional *& Federal Studies, 12(4), 13–3*6. doi:10.1080/714004774

Pacific Water and Wastewater A*ssociation. (2021). PWWA: Post-COVID recove*ry and new frontiers. Pacific Water and Wastewater Association. https://www.ib-net.org/doc/PWWA_2021_A4s.*pdf*

*Paige, K., Haggerty, B., & Comber, B. (2022). Water Literacies: Co-researching, Learning, and Act*ing for the Wetlands. In M. Häggström & C. Schmidt (Eds.), Relational and Critical Perspectives on Education for Sustainable Development (p. 66). Springer. doi:10.1007/978-3-030-84510-0_4

Pandey, P. (2019). Disciplines, Professions and the Sustainable De*velopment Goals (SDGs): Challenge*s *in* Higher Education in India. In Implementing the 2030 agenda at higher edu*cation institutions: Challenges and responses (pp. 47-53). Springer.*

Pantini, S., Verginelli, I., *& Lombardi, F. (2014). A n*ew screening model for leachate production assessment at l*andfill sites. International Journal of Envi*ronmenal Science and Technology, 11(6), 1503–1516. doi10.100713762-013-0344-7

Paolo, U. (2010). Public-Private Partnerships: Success and Failure Factors for In-Transition Countries. University Press of America.

Papoutsoglou, S. E. (1992). Possi*ble Effects of Climate Change on Fisheries and Aquaculture in Greece. Bank of* Greece.

Parker, A. (1986). Landfill gas-a potential environmental hazard. Disasters, 10(1), 65–69. doi:10.1111/j.1467-7717.1986.tb00569.x PMID:20958628

Parker, T., Dottridge, J., & Kelly, S. (2002). Investigation of the composition and emissions of trace components in landfill gas. R&D Technical Report P1-438/TR. Environment Agency.

Pathak, A. K., Singh, M. M., Kumar, V., & Trivedi, A. K. (2012). Phytoremediation of mun*icipal solid waste landfill site: A review. J. Chem. Chem. Sci*., 2(1), 77–92.

Pathak, S., Agarwal, A. V., & Pandey, V. C. (2020*). Phytoremediation—a holistic approach for remediation of heavy metals and metallo*ids. Bioremediation of Pollutants. doi:10.1016/B978-0-12-819025*-8.00001-6*

*Paul, G. (1999). Measuring the Effect of Municipal Enterpri*ses on the Budgets of Local Governments. The Western Journal of *Black Studies, 23(4), 217–228.*

*Pavlović, B., Ivezić, D., & Živković, M. (2022). Tra*nsition pathways of household heating in Serbia: Analysis based on an agent-based model. Renewable & Sustainable Energy R*eviews, 1*63, 163. doi:10.1016/j.rser.2022.112506

Pawłowska, M. (2014). Mitigation of landfill gas emissions. CRC Press. doi:10.1201/b16791

Pejčić, D., & Vranjanac, Ž. (2016). Environmental impact analysis of h*ygiene and cleaning* p*r*oducts packaging waste, Safety Engineering. Faculty of Occupation*al Safety in Niš.*

Perišić, M. (2003). Računovodstvo okoliša i održivi razvoj turizma. Academic Press.

Perkmann, M. (2007a). Construction of new territorial scales. A framework and case study of the EUREGIO cross-border region. Regional Studies, 41(2), *253–266. doi:10.1080/00343400600990517*

*P*erkmann, M. (2007b). Policy entrepreneurship and multilevel governance: A comparative study of European cross-border regions. Environment and Planning. C, *Governmnt & Policy, 25(6), 861–879. do*i:*10.*1068/c60m

Perović, D., & Radukić, S. (2017). Comparative ana*lysis of sustainable development com*ponents for the Republic of Serbia and neighbouring countries. Teme – *Journal for Social Sciences, 41(3), 747–765.*

Petrović, M. (2013). Conducting public utilities in Serbia: providing and maintaining services in Kragujevac. International Journal of Public Sector Management, 26(2), 116-126. doi:10.1108/09513551311317988

Pheakdey, D. V., Quan, N. V., Khanh, T. D., & Xuan, T. *D. (2022). Challenges and Priorities of Municipal So*l*id* Waste Management in Cambodia. International Journal of Enviro*nmental Research and Public Health, 19(14), 845*8. doi:10.3390/ijerph19148458 PMID:35886307

Poschenrieder, C., & Coll, J. B. (2003). Phytoremediation: Principles and perspectives. Contributi*ons in Science,* 2, *3*33–44.

Prasad, K., Kumar, H., Singh, L., Sawarkar, D., Kumar, M., & Kumar, S. (2022). Phytocapping technology for sustainable management of contaminated sites: case studie*s, challenges, and future prospects. Phytoremedi*atio*n Technology for the Removal of Heavy Metals and Other Contaminants from Soil and Water, 601-616 doi:10.1016/B978-0-323-85763-5.00041-6

Pérez-López, G., Prior, D., & Zafra-Gómez, J. *L. (2015). Rethinking New Public* Man*a*gement Delivery Forms and Efficiency: Long-Term Effects in Spanish Local Government. Journal of Public Administration: Rese*arch and Theory, 25(4), 1157–1183. doi10.1093/jopart/*muu088

Qasim, S. R., & Chiang, W. (1994). Sanitary Landfill Leachate: Generation, Control and Treatment. doi:10.1201/9780203740217

Queirós, A., Faria, D., & Almeida, F. (2017). Strengt*hs and Limitations of Qualitative and Quantitative Research Metho*ds, European Journal of Education Studies, 3 (9). www.oapub.org/edu

Radosavljević, J. (2010). Prostorno planiranje i zaštita životne sredine [Spa*tial planning and enviro*nm*e*ntal protection]. Fakultet zaštite na radu u Nišu, Niš.

Radukic, S., Perovic, D., & Vucetic, D. (2018). Economic and environmental effects from liberalizing utility service prices in the Republic of Serbia. Industrija, 46(4).

Radukić, S., Perović, D., & Vučetić, D. (2018). Economic and environmental effects from liberalizing utility service prices in the Republic of Serbia. Industrija, 46(4), 29*-46.. doi:10.5937/ industrija46-18444*

*Radulovic, B., & Dragu*tinovic, S. (2015). Efficiency of local self-governments in Serbia: An SFA approach. Industrija, 43(3), 123–142. doi:10.5937/industrija43-8846

Rakić, *B., & Rađenović, T. (2011a). Risks an*d *B*enefits of Private Capital Participation in Public Projects Financing under the Contemporary Economic Crisis Conditions. In B. Krstić (Ed.), Improving the Competitiveness o the Public and Private Sector by *Networking Competences (pp. 65–83). University of Niš, Faculty of Eco*nomics.

Rakić, B., & Rađenović, T. (2011b). The Impact of Global Economic Crisis on Public-Private Partnerships. In E. Petrović (Ed.), Science and World Economic Crisis (pp. 51–60). University of Niš, Faculty of Economics.

Rakić, B., & Rađenović, T. (2014). Real Options Methodology in Public-Private Partnership Projects Valuation. Economic Annals, 59(200), 91*-113. doi:10.22*98/EKA1400091R

Rakić, B., Milenković-Kerković, T., & Rađenović, T. (2014). Infrastructure Development through public-private partnership. Actual Problems of Economics, No. 2. National Academy of M*anagement.*

*Ra*mamurti, R. (2004). Developing countries and MNEs: Extending and enriching the research agenda. Journal of Intern*ational Busine*ss Studies, 35(4), 277–283. doi:10.1057/palgrave.jibs.8400087

Ranđelović, S., & Vukanović, S. (2021). Fiscal decentralization and local public investment *policy in the Repub*lic of Serbia. Ekonomski horizonti, 23(3), 197-213.

Rathod, M., Mishra, H., & Karmakar, S. (2013). *Leachate characterization and assessment of water pollution near municipal solid waste landfill s*ite. Int J Chem Phys Sci.

Rađenović, Ž., Krstić, B., & Marković, M. (2022). Economic Performance of Agriculture in the European Union Countries / Wyniki ekonomiczne w rolnictwie w krajach Unii Europejskiej. Zagadnienia Ek*onomiki Rolnej / Problems of Agricultural Economics, 370(1), 5–21. https://doi doi:org/1*0.30858/zer/145686

Rebecca, J., Jan, R., David, H., & Nikolaos, V. (2007). Household hazardous waste disposal to landfill: Using LandSim to model leachate migration. Environmental Po*llution, 501–509. PMID:17046126*

Region of Western Macedonia. (2012). Special Spatial Study of the Prespa area.

Region of Western Macedonia. (2015). Spatial Plan of the Region of Western *Macedonia.*

*Region of Western Macedonia. (20*17). Special Environmental Study of the Prespa Region.

Registry Agency of the Republic of Bulgaria. (2021). Commercial register and register of non-profit legal entities. Ret*rieved September 10, 20*22, from https://portal.registryagency.bg/CR/reports/ActiveCond*ition/*

Regulated Industries Commission. (2010, December). Improving transparency and accountability in the electricity and water. RIC. http://www.ric.org.tt/wp-content/uploads/2021/02/Improving-Transparency-and-Accountability-in-the-Electricity-and-Water-Sectors.Main_.*201.pdf*

*Reiff, M., Ivan*icova, Z., & Surmanova, K. (2018). Cluster analysis of selected *world development indicators in the fie*lds of agriculture and the food industry *in European Union countries. Agric. Econ. –.* Czech, 64(5), 197–205. doi:10.17221/198/*2016-AGRICECON*

*Reiff, M., Surmanová, K., Balcer*zak, A. P., & Pietrzak, M. B. (2016). Multiple criteria *analysi of European Union agriculture. Journal of Internationa*l Students, 9(3), 62–74. doi:10.4254/2071-8330.2016/9-3/5

Reinikka, R., & Svensson, J. (2011). The power of information in public services: Evidenc*e from education in Uganda. Journal of Public Economics, 95(7-8), 956–9*66. doi:10.1016/j.jpubeco.2011.02.006

Reisz, A., & Perlich, C. (2007). A market-based framework for bankruptcy prediction. Journal of Financial Stability, 3(2), 85–131. doi:10.1016/j.jfs.2007.02.001

Ren, J., Chen, C., Gao, B., & Zhang, J. (2019). Performance evaluation of pallet rental companies: A non-oriented super-efficiency integer-valued DEA mod*el. I*EEE Access: Practical Innovations, Open Solutions, 7, 151628–151637. doi:10.1109/ACCESS.2019.2948123

Rezaei, S. A., & Gilkes, R. J. (2005). The effects of landscape attributes an*d plant community on soil physica*l properties in rangelands. Geoderma, 125(1–2), 145–154. doi:10.1016/j.geoderma.2004.07.011

Richard, F., & Esther, G. (2008). Regulating Water and Sanitation for the *Poor: Economic Regulation f*or Public and Private Partnerships. Earthscan Publications Ltd.

Richardson, C. W. (2019). Obstacles to the implementation of the SDGs: Feel*ings over facts. In Implementin*g the 2030 agenda at higher education institutions: Challenges and responses (pp. 54-65). Global University Network for Innovation.

Richter, A. (2021). New geothermal district heating system in Höfn, Ic*eland. Think Geoenergy. Retrieved December 20, 2022*, from https://www.thinkgeoenergy.com/new-geothermal-district-heating-system-in-hofn-iceland/

Rieckmann, M., & Barth, M. (2022). Educators' Competence Frameworks in Education for Sustainab*le Deve*lopmen*t. In P. Vare, N. Lausselet, & M. Rieckmann (Eds.), Competences in Education for Susta*inable Development (pp. 27–34). Springer. doi:10.1007/978-3-030-91055-6_3*

Ripanti, E. F., Tjahjono, B., & Fan, I. S. (2015, September). Circular economy in reverse logistics: relationships and potential applications in product remanufacturing. 20th Logistics Research Network (LN) Conference.

Ritchie, H., & Roser, M. (2017). Water Use and Stress. Our World in Data. https://ourworldindat*a.org/water-use-stress*

*Rodrigo-Ilarri, J., & Rodrigo-C*lavero, M.-E. (2020). Mathematical modeling of the biogas production in MSW landfills. Impact of the implementation of organic matter and food waste selective collection systems. Atmosphere, 11(12), 11. doi:10.3390/atmos11121306

Rodrigo-Ilarri, J., Rodrigo-Clavero, M.-E., & Cassiraga, E. (2020). A n*ew decision support model for the real-time managemen*t of municipal solid waste bioreactor landfills. International Journal of Environmental Research and Public Health, 17(5), 17. doi:10.3390/ijerph17051675 PMID:32143477

Romano, G., & Guerrini, A. (2011). Measuring and comparing *the efficiency of water utility companies: A d*ata envelopment analysis approach. Utilities Policy, 19(3), *202–209. doi:10.*1016/j.jup.2011.05.005

Rothe, C., Schunk, M., Sothmann, P., Bretzel, G., Froeschl, G., Wallrauch, C., Zimmer, T., Thiel, V., Janke, C., Guggemos, W., Seilmaier, M., Drosten, C., Vollmar, P., Zirglmaier, K., Zange, S., Wölfel, R., & Hoelscher, M. (2020). *Transmissio*n *o*f 2019-nCoV Infection from an asymptomatic contact in Germany. The New England Journal of Medicine, 382(10), 970–971. doi:10.1056/NEJMc2001468 PMID:32003551

Rounaghi, M. (2019). Economic analysis of using gree*n accounting and environmental accounting to identify environment*al *c*osts and sustainability indicators. International Journal of Ethics and Systems, 35(4), 504–512. doi:10.1108/IJOES-03-2019-0056

Rowlett, R. (2005). A Dictionary of Units of Measurement. Russ *Rowlett and the* Uni*v*ersity of North Carolina at Chapel Hill.

Rubin, I. S. (1988). Municipal Enterprises: Exploring Budgetary and Political Implications. Public Administration Review, 48(1), 542–550. doi:10.2307/975517

Rusciano, V., Civero, G., & Scarpato, D. (2020). Social and ecological high influential factors in community gardens innovation: An empirical survey in I*taly. Sustainability, 12(11), 12. d*oi*:10.*3390u12114651

Rykala, W., Fabianska, M. J., & Dabrowska, D. (2022). The Influence of a Fire at an Illegal Landfill in Southern Poland on the Formation of Toxic Compounds and Their Impact on the Natural Environm*ent. International Journal of Environmental* Re*s*earch and Public Health, 19(20), 13613. doi:10.3390/ijerph1920136*13 PMID:36294191*

Sadoff, C., & Grey, D. (2005). Cooperation on International Rivers. A Continuum for Securing and Sharing Benefits. Water International, 30(4), 420–427. doi:10.1080/0250806050869188*6*

Sadowska-Rociek, A., Kurdziel, M., Szczepaniec-Cięciak, E., Riesenmey, C., Vaillant, H., Batton-Hubert, M., & Piejko, K. (2009). Analysis of odorous compounds at municipal landfill sites. Waste Management & Resarch, 27(10*), 966–975. d*oi*:10.*1177/0734242X09334616 PMID:19710115

Sadowsky, M. J. (1999). Phytoremediation: past promises and future practices. In Proc. 8th Int. Symp. on Microbial Ecology. Atlantic Canada Society for Microbial Ecology.

Saltelli, A. (2007). Co*mposite Indicators between Analysis and Advocacy. Social Indicato*rs *R*esearch, 1(81), 65–77. doi:10.100711205-006-0024-9

Sapuric, Z. (2014). The potentials for bio waste management in macedonia. International Journal of Ecosystems., 4, 513–*520.*

Sarwar, N., Imran, M., Shaheen, M. R., Ishaque, W., Kamran, M. A., Matloob, A., Rehim, A., & Hussain, S. (2017). Phytoremediation strategies for soils contaminated with heavy metals: Modifications and future prspectives. Chemosphere, 171, 710–721. d*oi:10.1016/j.chemosphere.20*16.*12*.116 PMID:28061428

Sathish, T. (2019). Profit maximization in reverse logistics based on disassembly scheduling using hybrid bee colony an*d bat optimization. Transactions of the* Canadian Society for Mechanical Engineering, 43(4), 551–559. doi:10.1139/tcsme-2019-0017

Sathish, T., & Jayaprakash, J. (20*17). Optimizing supply cha*in in reverse logistics. International Journal of Mechanical and Production Engineering Research and Development, 7(6), *551–560. doi:10.24247/ijmperddec2017*63

Savickas, R. (Ed.). (2019). Guidelines for Introduction Heat Metering in the City of Belgrade.

Schleup, J. (2008). How Does Cogeneration Provide Heat and Power? Scientific American. Retrieved December 20, 2022, from https://www.sci*entificameri*can.com/article/how-does-cogeneration-provide-heat-power/

Schwitzguébel, J. P., van der Lelie, D., Baker, A., Glass, D. J., & Vangronsveld, J. (2002). Phytoremediation: European and American trends success*es, obstacles and needs. Journal of Soils and Sediments, 2(2),* 91–99. doi:10.1007/BF02987877

Seetharaman, A., Ismail, M., & Saravanan, A. S. (2007). Environmental Accounting as a Tool for Enviro*nmental Management System. Journal of Applied Science & Environmental Management, 11(2), 1*37–145.

Senn, J., & Giordano-Spring, S. (2020). The limits of environmen*tal accounting disclosure: Enforcement of regulations, standards* and interpretative strategies. Accounting, Auditing & Accountability *Journal, 33(6), 136*7–1393. doi:10.1108/AAAJ-04-2018-3461

SEPA. (2021). Questionnaire to Western Balkan countries for providing information regarding municipal waste management and waste prevention and follow-up interview: Serbia. Serbia Environmental Protection Agency.

Sgarbossa, F., Grosse, E. H., Neumann, W. *P., Battini, D., & Glock, C. H. (*2020). Human factors in production and logistics systems of the future. Annual Reviews in Control, 49, 295–305. doi:10.1016/j.arcontrol.2020.04.007

Shammas, N. K., *& Wang, L. K. (2007). Land Application of Biosolids.* In L. K. Wang, N. K. Shammas, & Y. T. Hung (Eds.), Biosolids Treatment Processes. Handbook of Environmental Engineering (Vol. 6). Humana Press. doi:10.1007/978-1-5929-996-7_23

*Sharma, A., Pezzaniti, D., Myers, B., Cook, S., T*jandraatmadja, G., Chacko, P., & Chavoshi, S. (2016). Water S*ensitive Urban Design: An Investigation of Current Systems, Implementation Drivers, Community Perceptions and Potential to Supplement Urban Water Services.* Water, 8(7), 272. doi:10.3390/w8070272

Simović, O., Rađenović, Ž., Perović, D., & Vujačić, V. (2020), Tourism in the Digital Age: E-Booking Perspective. ENTRENOVA – ENTerprise REsearch InNOV*ation, 6(1), 616-627. htt*ps://hrcak.srce.hr/ojs/index.php/entrenova/ article/view/ 13515/6766

Singh, R., & Vutukuru, V. (2010). Enhancing Accountability in Public Service Delivery through Social A*udits: A case study of Andhra Pradesh. Accountability Initiative. Ce*ntre for Policy Research.

Skender, H. P., Zaninović, P. A., & Srića, E. (2019). Review of Modern Transportation Technologies with focus on Containerization. Annals of Maritime Studies/Pomorski Zbornik, 57(1), 111-121. Doi:10.18048/2019.57.08

Skoulikaris, C., Filali-Meknassi, Y., Aureli, A., Amani, A., & Jiménez-Cisneros, *B. E. (*2018). Information-Communication Technologies as an Integrated Water Resources Management (IWRM). Tool for Sustainable Development. Achievements an*d Challenges of Integrated River Basin Manage*ment., doi:10.5772/intechopen.74700

Society for the Protection of the Prespa. (2011). Protection and Sustainable Use of Biodiversity in the Region of the Large Lakes Prespa, Ohrid and Sckoder. Albania– Fyrom (2011-2014). https://www.spp.gr/

*Sofia Munic*ipality. (2022). Register of municipal commercial companies with 100% mun*icipal ownership of the capital. Retrieved November 06, 2022, from https://www.sofia.bg/register-of-municipal-companies*

Solid waste management law (Official Gazette of the Republic of Macedonia, no. 216/21).

Solomon, A., & Ayodeji, O. (2019). Environmental Cost and Financial Performance: Ana*lysis of Cement Companies in Nigeria. Inter*nat*io*nal Journal of Academic and Applied Research, 60-65.

Solovida, G., & Latan, H. (2017). Linking environmental strategy to environment*al performance. Sustainability Accounting. Management and Policy Journal, 8(5), 595–619.*

Sorensen, R. J. (2007). Does dispersed public ownership impair efficiency? The case of refuse collection in Norway. Public Administration, 85(4), 1045–1058. doi:10.1111/j.1467-9299.*2007.00681.x*

Spasov, S., & Arsov, S. (2004). Financial Management. Faculty of Economics.

*Spoann, V., Fuji*wara, T., Seng, B., Lay, C., & Yim, M. (2019). Assessment of public-private p*artnership in municipal solid waste management in Phnom Penh, Cambodia. Sustainability,* 11(5), 1228. doi:10.3390u1105122

Standard & Poor. (2010). Public finance system overview, Macedonian municipalities. Standard & Poor.

Stanković, J. J., Marjanović, I., & Stojković, N. (2021). DEA Assessment of Socio-economic Development of European Countries. Management: Journal of Sustainable Bu*siness and Management Soluions in Emerging Economies,* 26(1), 13–24.

Stanković, S., Vasović, D., & Trajković, S. (2019). Model of sustainable water resources m*anagement in the conditio*ns *of extreme hydrological phen*om*e*na. Journal of Environmental Protection and Ecology, 20(3), 1393-1401. Available at: https://scibulcom.net/en/journal/1311-5065/iss*ue/2019-20-3/*

State Prop*e*rty Act. (1996). State Official Journal: 44/1996. Retrieved September 10, 2022, from *https://www.lex.bg/b*g/laws/ldoc/2133874689

Stepanov, J. (2018). A model for the evaluation of the municipal waste management system using the life cycle assessment method. Faculty of Technica Sciences in Novi *Sad.*

*Stevanovi*ć, S., & Pucar, M. (2012). Financial measures Serbia should *offer for solar water heating systems. Energy and Buildin*g, 54, 519–526. doi:10.1016/j.enbuild.2012.02.054

Stević, M. (2006). Povećanje tačnosti merenja numerički upravljanih mernih mašina [Increasing the measurement accuray of *numerically controlled measuring machines]. Fakulte*t tehničkih nauka u Novom Sadu, Novi Sad.

Stoilova, D. (2022). Analysis of the financial management of municipal enterprises in Blagoevgrad with Z-score model. Economics & Law, 4(1), 1–14. doi:10.37708/el.swu.v4i1.1

*Stoyanov, A., & Gerganov, A. (2017). Anti-corruption: Implementation and Evaluation of A*nti-*c*orruption Measures and Policies. Center *for the Study of Democracy. Ret*rieved September 15, 2022, from https://csd.bg/publications/publication/anti-corruption-iplementation-*and-evaluation-of-anti-corruption-measures-and-policies-macpi/*

Stretch, D., Laister, G., Strachan, L., & Saner, M. (2001). Odour trails from landfill sites. Proceedings of the 8th International Waste Management & Landfill Symposium, 709-718.

Sun, X., Xu, Y.*, Liu, Y., Nai, C., D*ong, L., Liu, J., & Huang, Q. (2019). Evolution of geomembrane degradation and defects in a landfill:Impacts on long-term leachate leakage and groundwater quality. Journal of Cleaner Production,224, 335–345. doi:10.1016/j.jclepro.2019.03.200

Superservicios. (2022). Superintendency of Residential Public Services. Superservicios. https://www.superservicios.gov.co/

Takić, L., Živković, S., & Živković, N. (2013). Improvement of environmental management: a case study. Fresenius Environmental Bulletin, 22(12C), 3840-3847. Available at: https://www.prt-parlar.de/download_feb_2013/

Tan, C. H. (1992). Public Enterprises and Privatization: The Experience of Singapore. Annals of Public and Cooperative Economics, 63(1), 119–125. doi:10.1111/j.1467-8292.1992.tb02081.x

Tasić, D., & Živković, V. (2000). Osnovi metrologije [Basics of metrology]. Savezni zavod za mere i dragocene metale, Beograd.

Tavares, A. F., & Camões, P. J. (2007). Local service delivery choices in Portugal: A political transaction costs framework. Local Government Studies, 33(4), 535–553. doi:10.1080/03003930701417544

Tavares, A. F., & Camões, P. J. (2010). New Forms of Local Governance: A theoretical and empirical analysis of municipal corporations in Portugal. Public Managemnt Review, 12(5), 587–608. doi:10.1080/14719031003633193

Taylor, K. M. (2021). Effectiveness of Social Enterprises: Aligning Strategies and Supply Chains for Impact. Electronic Thesis and Dissertation Repository. 7850. https://ir.lib.uwo.ca/etd/7850

The Law on Accounting for Budgets and Budget Users ("Official Gazette of the Republic of Macedonia", no. 61/02, 98/02).

The Statistical Office of the Republic of Serbia. (2022). Progress Report on the Implementation of Sustainable Development Goals (SDG) for the Republic of Serbia for 2021. The Statistical Office of the Republic of Serbia.

The World Bank. (2022, October 05). Water resources management. World Bank. https://www.worldbank.org/en/topic/waterresourcesmanagement

Thieme, C., Giménez, V., & Prior, D. (2012). A comparative analysis of the efficiency of national education systems. Asia Pacific Education Review, 13(1), 1–15. doi:10.100712564-011-9177-6

Tian, G., Granato, T. C., Pietz, R. I., Carlson, C. R., & Abedin, Z. (2006). Effect of long-term application of biosolids for land reclamation on surface water chemistry. Journal of Environmental Quality, 35(1, 101–113. doi:10.2134/jeq2004.0354 PMID:16391281

Todea, N., Stanciu, I. C., & Udrea, A-M. (2011). Accounting Policies On Environmental Costs And Their Calculation Method In The Entity. Annals of DAAAM & Proceedings of the 22nd International DAAAM Symposium, 22, 653-654.

Todorovski, I. (2004). Functioning of the local self-government system in the Republic of Macedonia. Institute for Sociological and Political Legal Research, UKIM.

Topaloglou, L., & Petrakos, G. (2008b). *The economic geography of borders. A brief literature review. Research Paper Series*, University of Thessaly, 14(6), 105-118.

Tošić, N., & Vasović, D. (2020). Analysis of contemporary municipal waste management practice in the Republic of Serbia. Safety Engineering, X(2), 89–96. doi:10.5937/SE2002089T

Transboundary Waters Assessment Programme (TWAP), Transboundary Lakes and Reservoirs: *Status and Future Trends*. http://geftwap.org/

Transparency International (TI). (2022a). 2021 corruption perceptions index - Explore the results. Transparency.org. https://www.transparency.org/en/cpi/2021

Transparency International (TI). (2022b). *Ethics - Corruptionary A-Z*. Transparency.org. https://www.transparency.org/en/corruptionary/ethics

Transparency International (TI). (2022c). Transparency - Corruptionary A-Z. Transparency.org. https://www.transparency.org/en/corruptionary/transparency

Transparency International (TI). (2022d). What is corruption? Transparency.org. https://www.transparency.org/en/what-is-corruption

Transparency International Bulgaria. (2015). Index of the local integrity system – 2015. Retrieved September 15, 2022, from http://lisi.transparency.bg/years/2015/

Tsakalidis, A., Gkoumas, K., & Pekár, F. (2020). Digital transformation supporting transport decarbonisation: Technological developments in EU-funded research and innovation. Sustainability, 12(9), 3762. doi:10.3390u12093762

Turilli, M., & Floridi, L. (2009). The Ethics of Information Transparency. Ethics and Information Technology, 11(2), 105–112. doi:10.100710676-009-9187-9

UN-SDGs. (2022). United Nations Sustainable Development *Goals Platform. Available online:* https://sdgs.un.org/goals

UN. (2022, December 1). International Decade for Action on Water for Sustainable Development, 2018-2028. *Retrieved from United* Nations: https://www.un.org/en/events/waterdecade/

UNCITRAL. (2015). Legislative Guide. Author.

UNECE. (2018). *Identifying, assessing and communicating* the benefits of transboundary water cooperation: Lessons learned and recommendations. UNECE. https://unece.org/environment-policy/publications/identifying-assessing-and-communicating-benefits-transboundary

UNESCO. (2020). Education for Sustainable *Development: A roadmap. United Nations* Educational, Scientific and Cultural Organization.

UN General Assembly. (2022, October 28). General Assembly Adopts Resolution Recognizing Access to Clean Water, Sanitation as Human Right by Recorded Vote of 122 in Favour, Noe against, 41 Abstentions. *United Nations. h*ttps://press.un.org/en/2010/ga10967.doc.htm

United Nations. (2008). Achieving Sustainable Development and Pr*omoting Development Cooperation.* UN. https://www.un.org/en/ecosoc/docs/pdfs/fina_08-45773.pdf

United Nations. (2022). Go*al 4: Education. Retrieved from: https://www.un.org/ sustainabledevelopment/education/*

USEPA. (2012). A Handbook for Water and Wastewater Utilities. Seattle, WA 98101: U.S. Environmental Protection Agency.

Valvis, A. (2015). Transboundary Freshwa*ter Resources Management: Greece and its neighbors towards Cooperation or Confl*ict, [PhD Thesis, University of Peloponnese, Greece].

van Griensven, A., & Vanrolleghem, P. A. *(2006). The Cat*chMod toolbox: Easy and *guided access to ICT tools for Water Framework Directive implementation. Water Science and Technology, 53(10), 285–292. doi:10.*2166/ws.2006.323 PMID:16838714

Vangronsveld, J., & Cunningham, S. (1998). In situ Inactivation and Phytorestoration of Metal-Contaminated *Soils. Landes Biosciences.*

Vare, P., Rieckmann, M., & Lausselet, N. (2022). Introduction. In P. Vare, N. Lausselet, & M. Rieckmann (Eds.), C*ompetences in Education for Sustainable Development (pp. 3–10). Springer.* doi:10.1007/978-3-030-91055-6_1

Vargas-Terranova, C.-A., Rodrigo-Ilarri, J., Rodrig*o-Clavero, M.-E.,* & Parra-Saad, A. (2022). Implementing circular economy techniques for the optimal manag*ement of recyclablesolid waste using the M-GRCT decis*ion support model. Applied Sciences (Basel, Switzerland), 12(16), 12. doi:10.390/app12168072

Vaseashta, A. (2013). Ecosystem of Innovations in Nanomaterials Based CBRNE Sensors and Thr*eat Mitigation. In A. Vaseashta & S. Khudaverdyan (Eds.), Advanced Sensors for Safety and Security. NAT*O Science for Peace and Seurity Series B: Physics and Biophysics (pp. 3–25). Springer. doi:10.1007/978-94-007-7003-4_1

Vaseashta, A. (2014). Advanced sciences convergence-based methods for surveillance of *emerging trends in science,* technology, and intelligence. Foresight, 16(1), 17–36. doi:10.1108/ FS-10-2012-0074

Vaseashta, A. *(2021). Advanced Sensors for Real-time Infrastructure Integrity and Stru*ctural Health Monitoring. Proceedings of the 16th International Scientific Conference CIBv - Civil Engineering and Building Services.

*Vaseashta, A. (2021). Nexus of Advanced Technology P*latforms for Strengthening Cyber-Defense Capabilities. NATO Science for Peace and Security Series. doi:10.3233/NHSDP220003

Vaseashta, A. (2022). Applying Resilience to Hybrid Threats in Infrastructure, Digital, and Social Domains Using Multisectoral, Multidisciplinary, and Whole-of-G*overnment Approach. NATO Science for* Peace and Security Series - D: Information and Communication Security. Vol. 61: Building Cyber Resilience against Hybrid Threats, 42-59. doi:10.3233/NI*CSP220017*

*Vasiljević· Z. (2017). The Legal Regime of Utility Services and Public-Private Partnership in B*osnia and Herzegovina. Network Industries Quarterly., 19(1), 1–34.

Vasić, G. (2018). Application of multi criteria analysis in the design of energy policy: Space and water heating in households – City Novi Sad, Serbia. Energy Policy, 113, 410–419. doi:10.1016/j.enpol.2017.11.025

Vasović, D., Janaćković, G., Malenović Nikolić, J., Milošević, L., & Mušicki, S. (2018b). Promoting reflective practice in resources protection area: a step to forecast outcomes in uncertainty. Journal of Environmental Protection and Ecology, 19(3), 1320-1329. Available at: https://scibulcom.net/en/journal/1311-5065/issue/2018-19-3/

Vasović, D., Janaćković, G., Malenović Nikolić, J., Mušicki, S., & Mar*ković, S. (2018a). Multimodality in the field of resources protection. Journal of Environmental Protection and*Ecology, 19(4), 1519-1525. Available at: https://scibulcom.net/en/journal/1311-5065/issue/2018-19-4/

Vasović, D., Malenovic Nikolic, J., & Janackovic, G. (2016). Evaluation and Assessment Model for *Environme*ntal Management under the Seveso III, IPPC/IED and Water Framework Directive. Journal of Environmental Protection and Ecology, 17(1), 356-365. Available at: https://scibulcom.net/en/journal/131-50*65/issue/2016*-17-*1*/

Vassiliadou, I., Papadopoulos, A., Costopoulou, D., Vasiliadou, S., Christoforou, S., & Leondiadis, L. (2009). Dioxin contamination after an accidental fire in *the municipal landfill of Ta*gara*d*es, Thessaloniki, Greece. Chemosphere, 74(7), 879–884. doi:10.1016/j.chemosphere.2008.11.016 PMID:19101012

VAT Law (Official Gazette of the Republic of Macedonia, no. 44/99 with changes).

Vaverková, D. M. *(2019). Landfill Impacts on the Environment-Revie*w. Geosciences, 9(10), 431. doi:10.3390/geosciences9100431

Vaverková, D. M., & Adamcová, D. (2018). Case study of landfill reclamation at Czech landfill site. Environmental Engineering and Management Journal, 17(3), 64. doi:10.3063*8/eemj.2018.065*

Velasco-Muñoz, J., Aznar-Sánchez, J., Belmonte-Ureña, L., & Román-Sánchez, I. (2018). Sustainable Water Use in Agriculture: A Review of Worldwide Research. Sustainability, 10(4), 1084. doi:10.3390/su10041084

Venkatraman, K., & Ashwath, N. (2009). Phytocapping: Importance of Tree Selection and Soil Thickness. *Water, Air, and Soil Pollution, 9(5-6), 421–430.* doi:10.100711267-009-9236-8

Venkatraman, K., & Ashwath, N. (2016). Canopy Rainfall Intercepted by Nineteen Tree Species Grown on a Phytocapped Landfill. International Journal of Waste Resources, 6(1), 202. doi:10.4172/2252-5211.1000202Vergara, S. E., & Tchobanoglous, G. (2012). Municipal Solid Waste and *the Environment*: A Global Perspective. Annual Review of Environment and Resources, 37(1), 277–309. doi:10.1146/annurev-environ-050511-122532

Veselinović, N., Bugarčić, F. Ž., & Radonjić, Lj. (2020, December). Innovation, export, CO2 *emission and* economic growth: Panel analysis of selected Central and Eastern uropean countries. 6th International Scientific Conference on Contemporary Is*sues in Economics, Business and Management (EBM* 0*20)*, 233-244.

von Schönfeld, K., Ferreira, A., & Pinho, P. (2018). The dialectics between social acceleration and the growth paradigm: Innovation and transport in neoliberal planning. Proceedings *of the Institutio*nalisation of Degrowth & Post-growth: The European level, 17-19.

Voorn, B., Marieke, L. G., & Thiel, S. (2017). The efficiency and effec*tiveness of municipally owned* co*r*porations: A systematic review. Local Government Studies, 43(5), 820–841. doi:10.1080/03003930.2017.1319360

Vranjanac, Ž. (2015). Ekonomsko-ekološki uticaj otpada od hig*ijenskih sredstava na životnu sredinu [Eco*nomic-Environmental Impact of Household care Products on the environment]. Master rad, Fakultet zaštite na radu u Nišu, Niš.

Vranjanac, Ž. (2015). Qua*lity management of public lighting. Intern*acio*nal May Conference on Strategic Management – IMKSM 2015, pp. 373 - 382, Bor, Serbia.

Vranjanac, Ž. (2019). Overview of indicator development in the fields of sustainable development and environmental protection, Facta Universitatis, Series. Work*ing and Living Environmental Protection, 16(3), 193–198.*

*Vranjanac, Ž., & Spasić, D. (2017). Economic and Envi*ronmental Effects of Collection and Primary Recycling of Packaging Waste from Hygiene and Cleaning Products in Serbia, Serbian. Journal of Management, 12(2), 317–330.

Vranjanac, Ž., *Vasović, D., Janaćković, G., Živković, N., & Malenović-Nikolić, J. (2019). Comparati*ve Analysis of Selected Environmental Indicators within Adjusted Savings in Serbia and Romania. Journal of Environmental Protection and Ecology, 2*0(2), 906–911.*

*Vranjana*c, Ž., Velimirović, L., & Stanković, M. (2022). Guideline for constructing composite indicators that measure circular economy performance, Facta Universitatis, Series. Working and Living Environmental Protection, 19(1), 1–7.

Vranjanac, Ž., Živković, N., Djordjević, A., Janaćković, G., & Vasović, D. (2022). Correlation between Development of *the Country and Contribution to Air Pollution an Indicator-based* Analysis for EU and WBC. Fresenius Environmental Bulletin, 31(5), 5192–5169.

W&CC. (2010). Waste and Climate Change - Global Trends and Strategy Framework. https://wedocs.unep.org/20.500.11822/8648

Wada, Y., van Beek, L. P. H., & Bierkens, M. F. P. (2011). Modelling global water stress of the recent past: On the relative importance of trends in water demand and climate variability. Hydrology and Earth System Sciences, 15(12), 3785–3808. doi:10.5194/hess-15-3785-2011

Wang, C. H., Padmanabhan, P., & Huang, C. H. (2022). The impacts of the 1997 Asian financial crisis and the 2008 global financial crisis on renewable energy consumption and carbon dioxide emissions for developed and developing countries. Heliyon, 8(2), e08931. doi:10.1016/j.heliyon.2022.e08931 PMID:35243057

Wang, D. F., Dong, Q. L., Peng, Z. M., Khan, S. A. R., & Tarasov, A. (2018). The green logistics impact on international trade: Evidence from developed and developing countries. Sustainability, 10(7), 2235. doi:10.3390u10072235

Wang, J.-J., Chen, H., Rogers, D. S., Ellram, L. M., & Grawe, S. J. (2017). A bibliometric analysis of reverse logistics research (1992-2015) and opportunities for future research. International Journal of Physical Distribution & Logistics Management, 47(8), 666–687. doi:10.1108/IJPDLM-10-2016-0299

Wang, K., Fu, X., & Luo, M. (2015). Modeling the impacts of alternative emission trading schemes on international shipping. Transportation Research Part A, Policy and Practice, 77,35–49. doi:10.1016/j.tra.2015.04.006

Wasowicz, K. (2018). Assessment of the efficiency of municipal companies based on local collective transport. Zarządzanie Publiczne, 44(2), 56–70. doi:10.15678/ZP.2018.44.2.04

Water, U. N. (2022, November). Country activities and commitments. Water Action Decade: https://www.wateractiondecade.org/country-activities/

Water Integrity Network (WIN). (2021). Water integrity global outlook 2021. WIN. https://www.waterintegritynetwork.net/wigo2021/

Water Integrity Network (WIN). (2022). About win. WIN. https://www.waterintegritynetwork.net/about/

Water Law (Official Gazette of the Republic of Macedonia, no. 04/98).

WHO, JMP, & UNICEF. (2017). Progress on drinking water, sanitation and hygiene: 2017 update and SDG baselines. Available at: https://www.who.int/publications/i/item/9789241512893

WHO. (2012). Global Costs and Benefits of Drinking-Water Supply and Sanitation Interventions to Reach the MDG Target and Universal Coverage. Analytical report, WHO/HSE/WSH/12.01, WHO. Available at: https://apps.who.int/iris/handle/10665/75140

WHO Director-General's opening remarks at the media briefing on COVID-19. (2020, Mar. 11). https://www.who.int/dg/speeches/detail/who-director-general-s-opening-remarks-at-the-media-briefing-on-covid-19

Wichaisri, S., & Sopadang, A. (2018). Trends and future directions in sustainable development. Sustainable Development, 26(1), 1–17. doi:10.1002d.1687

Wiek, A., & Redman, A. (2022). What Do Key Competencies in Sustainability Offer, and How to Use Them. In P. Vare, N. Lausselet, & M. Rieckmann (Eds.), Competences in Education for Sustainable Develoment (pp. 27–34). Springer. doi:10.1007/978-3-030-91055-6_4

Wilson, M., Paschen, J., & Pitt, L. (2021). The circular economy meets artificial intelligence (AI): Understaning the opportunities of AI for reverse logistics. Management of Environmental Quality. Advance online publication. doi:10.1108/MEQ-10-2020-022

Wilson, M. A., & Carpenter, S. R. (1999). Economic Valuation of Freshwater Ecosystem Services In The United States: 1971-1997. Ecological Applications, 9, 772–783.

Windham, D. (1990). Improving the efficiency of educational systems. In Stratégie *du développement des ressources humaines: communications découlant du séminaire-atelier tenu à Yaoundé, Cameroun, 2-5 fév. 19*88. CRDI. Retrieved from: https://idl-bnc-idrc.dspacedirect.org/bitstream/handle/10625/18253/IDL-18253.pdf?sequence=1

Witte, K. D., & López-Torres, L. (2017). Efficiency in education: A review of literature and a way forward. The Journal of the Operational Research Society, 68(4), 339–363. doi:10.1057/jors.2015.92

Wolf, A. (2006). Conflict and Cooperation Over Transboundary Waters, UNDP (United Nations Development Programme). https://hdr.undp.org/

World-Health-Organization. (2019). Middle East respiratory syndrome coronavirus (MERS-CoV). https://www.who.int/emergencies/mers-cov/en/

World Bank. (2003). UNCAC. World Bank. https://star.worldbank.org/focus-area/uncac

World Bank. (2012). Inclusive Green Growth: The Pathway to Sustainable Development. Technical Report. World Bank Publications.

World Bank. (2022). Worldwide governance indicators. World Bank. https://info.worldbank.org/governance/wgi/

World Economic Forum (WEF). (2021). Clifford Chance, Delivering a Climate Trade Agenda: Industry Insights, 2021. Retrieved from: https://www.weforum.org/agenda/2021/09/how-can-policymakers-and-the-business-community-deliver-a-climate-focused-trade-policy-agenda-clifford-chance/

World Health Organization. (2003). Update 49 - SARS case fatality ratio, incubation period. https://www.who.int/csr/sars/archive/2003_05_07a/en/

World Tourism Organization. (2001). Sustainable Development of Tourism: A Compilation of Good Practices. World Tourism Organization.

Worthington, A. C. (2001). An empirical survey of frontier efficiency measurement techniques in education. Education Economics, 9(3), 245–268. doi:*10.1*080/09645290110086126

Wright, R. T. (2005). Environmental Science (International Edition). Pearson, Prentice Hall Inc.

Wu, Z., & McGoogan, J.M. (2020). Characteristics of and important lessons from the *coonavirus disease 2019 (COVID-19*) outbreak in China: Summary of a report of 72314 cases from the Chinese Center for Disease C*ontol and Prevention. Academic Press.*

Wuana, R. A., & Okieimen, F. E. (2011). Heavy Metals in Contaminated Soils: A Review of Sources, Chemistry, Risks and Best Available Strategies for Remediation. International Scholarly Research Notices. doi:10.5402/2011/402647

Yan, A., Wang, *Y., Tan, S. N., Mohd Yusof, M. L., Ghosh, S., & Chen,* Z. (2020). Phytoremediation: A Promising Approach for Revegetation of Heavy Metal-Polluted L*and. Front. Plant Sci., 11, 359. doi:10.3389/fpls.2020.00359 PMID:*32425957

Yang, F. C., Kao, R. H., Chen, Y. T., Ho, Y. F., Cho, C. *C., & Huang, S. W. (2018). A common weight approach to* construct composite indicators: The evaluation of fourtee emerging markets. Social Indicators Research, 137(2), 463–479. doi:10.100711205-017-1603-7

Yesc*ombe, E. R. (2007).* P*u*blic-Private Partnerships: Principles of Policy and Finance. Elsevi*er Ltd. doi:10.1016/B*978-075068054-7.50025-3

Yingfei, Y., Mengze, Z., Zeyu, L., Ki-Hyung, B., Avotra, A. A. *R. N., & Nawaz, A. (2022). Green logistics performance and infrastructure on service trade and environment-measurig firm's performance and service quality. Journal of King Saud University. Science,* 34(1), 101683. doi:10.1016/j.jksus.2021.101683

Yu, Y., Wang, X., Zhong, R. Y., & Huang, G. Q. (2017). E-commerce logistics in supply chain management: Implementations and future perspective in furniture industry. Industrial Management & Data Systems, 117(10), 2263–2286. doi:10.1108/IMDS-09-2016-0398

Zalesny, R. S. Jr, & Bauer, O. E. (2007b). Selecting and utilizing Populus and Salix for landfill covers: Imp*lications for lea*chat*e* irrigation. International Journal of Phytoremediation, 9(6), 497–511. doi:10.1080/15226510701709689 PMID:18246776

Zalesny, R. S. Jr, Wiese, A. H., Bauer, E. O., & Riemenschneider, D. E. (2006). Sapflow of hybrid poplar (Populus nigra L.×*P. maximowiczii A. Henry* 'N*M6'*) during phytoremediation of landfill leachate. Biomass and Bioener*gy, 30(8-9), 784–793. doi:10.1016/j.biombioe.2005.08.006*

*Zam*an, K., & Shamsuddin, S. (2017). Green logistics and national scale economic indicators: Evidence from a panel of selected European countries. Journal of Cleaner Production, 143, 51–63. doi:10.1016/j.jlepro.2016.12.150

Zaninović, P. A., Zaninović, V., & Skender, H. P. (202*0). The effects of logistics performanc*e *on* international trade: EU15 vs CEMS. Economic Research-Ekonomska Istraživanja, 1-17. do i:10.1080/1331677X.2020.1844582

Zhang, H., He, P., & Shao, L. (2009). N2O emissions at municipal solid waste landfill sites: *Effects of CH4 emissions and cover soil.* Atmospheric Environment, 43(16), 2623–2631. doi:10.1016/j.atmosenv.2009.02.011

Zhang, Q., Wu, X., & Chen, Y. (2022). Is economic crisis an opp*ortunity for realizing the low-c*arbon transition? A simulation study on the interaction between economic cycle and energy regulation policy. Energy Policy, 168, 113114. doi:10.1016/j.enpol.2022.113114

Zhou, F., Yu, T., Du, *R., Fan, G., Liu, Y., Liu, Z., Xiang, J.,* Wang, Y., Song, B., Gu, X., Guan, L., Wei, Y., Li, H., Wu, X., Xu, J., Tu, S., Zhang, Y., Chen, H., & Cao, B. (2020, March). Clinical course and risk factors for mor*tality of adu*lt i*npatients with* COVID-19 i Wuhan, China: A retrospective cohort study. Lancet, *395(10229), 1054–1062. do*i:10.1016/S0140-6736(20)30566-3 PMID:32171076

Ziemele, J., Talcis, N., Osis, U., & Dace, E. (2021). A methodology for selecting a sustainable development strategy for connecting low heat density co*nsumers to a district heating sys*tem by cascading of heat carriers. Energy, 230, 120776. doi:10.1016/j.energy.2021.120776

Zijm, H., & Klumpp, M. (2017). Future Logistics: What to expect, how to adapt. Dynamics *in logistics, 365-379. doi:10.1007/978-3-*319-45117-6_32

Çakar, N. D., Gedikli, A., Erdoğan, S., & Yıldırım, D. Ç. (2021). A comparative analysis of the relationship between innovation and transport sector carbon emis*sions in developed and* dev*e*loping Mediterranean countries. Environmental Science and Pollution Research International, 1(33), 45693–45713. Advance online publication. doi:10.100711356-021-13390-y

Đorđević, L., Redžić, N., Radovanović, N., & Jovanović, G. (2021). Waste management in *the Republic* of *Se*rbia in the period 2011-2020 years. Agency for Environmental Protection.

Đurović-Todorović, J., & Đorđević, M. (2011). Characteristics of the fiscal federalism of Bosnia and Herzegovina. Ekonomika (Nis), 57(2), 39–54.

Đurović Todorović & Đorđević. (2019). Public finance-Theory and practice. Faculty of Economics.

Şimşek, H., & Öztürk, G. (2021). Evaluation *of the rel*ationship between environmental accounting and business performance: The case of Istanbul province. Green Finance, 3(1), 46–58. doi:10.3934/GF.2021004

Šulskytė, D. (2019). The impact of logistics sector on sustainable development. Vilnius University Open Series, (2), 75–81. doi:10.15388/*OpenS*eries.2019.18407

Žalėnienė, I., & Pereira, P. (2021). Higher education for sustainability: A global perspective. Geography and Sustainability, 2(2), 99–106. doi:10.1016/j.geosus.2021.05.001

Živković, M., Pereverza, K., Pasichnyi, O., Madžarević, A., Ivezić, D., & Kordas, O. (2016). Exploring scenarios for more sustainable heating*: The cae of Niš, Serbia. Energy, 115, 1758–1770. doi:10.1*016/j.energy.2016.06.034

Živković, N., Takić, L., Djordjević, L., Djordjević, A., Mladenović-Ranisavljević, I., Golubović, T., & Božilov, A. (2019). Concentrations of Heavy Metal Cations and a Health Risk Assessment of S*ediments and River Surface Water: A Case* Study from a Serbian Mine. Polish Journal of Environmental Studies, 28(3), 2009–2020. doi:10.15244/pjoes/89986

Živković, S., Takić, L., & Živković, N. (2013). The improvement of environmental performances by applying ISO 14001 standard: A cas*e study. Ch*emical Industry and Chemical Engineering Quarterly/CICEQ, 19(4), 541-552. Available at: http://www.ache.org.rs/CICEQ/Arhiva/

Živković, S., Todorović, M., & Pejčić, D. (2016). Improvements in Environmental Protection Through Optimization of Production Processes: A Case Study. FEB-Fresenius Environmental Bulle*tin, 25(8), 2725-2735. Available at: ht*tps://www.prt-parlar.de/download_feb_2016/

About the Contributors

Jordan Gjorcev is a full-time professor at International Slavic University, North Macedonia. He holds a master's degree in the field of social psychology in Russia and social and political relations in Bulgaria, and a doctorate at the Tambov State University on a topic from the field of economic theories. From 2000-2005, he worked as the Mayor of the municipality of Sveti Nikole. In 2005 he founded the International Slavic University. Today, he works as the President of the Management Board of ISU.

Samoil Malcheski holds a Ph.D. degree in applied economy and economic statistics from Institute of Economics at Ss. Cyril and Methodious University in Skopje. He is associate professor at International Slavic University in Macedonia. Prof. Malceski is the author and co-author of a dozen university textbooks on mathematics, applied mathematics in economics and statistics, as well as the author and co-author of over 50 professional books. He has published over 70 professional and over 30 scientific papers. Prof. Malcheski has extensive experience in supporting start-ups and would-be entrepreneurs, more than 15 years he is working with start-ups, training and mentoring. Lately, he is working on various EU funded projects as a trainer and consultant, and also he is UNDP consultant for supporting SMEs and business start-ups. Mr. Malcheski is consultant of the Agency for Promotion of Entrepreneurship of the Republic of Macedonia in the field of product development, business planning and strategic planning.

Tamara Rađenović, PhD, is an Assistant Professor at Faculty of Occupational Safety, University of Niš. She earned her MA in Finance and Investments with Merit from Nottingham University Business School, the UK in 2007, and PhD in Economics from the Faculty of Economics, University of Niš, Serbia in 2018. From 2011 to 2018 she was a Teaching Assistant for Public Sector Economics at Faculty of Economics. He teaches Safety Economics at undergraduate studies, and Economics of Occupational Safety, Economics of Environmental Protection, Efficiency of Communal Systems at master studies. Her areas of interest include: safety economics, economics of sustainable development, intellectual capital management, performance management, macroeconomics, economic development, financial markets, public-private partnerships, competitiveness, and real options. She has published over 50 papers in the journals indexed in WoS and Scopus including Renewable and Sustainable Energy Reviews, Journal of Balkan and Near Eastern Studies, Proceedings of Rijeka Faculty of Economics, Acta Oeconomica. She is a co-author of two monographs in the field of Strategic and Operational Intellectual Capital Management.

Dejan Vasović, PhD, is an associate professor of the University of Niš, Faculty of Occupational Safety in Niš, Republic of Serbia. He is member of the Department for Working and Living Environment Quality Management. He is the author or co-author of several book chapters, and over one hundred and fifty scientific papers published in scientific journals and proceedings of scientific conferences. He took part in the realization of three national and one international research projects. With no less importance is his experience within teacher's mobility programs, such ERASMUS+ and CEEPUS. He was a member of organizational and program boards of more that dozen national and international scientific conferences. He peer reviewed a number of scientific and professional papers published in the proceedings of national and international conferences and scientific journals. His research interests include environmental protection in general, water protection and sustainable water resources management, environmental safety and security issues, emergency management, etc.

Snežana Živković is a Full Professor at Faculty of Occupational Safety, University of Niš. She received a PhD degree in Occupational Safety from Faculty of Occupational Safety, University of Niš. She has published over 250 papers in international monographs and leading scientific journals, including Renewable and Sustainable Energy Reviews, Environmental Science and Pollution Research and International Journal of Injury Control and Safety Promotion. Professor Živković has been the author of 4 international monographs, 3 national monographs and 5 handbooks. Her research interests include occupational safety, organizational behavior, management and human resources, emergency management, protection of living and working environment. She is an executive editor of the scientific journal "Economics of Sustainable Development". She has been the member of the organizing committee of numerous scientific conferences. In her rich scientific career, she worked as a reviewer for many scientific journals, including: Themes, Economics, International Journal of Injury Control and Safety Promotion, Safety Engineering, Economics of Sustainable Development, etc.

* * *

Filip Bugarčić holds Ph.D. in Economics, with a specialization in international trade logistics, trade policy, and industrial development. He teaches the following courses at undergraduate levels: International Economy, International Trade, and Economic Development.

Georgios Damianos is a PhD student in the Postgraduate Programme "Green leadership, organizational culture and sustainable innovative entrepreneurship" at the School of Economic Sciences, University of Western Macedonia, Greece. He graduated from the School of Rural and Surveying Engineering, Faculty of Engineering Aristotle University of Thessaloniki, Greece in 2020. His research interest includes sustainable development, circular economy, green entrepreneurship.

Marina Đorđević is a Full Professor at the Faculty of Economics, University of Niš, Republic of Serbia, in the Department of National Economy and Finance. She earned her PhD in Economics (scientific field: Finance and Banking) from the Faculty of Economics, University of Niš in 2009. Professor Đorđević teaches Public Finance and Monetary Economics at the undergraduate level, Public Finance II and Monetary Economics II at the master's level, and Financial Theory and Policy at the PhD level. Her areas of expertise include Public Finance, Monetary Policy, and Economic Development. She is a member of the Association of Economists of Serbia and has experience implementing projects in Serbia and abroad. To date, she has published numerous papers, 2 books, and 5 monographs.

Milica Đorđević, PhD, Associate Professor, was born in 1981 in Niš. She graduated from the Faculty of Economics in Nis and successfully defended her master's thesis in 2010. She defended her doctoral dissertation entitled Internal audit in the function of improving corporate governance in 2016 at the Faculty of Economics in Nis. Since 2008 he has been working at the Faculty of Economics in Nis. In 2022, she was elected associate professor. She is assigned to teach the following subjects: Financial Accounting and Auditing, Accounting Valuation of Financial Instruments and Public Sector Auditing. She is the author and co-author of several papers in scientific and professional journals and is a participant in several scientific conferences and conferences in the country and abroad.

Jadranka Đurović Todorović is a Full Professor at the Faculty of Economics, University of Niš, Republic of Serbia, in the Department of National Economy and Finance. Professor Djurović Todorović teaches Public Finance and Monetary Economy at the undergraduate level, Public Finance II and Monetary Economy II at the master's level, and Financial Theory and Policy at the PhD level at the Faculty of Economics, University of Niš, Republic of Serbia. She completed her postgraduate studies at the Faculty of Economics in Belgrade and earned her PhD at the Faculty of Economics in Niš in 2001. She is a member of the Association of Economists of Serbia and has experience implementing projects in Serbia and abroad. To date, she has published numerous papers, books, and monographs. Her areas of expertise include Public Finance, Monetary Policy, and Economic Development.

Tatjana Golubović is a full professor at the University of Niš, Faculty of Occupational Safety. She is the Head of Chair of Occupational and Environmental Quality. She received the diploma and the Ph.D. degree in chemistry from the University of Niš, Faculty of Sciences and Mathematics. Her main areas of research include chemistry, environmental chemistry, toxicology, ecotoxicology, and soil protection. She has published a number of scientific papers on this subject and took part in the realization of a number of national and international research projects.

Sreten Ilić has a master's degree in environmental science. He received a master's degree in environmental science from Faculty of Occupational Safety, University of Niš. His main areas of research include chemical accidents and problems of environmental pollutions. He published a number of scientific papers on this subject.

Milica Jovanović Vujatović is a Junior Teaching Assistant at the Faculty of Economics, University of Niš, Serbia and a PhD student at the Faculty of Economics, University of Niš, Serbia. She was a scholarship holder of the Ministry of Education, Science and Technological Development of the Republic of Serbia at all levels of study. Her areas of interest are based on the following: business performance management, competitiveness, intangible asset valuation, intangible asset management, and brand management. She has published over 40 articles, and one monograph, and has participated in a number of conferences. She is a member of the Society of Economists "Ekonomika" and Serbian Marketing Association "SeMA".

Bojan Krstić, PhD, is a Full Professor of Management of Business Performance and Management of Intellectual Capital, Strategic Control of Enterprises and Theory of Enterprises at Faculty of Economics, University of Niš. He received a PhD degree in Business Management from Faculty of Economics, University of Niš. He has published over 330 papers in international monographs and leading scientific journals, including Prague Economic Papers, Economic Research, Acta Oeconomica, Development Southern Africa. Professor Krstić has been the editor of 21 international monographs, and also the author of 4 handbooks and 8 national monographs. His research interests include business performance management, intellectual capital management, strategic management, theory of firm, performance management of non-profit organizations, corporate social responsibility, and economics of sustainable development. Professor Krstić is a member of the program committee of ten international conferences, a member of the editorial board of four scientific journals.

Carmen Maftei is Professor at the Civil Building Services Department and Vice dean for Academic Affairs at the Transilvania University of Brasov, Romania. She attended Polytechnic Institute of Iasi where she majored in Land Reclamation in 1988 and from 1996-1998 she attends a specialization in Water resources and protection of water resources, equivalent of Master of Science. In 2002 she finished the PhD studies in Civil Engineering. Her research activity is focused on: (i) hydrology and hydrological modelling.

Ivana Marjanović is a PhD candidate and a teaching assistant at the Faculty of Economics, University of Niš. Her field of scientific interest is the application of quantitative methods in economics, with the main focus on the application of operational research and decision theory methods and models. She has noteworthy experience in conducting quantitative and qualitative research in the area of urban studies and sustainable development.

Carlos Andrés Merlano is a public economics professor at Corporación Universitaria del Caribe - CECAR in Colombia. He graduated in economics from Pontificia Universidad Javeriana and obtained a master's degree in economics from this institution. He also completed a Master's in Business Administration from the University of Manchester and is currently doing a doctorate in technology at Purdue University. Prof. Merlano has 12+ years of experience in academia and research and 22+ years of experience in several public and private organizations in Colombia. Of his work in private and public companies, he has 7+ years of experience with public and private utility companies in Colombia. He works as a foundation director in educational activities, an expert in the think tank Altercontacts and a university professor in recognized universities in Colombia. His research interests are transparency and integrity in utility companies, novel technologies, and sustainability.

Vladimir Mićić, Ph.D., is a Full Professor at the Faculty of Economics, University of Kragujevac in Serbia, where he received his Ph.D. He teaches the subjects of the economics of the industry, economic development undergraduate studies and economics of growth and development. His research interests include relevant issues, industry policy, competitiveness, tourism and economic development.

Sandra Milanović is a junior teaching assistant of the Faculty of Economics, University of Niš, research assistant at the Innovation Center, University of Niš and a PhD student at the Faculty of Economics of the University of Niš. She has significant teaching and project experience. Currently she is involved in the Horizon Europe project, UR-DATA. She is the author of more than 60 scientific papers published in domestic and international journals and presented at conferences. Key area of her interest is a business management and human resource management.

Bojana Novićević Čečević, PhD, Assistant Professor, was born in 1983 in Niš. She graduated from the Faculty of Economics in Niš and successfully defended her master's thesis in the subject of Strategic Management Accounting. She defended her doctoral dissertation entitled Management and Accounting Support to Company Management in a Lean Business Environment in 2016 at the Faculty of Economics in Niš. Since October 2008, she has been working at the Faculty of Economics in Niš. She is the author of a large number of papers published in leading national journals and proceedings of scientific conferences, co-author of the monograph and workbook from Management Accounting and Cost Accounting.

Lence Petreska holds a Ph.D. degree in marketing from Faculty of Economy at Ss. Cyril and Methodious University in Skopje. She is full time professor at International Slavic University in North Macedonia and at this moment she is Rector of the University. Prof. Petreska is the author and co-author of a dozen university textbooks on marketing. She has published over 50 professional and over 35 scientific papers. Prof. Petreska is President of the Advisory board of Macedonian Association for Marketing.

Natalija Petrović received master diploma in Environmental safety at Faculty of Occupational Safety in Niš, University of Niš. Now she is at PhD study program of Environmental Safety Engineering at the Faculty of Occupational Safety in Nis, University of Niš. Her main areas of research include environmental protection, environmental management, and water protection. She is currently working as a teaching assistant at the Academy of Applied Tecnicla and Preschool Studies, Department Niš.

Žarko Rađenović is a Research Associate at the Innovation Center, University of Niš, Serbia. He obtained PhD in Economics from Faculty of Economics, University of Niš, Serbia and MSc in Industrial Engineering from Faculty of Engineering, University of Niš, Serbia. His scientific fields of interest include Applied statistics and informatics, Multi-criteria decision making tools, Sustainable Development,

Circular economy, Management of business information systems, Health economics, Data Science, eBusiness, Digitalization in Economics.

Dorin Radu is Vice Dean of Research at the at the Faculty of Civil Engineering of Transilvania University of Brasov. He has a Doctoral Degree in Civil Engineering - Structural Integrity of Steel Structures and has teaching and research activities in Civil Engineering since 2003. He holds lectures/courses in Static and Stability of the Structures, Theory of Elasticity and Plasticity and Building Information Modelling. He is author of books, articles and conference papers published in national and international publishing houses. R&D expertise: structural integrity; FEM modelling, assessment, and optimization of structural elements; assessment of buildings; neural networks applied in civil engineering, new materials for sustainable constructions, environmental protection and energy saving. He is organizer, editor and reviewer for international conferences and journals.

Milica Ristić Cakić is a Teaching Assistant at the Faculty of Economics, University of Nis in Serbia, in the Department of National Economy and Finance. She is working on her Ph.D. dissertation on "Dilemmas and Paradoxes Regarding Key Tax Elements - The Causes of Constant Corporate Income Tax Reforms". Milica has participated in various projects, including feasibility studies and business plans. Her areas of expertise include Public Finance, Monetary Policy, and Economic Development. She has published over 40 papers in national and international journals, 1 monograph, and 3 chapters in international monographs. She has also conducted research on the Russian state budget at Belgorod State Technological University "V.G.Shukhov" in Russia.

Sandra Stanković is a Teaching Assistant and Laboratory Supervisor at the Academy of Applied Technical and Preschool studies, Department Niš, Serbia since 2021. She obtained her Master's degree in Environmental Engineering - Utility Management System from Faculty of Occupational Safety in Niš, Serbia. She was awarded with a PhD research scholarship (CEEPUS, CIII-RS-1112) financed by Austrian Agency for International Cooperation in Education and Research (OeAD-GmbH) and Centre for International Cooperation & Mobility (ICM) at the University of Natural Resources and Life Sciences, Vienna (BOKU). Currently, she is pursuing PhD degree in Environmental Engineering - Water Management. Her research interest includes water management, climate change adaptation measures and sustainable development. Member of the European Society of Safety Engineers (ESSE), World Youth Parliament for Water and Balkan Environmental Association (B.E.N.A.)

Marina Stanojević is employed as an associate for scientific research and publishing at the Faculty of Economics, University of Niš, and is PhD student at the same Faculty. She also has teaching experience as teaching associate in the area of Business management and Business statistics. She is coordinator of International Summer School of Economics at the Faculty of Economics, University of Niš and member of organizing and programme committees of conferences. She is an author of articles published in journals, conference proceedings, monographs, etc. She has been an active member of numerous project teams of domestic and international projects.

Desislava Stoilova joined the Faculty of Economics at the South-West University "Neofit Rilski", Bulgaria after her graduation (Master's degree in Finance) in 1999 as an assistant professor. In 2006 she obtained Ph.D. in Finance with a thesis in the field of financial decentralization and intergovernmental fiscal relations. Since 2010 Desislava Stoilova is an associate professor at the South-West University "Neofit Rilski". Currently, she teaches financial subjects and participates in a variety of research projects. Desislava Stoilova is author of more than 50 publications primarily intended to promote the application of effective methods and tools for financial management in the public and private sector.

Georgios Tsaples is a Researcher at the University of Macedonia, working on EU funded projects. He obtained his PhD in Operational Research at the Department of Business Administration of the University of Macedonia, Greece. He received his MSc from the Delft University of Technology at the Department of Technology and Policy Management. He has worked as a Research Fellow at the Center for Cyber Intelligence and Information Security of the University of Sapienza in Rome (2014-2016), as a Research Associate Hellenic Institute of Transport (2018-2019) and at the University of Macedonia (ongoing). Current main interests: methodological aspects of operational research, simulation, scenario discovery, combination of machine learning techniques with established OR methods.

Ashok Vaseashta is a professor, researcher, and strategic advisor. He is CTO/CRO of the International Clean Water Institute. Concurrently, he serves as Chaired Professor of Nanotechnology at the Academy of Sciences of Moldova, Academician at EMAAS, Senior Strategic Research Advisor for several organizations, and Professor at the Transylvania University of Brasov. Inspired by nature and guided by societal necessities, he strives for innovations to address global challenges such as environment, human safety and security, and sustainability using advanced technological solution platforms. He is a scholar, dedicated futurist and visionary leader. He received PhD from the Virginia Tech, VA in 1990 followed by Kobe post-doctoral fellowship. He served the U.S. Department of State in two rotations, as strategic S&T advisor and U.S. diplomat. His research interests span nanotechnology, environmental/ ecological science and safety and security. He has authored over 300 research publications, edited/authored 12 books on nanotechnology, and presented many keynote and invited lectures worldwide. He serves on the editorial board of several highly reputed international journals.

Žarko Vranjanac is a Research Assistant at the Innovation Center, University of Niš, Serbia. He is a PhD student of the Faculty of Occupational Safety, University of Niš where he completed his bachelor studies and his masters studies in the field of Utility System Management. As a PhD scholar of the Ministry of Education, Science and Technological Development of the Republic of Serbia, he was engaged in the Mathematical Institute of the Serbian Academy of Sciences and Arts as well as in the Faculty of Occupational Safety in Niš. His areas of interest include: environmental indicators, public utilities, environmental performance, environmental economy, environmental innovations. He was published over 40 articles. Žarko Vranjanac is member of Balkan Environmental Association (B.EN.A.).

Index

A

B

C

D

E

F

G

H

I

L

M

N

O

P

Q

R

S

T

U

W

Z

www.ingramcontent.com/pod-product-compliance
Lightning Source LLC
LaVergne TN
LVHW080348011026
849161LV00009B/2229
9781668477304